# KALORIK MAXX
# AIR FRYER COOKBOOK

# 1001

## Delicious, Fast and Easy to Make Healthy Recipes in your Air Fryer Oven for Beginners

## *With 80 Super Fast "5-Minute" Ideas*

## Emily Finner

> "One cannot think well, love well, sleep well,
>
> if one has not dined well."

VIRGINIA WOOLF

# TABLE OF CONTENTS

# ABOUT THE AUTHOR

**EMILY FINNER**

A nutritionist with a lifelong passion for cooking, Emily Finner started cooking alongside her grandmother when she was a teen and it soon became her biggest passion. Her dream is to become a chef, but the most important thing for her is being a mom of two beautiful children.

She adopted a different approach in cooking to ensure a clean lifestyle to her family and quickly became an enthusiast of healthy and mindful eating.

Very passionate about new kitchen appliances and best diets, she has a long experience in air frying cooking, and she desires to share her passion with other women with the same interests.

## RECIPES ARE NEVER ENOUGH!

Do you want to receive a new
Air Fryer Recipe every week?

Scan the QR code with your mobile

SCAN ME

# INTRODUCTION

The Kalorik MAXX Air Fryer Oven is an "all-in-one" kitchen appliance that promises **to replace a deep fryer, convection oven and microwave**; it also lets you sauté your foods. The Kalorik MAXX Air Fryer Oven is a unique kitchen gadget designed to fry food in a special chamber using super-heated air. In fact, the hot air circulates inside the cooking chamber using the convection mechanism, cooking your food evenly from all sides. It uses the so-called Maillard effect – a chemical reaction that gives fried food that distinctive flavor. Simply put, thanks to the hot air, your foods get that crispy exterior and a moist interior and do not taste like fat.

Why use an Air Fryer? I'm asked this question time and time again, so my answer is always the same: it all boils down to **versatility**, **health**, and **speed**. It means that you can "set it and forget it" until it is done. Unlike most cooking methods, there's no need to keep an eye on it. **You can pick the ingredients, turn the machine on and walk away** – no worries about overcooked or burned food. Another great benefit of using an Air Fryer is that unlike the heat in your oven or on a stovetop, the heat in the cooking chamber is constant and it allows your food to cook evenly. Plus, it is an energy-efficient and space-saving solution.

Air fryers operate by cooking food with the flow of hot air. This is what makes the foods you put into them so crunchy when they come out! There is this thing called the "Maillard Effect" that happens, which is a chemically prompted reaction that happens to the high temperature that makes it proficient for this fryer to cook foods in such little time while the nutrients and flavor are intact.

# BENEFITS OF THE AIR FRYER

There are numerous benefits you'll get from using an Air Fryer.

Here are the top three:

## Fast cooking and convenience

The Air Fryer is an electric device, you just need to press the right buttons and go on with your business. It heats up in few minutes so you can cut down your usual cooking time; moreover, hot air circulates around your food, cooking it quickly and evenly. **Roast chicken is perfectly cooked in 30 minutes, baby back ribs in less than 25 minutes and beef chuck or steak in about 15 minutes.** You can use dividers and cook different foods at the same time. The Air Fryer is a real game-changer, it is a cost-saving solution in many ways. I also use my Air Fryer to keep my food warm. Air Fryer features include automatic temperature control that eliminates the need to slave over a hot stove.

## Healthy eating

Yes, there is such a thing as healthy fried food and the Air Fryer proves that!

The Air Fryer is so inspiring that I started to enjoy cooking healthy and well-balanced meals for my family every day. Recent studies have shown that **air-fried foods contain up to 80% less fat than deep-fried foods.** Deep-fried food contributes to obesity, type 2 diabetes, high cholesterol, increases the risk of heart disease, and so on. Plus, fats and oils become harmful at high temperature, which leads to increase inflammation in your body and speeds up aging. these oils also release cancer-causing toxic chemicals. In addition, spilling fats and oils in nature is pretty dangerous for the wildlife and produces other undesirable effects on planet Earth.

According to the leading experts, **you should not be afraid of healthy fats and oils, especially if you follow the ketogenic diet.** It is preferable to Avoid partially hydrogenated and genetically modified oils such as cottonseed oil, soybean oil, corn oil, and rice bran oil. You should also avoid margarine since it is loaded with trans-fats. Good fats and oils include olive oil, coconut oil, avocado oil, sesame oil, nuts and seeds. **Air-fried foods are delicious and have the texture of regular fried food, but they do not taste like fat**. French fries are just a starting point. Perfect ribs, hearty casseroles, snacks, and delicious desserts turn out great in this revolutionary kitchen gadget. When it comes to healthy dieting that does not compromise flavor, the Air Fryer is a real winner.

## The ultimate solution to lose pounds and maintain a healthy weight

One of the greatest benefits of having an Air Fryer is **the possibility to maintain an ideal weight in an easy and healthy way**. It doesn't mean that you must give up fried fish fillets, saucy steaks, and scrumptious desserts. Choosing a healthy-cooking technique is the key to success. Air frying requires less fat compared to many other cooking methods, making your weight loss diet more achievable.

# UNDERSTANDING KALORIK MAXX AIR FRYER OVEN

Before we get to the recipes, let's focus our discussion on what Kalorik Maxx Air Fryer really is, how it works and how to take good care of it.

This is a device equipped with a fan and heating elements to create hot air circulated inside in order to cook food (basically, all conventional air fryers work like this).

This specific air fryer heats up quickly as it has 1700 watts, and its temperature can be adjusted between 80° and 500°F with a time range of 1 to 30 minutes (the range depends on your cooking preset).

## The Presets

The Kalorik Air Fryer is equipped with 19 cooking presets:

- Pastry
- Bake
- Toast
- Reheat
- Wings
- Fish
- Ribs

- Shrimp
- Vegetables
- Chicken steak
- Bacon
- Eggs
- Corn
- Fries

- Defrost
- Roast broil
- Air fry
- Pizza
- Proof

Seven of the presets are in oven mode while fourteen are in air fry mode.

## The Accessories

The air fryer comes with 9 accessories:

- Rack handle
- Rotisserie spit
- Baking pan
- Two-in-one reversible steak and dehydration tray
- Crumb tray

- Rotisserie handle
- Bacon tray
- Rack
- An air frying basket

A great feature is that the baking sheet, steak pan, crisper tray, rack, and bacon tray can be kept inside the equipment - but you have to remove them when you need to use the air fryer. Also, the bacon tray has a wavy design to keep the draining grease away from the bacon as it cooks.

## The Dials

When it comes to functionality, the Kalorik Air Fryer is easy to wrap your head around as it doesn't have too many features, and its control panel is readily comprehensible. Here is a little intro to the controls to know what to expect from the air fryer:

*Timer Dial*

This dial is positioned on the outer front side of the device and can be set between 0 to 30 minutes. When the time is up, the fryer automatically shuts down - so you don't have to keep checking on your meals.

*Temperature Dial*

This dial is located at the top of the unit and can be adjusted between 175 to 400 degrees F.

*Power Light*

This lights up right after you set the time, and it is green in color.

*Preheat Light*

This lights up as the device heats up, and sometimes when cooking, it is orange in color.

*Rack Slots*

This section allows you to place the food racks and baskets mentioned above

Now that we have an overview of what the Kalorik Maxx is, let's look at how to actually use it.

## How to Use the Kalorik Maxx Air Fryer

Using this unit is straightforward.

At first use, after putting the air fryer out of the box, the manufacturer recommends to turn it on and let it run for approximately 20 minutes with no food in it. This is important to get rid of the plastic smell - if there are any.

When you are ready to make a meal:

1. Take out the basket and its holder and add your ingredients to the basket.
2. Place the basket with the ingredients back into the unit and choose your temperature and time by turning the respective dials.
3. As soon as you set the timer, the equipment will start heating up, and the orange and green lights will light up.
4. Once the unit reaches the set temperature, the orange light will switch off.

You are free to take out the basket and its holder at any time during the cooking process to give your meal a good shake.

You can also cook 2 layers of food at the same time using the dual-layer rack. It is pretty easy; add the rack to the basket and put your ingredients under and on it as desired.

That's it!

Next, we will move our focus to cleaning it well.

## Cleaning It

Cleaning the device is straightforward. You only need a damp cloth and light cleaning detergent spray to wipe down the interior and exterior. The racks and the baskets are dishwasher safe, it can be as easy as throwing them in with the next batch of dishes.

You can also hand-wash them gently but do not use abrasive washing tools which can wear down the non-stick coating.

### Tips for Cleaning

When cleaning the Kalorik Maxx Air Fryer, the following tips will come in handy:

- Make sure to unplug the machine before cleaning it to avoid an electric shock.
- Do not remove stuck-on food using utensils, especially metal ones. Use a non-abrasive kitchen sponge instead.
- If the food has hardened on the basket and pan, soak in soapy hot water to soften the food.
- Make sure to rinse then thoroughly dry after you clean the fryer.

## Deodorizing

Sometimes your air fryer might get a little stinky. When this happens, simply take half a lemon and place it on the pan or inside the basket and let it sit for 20 to 30 minutes. Once the time elapses, clean, rinse and dry the pan and the basket.

## Tips for Maintenance

In addition to properly cleaning your Kalorik Maxx, you also need to take care of it actively.

Here are a few tips on how to do this properly:

- *Read the Manual* - go through the manual before setting up and cooking, and use the manual as a reference point if you don't understand how to operate a certain feature.
- *Proper Storage* - always store it in an upright position and unplug from electrical outlets. Keep the cords somewhere safe until you are ready to use your fryer again.
- *Inspecting the Cords* - do this every time before use. Never plug in a frayed or damaged cord into an outlet; it can be fatal.
- *Positioning* - keep the air fryer away from other appliances or the wall. It will need about 4 inches of space behind and above it to adequately vent hot air and steam; an enclosed space may lead to overheating.
- *Inspection* - inspect each component thoroughly use and if you notice any damaged parts, contact the manufacturer to get replacements.

At this point, you have a clear understanding of what the Kalorik Maxx Air Fryer is, how to use it and how to keep it in top-notch condition!

# BREAKFAST RECIPES

## HAM & EGG POCKETS
*Prep time:10 min | Cook time:25 min | Serves: 2*

**Ingredients**
- 1 egg
- Crescent rolls from tube: 4 oz.
- Milk: 2 tsp.
- Cheddar cheese: 2 tbsp., shredded
- Butter: 2 tsp.
- Deli ham: 1 oz., chopped

**Instructions**
- Let the Kalorik Air Fryer Oven preheat to 300 F.
- In a bowl, whisk eggs with milk. Cook eggs in butter until set. Add cheese and ham.
- Make two rectangles from the crescent dough, add the egg mixture to each rectangle. Fold the dough and seal the edges.
- Place in the air fryer tray and cook for 8 to 10 minutes.
- Serve right away.

Cal 326 | Fat 20g | Carb 25g | Protein 12g

## AIR FRYER OMELETS
*Prep time:20 min | Cook time:10 min | Serves: 2*

**Ingredients**
- Milk: 1/4 cup
- Shredded cheese: 1/4 cup
- Salt, to taste
- Ham diced, as needed
- 2 eggs
- Vegetables diced, as needed
- Breakfast Seasoning: 1 tsp.

**Instructions**
- In a bowl, whisk eggs with milk.
- Add vegetables, ham and salt to the eggs.
- Take a six by 3" pan and oil spray it. Pour the mixture into the pan.
- Let the Kalorik Air Fryer Oven preheat to 350 F.
- Air fry the eggs for 8 to 10 minutes
- After 5 minutes, add cheese and cook for 5 to 3 minutes more.
- Serve with green onion on top.

Cal 156 | Carb 21 g | Protein 6g | Fat 8 g

## ROSEMARY PARMESAN HAYSTACK POTATOES
*Prep time:15 min | Cook time:10 min | Serves: 4-6*

**Ingredients**
- Kosher salt: 2 tsp.
- Peeled russet potatoes: 1 1/2 lbs.
- Grated parmesan: 1 tbsp.
- Olive oil: 1 tbsp.
- Fresh rosemary: 2 tsp., chopped

**Instructions**
- Spiralizer the potatoes into 8-inch-long spirals, put in the cold water for 5 to 10 minutes, take out and rinse. Soak on some paper towels.
- Toss the potatoes noodles with salt and olive oil
- Put the air fryer tray to the bottom, select temperature to 380 F.

- Add the noodles to the tray, air fry for ten minutes. Toss the noodles once.
- After ten minutes, keep checking them for doneness.
- Sprinkle with parmesan and rosemary, serve right away.

## TOAD IN A HOLE

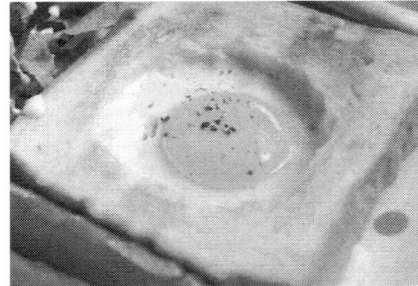

*Prep time:10 min | Cook time:5 min | Serves: 1*

**Ingredients**
- Butter: 1 tsp.
- Bread: 1 slice
- Salt & pepper, to taste
- 1 egg

**Instructions**
- In the centre of the bread, cut a two-inch hole.
- Butter the toast on both sides.
- Let the Kalorik Air Fryer Oven preheat to 300 F.
- Line the air fryer tray with foil and place the bread on foil; cook for 1 minute.
- Take out and crack an egg in the hole.
- Cook for two minutes. Serve right away.

Cal 144 | Carb 7g | Protein 13g | Fat 10g

## BOURBON BACON CINNAMON ROLLS
*Prep time:20 min | Cook time:10 min | Serves: 8*

**Ingredients**
- Bacon strips: 8
- Chopped pecans: half cup
- Bourbon: 3/4 cup
- Minced fresh gingerroot: 1 tsp.
- Cinnamon rolls with icing: 1 tube (~12 oz.)
- Maple syrup: 2 tbsp.

**Instructions**
- In a dish, add bacon and bourbon. Cover with plastic wrap and keep in the fridge overnight.
- Take the bacon out, pat dry and discard liquids.
- Cook bacon in a pan till crispy. Take out on paper towels.
- Let the Kalorik Air Fryer Oven preheat to 350 F.
- Cut the dough into eight rolls, save the icing.
- Roll the dough pieces into strips (6 by 1 inch). Put one bacon strip in each dough piece.
- Roll into a spiral just like cinnamon buns. Seal the edges.
- Place on the air fryer tray and air fry for five minutes.
- Flip and cook for 4 more minutes.
- In a bowl, mix maple syrup and pecans.
- In another bowl, mix the icing packet with ginger.
- Cook the pecan mixture on medium flame and cook for 2 to 3 minutes.

- Serve the buns with icing and pecans on top.
Cal 267 | Fat 14g | Carb 28g | Protein 5g

## MUSHROOM FRITTATA

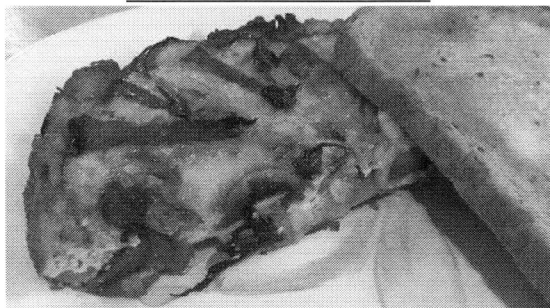

*Prep time: 10 min | Cook time: 13 min | Serves: 1*

### Ingredients
- 1 cup egg whites
- 1 cup spinach, chopped
- 2 mushrooms, sliced
- 2 tbsp parmesan cheese, grated
- Salt

### Directions
- Sprinkle pan with cooking spray and heat over medium heat. Add mushrooms and sauté for 2-3 minutes. Add spinach and cook for 1-2 minutes or until wilted.
- Transfer mushroom spinach mixture into the baking pan. Beat egg whites in a mixing bowl until frothy. Season it with a pinch of salt.
- Pour egg white mixture into the spinach and mushroom mixture and sprinkle with parmesan cheese. Place pan in air fryer and cook frittata at 350°F for 8 minutes
- Slice and serve.

Cal 176 | Fat 3g | Carb 4g | Protein 31 g

## BROCCOLI STUFFED PEPPERS

*Prep time: 10 min | Cook time: 40 min | Serves: 2*

### Ingredients
- 4 eggs
- 1/2 cup cheddar cheese, grated
- 2 bell peppers cut in half and remove seeds
- 1/2 tsp garlic powder
- 1 tsp dried thyme
- 1/4 cup feta cheese, crumbled
- 1/2 cup broccoli, cooked
- 1/4 tsp pepper
- 1/2 tsp salt

### Directions
- Preheat the Kalorik Air Fryer Oven to 325°F.
- Stuff feta and broccoli into the bell peppers halved.
- Beat egg in a bowl with seasoning and pour egg mixture into the pepper halved over feta and broccoli.
- Place bell pepper halved into your air fryer oven and cook for 35-40 minutes
- Top with grated cheddar cheese and cook until cheese melted.
- Serve and enjoy.

Cal 340 | Fat 22g | Carb 12g | Protein 22 g

## SAUSAGE, PEPPERS, & ONIONS

*Prep time:5 min | Cook time:10 min | Serves: 4*

### Ingredients
- Sausage: 1 lb.
- Olive Oil: 2 tbsp.
- 1 Onion, thinly sliced
- 1 Bell Pepper, thinly sliced

### Instructions
- Let the Kalorik Air Fryer Oven preheat to 400 F on the air fryer.
- Coat the vegetable in olive oil.
- On the tray, arrange the vegetables and sausage.
- Air fry for ten minutes. Toss halfway through.
- Cut in half to check if it's cooked through.
- Serve with buns.

Cal 101 | Carb 3g | Protein 8g | Fat 7g

## PIZZA DOUGH CINNAMON ROLLS

*Prep time:5 min | Cook time:10 min | Serves: 8*

### Ingredients
- Cinnamon: 2 tsp.
- Powdered sugar: 2 tsp.
- Brown sugar: 1/4 cup
- 1 pizza dough

### Instructions
- Roll the pizza dough into a rectangle.
- Melt the brown sugar with cinnamon for 20 seconds in the microwave.
- Let the Kalorik Air Fryer Oven preheat to 400 F with Bake.
- Spread the mixture on the pizza dough and roll. Cut them into small pieces, and place them on the air fryer tray.
- Bake in the Kalorik Air Fryer Oven for seven minutes, till golden brown. Add powdered sugar on top and serve.

Cal 150 | Carb 31g | Protein 4g | Fat 2g

## EGG, HAM, AND CHEESE BREAKFAST BISCUITS

*Prep time:5 min | Cook time:8 min | Serves: 4*

### Ingredients
- Salt & pepper: half tsp. each
- Ham: 2 slices (halved)
- Milk: 1 tbsp.
- Cheese: 1 slice, cut into fours
- 2 eggs
- biscuits from the vewccan: 4

### Instructions
- Preheat the Air Fryer to 350 F. Place the rack in the centre.
- Cook 4 biscuits on the rack for 8 minutes, flipping halfway through.
- Cook the egg in the microwave.
- Assemble the sandwiches until the biscuits are done: biscuit, ham, bacon, and cheese.

Cal 288 | Carb 29g | Protein 11g | Fat 15g

## HARD BOILED EGGS

*Prep time:1 min | Cook time:9 min | Serves: 1*

### Ingredients
- 2 large eggs

### Instructions
- Preheat your Kalorik Air Fryer Oven to BAKE mode at 300 F.

- Place the eggs in the middle of a rack. Cooking time for soft-boiled eggs is 7 minutes and for hard-boiled eggs is 9 minutes.
- Remove the eggs from the shells and put them in cold water.

Cal 63 | Carb 1g | Protein 6g | Fat 4g

## BLUEBERRY MUFFINS

*Prep time:10 min | Cook time:15 min | Serves: 12*

**Ingredients**

- Whole wheat flour 1 1/2 cups
- Old-fashioned oats 3/4 cup
- Brown sweetener 1/2 cup
- Baking powder 1 tbsp.
- Cinnamon 1/2 tsp.
- Salt 1/2 tsp.
- Milk 1 cup
- Melted unsalted butter 1/4 cup (at room temp)
- Eggs 2 (at room temp)
- Vanilla 2 tsp.
- Blueberries 1 cup

**Instructions**

- Add the flour, salt, cinnamon, rolled oats, brown sugar, and baking powder in a bowl and mix.
- Add the milk, vanilla, eggs, and butter to another bowl. Mix with a spoon.
- In the mixing bowl, combine the wet and dry ingredients. Mix it a little.
- Fold in the blueberries.
- Pour the batter into 12 silicone muffin cups and place them in the air fryer.
- Preheat the fryer to 350°F. Muffins will take 11 to 15 minutes to bake. Place a toothpick into the middle of a muffin; if it comes out clean, the muffins are finished baking.

Cal 127 | Protein 2.2g | Carb 24g | Fat 2.6g

## OMELET EGG BITES

*Prep time:10 min | Cook time:13 min | Serves: 12*

**Ingredients**

- 4 eggs
- Diced bell peppers: 1/4 cup
- Milk: half cup
- Salt: 1 tsp.
- Diced ham: 1/4 cup
- Black pepper: half tsp.
- Shredded cheese: 1/4 cup

**Instructions**

- In a bowl, add eggs and the rest of the ingredients, mix well.
- Oil spray a silicone muffin mold.
- Pour the mixture into the cups.
- Let the air fryer heat to 350 F, place the mold in the air fryer.
- Air fry for ten minutes, flip and air fry for three minutes more.
- Serve right away.

Cal 127 | Protein 2.2g | Carb 24g | Fat 2.6g

## FRENCH BREAD PIZZA

*Prep time:10 min | Cook time:7 min | Serves: 12*

**Ingredients**

- 1 jar of pizza sauce
- Pepperonis: ¼ cup, quartered
- 1 loaf of French Bread

- Butter: ¼ cup
- mozzarella cheese: 1 cup
- 1 minced garlic clove

**Instructions**

- In a bowl, melt the butter. Add garlic.
- Cut the loaf lengthwise and in half to get a total of four pieces.
- Brush the bread with melted butter.
- Preheat the Kalorik Air Fryer Oven to 400 F.
- Air fry the bread for four minutes. Take out and spread toppings on top.
- Put back in the air fryer and exchange position of the trays with each other.
- Serve right away.

Cal 127 | Protein 2.2g | Carb 24g | Fat 2.6g

## STRAWBERRY FRENCH TOAST BAKE

*Prep time:75 min | Cook time:25 min | Serves: 8*

**Ingredients**

- Vanilla extract: 2 tsp.
- Brioche bread loaf: 1 lb.
- Butter: 4 tsp.
- 8 eggs
- Milk: 2 cups
- Cinnamon: 1 tsp.
- Brown sugar: 2 tbsp.
- Fresh strawberries: 8 oz., quartered
- Heavy cream: 1 cup

**Instructions**

- In a baking dish, add chunks of brioche.
- In a bowl, add the rest of the ingredients except for strawberries.
- Pour the mixture over bread. Cover with foil and cool in the fridge for 1-12 hours.
- Take the tray out and add strawberries to the dish. Cover with foil and bake in the Kalorik Air Fryer Oven for 20 minutes. uncover and bake for 5 to 10 more minutes.
- Serve with syrup.

Cal 407 | Protein 14 g | Carb 37 g | Fat 23 g

## PEACH TURNOVERS

*Prep time:20 min | Cook time:10 min | Serves: 6*

**Ingredients**

- Peaches chopped: 10 oz.
- Sugar: 3 tbsp.
- Lemon juice: 1 tbsp.
- Pie crust: 14 oz., 2 crusts
- Vanilla: 1 tsp.
- Salt: 1/4 tsp.

- Cornstarch: 1 tsp.

**Instructions**

- In a bowl, add peaches, sugar (2 tbsp.), vanilla, lemon juice and salt. Mix and let it rest for 15 minutes.
- Drain all but one tbsp. of peach liquids. Add sugar and cornstarch and mix.
- Slice pie crust into four pieces to get a total of 8 pieces. Add the peach filling and seal the edges with water, make into triangle shapes. With a fork, poke holes in the turnovers.
- Air fry at the bottom for ten minutes at 350 F. Do not turn the food.
- Serve with powdered sugar on top.

## FRIED CHICKEN AND WAFFLES

*Prep time: 10 min | Cook time: 30 min | Serves: 4*

**Ingredients**

- 8 whole chicken wings
- 1 teaspoon garlic powder
- Chicken seasoning or rub
- Pepper
- ½ cup all-purpose flour
- Cooking oil
- 8 frozen waffles
- Maple syrup (optional)

**Directions**

- In a medium bowl, spice the chicken with the garlic powder and chicken seasoning and pepper to flavor.
- Put the chicken to a sealable plastic bag and add the flour. Shake to thoroughly coat the chicken.
- Sprinkle the air fryer basket with cooking oil.
- With the use of tongs, put the chicken from the bag to your air fryer oven. It is okay to pile the chicken wings on top of each other. Sprinkle them with cooking oil. Heat for five minutes
- Unlock the air fryer and shake the basket. Presume to cook the chicken. Keep shaking every 5 minutes until 20 minutes has passed and the chicken is completely cooked.
- Take out the cooked chicken from the air fryer and set aside.
- Wash the basket and base out with warm water. Put them back to the Air Fryer.
- Ease the temperature of the air fryer to 370°F.
- Put the frozen waffles in the air fryer. Do not pile. Depends on how big your air fryer is, you may need to cook the waffles in batches. Sprinkle the waffles with cooking oil. Cook for 6 minutes
- If necessary, take out the cooked waffles from the air fryer, then repeat step 9 for the leftover waffles.
- Serve the waffles with the chicken and a bit of maple syrup if desired.

Cal 461 | Fat 22g | Carb 45g | Protein 28g

## BACON CRESCENT ROLLS

*Prep time:10 min | Cook time:10 min | Serves: 8*

**Ingredients**

- Onion powder: 1 tsp.
- Crescent rolls: 8 oz.
- 6 cooked bacon strips, crumbled

**Instructions**

- Let the Kalorik Air Fryer Oven preheat to 350 F. Cut the dough into eight triangles.
- Toss the bacon with onion powder. Save the 1 tbsp. of bacon.
- Add the rest to the triangles and roll. Add 1 tbsp. of bacon on top and press into the dough.
- Air fry for 8 to 10 minutes' points side down. Serve right away.

Cal 133 | Protein 4 g | Carb 12 g | Fat 7 g

## MINI LOAF CHERRY CAKES

*Prep time:10 min | Cook time:22 min | Serves: 3-4*

**Ingredients**

- Baking powder: ¾ tsp.
- 2 eggs
- Vanilla extract: 1 tsp.
- Butter: half cup, softened
- Cherries: 1 cup, chopped
- All-purpose flour: 1 cup plus 2 tbsp.
- Cream cheese: 4 oz., softened
- Granulated sugar: ¾ cup
- Lemon extract: half tsp.

**Vanilla glaze**

- Vanilla extract: half tsp.
- Confectioner's sugar: 1 cup
- Milk: 2-3 tbsp.

**Instructions**

- In a bowl, add flour, baking powder and mix.
- In another bowl, add cream cheese and butter and mix. Add eggs gradually and beat.
- Add lemon extract, sugar and vanilla.
- Gradually add flour mixture and mix, fold in cherries.
- Take four mini loaf pans and oil spray.
- Bake at 300 F in the Kalorik Air Fryer Oven for 20 minutes.
- Check the doneness with a toothpick.
- In a bowl, add all ingredients of glaze, pour over mini loaves and serve.

Cal 407 | Protein 14 g | Carb 37 g | Fat 23 g

## BLACKBERRY PIES

*Prep time:15 min | Cook time:15 min | Serves: 3-4*

**Ingredients**

**Dough**

- Baking soda: 1/4 tsp.
- Vegetable oil: half cup
- Buttermilk: 1/3 cup
- Salt: 1/4 tsp.
- Flour: 2 cups

**Filling**

- Sugar: half cup
- Nutmeg: half tsp.

- Water: half cup
- Blackberries: 2 cups
- Cornstarch: 1 tbsp.
- Lemon juice: 1 tbsp.
- Cinnamon: 3/4 tsp.

**Instructions**

- In a bowl, add flour, salt and baking soda.
- In another bowl, add oil and buttermilk.
- Mix the wet into dry ingredients. Mix with hands until dough forms.
- Roll into ¼" of thickness.
- With a four-inch biscuit cutter, cut all the dough into circles.
- In a pan, add spices, cornstarch, lemon juice, sugar and water on medium flame.
- Add blackberries. Keep mixing and Let it come to a boil. Turn the heat off and let it cool.
- In each biscuit pie, add 1 tbsp. of blackberry filling and fold in half.
- Seal the edges.
- Preheat the Kalorik Air Fryer Oven to 350 F.
- Bake for five minutes on each side.
- Serve right away with a glaze on top.

## BREAKFAST PIZZA
*Prep time:5 min | Cook time:6 min | Serves: 4*

**Ingredients**

- 2 eggs
- Gravy: 4 tbsp.
- Mexican Cheese: 1/4 cup
- Biscuits: half can roll flat
- Smoked Sausage: 1/4 cup

**Instructions**

- Let the Kalorik Air Fryer Oven preheat to 390 F. Cook the eggs.
- Place biscuits on the tray and bake for five minutes, flip once.
- Add toppings (gravy first) and bake for 1 minute more,
- Serve right away.

Cal 318 | Carb 29g | Protein 10g | Fat 18g

## BREAKFAST CROQUETTES
*Prep time:30 min | Cook time:15 min | Serves: 6*

**Ingredients**

- Butter: 3 tbsp.
- All-purpose flour: 3 tbsp.
- Milk: 3/4 cup
- Chopped fresh asparagus: half cup
- Shredded cheddar cheese: 1/3 cup
- Chopped fresh tarragon: 1 tbsp.
- 3 eggs, whisked
- 1/4 tsp. Salt & pepper each
- Chopped green onions: half cup
- 6 eggs, boiled & chopped
- Panko bread crumbs: 1 to 3/4 cups

**Instructions**

- In a pan, on medium flame. Add butter and flour, cook for 1 to 2 minutes.
- Slowly add milk, and whisk until thickens. Add green onions, boiled eggs, tarragon, salt, cheese, asparagus and pepper. Mix and keep in the fridge for two hours.

- Let the Kalorik Air Fryer Oven preheat to 350 F.
- Make the mixture into small bites. In 2 bowls, add eggs and bread crumbs.
- Coat the bites in eggs then in crumbs.
- Oil spray the air fryer tray and place the coated bites. Oil spray the bites
- Air fry for 8 to 10 minutes, flip and spray with oil. Cook for 3 to 5 minutes more.
- Serve with spicy ketchup.

Cal 294 | Fat 17g | Carb18g | Protein 15 g

## SPINACH FRITTATA

*Prep time: 5 min | Cook time: 8 min | Serves: 1*

**Ingredients**

- 3 eggs
- 1 cup spinach, chopped
- 1 small onion, minced
- 2 tbsp mozzarella cheese, grated
- Pepper
- Salt

**Directions**

- Preheat the Kalorik Air Fryer Oven to 350°F. Spray air fryer pan with cooking spray.
- In a bowl, whisk eggs with remaining ingredients until well combined.
- Pour egg mixture into the prepared pan and place pan in the air fryer.
- Cook frittata for 8 minutes or until set. Serve and enjoy.

Cal 384 | Fat 23g | Carb 11g | Protein 34g

## CLASSIC HASH BROWNS
*Prep time: 15 min | Cook time: 20 min | Serves: 4*

**Ingredients**

- 4 russet potatoes
- 1 teaspoon paprika
- Salt
- Pepper
- Cooking oil

**Directions**

- Peel the potatoes using a vegetable peeler. Using a cheese grater shred the potatoes. If your grater has different-size holes, use the area of the tool with the largest holes.
- Put the shredded potatoes in a large bowl of cold water. Let sit for 5 minutes Cold water helps remove excess starch from the potatoes. Stir to help dissolve the starch.
- Dry out the potatoes and dry with paper towels or napkins. Make sure the potatoes are completely dry.
- Season the potatoes with the paprika and salt and pepper to taste.

- Spray the potatoes with cooking oil and transfer them to your air fryer oven. Cook for 20 minutes and shake the basket every 5 minutes (a total of 4 times).
- Cool before serving.

Cal 150 | Carb 34g | Fiber 5g | Protein 4g

## BREAKFAST SAUSAGE

*Prep time:2 min | Cook time:5 min | Serves: 2-3*

**Ingredients**

- Breakfast sausage: 3 to 4

**Instructions**

- Let the Kalorik Air Fryer Oven preheat to 329 F. Select air fry.
- Crumble the sausage and place it on the tray.
- Put tray at the bottom.
- Air fry for 4 to 5 minutes.
- Serve right away.

Cal 156 | Carb 21g | Protein 6g | Fat 8 g

## SWEET POTATO HASH BROWNS

*Prep time:40 min | Cook time:20 min | Serves: 4*

**Ingredients**

- Paprika: 1 tsp.
- 4 peeled sweet potatoes
- Olive oil: 2 tsp.
- 2 minced garlic cloves
- Cinnamon: 1 tsp.
- Salt & pepper to taste

**Instructions**

- Grate the potatoes in cold water. Let it rest for 20 to 25 minutes.
- Drain and completely dry the sweet potatoes on paper towels.
- In a bowl, add dried potatoes and toss with the rest of the ingredients.
- Let the Kalorik Air Fryer Oven preheat to 400 F.
- Place the potatoes in the air fryer, cook on air fry for ten minutes.
- Shake the tray and air fry for another 10 minutes.
- Serve right away.

Cal 134 | Fat 1g | Carb 23g | Protein 2g

## GRILLED CHEESE SANDWICH

*Prep time:5 min | Cook time:5 min | Serves: 1*

**Ingredients**

- Bread: 2 slices
- Turkey: 2 slices
- Butter: 1 tsp.
- Cheddar cheese: 2 slices

**Instructions**

- Preheat the Kalorik Air Fryer Oven to 350 F.
- Spread the butter on the surface of the loaf. If using, top with cheese and turkey, then top with another buttered bread slice.
- Place the sandwich inside the Air Fryer. Set a timer for 5 minutes. Flip halfway through.
- Serve right away.

Cal 346 | Fat 19g | Carb 31.6g | Protein 12g

## VEGGIE BALLS

*Prep time:5 min | Cook time:12 min | Serves: 4*

**Ingredients**

- Desiccated Coconut: half Cup
- Gluten-Free Oats 1 Cup
- Salt and Pepper, to taste
- Cauliflower: 7 oz.
- Sweet Potato: 3.5 oz.
- Carrot: 2.5 oz.
- Parsnips: 3 oz.
- Garlic Puree: 2 tsp.
- Chives: 1 tsp.
- Paprika: 1 tsp.
- Mixed Spice: 1 tsp.
- Oregano: 2 tsp.

**Instructions**

- Steam the vegetables.
- Place the cooked vegetables in a clean tea towel and squeeze out any excess water.
- In a mixing bowl, arrange them and season them. Blend thoroughly and roll into medium-sized balls.
- Place them in the fridge for 2 hours to allow them to firm up a little.
- In a mixer, combine the coconut and gluten-free oats and whizz until it resembles hard flour. Add it to a bowl.
- Roll the veggie balls in the mixture and place them in the air fryer tray.
- Bake for ten minutes at 400 F.
- Cook for another two minutes at the same temperature on the other side.

Cal 437 | Carb 64g | Protein 22g | Fat 12g

## SCRAMBLED EGGS

*Prep time:3 min | Cook time:9 min | Serves: 2*

**Ingredients**

- 2 eggs
- Cheddar cheese: 1/8 cup
- Milk: 2 tbsp.
- Unsalted butter: 1/3 tbsp.
- Salt & pepper to taste

**Instructions**

- Melt the butter.
- Whisk the eggs with milk and season with salt and pepper.
- In a pan, add eggs and butter. Bake in the Kalorik Air Fryer Oven for three minutes at 300 F.
- Take out and stir them.
- Cook for two minutes, add cheese and stir again.
- Air fry for two more minutes and serve.

Cal 126 | Fat 9g | Carb 1g | Protein 9g

## BREAKFAST DUMPLINGS

*Prep time:10 min | Cook time:10 min | Serves: 2*

**Ingredients**

- Swiss cheese: 1 tbsp.

- Wonton wrappers: 8
- Crumbled cooked bacon: 1 tbsp.
- Salt, to taste
- Egg whites: half cup

**Instructions**

- In a microwave-safe mug, add egg, salt and cheese. Microwave for 1 ½ minute until cheese melts and eggs are set.
- Add bacon and let it cool for five minutes. Add this mixture to each of the wrappers. Seal the edges with water.
- In the air fryer tray, place the dumplings and air fry for five minutes at 375 F, until crispy and golden.

## CHERRY TURNOVERS
*Prep time:15 min | Cook time:10 min | Serves: 8*

**Ingredients**

- Water: 2 tbsp.
- Cherry pie filling: 1 can (10 oz.)
- Puff pastry: 4 sheets
- 1 egg, whisked

**Instructions**

- Roll the puff pastry and cut it into four squares to get a total of 8 pieces.
- Whisk the egg with water. Brush the pastry edges with egg wash.
- Add 1-1 ½ tbsp. of cherry filling in the centre of the square. Fold into triangles.
- Make three cuts on the top of turnovers. Brush the top with egg wash.
- Preheat the Kalorik Air Fryer Oven to 370 F.
- Cook the turnovers for 8 minutes, do not flip.
- Cool for 2 to 3 minutes and serve.

## PUMPKIN SPICE MUFFINS
*Prep time:10 min | Cook time:10 min | Serves: 2*

**Ingredients**

- Flour: 1 Cup
- Pumpkin puree: ⅓ Cup
- Sugar: ⅓ Cup
- Vanilla extract: 1 tsp.
- Baking powder: 1 tsp.
- Oil: 3 tbsp.
- Pumpkin spice: 1 tbsp.
- 1 Egg
- Milk: ¼ Cup

**Instructions**

- In a bowl, add dry ingredients.
- In another bowl, add the wet ingredients and mix
- Add the wet to dry ingredients and mix well.
- Pour the batter into muffin cups.
- Let the Kalorik Air Fryer Oven preheat to 360 F on bake.
- Bake the muffins for 10-12 minutes.
- Serve warm.

## CINNAMON SUGAR DONUTS
*Prep time:5 min | Cook time:16 min | Serves: 8*

**Ingredients**

- Stevia: 1-2 tsp.
- Biscuits (canned): 8 oz.
- Ground cinnamon: 1 tsp.

**Instructions**

- Roll the biscuits and cut the centre with a small cookie cutter.
- Place the donuts in the preheated air fryer.
- Cook for four minutes at 360 F.
- On a plate, mix the cinnamon with stevia.
- Coat the warm donuts in a sugar mixture.
- Serve warm.

Cal 186 | Fat 9g | Carb 25g | Protein 3g

## AIR FRYER BAGELS
*Prep time:10 min | Cook time:15 min | Serves: 2*

**Ingredients**

- 1 egg white, whisked
- Plain Greek yogurt: 5.3 oz.
- Self-rising flour: half cup
- Salt: 1/4 tsp.

**Instructions**

- In a bowl, whisk salt and flour. Add yogurt and mix with a fork until dough forms.
- Knead dough on a floured surface until slightly tacky. Cut the dough in half.
- Make each portion into one" thick ropes and make it into a bagel.
- With the egg white, brush the bagels.
- Place bagels on the Kalorik Air Fryer Oven tray and bake for 15 minutes at 280 F.
- Serve warm.

## BREAKFAST SWEET POTATO SKINS
*Prep time:7 min | Cook time:23 min | Serves: 4*

**Ingredients**

- Olive oil: 2 tsp.
- 4 eggs
- 2 green onions, thinly sliced
- Whole milk: 1/4 cup
- Sweet potatoes: 2 medium
- Salt & pepper, to taste
- Cooked bacon: 4 slices

**Instructions**

- Make 3 to 4 cuts on the potatoes, microwave for 6 to 8 minutes, till they are soft.
- Cut the potatoes in half and take the flesh out; leave 1/4th of skin behind.
- Brush the skins with olive oil and add salt. Air fry in a preheated air fryer for ten minutes at 400 F.
- In a skillet, add milk, egg, salt and pepper, cook until eggs are set.
- In each skin, add the cooked egg mixture and crumbled bacon. Add cheese on top and air fry for three minutes.
- Serve with green onions on top.

Cal 208 | Fat 12g | Carb 14g | Protein 12g

## PEACH BREAD
*Prep time:7 min | Cook time:35 min | Serves: 4*

**Ingredients**

- Baking soda: 1 tsp.
- Vegetable oil: 1/3 cup
- Cinnamon: 1 tsp.
- Salt: 1/4 tsp.

- Flour: 1 1/2 cups
- Sugar: half cup
- 3 eggs
- 1 peach, diced with skin
- Baking powder: 1 tsp.

**Glaze**
- Milk: 2 tbsp.
- Powdered sugar: ⅓ cup

**Instructions**
- Let the Kalorik Air Fryer Oven preheat to 350 F to Bake.
- In a bowl, add all wet ingredients and sugar.
- In a bowl, add dry ingredients and mix.
- Add the wet ingredients to dry and mix until batter forms.
- Add diced peaches. Oil spray a loaf pan and pour the batter.
- Bake for 35 minutes at 350 F. cover with foil if tops become brown and not cooked yet.
- In a bowl, add all ingredients of glaze and mix.
- Pour over the bread and serve warm.

## BREAKFAST COOKIES
*Prep time:20 min | Cook time:10 min | Serves: 6*

**Ingredients**
- Old-fashioned oats: 1 cup
- Honey: half cup
- Chunky peanut butter: half cup
- Ground cinnamon: 2 tsp.
- Vanilla extract: 1 tsp.
- Whole wheat flour: half cup
- Mashed ripe bananas: 1 cup
- Milk powder: 1/4 cup
- Salt: half tsp.
- Baking soda: 1/4 tsp.
- Dried cranberries: 1 cup

**Instructions**
- Let the Kalorik Air Fryer Oven preheat to 300 F.
- In a blender, add honey, banana, vanilla and peanut butter.
- In another bowl, add the rest of the ingredients, except for dried cranberries, and mix into a banana mixture. Add dried cranberries.
- Oil spray the air fryer tray and add dollops of dough and flatten slightly.
- Bake for 6 to 8 minutes, until lightly browned.
- Cool and serve.

Cal 212 | Fat 6g | Carb 38g | Protein 5g

## BREAKFAST FRITTATA
*Prep time:10 min | Cook time:16 min | Serves: 2*

**Ingredients**
- 4 Eggs
- Salt & Pepper, to taste
- Feta crumbled: 1.7 oz.
- Milk: 4 tbsp.
- 1 Tomato, chopped without seeds
- Spinach chopped: 0.5 oz.
- Cheddar Cheese grated: 1.2 oz.
- Olive Oil: half tsp.
- Fresh Herbs: 1 tbsp., chopped

- 2 Spring Onion chopped

**Instructions**
- In a bowl, whisk eggs with milk.
- Add the rest of the ingredients, except for oil and whisk.
- Let the Kalorik Air Fryer Oven preheat to 350 F.
- Oil spray a spring foam that will fit in the air fryer and place baking paper inside.
- Pour the mixture into the pan and air fry for 16 minutes. Check after 12 minutes.
- Let it cool for five minutes' slice and serve. Cover with foil if it starts to get brown.

## SCOTCH EGGS W/ SMOKED SAUSAGE
*Prep time:5 min | Cook time:10 min | Serves: 12*

**Ingredients**
- Pork rinds: half cup
- 12 eggs
- Smoked Sausage: half lb.

**Instructions**
- Boil the eggs for ten minutes.
- In a food processor, add the sausage.
- Let the Kalorik Air Fryer Oven preheat to 390 F.
- Add bread crumbs to the sausage and mix.
- Roll the eggs in the sausage mixture, and wrap.
- Air fry for six minutes at the middle position. Flip hallway through.
- Cook until browned.
- Serve with sauce.

Cal 126 | Carb 1g | Protein 9g | Fat 10g

## SAUSAGE BREAKFAST CASSEROLE

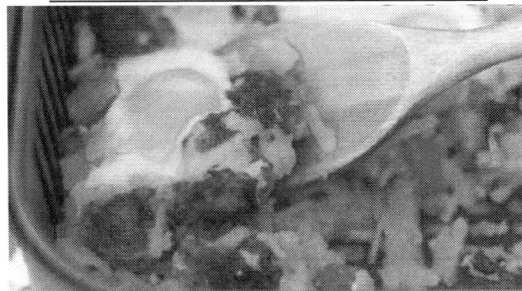

*Prep time:15 min | Cook time:20 min | Serves: 4*

**Ingredients**
- Hash Browns: 1 lb.
- Ground Breakfast Sausage: 1 lb.
- 1 each of Green, red, yellow Bell Peppers, Diced
- Onion: 1/4 Cup, Diced
- 4 Eggs

**Instructions**
- Foil two air fryer safe pan.
- Place hash browns on the bottom, place sausage on top in the same pan.
- Add onions, peppers on top.
- Air fry for ten minutes at 335 F.
- Toss the content if needed, for even cooking.
- In each pan, add eggs.
- Cook for ten minutes more
- Season with salt and pepper and serve.

## VEGAN BREAKFAST HASH BROWNS
*Prep time:15 min | Cook time:15 min | Serves: 4*

### Ingredients
- Chili flakes: 2 tsp.
- Corn flour: 2 tbsp.
- Salt, to taste
- 4 peeled potatoes, grated
- Vegetable Oil: 2 tsp.
- Pepper, to taste
- Garlic & garlic powder: 1 tsp. each

### Instructions
- Grate the potatoes in cold water, drain and dry on paper towels.
- In a pan, sauté the grated potatoes in 1 tsp. of oil for 3 to 4 minutes.
- Take out on a plate and cool.
- Add the rest of the ingredients to the potatoes. Mix well.
- Spread in a pan, and keep in the fridge for 20 minutes.
- Let the Kalorik Air Fryer Oven preheat to 356 F.
- Oil spray the potatoes and air fry for 10 to 15 minutes.
- Serve warm.

## CANDIED BACON
*Prep time:5 min | Cook time:8 min | Serves: 12*

### Ingredients
- Honey: 6 tbsp.
- Butter: 1 tbsp.
- Thick-cut bacon: 8 oz.
- White miso paste: 1/4 cup
- Rice wine vinegar: 1 tbsp.

### Instructions
- Let the Kalorik Air Fryer Oven preheat to 390 F.
- In a pan, add butter over medium flame. Melt and add the rest of the ingredients except for bacon; mix well on medium-high heat. Let it come to a boil; turn off the heat.
- Place bacon in the tray of the air fryer in one even layer. Air fry for 3 to 4 minutes.
- Brush with the glaze on cook for 1 minute.
- Serve with eggs.

Cal 131 | Carb 10g | Protein 3g | Fat 9g

## CHEESY BAKED EGGS
*Prep time:4 min | Cook time:16 min | Serves: 2*

### Ingredients
- Salt & pepper to taste
- 4 eggs
- Bagel (everything) seasoning, to taste
- Smoked gouda: 2 oz., chopped

### Instructions
- Oil spray 2 ramekins. Add two eggs in each ramekin, add gouda, salt, pepper equally in each.
- Add bagel seasoning on top.
- Air fry for 16 minutes at 400 F.
- Serve right away.

Cal 240 | Carb 1g | Protein 12g | Fat 16g

## BLUEBERRY BREAD
*Prep time:5 min | Cook time:30 min | Serves: 2-6*

### Ingredients
- Frozen blueberries: 1 ½ cups

- Bisquick: 3 cups
- Milk: 1 cup | Protein powder: ¼ cup
- 3 eggs

### Instructions
- In a bowl, add all ingredients and mix.
- Pour into a loaf pan.
- Let the Kalorik Air Fryer Oven preheat to 350 F on bake.
- Bake the bread for half an hour.
- Slice and serve.

Cal 140 | Total Fat 5g | Carb 18g | Protein 2 g

## PEANUT BUTTER & JELLY PANCAKE BAKE
*Prep time:5 min | Cook time:15 min | Serves: 2-4*

### Ingredients
- Peanut butter: 2 tbsp.
- Jelly/ jam: 2 tbsp.
- Pancake mix: 1 cup

### Instructions
- Microwave the jam and peanut butter for ten seconds in two different bowls.
- Let the Kalorik Air Fryer Oven preheat to 350 F on Bake.
- Make the pancake mix as per instructions on the pack.
- Take a cheesecake tin and spray with oil. Pour the pancake mixture.
- Add jam and peanut butter on top. Swirl the design as you want.
- Bake in the air fryer for ten minutes. Slice and serve.

Cal 138 | Carb 16g | Protein 5g | Fat 7g

## MONTE CRISTO SANDWICH
*Prep time:15 min | Cook time:10 min | Serves: 4*

### Ingredients
- Pancake mix: 1 cup
- Milk: half cup
- 1 egg
- Cheese Swiss: 16 slices
- Bread: 8 slices
- Water: 1/4 cup
- Ham: 16 slices

### Instructions
- Let the Kalorik Air Fryer Oven preheat to 380 F.
- In a bowl, add egg, water, milk and pancake mix. Mix well.
- On each bread, add cheese (2 slices), ham (4 slices), cheese (2 slices on top), and another slice of bread.
- Secure with toothpicks.
- Coat the sandwich in the batter, drip off excess batter.
- Place on the lined air fryer tray, air fry for seven minutes. Change the temperature to 360 F, flip and air fry on the other side.
- Take out from air fryer and serve right away.

Cal 980 | Fat 62g | Carb 40g | Protein 63g

## CHEDDAR BISCUITS
*Prep time:10 min | Cook time:15 min | Serves: 6*

### Ingredients
- Water: 1 1/3 cups
- Bisquik: 2 cups
- Cheddar cheese: 3/4 cup, shredded

**Topping Mixture:**
- garlic powder: half tsp.
- dried parsley: 1/8 tsp.

- dried parsley: 1/8 tsp.
- kosher salt: 1/8 tsp.
- butter melted: 3 tbsp.
- onion powder: 1/8 tsp.

**Instructions**

- In a bowl, add water, cheese and baking mix, mix into a dough.
- Line the trays with parchment paper and divide them into six places.
- Let the Kalorik Air Fryer Oven preheat to 320 F with a bake
- Place the trays in the air fryer.
- Do not turn the food.
- In a bowl, add all mixture toppings and mix.
- Brush the biscuits with toppings and serve with eggs.

## AIR FRYER GRANOLA

*Prep time:5 min | Cook time:40 min | Serves: 6*

**Ingredients**

- Olive Oil: 1/3 cup
- Rolled oats: 2 3/4 cup
- Maple syrup: 1/3 cup
- Mixed nuts: 1 cup
- Unsweetened coconut chips: 1 cup
- Light brown sugar: half cup
- Dried fruit: 3/4 cup
- Pumpkin seeds: 1/3 cup
- Sea salt: 1 tbsp.

**Instructions**

- Select 165 F and dehydrate in the air fryer, place the tray at the bottom.
- In the pan, add oil, syrup and sugar, heat until sugar dissolves.
- In a bowl, add the rest of the ingredients except for fruits.
- Add the liquid to the dry ingredients, mix well.
- In an air fryer-safe dish, spray with oil spray and spread the mixture.
- Dehydrate for 30 to 40 minutes. Stir every ten minutes.
- Add dried fruits and serve.

Cal 101 | Carb 3g | Protein 8g | Fat 7g

## MINI EGG, HAM, & CHEESE QUICHE

*Prep time:5 min | Cook time:26 min | Serves: 4-6*

**Ingredients**

- Milk: 2 tbsp.
- Cheese: half cup
- Diced ham: half cup
- 4 eggs
- Bread: 1 slice, chopped

- Salt & pepper, to taste

**Instructions**

- Let the Kalorik Air Fryer Oven preheat to 350 F with Bake.
- In a bowl, add all ingredients and mix.
- Pour this mixture into air fryer safe cups and distribute equally.
- Cover with foil and bake for 20 minutes; take the foil off and cover for five minutes.
- Serve right away.

Cal 106 | Carb 3g | Protein 8g | Fat 7g

## CHEESY BREAKFAST EGG ROLLS

*Prep time:30 min | Cook time:10 min | Serves: 12*

**Ingredients**

- Bulk pork sausage: half pound
- Pepper, to taste
- Cheddar cheese: half cup, shredded
- Salt: ¼ tsp.
- Green onions: 1 tbsp., chopped
- 4 eggs
- Monterey jack cheese: half cup, shredded
- Milk: 1 tbsp.
- Butter: 1 tbsp.
- Egg roll wrappers: 12

**Instructions**

- In a skillet, cook sausage for 4 to 6 minutes, drain. Add green onions and cheese; set it aside.
- In a bowl, whisk eggs with pepper, milk and salt.
- Cook eggs until set, and no liquid is present. Add in the sausage mixture.
- Let the Kalorik Air Fryer Oven preheat to 400 F.
- In each wrapper, add egg and sausage filling and wrap like an egg roll.
- Place egg rolls in one even layer in the air fryer tray and oil spray them.
- Cook for 3 to 4 minutes. Serve with salsa.

Cal 209 | Fat 10g | Carb19g | Protein10g

## BANANA BREAD PIZZA

*Prep time:10 min | Cook time:25 min | Serves: 12*

**Ingredients**

- Baking powder: 1 1/2 tsp.
- Brown sugar: 1 cup
- Flour: 3 1/2 cups
- Baking soda: 1/4 tsp.
- Bananas: 3 ripe, mashed
- Cinnamon: 1 tbsp.
- Powdered sugar: 1 cup
- 1 egg

**Cream cheese layer**

- Sugar: 2/3 cup
- Cream cheese: 8 oz., softened

**Instructions**

- In a bowl, add all ingredients except for flour and powder sugar. Mix and add flour.
- Mix until stiff dough forms.
- Cut the dough in half, make each half into a ball. Roll into a disk with powder sugar to prevent sticking.
- Place these two discs in a larger square parchment paper.

- In a bowl, add cream cheese topping ingredients. Mix well.
- Spread this topping mixture on each ball of dough.
- Add nuts on top, if you like.
- Let the Kalorik Air Fryer Oven preheat to 350 F at Bake.
- Bake each disc for 15 minutes, and serve.

## BREAKFAST POCKETS
*Prep time:20 min | Cook time:10 min | Serves: 2*

### Ingredients
- Cheddar cheese: half cup, shredded
- 5 eggs
- Puff pastry sheets: 1 pack
- Bacon: half cup, cooked
- Sausage crumbles: half cup, cooked

### Instructions
- In a skillet, cook eggs as scrambled eggs, add meat and cook.
- Roll the puff pastry and cut it into rectangles.
- Add egg mixture and cheese in each rectangle. Fold the pockets.
- Oil spray the packets and place them on air fryer trays.
- Let the Kalorik Air Fryer Oven preheat to 370 F.
- Air fry the pockets for 8 to 10 minutes.
- Keep an eye on them and serve.

## FLOURLESS BROCCOLI QUICHE
*Prep time:15 min | Cook time:20 min | Serves: 4*

### Ingredients
- Pie Crust: 10.5 oz.
- 3 Eggs
- Cheddar Cheese: 10.5 oz., shredded
- Salt & Pepper, to taste
- Cherry Tomatoes: 4
- Mixed Herbs: 2 tsp.
- Milk: 2.5 oz.
- Oregano: 1 tbsp.

### Instructions
- Roll the pie crust and add mixed herbs on top, and roll.
- Place the crust in the ramekins.
- Whisk eggs with milk, salt and pepper.
- In each ramekin, add cheese, pour the egg mixture until 3/4 full.
- Slice the tomatoes in half and add cherry tomatoes to each ramekin.
- Add oregano and cheese on top.
- Let the Kalorik Air Fryer Oven preheat to 360 F.
- Place the ramekins on the air fryer trays and air fry for 8 minutes.
- Change the temperature to 320 F and air fry for ten minutes.
- Serve right away

Cal 715 | Carb 40g | Protein 29g | Fat 49g

## VEGETABLE FRITTATA
*Prep time:5 min | Cook time:18 min | Serves: 2*

### Ingredients
- Skim milk: 2 tbsp.
- Black pepper, to taste
- Sliced tomato: ¼ cup
- Egg whites: 1 cup
- Sliced mushrooms: ¼ cup
- Chopped fresh chives: 2 tbsp.

### Instructions

- Let the Kalorik Air Fryer Oven preheat to 320 F on bake.
- In a bowl, add all ingredients and mix.
- Oil spray an air fryer safe pan and pour the mixture in the pan.
- Bake for 15 minutes, until cooked completely.
- Serve right away.

Cal 156 | Carb 21 g | Protein 6g | Fat 8 g

## EGG MCMUFFIN
*Prep time:15 min | Cook time:18 min | Serves: 4*

### Ingredients
- 2 muffins
- 2 Eggs
- cheese: 2 slices
- Bacon: 2 slices

### Instructions
- Let the Kalorik Air Fryer Oven preheat to 400 F.
- Foil line the air fryer trays and place rings from the mason jar on the trays.
- Spray with oil.
- Add bacon and egg to each ring. Air fry for ten minutes' flip halfway through.
- Toast the muffins, assemble the McMuffin and serve.

Cal 662 | Fat 36g | Carb 61g | Protein 22g

## BACON & EGG BREAKFAST PASTRIES
*Prep time:5 min | Cook time:20 min | Serves: 4*

### Ingredients
- Cooked bacon: 4 slices & crumbled
- Puff pastry: 8 oz.
- Chopped parsley
- Any shredded cheese: 2/3 cup
- 4 eggs

### Instructions
- Slice the puff pastry into four squares, and place two pieces on the air fryer tray.
- Select air fryer and 390 F. Select time to ten minutes.
- Place the tray in the air fryer. Cook for five minutes, take the tray out and make depressions in the puff pastry center.
- Add one egg in each depression, sprinkle some of the bacon and cheese on the sides of the egg.
- Cook for five more minutes, serve right away.

Cal 156 | Carb 21 g | Protein 6g | Fat 8 g

## BREAKFAST QUICHE
*Prep time:15 min | Cook time:15 min | Serves: 2*

### Ingredients
- Bread: 1 slice
- Cheese: half cup
- Sausage: 1 piece
- Half Bell Pepper
- 4 Eggs, whisked
- Half Onion
- Salt and pepper: 1 tsp. each

### Instructions
- Preheat the air fryer to 350 F
- In a pan, sauté onion and peppers. Cut the bread into cubes
- Season the eggs with salt and pepper.
- Add bread to the eggs and soak for few minutes.

- Spray the air fryer trays with oil spray. In the eggs, add the rest of the ingredients.
- Mix and cover with foil tightly.
- Put in the Kalorik Air Fryer Oven and select 10 minutes or less.
- Take the foil off; if it needs more cooking, cook for another 5-10 minutes.

Cal 156 | Carb 21 g | Protein 6g | Fat 8 g

## SCOTTISH SHORTBREAD

*Prep time:15 min | Cook time:10 min | Serves: 24*

**Ingredients**
- All-purpose flour: 4 cups
- Butter: 2 cups, softened
- Packed brown sugar: 1 cup

**Instructions**
- Let the Kalorik Air Fryer Oven preheat to 290 F on bake.
- Cream the brown sugar and butter. Add flour and mix well.
- Knead with hands for five minutes. Add more flour if necessary to make a soft dough.
- Make into half" thickness, slice into strips and prick with a fork.
- In the air fryer, trays place in one even layer, with some distance in between.
- Bake for 7 to 9 minutes, cool, and serve

1 cookie: Cal 123 | 8g Fat | 12g Carb | 1g Protein

## GREEK BREADSTICKS

*Prep time:20 min | Cook time:15 min | Serves: 16*

**Ingredients**
- Artichoke hearts: 1/4 cup, marinated & quartered
- Grated parmesan cheese: 2 tbsp.
- Pitted Greek olives: 2 tbsp.
- 1 pack of (~18 oz.) Puff pastry
- Water: 1 tbsp.
- Sesame seeds: 2 tsp.
- 1 can of (~7 oz.) cream cheese (spinach & artichoke)
- 1 egg

**Instructions**
- Let the Kalorik Air Fryer Oven preheat to 325 F.
- In a food processor, add olives and artichokes, pulse until chopped.
- On one pastry sheet, add half of the cream cheese and half of the olive mixture on top.
- Add cheese and fold the other half of the pastry. Seal the edges.
- Repeat the same with other puff pastries.
- In a mug, whisk the egg with water, brush the puff pastry with egg wash.
- Add sesame seeds on top. Cut each puff pastry in 16 wide strips. Twist the strips.
- Place the bread sticks on the air fryer tray and air fry for 12 to 15 minutes.
- Serve right away.

Cal 99 | Fat 6g | Carb 9g | Protein 2g

## BANANA PANCAKE DIPPERS

*Prep time:10 min | Cook time:15 min | Serves: 1*

**Ingredients**
- Pancake Mix: 1 pack
- Butter: 1 tbsp.
- 3 bananas, cut in half

- Melted chocolate

**Instructions**
- Make the pancake mix as per package instructions.
- Let the Kalorik Air Fryer Oven preheat to 350 F.
- Coat the bananas in pancake mix and place them on the air fryer tray.
- Air fry for 16 minutes.
- Serve with melted chocolate.

Cal 156 | Carb 21 g | Protein 6g | Fat 8 g

## SPINACH, PEPPER AND HAVARTI FRITTATA

*Prep time:15 min | Cook time:30 min | Serves: 4*

**Ingredients**
- 8 eggs
- Fresh herbs, chopped: 4 tbsp.
- Baby spinach leaves: 2 cups
- Chopped bell pepper: ¾ cup
- Salt & black pepper, to taste
- Parmesan: ¼ cup, grated
- 2 scallions, chopped
- Havarti: 1 cup, grated

**Instructions**
- Oil spray a cake pan.
- Whisk eggs with salt and pepper. Add the rest of the ingredients and mix.
- Let the Kalorik Air Fryer Oven preheat to 310 F.
- Pour the mixture into the cake pan and air fry for 25 minutes.
- Cool for 5 minutes, slice and serve.

Cal 156 | Carb 21 g | Protein 6g | Fat 8 g

## Breakfast Hash

*Prep time:10 min | Cook time:30 min | Serves: 4*

**Ingredients**
- 1 sweet potato, diced
- Thyme: 1 tsp.
- 1 onion, diced
- Salt: 1 tsp.
- Pepper: half tsp.
- 2 russet potatoes, diced
- Garlic powder: 2 tsp.
- Olive oil: 2 tbsp.

**Instructions**
- In a bowl, add all ingredients and toss.
- Place the mixture on the air fryer tray.
- Air fry for 20 to 30 minutes at 400 F. Keep an eye on them, so they do not burn.
- Serve with eggs.

Cal 175 | Fat 8g | Carb 23g | Protein 3g

## Delicious Frittata

*Prep time:3 min | Cook time:6 min | Serves: 2*

**Ingredients**
- 3 eggs
- Milk: 2 tbsp.
- 1/4 small onion, diced
- 2 mushrooms
- Shredded cheese: 2 tbsp.
- 1/4 bell pepper, chopped

- Salt & pepper, to taste

**Instructions**
- In a large bowl, add all ingredients, except for cheese, and whisk.
- Let the Kalorik Air Fryer Oven preheat to 400 F.
- Pour the mixture into a pan and air fry for 5 minutes.
- Take it out, add cheese on top and air fry for 1 minute more.
- Serve warm.

Cal 162 | Carb 4g | Protein 12g | Fat 10g

## SOUTHWEST EGG ROLLS

*Prep time:15 min | Cook time:10 min | Serves: 12*

**Ingredients**
- Corn kernels: 1 cup
- Bred bell pepper: half cup, diced
- Green onions: ¼ cup, diced
- Paprika: 1 tsp.
- Shredded chicken: 2 cups
- Monterey jack cheese: 3 cups, shredded
- Jalapeno pepper: ¼ cup, diced
- Lack beans: 1 cup, rinsed
- Ground cumin: half tsp.
- 1 egg
- 12 egg roll wrappers
- Chili powder: 1 tsp.
- Salt: half tsp.
- Water: 1 tbsp.

**Instructions**
- In a bowl, whisk the egg with water.
- In another bowl, add the rest of the ingredients, except for wrappers, and mix.
- In each wrapper, add the filling mixture and fold, seal the edges with egg wash.
- Oil spray the egg rolls and place them on the air fryer trays.
- Let the Kalorik Air Fryer Oven preheat to 375 F.
- Air fry the rolls for five minutes.
- Flip the rolls and air fry for 3 to 5 minutes more.
- Serve with any dipping sauce.

Cal 221 | Carb 14g | Protein 16g | Fat 11g

## OMELET

*Prep time:5 min | Cook time:10 min | Serves: 1*

**Ingredients**
- Salt & pepper, to taste
- 2 eggs
- shredded cheese: 1/4 cup
- Milk: 1/4 cup
- Onion, tomato & mushroom diced: half cup

**Instructions**
- In a bowl, add all ingredients and whisk.
- Let the Kalorik Air Fryer Oven preheat to 350 F.
- Pour the egg mixture into a pan and air fry for 8 to 10 minutes.
- Slice and serve.

Cal 156 | Carb 21 g | Protein 6g | Fat 8 g

## CRUNCHY CORN DOG BITES

*Prep time:10 min | Cook time:10 min | Serves: 4*

**Ingredients**
- Yellow mustard: 8 tsp.
- All-purpose flour: half cup
- 2 beef hot dogs
- Crushed cornflakes: 1 ½ cups
- 2 eggs, whisked
- Bamboo skewers: 12

**Instructions**
- Slice hot dogs in halves. Cut every half into 3 pieces.
- Thread them on bamboo skewers.
- Add flour to a bowl. Add eggs to another bowl.
- Add cornflakes to another bowl.
- Coat the hot dogs in flour, then in egg, and then coat in crushed corn flakes.
- Oil spray the air fryer's trays. Put hot dog skewers on the trays, in one even layer.
- Air fry for 10 minutes at 375 F. Flip them halfway through.
- Serve with mustard.

Cal 82 | Carb 8 g | Protein 5 g | Fat 3 g

## BREAKFAST CASSEROLE

*Prep time:10 min | Cook time:25 min | Serves: 8*

**Ingredients**
- Fennel Seed: 1 tsp.
- Garlic salt: half tsp.
- 1 lb. Ground sausage
- Shredded Jack Cheese: ½ cup
- 8 eggs, whisked
- 1 chopped green bell pepper
- Diced white onion: 1/4 cup

**Instructions**
- In a skillet, brown the beef with onions & pepper until tender and the meat are no longer pink.
- Take a small dish that is air fryer safe and add sausage mix at the bottom.
- Add cheese on top, and pour whisked eggs on top.
- Sprinkle with garlic salt and fennel seed.
- Place on the air fryer tray, air fry at 390 F for 15 minutes.
- Serve right away.

Cal 156 | Carb 21 g | Protein 6g | Fat 8 g

## CHEESY CHICKEN OMELET

*Prep time:5 min | Cook time:10 min | Serves: 2*

**Ingredients**
- Black pepper, to taste
- 4 eggs
- Chicken breast: half cup, cooked & diced
- Cheese: 2 tbsp., shredded

- Salt, to taste
- 1/4 tsp. of onion powder
- 1/4 tsp. of granulated garlic

**Instructions**
- Take 2 ramekins and spray them with oil.
- Add two eggs to each ramekin.
- Add seasonings and cheese in each ramekin, mix well.
- Add in ¼ cup of diced chicken to every ramekin.
- Let the Kalorik Air Fryer Oven preheat to 330 F.
- Air fry for 14-18 minutes at 330 F.
- Serve right away.

Cal 115 | Carb 5 g | Protein 10 g | Fat 7 g

## BACON & EGG BREAKFAST BOMBS
*Prep time:10 min | Cook time:25 min | Serves: 8*

**Ingredients**
- Black pepper, to taste
- Sharp cheddar cheese: 10 small cubes
- 4 bacon slices, cut in half-inch pieces
- 5 Buttermilk biscuits, (1 can)
- Butter: 1 tbsp.
- 1 egg mixed with 1 tbsp. water
- 2 eggs, whisked

**Instructions**
- In a skillet, cook bacon until crispy. Take out on a paper towel.
- Add butter into the skillet, melt the butter.
- Whisk eggs with black pepper.
- Pour eggs into the skillet and cook until still moist. Turn off the heat and add bacon. Let it cool for 5 minutes.
- Separate 5 biscuits into two layers.
- In each biscuit, add egg mixture. Add cheese cube on top.
- Fold pinch the edges.
- Brush each biscuit bomb with egg wash.
- Let the Kalorik Air Fryer Oven preheat to 325 F at Bake.
- Place the bombs in the air fryer tray
- Cook for 8 minutes or more

Cal 215 | Carb 11 g | Protein 9 g | Fat 9.9 g

## CHEESE & VEGGIE EGG CUPS
*Prep time:5 min | Cook time:10 min | Serves: 4*

**Ingredients**
- Minced cilantro: 1 tbsp.
- Cream: 4 tbsp.
- 4 eggs
- Vegetables: 1 cup, diced
- Shredded cheese: 1 cup
- Salt & black pepper, to taste

**Instructions**
- Take 4 ramekins, and coat them will oil spray.
- In a bowl, mix eggs with half cheese, cilantro, black pepper, salt, cream, and vegetables.
- Pour the mixture in all ramekins equally.
- Let the Kalorik Air Fryer Oven preheat to 300 F.
- Place ramekins in the air fryer and air fry for 12 minutes
- Add cheese on top & air fry for 2 minutes more at 400 F.

## MUSHROOM OATMEAL
*Prep time:10 min | Cook time:20 min | Serves: 4*

**Ingredients**
- Steel-cut oats: 1 cup
- 1 minced garlic cloves
- One onion, chopped
- Mushroom: 1 cup, sliced
- Butter: 2 tbsp.
- Water: half cup
- Gouda cheese: half cup, grated
- Chicken stock: 1 ½ cups
- Thyme springs, chopped
- olive oil: 2 tbsp.
- Salt & pepper to taste

**Instructions**
- Heat a pan over medium heat, add the butter, onions and garlic, cook for four minutes.
- Add oats, sugar, salt, pepper, stock, and thyme, stir.
- Let the Kalorik Air Fryer Oven preheat to 360 F.
- Place the pan in the air fryer for 16 minutes.
- In the meantime, prepare a skillet over medium heat with the olive oil, add mushrooms, cook them for 3 minutes, add oatmeal and cheese, whisk, divide into bowls and serve right away.

Cal 284 | Fat 8g | Carb 20g | Protein 17g

## BELL PEPPERS FRITTATA
*Prep time:10 min | Cook time:20 min | Serves: 4*

**Ingredients**
- Olive oil: 2 tbsp.
- Mozzarella cheese: half cup, shredded
- Chicken sausage: 2 cups, chopped
- One onion, chopped
- 2 teaspoons fresh oregano, chopped
- 1 each of red, orange, green bell pepper, chopped
- Salt & black pepper to taste
- 8 eggs, whisked

**Instructions**
- Cook bacon until crispy.
- In a pan, add the rest of the ingredients whisk.
- Pour in a pan.
- Let the Kalorik Air Fryer Oven preheat to 320 F to Bake.
- Bake for 10 to 15 minutes.
- Slice and serve.

Cal 212 | Fat 4g | Carb 8g | Protein 12g

## BUTTERMILK BISCUITS
*Prep time:12 min | Cook time:12 min | Serves: 10*

**Ingredients**
- All-purpose flour: 2 1/2 cups
- Salt: half tsp.
- Baking powder: 1 tbsp.
- Cold buttermilk: 1 cup
- Sugar: 2 tsp.
- Baking soda: half tsp.
- Cold salted butter: 8 tbsp., small cubes

**Instructions**
- In a bowl, add flour, salt, baking soda, powder, and salt. Whisk well.
- Add butter and mix with hands, so there are no big pieces of butter.

- Add buttermilk, and mix until just combined. Add more buttermilk if it is too dry.
- Take it out on a surface and make it into a half-inch-thick slab.
- With a biscuit cutter, cut as many biscuits as possible.
- Oil spray the air fryer basket.
- Let the Kalorik Air Fryer Oven preheat to 325 F. air fry the biscuits for 12-16 minutes.
- Brush with melted butter and serve.

Cal 213 | Fat 10g | Carb 26g | Protein 4g

## BAKED POTATOES
*Prep time:5 min | Cook time:40 min | Serves: 2*

**Ingredients**
- Olive oil, to taste
- Medium russet potatoes: 2 to 3
- Kosher salt, to taste

**Instructions**
- Toss the washed potatoes with olive oil and sprinkle salt on them.
- Pierce with a fork, all over.
- Let the Kalorik Air Fryer Oven preheat to 400 F.
- Air fry for half an hour, air fry for 10 to 15 minutes more, if not soft yet.
- Take out and cut a triangle piece lengthwise, drizzle olive oil and sprinkle salt and serve.

## AIR-FRIED ENGLISH BREAKFAST

*Prep time: 5 min | Cook time: 20 min | Serves: 4*

**Ingredients**
- 8 sausages
- 8 bacon slices
- 4 eggs
- 1 (16-ounce) can of baked beans
- 8 slices of toast

**Directions**
- Add the sausages and bacon slices to your air fryer and cook them for 10 minutes at a 320°F.
- Using a ramekin or heat-safe bowl, add the baked beans, then place another ramekin and add the eggs and whisk.
- Change the temperature to 290°F.
- Place it inside your air fryer and cook it for an additional 10 minutes or until everything is done.
- Serve and enjoy!

Cal 350 | Fat 40g | Carb 20g | Protein 48g

## BACON BBQ BURGERS
*Prep time:15 min | Cook time:8 min | Serves: 3*

**Ingredients**
- 6 slices of bacon
- Minced onion: 2 tbsp.
- Bbq sauce: 1 tbsp.
- Seasoned salt: half tsp.
- Ground beef: 1 pound
- 3 slices of cheese
- Pepper: half tsp.
- 3 buns

**Sauce**
- mayonnaise: 2 tbsp.
- BBQ sauce: 2 tbsp.

**Instructions**
- Let the Kalorik Air Fryer Oven preheat to 400 F.
- Air fry the bacon for 8-10 minutes, flipping halfway through.
- In a bowl, add the rest of the ingredients except for buns and cheese. Mix and make into 3 patties.
- Air fry for five minutes at 360 F, flip and cook for 3 to 4 minutes.
- Add cheese slices on each patty, air fry for 1 to 2 minutes.
- In a bowl, mix the sauce's ingredients and spread on one half of the bun.
- Add patty and desired toppings and serve.

Cal 748 | Fat 51g | Carb 26g | Protein 44g

## BREAKFAST STUFFED POBLANOS
*Prep time:20 min | Cook time:10 min | Serves: 4*

**Ingredients**
- Diced tomatoes & green chiles (canned): 1/3 cup
- Ground breakfast sausage: half-pound, spicy
- 4 eggs
- 4 large poblano peppers
- Cream cheese: 4 oz., softened
- Pepper jack cheese: half cup, shredded
- Sour cream: 1/4 cup

**Instructions**
- In a pan, cook sausage completely and take it out in a bowl.
- Add cream cheese and mix.
- Cook the eggs in the pan, do not completely cook them.
- Add eggs, tomatoes in the sausage mix and mix well.
- Cut the poblano in half, take the middle seeds out and stuff with the sausage mixture.
- Add cheese on top.
- Let the Kalorik Air Fryer Oven preheat to 350 F.
- Air fry for 10-12 minutes.
- Serve with sour cream.

Cal 400 | Fat 28g | Carb 12g | Protein 25g

## SIMPLE EGG SOUFFLÉ
*Prep Time: 5min | Cook Time: 8 min | Serves: 2*

**Ingredients**
- 2 eggs
- 1/4 tsp chili pepper
- 2 tbsp heavy cream
- 1/4 tsp pepper
- 1 tbsp parsley, chopped

- Salt

**Directions**

- In a bowl, whisk eggs with remaining ingredients.
- Spray two ramekins with cooking spray.
- Pour egg mixture into the prepared ramekins and place into your air fryer oven.
- Cook soufflé at 390°F for 8 minutes
- Serve and enjoy.

Cal 116 | Fat 10g | Carb 1.1g | Protein 6 g

## SAUSAGE AND EGG BREAKFAST BURRITO

*Prep time: 5 min | Cook time: 30 min | Serves: 6*

**Ingredients**

- 6 eggs
- Salt
- Pepper
- Cooking oil
- ½ cup chopped red bell pepper
- ½ cup chopped green bell pepper
- 8 ounces ground chicken sausage
- ½ cup salsa
- 6 medium (8-inch) flour tortillas
- ½ cup shredded Cheddar cheese

**Directions**

- In a medium bowl, whisk the eggs. Add salt and pepper to taste.
- Place a skillet on medium-high heat. Spray with cooking oil. Add the eggs. Scramble for 2 to 3 minutes, until the eggs are fluffy. Remove the eggs from the skillet and set aside.
- If needed, spray the skillet with more oil. Add the chopped red and green bell peppers. Cook for 2 to 3 minutes, once the peppers are soft.
- Add the ground sausage to the skillet. Break the sausage into smaller pieces using a spatula or spoon. Cook for 3 to 4 minutes, until the sausage is brown.
- Add the salsa and scrambled eggs. Stir to combine. Remove the skillet from heat.
- Spoon the mixture evenly onto the tortillas.
- To form the burritos, fold the sides of each tortilla in toward the middle and then roll up from the bottom. You can secure each burrito with a toothpick. Or you can moisten the outside edge of the tortilla with a small amount of water. I prefer to use a cooking brush, but you can also dab with your fingers.
- Spray the burritos with cooking oil and place them in the air fryer. Do not stack. Cook the burritos in batches if they do not all fit in the basket. Cook for 8 minutes
- Open the air fryer and flip the burritos. Heat it for an additional 2 minutes or until crisp.
- If necessary, repeat steps 8 and 9 for the remaining burritos.
- Sprinkle the Cheddar cheese over the burritos. Cool before serving.

Cal 236 | Fat 13g | Carb 16g | Protein 15g

## FRENCH TOAST STICKS

*Prep time: 5 min | Cook time: 15 min | Serves: 12*

**Ingredients**

- 4 slices Texas toast (or any thick bread, such as challah)
- 1 tablespoon butter
- 1 egg

- 1 teaspoon stevia
- 1 teaspoon ground cinnamon
- ¼ cup milk
- 1 teaspoon vanilla extract
- Cooking oil

**Directions**

- Cut each slice of bread into 3 pieces (for 12 sticks total).
- Place the butter in a small, microwave-safe bowl. Heat for 15 seconds, or until the butter has melted.
- Remove the bowl from the microwave. Add the egg, stevia, cinnamon, milk, and vanilla extract. Whisk until fully combined.
- Sprinkle the air fryer with cooking oil.
- Dredge each of the bread sticks in the egg mixture.
- Place the French toast sticks in the air fryer. It is okay to stack them. Spray the French toast sticks with cooking oil. Cook for 8 minutes
- Open the air fryer and flip each of the French toast sticks. Cook for an additional 4 minutes, or until the French toast sticks are crisp.
- Cool before serving.

Cal 52 | Fat 2g | Carb 7g | Protein 2g

## HOME-FRIED POTATOES

*Prep time: 5 min | Cook time: 25 min | Serves: 4*

**Ingredients**

- 3 large russet potatoes
- 1 tablespoon canola oil
- 1 tablespoon extra-virgin olive oil
- 1 teaspoon paprika
- Salt
- Pepper
- 1 cup chopped onion
- 1 cup chopped red bell pepper
- 1 cup chopped green bell pepper

**Directions**

- Cut the potatoes into ½-inch cubes. Place the potatoes in a large bowl of cold water and allow them to soak for at least 30 minutes, preferably an hour.
- Dry out the potatoes and wipe thoroughly with paper towels. Return them to the empty bowl.
- Add the canola and olive oils, paprika, and salt and pepper to flavor. Toss to fully coat the potatoes.
- Transfer the potatoes to your air fryer oven. Cook for 20 minutes, shaking the air fryer basket every 5 minutes (a total of 4 times).
- Put the onion and red and green bell peppers to the Air Fryer basket. Fry for an additional 3 to 4 minutes, or until the potatoes are cooked through and the peppers are soft.
- Cool before serving.

Cal 279 | Fat 8g | Carb 50g | Protein 6g

## JALAPENO BREAKFAST MUFFINS

*Prep time: 10 min | Cook time: 15 min | Serves: 8*

**Ingredients**

- 5 eggs
- 1/3 cup coconut oil, melted
- 2 tsp baking powder
- 3 tbsp erythritol

- 3 tbsp jalapenos, sliced
- 1/4 cup unsweetened coconut milk
- 2/3 cup coconut flour
- 3/4 tsp sea salt

**Directions**
- Preheat the Kalorik Air Fryer Oven to 325°F.
- In a large bowl, mix together coconut flour, baking powder, erythritol, and sea salt.
- Stir in eggs, jalapenos, coconut milk, and coconut oil until well combined.
- Pour batter into the silicone muffin molds and place into your air fryer oven.
- Cook muffins for 15 minutes
- Serve and enjoy.

Cal 125 | Fat 12g | Carb 7g | Protein 3 g

## STUFFED MUSHROOMS

*Prep time:20 min | Cook time:25 min | Serves: 16*

**Ingredients**
- 1/4 cup breadcrumbs
- Shredded mozzarella: 2 tbsp.
- 36 white button mushrooms, without stem
- Chopped fresh parsley: 1 tbsp.
- Grated pecorino-romano: ¼ cup
- Olive oil: 4 tbsp.
- Chopped fresh mint: 1 tsp.
- 1 minced garlic clove

**Instructions**
- In a bowl, add cheeses, mint, breadcrumbs, parsley, garlic, olive oil (2 tbsp.), salt and pepper. Toss to combine.
- Coat the mushrooms in the rest of the olive oil and place on the tray, cavity facing up.
- Add the crumbs mixture to the cavity.
- Let the Kalorik Air Fryer Oven preheat to 360 F.
- Air fry for ten minutes until bubbling.
- Serve right away.

## HOMEMADE CHERRY BREAKFAST TARTS

*Prep time: 15 min | Cook time: 20 min | Serves: 6*

**Ingredients**
**For the tarts:**
- 2 refrigerated piecrusts
- ⅓ Cup cherry preserves
- 1 teaspoon cornstarch
- Cooking oil

**For the frosting:**
- ½ cup vanilla yogurt
- 1-ounce cream cheese
- 1 teaspoon stevia

- Rainbow sprinkles

**Directions**
**To make the tarts:**
- Place the piecrusts on a flat surface. Make use of a knife or pizza cutter, cut each piecrust into 3 rectangles, for 6 in total. (I discard the unused dough left from slicing the edges.)
- In a small bowl, combine the preserves and cornstarch. Mix well.
- Scoop 1 tablespoon of the preserve mixture onto the top half of each piece of piecrust.
- Fold the bottom of each piece up to close the tart. Press along the edges of each tart to seal using the back of a fork.
- Sprinkle the breakfast tarts with cooking oil and place them in the air fryer. I do not recommend piling the breakfast tarts. They will stick together if piled. You may need to prepare them in two batches. Cook for 10 minutes
- Allow the breakfast tarts to cool fully before removing from the air fryer.
- If needed, repeat steps 5 and 6 for the remaining breakfast tarts.

**To make the frosting:**
- In a small bowl, mix the yogurt, cream cheese, and stevia. Mix well.
- Spread the breakfast tarts with frosting and top with sprinkles, and serve.

Cal 119 | Fat 4g | Carb 19g | Protein 2g

## VEGETABLE EGG SOUFFLÉ

*Prep time: 10 min | Cook time: 20 min | Serves: 4*

**Ingredients**
- 4 large eggs
- 1 tsp onion powder
- 1 tsp garlic powder
- 1 tsp red pepper, crushed
- 1/2 cup broccoli florets, chopped
- 1/2 cup mushrooms, chopped

**Directions**
- Sprinkle four ramekins with cooking spray and set aside.
- In a bowl, whisk eggs with onion powder, garlic powder, and red pepper.
- Add mushrooms and broccoli and stir well.
- Pour egg mixture into the prepared ramekins and place ramekins into your air fryer oven.
- Cook at 350°F for 15 minutes. Make sure soufflé is cooked if soufflé is not cooked then cook for 5 minutes more.
- Serve and enjoy.

Cal 91 | Fat 5.1g | Carb 4.7g | Protein 7.4g

## SPICY CAULIFLOWER RICE

*Prep time: 10 min | Cook time: 22 min | Serves: 2*

**Ingredients**
- 1 cauliflower head, cut into florets
- 1/2 tsp cumin
- 1/2 tsp chili powder
- 6 onion spring, chopped
- 2 jalapenos, chopped
- 4 tbsp olive oil
- 1 zucchini, trimmed and cut into cubes
- 1/2 tsp paprika
- 1/2 tsp garlic powder

- 1/2 tsp cayenne pepper
- 1/2 tsp pepper
- 1/2 tsp salt

**Directions**

- Preheat the air fryer to 370°F.
- Add cauliflower florets into the food processor and process until it looks like rice.
- Transfer cauliflower rice into the baking pan and rizzle with half oil.
- Place pan in the air fryer and cook for 12 minutes, stir halfway through.
- Heat the remaining oil in a small pan over medium heat.
- Add zucchini and cook for 5-8 minutes
- Add onion and jalapenos and cook for 5 minutes
- Add spices and stir well. Set aside.
- Add cauliflower rice in the zucchini mixture and stir well.
- Serve and enjoy.

Cal 254 | Fat 28g | Carb 12g | Protein 4.3 g

## ASPARAGUS FRITTATA

*Prep time: 10 min | Cook time: 10 min | Serves: 4*

**Ingredients**

- 6 eggs
- 3 mushrooms, sliced
- 10 asparagus, chopped
- 1/4 cup half and half
- 2 tsp butter, melted
- 1 cup mozzarella cheese, shredded
- 1 tsp pepper
- 1 tsp salt

**Directions**

- Toss mushrooms and asparagus with melted butter and add into your air fryer oven. Cook mushrooms and asparagus at 350°F for 5 minutes.
- Meanwhile, in a bowl, whisk together eggs, half and half, pepper, and salt. Transfer cook mushrooms and asparagus into a proper dish. Pour egg mixture over mushrooms and asparagus.
- Place dish in the Kalorik Air Fryer Oven and cook at 350°F for 5 minutes or until eggs are set. Slice and serve.

Cal 211 | Fat 13g | Carb 4g | Protein 16 g

## ZUCCHINI NOODLES

*Prep time: 10 min | Cook time: 44 min | Serves: 3*

**Ingredients**

- 1 egg

- 1/2 cup parmesan cheese, grated
- 1/2 cup feta cheese, crumbled
- 1 tbsp thyme
- 1 garlic clove, chopped
- 1 onion, chopped
- 2 medium zucchinis, trimmed and spiralized
- 2 tbsp olive oil
- 1 cup mozzarella cheese, grated
- 1/2 tsp pepper
- 1/2 tsp salt

**Directions**

- Preheat the Kalorik Air Fryer Oven to 350°F.
- Add spiralized zucchini and salt in a colander and set aside for 10 minutes. Wash zucchini noodles and pat dry with a paper towel.
- Heat the oil in a pan over medium heat. Add garlic and onion and sauté for 3-4 minutes
- Add zucchini noodles and cook for 4-5 minutes or until softened.
- Add zucchini mixture into the baking pan. Add egg, thyme, cheeses. Mix well and season.
- Place pan in the air fryer and cook for 30-35 minutes
- Serve and enjoy

Cal 435 | Fat 29g | Carb 10g | Protein 25 g

## EGG MUFFINS

*Prep time: 10 min | Cook time: 15 min | Serves: 12*

**Ingredients**

- 9 eggs
- 1/2 cup onion, sliced
- 1 tbsp olive oil
- 8 oz ground sausage
- 1/4 cup coconut milk
- 1/2 tsp oregano
- 1 1/2 cups spinach
- 3/4 cup bell peppers, chopped
- Pepper
- Salt

**Directions**

- Preheat the Kalorik Air Fryer Oven to 325°F.
- Add ground sausage in a pan and sauté over medium heat for 5 minutes
- Add olive oil, oregano, bell pepper, and onion and sauté until onion is translucent.
- Put spinach to the pan and cook for 30 seconds.
- Remove pan from heat and set aside.
- In a mixing bowl, whisk together eggs, coconut milk, pepper, and salt until well beaten.
- Add sausage and vegetable mixture into the egg mixture and mix well.
- Pour egg mixture into the silicone muffin molds and place into your air fryer oven. (Cook in batches)
- Cook muffins for 15 minutes
- Serve and enjoy.

Cal 135 | Fat 11g | Carb 1.5g | Protein 8 g

## YUMMY BREAKFAST ITALIAN FRITTATA

*Prep time: 5 min | Cook time: 10 min | Serves: 6*

### Ingredients

- 6 eggs
- 1/3 cup of milk
- 4-ounces of chopped Italian sausage
- 3 cups of stemmed and roughly chopped kale
- 1 red deseeded and chopped bell pepper
- ½ cup of a grated feta cheese
- 1 chopped zucchini
- 1 tablespoon of freshly chopped basil
- 1 teaspoon of garlic powder
- 1 teaspoon of onion powder
- 1 teaspoon of salt
- 1 teaspoon of black pepper

### Directions

- Turn on your Kalorik Air Fryer Oven to 360°F.
- Grease the air fryer pan with a nonstick cooking spray.
- Add the Italian sausage to the pan and cook it inside your air fryer for 5 minutes
- While doing that, add and stir in the remaining ingredients until it mixes properly.
- Add the egg mixture to the pan and allow it to cook inside your air fryer for 5 minutes
- Thereafter carefully remove the pan and allow it to cool off until it gets chill enough to serve.
- Serve and enjoy!

Cal 225 | Fat 14g | Carb 4.5g | Protein 20g

## SAVORY CHEESE AND BACON MUFFINS

*Prep time: 5 min | Cook time: 17 min | Serves: 4*

### Ingredients

- 1 ½ cup of all-purpose flour
- 2 teaspoons of baking powder
- ½ cup of milk
- 2 eggs
- 1 tablespoon of freshly chopped parsley
- 4 cooked and chopped bacon slices
- 1 thinly chopped onion
- ½ cup of shredded cheddar cheese
- ½ teaspoon of onion powder
- 1 teaspoon of salt
- 1 teaspoon of black pepper

### Directions

- Turn on your Kalorik Air Fryer Oven to 360°F.
- Using a large bowl, add and stir all the ingredients until it mixes properly.
- Then grease the muffin cups with a nonstick cooking spray or line it with a parchment paper. Pour the batter proportionally into each muffin cup.
- Place it inside your air fryer and bake it for 15 minutes
- Thereafter, carefully remove it from your air fryer and allow it to chill.
- Serve and enjoy!

Cal 180 | Fat 18g | Carb 16g | Protein 15g

## CHEESY TATER TOT BREAKFAST BAKE

*Prep time: 5 min | Cook time: 20 min | Serves: 4*

### Ingredients

- 4 eggs
- 1 cup milk
- 1 teaspoon onion powder
- Salt
- Pepper
- Cooking oil
- 12 ounces ground chicken sausage
- 1-pound frozen tater tots
- ¾ cup shredded Cheddar cheese

### Directions

- In a medium bowl, whisk the eggs. Add the milk, onion powder, and salt and pepper to taste. Stir to combine.
- Spray a skillet with cooking oil and set over medium-high heat. Add the ground sausage. Using a spatula or spoon, break the sausage into smaller pieces. Cook for 3 to 4 minutes, until the sausage is brown. Remove from heat and set aside.
- Spray a barrel pan with cooking oil. Make sure to cover the bottom and sides of the pan.
- Place the tater tots in the barrel pan. Cook for 6 minutes
- Open the air fryer and shake the pan, then add the egg mixture and cooked sausage. Cook for an additional 6 minutes. Open the air fryer and sprinkle the cheese over the tater tot bake. Cook for an additional 2 to 3 minutes.
- Cool before serving.

Cal 518 | Fat 30g | Carb 31g | Protein 30g

## SAUSAGE AND CREAM CHEESE BISCUITS

*Prep time: 5 minutes | Cook time: 15 minutes | Serves: 5*

### Ingredients

- 12 ounces chicken breakfast sausage
- 1 (6-ounce) can biscuits
- ⅛ cup cream cheese

### Directions

- Form the sausage into 5 small patties.
- Place the sausage patties in the air fryer. Cook for 5 minutes
- Open the air fryer. Flip the patties. Cook for an additional 5 minutes
- Remove the cooked sausages from the air fryer.
- Separate the biscuit dough into 5 biscuits.
- Place the biscuits in the air fryer. Cook for 3 minutes
- Open the air fryer. Flip the biscuits. Cook for an additional 2 minutes
- Remove the cooked biscuits from the air fryer.

- Split each biscuit in half. Spread 1 teaspoon of cream cheese onto the bottom of each biscuit. Top with a sausage patty and the other half of the biscuit, and serve.

Cal 120 | Fat 13g | Carb 7.3g | Protein 9g

## BREAKFAST GRILLED HAM AND CHEESE

*Prep time: 5 min | Cook time: 10 min | Serves: 2*

**Ingredients**
- 1 teaspoon butter
- 4 slices bread
- 4 slices smoked country ham
- 4 slices Cheddar cheese
- 4 thick slices tomato

**Directions**
- Spread ½ teaspoon of butter onto one side of 2 slices of bread. Each sandwich will have 1 slice of bread with butter and 1 slice without.
- Assemble each sandwich by layering 2 slices of ham, 2 slices of cheese, and 2 slices of tomato on the unbuttered pieces of bread. Top with the other bread slices, buttered side up.
- Place the sandwiches in the air fryer buttered-side down. Cook for 4 minutes
- Open the air fryer. Flip the grilled cheese sandwiches. Cook for an additional 4 minutes
- Cool before serving. Cut each sandwich in half and enjoy.

Cal 525 | Fat 25g | Carb 34g | Protein 41g

## CANADIAN BACON AND CHEESE MUFFINS

*Prep time: 5 min | Cook time: 10 min | Serves: 4*

**Ingredients**
- 4 English muffins
- 8 slices Canadian bacon
- 4 slices cheese
- Cooking oil

**Directions**
- Split each English muffin. Assemble the breakfast sandwiches by layering 2 slices of Canadian bacon and 1 slice of cheese onto each English muffin bottom. Put the other half on top of the English muffin. Place the sandwiches in the air fryer. Spray the top of each with cooking oil. Cook for 4 minutes
- Open the air fryer and flip the sandwiches. Cook for an additional 4 minutes
- Cool before serving.

Cal 333 | Fat 14g | Carb 27g | Protein 24g

## BREAKFAST SCRAMBLE CASSEROLE

*Prep time: 20 min | Cook time: 10 min | Serves: 4*

**Ingredients**
- 6 slices bacon
- 6 eggs
- Salt

- Pepper
- Cooking oil
- ½ cup chopped red bell pepper
- ½ cup chopped green bell pepper
- ½ cup chopped onion
- ¾ cup shredded Cheddar cheese

**Directions**
- In a pan, over medium-high heat, cook the bacon, 5 to 7 minutes, flipping to evenly crisp. Dry out on paper towels, crumble, and set aside. In a medium bowl, whisk the eggs. Add salt and pepper to taste.
- Spray a barrel pan with cooking oil. Make sure to cover the bottom and sides of the pan. Add the beaten eggs, crumbled bacon, red bell pepper, green bell pepper, and onion to the pan. Place the pan in the air fryer. Cook for 6 minutes Open the air fryer and sprinkle the cheese over the casserole. Cook for an additional 2 minutes. Cool before serving.

Cal 348 | Fat 26g | Carb 4g | Protein 25g

## RADISH HASH BROWNS

*Prep time: 10 min | Cook time: 13 min | Serves: 4*

**Ingredients**
- 1 lb. radishes, washed and cut off roots
- 1 tbsp olive oil
- 1/2 tsp paprika
- 1/2 tsp onion powder
- 1/2 tsp garlic powder
- 1 medium onion
- 1/4 tsp pepper
- 3/4 tsp sea salt

**Directions**
- Slice onion and radishes using a mandolin slicer.
- Add sliced onion and radishes in a large mixing bowl and toss with olive oil.
- Transfer onion and radish slices in air fryer and cook at 360°F for 8 minutes Shake basket twice.
- Return onion and radish slices in a mixing bowl and toss with seasonings.
- Again, cook onion and radish slices in air fryer for 5 minutes at 400°F. Shake the basket halfway through.
- Serve and enjoy.

Cal 62 | Fat 3.7g | Carb 7.1g | Protein 1.2g

## VEGETABLE EGG CUPS

*Prep time: 10 min | Cook time: 20 min | Serves: 4*

**Ingredients**
- 4 eggs
- 1 tbsp cilantro, chopped
- 4 tbsp half and half
- 1 cup cheddar cheese, shredded
- 1 cup vegetables, diced
- Pepper
- Salt

**Directions**
- Sprinkle four ramekins with cooking spray and set aside.
- In a mixing bowl, whisk eggs with cilantro, half and half, vegetables, 1/2 cup cheese, pepper, and salt.
- Pour egg mixture into the four ramekins.

- Place ramekins in air fryer and cook at 300°F for 12 minutes
- Top with remaining 1/2 cup cheese and cook for 2 minutes more at 400°F.
- Serve and enjoy.

Cal 194 | Fat 11.5g | Carb 6g | Protein 13g

## OMELET FRITTATA

*Prep time: 10 min | Cook time: 6 min | Serves: 2*

**Ingredients**
- 3 eggs, lightly beaten
- 2 tbsp cheddar cheese, shredded
- 2 tbsp heavy cream
- 2 mushrooms, sliced
- 1/4 small onion, chopped
- 1/4 bell pepper, diced
- Pepper
- Salt

**Directions**
- In a bowl, whisk eggs with cream, vegetables, pepper, and salt.
- Preheat the Kalorik Air Fryer Oven to 400°F.
- Pour egg mixture into the air fryer oven pan. Place pan in air fryer and cook for 5 minutes
- Add shredded cheese on top of the frittata and cook for 1 minute more.
- Serve and enjoy.

Cal 160 | Fat 10g | Carb 4g | Protein 12 g

## CHEESE SOUFFLÉS

*Prep time: 10 min | Cook time: 6 min | Serves: 8*

**Ingredients**
- 6 large eggs, separated
- 3/4 cup heavy cream
- 1/4 tsp cayenne pepper
- 1/2 tsp xanthan gum
- 1/2 tsp pepper
- 1/4 tsp cream of tartar
- 2 tbsp chives, chopped
- 2 cups cheddar cheese, shredded
- 1 tsp salt

**Directions**
- Preheat the Kalorik Air Fryer Oven to 325°F.
- Spray eight ramekins with cooking spray. Set aside.

- In a bowl, whisk together almond flour, cayenne pepper, pepper, salt, and xanthan gum.
- Slowly add heavy cream and mix to combine.
- Whisk in egg yolks, chives, and cheese until well combined.
- In a large bowl, add egg whites and cream of tartar and beat until stiff peaks form.
- Fold egg white mixture into the almond flour mixture until combined.
- Pour mixture into the prepared ramekins. Divide ramekins in batches.
- Place the first batch of ramekins into your air fryer oven.
- Cook soufflé for 20 minutes
- Serve and enjoy.

Cal 210 | Fat 16g | Carb 1g | Protein 12 g

## CHEESE AND RED PEPPER EGG CUPS

*Prep time: 10 min | Cook time: 15 min | Serves: 4*

**Ingredients**
- Large free-range eggs, 4.
- Shredded cheese, 1 cup
- Diced red pepper, 1 cup
- Half and half, 4 tbsps.
- Salt and Pepper.

**Directions**
- Preheat your air fryer to 300°F and grease four ramekins.
- Grab a medium bowl and add the eggs. Whisk well.
- Add the red pepper, half the cheese, half and half, and salt and pepper. Stir well to combine.
- Pour the mixture between the ramekins and pop into your air fryer oven.
- Cook for 15 minutes then serve and enjoy.

Cal 195 | Fat 12g | Carb 7g | Protein 13g

## COCONUT PORRIDGE WITH FLAX SEED

*Prep time: 5 min | Cook time: 30 min | Serves: 3*

**Ingredients**
- Unsweetened almond milk, 1 ½ cup
- Coconut flour, 2 tbsp.
- Vegan vanilla protein powder, 2 tbsp.
- Powdered erythritol, ¼ tsp.
- Golden flaxseed meal, 3 tbsp.

**Directions**
- Preheat your Air Fryer at a temperature of about 375°F
- Combine coconut flour with the golden flaxseed meal and the protein powder in a bowl
- Spray your Air Fryer with cooking spray, then pour the mixture in the air fryer pan
- Pour the milk and top with chopped blueberries and chopped raspberries
- Move the pan in the air fryer and seal the lid
- Set the temperature at about 375°F and the timer to about 30 minutes
- When the timer beeps, turn off your Air Fryer and remove the baking pan
- Serve and enjoy your delicious porridge!

Cal 249 | Fats: 14g | Carb 6g | Protein 17g

## CHEESY SPINACH OMELET

*Prep time: 5 min | Cook time: 10 min | Serves: 2*

**Ingredients**
- Eggs, 3
- Chopped fresh spinach, 2 tbsps.
- Shredded cheese, ½ cup
- Pepper.
- Salt.

**Directions**
- Mix the eggs with pepper and salt then whisk and put in an oven-safe tray.
- Add spinach and cheese but do not stir.
- Allow to cook in the air fryer for 8 minutes at 390°F.
- Cook for 2 more minutes to brown the omelet.
- Serve on plates to enjoy.

Cal 209 | Fat 15.9g | Carb 1g | Protein 15.4g

## ROASTED GARLIC AND THYME DIPPING SAUCE

*Prep time: 5 min | Cook time: 30 min | Serves: 1*

**Ingredients**
- Minced fresh thyme leaves, ½ tsp.
- Salt, 1/8 tsp.
- Light mayonnaise, ½ cup
- Crushed roasted garlic, 2 tbsps.
- Pepper, 1/8 tsp.

**Directions**
- Wrap garlic in foil. Put it in the cooking basket of the Air Fryer and roast for 30 minutes at 390°F.
- Combine all the ingredients to serve.

Cal 485 | Fat 39.4g | Carb 34.1g | Protein 2.2g

## EASY CHOCOLATE DOUGHNUT

*Prep time: 10 min | Cook time: 12 min | Serves: 6*

**Ingredients**
- Melted unsalted butter, 3 tbsps.
- Powdered sugar, ¼ cup
- Refrigerated biscuits, 8.
- Semisweet chocolate chips, 48

**Directions**
- Cut the biscuits into thirds then flatten them and place 2 chocolate chips at the center.
- Wrap the chocolate with dough to seal the edges.
- Rub each dough hole with some butter.
- Set the dough into your air fryer oven to cook for 12 minutes at 340°F.
- Set aside to add powdered sugar.
- Serve and enjoy.

Cal 393 | Fat 17g | Carb 55g | Protein 5g

## CHEESY SAUSAGE AND EGG ROLLS

*Prep time: 15 min | Cook time: 15 min | Serves: 8*

**Ingredients**
- Cooked breakfast sausage links, 8 pieces.
- Eggs, 3.
- Salt and Pepper,
- Cheddar cheese slices, 4.
- Refrigerated crescent rolls, 8 oz.

**Directions**
- Preheat the Kalorik Air Fryer Oven to 325°F.
- Beat the eggs; reserve one tablespoon as egg wash and scramble the rest.
- Halve the cheese slices.
- Separate the dough into 8 triangles.
- Fill each triangle with a half-slice of cheese, a tablespoon of scrambled eggs, and a sausage link.
- Loosely roll up all filled triangles before placing in the air fryer. Brush with the egg wash that was set aside and sprinkle all over with pepper and salt.
- Cook for 15 minutes.
- Serve right away.

Cal 270 | Fat 20.0g | Protein 10.0g | Carb 13.

## CHOPPED BONDIOLA

*Prep time: 5 min | Cook time: 10 min | Serves: 4*

**Ingredients**
- 1kg Bondiola in pieces
- Bread crumbs
- two eggs
- Seasoning to taste

**Directions**
- Cut the bondiola into small pieces, seasonings to taste.
- Beat the eggs.
- Pass the bondiola seasoned by beaten egg and then by breadcrumbs.
- Then we place in the air fryer for 20 minutes, in half time we turn and snacks of bondiola ready.

Cal 140 | Fat 4g | Carb 7g | Protein 11g

# APPETIZERS & SNACKS RECIPES

## AIR-FRYER PICKLES

*Prep time:20 min | Cook time:20 min | Serves: 32*

**Ingredients**

- 32 dill pickle slices
- Cayenne pepper: half tsp.
- Snipped fresh dill: 2 tbsp., chopped
- Salt: half tsp.
- 3 eggs, whisked
- Dill pickle juice: 2 tbsp.
- All-purpose flour: half cup
- Garlic powder: half tsp.
- Panko bread crumbs: 2 cups

**Instructions**

- Let the Kalorik Air Fryer Oven preheat to 400 F.
- Pat dry the pickles and let them rest for 15 minutes on towels.
- In a bowl, mix flour with salt.
- In another bowl, mix garlic powder, eggs, cayenne and juice.
- In a different bowl, add dill and panko.
- Coat pickles in flour, then in egg mixture and lastly in panko.
- Air fry the pickles for 7 to 10 minutes. Flip and oil spray, air fry for 7 to 10 minutes more.
- Serve with ranch.

1 slice: Cal 26 | Fat 1g | Carb 4g | Protein 1g

## POTATO CHIPS

*Prep time:30 min | Cook time:15 min | Serves: 6*

**Ingredients**

- Fresh herbs chopped
- 2 large potatoes
- Sea salt: half tsp.

**Instructions**

- Let the Kalorik Air Fryer Oven preheat to 360 F.
- With a mandolin, slice the potatoes in thin circles. Soak in water for 30 minutes, in cold water.
- Pat dry the potatoes and oil spray them. Place on the tray of the air fryer in a single layer.
- Sprinkle with salt, air fry got 15 to 17 minutes, flip every 5 to 7 minutes.
- Serve with fresh herbs on top.

## CAULIFLOWER TOTS

*Prep time:10 min | Cook time:10 min | Serves: 6*

**Ingredients**

- Cauliflower florets: 4 cups, steamed
- Salt & black pepper, to taste
- 1 egg, whisked
- Freshly grated parmesan: 1 cup
- Panko breadcrumbs: 2/3 cup
- Shredded cheddar: 1 cup
- Chopped fresh chives: 2 tbsp.

**Instructions**

- Let the Kalorik Air Fryer Oven preheat to 375 F.
- Oil spray a baking tray.
- Rice the cauliflower in the food processor. Take out on a towel and squeeze.
- In a bowl, add the rest of the ingredients, cauliflower and mix. Season with salt and pepper.
- Make tater tots with 1 tbsp. of mixture and place on the baking tray.
- Air fry for 10 minutes. serve with spicy ketchup

## ANTIPASTO EGG ROLLS

*Prep time:10 min | Cook time:30 min | Serves: 12*

**Ingredients**

- 12 egg roll wrappers
- Provolone: 12 slices
- Sliced pepperoncini: 1 cup
- Grated parmesan: ¼ cup
- Pepperoni: 36 slices
- Deli ham: 12 slices
- Shredded mozzarella: 1 cup

**Instructions**

- In each egg wrapper, add ham (1 slice), pepperoncini, pepperoni (3 slices), and some mozzarella. Fold tightly and seal the edges with water.
- Let the Kalorik Air Fryer Oven preheat to 390 F.
- Air fry the rolls for 12 minutes, flipping halfway through.

## BACON AVOCADO FRIES

*Prep time:10 min | Cook time:5 min | Serves: 24*

**Ingredients**

- Ranch dressing: 1/4 cup
- 3 avocados
- Bacon: 24 strips

**Instructions**

- Cut every avocado into 8 wedges. Wrap each wedge in the strip of bacon.
- Let the Kalorik Air Fryer Oven preheat to 400 F.
- Air fry the wedges for 8 minutes.
- Serve with ranch.

Cal 120 | Protein 4g | Carb 3 g | Fat 11g

## BLOOMING' APPLES

*Prep time:15 min | Cook time:5 min | Serves: 4*

**Ingredients**

- Packed brown sugar: 1 tbsp.
- 4 apples
- Granulated sugar: 1 tbsp.
- Melted butter: 4 tbsp.
- Ground cinnamon: half tsp.
- 8 chewy caramel squares

**Instructions**

- In a bowl, mix cinnamon, butter and sugar.
- Cut the top off of apples, scoop the centre out.
- Make 2 round cuts in apple, slice crosswise and do not cut all the way through core.
- Add caramel squares in every apple, brush with the butter mixer.
- Let the Kalorik Air Fryer Oven preheat to 350 F at Bake.
- Bake for 15 to 20 minutes.
- Serve with ice cream.

## CARIBBEAN WONTONS

*Prep time:30 min | Cook time:10 min | Serves: 12*

**Ingredients**
- Marshmallow crème: 1 cup
- 24 wonton wrappers
- Cream cheese: 4 oz., softened
- Mashed ripe banana: 1/4 cup
- Canned crushed pineapple: 2 tbsp.
- Chopped walnuts: 2 tbsp.
- Shredded coconut: 1/4 cup, sweetened

**Sauce**
- Fresh strawberries: 1 pound
- Cornstarch: 1 tsp.
- Sugar: 1/4 cup

**Instructions**
- Let the Kalorik Air Fryer Oven preheat to 350 F.
- Whisk the cream cheese until smooth. Add pineapple and other fruits and nuts.
- Fold the marshmallow crème.
- Add 2 tsp. of filling in each wonton wrapper, seal the edges with water.
- Place on the tray of air fryer, and spray with oil.
- Air fry for 10 to 12 minutes.
- In a food processor, add strawberries, and puree them.
- In a pan, add cornstarch, sugar, strawberries on medium flame.
- Cook for two minutes until thickened.
- Serve the wonton with sauce.

1 wonton: Cal 83 | Fat 3g | Carb 13g | Protein 1g

## GARLIC-ROSEMARY BRUSSELS SPROUTS

*Prep time:10 min | Cook time:20 min | Serves: 4*

**Ingredients**
- Minced fresh rosemary: 1 ½ tsp.
- Brussels sprouts: 1 pound, trimmed & halved
- Olive oil: 3 tbsp.
- 2 minced garlic cloves
- Pepper: ¼ tsp.
- Salt: half tsp.
- Panko bread crumbs: half cup

**Instructions**
- Let the Kalorik Air Fryer Oven preheat to 350 F.
- In a bowl, add olive oil, garlic, salt and pepper, microwave for 30 seconds.
- In a bowl, toss Brussels sprouts with oil mixture (2 tbsp.), and place on the tray of the air fryer. Air fry for 4 to 5 minutes, stir and cook for 8 minutes, stir again halfway.
- In the rest of the oil mixture, add crumbs and mix sprinkle over sprouts air fry for 3 to 5 minutes. Serve right away.

## APPLE CHIPS

*Prep time:5 min | Cook time:10 min | Serves: 2*

**Ingredients**
- Granulated sugar: 2 tsp.
- Cinnamon: half tsp.
- 2 apples, sliced thin

**Instructions**
- In a bowl, toss apples with sugar and cinnamon.
- Place the apples on the tray of the air fryer.
- Let the Kalorik Air Fryer Oven preheat to 350 F on bake.
- Bake for 12 minutes, flip every 4 minutes.

## AIR FRYER BACON

*Prep time:5 min | Cook time:10 min | Serves: 8*

**Ingredients**
- Thick-cut bacon: 3/4 lb.

**Instructions**
- Place bacon on the tray of the air fryer.
- Let the Kalorik Air Fryer Oven preheat to 400 F.
- Air fry bacon for ten minutes, check after 5 minutes and rearrange.

## NACHO HOT DOGS

*Prep time:20 min | Cook time:15 min | Serves: 6*

**Ingredients**
- Crushed tortilla chips (nacho-flavored): 1 cup
- Self-rising flour: 1-1/4 cups
- Greek yogurt: 1 cup
- Salsa: 1/4 cup
- 6 hot dogs
- 3 cheddar cheese sticks, cut in half, lengthwise
- Chili powder: ¼ tsp.
- Jalapeno pepper: 3 tbsp., chopped without seeds

**Instructions**
- Slice each hot dog in half, do not cut all the way through and add one half of cheese stick in the slit.
- Let the Kalorik Air Fryer Oven preheat to 350 F.
- In a bowl, add chili powder, flour, jalapenos, tortilla chips (1/4 cup), salsa and yogurt. Mix well into a dough.
- Divide the dough into 6 portions. Roll into long strips and wrap around the hot dog.
- Spray with oil and roll in the rest of the chips. Place on the tray of the air fryer.
- Air fry for 8 to 10 minutes.
- Serve with guacamole.

Cal 216 | Fat 9g | Carb 26g | Protein 9g

## CRISPY SRIRACHA SPRING ROLLS

*Prep time:50 min | Cook time:10 min | Serves: 12*

**Ingredients**

- Coleslaw mix: 3 cups
- Cream cheese: 16 oz., softened
- Soy sauce: 1 tbsp.
- Sesame oil: 1 tsp.
- 24 spring roll wrappers
- Chicken breasts: 1 pound, boneless & skinless
- 3 green onions, diced
- Seasoned salt: 1 tsp.
- Sriracha chili sauce: 2 tbsp.

**Instructions**

- Let the Kalorik Air Fryer Oven preheat to 360 F.
- In a bowl, mix soy sauce, sesame oil, coleslaw mix, and green onions.
- Place chicken on the tray of the air fryer. Cook for 18 to 20 minutes until the internal temperature, reaches 165 F.
- Take Chicken out, chop and season with salt.
- Change air fryer temperature to 400 F.
- In a bowl, mix cream cheese and sriracha. Add chicken and coleslaw mixture.
- In each wrapper, add some of the fillings. Seal the edges with water and roll tightly.
- Oil spray the rolls and Air fry the rolls for 5 to 6 minutes, flip and oil spray, air fry for 5 to 6 minutes.
- Serve with green onions on top.

Cal 127 | Fat 7g | Carb 10g | Protein 6g

## CHICKEN ZUCCHINI SKINS

*Prep time:15 min | Cook time:10 min | Serves: 25*

**Ingredients**

- Paprika: 1/4 tsp.
- 2 large zucchinis
- Garlic powder: 1/4 tsp.
- Salt: half tsp.

**Stuffing:**

- cream cheese: 1 oz., softened
- chopped scallions: 2 tbsp.
- Franks hot sauce: 1/4 cup
- chicken breasts: 7 oz., shredded & cooked
- crumbled blue cheese: 4 tsp.
- Ranch Dressing: 1/4 cup

**Instructions**

- In a bowl, whisk the hot sauce with cream cheese until smooth. Add chicken and mix.
- Slice the zucchini in half, then slice into eight pieces. Take the pulp out and leave the shells.
- Spray the zucchini with oil and sprinkle salt, paprika and garlic powder.
- Let the Kalorik Air Fryer Oven preheat to 350 F.
- Air fry the zucchini for 8 minutes.
- Add 3 to 4 tbsp. of chicken mixture in each zucchini bite, add cheese on top.
- Air fry for 2 minutes.
- Serve right away.

Cal 80 | Carb 3.5g | Protein 9.5g | Fat 3g

## SAUSAGE SANDWICH

*Prep time:10 min | Cook time:30 min | Serves: 6*

**Ingredients**

- 1 onion, sliced
- Salt, as needed
- Italian sausage: 1 ½ pound, 6 links
- Black pepper, as needed
- 1 bell pepper each yellow, green, & red sliced
- Marinara sauce: 1 cup
- 1 minced garlic clove
- Olive oil, as needed
- Italian seasoning: 1 tsp.
- 6 long crusty rolls
- Fresh parsley: 1 tbsp., chopped
- Provolone cheese: 18 slices

**Instructions**

- Let the Kalorik Air Fryer Oven preheat to 400 F.
- Air fry the sausage for 12 minutes, flipping halfway through.
- Take out and wrap in foil.
- Place onion on the tray of the air fryer and oil spray with oil. Sprinkle with salt and pepper, toss and air fry for five minutes, stirring halfway through.
- Add garlic, peppers and seasonings with the onion and toss. Air fry for ten minutes more.
- In the last three minutes, add the sausage back.
- Serve the sausage in rolls with cheese and vegetables.

## PIZZA BURGERS

*Prep time:10 min | Cook time:15 min | Serves: 4*

**Ingredients**

- Ground beef & pork: 1 pound
- Black pepper, to taste
- Chopped pepperoni: 1/3 cup
- Tomato paste: 1 tbsp.
- Minced onion: 1 tbsp.
- Round ciabatta rolls: 4
- Italian seasoning: 1 tsp.
- Salt: half tsp.
- Sliced mozzarella cheese: 6 oz.

**Instructions**

- In a bowl, add all ingredients except for buns, cheese. Mix until combined.
- Make into 4 burgers.
- Toast the buns after splitting them.
- Let the Kalorik Air Fryer Oven preheat to 370 F.
- Air fry the patties for 15 minutes, flipping halfway through.
- Add the patties on the buns with mozzarella, air fry for three minutes.
- Serve right away.

## PUMPKIN SEEDS

*Prep time:20 min | Cook time:35 min | Serves: 6*

**Ingredients**

- Pumpkin seeds: 1 ½ cups
- Smoked paprika: 1 tsp.
- Olive oil: 1 tsp.
- Salt: 1 ½ salt.

**Instructions**

- Boil the seeds for ten minutes. Drain and pat dry for 20 minutes.
- Let the Kalorik Air Fryer Oven preheat to 350 F.
- Toss the seeds with the rest of the ingredients and air fry for 35 minutes.
- Serve with your desired dish.

## STUFFED JALAPENO

*Prep time: 10 min | Cook time: 10 min | Serves: 4*

### Ingredients
- 1 lb. ground pork sausage
- 1 (8 oz.) package cream cheese, softened
- 1 cup shredded Parmesan cheese
- 1 lb. large fresh jalapeno peppers halved lengthwise and seeded
- 1 (8 oz.) bottle Ranch dressing

### Directions
- in Mix pork sausage ground with ranch dressing and cream cheese in a bowl. But the jalapeno in half and remove their seeds. Divide the cream cheese mixture into the jalapeno halves.
- Place the jalapeno pepper in a baking tray. Set the Baking tray inside the Air Fryer toaster oven and close the lid. Select the Bake mode at 350°F for 10 minutes. Serve warm.

Cal 168 | Protein 9.4g | Carb 12.1g | Fat 21.2g

## FLAX SEED CHIPS

*Prep time: 5 min | Cook time: 15 min | Serves: 4*

### Ingredients
- 1 Cup almond flour
- 1/2 Cup flax seeds
- 1 1/2 Teaspoons seasoned salt
- 1 Teaspoon sea salt
- 1/2 Cup water

### Directions
- Preheat the Air fryer toaster oven to 340°F.
- Combine almond flour, flax seeds, 1 1/2 teaspoons seasoned salt and sea salt in a container; Stir in the water up to the dough is completely mixed.
- Shape the dough into narrow size slices the size of a bite and place them on a baking sheet. Sprinkle the rounds with seasoned salt.
- Bake in preheated air fryer toaster oven up to crispy, about 15 minutes.
- Cool fully and store in an airtight box or in a sealed bag.

Cal 126.9 | Fat 6.1g | Carb 15.9g | Protein 2.9g

## PORK RIND NACHOS

*Prep time:5 min | Cook time:5 min | Serves: 2*

### Ingredients
- 2 tbsp. pork rinds
- 1/4 cup cooked chicken shredded
- 1/4 cup sour cream
- Shredded Monterey jack cheese: half cup
- 1/4 cup pickled jalapeños, sliced
- 1/4 cup guacamole

### Instructions
- Put pork rinds in a 6-inch round baking pan. Fill with grilled chicken and cheese. Put the pan in the basket with the air fryer.
- Let the Kalorik Air Fryer Oven preheat to 370 F.
- Air fry for 5 minutes or until the cheese has been melted.
- Serve with jalapeños, sour cream & guacamole.

Cal 295 | Protein 30.1g | Fat 27.5g | Carb3.0 g

## REUBEN EGG ROLLS

*Prep time:20 min | Cook time:20 min | Serves: 8*

### Ingredients
- 8 egg roll wrappers
- Russian dressing: 1 cup
- Corned beef: 12 oz., sliced
- Sauerkraut: 2 cups
- Swiss cheese: 16 slices

### Instructions
- In each egg wrapper, add cheese, corned beef (2 oz.), sauerkraut (1/4 cup), and Russian dressing (1/4 cup).
- Seal the edges with water and roll tightly.
- Let the Kalorik Air Fryer Oven preheat to 400 F.
- Oil spray the rolls and air fry for ten minutes.
- Serve right away

## CAULIFLOWER PIZZA BITES

*Prep time:20 min | Cook time:15 min | Serves: 8*

### Ingredients
**Crust**
- Grated Parmesan cheese: half cup
- 2 eggs
- Black pepper, to taste
- Cauliflower: 1 head
- All-purpose flour: ¼ cup
- Salt: 1 tsp.

**Pepperoni Pizza Bites**
- Dried oregano
- Pizza sauce: 1 cup
- Mini pepperoni: 1 cup
- Grated mozzarella cheese: 2 cups

### Instructions
- Rice the cauliflower in the chopper. Squeeze the water from the cauliflower.
- In a bowl, add cauliflower and the rest of the crust's ingredients.
- Let the Kalorik Air Fryer Oven preheat to 400 F.
- Make the cauliflower mixture into little patties, and air fryer the patties.
- Cook for 8 minutes after spraying with oil, flip and cook for 2 more minutes.
- Add the pizza sauce to the cauliflower crust. Add cheese and pepperoni slices.
- Air fry for 3-5 minutes at 360 F.
- Sprinkle oregano and serve.

## APPLE CRANBERRY MINI BRIE BITES
*Prep time:20 min | Cook time:20 min | Serves: 8-12*

### Ingredients
- 1 Smith apple
- Puff pastry: 2 sheets
- Whole cranberry sauce: 1 cup
- Brie cheese: 8 oz.
- chopped fresh rosemary: 2 tsp.
- 1 egg, whisked

### Instructions
- Cut the brie into 24 pieces.
- Cut the pastry into 12" squares.
- Cut the apple into thin slices and a further cut in half
- In a bowl, mix the cranberry sauce with rosemary.
- Brush the puff pastry with whisked eggs.
- Add some cranberry sauce, brie piece and apple piece.
- Wrap the pastry and seal the edges.
- With egg wash, brush the pastry and keep it in the fridge for half an hour.
- Let the Kalorik Air Fryer Oven preheat to 360 F.
- Air fry the bites for ten minutes.
- Serve warm.

## SOFT PRETZELS
*Prep time:60 min | Cook time:6 min | Serves: 12*

### Ingredients
- Water warm: 1 cup
- All-purpose flour: 2½ cups
- Yeast: 2 tsp.
- Sugar: 1 tsp.
- Baking soda: 1 tbsp.
- Salt: 1 tsp.
- Butter: 2 tbsp., melted
- Boiling water: 1 cup

### Instructions
- In a bowl, add warm water and yeast. Mix and rest it for five minutes.
- In a stand mixer, add flour, salt and sugar, use the hook and add yeast mixture slowly as it is running. Add butter, knead for ten minutes.
- Let it rest for 60 minutes. Divide the dough into 12 pieces.
- Roll and make into a knot, place on the parchment lined tray.
- Let the Kalorik Air Fryer Oven preheat to 350 F.
- In a bowl, mix baking soda with boiling water. Let it cool a little, soak the pretzels in this water for 1 minute and place them on the tray, sprinkle some salt on top.
- Air fry for three minutes on each side.
- Brush with butter and serve with mustard.

## CHEDDAR CHEESE BISCUITS
*Prep time:15 min | Cook time:22 min | Serves: 8*

### Ingredients
- Self-rising flour: 2 1/3 Cups
- Buttermilk: 1-1/3 Cups
- Sugar: 2 tbsp.
- Butter: half cup, frozen
- Butter: 1 tbsp., melted
- Cheddar cheese: half cup, grated

### Instructions
- In a bowl, add the sugar, cheese and flour. Grated the cold butter.
- Mix and add buttermilk, make it into a wet dough.
- Roll the dough thickly in some flour and cut into 8 pieces with a cookie-cutter.
- Place the biscuits on the air fryer tray.
- Let the Kalorik Air Fryer Oven preheat to 380 F.
- Air fry for 20 minutes; make sure they do not burn.
- Serve right away.

## ZUCCHINI FRIES

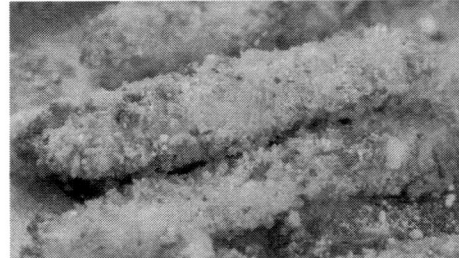

*Prep time:25 min | Cook time:12 min | Serves: 4*

### Ingredients
Garlic Aioli
- Olive oil: 2 tbsp.
- Salt & pepper, to taste
- Mayonnaise: half cup
- Roasted garlic: 1 tsp.
- Half lemon's juice

Zucchini Fries
- 1 large zucchini, sliced into half-inch sticks
- Flour: half cup
- seasoned breadcrumbs: 1 cup
- 2 eggs, whisked
- salt & pepper

### Instructions
- In a bowl, add all ingredients of aioli and mix. Adjust seasoning.
- In a bowl, add flour and season with salt and pepper.
- In another bowl, add whisked eggs.
- In the third bowl, add seasoned breadcrumbs.
- Coat the zucchini fries in flour, then in eggs and lastly in breadcrumbs.
- Place them on the air fryer tray. Let them rest for ten minutes.
- Let the Kalorik Air Fryer Oven preheat to 400 F.
- Oil spray the zucchini fries and air fry for 12 minutes, flipping halfway through.
- Serve with aioli.

## CAULIFLOWER PAN PIZZA
*Prep time:20 min | Cook time:20 min | Serves: 2*

### Ingredients
- Parmesan cheese: 1/3 Cup
- 1 egg
- Grated mozzarella: 1 ½ Cups
- Riced cauliflower: 2 cups
- Oregano: half tsp.
- Pizza sauce: ¼ Cup
- Fresh basil leaves

- Flour: 2 tbsp.
- Salt & black pepper, to taste

**Instructions**

- Let the Kalorik Air Fryer Oven preheat to 400 F.
- squeeze any moisture from riced cauliflower.
- In a bowl, add cauliflower, and the rest of the ingredients, except for pizza sauce, some mozzarella.
- Mix well.
- Add foil to the 7" baking pan, add the cauliflower mixture and press in the pan.
- Air fry for ten minutes, take out, flip and air fry for five minutes.
- Take out and spread the pizza sauce, add mozzarella cheese and oregano on top.
- Air fry for five minutes at 360 F, till cheese melts.
- Serve right away.

## BACON-CHEDDAR STUFFED POTATO SKINS

*Prep time:30 min | Cook time:42 min | Serves: 2-4*

**Ingredients**

- 2 russet potatoes, medium-sized
- Sour cream
- Grated cheddar cheese: 2 cups
- Bacon cooked: 1/4 pound, chopped
- Salt & black pepper, to taste
- Scallions chopped

**Instructions**

- Let the Kalorik Air Fryer Oven preheat to 400 F.
- Cut the potatoes in length half. Oil spray and season with salt and pepper.
- Air fry for 20 minutes cut side up. Flip and air fry for ten minutes.
- Take the flesh out and leave a shell.
- Oil spray with oil, sprinkle salt and pepper, air fry for ten minutes.
- Add bacon and cheese, air fry for 1-2 minutes.
- Serve with sour cream and scallions.

Cal 860 | Fat 60g | Carb 41g | Protein 40g

## AIR FRYER BREAD

*Prep time:70 min | Cook time:25 min | Serves: 1 loaf*

**Ingredients**

- Sugar: 1 ½ tsp.
- Unsalted butter: 2 tbsp., melted
- All-purpose flour: 2 2/3 cups
- Active dry yeast: 1 ½ tsp.
- Kosher salt: 1 ½ tsp.

**Instructions**

- Oil spray a 6 by 3" round pan.
- In a stand mixer, add sugar, warm water (1 cup), salt, yeast and mix with the dough hook. At low speed, add flour gradually.
- Knead for 8 minutes at medium speed.
- Let it rest for 1 hour.
- Let the Kalorik Air Fryer Oven preheat to 380 F.
- Place the dough in the pan, air fry for 20 minutes, or the internal temperature reaches 200 F.
- Rest it for five minutes.
- Slice and serve.

## BACON-BURGER BITES

*Prep time:10 min | Cook time:20 min | Serves: 15*

**Ingredients**

- 90% beef: 2 lbs.
- Yellow mustard: 2 tbsp.
- Kosher salt: half tsp.
- 30 jalapenos slices
- 1 head of butter lettuce
- Raw bacon: 4 oz., minced
- Onion powder: half tsp.
- Black pepper: 1/4 tsp.
- Cherry tomatoes: 30
- 30 dill pickle slices

**Instructions**

- In a bowl, add bacon, onion powder, salt, beef, pepper and mustard. Mix gently. Make into 30 small balls.
- Let the Kalorik Air Fryer Oven preheat to 400 F.
- Air fry the burger balls for 8-10 minutes.
- Thread the burger balls with the rest of the ingredients alternatively and serve.

Cal: 63 | Carb 1g | Protein 7g | Fat 4g

## SHISHITO PEPPERS

*Prep time:2 min | Cook time:8 min | Serves: 4*

**Ingredients**

- 1 lemon, sliced into wedges
- Shishito peppers: 8 oz.
- Kosher salt: 1/4 tsp.

**Instructions**

- Oil spray the peppers.
- Let the Kalorik Air Fryer Oven preheat to 400 F.
- Air fry for 8 minutes, flipping halfway through until charred.
- Sprinkle salt and serve right away.

Cal 15 | Protein 1.5g | Carb 2.5g | Fats 0g

## GREEN TOMATO STACKS

*Prep time:20 min | Cook time:15 min | Serves: 8*

**Ingredients**

- Mayonnaise: 1/4 cup
- Lime zest: 1/4 tsp.
- Minced fresh thyme: 1 tsp.
- Pepper: half tsp.
- Salt: 1/4 tsp.
- Lime juice: 2 tbsp.
- Cornmeal: 3/4 cup
- All-purpose flour: 1/4 cup
- 2 red tomatoes
- 2 egg whites, whisked
- 2 green tomatoes
- Canadian bacon: 8 slices

**Instructions**

- Let the Kalorik Air Fryer Oven preheat to 375 F.
- In a bowl, mix thyme, mayo, lime juice, zest and pepper (1/4 tsp.).
- In a bowl, add flour.
- In another bowl, add the egg whites.
- In the fourth bowl, add salt, the rest of the pepper and cornmeal.

- Slice each tomato in four slices, coat in flour, then in egg and lastly in cornmeal.
- Oil spray the tomatoes.
- Place on the tray, air fry for 4 to 6 minutes, flip, oil spray and air fry for 4 to 6 minutes more.
- Serve alternate color tomato
- Serve with mayo sauce.

Cal 114 | Fat 2g | Carb 18g | Protein 6g

## AVOCADO EGG ROLLS

*Prep time:15 min | Cook time:15 min | Serves: 4-6*

### Ingredients
- 10 egg roll wrappers
- 3 medium avocados, cut into cubes
- Limes juice from 1 to 2 limes
- Diced red onion: 2/3 cup
- Chopped cilantro: 1/3 cup
- Sundried tomatoes: ¼ cup, chopped without oil
- Salt & black pepper, to taste

### Instructions
- In a bowl, add all ingredients except for egg rolls and mix.
- In each egg roll, place some filling and roll tightly seal the edges with water.
- Oil spray the egg rolls.
- Let the Kalorik Air Fryer Oven preheat to 400 F
- Cook for 12 minutes, flipping halfway through, and oil spray again.
- Serve right away.

Cal 148 | Protein 3.5g | Carb 17.5g | Fats 8g

## HAM & CHEESE TURNOVERS

*Prep time:20 min | Cook time:10 min | Serves: 4*

### Ingredients
- Crumbled blue cheese: 2 tbsp.
- Deli ham: 1/4 pound, sliced thin
- 1 pear, sliced thin
- 1 tube of pizza crust, 13 oz.
- Chopped walnuts: 1/4 cup, toasted

### Instructions
- Let the Kalorik Air Fryer Oven preheat to 400 F.
- Roll the pizza dough to a 12-inch square. Slice into four squares.
- In each square, add ham, walnuts, cheese and pear. Fold the dough and seal the edges, make into a triangle.
- Air fry the turnovers for 4 to 6 minutes after spraying with oil on each side.
- Serve right away.

Cal 357 | Fat 10g | Carb 55g | Protein 15g

## TORTELLINI WITH PROSCIUTTO

*Prep time:25 min | Cook time:10 min | Serves: 3 ½ dozen*

### Ingredients
- Chopped onion: 3 tbsp.
- Olive oil: 1 tbsp.
- Tomato puree: 15 oz.
- Chopped fresh basil: 1 tbsp.
- 1/4 tsp each, salt & pepper
- 4 minced garlic cloves

### Tortellini
- Minced fresh parsley: 1 tbsp.

- Milk: 2 tbsp.
- Seasoned bread crumbs: 2/3 cup
- Garlic powder: 1 tsp.
- 2 eggs
- Prosciutto ricotta: 1 pack tortellini
- Pecorino romano cheese: 2 tbsp., grated
- Salt: half tsp.

### Instructions
- In a pan, add oil on medium flame.
- Sauté garlic, onion for 3 to 4 minutes.
- Add puree, salt, basil and pepper. Let it come to a boil. Simmer for ten minutes.
- Let the Kalorik Air Fryer Oven preheat to 350 F.
- In a bowl, whisk eggs with milk.
- In the other bowl, add garlic powder, parsley, salt, cheese and bread crumbs.
- Coat the tortellini in egg then in crumbs. Oil spray them and air fry for 4 to 5 minutes on each side.
  Serve with sauce

## DEEP DISH PIZZA

*Prep time:20 min | Cook time:22 min | Serves: 2*

### Ingredients
- Button mushrooms: 3 oz., sliced
- Pizza dough: 12 oz.
- Spinach: half cup
- Olive oil: 1 tbsp.
- Prosciutto: 3 oz., sliced
- Italian seasoning: ¼ tsp.
- Pizza sauce: 1/3 cup
- Grated mozzarella cheese: 1½ cups

### Instructions
- Coat the mushrooms with olive oil, Italian seasonings. Let it rest for 15 minutes.
- Let the Kalorik Air Fryer Oven preheat to 370 F.
- Oil spray a 7" baking pan and roll the dough, and place in the pan.
- Pierce with a fork, air fry for five minutes.
- Take out and flip the crust, air fry for five minutes.
- Add sauce and cheese on top.
- On half of the pizza, add spinach and add mushrooms to the other half.
- Add prosciutto on top.
- Air fry for 10-12 minutes.
- Slice and serve.

Cal 941 | Fat 48g | Carb 89g | Protein 40g

## AVOCADO FRIES WITH LIME DIPPING SAUCE

*Prep time:10 min | Cook time:10 min | Serves: 4-5*

**Ingredients**

- Panko breadcrumbs: 3/4 cup
- 2 small avocados, sliced into 16 wedges
- seasoning salt (lime chili): 1 1/4 tsp.
- 1 egg, whisked

**Lime dipping sauce**

- Mayonnaise: 3 tbsp.
- kosher salt: 1/8 tsp.
- Greek Yogurt: 1/4 cup
- lime juice: 2 tsp.
- seasoning salt (lime chili): half tsp.

**Instructions**

- Let the Kalorik Air Fryer Oven preheat to 390 F.
- In a bowl, whisk egg.
- In another bowl, add panko with seasoned salt.
- Season the avocado with seasoned salt, coat in egg and then in crumbs.
- Spray with oil and air fry for 7-8 minutes, flip halfway through.
- Serve with dipping sauce.
- In a bowl, add all ingredients of dipping sauce and mix.

Cal 197 | Protein 7g | Carb 15g | Fats 12.5g

## STUFFED BAGEL BALLS

*Prep time:10 min | Cook time:25 min | Serves: 4-5*

**Ingredients**

- All-purpose flour: 1 cup
- Greek yogurt: 1 cup
- Baking powder: 2 tsp.
- 1 egg white, whisked
- Kosher salt: ¾ tsp.
- Cream cheese: 4 oz., cut into 8 cubes

**Instructions**

- In a bowl, add flour, salt and baking powder and mix.
- Add yogurt and mix until it crumbles.
- Knead the dough for 15 turns.
- Make into 8 balls.
- Roll into a circle and add half tbsp. of cream cheese. Roll in a ball.
- Brush the top with egg wash.
- Let the Kalorik Air Fryer Oven preheat to 325 F on bake.
- Bake for 11-12 minutes. Serve warm.

Cal 173 | Protein 10.5 g | Carb 25 g | Fats 3 g

## GARLIC KNOTS

*Prep time:10 min | Cook time:20 min | Serves: 4-5*

**Ingredients**

- Kosher salt: ¾ tsp.
- 3 minced garlic cloves
- Whole wheat flour: 1 cup
- Greek yogurt: 1 cup
- Butter: 2 tsp.
- Parmesan cheese: 1 tbsp., grated
- Baking powder: 2 tsp.
- Fresh parsley: 1 tbsp., chopped

**Instructions**

- Let the Kalorik Air Fryer Oven preheat to 375 F.

- In a bowl, add flour, salt and baking powder and mix.
- Add yogurt and make it into a soft dough.
- Divide into 8 pieces and roll each piece into 9" long strip.
- Make each strip into a knotted ball, and place it on the tray.
- Oil spray the buns.
- Let the Kalorik Air Fryer Oven preheat to 325 F.
- Air fry the knots for 11-12 minutes.
- In a pan, add butter and garlic cook for few minutes.
- Brush the knots with garlic butter and serve.

Cal 87 | Protein 5g | Carb 14g | Fat 1.5g

## HALOUMI POPCORN

*Prep time:20 min | Cook time:10 min | Serves: 10-12*

**Ingredients**

- Brown sugar: 1 tsp.
- Mustard powder: 1 tsp.
- Smoked paprika: 2 tsp.
- 2 eggs
- Onion powder: 1 tsp.
- Thyme fresh leaves: 1 tbsp.
- Garlic powder: half tsp.
- Corn flour: 1 tsp.
- Haloumi: 1 cup, 1-inch pieces
- Panko breadcrumbs: 1 1/4 cups

**Instructions**

- Let the Kalorik Air Fryer Oven preheat to 356 F.
- In a bowl, add all spices, cornflour and sugar. Mix and add halloumi stir to coat.
- Place on the tray.
- In a bowl, whisk eggs and coat the halloumi in eggs.
- In a bowl, mix thyme with bread crumbs and coat the halloumi in crumbs. Keep in the freezer for five minutes.
- Air fry the halloumi for 6 to 8 minutes, until soft.
- Serve right away.

## PEACH, PROSCIUTTO & BURRATA FLATBREAD

*Prep time:10 min | Cook time:12 min | Serves: 2*

**Ingredients**

- 1 peach, sliced
- Burrata cheese: 2 oz.
- Dark brown sugar: 2 tbsp.
- Serrano ham: 3 slices, sliced
- Olive oil, to taste
- Butter: 1 tbsp., melted
- Mint leaves
- 1 flat bread crust (pre made), 7 inches
- Balsamic glaze

**Instructions**

- Toss the peach slices in butter and sprinkle brown sugar.
- Let the Kalorik Air Fryer Oven preheat to 400 F.
- Air fry peaches for five minutes. Take out and air fry the ham after spraying with oil.
- Air fry for 2 minutes.
- Brush the flatbread with oil, air fry for three minutes, flip and air fry for 2 minutes.
- Add ham and peaches to the bread, add burrata cheese on top.
- Air fry for two minutes.

- Drizzle balsamic and serve.
Cal 428 | Fat 20g | Carb 48g | Protein 17g

## TOSTONES
*Prep time:5 min | Cook time:20 min | Serves: 4-5*

### Ingredients
- Garlic powder: 3/4 tsp.
- 1 plantain (large green), trimmed & peeled
- Kosher salt: 1 tsp.
- Water: 1 cup

### Instructions
- Cut the plantain in half, lengthwise, cut it into one" pieces. Total 8 pieces.
- In a bowl, add the rest of the ingredients.
- Let the Kalorik Air Fryer Oven preheat to 400 F.
- Oil spray the plantain and air fry for 6 minutes.
- Mash the plantain.
- Dip in the water mixture.
- Air fry for five minutes.
- Season with salt and serve.
Cal 102 | Protein 1 g | Carb 27 g

## PUMPKIN FRIES
*Prep time:25 min | Cook time:15 min | Serves: 4*

### Ingredients
- Greek yogurt: half cup
- Pepper: ¼ tsp.
- Chopped chipotle peppers: 2-3 tsp., in adobo sauce
- Ground cumin: ¼ tsp.
- Salt, to taste
- Maple syrup: 2 tbsp.
- 1 pumpkin
- Garlic powder: ¼ tsp.
- Chili powder: ¼ tsp.

### Instructions
- In a bowl, add maple syrup, salt, yogurt, chipotle peppers mix and keep in the fridge.
- Let the Kalorik Air Fryer Oven preheat to 400 F.
- Peel and slice the pumpkin in half. Cut into half-inch strips.
- Toss with salt and all other spices.
- Air fry the pumpkin for 6 to 8 minutes. Stir and air fry for 3 to 5 minutes.
- Serve with sauce.
Cal 151 | Fat 3g | Carb 31g | Protein 5g

## MINI CALZONES

*Prep time:25 min | Cook time:10-15 min | Serves: 16*

### Ingredients
- Pizza dough: 1 pound
- Mini pepperoni: 6 oz., chopped
- Pizza sauce: 1 cup
- Mozzarella cheese: 8 oz., shredded

### Instructions
- Roll the dough into 1/4" thick.
- Slice into 8-10 circles. Make a total of 16 circles.
- Add pizza sauce, pepperoni and cheese to each circle.
- Fold the circle in half and seal the edges.
- Let the Kalorik Air Fryer Oven preheat to 374 F.
- Air fry the calzones for 8 minutes. Serve right away.
Cal 185 | Fat 9.3g | Carb 16.4g | Protein 8.4g

## PEPPER POPPERS
*Prep time:20 min | Cook time:15 min | Serves: 12*

### Ingredients
- Cream cheese: 8 oz., softened
- Smoked paprika: ¼ tsp.
- Shredded cheddar cheese: 3/4 cup
- 6 cooked bacon strips, crumbled
- Jalapenos: 1 pound, halved without seeds
- Salt: ¼ tsp.
- Garlic powder: ¼ tsp.
- Monterey jack cheese: 3/4 cup, shredded
- Chili powder: ¼ tsp.
- Bread crumbs: half cup

### Instructions
- Let the Kalorik Air Fryer Oven preheat to 325 F.
- In a bowl, add seasonings, bacon and chess. Mix and spoon into each pepper half. Coat in bread crumbs.
- Oil spray the peppers.
- Air fry for 15 to 20 minutes.
Cal 81 | Fat 6g | Carb 3g | Protein 3g

## THYME GARLIC TOMATOES
*Prep time:10 min | Cook time:10 min | Serves: 4*

### Ingredients
- Salt & black pepper
- 4 roma tomatoes
- Dried thyme: half tsp.
- Olive oil: 1 tbsp.
- 1 garlic clove minced

### Instructions
- Let the Kalorik Air Fryer Oven preheat to 390 F.
- Slice the tomatoes in half and take the flesh out.
- Toss with olive oil and other ingredients.
- Air fry for 15 minutes cut side up.
- Serve with pasta.
Cal 43 | Fat 3g | Carb 2g

## STUFFING HUSHPUPPIES
*Prep time:10 min | Cook time:12 min | Serves: 15*

### Ingredients
- Cold stuffing: 3 cups
- 1 egg

### Instructions
- In a bowl, whisk eggs. Add stuffing and mix until combined.
- Make into 1-inch balls.
- Let the Kalorik Air Fryer Oven preheat to 375 F.
- Air fry the balls for 12 minutes rotate the tray halfway.

Cal 238 | Fat 16.6g | Carb 18.8g | Protein 3.2g

## MAC & CHEESE BALLS

*Prep time:60 min | Cook time:12 min | Serves: 16*

### Ingredients

- Seasoned bread crumbs: 2 cups
- Leftover mac & cheese: 4 cups
- 2 eggs whisked

### Instructions

- Keep the leftovers in the fridge for 3 hours.
- Make into 16 balls. Coat the ball in egg then in crumbs.
- Keep in the fridge for half an hour.
- Let the Kalorik Air Fryer Oven preheat to 360 F.
- Air fry the balls for 10 to 12 minutes.
- Serve with spicy ketchup.

## SWEET AND SALTY SNACK MIX

*Prep time:5 min | Cook time:12 min | Serves: 10*

### Ingredients

- Honey ½ cup
- Cashews 1 cup
- Crispy corn puff cereal/corn pops 2 cups
- Mini pretzel crisps 2 cup
- Butter melted 3 tablespoons.
- Salt 1 teaspoon
- Sesame sticks 2 cups.
- Pepitas pumpkin seeds 1 cup
- Granola 2 cups

### Instructions

- Put the butter, honey, and salt together. Until combined, stir.
- Mix the sesame sticks, granola, cashews, corn puff cereal, pepitas, and pretzel crisps in a large bowl. To combine, pour over the surface the honey mixture and toss.
- Preheat Air Fryer to 370 F
- Air fry in two batches the snack mix. Place half of the mixture in the air fryer and fry for 10 - 12 minutes, or until the mixture is lightly toasted
- To a cookie sheet, move the snack mix & let it cool down. Keep in an airtight jar for up to 1 week or box in gift bags for a holiday gift.

Cal 198 | Fat 9.6 g | Carb 27.9 g | Protein 4.1g

## CRISPY ARTICHOKE HEARTS WITH HORSERADISH AIOLI

*Prep time:5 min | Cook time:45min | Serves: 2*

### Ingredients

- 3 cups (1 to 12-ounce bag) of Frozen artichoke hearts
- 1/4 teaspoon of coarsely ground black pepper
- 1 tablespoon of Fresh squeezed lemon juice
- 2 tablespoons of Olive oil
- 1/2 teaspoon of Homemade seasoned salt

### Instructions

- Preheat the air fryer to 400 F.
- Break the frozen artichoke heart bag open; drizzle with olive oil & lemon juice; mix well to cover the heart. Sprinkle with black pepper and seasoned salt and toss again to blend.
- Arrange artichoke hearts on a cookie sheet parchment-lined in a single layer and bake at 400 for 33 minutes.

- when they cool, the hearts can crisp up more. Move to a plate & serve as a dip of chilled horseradish sauce.

Cal 67 | Protein 2.8g | Carb 7.3g | Fat 3.1g

## PROSCIUTTO WRAPPED BRIE

*Prep time:3-4 min | Cook time:23-25 min | Serves: 6*

### Ingredients

- Brie Cheese Wheel 1 Double, small
- Prosciutto 4 ounces thinly sliced.
- Sugar-Free Preserves 2 tablespoons.

### Instructions

- In a 5" pie pan, lie prosciutto four slices.
- Place two slices that go the other direction.
- Over the first half, break the brie in half, sprinkle sugar-free preserves 1tablespoon, then place the latter half back on & spread the preserves on top.
- Fill the brie with six bacon slices.
- Bake for 20 minutes at 400F, then broil 2 to 3 minutes.
- To make this possible in the air fryer, the air fryer is set to 350F and carefully track. The cheese is undoubtedly melting once you see the crisping up of prosciutto. In order to keep the cheese in place, you would need to bring it into a tiny pan.

Cal 470 | Fat 47g | Carb 43g | Protein 21g

## AIR FRYER TATER TOTS

*Prep time:4 min | Cook time:15 min | Serves: 4*

### Ingredients

- Russet potatoes 1 1/2 lbs.
- Garlic powder 1 teaspoon
- Thyme 1/4 teaspoon
- Smoked paprika 1 teaspoon
- All-purpose flour 2 teaspoons cooking oil
- Salt & pepper
- Optional spices/seasoning

### Instructions

- Bring a saucepan or pot 3/4 of the way full of cold water to a boil with a pinch of salt. Add enough water to cover the potatoes.
- Add the potatoes and simmer for 6-12 minutes. You should be able to pierce the potatoes easily on the outside and tell that the inside of the potatoes is still firm.
- Remove the potatoes from the water. Dry and allow them to cool. Wait for about 10 minutes.
- Once cooled, use the large area of a cheese grater to grate the potatoes. Squeeze out any excess water from the potatoes.
- In a bowl, place the grated potatoes with the flour & seasonings. Russet potatoes are bland. Salt according to taste. Then stir.
- Use your hands to form tots with the mixture. I like larger tots and made 16 tater tots. You can make smaller tots if you wish.
- Spray both sides of the tots with cooking oil. Place the tots in the air fryer. Air fry for 10 minutes at 400 F
- Open the air fryer and flip the tots. Cook for an additional 5 minutes or until the tots have reached your desired crisp.

Cal 110 | Protein 1.5g | Carb 15.9g | Fat 6.1g

## GREEK BAKED FETA PISTIL

*Prep time:7-8 min | Cook time:10 min | Serves: 4*

### Ingredients

- Feta cheese 8 ounces, in a block
- Dried Oregano 1 tablespoons

- Honey/Choc zero Syrup for Keto 2 tablespoons.
- Olive oil 2 tablespoons.
- Crushed red pepper 1 tablespoons

**Instructions**

- Cut the feta block in half and then cut half of each thinner slice to produce four pieces.
- On a serving bowl (heatproof), arrange these.
- Using a basting brush (silicone) to disperse the oil uniformly. With olive oil, drizzle the cheese. Then sprinkle with the oregano and red pepper flakes.
- Using a basting brush (silicone), cover with honey and uniformly scatter the honey throughout.
- Put the dish in the air fryer.
- For 10 minutes, to 400F, set the air fryer.
- When finished, remove and serve with the basting brush to disperse any honey and oil that has been transferred to the bottom.

Cal 35 | Carb 8g | Protein 1g | Fat 1g

## GERMAN CURRYWURST RECIPE

*Prep time:10 min | Cook time:12 min | Serves: 4*

**Ingredients**

- Canned tomato sauce 1 cup
- Cayenne pepper ¼ teaspoon
- Diced onion ½ cup.
- Bratwurst 1 lb.
- Vinegar 2 tablespoons.
- Curry powder 2 teaspoons
- Sweet paprika 2 teaspoons
- Truvia 1/2 teaspoon, or sugar 1 teaspoons

**Instructions**

- Whisk together the tomato sauce, curry powder, paprika, vinegar, sugar, & cayenne pepper in a heatproof container 6 x 3. Stir the onions in.
- Slice the bratwurst into 1" thick chunks on the diagonal. To the sauce, apply bratwurst and mix well.
- The pan is placed in the air fryer.
- Till the sausage is cooked & the sauce is bubbling, to 400F, set the air fryer for 12 minutes.

Cal 451 | Protein 18.4g | Carb 26.1g | Fat 31.7g

## AIR-FRYER RAVIOLI

*Prep time:10 min | Cook time 10 min | Serves: 17*

**Ingredients**

- Seasoned bread crumbs 1 cup
- Optional fresh minced basil cooking spray
- Marinara sauce 1 cup, warmed.
- Shredded parmesan cheese 1/4 cup
- Dried basil 2 teaspoon
- All-purpose flour 1/2 cup
- Eggs 2 large, lightly beaten.
- Frozen beef ravioli 9 ounces, thawed.

**Instructions**

- Preheat the fryer to 350 F.
- Mix the bread crumbs, the parmesan cheese, and the basil in a bowl. In different bowls, position the flour & eggs.
- To cover all ends, dip the ravioli in flour; shake off the waste. Dip in the eggs, then pat in the crumb mixture to help adhere to the coating.

- Arrange the ravioli in batches in the air-fryer in a single layer, dust with cooking spray. Then Cook until crispy brown, 3 to 4 minutes. Flip; spritz with spray for cooking. Cook until crispy brown, 3 to 4 minutes longer. Sprinkle instantly with basil and extra Parmesan cheese if needed. With marinara sauce, serve warm.

Cal 373 | Protein 17.6g | Carb 45.6g | Fat 13.4g

## AIR FRYER FRENCH TOAST STICKS

*Prep time:10 min | Cook time:8 min | Serves: 12*

**Ingredients**

- Granulated sugar 1/4 cup
- Cinnamon 1 tablespoons
- Optional Maple syrup
- Texas Toast 12 slices
- Milk 1 cup
- Eggs 5 large
- Butter 4, melted.
- Vanilla extract 1 teaspoon

**Instructions**

- Slice each slice of bread into thirds.
- Add the milk, butter, eggs, and vanilla to a cup. Whisk until they're mixed.
- Add the sugar and the cinnamon to a separate bowl.
- Dip each stick of bread into the mixture of eggs easily.
- Sprinkle both sides with the sugar mixture.
- Put in the air-fryer & cook for around 8 minutes or until only crispy at 350 °F.
- Remove and allow to cool. If desired, serve it with maple syrup.

Cal 48 | Protein 1.9g | Carb 5g | Fat 2.2g

## BACON-WRAPPED CRACKERS

*Prep time:5 min | Cook time:8 min | Serves: 4-5*

**Ingredients**

- Brown sugar: 2 tbsp.
- 14 club crackers
- Cayenne pepper, a pinch
- Bacon: 7 slices, cut in half lengthwise

**Instructions**

- Around every cracker, wrap a piece of bacon.
- Sprinkle sugar and cayenne pepper on bacon.
- Oil spray the basket of the air fryer.
- Let the Kalorik Air Fryer Oven preheat to 350 F.
- Air fry for 8-10 minutes, flipping halfway through.

## AVOCADO WEDGES

*Prep time:10 min | Cook time:30 min | Serves: 1 dozen*

**Ingredients**

- Lime juice 1 to 2 tablespoons
- Grated lime zest 1 teaspoon

- Ripe avocados 2 med
- Bacon strips 12
- Sauce:
- Mayonnaise 1/2 cup
- Sriracha chili sauce 2 to 3 tablespoons.

**Instructions**

- Preheat to 400 the air fryer. Cut in half each avocado; peel and extract the pit. Cut the halves into thirds each. Wrap around every avocado wedge with 1 bacon slice. If required, operate in batches, put wedges in one layer in the fryer & cook 10-15 minutes until the bacon is fried through.
- Meanwhile, whisk together the mayonnaise, lime juice, sriracha sauce, and zest in a bowl. With sauce on the wedges, serves.

Cal 243 | Carb 6.3g | Protein 10.4g | Fat 20.4g

## AIR-FRYER CRUMB-TOPPED SOLE
*Prep time:5 min | Cook time:10 min | Serves: 4*

**Ingredients**

- Ground Mustard 1/2 teaspoon
- Butter 2 teaspoons., melted.
- Reduced-Fat mayonnaise 3 tablespoons
- Grated parmesan cheese 3 tablespoons
- Mustard seed 2 teaspoons
- Pepper 1/4 teaspoon
- Sole fillets 4 (6 ounces each)
- Soft bread crumbs 1 cup
- Green onion 1, finely chopped.

**Instructions**

- Preheat the fryer to 375 F. Combine the mayonnaise, 2 tablespoons. of cheese, mustard seeds, and pepper; add to the tops of the fillets.
- In an air-fryer, Cook until the fish easily flakes, 3-5 minutes, with a fork.
- Combine the bread crumbs, ground mustard, onion, and the remaining 1 tablespoon of cheese in a small bowl; whisk in the butter. Spoon over the fillets, patting to stick gently; spritz topping with spray for frying. Cook until crispy brown, 2-3 minutes longer. Sprinkle with extra green onions if desired.

Cal 233 | Fat 11g | Carb8g | Protein 24g

## QUESO FUNDIDO
*Prep time:2-3 min | Cook time:25 min | Serves: 3-4*

**Ingredients**

- Mexican-style chorizo 4 ounces, casings removed.
- Onions 1 cup, chopped.
- Minced Garlic 1 tablespoon
- Diced tomatoes 1 cup.
- Jalapenos 2, diced.
- Ground Cumin 2 teaspoons
- Grated Oaxaca cheese/Mozzarella 2 cups
- Half and Half 1/2 cup

**Instructions**

- Mix the chorizo, garlic, tomatoes, onion, jalapenos & ground cumin together in a heatproof pan 6 x 3. Place the pan in the in the air fryer.
- For 15 minutes or till the sausage is fried, to 400F, set the air fryer. Stir the mixture halfway through cooking to break the sausage.
- The cheese, half and half are added, then swirl again.

- For 10 minutes, to 320F, set the air fryer before the cheese melts.
- Serve with chips or tortillas.
- Cut the onions in half & use cherry tomatoes rather than normal tomatoes to reduce Carb.

Cal 160 | Carb 3g | Protein 9g

## ONION RINGS
*Prep time:10 min | Cook time:10 min | Serves: 4*

**Ingredients**

- Mayo 1/3 cup
- Ketchup 1 1/2 -2 tablespoons
- Creamy horseradish 1-2 tablespoons
- Smoked paprika 1/2 teaspoon.
- Oregano 1/2 teaspoon
- Salt n pepper
- Vidalia onion 1 large (peeled) Mine weighed 12oz.
- Panko breadcrumbs 1 1/2 cup
- Buttermilk 1 cup
- Beaten 1 egg.
- Flour 1 cup
- Smoked paprika 1 teaspoon.
- Garlic powder 1 teaspoon
- Optional Dipping Sauce

**Instructions**

- Spray the air fryer with cooking oil.
- Cut stems off all onion sides. Cut onion into rounds that are 1/2" thick. There are wobbly onions. When chopping, be patient and if necessary, use a mandolin. Before you slice, attempt to stabilize the onion.
- In a large bowl, add the flour. With the garlic powder, smoked paprika, salt, & pepper to taste, season the flour.
- To seasoned flour, add the egg and buttermilk. Beat & stir to blend together.
- In a separate bowl, add the panko breadcrumbs.
- Dredge the sliced onions and the panko breadcrumbs in the flour buttermilk blend.
- On a tray, put the onion rings. For 15 minutes, Freeze the onion rings after onions breading.
- In an air fryer, put the onions. Don't leave them stacked. If required, cook in batches.
- With cooking oil, spray it.
- Cook at 370o for 10-12 minutes. To determine that both sides are crisp & golden brown, check in on yours. If required, flip.

Cal 152 | Fat 6g | Carb 18g | Protein 4g

## BACON WRAPPED CHICKEN BITES
*Prep time: 10 min | Cook time:8 min | Serves: 10*

**Ingredients**

- Skinless, boneless chicken breast 1.25 lbs. 3, cut in 1" chunks (30 pieces)
- Optional, for dipping duck sauce/Thai sweet chili sauce
- Centre cut bacon 10 slices, cut into thirds.

**Instructions**

- Preheat the fryer.
- Wrap a bacon piece around each chicken piece and secure it with a toothpick.
- For 8 minutes in batches, Air fry in an even 400F layer, rotating halfway till chicken is cooked & browned is the bacon.
- Blot it on a paper towel & serve it immediately.

Cal 453 | Protein 33.4g | Carb 1g | Fat 34.3g

## NEW YORK STYLE EGG ROLLS
*Prep time:10 min | Cook time:10 min | Serves: 12*

**Ingredients**
- Egg Roll Wrappers 12
- Egg 1
- Oil Mister 1
- Egg Roll Bowls 4 cups
- Sweet 'N Sour Sauce 1 cup
- Hamburger Hamlet Apricot Dipping Sauce 1 cup

**Instructions**
- Prepare the dipping sauce
- Crack the egg and whisk it in a shallow bowl. Spread out the wrapping of an egg roll with one of the corners pointed towards you.
- Slightly moistened with Egg Wash Wrapper sides. To compact the filling, take a decent Egg Roll filling one-third cup and squeeze out excess liquid. Place the filling slightly below the wrapper centre.
- Tuck under the filling and fold the bottom point over the filling. Fold all sides in to make sure the first flap holds to them. Close up firmly and seal the wrapper with Egg Wash. Repeat until you have finished all the Egg Rolls.
- In the Air Fryer, bring the Egg Rolls in. Spray the egg rolls generously with oil.
- Cook for 10 minutes at 390 F, turning halfway through & shaking if required.

Cal 216 | Protein 10.6g | Carb 27g | Fat 7.7g

## BAKED ZUCCHINI STICKS
*Prep time: 5 min | Cook time:25 min | Serves: 4*

**Ingredients**
- Cooking spray
- Grated pecorino Romano cheese 2 tablespoons
- Garlic powder 1/4 teaspoon
- For dipping marinara sauce, 1/2 cups optional
- 7 oz. each zucchini 4 meds, ends trimmed.
- Egg whites 3 large, beaten.
- Kosher salt 1/4 teaspoon
- Fresh black pepper, to taste.
- Whole wheat bread crumbs 1 cup

**Instructions**
- Preheat to 400F the air fryer.
- Air fry in batches in a single layer, 12-14 minutes, turning halfway till golden.

Cal 219 | Carb 26g | Protein 6g | Fat 9g

## TAQUITOS
*Prep time:10 min | Cook time:15 min | Serves: 10*

**Ingredients**
- Corn tortillas 10 (6 inches), warmed.
- Salsa & guacamole Optional cooking spray
- Eggs 2 large
- Dry bread crumbs 1/2 cup
- Taco seasoning 3 tablespoons
- Lean ground beef 1 lb.

**Instructions**
- Preheat the fryer to 350 F. Combine the eggs, bread crumbs & taco seasoning in a wide bowl. Add beef, blend thoroughly but lightly.
- Spoon the beef mixture 1/4 cup down the middle of each tortilla. With toothpicks, roll up tightly & secure. Arrange taquitos in batches on an oiled tray in the air-fryer in a single layer; spritz with the cooking spray.
- Cook for 6 minutes; switch and cook till meat is cooked & taquitos are 6-7 minutes longer, golden brown & crispy. Before serving, remove the toothpicks. Serve with salsa & guacamole if desired.

Cal 174 | Protein 10.3g | Carb 12.9g | Fat 9.2g

## ACORN SQUASH SLICES
*Prep time:10 min | Cook time:15 min. | Serves: 6*

**Ingredients**
- Butter 1/2 cup, softened.
- Acorn squash 2 med
- Packed brown sugar 2/3 cup.

**Instructions**
- Preheat the fryer to 350 F. Slice the squash lengthwise in half; cut and discard the seeds. Cut crosswise each half to 1/2" slices; discard the ends. in a single layer Arrange squash in batches on an oiled tray in an air-fryer. Cook till about warm, 5 minutes on either side.
- Combine the butter and sugar; spread the squash. Cook for 3 minutes longer.

Cal 148 | Carb 11g | Protein 1g | Fat 3g

## RATATOUILLE
*Prep time:10 min | Cook time:25 min | Serves: 4*

**Ingredient**
- White wine 1 tablespoon
- Vinegar 1 teaspoon
- Eggplant ½ small, in cubes
- Zucchini 1, in cubes
- Tomato 1 med, in cubes
- Yellow bell pepper ½ large, in cubes
- Red bell pepper ½ large, in cubes
- Onion ½, in cubes
- Cayenne pepper 1 fresh, diced.
- Fresh basil 5 sprigs stemmed and chopped.
- Fresh oregano 2 sprigs stemmed and chopped.
- Clove garlic 1, crushed.
- Salt & ground black pepper
- Olive oil 1 tablespoon

**Instructions**
- Preheat the air fryer to a temperature of 400º F.
- In a bowl, combine the eggplant, zucchini, tomatoes, bell peppers, & onion. Add the cayenne pepper, oregano, basil, salt, pepper, and garlic. Mix well and equally disperse everything. Drizzle with oil, wine, & vinegar, blending for coating all the vegetables.
- Pour the mixture of vegetables into a baking dish & put it in the air fryer's. For 8 minutes, cook. Stir; cook for an additional 8 minutes. Stir again & begin to cook until soft, stirring for another 10 to 15 minutes every 5 minutes. Switch the air fryer off, keeping the dish inside. Leave to rest before serving for 5 minutes.

Cal 79 | Protein 2.1g | Carb 10.2g | Fat 3.8g

## CHICKPEA FRITTERS WITH SWEET-SPICY SAUCE

*Prep time:10 min | Cook time:5 min | Serves: 2 dozen*

**Ingredients**

- Plain yogurt 1 cup
- Egg 1 large
- Baking soda 1/2 teaspoons
- Chopped fresh cilantro 1/2 cup.
- Green onions 2, thinly sliced.
- Sugar 2 tablespoons
- Honey 1 tablespoon
- Salt 1/2 teaspoons
- Pepper 1/2 teaspoons
- Crushed red pepper flakes 1/2 teaspoons
- Chickpeas/garbanzo beans 1 can (15 ounces), rinsed & drained.
- Ground cumin 1 teaspoons
- Salt 1/2 teaspoons
- Garlic powder 1/2 teaspoons
- Ground ginger 1/2 teaspoons

**Instructions**

- Preheat the air-fryer to 400 F
- Combine the 1st 6 ingredients in a small bowl; refrigerate before they are served.
- Put in a food processor, chickpeas and seasonings; process till finely ground. Add the baking soda and egg, pulse until combined. Move to a bowl, whisk in the green onions and cilantro.
- Drop rounded tablespoons of bean mixture into the oiled tray in the air-fryer in batches. Cook for 5-6 minutes, till lightly browned. Serve with the sauce.

Cal 46 | Fat 2g | Carb 5g | Protein 1g

## PERFECT BAKED PLANTAINS

*Prep time: 20 min | Cook time:20 min | Serves: 6*

**Ingredient**

- 1 tablespoon salt
- Olive oil 3 tablespoons. /melted coconut oil.
- Ripe plantains 3 (dark yellow having black spots)

**Instructions**

- Let the Kalorik Air Fryer Oven preheat to 400 F.
- Cut the ends of each plantain off and from end to end score the peels, ensuring sure the plantains are not cut through. Pull and discard the peels.
- Slice the plantains at an angle, 1/4-1/3" thick, to create longer pieces.
- Pile the plantain slices & drizzle them with oil on the baking sheet. Toss on all sides to cover all plantain strips. In one layer, spread them. Then sprinkle with salt generously.
- Bake 10 minutes the plantains. Then flip & bake for 10 more minutes. Serve at room temperature or warmer.

Cal 171 | Carb 28g | Protein 1g | Fat 7g

## RADISHES O'BRIEN

*Prep time:10 min | Cook time:23 min | Serves: 4*

**Ingredients**

- Garlic Cloves 4-6 sliced thinly.
- Kosher Salt 1/2-1 teaspoon
- Pepper 1/2-1 teaspoon
- Onion 1 cup, diced.
- Bell Peppers 1 cup, diced.
- Melted Butter 2 tablespoons
- Radishes 2 cups, diced.

**Instructions**

- Mix the radishes, onions, garlic, salt, peppers, and pepper together in a large bowl. Ensure that all the vegetables are of the same size in order to cook them evenly. Pour the molten butter over and blend well.
- Through the Air Fryer, put the mixture directly.
- For 20 minutes, to 360F, set the Air Fryer. Then, to crisp the vegetable edges, lift the temp for 3 minutes to 400F.

Cal 88 | Carb 9g | Protein 1g | Fat 6g

## STUFFED JALAPENO POPPERS

*Prep time:2 min | Cook time:5 min | Serves: 5*

**Ingredients**

- Bacon 2 slices cooked & crumbled.
- Fresh jalapenos 10
- Cream cheese 6 oz.
- Shredded cheddar cheese 1/4 cup

**Instructions**

- To produce 2 halves per jalapeno, break the jalapenos in two, vertically.
- In a bowl, put the cream cheese. 15 secs in the microwave for softening.
- Remove the seeds & the jalapeno inside.
- In a bowl, mix together the cream cheese, shredded cheese, and crumbled bacon. Mix well.
- For spicier poppers, add some seeds to the mixture of cream cheese, and blend well.
- With the mixture of cream cheese, stuff each jalapeno.
- Through the Air Fryer, load the poppers. With cooking oil, spray the poppers.
- Air Fryer is Closed now. Cook the poppers for 5 minutes at 370 F.
- Remove it from the Air Fryer & cool before serving.

Cal 96 | Fat 8g | Carb 1g | Protein 4g

## TORTILLA CHIPS

*Prep time:2 min | Cook time:6 min | Serves: 6*

**Ingredients**

- Corn tortillas 6
- Kosher salt

**Instructions**

- Using cooking oil to spray all sides of each tortilla.
- In 1 stack, position the tortillas. Using a pizza cutter or knife to cut the stack in two.
- To make 4 bits, then flip the stack & cut again.
- Then, both horizontally & vertically, you'll cut down the centre again to form per layer Eight total chips.

- Sprinkle salt all over the chips. If you like, you may add some additional seasonings.
- In the air fryer, Load the chips. And do not overload. If possible, cook in batches.
- Air-fry the chips at 370 F for 6 minutes.
- When they're golden brown, solid, and no longer pliable & flexible, the chips have done frying.

Cal 120 | Fat 1.5g | Carb 24g

## ROASTED RATATOUILLE RECIPE

*Prep time:15 min | Cook time:35 min | Serves: 2*

### Ingredients

- Eggplant 2 cups peeled & diced to 3/4" cubes.
- Cherry Tomatoes 1 cup left whole.
- Garlic Cloves 6-8, sliced in half lengthwise
- Oil 3 tablespoons
- Dried Oregano 1 teaspoon
- Kosher Salt 1 teaspoon
- Ground Black Pepper 1/2 teaspoons
- Dried Thyme 1/2 teaspoon
- Sweet Bell Peppers 1 cup, diced.

### Instructions

- Toss the eggplant, tomato, garlic, pepper, oil, oregano, pepper, salt, and thyme together in a medium dish.
- Put your vegetables in the air fryer. For 20 minutes or till the vegetables are soft and roasted, to 400 °F sets the air fryer.

Cal 180 | Fat 0g | Carb 43g | Protein 8g

## PARMESAN "FRIED" TORTELLINI

*Prep time: 15 min | Cook time:20 min | Serves: 6*

### Ingredients

- Kosher salt
- Black pepper
- All-purpose flour 1 cup
- Eggs 2 large
- For serving marinara
- 1 package cheese tortellini 9-oz.
- Panko breadcrumbs 1 c.
- Freshly grated parmesan 1/3 c.
- Dried oregano 1 teaspoon.
- Garlic powder 1/2 teaspoon
- Crushed red pepper flakes 1/2 teaspoon

### Instructions

- Cook the tortellini in a big pot of boiling salted water, according to product directions, until al dente. Then drain.
- Mix together the Panko, Parmesan, garlic powder, oregano, & red pepper flakes in a bowl. With salt & pepper, season. Beat the eggs in another bowl and add the flour to the 3rd small bowl.
- Coat the tortellini in the flour, and dredge them in the eggs, then in the mixture of Panko. Continue until they are all coated with tortellini.
- Put in an air fryer, then fry for 10 minutes at 370° till crispy.

Cal 108 | Carb 14g | Protein 5g | Fat 3g

## BRUSSELS SPROUTS

*Prep time:5 min | Cooking: 10 min | Serves: 2*

### Ingredients

- 1 teaspoon. Avocado oil
- 1 teaspoon Balsamic vinegar
- 2 teaspoon Crumbled cooked bacon (optional)
- 1/2 teaspoon. Salt
- 1/2 teaspoon. Ground black pepper
- 10 ounces Brussels sprouts, trimmed & halved lengthwise

### Instructions

- Preheat your air fryer to 350°F
- In a mixing bowl, combine the oil, salt, and pepper. Toss in the Brussels sprouts and toss to cover.
- Cook for 5 minutes in the air, then shake the sprouts and cook for another 5 minutes.
- Sprinkle balsamic vinegar over sprouts in a serving dish and toss to cover. Bacon should be sprinkled.
- Cal94 | Carb 13.3g | Protein 5.8g | Fat 3.4g

## SWEET AND SPICY ROASTED CARROTS

*Prep time:5 min | Cooking: 20 min | Serves: 2*

### Ingredients

- 1 tablespoon orange juice
- 1 pinch of salt & ground black pepper
- 1 serving cooking spray
- 1 tablespoon butter, melted
- 1 tablespoon hot honey
- 1/2 teaspoon ground cardamom
- 1/2 lb. baby carrots
- 1 teaspoon. grated orange zest

### Instructions

- Preheat your air fryer to 400°F
- In a mixing bowl, combine the butter, orange zest, honey, and cardamom. 1 tablespoon of the sauce should be set aside in a separate bowl. Toss in the carrots with the remaining sauce until they are evenly coated. Place the carrots in the air fryer.
- For 15 to 22 minutes, air fry until it gets roasted and tossing it after 7 minutes. Combine the orange juice and the honey-butter sauce that has been set aside. Toss with the carrots until everything is well combined. Salt and pepper to taste.

Cal 129 | Carb19.3g | Protein 0.9g | Fat 6.1g

## FRENCH FRIES

*Prep time:10 min | Cook time: 25 min | Serves: 4*

### Ingredients

- 1/2 teaspoons Kosher salt
- 1 lb. russet potatoes, peeled
- 2 teaspoons Vegetable oil
- 1 pinch cayenne pepper

### Instructions

- Each potato should be sliced lengthwise into 3/8-inch thick slices. Sections should be cut into 3/8-inch-wide sticks.
- To release excess starches, cover potatoes with water and soak for 5 minutes. Drain and cover with a few inches of boiling water (or place in a bowl of boiling water). Allow for a 10-minute rest period.
- Drain the potatoes and place them on paper towels. Blot excess water and set aside to cool for at least 10 minutes. Drizzle with oil, season with cayenne, and toss to coat in a mixing bowl.
- Preheat the air fryer to 375 F in the fryer, stack the potatoes in a double layer. Cook for 15 minutes at 350°F. Continue to fry for another 10 minutes or until golden brown. In a mixing bowl, toss the fries with salt. Serve right away.
- Notes: Go with russet potatoes for best results.

- Season these however you like, but I like to wait till the end to add salt.

Cal 106 | Carb19.9g | Protein2.3g | Fat2.4g

## POTATO HAY

*Prep time:10 min | Cook time:30 min | Serves: 4*

### Ingredients

- Kosher salt & ground black pepper
- 1 tablespoon canola oil
- 2 russet potatoes

### Instructions

- Using the medium grating attachment on a spiralizer, spiralize potatoes into spirals, cutting the spirals with kitchen shears after 4 or 5 rotations.
- Soak potato spirals for 20 minutes in a bowl of water. Drain and clean thoroughly. Using paper towels, pat potatoes dry to remove as much moisture as possible.
- Fill a big resealable plastic bag halfway with potato spirals. Toss in the oil, salt, and pepper to coat.
- Preheat the air fryer to 360°F
- Half of the potato spirals should be placed in the fry and placed in the air fryer. Cook for about 5 minutes, or until golden.
- Boost the temperature to 390 F, Toss the potato spirals with tongs after removing the fry. Return the air fryer to the heat and cook for another 10 to 12 minutes, flipping periodically.
- Reduce the temperature to 360°F and continue with the remaining potato spirals.

Cal 113 | Carb 18.6g | Protein 2.2g | Fat 3.6g

## LOADED GREEK FRIES

*Prep time:10 min | Cook time:30 min | Serves: 4*

### Ingredients

- 2 teaspoon Greek seasoning
- ½ (16 ounce) container Greek yogurt
- 1 small red onion, cut in thin strips
- ¼ cup sliced Kalamata olives
- 12 grape tomatoes, halved
- ½ English cucumber, shredded
- 1 tablespoons Lemon juice
- 2 teaspoons Freeze-dried dill
- ½ teaspoon Salt
- 1 teaspoon Minced garlic
- 1 teaspoon Apple cider vinegar
- ½ (4 ounce) package crumbled feta cheese
- 4 med russet potatoes, peeled and cut in fries
- 2 teaspoon Olive oil

### Instructions

- Sprinkle salt over the shredded cucumber in a colander. Drain for 10 minutes.
- In a small bowl, combine the yoghurt, lemon juice, dill, garlic, vinegar, and feta to make the rest of the tzatziki. Stir until everything is well combined. Set aside until ready to use, then stir in the shredded cucumber.
- Preheat your air fryer to 400°F
- In a large mixing bowl, combine the fries, olive oil, and Greek seasoning and stir to combine evenly. Half of the fries should be fried in the air fryer.

- 10 minutes in the air fryer Cook for another 5 minutes on the other side, or until desired crispiness is achieved. Continue with the remaining fries.
- Serve the fries on four plates. Drizzle the cucumber sauce over the fries. Red onion strips, Kalamata olives, and grape tomatoes should be garnished on each plate.

Cal 350 | Carb 47.5g | Protein 11g | Fat 13.8g

## HASSEL BACK POTATOES

*Prep time:10 min | Cooking: 30 min | Serves: 4*

### Ingredients

- 4 tablespoons. olive oil, or as needed
- salt and ground black pepper to taste
- ½ teaspoon. chopped fresh chives (Optional)
- 4 (6 ounce) russet potatoes, dried & scrubbed
- 2 chopsticks

### Instructions

- Preheat the air fryer to 350 F
- Take 1 potato and cut a very thin slice lengthwise from the flattest edge. Place the potato cut-side down on a cutting board so that it lies uniformly without rolling. Place chopsticks along the top and bottom edges of the potato lengthwise. Slice uniformly around the length of the potato to make 1/4-inch slices, resting the knife on chopsticks each time to keep the potato's bottom intact. Continue with the remaining potatoes. Oil the outsides and the gaps between the slices. Season to taste with salt and pepper.
- Cook the potatoes for 15 minutes in the air fryer's tank. Brush with oil and cook for another 15 minutes, or until crispy on the edges and soft in the middles. Serve with a sprinkling of chives.

Cal 250 | Carb 29.7g; | Protein 3.4g; | Fat 13.7g;

## BACON WRAPPED AVOCADOS

*Prep time: 10 min | Cook time: 30 min | Serves: 4*

### Ingredients

- 12 thick strips bacon
- large avocados, sliced
- ⅓ tsp salt
- ⅓ tsp chili powder
- ⅓ tsp cumin powder

### Directions

- Stretch the bacon strips to elongate and use a knife to cut in half to make 24 pieces. Wrap each bacon piece around a slice of avocado from one end to the other end. Tuck the end of bacon into the wrap. Arrange on a flat surface and season with salt, chili and cumin on both sides.
- Arrange 4 to 8 wrapped pieces in the air fryer and cook at 350°F for 8 minutes, or until the bacon is browned and crunchy, flipping halfway through to cook evenly. Remove onto a wire rack and repeat the process for the remaining avocado pieces.

Cal 193 | Carb 10g | Fat 16g | Protein 4g

## GARLIC AND PARSLEY BABY POTATOES

*Prep time:5 min | Cook time:20 min | Serves: 4*

**Ingredients**

- 1 tablespoon. Avocado oil
- ¼ teaspoon. Salt
- ½ teaspoon Granulated garlic
- ½ teaspoon Dried parsley
- 1 lb. baby potatoes, cut in quarters

**Instructions**

- Preheat your air fryer to 350°F
- In a mixing bowl, toss the potatoes with the oil to coat them. Toss in 1/4 teaspoon garlic granules and 1/4 teaspoon parsley to coat. Rep with the rest of the garlic and parsley. Place the potatoes in the air fryer.
- Cook, tossing occasionally, until golden brown in the air fryer, about 20 to 25 minutes.

Cal 120 | Carb 20.1g | Protein 2.4g | Fat 3.6g

## TRUFFLE FRIES

*Prep time:10 min | Cook:20 min | Serves: 4*

**Ingredients**

- 1 tablespoon of grated Parmesan cheese
- 1 ¾ lbs. russet potatoes,
- 2 teaspoon chopped fresh parsley
- ½ teaspoon. Paprika
- 2 tablespoons. truffle olive oil
- 1 teaspoon black truffle sea salt

**Instructions**

- Fries should be placed in a bowl. Soak for 30 minutes after covering with water. Drain the water and pat it dry.
- Preheat the air fryer to 400 F
- Drain the fries and place them in a big mixing bowl. Stir in the truffle paprika and olive oil until well combined. Place the fries in the air fryer.
- Cook for 20 minutes in the cold, shaking every 5 minutes. Place the fries in a bowl. Combine the Parmesan cheese, parsley, and truffle salt in a mixing bowl. Toss to evenly coat.

Cal 226; | Carb 36.1g; | Protein 4.8g; | Fat 7.6g;

## NASHVILLE CAULIFLOWER BITES

*Prep time:35 min | Cook time:20 min | Serves: 4*

**Ingredients**
**Spice Mix**

- Cayenne: 2 tsp.
- Paprika: 1 tbsp.
- Garlic powder: 2 tsp.
- Mustard powder: 2 tsp.
- Onion powder: 2 tsp.
- Freshly ground black pepper: 2 tsp.

**Cauliflower**

- Cauliflower florets: 1 lb.
- Salt, to taste

**Batter**

- Hot sauce: 1 tbsp.
- Buttermilk: 1 cup
- Dry breadcrumbs: 1 cup

- Flour: ½ cup

**Instructions**

- Add all spices to a bowl and mix.
- Add cauliflower in a different bowl and toss with salt. Add to the spice bowl and toss. Marinate in the fridge for 30 minutes, covered.
- Let your air fryer preheat to 350 F.
- In a dish, add the batter ingredients and mix. In a separate bowl, add the bread crumbs.
- Coat the vegetable in the batter, and then in breadcrumbs. Oil spray the basket.
- Cook in air fry for 15 minutes and serve.

Cal 362 | Fat 15g | Carb 45g | Protein 9g

## STROMBOLI ROLLS

*Prep time:10 min | Cook time:10 min | Serves: 6*

**Ingredients**

- 1/2 cup sausage
- 1 cup marinara or spaghetti sauce
- 1/4 cup olive oil or butter
- 1 cup mozzarella cheese
- 1 Pizza Dough
- 1/2 cup pepperoni slices

**Instructions**

- Preheat the air fryer to 400 F.
- Roll out the pizza dough until it is fully smooth.
- Stack the meats on top of the dough in layers.
- Add cheese to the top.
- Roll up your sleeves
- Cook for 10 minutes, checking often to ensure that it does not burn.

Cal 412 | Carb 34g | Protein 15g | Fat 25g

## CHICKEN POT PIE

*Prep time:10 min | Cook time:25 min | Serves: 4*

**Ingredients**

- 3 tablespoons all-purpose flour
- 1-3/4 teaspoons salt
- 1 teaspoon dried thyme
- 3/4 teaspoon pepper
- 1/2 cups whole milk
- 1 cup diced chicken 1
- 1 refrigerated pie crust
- 1/2 cup sliced carrots
- 1/2 cup green peas
- 1/2 cup corn
- 3 tablespoons of butter
- 1/3 cup chopped onion

**Instructions**

- Preheat your air fryer to 350°F with the BAKE mode. The rack should be set to the lowest level possible.
- Cut the pie crust to match the pan you're using. Cover the bottom of your plate with the leftovers.
- Bake for 5 minutes, or until the bottom pie crust is golden brown.
- While the crust is baking, melt one tablespoon of butter in a pan and sauté the carrots and onions.

- Stir in the remaining butter, flour, and seasonings until well combined. Stir in the broth and milk gradually. Cook, stirring constantly, for 2 minutes, or until the sauce has thickened. Combine the chicken, peas, and corn in a mixing bowl. Remove the pan from the sun.
- Spread out the chicken and vegetable mixture to fill the entire dish. Place the remaining pie crust on top. Brush lightly with melted butter or egg wash, as desired.
- Bake for 20-30 minutes, or until lightly browned crust. The length of time will be determined by the size of your pan. Allow for a 15-minute rest before cutting.

Cal 356 | Carb 36g | Protein 6g | Fat 21g

## STUFFED PORTOBELLO MUSHROOM

*Prep time:10 min | Cook time:15 min | Serves: 2*

**Ingredients**

- 2 cloves garlic minced
- 1 cup spinach
- 2 tablespoons balsamic vinegar
- 4-6 slices Swiss cheese
- 4-6 Portobello mushroom caps
- 1 tablespoon olive oil
- 1 lb. smoked sausage - we Bradley's
- 1 cup minced onion about 1/2 of 1 large
- 1 red bell pepper finely diced

**Instructions**

- Preheat the Vortex on AIRFRY to 350°F. For this recipe, the rack should be set to Centre.
- Sausage, tomatoes, and onions can all be diced up. Place onions on a tray and roast in an air fryer for 4 minutes, or until wilted.
- During the preparation of the sausage. Clean the mushrooms just enough to remove some dirt. Scrape the interior of the mushrooms with a spoon and remove the gills. Place the mushrooms that have been cleaned to the side.
- Take the sausage mixture out of the pan and into a mixing bowl. Add the spinach and mix thoroughly. The sausage's heat will cause it to wilt.
- Carefully place the caps on the trays; they will be hot. Fill the mushroom caps to the brim with the filling.
- 10 minutes of air-frying the caps Make sure they don't burn by keeping a close eye on them.
- Cook for an additional 1-2 minutes after adding a slice of cheese to each.

Cal 202 | Protein 10.7g | Carb 8.2g | Fat 14.9g

## STYLE PINTO BEANS

*Prep time: 5 min | Cook time:1-hour | Serves: 6*

**Ingredients**

- 1 teaspoon cumin
- 1 teaspoon black pepper plus more to taste
- Salt to taste
- 1 tablespoon garlic
- 2 cups chicken stock
- 1 onion
- 1 bag dried pinto beans small bag
- 1 teaspoon garlic powder plus more to taste
- 1 leftover ham hock
- 1 bay leaf
- 2 cups water

**Instructions**

- Pinto beans should be soaked overnight.
- Cook the onion and garlic in the Air Fryer until they are translucent.
- Combine the stock, water, beans, ham hock, and seasonings in a large mixing bowl. Make sure the beans and hock are covered in water; if not, add more.
- Allow time for the beans/chili to cook. Release the pressure gradually.
- To taste, season with pepper, garlic powder, and salt. Serve the food.

Cal 110 | Carb 5g | Protein 8g | Fat 6g

## CROUTONS

*Prep time:5 min | Cook time:5 min | Serves: 4*

**Ingredients**

- 2 slices bread day old, brioche
- 2 tablespoon Olive Oil
- 2 teaspoon Cajun seasoning

**Instructions**

- Preheat the air fryer to 390 F
- Make squares out of the bread. About 1/2 inch thick.
- Pour the EVOO and seasoning into a mixing dish. Coat the bread cubes in the sauce.
- Place on a rack in a single layer. Place in the air fryer's middle. Look OUT FOR THESE. They are easy to cook. After a minute or two, search again. As needed, flip.
- If you make too many, freeze them and reheat them later!

Cal 103 | Carb 7g | Protein 2g | Fat 8g

## MOZZARELLA STICKS

*Prep time:40 min | Cook time:20min | Serves: 4*

**Ingredients**

- 1 egg beaten
- 2 tablespoon milk
- 4 mozzarella cheese sticks cut in half
- 1 teaspoon Italian seasoning
- 1/2 teaspoon salt
- 1 cup panko breadcrumbs

**Instructions**

- Cut the mozzarella sticks in half and place them in the freezer for at least 30 minutes.
- 3 bowls are required. In one bowl, whisk together the egg and milk; in another, combine everything else.
- Preheat your Air Fryer to 400 F. Dip the stick in the egg mixture first, then the panko crumbs, then back in the egg and crumbs until fully coated. Place the dish on the rack.
- Continue until all of the other sticks have been completed.
- Return for another 8 minutes, flipping halfway through. When they turn brownish, keep an eye on them and remove them.

- Toss with marinara sauce and serve.

Cal 161 | Carb 13g | Protein 10g | Fat 8g

## CHEESY BISCUIT BALLS

*Prep time:5 min | Cook time:10 min | Serves: 8*

### Ingredients

- ½ cup Marinara sauce for dipping cooking Spray
- 1 can jumbo biscuit
- 8 cubes mozzarella cheese

### Instructions

- Spread biscuits out on a non-stick surface and use a rolling pin to slightly flatten them.
- Each flattened biscuit should have a cheese cube on it.
- Shape a ball with the dough. Cooking spray should be used.
- Air fry for 10-12 minutes at 375°F.
- Enjoy with a side of marinara sauce.

Cal 217 | Carb 29g | Protein 4g | Fat 10g

## CORNBREAD STICKS

*Prep time:10 min | Cook time:10 min | Serves: 5*

### Ingredients

- 1/4 teaspoon salt
- 3/4 cup buttermilk
- 1 cup self-rising cornmeal mix
- 1/4 cup sugar Omit if you don't like sweet cornbread
- 1/4 cup butter melted
- 1 egg beaten

### Instructions

- Add the, salt, cornmeal and sweetener to a mixing bowl and stir. Add in the, buttermilk butter, and egg and mix tile combined.
- Preheat the air fryer to 330 on BAKE
- Spray the cast iron and pour the mixture into the tray.
- Put the tray on the lowest level and bake for 10 minutes. If not done, add another 5 minutes and check again. You may need to add a cover to keep the tops from over browning.

Cal 273 | Carb 37g | Protein 5g | Fat 12g

## PULL APART CHEESE BREAD

*Prep time:5 min | Cook time:5 min | Serves: 3*

### Ingredients

- 1 teaspoon garlic
- 6-inch bread Any variation will work - I used French
- 2 tbsp. butter melted
- 1/2 cup Mozzarella Cheese
- 1/2 cup Marinara for serving

### Instructions

- Preheat the Air Fryer to 350 F
- Break the bread into strips. Use a grid pattern but stop short of cutting all the way to the bottom.
- Melt the butter and add the garlic. Fill the slits with the mixture. Coat the bread as much as possible with a spoon or brush.
- Cheese should be stuffed into the slits.
- 5 minutes in the air fryer
- Toss with marinara sauce and serve.

Cal 148 | Carb 5g | Protein 5g | Fat 12g

## BURRATA-STUFFED TOMATOES

*Prep time: 5 min | Cook time: 5 min | Serves: 4*

### Ingredients

- 4 medium tomatoes
- ½ teaspoon fine sea salt
- 4 (2-ounce) Burrata balls
- Fresh basil leaves, for garnish
- Extra-virgin olive oil, for drizzling

### Directions

- Preparing the Ingredients. Preheat the air fryer to 300°F.
- Scoop out the tomato seeds and membranes using a melon baller or spoon. Sprinkle the insides of the tomatoes with the salt. Stuff each tomato with a ball of Burrata.
- Air Frying. Put it in the fryer and cook for 5 minutes, or until the cheese has softened.
- Garnish with olive oil and basil leaves. Serve warm.

Cal 108 | Fat 7g | Protein 6g | Carb 5g | Fiber 2g

## CHEESEBURGER SLIDERS

*Prep time:5 min | Cook time:6 min | Serves: 4*

### Ingredients

- 1 teaspoon garlic powder
- 1 ranch powder
- salt to taste
- pepper to taste
- 1 tbsp. Worcestershire sauce
- 1 lb. ground beef or pork or turkey a mixture of all is even better
- 1 pig Hawaiian rolls
- 1/2 onion finely chopped

### Instructions

- Preheat the Air Fryer to 400 F
- In a mixing bowl, combine all of the ingredients.
- Roll into a disc the size of a golf ball. When you have them all, flatten them with a plate or other flat surface.
- Place in the air fryer and cook for 4 minutes before flipping. Cook time:can vary between 8 and 15 minutes, depending on how done you want them.
- Attach the cheese and toast for another minute.
- Butter your buns and toast them for 2-3 minutes.
- Create your burgers! | Cook time:varies between 8 and 15 minutes. To scan for doneness, use a thermometer.

Cal 322 | Carb 7g | Protein 20g | Fat 23g

## LOADED TATER TOT SKEWERS

*Prep time:10 min | Cook time:15 min | Serves: 6*

### Ingredients

- 1/2 cup Shredded Cheddar Cheese
- Skewers cut to 7 inches or shorter

- 1 bag Tater Tots
- 3 tbsp. Bacon Bit
- 1/4 cup Chopped Green Onions
- 1/2 cup Sour Cream

**Instructions**
- Preheat the air fryer to 400 F.
- If necessary, shorten the skewers to 7 inches.
- Cook for 5 minutes before flipping. Cook for a few more minutes, just until the bacon is crispy.
- Add 4 to 6 tater tots to each skewer once they've cooled.
- To capture the topping, place the skewers on a rack on parchment paper or a pan. You can fit three on one, but they shouldn't touch. Bacon bits and sliced green onion are sprinkled on top, followed by shredded cheese.
- Return the skewers to the air fryer for another 2-3 minutes, or until the cheese has melted.
- Remove from the air fryer and serve with sour cream.

Cal 361 | Carb 40g | Protein 7g | Fat 20g

## KIMCHI STEW
*Prep time:10 min | Cook time:10 min | Serves: 4*

**Ingredients**
- 1 tbsp. minced fresh ginger
- 1 tbsp. toasted sesame oil
- 1 tbsp. dark soy sauce
- 1 tbsp. gochujang (Korean ground red pepper)
- 1/2 teaspoon granulated sugar
- 1/2 teaspoon kosher salt
- 2 cups kimchi
- 1 package firm tofu diced, 8-ounce
- 1 cup chopped onion
- 1 cup dried shiitake mushrooms
- 3 garlic cloves minced
- 2 cups Water
- 1/2 cup Chopped green onions

**Instructions**
- Combine the kimchi, onions, garlic, ginger, mushrooms, sesame oil, gochujang, sugar, soy sauce salt, and water in the Air Fryer.
- Cook it for 3 minutes.
- Enable the pot to sit undisturbed for 10 minutes after the Cook time:has ended, then quickly release any remaining strain.

Cal 295 | Carb: 7g | Protein 10g | Fat 26g

## BACON-WRAPPED JALAPENOS
*Prep time:10 min | Cook time:12 min | Serves: 6*

**Ingredients**
- Garlic powder: ¼ tsp.
- Cream cheese: 8 oz., softened
- Bacon: 6 slices
- Mayonnaise: 1 tbsp.
- Salt
- 12 jalapenos (fresh or pickled)

**Instructions**
- With a hand mixer, whisk the cream cheese, salt, mayo and garlic powder till smooth.
- Slice the jalapenos in half, lengthwise and take the seeds out.
- Stuff the jalapenos with cream cheese mixture and wrap in bacon. Secure with a toothpick.

- Let the Kalorik Air Fryer Oven preheat to 400 F.
- Air fry for 12 minutes, serve.

Cal 245 | Fat 10g | Carb 5g | Protein 8g

## WILD RICE AND MUSHROOM SOUP
*Prep time:15 min | Cook time:30 min | Serves: 4*

**Ingredients**
- 1 1/2 teaspoon poultry seasoning
- 1 1/2 teaspoon kosher salt
- 4 cups Water
- 1 can evaporated milk 5-ounce
- 2 cups baby carrots chopped lengthwise
- 2 cups sliced mushrooms
- 1 cup chopped onion
- 1 cup chopped celery
- 1/2 cup wild rice
- 3 cloves garlic minced

**Instructions**
- Combine the carrots, onion, celery, mushrooms rice, garlic, salt, poultry seasoning and water in the air fryer
- Cook for 10 minutes.
- Add the evaporated milk and mix well.
- Puree about half of the mixture using an immersion blender.
- Serve

Cal 180 | Fat 4g | Carb 31g | Protein 8g

## ROASTED GARLIC

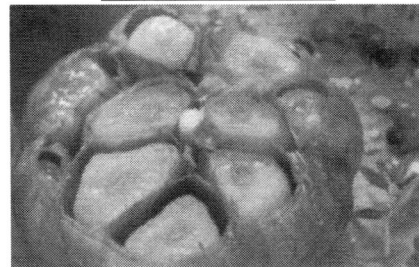

*Prep time:10 min | Cook time:25 min | Serves: 3-4*

**Ingredients**
- 1 garlic bulb
- Olive oil

**Instructions**
- Cut the top off the bulb.
- Coat in olive oil and wrap in foil.
- Let the Kalorik Air Fryer Oven preheat to 390 F.
- Air fry for 20 to 25 minutes, let it cool slightly.
- Take out the cloves, mash and serve with bread with a sprinkle of salt.

## BACON-WRAPPED ONION RINGS
*Prep time:10 min | Cook time:9 min | Serves: 4*

**Ingredients**
- Bacon slices: 8 to 10
- 2 sweet onions, large
- Sriracha: 1 tsp.

**Instructions**
- Slice the onions into half-inch slices. For every onion ring, 2 rings need to stick together.
- Coat the onion with sriracha.

- On every onion piece, wrap the bacon. Use a toothpick to secure.
- Air fry for 9 nine minutes at 370 F, flipping halfway through.

Cal 213 | Fat 17g | Carb 7g | Protein 6g

## SWEET & SPICY BACON WRAPPED CHICKEN BITES

*Prep time:10 min | Cook time:8 min | Serves: 8*

### Ingredients

- Honey: 1 ½ tbsp.
- 2 chicken breasts boneless & skinless
- Cayenne pepper: half tsp.
- Bacon 10 to 12 slices, halved
- Paprika: half tsp.

### Instructions

- Slice chicken in larger than one" pieces and wrap in bacon; use a toothpick to secure.
- Let the Kalorik Air Fryer Oven preheat to 400 F.
- Air fry for 8 minutes, flipping halfway through.
- In a bowl, whisk the rest of the ingredients.
- Brush the chicken with this mixture and serve.

Cal 159 | Fat 11g | Carb 3g | Protein 9g

## SWEET & SPICY CANDIED PECANS

*Prep time:8 min | Cook time:8 min | Serves: 8*

### Ingredients

- Pecans halves: 2 cups
- Paprika: 1 tsp.
- 1 egg white
- Salt: half tsp.
- Light brown sugar: ¼ cup, packed
- cinnamon: ¼ tsp.
- Ground cumin: half tsp.
- Cayenne pepper: half tsp.

### Instructions

- In a bowl, mix pecans with egg white.
- Add the rest of the ingredients and mix.
- Oil spray the basket and add the pecan mixture.
- Let the Kalorik Air Fryer Oven preheat to 300 F.
- Air fry for 8-10 minutes, shake the basket a few times.

Cal 226 | Fat 20g | Carb 11g | Protein 3g

## AIR-FRYER ASPARAGUS

*Prep time:10 min | Cook time:10 min | Serves: 4*

### Ingredients

- Lemon zest: 1 ½ tsp.
- Mayonnaise: 1/4 cup
- Parmesan cheese: 2 tbsp.
- 1 minced garlic clove
- Olive oil: 4 tsp.
- Salt & pepper
- Trimmed asparagus: 1 pound

### Instructions

- Let the Kalorik Air Fryer Oven preheat to 375 F.
- In a bowl, add all ingredients and toss well.
- Air fry for 4 to 6 minutes.
- Serve with parmesan cheese on top.

Cal 156 | Fat 15g | Protein 2g | Carb 3g

## JICAMA FRIES

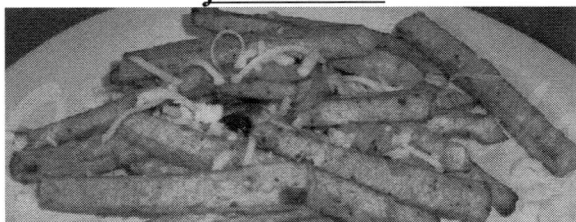

*Prep time: 10 min | Cook time: 5 min | Serves: 4*

### Ingredients

- 1 tbsp. dried thyme
- ¾ C. arrowroot flour
- ½ large Jicama
- eggs

### Directions

- Preparing the Ingredients. Sliced jicama into fries.
- Whisk eggs together and pour over fries. Toss to coat.
- Mix a pinch of salt, thyme, and arrowroot flour together. Toss egg-coated jicama into dry mixture, tossing to coat well.
- Air Frying. Spray the air fryer basket with olive oil and add fries. Set temperature to 350°F, and set time to 5 minutes. Toss halfway into the cooking process.

Cal 211 | Fat 19g | Carbs 16g | Protein 9g

## TURMERIC CARROT CHIPS

*Prep time: 5 min | Cook time: 25 min | Serves: 4*

### Ingredients

- carrots, thinly sliced
- Salt and black pepper to taste
- ½ teaspoon turmeric powder
- ½ teaspoon chaat masala
- 1 teaspoon olive oil

### Directions

- Put all of the ingredients in a bowl and toss well.
- Put the mixture in your air fryer's basket and cook at 370°F for 25 minutes, shaking the fryer from time to time.
- Serve as a snack.

Cal 161 | Fat 1g | Fiber 2g | Carb 5g | Protein 3g

## BALSAMIC ZUCCHINI SLICES

*Prep time: 5 min | Cook time: 50 min | Serves: 6*

### Ingredients

- zucchinis, thinly sliced
- Salt and black pepper to taste
- tablespoons avocado oil
- tablespoons balsamic vinegar

### Directions

- Put all of the ingredients into a bowl and mix.
- Put the zucchini mixture in your air fryer's basket and cook at 220°F for 50 minutes.
- Serve as a snack and enjoy!

Cal 40 | Fat 3g | Fiber 7g | Carb 3g | Protein 7g

## PESTO TOMATOES

*Prep time: 5 min | Cook time: 10 min | Serves: 4*

### Ingredients

- Large heirloom tomatoes – 3, cut into ½ inch thick slices.
- Pesto – 1 cup

- Feta cheese – 8 oz. cut into ½ inch thick slices
- Red onion – ½ cup, sliced thinly
- Olive oil – 1 tbsp.

**Directions**

- Spread some pesto on each slice of tomato. Top each tomato slice with a feta slice and onion and drizzle with oil. Arrange the tomatoes onto the greased rack and spray with cooking spray.
- Preheat the Air Fryer to 390°F.
- Arrange the drip pan in the bottom of Air Fryer Oven cooking chamber and cook for 14 minutes.
- Serve warm.

Cal 480 | Carb 13g | Fat 41.9g | Protein 15.4g

## CRISP KALE

*Prep time: 5 Min | Cook time: 8 Min | Serves: 2*

**Ingredients**

- 4 Handfuls Kale, Washed & Stemless
- 1 Tablespoon Olive Oil
- Pinch Sea Salt

**Directions**

- Start by heating it to 360°F, and then combine your ingredients together making sure your kale is coated evenly.
- Place the kale in your fryer and cook for 8 minutes.

Cal 121 | Fat 4g | Carb 5g | Protein 8g

## CHIVES RADISH SNACK

*Prep time: 5 min | Cook time: 10 min | Serves: 4*

**Ingredients**

- 16 radishes, sliced
- A drizzle of olive oil
- Salt and black pepper to taste
- 1 tablespoon chives, chopped

**Directions**

- In a bowl, mix the radishes, salt, pepper, and oil; toss well.
- Place the radishes in your air fryer's basket and cook at 350°F for 10 minutes.
- Divide into bowls and serve with chives sprinkled on top.

Cal 100 | Fat 1g | Fiber 2g | Carb 4g | Protein 1g

## AIR FRIED CORN

*Prep time: 5 min | Cook time: 10 min | Serves: 4*

**Ingredients**

- tablespoons corn kernels
- 2½ tablespoons butter

**Directions**

- In a saucepan that fits your air fryer, mix the corn with the butter.
- Place the pan inside the air fryer and cook at 400°F for 10 minutes.
- Serve as a snack and enjoy!

Cal 70 | Fat 2g | Fiber 2g | Carb 7g | Protein 3g

## TUNA ZUCCHINI MELTS

*Prep time: 15 min | Cook time: 5 min | Serves: 4*

**Ingredients**

- corn tortillas
- tablespoons softened butter
- 1 (6-ounce) can chunk light tuna, drained
- 1 cup shredded zucchini, drained by squeezing in a kitchen towel

- ⅓ cup mayonnaise
- tablespoons mustard
- 1 cup shredded Cheddar or Colby cheese

**Directions**

- Spread the tortillas with the softened butter. Place in the air fryer basket and grill for 2 to 3 minutes or until the tortillas are crisp. Remove from basket and set aside.
- In a medium bowl, combine the tuna, zucchini, mayonnaise, and mustard, and mix well.
- Divide the tuna mixture among the toasted tortillas. Top each with some of the shredded cheese.
- Grill in the air fryer for 2 to 4 minutes or until the tuna mixture is hot, and the cheese melts and starts to brown. Serve.

Cal 428 | Fat 30g | Carb 19g | Fiber 3g | Protein 22g

## BREADED MUSHROOMS

*Prep time: 10 min | Cook time: 45 min | Serves: 4*

**Ingredients**

- 1 lb. small Button mushrooms, cleaned
- cups breadcrumbs
- eggs, beaten
- Salt and pepper to taste
- 2 cups Parmigiano Reggiano cheese, grated

**Directions**

- Preheat the Air Fryer to 360°F. Pour the breadcrumbs in a bowl, add salt and pepper and mix well. Pour the cheese in a separate bowl and set aside. Dip each mushroom in the eggs, then in the crumbs, and then in the cheese.
- Slide out the fryer basket and add 6 to 10 mushrooms. Cook them for 20 minutes, in batches, if needed. Serve with cheese dip.

Cal 487 | Carb 49g | Fat 22g | Protein 31g

## HOT CHICKEN WINGETTES

*Prep time: 10 min | Cook time: 40 min | Serves: 4*

**Ingredients**

- 15 chicken wingettes
- Salt and pepper to taste
- ⅓ cup hot sauce
- ⅓ cup butter
- ½ tbsp vinegar

**Directions**

- Preheat the Air Fryer to 360°F. Season the vignettes with pepper and salt.
- Add them to your air fryer oven and cook for 35 minutes. Toss every 5 minutes. Once ready, remove them into a bowl. Over low heat melt the butter in a saucepan.
- Add the vinegar and hot sauce. Stir and cook for a minute.
- Turn the heat off. Pour the sauce over the chicken. Toss to coat well. Transfer the chicken to a serving platter.
- Serve with blue cheese dressing.

Cal 563 | Carb 2g | Fat 28g | Protein 35g

## CHEESY STICKS WITH SWEET THAI SAUCE

*Prep time: 2 hours | Cook time: 20 min | Serves: 4*

**Ingredients**

- 12 mozzarella string cheese
- cups breadcrumbs
- eggs
- 1 cup sweet Thai sauce
- tbsp skimmed milk

**Directions**

- Pour the crumbs in a medium bowl. Break the eggs into a different bowl and beat with the milk. One after the other, dip each cheese sticks in the egg mixture, in the crumbs, then egg mixture again and then in the crumbs again.
- Place the coated cheese sticks on a cookie sheet and freeze for 1 to 2 hours. Preheat the Air Fryer to 380°F.
- Arrange the sticks in the fryer without overcrowding. Cook for 5 minutes, flipping them halfway through cooking to brown evenly. Cook in batches.
- Serve with a sweet Thai sauce.

Cal 158 | Carb 14g | Fat 7g | Protein 9g

## CRISPY BRUSSELS SPROUTS

*Prep time: 5 min | Cook time: 10 min | Serves: 2*

**Ingredients**

- ½ pound brussels sprouts, cut in half
- ½ tablespoon oil
- ½ tablespoon unsalted butter, melted

**Directions**

- Rub sprouts with oil and place into your air fryer oven basket.
- Cook at 400°F for 10 minutes. Stir once at the halfway mark.
- Remove the air fryer basket and drizzle with melted butter.
- Serve.

Cal 90 | Fat 6.1g | Carb 4g | Protein 2.9g

## LENTILS SNACK

*Prep time: 5 Min | Cook time: 12 min | Serves: 4*

**Ingredients**

- 15 ounces canned lentils, drained
- ½ teaspoon cumin, ground
- 1 tablespoon olive oil
- 1 teaspoon sweet paprika
- Salt and black pepper to taste

**Directions**

- Place all ingredients in a bowl and blend it well.
- Transfer the mixture to your air fryer and cook at 400°F for 12 minutes.
- Divide into bowls and serve as a snack or a side, or appetizer!

Cal 151 | Fat 1g | Fiber 6g | Carb 10g | Protein 6g

## CARROT CRISPS

*Prep time: 10 min | Cook time: 10 min | Serves: 4*

**Ingredients**

- large carrots, washed and peeled
- Salt to taste
- Cooking spray

**Directions**

- Using a mandolin slicer, slice the carrots very thinly height wise. Put the carrot strips in a bowl and season with salt to taste. Grease the fryer basket lightly with cooking spray, and add the carrot strips.
- Cook at 350°F for 10 minutes, stirring once halfway through.

Cal 35 | Carb 8g | Fat 3g | Protein 1g

## BACON-WRAPPED ASPARAGUS

*Prep time: 5 min | Cook time: 10 min | Serves: 4*

**Ingredients**

- 1 pound asparagus, trimmed (about 24 spears)
- 4slices bacon or beef bacon
- ½ cup Ranch Dressin for serving
- 3 tablespoons chopped fresh chives, for garnish

**Directions**

- Preparing the Ingredients. Grease the air fryer basket with avocado oil. Preheat the air fryer to 400°F.
- Slice the bacon down the middle, making long, thin strips. Wrap 1 slice of bacon around 3 asparagus spears and secure each end with a toothpick. Repeat with the remaining bacon and asparagus.
- Air Frying. Place the asparagus bundles in the air fryer in a single layer.
- Cook for 8 minutes for thin stalks, 10 minutes for medium to thick stalks, or until the asparagus is slightly charred on the ends and the bacon is crispy.
- Serve with ranch dressing and garnish with chives. Best served fresh.

Cal 241 | Fat 22g | Protein 7g | Carb 6g | Fiber 3g

## GARLICKY BOK CHOY

*Prep time: 10 min | Cook time: 10 min | Serves: 2*

**Ingredients**

- bunches baby bok choy
- spray oil
- 1 tsp garlic powder

**Directions**

- Toss bok choy with garlic powder and spread them in the Air fryer. Spray them with cooking oil.
- Select the Air Fry mode at 350°F temperature for 6 minutes.
- Serve fresh.

Cal 81 | Protein 0.4g | Carb 4.7g | Fat 8.3g

## QUICK CHEESE STICKS

*Prep time: 5 min | Cook time: 10 min | Serves: 4*

**Ingredients**

- 6 oz bread cheese
- tbsp butter
- cups panko crumbs

**Directions**

- Place the butter in a dish and melt it in the microwave, for 2 minutes; set aside. With a knife, cut the cheese into equal sized sticks.
- Brush each stick with butter and dip into panko crumbs. Arrange the cheese sticks in a single layer on the fryer basket.
- Cook at 390°F for 10 minutes. Flip them halfway through, to brown evenly; serve warm.

Cal 256 | Carb 8g | Fat 21g | Protein 16g

## RADISH CHIPS

*Prep time: 10 min | Cook time: 20 min | Serves: 4*

**Ingredients**
- radishes, leaves removed and cleaned
- Salt to season
- Water
- Cooking spray

**Directions**
- Using a mandolin, slice the radishes thinly. Put them in a pot and pour water on them. Heat the pot on a stovetop, and bring to boil, until the radishes are translucent, for 4 minutes. After 4 minutes, drain the radishes through a sieve; set aside. Grease the fryer basket with cooking spray.
- Add in the radish slices and cook for 8 minutes, flipping once halfway through. Cook until golden brown, at 400°F. Meanwhile, prepare a paper towel-lined plate. Once the radishes are ready, transfer them to the paper towel-lined plate. Season with salt, and serve with ketchup or garlic mayo.

Cal 25 | Carb 0.2g | Fat 2g | Protein 0.1g

## HERBED CROUTONS WITH BRIE CHEESE

*Prep time: 10 min | Cook time: 10 min | Serves: 4*

**Ingredients**
- tbsp olive oil
- 1 tbsp french herbs
- oz brie cheese, chopped
- slices bread, halved

**Directions**
- Warm up your Air Fryer to 340° F.
- Using a bowl, mix oil with herbs.
- Dip the bread slices in the oil mixture to coat.
- Place the coated slices on a flat surface. Lay the brie cheese on the slices.
- Place the slices into your air fryer's basket and cook for 7 minutes.
- Once the bread is ready, cut into cubes.

Cal 20 | Carb 1.5g | Fat 1.3g | Protein 0.5g

## CHIA SEED CRACKERS

*Prep time: 15 min | Cook time: 45 min | Serves: 48*

**Ingredients**
- 1 Cup raw chia seed
- 3/4 Teaspoon salt
- 1/4 Teaspoon garlic powder
- 1/4 Teaspoon onion powder
- 1 Cup cold water

**Directions**
- Put the chia seeds in a bowl. Add salt, garlic powder, and onion powder.

- Pour into the water. Stir. Cover with plastic wrap. Store in the fridge overnight.
- Preheat the Air fryer toaster oven to 200°F. Cover a baking sheet with a silicone mat or parchment.
- Transfer the soaked linseed to a prepared baking sheet. Scatter it out with a spatula in a thin, flat rectangle about 1 cm thick. Rate the rectangle in about 32 small rectangles.
- Bake in the preheated Air fryer toaster oven up to the chia seeds have darkened and contract slightly, about 3 hours. Let it cool. Break individual cookies.

Cal 120 | Fat 3.9g | Carb 1.9g | Protein 1.9g

## SALTED HAZELNUTS

*Prep time: 15 min | Cook time: 10 min | Serves: 8*

**Ingredients**
- Cups dry roasted Hazelnuts, no salt added
- Tablespoons coconut oil
- 1 Teaspoon garlic powder
- 1 Sprig fresh Thyme, chopped
- 1 1/2 Teaspoons salt

**Directions**
- Preheat the Air fryer toaster oven to 350°F.
- Mix the Hazelnuts, coconut oil, garlic powder and thyme in a bowl until the nuts are fully covered. Sprinkle with salt. Spread evenly on a baking sheet.
- Bake in the preheated Air fryer toaster oven for 10 minutes.

Cal 237 | Fat 21.3g | Carb 5.9g | Protein 7.4g

## CAJUN OLIVES AND PEPPERS

*Prep time: 4 min | Cook time: 12 min | Serves: 4*

**Ingredients**
- 1 tablespoon olive oil
- ½ pound mixed bell peppers, sliced
- 1 cup black olives, pitted and halved
- ½ tablespoon Cajun seasoning

**Directions**
- In a pan that fits the air fryer, combine all the ingredients.
- Put the pan it in your air fryer and cook at 390°F for 12 minutes.
- Divide the mix between plates and serve.

Cal 151 | Fat 3g | Fiber 2g | Carb 4g | Protein 5g

## GREEN BEANS & BACON

*Prep time: 15 min | Cook time: 20 min | Serves: 4*

**Ingredients**
- 3 cups frozen cut green beans
- 1 medium onion, chopped
- 3slices bacon, chopped
- ¼ cup water
- Kosher salt and black pepper

**Directions**

- In a 6 × 3-inch round heatproof pan, combine the frozen green beans, onion, bacon, and water. Toss to combine. Place the saucepan in the basket.
- Air Frying . Set the air fryer to 375°F for 15 minutes.
- Raise the air fryer temperature to 400°F for 5 minutes. Season the beans with salt and pepper to taste and toss well.
- Remove the pan from the air fryer basket and cover with foil. Let it rest for 5 minutes then serve.

Cal 230 | Fat 10g | Carb 14g | Protein 17g

## WRAPPED ASPARAGUS
*Prep time: 10 min | Cook time: 5 min | Serves: 4*

**Ingredients**
- 12 ounces asparagus
- ½ teaspoon ground black pepper
- 3-ounce turkey fillet, sliced
- ¼ teaspoon chili flakes

**Directions**
- Sprinkle the asparagus with the ground black pepper and chili flakes.
- Stir carefully.
- Wrap the asparagus in the sliced turkey fillet and place in the air fryer basket.
- Cook the asparagus at 400° F for 5 minutes, turning halfway through cooking.
- Let the wrapped asparagus cool for 2 minutes before serving.

Cal 133 | Fat 9g | Fiber 1.9g | Carbs 3.8g | Protein 9.8g

## YOGURT BREAD
*Prep time: 20 min | Cook time: 40 min | Serves: 10*

**Ingredients**
- 1½ cups warm water, divided
- 1½ teaspoons active dry yeast
- 1 teaspoon sugar
- 3 cups all-purpose flour
- 1 cup plain Greek yogurt
- 2 teaspoons kosher salt

**Directions**
- Add ½ cup of the warm water, yeast and sugar in the bowl of a stand mixer, fitted with the dough hook attachment and mix well.
- Set aside for about 5 minutes
- Add the flour, yogurt, and salt and mix on medium-low speed until the dough comes together.
- Then, mix on medium speed for 5 minutes
- Place the dough into a bowl.
- With a plastic wrap, cover the bowl and place in a warm place for about 2-3 hours or until doubled in size.
- Transfer the dough onto a lightly floured surface and shape into a smooth ball.
- Place the dough onto a greased parchment paper-lined rack.
- With a kitchen towel, cover the dough and let rest for 15 minutes
- With a very sharp knife, cut a 4x½-inch deep cut down the center of the dough.
- Take to the preheated air fryer at 325°F for 40 minutes.
- Carefully, invert the bread to cool completely before slicing.
- Cut the bread into desired-sized slices and serve.

Cal 157 | Fat 0.7g | Carb 31g | Protein 5.5g

## FRIED PLANTAINS
*Prep time: 5 min | Cook time: 10 min | Serves: 2*

**Ingredients**
- 2 ripe plantains, peeled and cut at a diagonal into ½-inch-thick pieces
- 3 tablespoons ghee, melted
- ¼ teaspoon kosher salt

**Directions**
- Preparing the Ingredients. In a bowl, mix the plantains with the ghee and salt.
- Air Frying. Arrange the plantain pieces in the air fryer basket. Set the air fryer to 400°F for 8 minutes. The plantains are done when they are soft and tender on the inside, and have plenty of crisp, sweet, brown spots on the outside.

Cal 180 | Fat 5g | Carb 10g | Protein 7g

## ALLSPICE CHICKEN WINGS

*Prep time: | Cook time: 45 min | Serves: 8*

**Ingredients**
- ½ tsp celery salt
- ½ tsp bay leaf powder
- ½ tsp ground black pepper
- ½ tsp paprika
- ¼ tsp dry mustard
- ¼ tsp cayenne pepper
- ¼ tsp allspice
- 2 pounds chicken wings

**Directions**
- Grease the air fryer basket and preheat to 340°F. In a bowl, mix celery salt, bay leaf powder, black pepper, paprika, dry mustard, cayenne pepper, and allspice. Coat the wings thoroughly in this mixture.
- Arrange the wings in an even layer in the basket of the air fryer. Cook the chicken until it's no longer pinks around the bone, for 30 minutes then, increase the temperature to 380°F and cook for 6 minutes more, until crispy on the outside.

Cal 332 | Fat 10.1g | Carb 31.3g | Protein 12 g

## CHILI CORN ON THE COB
*Prep time: 10 min | Cook time: 15 min | Serves: 4*

**Ingredients**
- 2 tablespoon olive oil, divided
- 2 tablespoons grated Parmesan cheese
- 1 teaspoon garlic powder
- 1 teaspoon chili powder
- 1 teaspoon ground cumin
- 1 teaspoon paprika
- 1 teaspoon salt
- ¼ teaspoon cayenne pepper (optional)
- 4 ears fresh corn, shucked

## Directions

- Grease the air fryer basket with 1 tablespoon of olive oil. Set aside.
- Combine the Parmesan cheese, garlic powder, chili powder, cumin, paprika, salt, and cayenne pepper (if desired) in a small bowl and stir to mix well.
- Lightly coat the ears of corn with the remaining 1 tablespoon of olive oil. Rub the cheese mixture all over the ears of corn until completely coated.
- Arrange the ears of corn in the greased basket in a single layer.
- Put in the air fryer basket and cook at 400°F for 15 minutes.
- Flip the ears of corn halfway through the cooking time.
- When cooking is complete, they should be lightly browned. Remove from the oven and let them cool for 5 minutes before serving.

Cal 172 | Fat 9.8g | Carb 17.5g | Protein 3.9g

## SIMPLE STUFFED POTATOES

*Prep time: 15 Min | Cook time: 35 Min | Serves: 4*

**Ingredients**

- 4 Large Potatoes, Peeled
- 2 Bacon, Rashers
- ½ Brown Onion, Diced
- ¼ Cup Cheese, Grated

**Directions**

- Start by heating your air fryer to 350°F.
- Cut your potatoes in half, and then brush the potatoes with oil.
- Put it in your air fryer, and cook for ten minutes. Brush the potatoes with oil again and bake for another ten minutes.
- Make a whole in the baked potato to get them ready to stuff.
- Sauté the bacon and onion in a frying pan. You should do this over medium heat, adding cheese and stir. Remove from heat.
- Stuff your potatoes, and cook for four to five minutes.

Cal 180 | Fat 8g | Carb 10g | Protein 11g

## RAVISHING CARROTS WITH HONEY GLAZE

*Prep time: 5 min | Cook time: 11 min | Serves: 1*

**Ingredients**

- 3 cups of chopped into ½-inch pieces carrots
- 1 tablespoon of olive oil
- 2 tablespoons of honey
- 1 tablespoon of brown sugar
- salt and black pepper

**Directions**

- Heat up your air fryer to 390°F.
- Using a bowl, add and toss the carrot pieces, olive oil, honey, brown sugar, salt, and the black pepper until it is properly covered.
- Place it inside your air fryer and add the seasoned glazed carrots.
- Cook it for 5 minutes at 390°F, and then shake after 6 minutes. Serve and enjoy!

Cal 90 | Fat 3.5g | Fiber 2g | Carb 13g | Protein 1g

## SWEET POTATO FRIES

*Prep time: 10 Min | Cook time: 12 Min | Serves: 2*

**Ingredients**

- 3 Large Sweet Potatoes, Peeled
- 1 Tablespoon Olive Oil
- A Pinch Teaspoon Sea Salt

**Directions**

- Turn on your air fryer to 390°F.
- Start by cutting your sweet potatoes in quarters, cutting them lengthwise to make fries.
- Combine the uncooked fries with a tablespoon of sea salt and olive oil. Make sure all of your fries are coated well.
- Place your sweet potato pieces in your air fryer, cooking for 12 minutes.
- Cook for two to three minutes more if you want it to be crispier.
- Add more salt to taste, and serve when cooled.

Cal 150 | Fat: 6g | Carbs: 8g | Protein: 9g

## PERFECT VORTEX BACON

*Prep time:1 min | Cook time:8 min*

**Ingredients**

- 1/2 lb. bacon

**Instructions**

- Preheat the air fryer to 390°F.
- On a rack, arrange the bacon in a single sheet. Two racks can be cooked at the same time.
- Cook for another 4 minutes before tossing. When you turn the pan, move the racks as well so that it cooks evenly. Cook for an additional 4 minutes.
- Depending on the crispness needed, you will need to cook for a few minutes longer.

Cal 946 | Carb 3g | Protein 29g | Fat 90g

## SEASONED POTATOES

*Prep time: 5 min | Cook time: 40 min | Serves: 2*

**Ingredients**

- Russet potatoes – 2, scrubbed
- Butter – ½ tbsp. melted
- Garlic & herb blend seasoning – ½ tsp.
- Garlic powder – ½ tsp.
- Salt, as required

**Directions**

- In a bowl, mix all of the spices and salt.
- With a fork, prick the potatoes. Coat the potatoes with butter and sprinkle with spice mixture.
- Preheat the Kalorik Air Fryer Oven to 400°F.
- Arrange the potatoes onto the cooking rack, insert the cooking rack in the center position and cook for 40 minutes. Serve hot.

Cal 176 | Carb 34g | Fat 2.1g | Protein 3.8g

# SEAFOOD RECIPES

## SEAFOOD LASAGNA W/ PASTA

*Prep time:20 min | Cook time:20 min | Serves: 4*

**Ingredients**

- 1/2 lb. lasagne noodles
- Salt & pepper
- 2 tbsp. olive oil
- 1/2 lb. Shrimp peeled & deveined, tails removed
- 1/4 lb. Scallops
- 1/4 lb. Crab meat
- Spaghetti sauce: 1 cup
- Alfredo sauce: 1 cup
- Fresh herbs
- 1 clove garlic minced
- chopped parsley: 2 tbsp.
- Ricotta: 16 oz.
- 1/4 cup Parmesan
- 1 egg
- 1 cup Mozzarella Grated
- 1 cup Mexican Cheese

**Instructions**

- Preheat the air fryer to 350°F with the Bake setting. Cook spaghetti sauce, Alfredo, and garlic for 10 minutes.
- Cook noodles as per package instructions.
- Cook for 5 minutes after adding the seafood to the sauce.
- Combine ricotta, egg, Parmesan, parsley, salt, and pepper in a mixing bowl.
- In a separate dish, combine the Mexican cheese and mozzarella. Any pan that will fit in your air fryer can be used.
- Spread a thin layer of sauce across the bottom of the pan. Place a layer of noodles on top. Spread the ricotta mixture over the noodles and top with a layer of cheese. Repeat until the pan is finished.
- Bake for 20 minutes. Cool before serving.

## COCONUT SHRIMP

*Prep time:10 min | Cook time:5 min | Serves: 2*

**Ingredients**

- 1/2 lb. shrimp
- 1 egg whisked
- ½ cup All-Purpose Flour
- ½ cup shredded coconut, unsweetened
- ¼ cup Panko Breadcrumbs
- 1 tsp. Cajun Seasoning
- 1 tsp. salt
- ¼ tsp. black pepper

**Instructions**

- Preheat the air fryer to 390°F on AIRFRY mode.
- Leave the tails on the shrimp and peel them.
- 3 bowls are required. In one dish, combine the flour with all of the seasonings; in another, combine the egg; and in the third, combine the coconut and breadcrumbs.
- Every shrimp should be dipped in flour, then egg, and finally coconut mixture, ensuring that all sides of the shrimp are coated.
- Arrange the shrimp on the rack in a single layer.

- Cook for 3 minutes after gently spraying the shrimp with oil in the middle position.
- Cook for another minute or two after flipping the shrimp after 3 minutes. The shrimp's size will determine the length of time.
- Serve with the sauce

Cal 445 | Carb 36g | Protein 32g | Fat 19g

## SHRIMP TIKKA

*Prep time:25 min | Cook time:10 min | Serves: 1*

**Ingredients**

- 2.5 cups shrimp (deveined)
- 1/2 cup Greek yogurt
- 1.5 tsp. ginger garlic paste
- 1 tsp. cilantro
- 2 tsp. heavy whipping cream
- 1/2 tsp. carom seeds
- 1 and 1/4 tsp. salt
- 2 tsp. red chili powder
- 1 tsp. garam masala
- 2 tsp. dried fenugreek leaves
- 1/4 tsp. ground mustard
- 2 tbsp. oil

**Instructions**

- Combine all of the ingredients, except the shrimp, in a mixing bowl with 1 tablespoon of oil. Mix well.
- Toss the shrimp in the marinade. Refrigerate it for 20 minutes.
- When you're ready to cook, rub the remaining oil on the air fryer tray
- Preheat the air fryer at 350°F.
- Add the shrimp and arrange them in a single layer in the air fryer tray.
- Air fry for 7 minutes. Flip the shrimp and cook for another 2 minutes. Serve immediately.

Cal 163 | Fat 5g | Carb 3g | Protein25g

## SHRIMP QUESADILLAS

*Prep time:10 min | Cook time:5 min | Serves: 1*

**Ingredients**

- 2 Tortilla
- 1/4 cup Mexican cheese

**Toppings, as needed**

- Tomatoes
- 12 cooked Shrimp diced
- Lettuce

- Avocado
- Sour Cream

**Instructions**
- Preheat the air fryer to 350 F.
- Place the tortilla on a rack and spread cheese on one. Place in the middle rack of the air fryer.
- Remove after 2 minutes. Fold in half after adding your toppings.

Cal 353 | Carb 31g | Protein 26g | Fat 13g

## GARLIC BUTTER SALMON
*Prep time:5 min | Cook time:10 min | Serves: 2*

**Ingredients**
- Garlic minced: 1 tsp.
- 2 salmon fillets, boneless & skin-on
- Salt & pepper, to taste
- Butter: 2 tbsp., melted
- Fresh italian parsley: 1 tsp.

**Instructions**
- Let the Kalorik Air Fryer Oven preheat to 360 F.
- With salt and pepper, season the salmon. Add the rest of the ingredients to a bowl.
- Coat the fish in the butter mixture, and place on the air fryer tray, skin side down.
- Cook for ten minutes.
- Serve right away.

Cal 338 | Fat 26g | Carb 1g | Protein 25g

## CRUMB-TOPPED SOLE
*Prep time:10 min | Cook time:10 min | Serves: 4*

**Ingredients**
- Mayonnaise: 3 tbsp.
- 4 sole fillets
- Parmesan cheese: 3 tbsp., divided
- black pepper, to taste
- Butter: 2 tsp., melted
- Soft bread crumbs: 1 cup
- 1 green onion, diced
- Mustard seed: 2 tsp.
- Ground mustard: half tsp.

**Instructions**
- Let the Kalorik Air Fryer Oven preheat to 375 F.
- In a bowl, mix mustard seed, mayonnaise, cheese (2 tbsp.) and black pepper. Mix and coat the fish in this mixture.
- Oil spray the air fryer tray. Place fish and cook for 3 to 5 minutes.
- In a bowl, add the rest of the ingredients. Mix and place on fish pat to adhere.
- Spray with oil and air fry for 2 to 3 minutes more.
- Serve right away.

Cal 233 | Fat 11g | Carb 8g | Protein 24g

## AIR FRYER TILAPIA FILLETS
*Prep time:15 min | Cook time:10 min | Serves: 2*

**Ingredients**
- Black pepper: half tsp.
- 2 tilapia filets
- Olive oil: 1 tbsp.
- Ground thyme: half tsp.
- Smoked paprika: 1 ½ tbsp.

- Garlic powder: 1/4 tsp.
- Dried oregano: half tsp.
- Onion powder: 1 ½ tsp.
- Cayenne pepper: half tsp.
- Sea salt: half tsp.
- Lemon wedges

**Instructions**
- In a bowl, add all spices and mix.
- Coat the fish with oil and sprinkle spice mix on top, and coat the fish. let it rest for 15 minutes.
- Let the Kalorik Air Fryer Oven preheat to 350 F.
- Put the fish on the air fryer tray. Air fry for six minutes.
- Flip and air fry for 4-6 minutes. (or do not flip).
- Serve with lemon wedges.

## BREADED SHRIMP
*Prep time:10 min | Cook time:7 min | Serves: 4*

**Ingredients**
- 1 Pound of Shrimp
- Salt: half tsp.
- Corn starch: 1 tsp.
- Garlic powder: half tsp.
- Flour: 4 tsp.
- Fine breadcrumbs: 2/3 Cup
- Onion powder: half tsp.
- 2 Eggs
- Water: 2 tbsp.
- Panko breadcrumbs: 2/3 Cup

**Instructions**
- In a bowl, mix onion powder, flour, salt, cornstarch, and garlic powder.
- Add shrimps and toss to coat.
- In a bowl, whisk eggs with water.
- In a bowl, mix the breadcrumbs.
- Coat the shrimps in egg then in breadcrumbs, till all shrimps are coated.
- Let the Kalorik Air Fryer Oven preheat to 370 F.
- Oil spray the air fryer tray, place the shrimps on the tray.
- Air fry for 7 minutes. Serve with spicy sauce.

Cal 271 | Carb 23g | Protein 30g | Fat 5g

## CATFISH & GREEN BEANS
*Prep time:10 min | Cook time:25 min | Serves: 2*

**Ingredients**
- 2 catfish fillets
- Fresh green beans: 12 oz., trimmed
- Light brown sugar: 1 tsp.
- All-purpose flour: ¼ cup
- 1 egg, whisked
- Panko bread crumbs: ⅓ cup
- Dill pickle relish: ¾ tsp.
- Kosher salt: to taste
- Black pepper: ¼ tsp.
- Granulated sugar: ⅛ tsp.
- Mayonnaise: 2 tbsp.
- Fresh dill, chopped
- Cider vinegar: half tsp.

## Instructions

- Let the Kalorik Air Fryer Oven preheat to 400 F.
- Spray the beans with oil. Add brown sugar, salt toss to coat.
- Air fry for 12 minutes, take out in a bowl and keep warm.
- Coat the fish in flour, dip in egg and add panko on top.
- Place the breaded fish on the tray and spray with oil.
- Air fry for 8 minutes at 400 F.
- In a bowl, add the rest of the ingredients and mix.
- Add salt and pepper on top of fish and serve with green beans and relish mix.

Cal 416 | Fat 18g | Carb 31g | Protein 33g

## LIGHTLY BREADED TILAPIA FILETS

*Prep time:10 min | Cook time:11 min | Serves: 2*

### Ingredients

- 2 tilapia filets
- Fine breadcrumbs: ¾ cup
- Cayenne pepper, a pinch
- Dried basil: half tsp.
- Garlic powder: 1/4 tsp.
- Mayonnaise: 1 tbsp.
- Dried oregano: half tsp.
- Coarse sea salt: half tsp.

### Instructions

- In a bowl, add garlic powder, breadcrumbs, cayenne, basil, salt, and oregano.
- Coat the fish in mayonnaise.
- Let the Kalorik Air Fryer Oven preheat to 350 F.
- Coat the fish in the breadcrumb mixture.
- Place the fish on the air fryer tray and air fry for six minutes.
- Cook for 4-6 minutes more.
- Serve with tartar sauce.

## COD WITH LEMON & DILL

*Prep time:10 min | Cook time:10 min | Serves: 4*

### Ingredients

- 4 cod fillet
- Salt: half tsp.
- 6 minced garlic cloves
- Lemon juice: 2 tbsp.
- Butter: 4 tbsp., melted
- Dried dill: 1 tsp.

### Instructions

- Let the Kalorik Air Fryer Oven preheat to 370 F.
- In a bowl, add all ingredients except for fish and garlic mix well.
- Add fish and coat it well. Press garlic in the fish.
- Place the fish on the air fry tray and air fry for ten minutes.
- Serve with lemon wedges.

Cal 302 | Fat 13g | Carb 3 g | Protein 42g

## FISH & CHIPS

*Prep time:15 min | Cook time:25 min | Serves: 2*

### Ingredients

- 1 potato
- Grated Parmesan cheese: 1 1/2 tsp.
- Olive oil: 1 tbsp.
- All-purpose flour: 3 tbsp.
- Haddock fillets: half pound

- 1 egg
- Water: 2 tbsp.
- Cayenne pepper, a pinch
- Salt & pepper: to taste
- Crushed cornflakes: 1/3 cup

### Instructions

- Let the Kalorik Air Fryer Oven preheat to 400 F.
- Cut the potato into half-inch sticks.
- Toss the potatoes with oil, salt and pepper.
- Spread the chips on the air fry tray and air fry for 5 to 10 minutes, until crispy and light brown.
- In a bowl, add black pepper and flour. In another bowl, whisk the egg with water.
- In another bowl, add cheese, cayenne and cornflakes.
- Season the fish with salt, coat the fish in flour, then egg, and finally in cornflakes mixture.
- Place the fish on the tray and air fry for 8 to 10 minutes.
- Serve with chips.

Cal 304 | Fat 9g | Carb 33g | Protein 23g

## BUTTER SALMON BITES

*Prep time:75 min | Cook time:25 min | Serves: 6*

### Ingredients

- Salmon: 8 Oz.
- Minced garlic: 1 tbsp.
- Lemon juice: 2 tbsp.
- Salt & pepper, 1 tsp. each
- Butter: ⅓ Cup, Softened
- Rice vinegar: 1 tbsp.

### Instructions

- In a bowl, add all ingredients except for fish. Mix well.
- Cut the salmon into 1 by 1 inch cubes.
- Add the cubes to the marinade and toss well. Keep in the fridge for 1 hour.
- Let the Kalorik Air Fryer Oven preheat to 350 F.
- Place the salmon cubes on the tray of the air fryer.
- Air fry for ten minutes, serve right away.

## POPCORN SHRIMP

*Prep time:10 min | Cook time:10 min | Serves: 4*

### Ingredients

- 2 eggs, whisked
- Small shrimps: 1 pound, peeled & deveined
- Water: 2 tbsp.
- Panko breadcrumbs: 1 ½ cups
- All-purpose flour: half cup
- Garlic powder: 1 tbsp.
- Ketchup: half cup
- Kosher salt, to taste
- Chipotle chiles: 2 tbsp., in adobo

- Ground cumin: 1 tbsp.
- Chopped fresh cilantro: 2 tbsp.
- Lime juice: 2 tbsp.

**Instructions**

- In a bowl, whisk eggs with water. In another bowl, add flour.
- In a 3rd bowl, add garlic powder, cumin and panko.
- Coat the shrimps in the flour, then in egg and lastly in panko mixture.
- Let the Kalorik Air Fryer Oven preheat to 360 F. Place the shrimps on the air fryer's tray.
- Air fry for 8 minutes.
- In a bowl, add the rest of the ingredients and whisk. Serve with shrimps.

Cal 297 | Fat 4g | Carb 35g | Protein 29g

## CRAB CAKES

*Prep time:15 min | Cook time:10 min | Serves: 2*

**Ingredients**

- 1 scallion, diced
- 1 egg, whisked
- Lump crab meat: half pound
- Milk: 1 tbsp.
- Panko breadcrumbs: half cup
- Old bay seasoning: 1/4 tsp.
- Dijon mustard: 1 tsp.
- Hot sauce, a dash
- Diced red bell pepper: 1/4 cup
- Lemon juice: 1 1/2 tsp.
- Worcestershire sauce: half tsp.
- Salt & black pepper, to taste

**Instructions**

- In a bowl, whisk the eggs with milk. Add breadcrumbs (1/4 cup).
- In a bowl, add the rest of the ingredients except for crab meat and breadcrumbs.
- Mix and add crab meat; add breadcrumb mixture. Make into four patties.
- Let the Kalorik Air Fryer Oven preheat to 375 F.
- On a plate, add the rest of the breadcrumbs. Coat the patties in breadcrumbs.
- Spray the patties with oil and place them on the air fryer tray.
- Air fry for five minutes, flip and cook for 5 more minutes.
- Serve with tartar sauce.

## LEMON & PEPPER SHRIMPS

*Prep time:5 min | Cook time:8 min | Serves: 4*

**Ingredients**

- Raw shrimp: 1 pound, peeled & deveined
- Pasta: 8 oz., cooked
- Lemon juice: 2 tbsp.
- Olive oil: half cup
- Black pepper: 1 tsp.
- Salt: half tsp.

**Instructions**

- Let the Kalorik Air Fryer Oven preheat to 400 F.
- In a bowl, add all ingredients and toss to coat.
- Line the air fryer tray with parchment paper and place the shrimp on it.
- Air fry for 8 minutes and serve with pasta.

Cal 322 | Fat 28g | Carb 2g | Protein 16g

## SHRIMP PO'BOY

*Prep time:35 min | Cook time:10 n*

**Ingredients**

- Creole mustard: 1 tbsp.
- Cayenne pepper: 1/8 tsp.
- Chopped dill pickles: 1 tbsp.
- Mayonnaise: half cup
- 1 tomato, sliced
- Coconut shrimp: recipe no. 2
- Minced shallot: 1 tbsp.
- Lemon juice: 1 1/2 tsp.
- 4 buns, split
- Lettuce shredded: 2 cups

**Instructions**

- Cook the coconut shrimps.
- In a bowl, add the rest of the ingredients, except for buns, tomato and lettuce. Mix well.
- Cut the buns in half, place them on the air fryer tray. Oil spray the buns.
- Air fry for 4 to 5 minutes at 350 F.
- Add shrimps and sauce on the buns, add toppings and serve.

Cal 716 | Fat 40g | Carb 60g | Protein 31g

## HONEY SRIRACHA SALMON

*Prep time:25 min | Cook time:7 min | Serves: 2*

**Ingredients**

- Honey: 3 tbsp.
- Salmon: 1.5 lbs.
- Salt, to taste
- Sriracha: 2 tbsp.

**Instructions**

- In a bowl, mix honey and sriracha.
- Season the fish with salt and pour the sriracha mixture on the fish.
- Let it rest for 20 minutes.
- Let the Kalorik Air Fryer Oven preheat to 400 F.
- Place the fish on the air fryer tray and air fry for 7 minutes.
- Serve right away.

Cal 580 | Carb 26g | Protein 68g | Fat 22g

## SCALLOPS WITH LEMON-HERB SAUCE

*Prep time:10 min | Cook time:10 min | Serves: 2*

**Ingredients**

- Black pepper: ¼ tsp.
- Salt: ⅛ tsp.
- Lemon zest: 1 tsp.
- Olive oil: ¼ cup
- sea scallops: 8 large
- Chopped garlic: half tsp.
- Flat-leaf parsley: 2 tbsp., chopped
- Capers: 2 tsp., chopped

**Instructions**

- Season the scallops with salt and pepper.
- Place scallops on the oil sprayed tray of the air fryer.
- Let the Kalorik Air Fryer Oven preheat to 400 F.
- Air fry the scallops for six minutes until the scallops' internal temperature reaches 120 F.

...d the rest of the ingredients whisk well. Pour over
... d serve.

...t 30g | Carb 5g | Protein 14g

## AIR FRYER SEASONED SHRIMP

*Prep time:10 min | Cook time:4 min | Serves: 6*

**...edients**

- 3 minced garlic cloves
- Cooked shrimp: 2 pounds, peeled & deveined
- Sea salt: half tsp.
- Olive oil: 2 tbsp.
- Lemon juice: 2 tsp.
- Black pepper: 1 tsp.
- Salad greens, as needed

**Instructions**

- In a bowl, add all ingredients and toss to coat. Let them rest for few minutes.
- Let the Kalorik Air Fryer Oven preheat to 350 F.
- Place the shrimps on the air fryer tray and air fry for three minutes. Cook in batches and serve right away.

## TUNA STEAKS

*Prep time:20 min | Cook time:5 min | Serves: 6*

**Ingredients**

- 2 tuna steaks, boneless & skinless
- Rice vinegar: half tsp.
- Honey: 2 tsp.
- Grated ginger: 1 tsp.
- Soy sauce: 1/4 cup
- Sesame oil: 1 tsp.

**Instructions**

- In a bowl, add all ingredients except for fish, mix well.
- Add tuna, coat well and let it rest for 20 to 30 minutes.
- Let the Kalorik Air Fryer Oven preheat to 380 F.
- Place the steaks on the air fryer tray and cook for four minutes.
- Slice and serve.

## WASABI CRAB CAKES

*Prep time:20 min | Cook time:10 min | Serves: 12*

**Ingredients**

- Wasabi: ¼ tsp.
- 1 sweet red pepper, diced
- Dry bread crumbs: 1/3 + half cup
- 1 celery rib, diced
- 2 egg whites
- Mayonnaise: 3 tbsp.
- 3 green onions, diced
- Salt: ¼ tsp.
- Lump crabmeat: 1 1/2 cups

**Instructions**

- Let the Kalorik Air Fryer Oven preheat to 375 F.
- In a bowl, add all ingredients except for a half cup of breadcrumbs and crab.
- Mix and fold in crab.
- In a bowl, add the breadcrumbs. Make the mixture into patties, coat in breadcrumbs.
- Place the patties on the air fryer tray and air fry for 8 to 12 minutes.
- Serve with any dipping sauce.

Cal 49 | Fat 2g | Carb 4g | Protein 3g

## FISH STICKS

*Prep time:10 min | Cook time:30 min | Serves: 2*

**Ingredients**

- Cod: 1 1/2 pound
- Onion powder: 1 1/2 tsp.
- 2 eggs
- Almond flour: 1 cup
- Tapioca starch: half cup
- Dried dill: 1 1/2 tsp.
- Sea salt: 1 tsp.
- Black pepper: 1 tsp.
- Mustard powder: half tsp.

**For tartar sauce**

- Dill relish: 1 tbsp.
- Salt: ¼ tsp.
- Dried herbs: 1 tbsp.
- Avocado oil mayo: 1/3 cup
- Lemon juice: 2 tsp.

**Instructions**

- Let the Kalorik Air Fryer Oven preheat to 390 F.
- Season the fish with salt and pepper.
- Slice the fish into sticks (half an inch by half an inch)
- In a bowl, add starch. In another bowl, whisk the eggs.
- In a bowl, whisk onion powder, almond flour, mustard powder, dill, salt and pepper.
- Coat the fish in starch, then in eggs and lastly in a flour mixture.
- Oil spray the air fry tray generously and place the fish sticks on it.
- Spray the fish sticks with oil.
- Air fry for 11 minutes, flipping halfway through.
- In a bowl, add all the ingredients of tartar sauce, mix and serve with fish sticks.

Cal 598 | Fat 22.5g | Carb 35.2g | Protein 61.7g

## SHRIMP FAJITAS

*Prep time:5 min | Cook time:10 min | Serves: 2*

**Ingredients**

- 1 yellow onion, sliced
- 1-pound raw shrimp
- Fajita seasoning: 1 tbsp.
- 3 bell peppers, sliced
- Vegetable oil: 1 tbsp.

**For serving**

- Avocado slices
- 4 tortillas
- Pico de gallo

**Instructions**

- Let the Kalorik Air Fryer Oven preheat to 375 F.
- In a bowl, add vegetables, half of the seasonings and half the oil. toss well.
- Air fry for three minutes.
- In a bowl, add shrimps and the rest of the oil and seasonings. Toss well
- After three minutes, add the shrimp tray to the air fryer.
- Air fry for six minutes, flip halfway through, keep an eye on vegetables.

- Serve the shrimps in a tortilla, vegetables and desired toppings.

Cal 338 | Carb 25g | Protein 27g | Fat 15g

## GREEK SALMON BURGERS

*Prep time:10 min | Cook time:15 min | Serves: 2*

### Ingredients

- Ground salmon: 8 oz.
- Chopped fresh oregano: 2 tsp.
- Red onion: ¼ cup, sliced
- Crushed red pepper: half tsp.
- Salt: ¼ tsp.
- Crumbled feta cheese: ¼ cup
- 2 minced garlic cloves
- 2 burger buns, halved & toasted
- Olive oil: 1 ½ tbsp.
- Baby spinach leaves: half cup
- Red-wine vinegar: half tbsp.

### Instructions

- In a bowl, add salmon, garlic, oil, salt, red pepper, and oregano. Mix well.
- Make into half-inch patties.
- Let the Kalorik Air Fryer Oven preheat to 360 F.
- Place on the air fryer tray and air fry for 13-15 minutes until internal temperature reaches 155 F. Flip halfway through.
- In a bowl, add vinegar, spinach and onion. Toss well
- Add feta on buns. Add burgers, add spinach mixture and serve.

Cal 351 | Fat 16g | Carb 26g | Protein 28g

## SALMON WITH SPINACH PESTO

*Prep time:5 min | Cook time:8-10 min | Serves: 4*

### Ingredients

- 4 salmon fillets, without skin
- Black pepper: half tsp.
- Olive oil: 1 tbsp.
- Pesto, as needed
- Kosher salt: half tsp.

### Instructions

- Season the fillets with pepper, oil and salt.
- Let the Kalorik Air Fryer Oven preheat to 390 F.
- Air fry the fillets for 7-10 minutes until the internal temperature reaches 145 F.
- Take salmon out, and spread pesto on top and serve with lemon wedges.

## CAJUN CATFISH

*Prep time:5 min | Cook time:20 min | Serves: 4*

### Ingredients

- 4 catfish fillets
- Cornmeal: 3/4 cup
- Spicy Tartar Sauce, as needed
- Cajun seasoning: 3 tsp.

### Instructions

- In a zip lock bag, add Cajun seasoning and cornmeal. Mix well.
- Add the fish to the bag. Shake to coat.
- Let the Kalorik Air Fryer Oven preheat to 390 F.
- Place the fish on the air fryer tray and air fry for 15 minutes. Flip hallway through.
- Change the temperature to 400 F, air fry for 5 minutes

- Serve with spicy tartar sauce.

Cal 481 | Fat 32g | Carb 19g | Protein 29g

## MAPLE-DIJON SALMON

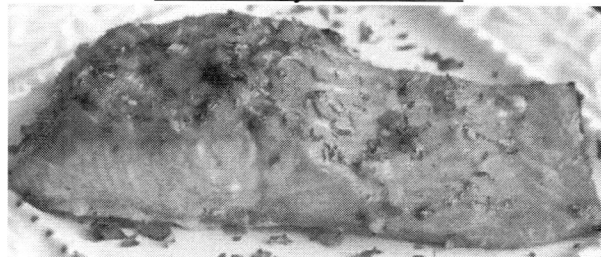

*Prep time:5 min | Cook time:10 min | Serves: 4*

### Ingredients

- Salt & pepper, to taste
- Butter: 3 tbsp.
- 1 lemon's juice
- Maple syrup: 3 tbsp.
- 1 minced garlic clove
- Dijon mustard: 1 tbsp.
- Olive oil: 1 tbsp.
- 4 salmon fillets

### Instructions

- Let the Kalorik Air Fryer Oven preheat to 400 F.
- In a pan, melt butter, add minced garlic, mustard, maple syrup and lemon juice.
- Mix on medium flame until thickness, for 2 to 3 minutes. Turn off the heat.
- Season the salmon with salt, pepper and oil.
- Air fry the fish for 5 to 7 minutes.
- Pour sauce over and serve.

Cal 329 | Fat 23g | Carb 11g | Protein 19g

## PERFECT AIR FRYER SALMON

*Prep time:5 min | Cook time:7-10 min | Serves: 2*

### Ingredients

- 2 salmon fillets
- Salt & coarse black pepper, to taste
- Avocado oil: 2 tsp.
- Paprika: 2 tsp.

### Instructions

- Season the salmon with oil, pepper, salt and paprika.
- Let the Kalorik Air Fryer Oven preheat to 390 F.
- Place the fish on the air fryer tray and air fry for 7 minutes.
- Serve with salad greens or rice.

Cal 288 | Fat 18g | Carb 1.4g | Protein 28.3g

## TILAPIA WITH HERBS & GARLIC

*Prep time:5 min | Cook time:10 min | Serves: 2*

### Ingredients

- Olive oil: 2 tsp.
- Fresh chives chopped: 2 tsp.
- Salt & pepper, to taste
- Fresh parsley chopped: 2 tsp.
- 2 tilapia filets
- Minced garlic: 1 tsp.

### Instructions

- Let the Kalorik Air Fryer Oven preheat to 400 F.
- In a bowl, add all ingredients except for fish.

- Mix well and brush the fish with this mixture.
- Oil spray the air fryer tray.
- Air fry the fish for 8-10 minutes.
- Serve right away.

## FISH CAKES

*Prep time:10 min | Cook time:10 min | Serves: 2*

### Ingredients

- Chopped white fish: 10 oz.
- Chopped fresh cilantro: 3 tbsp.
- Ground pepper: ¼ tsp.
- Thai sweet chili sauce: 2 tbsp.
- Panko breadcrumbs: ⅔ cup
- Mayonnaise: 2 tbsp.
- 1 egg
- Salt, to taste

### Instructions

- In a bowl, add all ingredients and mix.
- Make into four small cakes.
- Let the Kalorik Air Fryer Oven preheat to 400 F.
- Oil spray the cakes and air fry for 9-10 minutes until internal temperature reaches 140 F.
- Drizzle lime juice and serve.

Cal 399 | Fat 16g | Carb 28g | Protein 35g

## INDIAN BUTTER SHRIMP

*Prep time:10 min | Cook time:5 min | Serves: 2*

### Ingredients

- 1-pound shrimp, peeled and deveined
- 1/4 cup scallions, white only
- 2 tablespoons tomato paste
- 2 tablespoons tomato chutney
- 1/4 cup sliced Polanco peppers
- 2 tablespoons butter

### Instructions

- Remove the tails from your shrimp first.
- In a large mixing bowl, combine all of the ingredients, except for butter and mix.
- Pour the shrimp mixture into the air fryer tray and cook for 5 minutes at 400 F.
- When the shrimp is finished air fried, add the butter and stir until it is melted.
- Serve right away

Cal 224 | Fat 10g | Carb 1.3g | Protein 32g

## LOBSTER TAILS WITH LEMON-GARLIC BUTTER

*Prep time:10 min | Cook time:10 min | Serves: 2*

### Ingredients

- 2 lobster tails
- 4 tablespoons butter
- 1 teaspoon lemon zest
- 1 clove garlic, grated
- Salt & pepper to taste
- 1 teaspoon chopped fresh parsley

### Instructions

- Butter lobster tails use kitchen shears to cut lengthwise through the hard top shells and meat centres. Cut to the bottoms of the eggs, but not into them. Separate the tail halves. With the lobster meat facing up, place the tails in the air fryer basket.

- In a small saucepan over medium heat, melt the butter. Heat the lemon zest and garlic for around 30 seconds or until the garlic is tender. Brush 2 tablespoons of the butter mixture onto lobster tails in a small bowl; discard any remaining brushed butter to prevent contamination from raw lobster. Season the lobster with salt and pepper before eating.
- Cook for 5 to 7 minutes in an air fryer at 380 F until lobster meat is opaque. Place the lobster meat on a plate with the reserved butter from the saucepan. Serve with lemon wedges and parsley on top.

Cal 313 | Protein 18.1g | Carb 3.3g | Fat 25.8g

## CHINESE CRAB RANGOON

*Prep time:5 min | Cook time:8 min | Serves: 6*

### Ingredients

- 8 oz. cream cheese
- 8 oz. crab meat
- 1 teaspoon minced garlic
- 1 teaspoon garlic salt
- 1 teaspoon Worcestershire
- 2–3 scallions, diced
- 1 package Wonton wrappers

### Instructions

- Add the cream cheese, crab meat, minced garlic, garlic salt, Worcestershire sauce, and sliced scallions in a large mixing bowl.
- In the centre of the wrapper, place a tablespoon of filling.
- Pinch them to fold them up.
- Drizzle olive oil over on the tray.
- Drizzle olive oil over the tops of the crab Rangoon's. Place the tray of the air fryer cook for 5 minutes at 330 F.
- Serve right away

Cal 98 | Carb 12g | Protein 7g | Fat 3g

## SALMON SPRING ROLLS

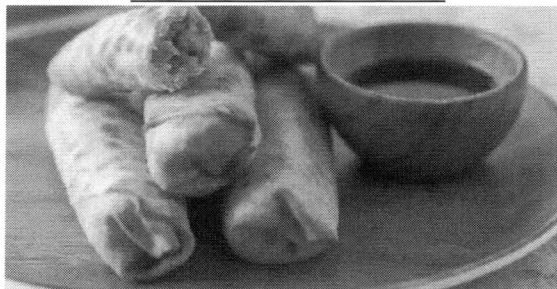

*Prep time:10 min | Cook time:8 min | Serves: 6*

### Ingredients

- 2 Salmon fillets
- butter: 1 to 2 tbsp.
- Minced Mint: 1 to 2 tsp.
- Diced Chinese Mushrooms: half cup
- Diced Onions: half cup
- Shredded Carrots: 1 cup
- Minced Basil: 1 to 2 tsp.
- Spring Roll Wrapper: 12 to 16

### Instructions

- In a skillet, sauté all ingredients, for 7 to 8 minutes, until tender.
- In the spring roll wrappers, add the filling and fold them.
- Let the Kalorik Air Fryer Oven preheat to 400 F.
- Place the rolls on the air fryer tray and air fry for 5 to 7 minutes, flipping halfway through.

- Serve right away

Cal 180 | Fat 9g | Protein 7g | Carb 19g

## CAJUN CRAB LEGS

*Prep time:5 min | Cook time:5 min | Serves: 2*

**Ingredients**

- 1 cluster Snow Crab legs
- 2 tablespoons olive oil
- 1 tablespoon Cajun seasoning

**Instructions**

- In a big mixing bowl, add all ingredients and toss well.
- Let the Kalorik Air Fryer Oven preheat to 350 F.
- Transfer to an air fryer tray and cook for 3 to 5 minutes.
- Serve right away.

Cal 790 | Fat 41g | Carb 51g | Protein 55g

## SALMON WITH HORSERADISH RUB

*Prep time:10 min | Cook time:20 min | Serves: 2*

**Ingredients**

- Skinless salmon fillet: 12 oz.
- Chopped flat-leaf parsley: 1 tbsp.
- Capers: 1 tbsp., chopped
- Grated horseradish: 2 tbsp.
- olive oil: 1 tbsp.
- Salt & pepper, to taste

**Instructions**

- In a bowl, mix oil, horseradish, capers and parsley. Add salt and pepper.
- Coat the salmon in this mixture and place it on the air fryer tray.
- Let the Kalorik Air Fryer Oven preheat to 375 F.
- Air fry for 15 minutes until the internal temperature reaches 130°F.
- Serve right away.

Cal 305 | Fat 15g | Carb 7g | Protein 35g

## SHRIMP CAESAR SALAD

*Prep time:15 min | Cook time:5 min | Serves: 2*

**Ingredients**

- 2 romaine hearts, chopped
- Parmesan cheese: ¼ cup, shredded
- Caesar salad dressing: half cup
- Flour: half cup
- Uncooked shrimp: 1 pound, peeled & deveined
- Cherry tomatoes: 1 cup, halved
- Salt & black pepper, to taste

**Instructions**

- Let the Kalorik Air Fryer Oven preheat to 375 F.
- In a bowl, add cheese, romaine, and tomatoes. Toss.
- In a bowl, add salt, flour and pepper. Add shrimps and coat.
- In the air fryer tray, add shrimps, spray with oil and air fry for 2 to 3 minutes.
- Flip and oil spray, air fry for 2 to 3 minutes.
- In the romaine bowl, add salad dressing, coat and add shrimps. Toss and serve.

Cal 313 | Fat 21g | Carb 8g | Protein 23g

## KOREAN GRILLED SHRIMP SKEWERS

*Prep time:5 min | Cook time:6 min | Serves: 2*

**Ingredients**

- Olive oil: 1 tbsp.

- Minced garlic: 1 tsp.
- Honey: 2 tbsp.
- Korean gochujang: 2 tbsp.
- Soy sauce: 2 tbsp.
- 2 pounds, peeled
- Lemon juice: 1 tbsp.
- Pepper flakes, to taste

**Instructions**

- Soak the skewers for half an hour.
- In a bowl, add all ingredients, except for shrimps and mix.
- Add shrimps and toss.
- Let the Kalorik Air Fryer Oven preheat to 350 F.
- Thread the shrimps onto the skewers.
- Air fry for 5 to 8 minutes, flipping halfway though.
- Serve right away

Cal 76 | Carb 3g | Protein 12g | Fat 2g

## BLACKENED AIR FRYER SHRIMP

*Prep time:5 min | Cook time:6 min | Serves: 2*

**Ingredients**

- Blackened seasoning: 1 tbsp.
- Olive oil: 2 tbsp.
- Large shrimp: 1 pound, peeled & deveined
- Parsley, chopped

**Instructions**

- Let the Kalorik Air Fryer Oven preheat to 400 F on Bake
- In a bowl, add all ingredients and toss well.
- Place the shrimps on the air fryer tray.
- Bake for 5 to 6 minutes, flipping halfway through.
- Serve with any dipping sauce.

Cal 175 | Protein 23g | Fat 9g

## CHEESY TUNA FLAUTIST

*Prep time:15 min | Cook time:5-7 min | Serves: 2*

**Ingredients**

- 8 flour tortillas
- Wild tuna: 1 can
- Cheddar cheese: half cup, shredded
- Garlic powder: 1/8 tsp.
- Salt: 1/8 tsp.
- Ancho chili powder: 1/8 tsp.
- Cilantro: half tsp., chopped

**Instructions**

- In a bowl, add the tuna, cilantro, garlic powder, salt, and ancho chili powder.
- In every tortilla, add cheese and add tuna mixture, roll them.
- Let the Kalorik Air Fryer Oven preheat to 350 F.
- Air fry for 5 to 7 minutes.
- Slice and serve.

Cal 174 | Protein 10.3g | Carb 12.9g | Fat 9.2g

## FISH FINGERS

*Prep time:10 min | Cook time:15 min | Serves: 2*

**Ingredients**

- 2 eggs
- Fish fillets: 1 pound
- Salt: 1 tsp.
- Black pepper: half tsp.

- All-purpose flour: half cup
- Dried breadcrumbs: 1 cup
- Fresh herbs

**Instructions**

- In a bowl, add flour with salt, fresh herbs and pepper.
- In a bowl, add whisked eggs, and in another bowl, add breadcrumbs.
- Cut the fish fillets into fish sticks.
- Coat the fish sticks in flour, then in egg and lastly in breadcrumbs.
- Oil spray the fish sticks and place them on the air fryer tray.
- Let the Kalorik Air Fryer Oven preheat to 400 F.
- Air fry the fish sticks for ten minutes, flip them halfway through.
- Serve with tartar sauce.

Calories: 99 | Carb 6g | Protein 12g | Fat 3g

## FURIKAKE SALMON

*Prep time:10 min | Cook time:10 min | Serves: 2*

**Ingredients**

- Salmon fillet: 1 pound
- Mayonnaise: half cup
- Furikake: 2 tbsp.
- Shout: 1 tbsp.
- Salt & pepper to taste

**Instructions**

- Let the Kalorik Air Fryer Oven preheat to 400 F.
- In a bowl, mix shout and mayo. Mix well.
- Season the salmon with salt and pepper.
- Spread the shout mix on the salmon and spread furikake on the salmon.
- Oil spray the salmon.
- Air fry for 8 to 10 minutes. Serve right away.

Cal 578 | Fat 47g | Carb 2g | Protein 34g

## CAJUN SCALLOPS

*Prep time:5 min | Cook time:6 min | Serves: 2*

**Ingredients**

- 6 Sea scallops
- Cajun seasoning, as needed
- Kosher salt, to taste

**Instructions**

- Let the Kalorik Air Fryer Oven preheat to 400 F.
- Season the scallops with Cajun seasoning and salt.
- Oil spray the seasoned scallops.
- Air fry for three minutes
- Serve with pasta.

Cal 348 | Protein 13.9g | Carb 4.6g | Fat 29.8g

## CRAB STUFFED MUSHROOMS

*Prep time:15 min | Cook time:18 min | Serves: 2*

**Ingredients**

- Baby Bella Mushrooms: 2 pounds
- Bread Crumbs: half cup, seasoned
- ¼ Red Onion chopped
- Salt Blend: 2 tsp.
- Lump Crab: 8 oz.
- 1 egg
- 2 Celery Ribs, diced

- Hot Sauce: 1 tsp.
- Parmesan Cheese: half cup, shredded
- Oregano: 1 tsp.

**Instructions**

- Let the Kalorik Air Fryer Oven preheat to 400 F on Bake.
- Take the stems off the mushrooms, and spray them with oil.
- Sprinkle salt blend on the mushrooms.
- Chop the onion and celery into small pieces.
- Combine the celery, lobster, breadcrumbs, egg, onions, shredded Parmesan (half), oregano, and hot sauce in a bowl.
- On every mushroom, stuff with mixture.
- Add the rest of the cheese on top.
- Bake for 8 to 9 minutes, serve right away.

Cal 33 | Fat 1g | Carb 3g | Protein 4g

## BLACKENED SALMON

*Prep time:10 min | Cook time:18 min | Serves: 2*

**Ingredients**

- Olive oil: 1 tbsp.
- Blackened seasoning: 1 tbsp.
- Salmon: 1 lb., cut into 3 to 4 filets

**Instructions**

- Let the Kalorik Air Fryer Oven preheat to 400 F.
- Coat the salmon in olive oil.
- Sprinkle blackened seasoning on the salmon. Coat well.
- Air fry for 7 to 10 minutes.
- Serve right away.

Cal 498 | Fat 32g | Carb 0g | Protein 48g

## POPCORN SHRIMP TACOS

*Prep time:10 min | Cook time:20 min | Serves: 4*

**Ingredients**

- Coleslaw mix: 2 cups
- Lime juice: 2 tbsp.
- Salt: 1/4 tsp.
- Minced fresh cilantro: 1/4 cup
- Panko bread crumbs: 1-1/2 cups
- 1 jalapeno pepper, chopped without seeds
- Honey: 2 tbsp.
- Uncooked small shrimp: 1 pound, peeled & deveined
- 2 eggs
- Milk: 2 tbsp.
- All-purpose flour: half cup
- 8 corn tortillas small
- Ground cumin: 1 tbsp.
- Garlic powder: 1 tbsp.
- Avocado slices

**Instructions**

- In a bowl, add jalapeno, coleslaw mix, honey, salt, cilantro, and lime juice. Toss and set it aside.
- Let the Kalorik Air Fryer Oven preheat to 375 F.
- In a bowl, whisk eggs with milk. In another bowl, add flour. Add garlic powder, panko, and cumin to another bowl and mix.
- Coat shrimps in flour, then in egg and lastly in panko. Oil spray the shrimps.
- Air fry the shrimps for 2 to 3 minutes on each side.
- In a tortilla, add shrimps, avocado slices and coleslaw mix.

Cal | Fat 6g | Carb 29g | Protein 15g

# Cajun Salmon

*Prep time: 5 min | Cook time: 10 min | Serves: 2*

**Ingredients**

- Salmon fillet (1 - 7 oz.) 0.75-inches thick
- Cajun seasoning
- Juice (¼ of a lemon)
- Optional: Sprinkle of sugar

**Directions**

- Set the Air Fryer at 356º F to preheat for five minutes.
- Rinse and dry the salmon with a paper towel. Cover the fish with the Cajun coating mix.
- Place the fillet in the air fryer for seven minutes with the skin side up.
- Serve with a sprinkle of lemon and dusting of sugar if desired.

Cal 285 | Fat 17.8g | Carb 6.8g | Protein 42.1g

## Bacon Wrapped Shrimp

*Prep time:40 min | Cook time:10 min | Serves: 8*

**Ingredients**

- Raw shrimp: 24 jumbos, deveined
- Fresh parsley: 1 tbsp., chopped
- Olive oil: 1 tbsp.
- Bacon: 8 slices, cut into thirds
- Paprika: 1 tsp.
- Minced garlic: 1 to 2 cloves

**Instructions**

- In a bowl, add paprika, parsley, garlic and olive oil.
- In a bowl, add shrimps and pour the garlic mixture toss to coat.
- With bacon pieces, wrap the shrimps and place them in the tray. Keep in the fridge for half an hour.
- Let the Kalorik Air Fryer Oven preheat to 400 F.
- Air fry the shrimps for 8-10 minutes, serve right away.

## Parmesan Shrimp

*Prep time:10 min | Cook time:10 min | Serves: 8*

**Ingredients**

- Jumbo shrimp, cooked: 2 pounds, peeled & deveined
- Oregano: half tsp.
- 4 minced garlic cloves
- Parmesan cheese: 2/3 cup, grated
- Basil: 1 tsp.
- Olive oil: 2 tbsp.
- Pepper, to taste
- Onion powder: 1 tsp.

**Instructions**

- In a bowl, add all ingredients and coat well.
- Let the Kalorik Air Fryer Oven preheat to 350 F.
- Place the shrimps on the air fryer tray.

- Air fry for 8 to 10 minutes.
- Serve with a drizzle of lemon juice.

## Foil Packet Salmon

*Prep time:10 min | Cook time:15 min | Serves: 4*

**Ingredients**

- Salmon 4 fillets
- Soy sauce: 4 tbsp.
- Green beans: 4 cups
- Kosher salt: half tsp.
- Sesame seeds: 2 tsp.
- Garlic powder: 1 tsp.
- Red pepper flakes: ¼ tsp.
- Ginger powder: half tsp.
- Honey: 2 tbsp.
- White pepper: ¼ tsp.

**Instructions**

- In a bowl, add all ingredients except for beans and salmon. Mix well.
- Cut out four sheets of 12 by 11 inches' foil sheets.
- Oil spray the beans and fillets and sprinkle salt on them.
- Let the Kalorik Air Fryer Oven preheat to 390 F
- Place beans in the centre of the foil, place a fish fillet on top.
- Add sauce over every fish fillet and seal the packet.
- Place the packets in the air fryer.
- Air fry for 12 minutes, rest for five minutes. Serve.

Cal 245 | Carb 19g | Protein 26g | Fat 8g

## Tuna Burgers

*Prep time:10 min | Cook time:20 min | Serves: 4*

**Ingredients**

- 1 egg, whisked
- Finely chopped celery: half cup
- Mayonnaise: 1/3 cup
- Chopped onion: 1/4 cup
- Dry bread crumbs: half cup
- Tuna in water: ~7 oz.
- Chili sauce: 2 tbsp.
- 4 buns, split and toasted

**Instructions**

- Let the Kalorik Air Fryer Oven preheat to 350 F
- In a bowl, add all ingredients except for buns, and mix. Make into four patties.
- Air fry the patties for 5 to 6 minutes on each side.
- Serve on buns with tomato and lettuce.

Cal 366 | Fat 17g | Carb 35g | Protein 17g

## Salt & Pepper Shrimp

*Prep time:10 min | Cook time:10 min | Serves: 4*

**Ingredients**

- Shrimp: 1 pound
- Black Peppercorns: 2 tsp., ground
- Kosher Salt: 1 tsp.
- Oil: 2 tbsp.
- Sichuan peppercorns:2 tsp., ground
- Sugar: 1 tsp.
- Rice Flour: 3 tbsp.

**Instructions**

- In a pan, roast the peppercorns for 1 to 2 minutes, let them cool.
- In a mortar and pestle, add peppercorns, salt and sugar, spices, crush until coarse powder forms.
- In a bowl, add shrimps, oil, rice flour and spices coat well.
- Let the Kalorik Air Fryer Oven preheat to 325 F.
- Place the shrimps on the air fryer tray, spray with oil, and air fry for 8 to 10 minutes. Flip halfway through.

Cal 178 | Carb 9g | Protein 16g | Fat 8g

## SOUTHERN FRIED CATFISH
*Prep time:15 min | Cook time:13 min | Serves: 4*

### Ingredients
- 1 Lemon
- Catfish Fillets: 2 pounds
- Yellow Mustard: half cup
- Milk: 1 cup

### Seasoning Mix
- Dried Parsley Flakes: 2 tbsp.
- Garlic Powder: 1/4 tsp.
- Kosher Salt: half tsp.
- All-Purpose Flour: 1/4 cup
- Black Pepper: 1/4 tsp.
- Cayenne Pepper: 1/4 tsp.
- Cornmeal: half cup
- Chili Powder: 1/4 tsp.
- Onion Powder: 1/4 tsp.

### Instructions
- In a dish, add fish and milk.
- Add lemon juice. Coat and keep in the fridge for 15 minutes.
- In a bowl, add all ingredients of seasonings.
- Let the Kalorik Air Fryer Oven preheat to 390-400 F.
- Take fish out and pat dry.
- Spread mustard all over the fillets. Coat the fish in seasoning mix and spray with oil.
- Place the fish on the tray of the air fryer.
- Air fry for ten minutes.
- Serve right away.

Cal 391 | Fat 11g | Carb 29g | Protein 44g

## GINGERED HONEY SALMON
*Prep time:20 min | Cook time:10 min | Serves: 1*

### Ingredients
- Garlic powder: 1 tsp.
- Orange juice: 1/3 cup
- Honey: 1/4 cup
- 1 green onion, diced
- 1 salmon fillet
- Soy sauce: 1/3 cup
- Ground ginger: 1 tsp.

### Instructions
- In a bowl, add all ingredients and coat the fish well. Keep in the fridge for half an hour.
- Take fish out and save the marinade.
- Let the Kalorik Air Fryer Oven preheat to 325 F.
- Place the fish on the air fryer tray, air fry for 15 to 18 minutes.
- Baste with the reserved marinade in the last five minutes.
- Serve right away.

Cal 237 | Fat 10g | Carb 15g | Protein 20g

## CRISPY COD NUGGETS
*Prep time:10 min | Cook time:15 min | Serves: 3-4*

### Ingredients
- Cod fillets: 1 1/2 pounds, cut into chunks
- 1 egg + 1 tbsp. Water
- Salt & pepper, to season
- Oil: 1 tbsp.
- Flour: half cup
- Cornflake crumbs: half cup

### Instructions
- In a food processor, crush the cornflakes. Add oil and mix.
- Season the fish with salt and black pepper, coat the seasoned fish in flour.
- Coat the fish in egg wash, and lastly in crumb mixture.
- Let the Kalorik Air Fryer Oven preheat to 356 F.
- Air fry for 15 minutes, serve with French fries.

## HONEY TERIYAKI SALMON
*Prep time:15 min | Cook time:13 min | Serves: 3*

### Ingredients
- Wild-caught Salmon: 3 fillets
- Honey: 3 tbsp.
- Teriyaki: 8 tbsp.
- Extra virgin olive oil: 2 tbsp.
- 2 garlic cloves

### Instructions
- In a bowl, add all ingredients except for fish, whisk well and pour over the fillets.
- Coat and let it rest for 20 minutes.
- Let the Kalorik Air Fryer Oven preheat to 350 F.
- Air fry the salmon for 12 minutes, flipping halfway through.
- Serve right away.

## BAJA FISH TACOS
*Prep time:30 min | Cook time:15 min | Serves: 6-8*

### Ingredients
- Mahi Mahi Filets: 2 pounds, cut into strips
- 2 Eggs
- Sea Salt: 1 tsp.
- Black Pepper: half tsp.
- Milk: 1 cup
- Mayonnaise: 1 ½ tbsp.
- All-Purpose Flour: half cup
- Potato Starch: half cup
- 2 Limes
- Baking Soda: 1 tsp.
- Garlic Powder: 2 tsp.
- 8 Corn Tortillas

### Instructions
- In a bowl, add fish strips and lime juice, and milk. Mix and keep in the fridge for 15 minutes.
- In a bowl, whisk the egg with mayo and baking soda.
- In another bowl, add all spices, flour and potato stretch.
- Dip fish in egg mixture, then in the starch mixture.
- Keep them in the fridge for half an hour.
- Let the Kalorik Air Fryer Oven preheat to 390 F.
- Oil spray the strips and air fry for seven minutes, flip them, spray with oil and air fry for five minutes more.

- Serve in a tortilla, with salsa and other desired toppings.

Cal 405 | Fat 9g | Carb 48g | Protein 30g

## GARLIC SHRIMP

*Prep time:5 min | Cook time:10 min | Serves: 4*

**Ingredients**

- Avocado oil: 1 tbsp.
- Jumbo shrimp: 1 Pound, peeled & deveined
- Pepper: half tsp.
- Garlic powder: 1 tsp.
- Kosher salt: half tsp.

**Instructions**

- In a bowl, add all ingredients and toss to coat well.
- Let the Kalorik Air Fryer Oven preheat to 400 F.
- Place the shrimps in the tray of the air fryer, air fry for ten minutes.
- Serve right away.

## PRETZEL-CRUSTED CATFISH

*Prep time:15 min | Cook time:10 min | Serves: 4*

**Ingredients for 4 catfish fillets**

- milk: 2 tbsp.
- pepper: half tsp.
- 2 eggs
- mini honey mustard pretzels: 4 cups, crushed
- Dijon mustard: 1/3 cup
- salt: half tsp.
- all-purpose flour: half cup

**Instructions**

- Let the Kalorik Air Fryer Oven preheat to 325 F.
- Season the fish with salt and pepper.
- In a bowl, whisk the egg with mustard.
- In two different bowls, add flour and pretzels.
- Coat the fish in flour, then in egg and last in pretzels. Oil spray the fish
- Air fry the fish for 10 to 12 minutes, serve with lemon wedges

1 fillet: Cal 466 | Fat 14g | Carb 45g | Protein 33g

## TORTILLA CRUSTED TILAPIA SALAD

*Prep time:15 min | Cook time:15 min | Serves: 2*

**Ingredients**

- 1 avocado
- mixed greens: 6 cups
- Tortilla Crusted: 2 Tilapia fillets
- cherry tomatoes: 1 cup
- red onion: 1/3 cup, chopped
- Chipotle Lime Dressing: half cup

**Instructions**

- Oil spray the fillets and Let the Kalorik Air Fryer Oven preheat to 390 F.
- Air fry the fillets for 15 to 18 minutes.
- In two bowls, add the rest of the ingredients equally. Toss and add baked fillets on top and serve right away.

## BANG BANG SHRIMP

*Prep time:15 min | Cook time:15 min | Serves: 2*

**Ingredients**

**For shrimp**

- Buttermilk: 1 cup
- Cornstarch with salt & pepper: 1 cup
- 1 egg + 1 tsp. Water
- Shrimp: 2 pounds, peeled & deveined

**For the sauce**

- Sour cream: ¼ cup
- Sriracha: 1 tbsp.
- Mayonnaise: ¼ cup
- Dill weed, a pinch
- Thai chile sweet sauce: 1/3 cup
- Buttermilk: 2 tbsp.

**Instructions**

- In a bowl, add corn starch.
- In a bowl, add shrimps and buttermilk, toss to coat.
- Coat the shrimps in corn starch and place them on the air fryer tray.
- Brush the shrimps with egg wash and oil spray the shrimps
- Let the Kalorik Air Fryer Oven preheat to 450 F.
- Air fry for five minutes. Flip them.
- Oil spray again, egg wash, air fry for 4-5 minutes.
- In a bowl, add all ingredients of the sauce and mix well.
- Serve with shrimps.

Cal 415 | Fat 15g | Carb 28g

## LEMON BUTTER BAKED FISH

*Prep time:5 min | Cook time:10 min | Serves: 2*

**Ingredients**

- White fish, boned: 1.7 lb.
- Asparagus, trimmed
- 4 minced garlic cloves
- Lemon juice: 3 tbsp.
- Butter: 3 tbsp.
- Dried oregano: 2 tsp.
- Salt & pepper to taste

**Instructions**

- Let the Kalorik Air Fryer Oven preheat to 375 F.
- In a pan, add herbs, butter, garlic and lemon, let it simmer. Turn off the heat and let it cool.
- Line the air fryer trays with foil.
- On the tray of the air fryer, place asparagus and fish. Sprinkle salt and pepper.
- Pour the butter mixture all over fish and asparagus.
- Air fry for 8-10 minutes. Serve right away.

Cal 275 | Carb 1g | Protein 40g | Fat 12g

## FISH WITH GARLIC & BASIL

*Prep time:15 min | Cook time:15 min | Serves: 2*

**Ingredients**

- Fish fillet: 2 lb.
- Olive oil: 6 tbsp.
- Ground coriander: 1 tsp.
- Sweet paprika: 1 tsp.
- Dry oregano: 1 ½ tsp.
- 10 minced garlic cloves
- 2 shallots, sliced
- Salt & pepper, to taste
- 10 basil leaves, thinly sliced
- 1 lemon's juice

**Instructions**

- Season the fish with salt and pepper.
- In a zip lock bag, add all ingredients and toss well. Keep in the fridge for half an hour.
- Let the Kalorik Air Fryer Oven preheat to 400 F.
- Place onions on the bottom and fish on top in a baking dish.
- Pour the marinade over.
- Air fry for 10 to 12 minutes; keep an eye on it.
- Serve right away.

Cal 280 | Fat 16.2 g | Carb 5.2 g | Protein 28 g

## FISH IN GARLIC-CHILE SAUCE

*Prep time:15 min | Cook time:15 min | Serves: 2*

**Ingredients**

- Oyster sauce: 1/4 cup
- Brown sugar: 2 tbsp.
- Soy sauce: 1/4 cup
- 8 minced garlic cloves
- 1-3 chile peppers, sliced
- Fish sauce: 1 tbsp.
- Black pepper, to taste
- lime juice: 1 tbsp.
- 1 whole red snapper

**Instructions**

- Let the Kalorik Air Fryer Oven preheat to 350 F on Bake.
- In a bowl, add all ingredients and mix well.
- Make cuts on the fish and coat the fish in the marinade.
- Wrap the fish in foil and bake for 12-17 minutes.
- Serve right away.

## MEXICAN BAKED FISH

*Prep time:15 min | Cook time:15 min | Serves: 2*

**Ingredients**

- Cod: 1 ½ pound
- Crushed corn chips: half cup
- Salsa: 1 cup
- sour cream: ¼ cup
- Cheddar cheese: 1 cup, shredded
- 1 avocado, sliced

**Instructions**

- Let the Kalorik Air Fryer Oven preheat to 375 F on bake.
- Oil spray a baking dish.
- Place fish in the baking tray, add salsa on top. Add cheese and lastly corn chips.
- Bake for 10-11 minutes.
- Serve with sour cream and avocado.

Cal 311 | Protein 27.6g | Carb 11.3g | Fat 17.6g

## SARDINES WITH GARLIC AND OREGANO

*Prep time:15 min | Cook time:30 min | Serves: 6*

**Ingredients**

- Sardines: 2 to 2 ½ pound
- Lemon juice: half cup
- Salt & black pepper, to taste
- Water: half cup
- 5-6 garlic cloves, sliced
- Greek oregano: 2 tbsp.
- Olive oil: half cup

**Instructions**

- Let the Kalorik Air Fryer Oven preheat to 330 F on bake.
- Clean the sardines.
- In a baking tray, add sardines and add the rest of the ingredients and coat well.
- Bake for 30 to 35 minutes.
- Serve right away.

Cal 341 | Fat 19g | Carb 35g | Protein 11g

## BREADED COD STICKS

*Prep time: 5 min | Cook time: 20 min | Serves: 4*

**Ingredients**

- Large eggs (2)
- Milk (3 tbsp.)
- Breadcrumbs (2 cups)
- Almond flour (1 cup)
- Cod (1 lb.)

**Directions**

- Heat the Air Fryer at 350° F.
- Prepare three bowls; one with the milk and eggs, one with the breadcrumbs (salt and pepper if desired), and another with almond flour.
- Dip the sticks in the flour, egg mixture, and breadcrumbs.
- Place in the basket and set the timer for 12 minutes. Toss the basket halfway through the cooking process.
- Serve with your favorite sauce.

Cal 254 | Fat 14.2g | Carb 5.7g | Protein 39.1g

## BAKED HALIBUT STEAKS

*Prep time:15 min | Cook time:15 min | Serves: 4*

**Ingredients**

- Diced zucchini: 1 cup
- Chopped fresh basil: 2 tbsp.
- Onion: half cup, diced
- 1 minced garlic clove
- Crumbled feta cheese: ⅓ cup
- Olive oil: 1 tsp.
- Fresh tomatoes: 2 cups, diced
- Salt & pepper, to taste
- 4 halibut steaks

**Instructions**

- Let the Kalorik Air Fryer Oven preheat to 375 F.
- In a pan, add olive oil on medium flame. Sauté onion, garlic, and zucchini for five minutes. Turn off the heat and add pepper, salt, tomatoes and basil.
- In a baking dish, add the fish. Pour the zucchini mixture on the fish. Add cheese on top.
- Air fry for 10-12 minutes.
- Serve right away.

## FLOUNDER WITH LEMON AND BUTTER

*Prep time:10 min | Cook time:15 min | Serves: 4*

**Ingredients**

- Salt, to taste
- Black pepper
- Minced onion: 2 tsp.
- Flounder fillets: 1 1/2 pounds, cut into portions
- Butter: 4 tbsp., melted
- Lemon juice: 2 tbsp.
- Paprika: 1 tsp.

**Instructions**

- Let the Kalorik Air Fryer Oven preheat to 300 F on bake.
- In a baking dish, place the fish and season with salt and pepper.
- Add the rest of the ingredients on top of the fish.
- Bake for 10-15 minutes.
- Serve with lemon wedges.

Cal 302 | Fat 16g | Carb 17g | Protein 28g

## PERFECT TEN BAKED COD

*Prep time:10 min | Cook time:15 min | Serves: 4*

**Ingredients**

- Thick-cut cod loin: 1 pound
- Butter: 4 tbsp.
- Half pack round crackers, crushed
- Fresh parsley: 1 tbsp., chopped
- Half lemon, juiced
- Green onion: 1 tbsp., chopped
- Dry white wine: ¼ cup

**Instructions**

- Let the Kalorik Air Fryer Oven preheat to 375 F.
- In a mug, add butter (2 tbsp.) and melt; add crackers in the butter.
- In a baking dish, add the rest of the melted butter. Coat the cod in the butter.
- Air fry for 7-8 minutes.
- Take out from the air fryer and pour the cracker mixture, wine and lemon juice over.
- Air fry for 7 minutes more or till it flakes.
- Serve with green onion on top.

## STUFFED HADDOCK

*Prep time:10 min | Cook time:30-40 min | Serves: 4*

**Ingredients**

- Kosher salt, to taste
- Whole haddock
- Bacon strips: 8-10
- Stuffing of your choice

**Instructions**

- Clean and trim the fish. Season with salt and place on the baking dish.
- Let the Kalorik Air Fryer Oven preheat to 375 F.
- Stuff the fish with stuffing, add more stuffing around the fish on the baking dish.
- Place bacon strips on the fish.
- Air fry for 30-40 minutes.
- Serve with potatoes.

Cal 100 | Fat 5 g | Protein 7g | Carb 6 g

## ROSEMARY GARLIC GRILLED PRAWNS

*Prep time:75 min | Cook time:10 min | Serves: 2*

**Ingredients**

- Eight prawns
- Melted butter: 1/2 tbsp.
- Rosemary leaves
- Kosher salt & black pepper
- Green capsicum: slices
- 3-4 cloves of minced garlic

**Instructions**

- In a bowl, mix all the ingredients and marinate the prawns in it for at least 60 minutes or more
- Add 2 prawns and 2 slices of capsicum on each skewer.
- Let the Kalorik Air Fryer Oven preheat to 356 F.
- Air fry the skewers for 5 to 6 minutes. Then change the temperature to 390 F and cook for 1 minute.
- Serve with lemon wedges.

Cal 194 | Fat 10g | Carb 12g | Protein 26g

## LOBSTER JALAPEÑO EMPANADAS

*Prep time:10 min | Cook time:10 min | Serves: 4*

**Ingredients**

- 1 jalapeno, minced
- 8 empanada discs
- 1 egg white, whisked
- Diced onion: 2 tbsp.
- Unsalted butter: 1 tsp.
- Lobster meat: 8 oz.
- Chopped chives: 2 tbsp.

**Instructions**

- In a pan, add butter and melt on medium flame.
- Add onion, jalapenos and cook for 2-3 minutes.
- Add lobster and cook for 1-2 minutes. Turn off the heat, add chives.
- Drain any liquids.
- Add the crab filling in each of the dough pieces, seal the edges with egg white.
- Brush the tops with egg wash.
- Let the Kalorik Air Fryer Oven preheat to 325 F.
- Ai fry the empanadas for 8 minutes, flipping halfway through.
- Serve with spicy sauce.

**Cal 165 | Protein 5g | Carb 5g | Fat 5g**

## BALSAMIC BBQ SALMON

*Prep time:5 min | Cook time:10 min | Serves: 4*

**Ingredients**

- Salt & black pepper, to taste
- 4 salmon fillets
- Olive oil, as needed

**Balsamic bbq sauce**

- Worcestershire sauce: 2 tsp.
- Tomato ketchup: ¾ cup
- Balsamic vinegar: 3 tbsp.
- Brown sugar: 3 tbsp.
- Black pepper, to taste

**Instructions**

- Let the Kalorik Air Fryer Oven preheat to 380 F.

- In a pan, add all ingredients of the sauce and mix well. Let it come to a boil over medium flame.
- Simmer for 15 minutes, turn off the heat.
- Coat the fillet in olive oil, salt and pepper.
- Air fry the fish for five minutes.
- Brush with the sauce and air fry for 5 more minutes.
- Serve with salsa.

## SHRIMP EGG ROLLS

*Prep time:20 min | Cook time:10 min | Serves: 4*

### Ingredients

- Vegetable oil: 1 tbsp.
- Hoisin sauce: ¼ cup
- Cabbage: half head, shredded
- Cooked shrimp: 1 pound, diced
- Shredded carrots: 1 cup
- Soy sauce: 1 tbsp.
- Sugar: half tsp.
- Bean sprouts: 1 cup
- Sesame oil: 1 tsp.
- Black pepper, to taste
- Scallions: ¼ cup
- 8 egg roll wrappers

### Instructions

- Sauté the vegetables in oil over medium flame for 3 minutes.
- Add all the seasonings and cook for few minutes, turn off the heat and let it cool.
- Drain any liquids.
- Add this filling into each egg roll wrapper, seal the edges with water.
- Let the Kalorik Air Fryer Oven preheat to 370 F.
- Oil spray the egg rolls.
- Air fry for ten minutes, flip hallway through.
- Serve with sauce.

## LEMON-DILL SALMON BURGERS

*Prep time:10 min | Cook time:10 min | Serves: 4*

### Ingredients

- 2 salmon fillets, chopped
- 2 eggs, whisked
- Lemon zest: 1 tsp.
- Fresh dill weed: 2 tbsp., chopped
- Fine breadcrumbs: 1 cup
- Salt: 1 tsp.
- Black pepper, to taste
- 4 brioche buns

### Instructions

- Let the Kalorik Air Fryer Oven preheat to 400 F.
- Add all ingredients to a bowl, mix and make into four patties.
- Air fry the patties for four minutes on each side.
- Serve with buns and your desired toppings.

## SALMON WITH MAPLE SOY GLAZE

*Prep time:30 min | Cook time:10 min | Serves: 4*

### Ingredients

- Sriracha hot sauce: 1 tbsp.
- Maple syrup: 3 tbsp.
- 4 salmon fillets, skinless

- Soy sauce: 3 tbsp.
- 1 minced garlic clove

### Instructions

- In a bowl, add all ingredients and coat the fish well.
- Let it rest for 20-30 minutes.
- Let the Kalorik Air Fryer Oven preheat to 400 F.
- Take fish out and pat dry.
- Air fry the fish for 7-8 minutes.
- In a pan, add the leftover marinade and simmer for 1-2 minutes until it thickens.
- Pour over salmon and serve

Cal 292 | Protein 35g | Carb 12g | Fat 11g

## BASIL-PARMESAN CRUSTED SALMON

*Prep time:5 min | Cook time:15 min | Serves: 4*

### Ingredients

- 4 salmon fillets without skin
- Mayonnaise: 3 tbsp.
- Half lemon
- grated Parmesan: 3 tbsp.
- Kosher salt & black pepper, to taste
- Fresh basil leaves

### Instructions

- Let the Kalorik Air Fryer Oven preheat to 400 F
- Season the fish with salt, pepper and lemon juice.
- In a bowl, add mayo, cheese and basil leaves. Mix and spread all over the fish.
- Air fry the fish for 7 minutes.

Cal 289 | Protein 30g | Carb 1.5g | Fat 18.5g

## LEMON ALMOND TILAPIA

*Prep time:15 min | Cook time:15 min | Serves: 4*

### Ingredients

- Dried thyme: ¼ tsp.
- Flour: 2 tbsp.
- 2 egg whites, whisked
- 2 tilapia fillets
- Salt & black pepper, to taste
- Lemon zest: half tsp.
- Almonds: half cup, ground
- salt: ¼ tsp.

### Instructions

- In three different bowls, add flour, whisked eggs and the rest of the ingredients in the third bowl.
- Let the Kalorik Air Fryer Oven preheat to 400 F.
- Coat the fish in flour, then in egg and lastly in the third bowl.
- Oil spray the breaded fish and place it on the air fryer tray.
- Air fry for 8-10 minutes. Flip the fish halfway through.
- Serve right away.

## FISH STICKS WITH LEMON CAPER SAUCE

*Prep time:15 min | Cook time:15 min | Serves: 4*

### Ingredients

Lemon Caper Sauce

- Mayonnaise: 3 tbsp.
- Drained capers: 1 tbsp.
- Fresh minced chives: 1 tbsp.
- Black pepper: 1/8 tsp.

- Kosher salt: ¼ tsp.
- Greek yogurt: 1/4 cup
- Lemon juice: 1 tsp.

**Fish sticks**

- Half lemon's juice
- Cod fillet: 1 pound, 1-inch thick sticks
- Kosher salt & black pepper, to taste
- 3 egg whites
- Dijon mustard: 1 tbsp.
- Paprika: 1/8 tsp.
- Bread crumbs, as needed

**Instructions**

- In a bowl, add all ingredients of the sauce, mix and set it aside.
- Let the Kalorik Air Fryer Oven preheat to 370 F.
- In a bowl, add pepper, egg whites, paprika, mustard, and salt.
- In another bowl, add the bread crumbs.
- Coat fish sticks in the egg mixture then in crumbs. Oil spray the sticks.
- Air fry the sticks for 7-8 minutes, flipping halfway through.

Cal 229 | Protein 31 g | Carb 15g | Fat 4g

## BLACK COD WITH GRAPES & KALE

*Prep time:10 min | Cook time:15 min | Serves: 2*

**Ingredients**

- White balsamic vinegar: 2 tsp
- Salt & black pepper, to taste
- Olive oil: 2 tbsp. + 1 tsp.
- Black cod: 2 fillets
- Grapes: 1 cup, halved
- Pecans: half cup
- 1 fennel bulb sliced into ¼-inch thick
- Shredded kale: 3 cups

**Instructions**

- Let the Kalorik Air Fryer Oven preheat to 400 F.
- Season the fish with oil (1 tsp.), salt and pepper.
- Air fry for ten minutes.
- In a bowl, add the rest of the ingredients, toss and air fry for five minutes.
- Serve with the fish.

Cal 591 | Fat 36g | Carb 35g | Protein 39g

## CHILEAN SEA BASS

*Prep time:5 min | Cook time:20 min | Serves: 2*

**Ingredients**

- 2 sea bass fillets
- Maple syrup: 4 tbsp.
- Unsalted butter: 1 tbsp.
- White miso paste: 1/4 cup
- Ginger paste: half tsp.
- Rice wine vinegar: 1 tbsp.
- Mirin: 2 tbsp.

**Instructions**

- Let the Kalorik Air Fryer Oven preheat to 375 F.
- Season the fish with oil, salt and pepper.
- Air fry the fish for 12 to 15 minutes until the internal temperature reaches 135 F.
- In a pan, add butter on medium flame. Add the rest of the ingredients and mix well. Turn off the heat.

- Take fish out and brush with the sauce. Air fry for 1 to 2 minutes.
- Serve right away.

Cal 524 | Carb 23g | Protein 24g | Fat 29g

## SPECIAL SHRIMP FAJITAS

*Prep time:10 min | Cook time:20 min | Serves: 12*

**Ingredients**

- Onion: half cup, Diced
- Cooked Shrimp: 1 pound, without tail
- Flour Tortillas: 12
- 1 Red, 1 green Bell Pepper, chopped
- Taco Seasoning: 2 tbsp.

**Instructions**

- In a bowl, add shrimps, seasoning, onion and peppers. Toss well
- Place on the air fryer tray and spray with oil.
- Let the Kalorik Air Fryer Oven preheat to 390 F.
- Air fry for 12 minutes, take out the tray and oil spray again.
- Air fry for ten minutes more.
- In each tortilla, add the shrimp mixture and serve.

Cal 86 | Fat 2g | Carb 6g | Protein 10g

## CHILI LIME COD

*Prep time:10 min | Cook time:10 min | Serves: 2*

**Ingredients**

- Paprika: 1 tsp.
- Dried Parsley: 1 tsp.
- 1 Tablespoon Oil: 1 tbsp.
- Chili Powder: half tsp.
- Garlic Powder: half tsp.
- Dried Oregano: half tsp.
- Ground Cumin: ¼ tsp.
- 1 Lime's zest
- Black Pepper: ¼ tsp.
- Cayenne Pepper: 1/8 tsp.
- 2 Cod Fillets

**Instructions**

- In a bowl, add all spices and mix well.
- Brush the fish fillet with oil. Coat the fish in a spice mixture.
- Keep in the fridge for half an hour.
- Let the Kalorik Air Fryer Oven preheat to 380 F.
- Air fry the fillets for 8 to 13 minutes until the internal temperature reaches 145 F.
- Serve with lime zest on top.

Cal 810 | Carb 2g | Protein 16g | Fat 13g

## ROASTED SALMON WITH FENNEL SALAD

*Prep time:15 min | Cook time:20 min | Serves: 3*

**Ingredients**

- Fresh parsley: 2 tsp.
- Olive oil: 2 tbsp.
- Lemon juice: 1 tsp.
- Greek yogurt: 2/3 cup
- Fresh thyme: 1 tsp., minced
- 1 garlic clove, chopped
- Salt
- 4 salmon fillets, skinless

- Sliced fennel: 4 cups
- Orange juice: 2 tbsp.
- Fresh dill: 2 tbsp.

**Instructions**
- Let your vortex preheat to 350 F.
- In a dish, add herbs and salt. Toss.
- Oil spray the fish and rub with herb mixture.
- Cook in air fryer for 10 minutes.
- In a different bowl, add the rest of the ingredients. toss and serve with salmon.

Cal 434 | Fat 31g | Protein 37g | Carb 5g

## CHEESY LEMON HALIBUT
*Prep time: 5 min | Cook time: 10 min | Serves: 4*

**Ingredients**
- 1 lb. halibut fillet
- ½ cup butter
- 2 ½ tbsp. mayonnaise
- 2 ½ tbsp. lemon juice
- ¾ cup parmesan cheese, grated

**Directions**
- Pre-heat your fryer at 375°F.
- Spritz the halibut fillets with cooking spray and season as desired.
- Put the halibut in the fryer and cook for twelve minutes.
- In the meantime, combine the butter, mayonnaise, and lemon juice in a bowl with a hand mixer. Ensure a creamy texture is achieved.
- Stir in the grated parmesan.
- When the halibut is ready, open the drawer and spread the butter over the fish with a butter knife. Let it cook for a couple more minutes, then serve hot.

Cal 354 | Fat 21g | Carb 23g | Protein 19g

## SHRIMP CROQUETTES

*Prep time: 12 min | Cook time: 6 min | Serves: 3-4*

**Ingredients**:
- ⅔ pound cooked shrimp, shelled and deveined
- 1½ cups bread crumbs, divided
- 1 egg, beaten
- tablespoon lemon juice
- green onions, finely chopped
- ½ teaspoon dried basil
- Pinch salt
- Freshly ground black pepper
- tablespoons olive oil

**Directions**:
- Finely chop the shrimp. Take about 1 tablespoon of the finely chopped shrimp and chop it further until it's almost a paste. Set aside.

- In a medium bowl, combine ½ cup of the bread crumbs with the egg and lemon juice. Let stand for 5 minutes.
- Stir the shrimp, green onions, basil, salt, and pepper into the bread crumb mixture.
- Combine the remaining 1 cup of bread crumbs with the olive oil on a shallow plate; mix well.
- Form the shrimp mixture into 1½-inch round balls and press firmly with your hands. Roll in the bread crumb mixture to coat.
- Air-fry the little croquettes in batches for 6 to 8 minutes or until they are brown and crisp. Serve with cocktail sauce for dipping, if desired.

Cal 330 | Fat 12g | Carb 31g | Fiber 2g | Protein 24g

## SPICY MACKEREL
*Prep time: 5 min | Cook time: 10 min | Serves: 4*

**Ingredients**
- 2 mackerel fillets
- 2 tbsp. red chili flakes
- 2 tsp. garlic, minced
- 1 tsp. lemon juice

**Directions**
- Season the mackerel fillets with the red pepper flakes, minced garlic, and a drizzle of lemon juice. Allow to sit for five minutes.
- Preheat your fryer at 350°F.
- Cook the mackerel for five minutes, before opening the drawer, flipping the fillets, and allowing to cook on the other side for another five minutes.
- Plate the fillets, making sure to spoon any remaining juice over them before serving.

Cal 393 | Fat 12g | Carb 13g | Protein 35g

## THYME SCALLOPS
*Prep time: 5 min | Cook time: 10 min | Serves: 4*

**Ingredients**
- 1 lb. scallops
- Salt and pepper
- ½ tbsp. butter
- ½ cup thyme, chopped

**Directions**
- Wash the scallops and dry them completely. Season with pepper and salt, then set aside while you prepare the pan.
- Grease a foil pan in several spots with the butter and cover the bottom with the thyme. Place the scallops on top.
- Pre-heat the fryer at 400°F and set the rack inside.
- Place the foil pan on the rack and allow to cook for seven minutes.
- Take care when removing the pan from the fryer and transfer the scallops to a serving dish. Spoon any remaining butter in the pan over the fish and enjoy.

Cal 454 | Fat 18g | Carb 27g | Protein 34g

## BUTTERY SHRIMP SKEWERS
*Prep time: 5 min | Cook time: 10 min | Serves: 4*

**Ingredients**
- 8 shrimps; peeled and deveined
- 8 green bell pepper slices
- 1 tbsp. butter; melted
- 4 garlic cloves; minced
- Salt and black pepper to the taste

## Directions

- In a bowl mix shrimp with garlic, butter, salt, pepper and bell pepper slices; toss to coat and leave aside for 10 minutes.
- Arrange 2 shrimp and 2 bell pepper slices on a skewer and repeat with the rest of the shrimp and bell pepper pieces.
- Place them all in your air fryer's basket and cook at 360°F, for 6 minutes. Divide among plates and serve right away.

Cal 140 | Fat 1g | Fiber 12g | Carb 15g | Protein 7g

## MUSTARD SALMON

*Prep time: 5 min | Cook time: 10 min | Serves: 4*

### Ingredients

- 1 big salmon fillet; boneless
- 2 tbsp. mustard
- 1 tbsp. coconut oil
- 1 tbsp. maple extract
- Salt and black pepper to the taste

### Directions

- In a bowl mix maple extract with mustard, whisk well, season salmon with salt and pepper and brush salmon with this mix.
- Spray some cooking spray over fish; place in your air fryer and cook at 370°F, for 10 minutes; flipping halfway. Serve with a tasty side salad.

Cal 300 | Fat 7g | Fiber 14g | Carb 16g | Protein 20g

## CHINESE STYLE COD

*Prep time: 5 min | Cook time: 10 min | Serves: 2*

### Ingredients

- 2 medium cod fillets; boneless
- 1 tbsp. light soy sauce
- 1/2 tsp. ginger; grated
- 1 tsp. peanuts; crushed
- 2 tsp. garlic powder

### Directions

- Put fish fillets in a heat proof dish that fits your air fryer, add garlic powder, soy sauce and ginger; toss well, put in your air fryer and cook at 350°F, for 10 minutes.
- Divide fish on plates, sprinkle peanuts on top and serve.

Cal 254 | Fat 10g | Fiber 11g | Carb 14g | Protein 23g

## SALMON AND ORANGE MARMALADE

*Prep time: 5 min | Cook time: 20 min | Serves: 4*

### Ingredients

- 1 lb. wild salmon; skinless, boneless and cubed
- 1/4 cup orange juice
- 1/3 cup orange marmalade
- 1/4 cup balsamic vinegar
- A pinch of salt and black pepper

### Directions

- Heat up a pot with the vinegar over medium heat; add marmalade and orange juice; stir, bring to a simmer, cook for 1 minute and take off heat.
- Thread salmon cubes on skewers, season with salt and black pepper, brush them with half of the orange marmalade mix, arrange in your air fryer's basket and cook at 360°F, for 3 minutes on each side. Brush skewers with the rest of the vinegar mix; divide among plates and serve right away with a side salad.

Cal 240 | Fat 9g | Fiber 12g | Carb 14g | Protein 10g

## TILAPIA & CHIVES SAUCE

*Prep time: 5 min | Cook time: 10 min | Serves: 4*

### Ingredients

- 4 medium tilapia fillets
- 2 tsp. honey
- Juice from 1 lemon
- 2 tbsp. chives; chopped
- Salt and black pepper to the taste

### Directions

- Flavor fish with salt and pepper, spray with cooking spray, place in preheated air fryer 350°F and cook for 8 minutes; flipping halfway.
- Meanwhile in a bowl, mix honey, salt, pepper, chives and lemon juice and whisk really well. Divide air fryer fish on plates, drizzle yogurt sauce all over and serve right away.

Cal 261 | Fat 8g | Fiber 18g | Carb 24g | Protein 21g

## MARINATED SALMON RECIPE

*Prep time: 65 min | Cook time: 30 min | Serves: 4*

### Ingredients

- 1 whole salmon
- 1 tbsp. tarragon; chopped
- 1 tbsp. garlic; minced
- Juice from 2 lemons
- A pinch of salt and black pepper

### Directions

- In a large fish, mix fish with salt, pepper and lemon juice; toss well and keep in the fridge for 1 hour.
- Stuff salmon with garlic and place in your air fryer's basket and cook at 320°F, for 25 minutes. Divide among plates and serve with a tasty coleslaw on the side.

Cal 300 | Fat 8g | Fiber 9g | Carb 19g | Protein 27g

## TASTY GRILLED RED MULLET

*Prep time: 5 min | Cook time: 10 min | Serves: 8*

### Ingredients

- 8 whole red mullets, gutted and scales removed
- Salt and pepper to taste
- Juice from 1 lemon
- 1 tablespoon olive oil

### Directions

- Preheat the air fryer at 390°F.
- Place the grill pan attachment in the air fryer.
- Season the red mullet with salt, pepper, and lemon juice.
- Brush with olive oil.
- Grill for 15 minutes.

Cal 152 | Carb 0.9g | Protein 23.1g | Fat 6.2g

## GARLICKY-GRILLED TURBOT

*Prep time: 5 min | Cook time: 20 min | Serves: 2*

### Ingredients

- 2 whole turbot, scaled and head removed
- Salt and pepper to taste
- 1 clove of garlic, minced
- ½ cup chopped celery leaves
- 2 tablespoons olive oil

### Directions

- Preheat the air fryer at 390°F.

- Place the grill pan attachment in the air fryer.
- Flavor the turbot with salt, pepper, garlic, and celery leaves.
- Brush with oil.
- Cook in the grill pan for 20 minutes until the fish becomes flaky.

Cal 269 | Carb 3.3g | Protein 66.2g | Fat 25.6g

## CHAR-GRILLED SPICY HALIBUT

*Prep time: 5 min | Cook time: 20 min | Serves: 4*

**Ingredients**

- 3 pounds halibut fillet, skin removed
- Salt and pepper to taste
- 4 tablespoons olive oil
- 2 cloves of garlic, minced
- 1 tablespoon chili powder

**Directions**

- Place all ingredients in a Ziploc bag.
- Keep it in the fridge for at least 2 hours.
- Preheat the air fryer at 390°F. Place the grill pan attachment in the air fryer.
- Grill the fish for 20 minutes while flipping every 5 minutes.

Cal 385 | Carb 1.7g | Protein 33g | Fat 40.6g

## SWORDFISH WITH CHARRED LEEKS

*Prep time: 5 min | Cook time: 20 min | Serves: 4*

**Ingredients**

- 4 swordfish steaks
- Salt and pepper to taste
- 3 tablespoons lime juice
- 2 tablespoons olive oil
- 4 medium leeks, cut into an inch long

**Directions**

- Preheat the air fryer at 390°F.
- Place the grill pan attachment in the air fryer.
- Season the swordfish with salt, pepper and lime juice.
- Brush the fish with olive oil. Place fish fillets on grill pan and top with leeks.
- Grill for 20 minutes.

Cal 611 | Carb 14.6g | Protein 48g | Fat 40g

## BREADED COCONUT SHRIMP

*Prep time: 5 min | Cook time: 15 min | Serves: 4*

**Ingredients**

- Shrimp (1 lb.)
- Panko breadcrumbs (1 cup)
- Shredded coconut (1 cup)
- Eggs (2)
- All-purpose flour (.33 cup)

**Directions**

- Fix the temperature of the Air Fryer at 360°F.
- Peel and devein the shrimp.
- Whisk the seasonings with the flour as desired. In another dish, whisk the eggs, and in the third container, combine the breadcrumbs and coconut.
- Dip the cleaned shrimp into the flour, egg wash, and finish it off with the coconut mixture.
- Lightly spray the basket of the fryer and set the timer for 10-15 minutes.
- Air-fry until it's a golden brown before serving.

Cal 285 | Fat 12.8g | Carb 3.7g | Protein 38.1g

## COD FISH NUGGETS

*Prep time: 5 min | Cook time: 20 min | Serves: 4*

**Ingredients**

- Cod fillet (1 lb.)
- Eggs (3)
- Olive oil (4 tbsp.)
- Almond flour (1 cup)
- Gluten-free breadcrumbs (1 cup)

**Directions**

- Warm the Air Fryer at 390° F.
- Slice the cod into nuggets.
- Prepare three bowls. Whisk the eggs in one. Combine the salt, oil, and breadcrumbs in another. Sift the almond flour into the third one.
- Cover each of the nuggets with the flour, dip in the eggs, and the breadcrumbs.
- Arrange the nuggets in the basket and set the timer for 20 minutes.
- Serve the fish with your favorite dips or sides.

Cal 334 | Fat 10g | Carb 8g | Protein 32g

## GRILLED SARDINES

*Prep time: 5 min | Cook time: 20 min | Serves: 4*

**Ingredients**

- 5 sardines
- Herbs of Provence

**Direction:**

- Preheat the air fryer to 320°F.
- Spray the basket and place your sardines in the basket of your fryer.
- Set the timer for 14 minutes. After 7 minutes, remember to turn the sardines so that they are roasted on both sides.

Cal 189g | Fat 10g | Carb 0g | Sugars 0g | Protein 22g

## FRIED CATFISH

*Prep time: 5 min | Cook time: 15 min | Serves: 4*

**Ingredients**

- Olive oil (1 tbsp.)
- Seasoned fish fry (.25 cup)
- Catfish fillets (4)

**Directions**

- Heat the Air Fryer to reach 400° F before fry time.
- Rinse the catfish and pat dry using a paper towel.
- Dump the seasoning into a sizeable zipper-type bag. Add the fish and shake to cover each fillet. Spray with a spritz of cooking oil spray and add to the basket.
- Set the timer for 10 minutes. Flip, and reset the timer for ten additional minutes. Turn the fish once more and cook for 2-3 minutes.
- Once it reaches the desired crispiness, transfer to a plate, and serve.

Cal 376 | Fat 9g | Carb 10g | Protein 28g

## CREAMY SALMON

*Prep time: 5 min | Cook time: 20 min | Serves: 4*

**Ingredients**

- Chopped dill (1 tbsp.)

- Olive oil (1 tbsp.)
- Sour cream (3 tbsp.)
- Plain yogurt (1.76 oz.)
- Salmon (6 pieces)/.75 lb.)

**Directions**

- Heat the Air Fryer and wait for it to reach 285° F.
- Shake the salt over the salmon and add them to the fryer basket with the olive oil to air-fry for 10 minutes.
- Whisk the yogurt, salt, and dill.
- Serve the salmon with the sauce with your favorite sides.

Cal 340 | Carb 5g | Fat 16g | Protein 32 g

## CRUMBLED FISH

*Prep time: 5 min | Cook time: 15 min | Serves: 4*

**Ingredients**

- Breadcrumbs (.5 cup)
- Vegetable oil (4 tbsp.)
- Egg (1)
- Fish fillets (4)
- Lemon (1)

**Directions**

- Heat the Air Fryer to reach 350° F.
- Whisk the oil and breadcrumbs until crumbly.
- Dip the fish into the egg, then the crumb mixture.
- Arrange the fish in the cooker and air-fry for 12 minutes. Garnish using the lemon.

Cal 320 | Carb 8g | Fat 10g | Protein 28 g

## EASY CRAB STICKS

*Prep time: 5 min | Cook time: 10 min | Serves: 4*

**Ingredients**

- Crab sticks (1 package)
- Cooking oil spray (as needed)

**Directions**

- Take each of the sticks out of the package and unroll it until the stick is flat. Tear the sheets into thirds.
- Arrange them on the air fryer basket and lightly spritz using cooking spray. Set the timer for 10 minutes.
- Note: If you shred the crab meat, you can cut the time in half, but they will also easily fall through the holes in the basket.

Cal 285 | Fat 12.8g | Carb 3.7g | Protein 38.1 g

## DEEP FRIED PRAWNS

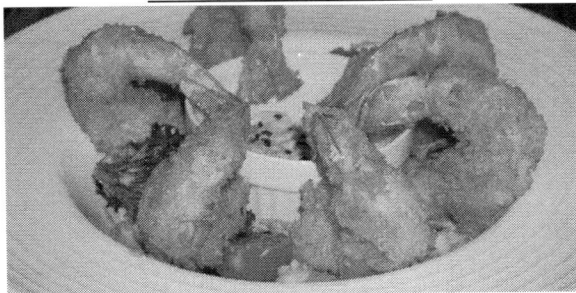

*Prep time: 15 min | Cook time: 20 min | Serves: 6*

**Ingredients**

- 12 prawns
- 2 eggs
- Flour to taste

- Breadcrumbs
- 1 tsp oil

**Direction**:

- Remove the head of the prawns and shell carefully.
- Pass the prawns first in the flour, then in the beaten egg and then in the breadcrumbs.
- Preheat the air fryer for 1 minute at 300°F.
- Add the prawns and cook for 4 minutes. If the prawns are large, cook 6 at a time.
- Turn the prawns and cook for another 4 minutes.
- They should be served with a yogurt or mayonnaise sauce.

Cal 2385.1 | Fat 23g | Carb 52.3g | Protein 21.4g

## ZUCCHINI WITH TUNA

*Prep time: 10 min | Cook time: 30 min | Serves: 4*

**Ingredients**

- 4 medium zucchinis
- 120g of tuna in oil (canned) drained
- 30g grated cheese
- 1 tsp pine nuts
- Salt, pepper to taste

**Direction**:

- Cut the zucchini in half laterally and empty it with a small spoon (set aside the pulp that will be used for filling); place them in the basket.
- In a food processor, put the zucchini pulp, drained tuna, pine nuts and grated cheese. Mix everything until you get a homogeneous and dense mixture.
- Fill the zucchini. Set the air fryer to 350°F.
- Simmer for 20 min. depending on the size of the zucchini. Let cool before serving.

Cal 389 | Carb 10g | Fat 29g | Protein 23g

## CARAMELIZED SALMON FILLET

*Prep time: 5 min | Cook time: 25 min | Serves: 4*

**Ingredients**

- 2 salmon fillets
- 60g cane sugar
- 4 tbsp soy sauce
- 50g sesame seeds
- Unlimited Ginger

**Direction**:

- Preheat the air fryer at 350°F for 5 minutes.
- Put the sugar and soy sauce in the basket.
- Cook everything for 5 minutes.
- In the meantime, wash the fish well, pass it through sesame to cover it completely and place it inside the tank and add the fresh ginger.
- Cook for 12 minutes.
- Turn the fish over and finish cooking for another 8 minutes.

Cal 569 | Fat 14.9 g | Carb 40g | Protein 66.9g

## MUSSELS WITH PEPPER

*Prep time: 15 min | Cook time: 20 min | Serves: 5*

**Ingredients**

- 700g mussels
- 1 clove garlic
- 1 tsp oil

- Pepper to taste
- Parsley Taste

**Direction:**

- Clean and scrape the mold cover and remove the byssus (the "beard" that comes out of the mold).
- Pour the oil, clean the mussels and the crushed garlic in the air fryer basket. Set the temperature to 390°F and simmer for 12 minutes. Towards the end of cooking, add black pepper and chopped parsley.
- Finally, distribute the mussel juice well at the bottom of the basket, stirring the basket.

Cal 150 | Carb 2g | Fat 8g | Sugars 0g | Protein 15g

## MONKFISH WITH OLIVES AND CAPERS
*Prep time: 25 min | Cook time: 40 min | Serves: 4*

**Ingredients**

- 1 monkfish
- 10 cherry tomatoes
- 50 g cailletier olives
- 5 capers

**Direction:**

- Spread aluminium foil inside the air fryer basket and place the monkfish clean and skinless.
- Add chopped tomatoes, olives, capers, oil, and salt.
- Set the temperature to 320°F. Cook the monkfish for about 40 minutes.

Cal 404 | Fat 29g | Carb 36g | Sugars 7g | Protein 24g

## SHRIMP, ZUCCHINI AND CHERRY TOMATO
*Prep time: 5 min | Cook time: 30 min | Serves: 4*

**Ingredients**

- 2 zucchinis
- 300 shrimp
- 7 cherry tomatoes
- Salt and pepper to taste
- 1 clove garlic

**Direction:**

- Pour the oil in the air fryer, add the garlic clove and diced zucchini.
- Cook for 15 minutes at 300°F.
- Add the shrimp and the pieces of tomato, salt, and spices.
- Cook for another 5 to 10 minutes or until the shrimp water evaporates.

Cal 214.3 | Fat 8.6g | Carb 7.8g | Protein 27.0g

## SALTED MARINATED SALMON
*Prep time: 10 min | Cook time: 30 min | Serves: 4*

**Ingredients**

- 500g salmon fillet
- 1 kg coarse salt

**Direction:**

- Place the baking paper on the air fryer basket and the salmon on top (skin side up) covered with coarse salt. Set the air fryer to 300°F.
- Cook everything for 25 to 30 minutes. At the end of cooking, remove the salt from the fish and serve with a drizzle of oil.

Cal 290 | Fat 13g | Carb 3g | Fiber 0g | Protein 40g

## SALMON WITH PISTACHIO BARK
*Prep time: 10 min | Cook time: 30 min | Serves: 4*

**Ingredients**

- 600 g salmon fillet
- 50g pistachios
- Salt to taste

**Direction:**

- Put the parchment paper on the bottom of the air fryer basket and place the salmon fillet in it (it can be cooked whole or already divided into four portions).
- Cut the pistachios in thick pieces; grease the top of the fish, salt (little because the pistachios are already salted) and cover everything with the pistachios.
- Set the air fryer to 350°F and simmer for 25 minutes.

Cal 371.7 | Fat 21.8g | Carb 9.4g Protein 34.7g

## SAUTÉED TROUT WITH ALMONDS
*Prep time: 35 min | Cook time: 20 min | Serves: 4*

**Ingredients**

- 700 g salmon trout
- 15 black peppercorns
- Dill leaves to taste
- 30g almonds
- Salt to taste

**Direction:**

- Cut the trout into cubes and marinate it for half an hour with the rest of the ingredients (except salt).
- Cook in air fryer for 17 minutes at 320°F. Pour a drizzle of oil and serve.

Cal 238.5 | Fat 20.1g | Carb 11.5g | Protein4.0 g

## AIR FRYER SHRIMP A LA BANG
*Prep time: 10 min | Cook time: 12 min | Serves: 2*

**Ingredients**

- 1/2 cup mayonnaise
- 1/4 cup sweet chili sauce
- 1 tablespoon. sriracha sauce
- 1/4 cup all-purpose flour
- 1 cup panko bread crumbs
- Raw shrimp: 1 pound, peeled and deveined
- 1 leaf lettuce
- 2green, chopped onions or to taste (optional)

**Directions**

- Set temperature of air fryer to 400°F.
- In a bowl, stir in mayonnaise, chili sauce, and sriracha sauce until smooth. Put some bang sauce, if desired, in a separate bowl for dipping.
- Take a plate and place flour on it. Use a separate plate and place panko bread crumbs on it.
- First coat the shrimp with flour, then mayonnaise mixture, then panko. Place shrimp covered on a baking sheet.
- Place shrimp, without overcrowding, in the air fryer basket.
- Cook for approximately 12 minutes. Repeat with shrimp leftover.
- Use lettuce wraps for serving, garnished with green onion.

Cal 415 | Fat 23.9g | Carb 32.7g | Protein 23.9 g

## AIR FRIED CRUMBED FISH

*Prep time: 10 min | Cook time: 12 min | Serves: 4*

### Ingredients

- Bread crumbs: 1 cup
- Vegetable oil: ¼ cup
- 4 Flounder fillets
- 1 Beaten egg
- 1 Sliced Lemon

### Directions

- Preheat an air fryer to 350°F.
- In a cup add the bread crumbs and the oil. Stir until the mixture becomes crumbly and loose.
- Dip the fish fillets in the egg mixture; shake off any excesses. Dip the fillets into a mixture of bread crumbs; until evenly and thoroughly coated.
- Gently lay coated fillets in the preheated air fryer. Cook, about 12 minutes, with a fork, until fish flakes easily. Garnish with sliced lemon.

Cal 354 Cal | Fat 17.7g | Carb 22.5g | Protein 26.9 g

## RABAS

*Prep time: 5 min | Cook time: 12 min | Serves: 4*

### Ingredients

- 16 rabas
- 1 egg
- Breadcrumbs
- Salt, pepper, sweet paprika

### Direction:

- Put the rabas in the air fryer to boil for 2 minutes. Remove and dry well.
- Beat the egg and season to taste. You can put salt, pepper and sweet paprika. Place in the egg.
- Bread with breadcrumbs. Place in sticks.

Cal 356 | Fat 18g | Carb 5g | Protein 34g

## HONEY GLAZED SALMON

*Prep time: 10 min | Cook time: 8 min | Serves: 2*

### Ingredients

- 2 (6-oz.) salmon fillets
- Salt, as required
- 2 tablespoons honey

### Directions

- Sprinkle the salmon fillets with salt and then, coat with honey.
- Take to your air fryer oven at 355°F for 8 minutes.
- Serve hot.

Cal 289 | Fat 10.5g | Carb 17.3g | Protein 33.1 g

## SWEET & SOUR GLAZED SALMON

*Prep time: 12 min | Cook time: 20 min | Serves: 2*

### Ingredients

- 1/3 cup soy sauce
- 1/3 cup honey
- 3 teaspoons rice wine vinegar
- 1 teaspoon water
- 4 (3½-oz.) salmon fillets

### Directions

- Mix the soy sauce, honey, vinegar, and water together in a bowl.
- In another small bowl, reserve about half of the mixture.
- Add salmon fillets in the remaining mixture and coat well.
- Cover the bowl and refrigerate to marinate for about 2 hours.
- Arrange the salmon fillets in greased "Air Fry Basket" and cook at 355°F for 12 minutes
- Flip the salmon fillets once halfway through and coat with the reserved marinade after every 3 minutes. Serve hot.

Cal 462 | Fat 12.3g | Carb 49.8g | Protein 41.3 g

# POULTRY RECIPES

## NASHVILLE HOT CHICKEN

*Prep time:40 min | Cook time:15 min | Serves: 6*

### Ingredients

- Dill pickle juice: 2 tbsp.
- Salt: 1 tsp.
- Chicken tenderloins: 2 pounds
- Olive oil: half cup
- Hot pepper sauce: 2 tbsp.
- Pepper: half tsp.
- 1 egg
- Buttermilk: half cup
- Chili powder: 1 tsp.
- All-purpose flour: 1 cup
- Cayenne pepper: 2 tbsp.
- Garlic powder: half tsp.
- Dark brown sugar: 2 tbsp.
- 1 teaspoon paprika: 1 tsp.
- Dill pickle slices

### Instructions

- In a bowl, add salt (half tsp.), pickle juice (1 tbsp.), and hot sauce (1 tbsp.), mix and add chicken. Coat well, keep in the fridge for 60 minutes, covered.
- Let the Kalorik Air Fryer Oven preheat to 375 F.
- In a bowl, add salt (half tsp.), pepper and flour.
- In another bowl, add the hot sauce, pickle juice, egg and butter milk. Mix.
- Coat the chicken in flour, then in the egg mixture and again in the flour. Oil spray the chicken.
- Air fry the chicken for 5 to 6 minutes, flip, oil spray and air fry for 5 to 6 minutes.
- In a bowl, mix the rest of the ingredients, pour over chicken and serve.

## CHICKEN WINGS WITH BUFFALO SAUCE

*Prep time:5 min | Cook time:30 min | Serves: 6*

### Ingredients

- Salt & pepper to taste
- Buffalo sauce, as needed
- Chicken drumettes & flats: 1 pound

### Instructions

- Let the Kalorik Air Fryer Oven preheat to 380 F.
- Cut the tips off of the chicken.
- Dry the chicken well.
- Season with salt and pepper.
- Air fry the wings for 20 to 22 minutes, flipping halfway through.
- Change the temperature to 400 F.
- Air fry for five minutes.
- Coat in buffalo sauce and serve.

## SOUTHERN-STYLE CHICKEN

*Prep time:15 min | Cook time:20-30 min | Serves: 6*

### Ingredients

- Crushed Ritz crackers: 2 cups
- Ground cumin: ¼ tsp.
- Garlic salt: 1 tsp.

- Paprika: 1 tsp.
- Fresh parsley: 1 tbsp., minced
- 1 chicken (3 -4 pounds), cut up
- Pepper: half tsp.
- Rubbed sage: ¼ tsp.
- 1 egg, whisked

### Instructions

- Let the Kalorik Air Fryer Oven preheat to 375 F.
- In a bowl, add the whisked egg. Add the rest of the ingredients to the other bowl.
- Coat the chicken in egg then in the other bowl.
- Place on the air fryer tray, oil spray the chicken.
- Air fry for ten minutes, flip, oil spray and cook for 10 to 20 minutes more.
- Serve right away.

## CHICKEN PARMESAN

*Prep time:10 min | Cook time:20 min | Serves: 4*

### Ingredients

- Dried oregano: 1 tsp.
- 2 chicken breasts, boneless
- All-purpose flour: 1/3 cup
- Red pepper flakes: half tsp.
- 2 eggs
- Salt & black pepper, to taste
- Panko bread crumbs: 1 cup
- Grated parmesan: 1/4 cup
- Shredded mozzarella: 1 cup
- Garlic powder: half tsp.
- Marinara sauce: 1 cup

### Instructions

- Make four pieces of chicken after butter the chicken. Season with salt and pepper.
- In a bowl, add flour with salt and pepper. In the other bowl, add whisked eggs and add pepper flakes, crumbs, garlic powder, Parmesan, and oregano in a different bowl.
- Coat the chicken in flour, then in egg and lastly in the third bowl.
- Let the Kalorik Air Fryer Oven preheat to 400 F.
- Air fry the chicken for five minutes on each side.
- Add sauce and cheese on top of the chicken, air fry for three minutes and serve.

## CRISPY CURRY DRUMSTICKS

*Prep time:35 min | Cook time:20 min | Serves: 4*

### Ingredients

- Salt: ¾ tsp.

- Onion salt: half tsp.
- Chicken drumsticks: 1 pound
- Olive oil: 2 tbsp.
- Curry powder: 2 tsp.
- Garlic powder: half tsp.

**Instructions**

- In a bowl, add chicken and water to cover it. Add half tsp. of salt and let it rest for 15 minutes.
- Take out and pat dry the chicken.
- Let the Kalorik Air Fryer Oven preheat to 375 F.
- In a bowl, add the rest of the ingredients and add chicken and toss.
- Air fry the chicken for 15 to 17 minutes until the internal temperature reaches 170 to 175 F.

Cal 180 | Fat 13g | Carb 1g | Protein 15g

## GARLIC HERB TURKEY BREAST

*Prep time:10 min | Cook time:40 min | Serves: 6*

**Ingredients**

- Salt & black pepper, to taste
- Chopped fresh thyme: 1 tsp.
- Butter: 4 tbsp., melted
- Turkey breast: 2 lb., skin on
- 3 minced garlic cloves
- Chopped fresh rosemary: 1 tsp.

**Instructions**

- Season the turkey with salt and pepper.
- In a bowl, add the rest of the ingredients, mix and brush all over the turkey.
- Let the Kalorik Air Fryer Oven preheat to 375 F.
- Air fry the turkey for 40 minutes, flip halfway through until the internal temperature reaches 160 F.
- Slice and serve.

## THANKSGIVING TURKEY

*Prep time:10 min | Cook time:45 min | Serves: 4*

**Ingredients**

- 1 (2-lb.) turkey breast
- Chopped fresh thyme: 1 tsp.
- Dijon mustard: 2 tbsp.
- Chopped fresh rosemary: 1 tsp.
- Salt & black pepper
- Chopped fresh sage: 1 tsp.
- Maple syrup: 1/4 cup
- Butter: 1 tbsp., melted

**Instructions**

- Season the turkey with salt and pepper, and rub with fresh herbs.
- Let the Kalorik Air Fryer Oven preheat to 390 F.
- Air fry the turkey for 30-35 minutes until the internal temperature reaches 160 F.
- In a bowl, whisk the rest of the ingredients.
- Brush the turkey with this mixture and air fry for 2 minutes at 330 F.
- Let it rest for a few minutes, slice and serve.

## FIESTA CHICKEN FINGERS

*Prep time:20 min | Cook time:15 min | Serves: 4*

**Ingredients**

- Chicken breasts: 3/4 pound, boneless & skinless

- All-purpose flour: 1 cup
- Buttermilk: half cup
- 1 envelope of taco seasoning
- Pepper: 1/4 tsp.
- Corn chips: 3 cups, crushed

**Instructions**

- Let the Kalorik Air Fryer Oven preheat to 400 F.
- Pound the chicken into half-inch thickness. Slice into one" strips.
- In a bowl, mix buttermilk with black pepper.
- In a bowl, add flour. In the third bowl, mix taco seasoning with corn chips.
- Coat the chicken in flour, then in buttermilk and lastly in corn chips.
- Oil spray the basket of air fryer and air fry for 7 to 8 on each side.
- Serve with salsa.

Cal 676 | Fat 36g | Carb 60g | Protein 24g

-

## LEMON CHICKEN THIGHS

*Prep time:10 min | Cook time:25 min | Serves: 4*

**Ingredients**

- Butter: ¼ cup, softened
- Lemon juice: 1 tbsp.
- Minced fresh rosemary: 2 tsp.
- 3 minced garlic cloves
- Minced fresh thyme: 1 tsp.
- 1/8 tsp. Each salt & pepper
- Lemon zest: 1 tsp.
- 4 chicken thighs, bone-in

**Instructions**

- Let the Kalorik Air Fryer Oven preheat to 400 F.
- In a bowl, add all ingredients except for chicken, mix and spread on chicken under the skin.
- Sprinkle salt and pepper.
- Place on the oil sprayed basket and air fry for 20 minutes, flip halfway through until the internal temperature of the meat reaches 170-175 F.

Cal 329 | Fat 26g | Carb 1g | Protein 23g

## LEMON PEPPER WINGS

*Prep time:5 min | Cook time:25 min | Serves: 4*

**Ingredients**

- Cayenne pepper: 1/4 tsp.
- Chicken wings: 1 1/2 pounds
- Lemon pepper seasoning: 2 tsp.

**Lemon pepper sauce**

- Lemon pepper seasoning: 1 tsp.
- Honey: 1 tsp.
- Butter: 3 tbsp.

**Instructions**

- Let the Kalorik Air Fryer Oven preheat to 380 F.
- Season the chicken with cayenne and lemon pepper seasoning.
- Air fry the wings for 20 to 22 minutes, flipping halfway through.
- Change the air fryer temperature to 400 F, air fry for 3 to 5 minutes more.
- In a bowl, add the rest of the ingredients, drizzle over wings and serve.

## CHICKEN SANDWICH

*Prep time:55 min | Cook time:35 min | Serves: 4*

**Ingredients**

- 2 boneless chicken breasts
- Buttermilk: 1 cup
- Half lemon's juice
- Cayenne pepper: ¼ tsp.
- 2 eggs, whisked
- All-purpose flour: 1 cup
- Black pepper: 1 tsp.
- Baking powder: half tsp.
- Celery seeds: half tsp.
- Powdered sugar: 2 tbsp.
- Dried thyme: half tsp.
- Salt: 2 tsp.
- 4 brioche rolls
- Dried sage: ¼ tsp.
- Butter: 1 tbsp., softened
- Coleslaw: 1½ Cup

**Instructions**

- Slice the chicken breast into 2 pieces, make it thinner with a mallet.
- In a bowl, add buttermilk, cayenne pepper and lemon juice, mix and add chicken, coat well. Keep in the fridge for 3 hours.
- In a bowl, add eggs. In another bowl, add the rest of the ingredients.
- Take chicken out, coat in the flour bowl, and dip in egg mixture, coat again in flour and place on the air sprayed air fryer basket.
- Let the Kalorik Air Fryer Oven preheat to 380 F.
- Oil spray the chicken and air fry for 12 minutes, flip and oil spray. Change the temperature to 400 F.
- Air fry for 4 minutes, flip and cook for 4 to 5 minutes until the internal temperature of chicken reaches 165 F.
- Serve the chicken in buns with desired toppings.

## TURKEY BREAST WITH HERB BUTTER

*Prep time:15 min | Cook time:50 min | Serves: 8*

**Ingredients**

- Chopped fresh parsley: 1 tbsp.
- Turkey breast: 5 to 6 pounds, trimmed
- Unsalted butter: half cup, softened
- Black pepper: half tsp.
- Chopped fresh rosemary: 1 tbsp.
- Salt: 1 tsp.
- Chopped fresh thyme: 1 tbsp.
- Chopped fresh sage: 1 tbsp.

**Instructions**

- Make sure turkey will fit in the air fryer so trim accordingly.
- In a bowl, add the rest of the ingredients, mix and massage under and above the turkey skin. Cover all the turkey.
- Let the Kalorik Air Fryer Oven preheat to 350 F.
- Air fry the turkey, skin side up for 20 minutes.
- Flip and air fry for 20 minutes more.
- Baste with the bottom juices, and cook for ten minutes more until the turkey's internal temperature reaches 165 F.
- Rest it for 15 minutes, slice and serve.

## TURKEY CROQUETTES

*Prep time:20 min | Cook time:10 min | Serves: 6*

**Ingredients**

- Mashed potatoes with milk, butter: 2 cups
- Swiss cheese: half cup, grated
- Pepper: ¼ tsp.
- 1 shallot, diced
- Minced fresh rosemary: 2 tsp.
- Parmesan cheese: half cup, grated
- Minced fresh sage: 1 tsp.
- Panko bread crumbs: 1-1/4 cups
- Salt: half tsp.
- Cooked turkey: 3 cups, diced
- 1 egg
- Water: 2 tbsp.

**Instructions**

- Let the Kalorik Air Fryer Oven preheat to 350 F.
- In a bowl, whisk the egg with water; in another bowl, add bread crumbs.
- In a large bowl, add the rest of the ingredients, mix and make into 1" thick patties.
- Coat the croquette in egg then in crumbs.
- Place the croquettes in the oil sprayed basket and air fry for 4 to 5 minutes.
- Flip, spray them with oil and cook for 4 to 5 more minutes.
- Serve with sour cream.

Cal 322 | Fat 12g | Carb 22g | Protein 29g

## ORANGE-SESAME CHICKEN WINGS

*Prep time:10 min | Cook time:25 min | Serves: 4*

**Ingredients**

- Chicken wings: 2 Pounds
- Hoisin sauce: 2 tbsp.
- Sesame oil: 1 tsp.
- Orange marmalade: 12 oz.
- Soy sauce: 1 tbsp.
- Chinese five spice seasoning: 1 tsp.
- Minced ginger: 1 tsp.
- Olive oil
- Sesame oil: 1 tbsp.
- Red pepper flakes, to taste optional

**Instructions**

- Coat the wings in olive oil and sesame oil. Season with 5 spices.
- In a saucepan, add the rest of the ingredients, let it come to a boil, simmer for 5-10 minutes until thickens.
- Let the Kalorik Air Fryer Oven preheat to 400 F.
- Air fry the wings for 12-15 minutes, flipping halfway through.

- Toss the air-fried wings in the sauce and air fry for 3-5 minutes more.
- Serve with sesame seeds on top.

## CHICKEN STUFFED TORTILLAS
*Prep time:20 min | Cook time:20 min | Serves: 12*

**Ingredients**
- Cream cheese: 4 oz., room temperature
- Cooked chicken: 2 cups, shredded
- Salt & black pepper
- Roasted peppers: half cup, diced
- Grated cheddar cheese: 2 ½ cups
- 1 jalapeño, chopped without seeds
- Olive oil: ¼ cup
- Corn kernels: 1 cup
- 3 scallions, diced
- 12 flour (8") tortillas
- Chili powder: 1 tsp.

**Instructions**
- In a bowl, add cheddar cheese, chicken, scallions, cream cheese, corn, salt, roasted pepper and pepper. Mix well.
- In another bowl, mix oil with chili powder.
- Slice the tortilla in half, and make it into a cone, fill with the filling (2 tbsp.).
- Flatten it into a triangle, and brush with chili oil.
- Let the Kalorik Air Fryer Oven preheat to 370 F.
- Air fry the tortilla for 6-7 minutes.
- Serve with salsa.

## TURKEY BREAST WITH CHERRY GLAZE
*Prep time:10 min | Cook time:55 min | Serves: 8*

**Ingredients**
- Olive oil: 2 tsp.
- Dried thyme: 1 tsp.
- Black pepper: half tsp.
- Bone-in turkey breast: 5 pound
- Fresh thyme leaves: 1 tbsp.
- Dried sage: half tsp.
- Salt: 1 tsp.
- Cherry preserves: half cup
- Soy sauce: 1 tsp.

**Instructions**
- In a bowl, mix soy sauce, cherry and fresh thyme mix and set it aside.
- Let the Kalorik Air Fryer Oven preheat to 350 F.
- with olive oil, brush the turkey. In a bowl, add the rest of the ingredients and rub all over the turkey.
- Place the turkey in the basket of air fryer, breast side up, air fry for 25 minutes.
- Turn it on the side and air fry for 12 minutes.
- Place the breast side down and air fry for 12 minutes until the internal temperature of the meat reaches 165 F.
- Brush the turkey with cherry glaze and air fry for five minutes until crispy. Slice and serve.

## ITALIAN CHICKEN MEATBALLS
*Prep time:20 min | Cook time:20 min | Serves: 6*

**Ingredients**
- Minced onion: 1/3 cup
- Seasoned panko breadcrumbs: ¾ cup
- Ground chicken: 1 ½ pound
- Chopped fresh parsley: 1 tbsp.
- Grated parmesan cheese: 2/3 cup
- black pepper: ¼ tsp.
- Italian seasoning: 1 tsp.
- Salt: 1 tsp.
- 1 egg, whisked

**Instructions**
- In a bowl, add all the ingredients and mix until combined, do not over mix.
- Make into 18 meat balls.
- Let the Kalorik Air Fryer Oven preheat to 350 F.
- Air fry the meatballs for 11-13 minutes, flipping halfway through.
- Serve with any dipping sauce

## CHICKEN PAILLARD
*Prep time:20 min | Cook time:15 min | Serves: 2*

**Ingredients**
- 2 chicken breasts, boneless & skinless
- Salt & black pepper
- Baby arugula: 4 cups
- Half lemon's juice
- 1 egg whisked
- Panko bread crumbs: 1¼ cups
- Burrata: 6 oz.
- Flour: 2 tbsp.
- Olive oil
- Cherry tomatoes: 1 cup

**Instructions**
- Butter and pound the chicken into half-inch thickness.
- In a bowl, add flour with salt and pepper. In another bowl, add eggs.
- In the third bowl, combine crumbs with salt and pepper.
- Coat the chicken in flour, then in eggs and lastly in the crumb mixture.
- Let the Kalorik Air Fryer Oven preheat to 400 F.
- Spray the chicken with oil and air fry for 5-8 minutes, flip halfway through.
- Take chicken out and add cherry tomatoes in the air fryer, spray with oil, sprinkle salt and pepper. Air fry for 3 to 4 minutes at 390 F.
- Toss arugula with lemon juice, olive oil, salt and pepper.
- Serve the chicken with arugula and cherry tomatoes.

## GLUTEN-FREE CHICKEN CUTLETS
*Prep time:15 min | Cook time:17 min | Serves: 4*

**Ingredients**
**Basil Buttermilk Sauce**
- Buttermilk: half cup
- Chopped fresh basil: 2 tbsp.
- Hot sauce, 2 dashes
- Mayonnaise: half cup
- Half lemon's juice
- Salt & black pepper, to taste

**Chicken cutlets**
- Butter: 1 tbsp.
- 4 chicken breasts, boneless & skinless

- Dried potato flakes: 1 cup
- Parmesan cheese: half cup, grated
- 2 eggs, whisked
- Salt: half tsp.
- Canola oil: 1 tbsp.

**Instructions**

- In a bowl, add all ingredients of the sauce, whisk well and set it aside.
- Let the Kalorik Air Fryer Oven preheat to 400 F.
- Pound the chicken and season with salt and pepper.
- In the food processor, add potato flakes (1/4 cup), make them into a powder, and take them out in a bowl.
- In a different bowl, add eggs. In another bowl, add the rest of the potato flakes, salt, cheese and pepper.
- Coat the chicken in flakes powder, then in egg and lastly in potato flakes.
- Oil spray the chicken and air fry for 5 to 8 minutes, flipping halfway through.
- Serve with basil sauce.

## PICKLE BRINED FRIED CHICKEN

*Prep time:6 hours & 20 min | Cook time:22 min | Serves: 4*

**Ingredients**

- 4 chicken legs, drumsticks & thighs, with skin & bone
- Flour: half cup
- Fine breadcrumbs: 1 cup
- Salt & black pepper
- 2 eggs
- Pickle juice
- Cayenne pepper: 1/8 tsp.
- Vegetable or canola oil: 2 tbsp.
- Ground paprika: half tsp.

**Instructions**

- In a bowl, add chicken and add pickle juice. Cover and keep in the fridge for 3-8 hours.
- Let the chicken come to room temperature.
- In a bowl, add flour, salt and pepper.
- In another bowl, whisk eggs with oil.
- In the third bowl, add crumbs, salt, cayenne, paprika, and pepper.
- Let the Kalorik Air Fryer Oven preheat to 370 F.
- Pat fry the chicken and coat in flour, then in eggs and lastly in crumb mixture.
- Oil spray the chicken and air fry for ten minutes. Flip and air fry for ten minutes.
- Serve right away.

## SUMMER ALE CHICKEN

*Prep time:15 min | Cook time:1 hour & 5 min | Serves: 4*

**Ingredients**

- Paprika: 2 tbsp.
- Dry mustard powder: 1 tsp.
- Butter melted: 2 tbsp.
- 1 whole chicken, cut in half with no backbone
- Brown sugar: 2 tbsp.
- Summer ale beer: 12 oz.
- Salt & black pepper
- 2-3 sweet onions, sliced
- 3 sprigs fresh thyme

- Chopped fresh chives: 1 tbsp.
- Baby red potatoes: 1½ pounds, halved

**Instructions**

- Let the Kalorik Air Fryer Oven preheat to 400 F.
- In a bowl, add salt, pepper, brown sugar, mustard and paprika. Mix, keep 1 tbsp. of spice mixture safe.
- Oil spray the chicken. Season, the chicken with the rest of the spice mixture. Let it rest.
- Toss the potatoes with oil, salt and pepper. Air fry for ten minutes. Take the potatoes and set them aside.
- Toss onion with butter, salt and pepper, air fry for 8 minutes.
- Add beer to the air fryer, let it go to the drawer below, place chicken on the onion, skin side down.
- Air fry for 20 minutes at 360 F.
- Flip and add the spice mixture on top, air fry for 15-20 minutes, until the internal temperature reaches 165 F.
- Serve the chicken with onions and potatoes.

## SPICY BLACK BEAN TURKEY BURGERS

*Prep time:10 min | Cook time:25 min | Serves: 2*

**Ingredients**

- Canned black beans: 1 cup, rinsed
- Minced red onion: 2 tbsp.
- Cayenne pepper: ¼ tsp.
- 1 jalapeño, chopped without seeds
- Plain breadcrumbs: 2 tbsp.
- Ground turkey: ¾ pound
- Pepper jack cheese: 2 slices
- Salt: half tsp.
- Chili powder: half tsp.

**Cumin-avocado spread**

- 1 lime's juice
- Chopped fresh cilantro: 1 tbsp.
- Ground cumin: 1 tsp.
- Salt: half tsp.
- 1 ripe avocado
- Black pepper, to taste

**Instructions**

- In a bowl, add black beans and smash lightly. Add turkey, cayenne pepper, onion, crumbs, jalapenos, salt, and chili powder.
- Mix and make into 2 patties, oil spray the patties.
- Let the Kalorik Air Fryer Oven preheat to 380 F.
- Air fry for 20 minutes, flipping halfway through. Add cheese slices on top and cook for 2 minutes.
- In a food processor, add avocado, salt, cumin and lime juice. Pulse until smooth.
- Add cilantro and black pepper, mix.
- Serve the burgers in burgers with avocado sauce and desired toppings.

Cal 705 | Fat 29g | Carb 53g | Protein 60g

## CHICKEN CORDON BLEU

*Prep time:35 min | Cook time:14 min | Serves: 4*

**Ingredients**

- 2 chicken breasts, boneless & skinless
- Panko breadcrumbs: ¾ cup
- Salt & black pepper
- Swiss cheese: 4 slices

- 1 egg whisked
- Deli-sliced ham: 4 slices
- Dijon mustard: 1 tbsp.
- All-purpose flour: ¼ cup
- Grated parmesan cheese: 1/3 cup

**Instructions**

- Butter the chicken and pound with a mallet.
- Season with salt and pepper. Add mustard on the inside of the chicken, add one cheese slice, ham (2 slices), and one slice one cheese on top.
- Roll and secure with 1-2 toothpicks.
- Let the Kalorik Air Fryer Oven preheat to 350 F.
- In a bowl, add flour. In another bowl, add whisked eggs and add parmesan cheese and crumbs in the third bowl.
- Coat the chicken in flour, then in egg and lastly in crumbs mixture.
- Spray the chicken with olive oil.
- Air fry for 14 minutes, flipping halfway through.

Cal 732 | Fat 36g | Carb 32g | Protein 65g

## HERBED BUTTERMILK CHICKEN BREAST

*Prep time:30 min | Cook time:55 min | Serves: 2-3*

**Ingredients**

- 1 split chicken breast, with skin & bone (1 ¼-1 1/2 lb.)
- Dried parsley: 1 1/2 tsp.
- Garlic powder: 1/4 tsp.
- Fresh: 1 1/2 tsp.
- Kosher salt: 3/4 tsp.
- Buttermilk: 1 cup
- Dried dill: half tsp.
- Onion powder: half tsp.

**Instructions**

- In a bowl, add chicken and buttermilk, coat the chicken and keep in the fridge for 4 hours, or at room temperature for 20 minutes.
- In another bowl, add the rest of the spices.
- Take the chicken out, drip off the excess, and air fry it, skin side up.
- Sprinkle spice mix on top of the chicken let it rest for five minutes.
- Oil spray the chicken and Let the Kalorik Air Fryer Oven preheat to 300 F.
- Air fry chicken for ten minutes, change the temperature to 350 F, cook for 30-35 minutes until the internal temperature of the meat reaches 160 F.
- Let it rest for ten minutes, slice and serve.

Cal 243 | Carb 2g | Protein 34.5g | Fat 9.5g

## CHICKEN MILANESE

*Prep time:15 min | Cook time:15 min | Serves: 2-3*

**Ingredients**

- 2 chicken breasts, boneless & skinless
- Black pepper, to taste
- Baby arugula: 6 cups
- Whole wheat seasoned breadcrumbs: half cup
- Kosher salt: ¾ tsp.
- Grated parmesan cheese: 2 tbsp.
- 1 egg, whisked

**Instructions**

- Slice the chicken into four cutlets, and pound into 1/4" of thickness.
- Season with salt and pepper.
- In a bowl, whisk the egg with 1 tsp. of water.
- In another bowl, mix cheese and crumbs.
- Coat the chicken in egg then in crumbs mixture. Oil spray the breaded chicken.
- Let the Kalorik Air Fryer Oven preheat to 400 F.
- Air fry for 7 minutes, flipping halfway through.
- Serve with arugula and lemon wedges.

Cal 219 | Protein 31g | Carb 10.5g | Fats 6g

## CHICKEN CAESAR SALAD

*Prep time:10 min | Cook time:17 min | Serves: 4*

**Ingredients**

- Olive oil: 2 tbsp.
- Worcestershire sauce: 2 tbsp.
- Dried thyme: half tsp.
- Black pepper: ¼ tsp.
- Dried oregano: half tsp.
- Lemon juice: 2 tbsp.
- Parmigiano-reggiano, grated
- Salt: 1 tsp.
- Honey: 2 tbsp.
- Chicken breasts: 12 oz.
- Romaine lettuce: 3 hearts, washed & cut into pieces

**Caesar dressing**

- Half lemon's juice
- 2 egg yolks
- Black pepper
- Anchovy paste: 1 tsp.
- Olive oil: ¼ cup
- 1 minced garlic clove
- Salt: ¼ tsp.
- Canola oil: half cup

**Instructions**

- In a bowl, add all ingredients except for chicken, lettuce, cheese and mix.
- In a zip lock bag, add chicken and add the marinade, coat well and keep in the fridge for 6 hours.
- In a bowl, add lemon juice, yolks, salt, pepper, whisk and add anchovy paste, garlic and mix well.
- Gradually add oils while whisking, keep in the fridge.
- Let the Kalorik Air Fryer Oven preheat to 380 F.
- Air fry the chicken for 12 minutes, flipping halfway through.
- In a bowl, add lettuce at the bottom, add dressing and coat, add cheese, toss well. Add croutons.
- Slice and place the chicken on top. Drizzle dressing and serve.

## DUCK BREAST

*Prep time:25 min | Cook time:12 min | Serves: 2*

**Ingredients**

- Pomegranate juice: 2 cups
- Brown sugar: 3 tbsp.
- Duck breast: 1 pound, boneless
- Salt & black pepper, to taste
- Lemon juice: 2 tbsp.
- 6 figs, cut in half

- Olive oil, to taste
- Thyme fresh sprigs

**Instructions**

- In a saucepan, add brown sugar, pomegranate juice, and lemon juice. Mix and let it come to a boil, turn the heat low and simmer for 25 minutes until it thickens. Turn off the heat.
- Let the Kalorik Air Fryer Oven preheat to 400 F.
- Make four slices on the duck breast, make four more diagonally.
- Season with salt and pepper.
- Air fry the duck breast, skin side up for 8-9 minutes, flip and air fry for 4-6 minutes, depends upon the doneness of the meat.
- Take the duck out and let it rest.
- Coat the figs with oil, salt and pepper. Air fry for five minutes.
- Slice and serve the duck breast with pomegranate molasses, thyme, and roasted figs.

### PROSCIUTTO STUFFED CHICKEN BREAST
*Prep time:15 min | Cook time:25 min | Serves: 4*

**Ingredients**

- 8 chicken thin cutlets
- Seasoned breadcrumbs: half cup
- Prosciutto, thin lean: 4 slices, halved
- Mozzarella: 4 slices, halved
- Baby spinach leaves, 1 oz.
- Olive oil: 1 tbsp.
- Roasted peppers: 8 slices
- 1 lemon's juice
- Salt & black pepper, to taste

**Instructions**

- In a bowl, add breadcrumbs; in another bowl, add lemon juice, olive oil and pepper.
- Let the Kalorik Air Fryer Oven preheat to 400 F.
- On each piece of chicken, add half slice of prosciutto, roasted pepper (1 slice), spinach leaves (3 leaves), half a slice of cheese, roll and secure with toothpicks.
- Coat the chicken in lemon juice mixture, then in breadcrumbs.
- Air fry for 12 minutes. Flip halfway through.

Cal 90 | Protein 27g | Carb 7g | Fats 6g

### CHIPOTLE BBQ CHICKEN WINGS
*Prep time:10 min | Cook time:25 min | Serves: 4*

**Ingredients**
**Spice Mix**

- Smoked paprika: 1 tsp.
- Dried oregano: 1 tsp.
- Salt & black pepper, to taste
- Dry mustard powder: half tsp.
- Chili powder: half tsp.
- Dried thyme: 1 tsp.
- Salt: 1 tsp.
- Chicken wings: 2 pounds

**Chipotle bbq sauce**

- Adobo sauce: 2 tsp.
- Apple cider vinegar: ¼ cup
- Tomato ketchup: half cup
- Water: ¼ cup
- Chopped chipotle peppers: 3-4 tbsp., in adobo sauce
- Brown sugar: ¼ cup

- Worcestershire sauce: 1 tbsp.

**Instructions**

- In a bowl, add the spice mix ingredients. Add wings and toss to coat.
- Let the Kalorik Air Fryer Oven preheat to 400 F.
- Oil spray the wings and air fry for ten minutes, shake the basket after half time.
- In a saucepan, add the ingredients of BBQ sauce. let it come to a boil, turn the heat low and simmer for ten minutes.
- Toss the air fried wings in BBQ sauce and serve

Cal 515 | Fat 31g | Carb 33g | Protein 25g

### PHILLY CHICKEN CHEESESTEAK
*Prep time:20 min | Cook time:12 min | Serves: 3-4*

**Ingredients**

- Vegetable oil: 1 tsp.
- Pizza dough: 14 oz.
- 2 chicken breasts, boneless & skinless thinly sliced
- Half onion, sliced
- Worcestershire sauce: 1 tbsp.
- Jarred warmed cheese sauce: half cup
- Salt & black pepper
- Grated cheddar cheese: 1½ cup
- Jarred warmed cheese sauce: half cup

**Instructions**

- In a bowl, add onions, toss with oil and air fry for 8 minutes; shake the basket halfway through.
- Add chicken and Worcestershire in the basket, add salt and pepper, air fry for 8 minutes, shake the basket for few times.
- Take out from the basket.
- Roll the dough into 13 by 11" rectangle. Add cheddar cheese to the dough, add onion, chicken mixture, add cheese sauce, add cheddar cheese again.
- Roll the pizza dough and place it in the air fryer's basket make it into a U shape.
- Make cuts on top and oil spray it.
- Let the Kalorik Air Fryer Oven preheat to 370 F.
- Air fry for 12 minutes, rotating halfway through.
- Slice and serve.

Cal 578 | Fat 25g | Carb 52g | Protein 33g

### CHICKEN FRIED STEAK
*Prep time:5 min | Cook time:12 min | Serves: 3-4*

**Ingredients**

- Cube steak: 1 pound, cut into 4-6 portions
- Pepper: ¼ tsp.
- All-purpose flour: half cup
- Paprika: half tsp.
- Salt: half tsp.
- 1 egg
- Garlic powder: 1 tsp.
- Water: ¼ cup

**The gravy**

- Flour: 2 tbsp.
- Milk: ¾ cup
- Butter: 2 tbsp.
- Salt & pepper to taste

**Instructions**

- Let the Kalorik Air Fryer Oven preheat to 370 F
- In a bowl, add flour and all spices.
- In another bowl, add the egg and water, whisk.
- Coat the steak in flour mixture, then in egg and back in flour mixture.
- Air fry the steaks for 12-15 minutes, flipping halfway through.
- In a pan, melt butter, whisk the rest of the gravy ingredients. Cook until it thickens; add more milk if it is too thick.
- Serve with steak

## SESAME CHICKEN

*Prep time:10 min | Cook time:20 min | Serves: 2*

**Ingredients**

- Cornstarch: half cup
- 6 Chicken Thighs Boneless & Skinless

**Sauce**

- Brown Sugar: 2 tbsp.
- Hoisin Sauce: 5 tsp.
- Soy Sauce: ¼ cup
- Ground Ginger: half tsp.
- 1 minced garlic clove
- Cornstarch: 1 tbsp.
- Orange Juice: 2 tbsp.
- Cold Water: 1 tbsp.
- Sesame Seeds: 2 tsp.

**Instructions**

- Slice the chicken into cubes, and toss with cornstarch.
- Let the Kalorik Air Fryer Oven preheat to 390 F.  oil spray the chicken.
- Air fry the chicken for 24 minutes' flip halfway through oil spray again.
- In a pan, add all sauce ingredients, except for starch and water, sesame seeds, whisk until combined.
- As sugar is dissolved, add water whisked with cornstarch.
- Add sesame seeds turn off the heat.
- Add chicken and coat well. Serve with rice.

**Cal 335 | Fat 12g | Carb 28g**

## SWEET CHILI CHICKEN WINGS

*Prep time:10 min | Cook time:20 min | Serves: 2*

**Ingredients**

- 12 Chicken Wings
- Garlic Powder: 1 tsp.
- Baking Powder: half tsp.
- Black Pepper: 1 tsp.
- Paprika: ¼ tsp.
- Sea Salt: half tsp.
- Onion Powder: ¼ tsp.

**Thai Sweet Chili Sauce**

- Soy Sauce: 1 tbsp.
- Sweet Chili Sauce: 3 ½ tbsp.
- 2 minced garlic cloves
- Rice Wine Vinegar: half tbsp.
- Hoisin Sauce: 1 ½ tbsp.
- Sesame Oil: half tbsp.
- Brown Sugar: 1 tbsp.
- Water: ¼ Cup
- Lime Juice: half tbsp.

- Ground Ginger: half tsp.
- Sea Salt: ¼ tsp.

**Instructions**

- In a zip lock bag, add chicken, baking powder and spices. Toss to coat.
- Let the Kalorik Air Fryer Oven preheat to 400 F.
- Oil spray the wings and air fry for 20 minutes, flipping halfway through.
- In a saucepan, add all ingredients of the sauce on medium flame. Let it come to a boil, turn the heat low and simmer until it thickens slightly.
- Toss the air-fried wings in the sauce, broil the wings for 2 to 4 minutes.
- Serve right away.

## BANG BANG CHICKEN

*Prep time:15 min | Cook time:15 min | Serves: 4*

**Ingredients**

- Sriracha sauce: half tbsp.
- Mayonnaise: half cup
- Honey: 2 tbsp.

**Chicken batter**

- Buttermilk: 1 cup
- Boneless & skinless chicken breast: 1 lb., bite size pieces
- Cornstarch: half cup
- Salt & pepper to taste
- All-purpose flour: 2/3 cup
- 1 egg
- Sriracha sauce: 1 tsp.
- Panko bread crumbs: 1 cup

**Instructions**

- In a bowl, add all ingredients of the sauce, mix well and set it aside.
- In a bowl, add the ingredients of batter, except for crumbs, whisk well.
- Oil spray the air fryer basket, add chicken to the batter, coat in crumbs and place in the basket.
- Air fry for 8 to 10 minutes, at 375 F. shake the basket halfway through.
- Serve the chicken with bang bang sauce.

Cal 1886 | Carb 213g | Protein 31g | Fat 20g

## EVERYTHING BAGEL CHICKEN STRIPS

*Prep time:10 min | Cook time:15 min | Serves: 4*

**Ingredients**

- Parmesan cheese: half cup, grated
- 1 everything bagel, torn
- Chicken tenderloins: 1 pound
- Red pepper flakes: ¼ tsp.
- Panko bread crumbs: half cup
- Butter: 1/4 cup, cubed
- Salt: half tsp.

**Instructions**

- Let the Kalorik Air Fryer Oven preheat to 400 F.
- In a food processor, add bagel and pulse until coarse crumbs form.
- In a bowl, add half a cup of crumbs, add pepper flakes, cheese and panko.

- In a bowl, melt butter.
- Season chicken with salt, and coat in butter, then in crumb mixture.
- Air fry in oil sprayed basket for 7 minutes, on each side.
- Serve right away.

Cal 269 | Fat 13g | Carb 8g | Protein 31g

## HONEY SOY CHICKEN
*Prep time:5 min | Cook time:10 min | Serves: 4*

### Ingredients
- Chicken thighs: 1.5 lb., boneless & skinless

**Honey Soy Marinade**
- Oil: ¼ cup
- Ground ginger: ¼ tsp.
- Honey: 3 tbsp.
- Soy sauce: 1/3 cup
- Garlic powder: half tsp.
- Salt and pepper, to taste

### Instructions
- In a bowl, add all the ingredients of marinade, mix well.
- In a different bowl, add half of the marinade, add chicken and coat well.
- Cover and keep in the fridge for half an hour.
- Let the Kalorik Air Fryer Oven preheat to 400 F.
- Air fry the chicken for 10 to 15 minutes until the internal temperature of the chicken reaches 165 F.
- Baste with the reserved marinade and serve.

## CHICKEN QUESADILLA
*Prep time:5 min | Cook time:10 min | Serves: 1-2*

### Ingredients
- Cheddar cheese: 1/3 cup, grated
- 2 corn tortillas
- Cooked chicken breast: half cup, cubed
- Guacamole: 3 tbsp.

### Instructions
- Let the Kalorik Air Fryer Oven preheat to 325 F.
- Oil spray the air fryer's basket, place the tortilla in the basket. Spread guacamole, add cheese, then chicken, place the second tortilla on top.
- Air fry for 6 to 10 minutes. Flip halfway through.
- Slice and serve.

Cal 106 | Carb 7g | Protein 7g | Fat 6g

## CHEESY CHICKEN DINNER
*Prep time:10 min | Cook time:8 min | Serves: 4*

### Ingredients
- 4 thin chicken breasts
- Parmesan-Asiago cheese blend: ¾ to 1 cup
- Milk: 1 cup
- Panko bread crumbs: half cup
- Salt & pepper, to taste

### Instructions
- Let the Kalorik Air Fryer Oven preheat to 400 F.
- In a bowl, add milk and chicken. Coat well and season with salt and pepper; let it rest for ten minutes.
- In a bowl, add crumbs and cheese.
- Coat the chicken in a crumb mixture and place in the oil sprayed air fryer.

- Air fry for 8 minutes, flipping halfway through.

Cal 570 | Carb 49g | Protein 55g | Fat 16g

## PEANUT CHICKEN EGG THAI ROLLS
*Prep time:10 min | Cook time:10 min | Serves: 2*

### Ingredients
- 1 carrot, thinly sliced
- Thai peanut sauce: 1/4 cup
- Egg roll wrappers: 4
- Shredded rotisserie chicken: 2 cups
- 1/4 red bell pepper, thinly sliced
- 3 green onions, chopped

### Instructions
- Let the Kalorik Air Fryer Oven preheat to 390 F
- In a bowl, add shredded chicken with peanut sauce and mix.
- Place 1 egg roll wrapper on a plate, and on the bottom, place vegetables with half tsp. of chicken mix.
- Fold the wrapper tightly and seal the edges with water.
- Spray the egg rolls with oil spray.
- Put rolls in one layer in the air fryer and air fry for 6-8 minutes.
- Serve and enjoy.

Cal 235 | Carb 17 g | Protein 7 g | Fat 7 g

## BRAZILIAN-STYLE DRUMSTICKS
*Prep time:5 min | Cook time:25 min | Serves: 2*

### Ingredients
- Cumin seeds: 1 tsp.
- Kosher salt: 1 tsp.
- Dried oregano: 1 tsp.
- Chicken drumsticks: 1 1/2 pounds
- Ground turmeric: 1 tsp.
- Coriander seeds: half tsp.
- Dried parsley: 1 tsp.
- Black peppercorns: half tsp.
- Cayenne pepper: half tsp.
- Lime juice: 1/4 cup
- Olive oil: 2 tbsp.

### Instructions
- In a grinder, add all dry spices and pulse until a fine powder.
- In a bowl, add ground spices, oil and lime juice. Mix and add in a zip lock bag, add the chicken coat well and let it rest at room temperature for half an hour.
- Let the Kalorik Air Fryer Oven preheat to 400 F.
- Air fry the chicken for 20 to 25 minutes, skin side up, flip halfway through until the internal temperature of the meat reaches 165 F.
- Serve right away

Cal 255 | Carb 3g | Protein 20g | Fat 18g

## STUFFED TURKEY BREAST
*Prep time:15 min | Cook time:45 min | Serves: 8*

### Ingredients
- Turkey breasts: 1.5 to 2 lb., with no bones
- Salt & black pepper, to taste

**Filling**
- Bacon: 4 slices, bite-sized pieces
- Dried sage: ¼ tsp.
- Half onion, diced
- 2 minced garlic cloves

- Mushrooms: 4oz., sliced
- Chopped fresh spinach: 2 cups
- Dried thyme: half tsp.
- Parmesan cheese or feta: ¼ cup

**Instructions**

- Cook bacon until crispy, add mushrooms, garlic and onion. Cook until softens.
- Add spinach, cook until wilts. Add herbs, pepper and salt, cook for a minute or two. Turn off the heat.
- Add cheese and mix.
- Pound the turkey breast into half-inch of thickness.
- Put turkey skin side down and add filling on top, fold it and tie.
- Sprinkle salt and pepper on top.
- Let the Kalorik Air Fryer Oven preheat to 360 F.
- Oil spray the air fryer basket and air fry turkey for 20 minutes.
- Flip and cook for 10 to 20 minutes more until the turkey's internal temperature reaches 165 F.
- Slice and serve.

## CHICKEN AND VEGGIES
*Prep time:10 min | Cook time:15 min | Serves: 4*

**Ingredients**

- Chicken breast: 1 pound, bite-size pieces
- 1 zucchini, chopped
- Bell pepper chopped: 1 cup
- Chili powder, salt, garlic powder, & pepper: half tsp., each
- Half onion, chopped
- Broccoli florets: 1 cup
- 2 minced garlic cloves
- Olive oil: 2 tbsp.
- Italian seasoning: 1 tbsp.

**Instructions**

- Let the Kalorik Air Fryer Oven preheat to 400 F.
- In a bowl, add chicken and vegetables.
- Add oil, seasonings and toss to combine.
- Air fry for ten minutes, shake the basket cook until charred.
- Serve with rice

Cal 230 | Carb 8g | Protein 26g | Fat 10g

## LEMON ROSEMARY CHICKEN
*Prep time:30 min | Cook time:20 min | Serves: 2*

**Ingredients**

**For marinade**

- Olive oil: half tbsp.
- Chicken: 2 ½ cups
- Ginger: 1 tsp., minced
- Soy sauce: 1 tbsp.

**For the sauce**

- Half lemon
- Fresh rosemary: half cup, chopped
- Honey: 3 tbsp.
- Oyster sauce: 1 tbsp.

**Instructions**

- In a big mixing bowl, add the marinade ingredients with chicken, and mix well.
- Keep in the fridge for 30 minutes
- Let the air fry preheat to 390 F.
- Place the marinated chicken in the air fryer. Air fry for 6 minutes.

- Add all the sauces ingredients in a bowl and mix well except for lemon wedges.
- Brush the sauce over half-baked chicken add lemon juice on top.
- Cook for another 13 minutes, flip the chicken halfway through. Let the chicken evenly brown.
- Serve right away.

Cal 308 | Proteins 25g | Carb 7g | Fat 12 g

## CHICKEN FRIED BROWN RICE
*Prep time:10 min | Cook time:20 min | Serves: 2*

**Ingredients**

- Chicken Breast: 1 Cup, Diced & Cooked
- Carrots: 1/4 cup diced
- Onion: 1/4 cup, chopped
- Celery: 1/4 Cup, diced
- Cooked brown rice: 4 Cups

**Instructions**

- Place foil on the air fryer basket, leave room for air to flow, roll up on the sides
- Spray the foil with olive oil. Mix all ingredients.
- Add all ingredients to the air fryer basket.
- Give an olive oil spray.
- Cook for 5 minutes at 390F.
- Open the air fryer and shake the basket
- Cook for 5 more minutes at 390F.
- Serve hot.

Cal 350 | Fat 6g | Carb 20g | Protein 22g

## TURKEY BREAST WITH MAPLE MUSTARD GLAZE
*Prep time:10 min | Cook time:55 min | Serves: 6*

**Ingredients**

- Olive oil: 2 tsp.
- Dijon mustard: 2 tbsp.
- Whole turkey breast
- Dried sage: half tsp.
- Salt: 1 tsp.
- Black pepper: half tsp.
- Smoked paprika: half tsp.
- Dried thyme: 1 tsp.
- Maple syrup: ¼ cup
- Butter: 1 tbsp.

**Instructions**

- Let the Kalorik Air Fryer Oven preheat to 350 F.
- Coat the turkey in olive oil.
- In a bowl, add all the spices and herbs. Rub all over the turkey breast.
- Air fry for 25 minutes, flip and cook for 12 minutes more.
- Rotate and air fry for 12 minutes until the internal temperature of the turkey reaches 165 F.
- In a pan, add butter, maple syrup and mustard.
- Brush the turkey with this glaze and air fry for five minutes; rest it for 5 minutes.
- Slice and serve.

## CHICKEN THIGHS
*Prep time:10 min | Cook time:20 min | Serves: 4*

**Ingredients**

- 4 chicken thighs skin-on, boneless
- 2 teaspoons. olive oil

- 1 teaspoon. smoked paprika
- ¾ teaspoon. garlic powder
- ½ teaspoon. salt
- ½ teaspoon. ground black pepper

**Instructions**
- Preheat your air fryer to 400 F
- Brush the skin side of each slice of chicken thighs with olive oil after patting them dry with a paper towel. On a tray, arrange chicken thighs in a single sheet, skin-side down.
- In a cup, combine the smoked paprika, garlic powder, salt, and pepper; evenly sprinkle half of the seasoning mixture over the 4 chicken thighs. Turn the thighs over and uniformly coat them with the remaining seasoning mixture. Place skin-side up chicken thighs in a single layer in the air fryer basket.
- Cook for 18 minutes in a preheated air fryer until the chicken is golden brown and the juices run clear. At least 165 F should be read on an instant-read thermometer inserted into the middle

Cal 226 | Carb 0.9g | Protein 19.3g | Fat 14.2g

## CRUMBED CHICKEN TENDERLOINS

*Prep time:15 min | Cook time:12 min | Serves: 4*

**Ingredients**
- 1 egg
- ½ cup of dry bread crumbs
- 2 tablespoons. Vegetable oil
- 8 chicken tenderloins

**Instructions**
- Preheat your air fryer to 350°F
- In a small bowl, whisk the egg.
- In a second cup, combine bread crumbs and oil until the mixture is loose and crumbly.
- Shake off any excess egg after dipping each chicken tenderloin in the egg. Make sure the chicken is uniformly and fully coated in the crumb mixture. Place chicken tenderloins in the air fryer basket. Cook for 12 minutes or until the centre is no longer pink. At least 165 F should be read on an instant-read thermometer inserted into the middle.

Cal 253 | Carb 9.8g | Protein 26.2g | Fat 11.4g

## MAPLE CHICKEN THIGHS
*Prep time:10 min | Cook time:25 min | Serves: 4*

**Ingredients**
- 1 cup of buttermilk
- ½ cup of maple syrup
- 1 egg
- 1 teaspoon. granulated garlic
- 4 skin-on, bone-in chicken thighs

**Dry Mix:**
- ½ teaspoon. granulated garlic

- ½ cup of all-purpose flour
- ¼ cup of tapioca flour
- 1 tablespoon. salt
- 1 teaspoon. sweet paprika
- ½ teaspoon. smoked paprika
- 1 teaspoon. granulated onion
- ¼ teaspoon. ground black pepper
- ¼ teaspoon. cayenne pepper
- ½ teaspoon. honey powder

**Instructions**
- In a resalable container, combine buttermilk, egg, maple syrup and 1 teaspoon granulated garlic. Add the chicken thighs and marinate them overnight.
- In a shallow cup, combine rice, tapioca flour, salt, sweet paprika, smoked paprika, cayenne pepper, granulated onion, pepper, 1/2 teaspoon garlic powder, and honey powder.
- Preheat your air fryer to 380°F
- Chicken thighs should be drained and the marinade discarded. Dredge the chicken in the flour mixture, shaking off any excess. Cook for 12 minutes with the skin side down in a preheated air fryer. Turn the thighs and cook for another 13 minutes.

Cal225 | Carb 50.8g | Protein 23.3g | Fat 13.4g

## BUTTERMILK CHICKEN
*Prep time:15 min | Cook time:20 min | Serves: 4*

**Ingredients**
- 1 cup of buttermilk
- ½ teaspoon. hot sauce
- ⅓ cup of tapioca flour
- ½ teaspoon. garlic salt
- ⅛ teaspoon. ground black pepper
- 1 egg
- ½ cup of all-purpose flour
- 2 teaspoons. salt
- 1 ½ teaspoon. brown sugar
- 1 teaspoon. garlic powder
- ½ teaspoon. paprika
- ½ teaspoon. onion powder
- ¼ teaspoon. oregano
- ¼ teaspoon. black pepper
- 1 lb. chicken thighs skinless, boneless

**Instructions**
- In a shallow dish, combine buttermilk and hot sauce and stir to combine.
- In a resalable plastic container, combine tapioca flour, garlic salt, and 1/8 teaspoon black pepper and shake to combine.
- In a shallow dish, beat the egg
- In a gallon-sized resalable container, add flour, salt, brown sugar, garlic powder, paprika, onion powder, oregano, and 1/4 teaspoon black pepper.
- Buttermilk mixture, tapioca mixture, egg, and flour mixture, in that order, dip chicken thighs in the prepared ingredients, shaking off excess after each dipping
- Preheat your air fryer to 380°F. Using parchment paper, line the air fryer basket.
- Place the coated chicken thighs in the air fryer basket in batches and cook for 10 minutes. Turn the chicken thighs and fry for

another 10 minutes, or until the chicken is no longer pink in the center and the juices run clear.

Cal 335 | Carb27.4g | Protein 24.3g | Fat 13.6g

## CHICKEN THIGH SCHNITZEL

*Prep time:15 min | Cook time:10 min | Serves: 4*

### Ingredients

- 1 lb. chicken thighs
- ½ cup of bread crumbs
- 1 teaspoon. Salt
- ½ teaspoon. Ground black pepper
- ¼ cup of flour
- 1 egg, beaten

### Instructions

- Place one chicken thigh between two sheets of parchment paper at a time and flatten with a mallet.
- In a small cup, combine bread crumbs, salt, and black pepper. In a third shallow dish, whisk together the flour and the beaten egg. First, cover the chicken thighs in flour, then in beaten egg, and then in the bread crumb mixture.
- Preheat your air fryer to 375°F
- Place the breaded thighs in the air fryer basket, making sure they don't touch; if possible, operate in batches. Cook for 6 minutes after misting with avocado oil. Cook for an additional 3 to 4 minutes after flipping each thigh and misting with oil.

Cal 293 | Carb 16.5g | Protein 23.6g | Fat 14g

## SESAME CHICKEN THIGHS

*Prep time:5 min | Cook time:15 min | Serves: 4*

### Ingredients

- 2 tablespoons. Sesame oil
- 2 tablespoons. Soy sauce
- 1 tablespoon. Honey
- 1 tablespoon. Sriracha sauce
- 1 teaspoon. Rice vinegar
- 2 lbs. chicken thighs
- 1 green onion, chopped
- 2 tablespoons. Toasted sesame seeds

### Instructions

- In a big mixing bowl, combine sesame oil, soy sauce, butter, sriracha, and vinegar. Stir in the chicken until it is well combined. Refrigerate for at least 30 minutes after covering.
- Preheat your air fryer to 400°F. Remove the chicken from the marinade.
- Place the skin-side-up chicken thighs in the air fryer basket. 5 minutes in the air fryer Cook for another 10 minutes on the other hand.
- Place the chicken on a plate and set aside for 5 minutes before serving. Serve with green onion and sesame seeds as garnish.

Cal 485 | Carb 6.6g | Protein 39.5g | Fat 32.6g

## BLACKENED CHICKEN BREAST

*Prep time:10 min | Cook time:20 min | Serves: 2*

### Ingredients

- 2 teaspoons. paprika
- 1 teaspoon. ground thyme
- 1 teaspoon. cumin
- ½ teaspoon. cayenne pepper
- ½ teaspoon. onion powder
- ½ teaspoon. black pepper
- ¼ teaspoon. salt
- 2 teaspoons. vegetable oil
- 2 (12 ounces) chicken breast halves skinless, boneless

### Instructions

- In a mixing bowl, combine paprika, thyme, cumin, cayenne pepper, onion powder, black pepper, and salt. Place the spice mixture on a smooth plate.
- Coat each chicken breast in oil until it is fully covered. Roll each piece of chicken in the blackening spice mixture, pressing down, so the spice adheres to all sides. Allow sitting for 5 minutes while the air fryer heats up.
- Preheat an air fryer for 5 minutes at 360 F
- Cook for 10 minutes with the chicken in the air fryer basket. Cook for another 10 minutes on the other hand. Until serving, move the chicken to a plate and set aside for 5 minutes to rest.

Cal 432 | Carb 3.2g | Protein 79.4g | Fat 9.5g

## BBQ CHEDDAR-STUFFED CHICKEN BREASTS

*Prep time:10 min | Cook time:25 min | Serves: 2*

### Ingredients

- 3 strips bacon
- 2 ounces Cheddar cheese, cubed
- ¼ cup of barbeque sauce
- 2 chicken breasts skinless, boneless
- salt & ground black pepper

### Instructions

- Preheat your air fryer to 380°F. In the air fryer, cook 1 strip of bacon for 2 minutes. Split into tiny parts after removing from the air fryer. Preheat the air fryer to 400 F and line the basket with parchment paper
- In a mixing bowl, combine cooked bacon, Cheddar cheese, and 1 tablespoon barbeque sauce.
- Make a horizontal 1-inch cut at the top of each chicken breast with a long, sharp knife to create a small internal pouch. Fill each breast with an equal amount of the bacon-cheese mixture. Wrap the remaining bacon strips around each chicken breast. Coat the remaining barbecue sauce on the chicken breasts and put them in the air fryer basket that has been prepared.
- Cook for 10 minutes in the air fryer, then turn and cook for another 10 minutes, or until the chicken is no longer pink in the centre and the juices run clear. At least 165 F should be read on an instant-read thermometer inserted into the middle

Cal 379 | Carb 12.3g | Protein 37.7g | Fat 18.9g

## MEXICAN-STYLE STUFFED CHICKEN BREASTS

*Prep time:20 min | Cook time:10 min | Serves: 2*

### Ingredients

- 4 extra-long toothpicks
- 4 teaspoons. Chili powder
- 4 teaspoons. Ground cumin
- 1 chicken breast skinless, boneless
- 2 teaspoons. Chipotle flakes
- 2 teaspoons. Mexican oregano
- Salt and ground black pepper
- ½ red bell pepper, sliced
- ½ onion, sliced
- 1 fresh jalapeno pepper, sliced
- 2 teaspoons. Corn oil
- ½ lime, juiced

## Instructions

- Soak toothpicks in water in a small bowl to prevent them from burning during the cooking process.
- In a shallow dish, combine 2 teaspoons chili powder and 2 teaspoons cumin
- Preheat your air fryer to 400°F
- Place the chicken breasts on a smooth work surface. Cut a horizontal slit into the middle of the pie. Using a kitchen mallet or rolling pin, pound each half until it is around 1/4-inch thick.
- Sprinkle the remaining chili powder, cumin, chipotle flakes, oregano, salt, and pepper evenly over each breast half. In the centre of one breast half, position 1/2 of the bell pepper, onion, and jalapeno. Roll the chicken from the tapered end upward, securing it with two toothpicks. Rep with the remaining breasts, herbs, and fruits, securing with toothpicks. In a shallow dish, roll each roll-up in the chili-cumin mixture while drizzling with olive oil until evenly coated.
- Place the toothpick side up in the air-fryer basket with the roll-ups. Preheat the air fryer to 350°F and set the timer for 6 minutes.
- Overturn the roll-ups. Cook for another 5 minutes in the air fryer, or until the juices run clear and an instant-read thermometer inserted into the middle registers at least 165 F
- Until eating, drizzle lime juice uniformly over the roll-ups.

Cal 185 | Carb 15.2g | Protein 14.8g | Fat 8.5g

### GREEK BUFFALO CHICKEN

*Prep time:20 min | Cook time:16 min | Serves: 4*

#### Ingredients

- ½ cup of Greek yogurt
- ¼ cup of egg
- 1 tablespoon. hot sauce
- 1 teaspoon. hot sauce
- 1 cup of panko bread crumbs
- 1 tablespoon. sweet paprika
- 1 tablespoon. garlic pepper seasoning
- 1 tablespoon. cayenne pepper
- 1 lb. chicken breasts skinless, boneless, cut in 1-inch strips

#### Instructions

- Combine Greek yogurt, egg substitute, hot sauce
- In a separate cup, combine panko bread crumbs, paprika, garlic powder, and cayenne pepper.
- Coat chicken strips in panko bread crumb mixture after dipping them in yogurt.
- In an air fryer, arrange coated chicken strips in a single sheet. Cook for around 8 minutes until evenly browned.

Cal 234 | Protein 31.2g | Carb 22.1g | Fat 4.6g

### CRISPY RANCH NUGGETS

*Prep time:15 min | Cook time:10 min | Serves: 4*

#### Ingredients

- 1 (1 ounce) package dry ranch salad dressing mix
- 2 tablespoons. flour
- 1 egg
- 1 lb. chicken tenders
- 1 cup of panko bread crumbs

#### Instructions

- Toss the chicken with the ranch seasoning in a large mixing bowl. Allow for 5-10 minutes of resting time.

- Fill a resalable bag halfway with flour. In a small cup, crack an egg and spread panko bread crumbs on a plate. Preheat the air fryer to 390°F.
- Toss the chicken in the bag to coat it. Dip the chicken in the egg mixture lightly, allowing excess to drip off. Roll the chicken parts in panko crumbs, pushing them into the meat.
- Spray the air fryer basket with oil and arrange the chicken parts inside, making sure they don't overlap. Depending on the size of your air fryer, you will need to do two batches. Using a light mist of cooking spray, lightly coat the chicken.
- 4 minutes in the air fryer Cook for another 4 minutes, or until the chicken parts are no longer pink on the inside. Serve right away.

Cal 244 | Carb 25.3g | Protein 31g | Fat 3.6g

### BUFFALO CHICKEN TENDERS

*Prep time: 5 min | Cook time: 20 min | Serves: 4*

#### Ingredients

- Boneless, skinless chicken tenders – 1 pound
- Hot sauce – ¼ cup
- Pork rinds – 1 ½ ounces, finely ground
- Chili powder – 1 tsp.
- Garlic powder – 1 tsp.

#### Directions

- Put the chicken breasts in a bowl and pour hot sauce over them. Toss to coat. Mix ground pork rinds, chili powder and garlic powder in another bowl.
- Place each tender in the ground pork rinds, and coat well. With wet hands, press down the pork rinds into the chicken. Place the tender in a single layer into your air fryer oven basket. Cook at 375°F for 20 minutes. Flip once. Serve.

Cal 160 | Carb 0.6g | Fat 4.4g | Protein 27.3g

### BACON-WRAPPED CHICKEN BREASTS

*Prep time:15 min | Cook time:30 min | Serves: 3*

#### Ingredients

- 3 chicken breasts skinless, boneless
- 1 teaspoon. lemon-pepper seasoning
- 3 slices Monterey Jack cheese
- 6 spears of fresh asparagus
- 9 slices bacon

#### Instructions

- Preheat the air fryer to 350 F
- Dry the chicken bits with paper towels. With a sharp knife, cut horizontally through the centre, beginning at the thickest part and not across to the other side. Spread out the two sides as if they were a novel.
- Lemon-pepper seasoning should be used on both sides. Place 1 slice of cheese on each chicken breast. Arrange four asparagus spear halves on top of the cheese. Roll the chicken up and then

over the cheese and asparagus to keep the stuffing within each roll. Wrap several pieces of bacon on each chicken breast and protect the overlap with wooden toothpicks.

- In the air fryer, put each bacon-wrapped breast and air fry for 15 minutes. On the other side, cook for another 15 minutes. Insert an instant-read thermometer into the middle of the chicken to check for doneness; it should read 165 F

Cal 393 | Carb 2g; | Protein 42.4g | Fat23g

## STUFFED CHICKEN THIGHS
*Prep time:5-6min | Cook time:10 min | Serves: 6*

### Ingredients
- 6 ounces' Swiss cheese
- 1 cup of panko bread crumbs
- 1 tablespoon. Sazon seasoning
- ½ cup of flour, divided
- 2 large eggs
- Salt & black pepper
- 6 slices turkey lunch meat
- 6 med boneless skinless chicken thighs
- Nonstick cooking spray

### Instructions
- Preheat your air fryer to 400°F
- Swiss cheese should be cut into six 2 1/2 x 1/2 x 1/2-inch bits.
- Prepare the breading station by putting bread crumbs, 2 teaspoons sazonador seasoning, and 1 tablespoon flour in one shallow dish, remaining flour and sazonador seasoning in another shallow dish, and eggs in a third shallow dish. Whip the eggs until they are light yellow and frothy. Using salt and pepper, season the eggs.
- Place one slice of Swiss cheese on top of each piece of turkey meat. Wrap Swiss cheese around luncheon meat.
- Place a turkey cheese bundle in the centre of each of the opened chicken thighs. Bundles of chicken thighs should be rolled around them. To coat, dip each in the flour mixture and shake off the excess. Shake off excess egg after dipping. Finally, dip the chicken in the bread crumb mixture and press it into the breading.
- Place the chicken bundles in the air fryer seam-side down. Using a non-stick spray, coat the chicken packages.
- Reduce the temperature of the air fryer to 380°F and air fry the chicken for 15 minutes, reduce the temperature of the air fryer to 370 F. Cook for an additional 8 minutes in the air fryer until the chicken is cooked through. Serve right away

Cal 997 | Carb 23.1g | Protein 93.9g | Fat 58g

## HONEY-CAJUN CHICKEN THIGHS
*Prep time:10 min | Cook time:25 min | Serves: 6*

### Ingredients
- ½ Cup of buttermilk
- 1 teaspoon. Hot sauce
- 1 ½ lb. skinless, boneless chicken thighs
- ¼ cup of all-purpose flour
- ⅓ cup of tapioca flour
- 2 ½ teaspoon. Cajun seasoning
- ½ teaspoon. Garlic salt
- ½ teaspoon. Honey powder
- ¼ teaspoon. Ground paprika
- ⅛ teaspoon. Cayenne pepper

- 4 teaspoons. Honey

### Instructions
- In a resalable plastic container, combine buttermilk and hot sauce. Marinate the chicken thighs for 30 minutes.
- In a small mixing bowl, combine rice, tapioca flour, garlic salt, honey powder, Cajun seasoning, paprika, and cayenne pepper. Remove the thighs from the buttermilk mixture and dredge them in the flour. Remove any extra flour by shaking it off.
- Preheat the air fryer to 360°F
- Cook for about 15 minutes in the air fryer basket with chicken thighs. Cook for another 10 minutes, or until the chicken thighs are no longer pink in the middle and the juices run clear. At least 165 F should be read on an instant-read thermometer inserted into the middle Remove the chicken thighs from the air fryer and drizzle 1 teaspoon honey over each one.

Cal 248 | Carb 16.4g | Protein 19.1g | Fat 11.5g

## BACON-WRAPPED CHICKEN THIGHS
*Prep time:10 min | Cook time:25 min | Serves: 4*

### Ingredients
**Finishing Butter:**
- ½ Stick butter, softened
- ½ clove minced garlic
- ¼ teaspoon. Dried thyme
- ¼ teaspoon. Dried basil
- ⅛ teaspoon. Coarse salt
- black pepper
- ⅓ lb. thick-cut bacon
- 1 ½ lb. chicken thighs boneless skinless
- 2 teaspoons. Minced garlic

### Instructions
- In a mixing bowl, combine melted butter, garlic, thyme, basil, salt, and pepper. To make a butter log, spread butter on wax paper and roll it up tightly. Refrigerate for 2 hours or until strong.
- On a piece of wax paper, lay one bacon strip flat. Sprinkle the chicken thigh with garlic and place it on top of the bacon. Remove the chicken thigh and cut it open. In the middle of the chicken thigh, spread 1-2 teaspoons of the cold finishing butter. One end of the bacon should be tucked into the middle of the chicken leg. Roll the bacon around the chicken thigh after folding it over. Rep with the rest of the thighs and bacon.
- Preheat your air fryer to 370°F
- Place the chicken thighs in the air fryer basket and cook for about 25 minutes, or until the chicken is no longer pink and the juices run clear. A thermometer inserted near the bone can read 165 F

Cal 453 | Carb 1g | Protein 33.4g | Fat 34.3g

## BUTTERMILK FRIED CHICKEN
*Prep time:5 min | Cook time:30 min | Serves: 6*

### Ingredients
- 1 ½ lb. chicken thighs boneless, skinless
- 2 cups of buttermilk
- 1 cup of all-purpose flour
- 1 tablespoon. Seasoned salt
- ½ tablespoon. Ground black pepper
- 1 cup of panko bread crumbs
- 1 serving cooking spray

### Instructions

- In a shallow casserole dish, position the chicken thighs. Refrigerate for 4 hours or overnight after pouring buttermilk over the chicken.
- Preheat your air fryer to 380°F
- In a big gallon-sized resalable container, combine flour, seasoned salt, and pepper. Chicken thighs should be dredged in seasoned flour. Dip in buttermilk again, then coat in panko bread crumbs.
- Using nonstick cooking oil, spray the air fryer basket. Place half of the chicken thighs in the basket, making sure they don't hit. Using cooking spray, coat the tops of each chicken thigh.
- Cook for 15 minutes in a preheated air fryer. Toss the coin. Re-spray the chicken's tops. Cook for another 10 minutes or until the chicken is no longer pink in the centre and the juices run clear. At least 165 F should be read on an instant-read thermometer inserted into the middle.

Cal 335 | Carb 33.2g | Protein 24.5g | Fat 12.8g

## PEACH-BOURBON WINGS
*Prep time:35 min | Cook time:15 min | Serves: 6-8*

### Ingredients
- peach preserves: half cup
- water: 1 ½ tsp.
- brown sugar: 1 tbsp.
- salt
- chicken wings: 2 lbs.
- white vinegar: 2 tbsp.
- 1 garlic clove minced
- corn starch: 1 tsp.
- whiskey: 2 tbsp.

### Instructions
- Let the Kalorik Air Fryer Oven preheat to 400 F.
- In a food processor, add salt, garlic, peach, and sugar, pulse until smooth.
- Transfer in a pan, and add bourbon. Simmer for 4-6 minutes.
- In a bowl, mix water with corn-starch. Add to the pan. Cook for 1 to 2 minutes.
- Cook the wings in air fry after oil spraying them for 6 minutes.
- Toss with sauce and cook for 5 minutes more. Serve.

Cal 77 | Carb 7 g | Protein 6 g | Fat 5 g

## CHICKEN KATSU
*Prep time:20 min | Cook time:20 min | Serves: 4*

### Ingredients
**Katsu Sauce:**
- ½ cup ketchup
- 2 tablespoons soy sauce
- 1 tablespoon brown sugar
- 1 tablespoon sherry
- 2 teaspoons Worcestershire sauce
- 1 teaspoon minced garlic

**Chicken:**
- 1-pound boneless skinless chicken breast, sliced in half horizontally
- 1 pinch salt and ground black pepper to taste
- 2 large eggs, beaten
- 1 ½ cups panko bread crumbs
- 1 serving cooking spray

### Instructions

- In a mixing bowl, whisk together ketchup, brown sugar, sherry, soy sauce, Worcestershire sauce, and garlic until the sugar gets dissolved. Set aside the katsu sauce.
- Preheat your air fryer to 350°F
- Place the chicken parts on a clean work surface in the meantime. Salt and pepper to taste.
- In a flat dish, beat the eggs. Fill a second flat dish halfway with bread crumbs. Dredge the chicken in the potato, then in the bread crumbs. Dig the chicken in the egg, then in the bread crumbs again, applying pressure to ensure the bread crumbs stick.
- Place the preheated air fryer basket with the chicken pieces in it. Cover the tops with nonstick cooking oil.
- Cook for 10 minutes in an air fryer. Flip the chicken parts over with a spatula and coat the tops with nonstick cooking spray. Cook for an additional 8 minutes. Put the chicken on a cutting board and thinly slice it. Serve with a side of katsu sauce.

Cal 318 | Carb 41.2g | Protein 32g | Fat 6.7g

## CHICKEN AND CHEESE TACO QUESADILLAS
*Prep time:2-3 min | Cook time:6 min | Serves: 4*

### Ingredients
- Soft tortilla shells 4
- Chopped tomatoes ¼ cup.
- Chopped onion ¼ cup.
- Shredded cheese 1 cup
- Cooked shredded 8-10 ounces/cubed chicken.
- Chili powder 1 teaspoon
- Cumin 1 teaspoon

### Instructions
- Flavor the chicken with chili powder & cumin. If not used, cooked rotisserie will have flavor chicken with pepper & salt.
- Line air fryer with the tortilla shell. Not use any oil in the basket & quesadilla does not stick to the basket.
- Put ½ cup cheese on the tortilla.
- The following number put all of the remaining ingredients: first onion, then tomatoes & at the end, chicken.
- Top with one extra tortilla.
- Cook for three minutes at 370 F
- Open air fryer & flip quesadilla.
- Cook for extra three minutes. Must be cook for a long time so that the cheese will melt & if you want crunchy quesadillas, then cook for a long time.
- Remove quesadilla from the air fryer. Slice it & serve.

Cal 317 | Carb 25g | Protein 28g | Fat 14g

## CILANTRO PESTO CHICKEN LEGS
*Prep time:2-3 min | Cook time:20 min | Serves: 2*

### Ingredients
- Chicken drumsticks 4
- Kosher Salt 1 teaspoon
- Lemon Juice 2 tablespoon.
- Jalapeño Peppers 1/2
- Garlic 8 cloves
- Ginger 2 thin slices
- Cilantro 1/2 cup
- Oil 2 tablespoon s.

### Instructions

- Put drumsticks in the flat tray. Use the sharp knife's tip, cut small slashes in the chicken at steady intervals so the marinade can easily penetrate the chicken.
- Equally chop pepper, ginger, cilantro, garlic & put it in a bowl.
- Put oil, salt & lemon juice in the chopped vegetables & combine well.
- Spread this combination on the chicken.
- Allow chicken to marinate at least for thirty minutes / up to twenty-four hours in the refrigerator.
- When completely ready to cook, put chicken legs in the air fryer basket; skin must be side up.
- Adjust air fryer at 390F for twenty minutes for the meaty legs of chicken. In the centre, turn the legs of the chicken over.
- Use a meat thermometer to confirm that the chicken has touched the internal temp of 165 F. Remove & serve with sufficient napkins.

Cal 372 | Carb 30g | Protein 28g | Fat 17g

## CHICKEN JALFREZI
*Prep time:20 min | Cook time:15 min | Serves: 4*

### Ingredients
- Boneless Chicken Thighs 1 lb. & cut it into the large, two-inch pieces.
- Cayenne Pepper 1/2 teaspoon
- Chopped Bell Peppers 2 cup
- Onions chopped 1 cup.
- Kosher Salt 1 teaspoon
- Turmeric 1 teaspoon
- Gram Masala 1 teaspoon
- Cayenne Pepper 1/2-1 teaspoon
- Oil 2 tablespoons.

### For the Sauce
- Tomato sauce 1/4 cup
- Kosher Salt 1/2 teaspoon
- Garam Masala 1 teaspoon
- Water 1 tablespoon

### Instructions
- In the bowl, combine onions, pepper, chicken, salt, oil, garam masala, turmeric & cayenne.
- Put vegetables & chicken in the basket of an air fryer.
- Adjust the air fryer at 360F for fifteen minutes. Mix & toss midway thru cooking time.
- In the meantime, make the sauce: In a microwave bowl, mix water, cayenne, garam masala & tomato sauce.
- Microwave it for one minute. Remove & mix for one minute. Put aside.
- When chicken is prepared take away & put chicken & vegetables in the bowl. Put prepared sauce on them & toss to cover chicken & vegetables equally with sauce. Enjoy with the naan, side salad/ rice.

Cal 265 | Protein 20.4g; | Carb 6.7g | Fat 16.9g;

## ASIAN-GLAZED BONELESS CHICKEN THIGHS
*Prep time:5 min | Cook time:30 min | Serves: 4*

### Ingredients
- Honey 1 tablespoon
- skinless chicken thighs eight boneless
- Balsamic vinegar 2 1/2 tablespoon s.
- Garlic three cloves, crushed.

- Sriracha hot sauce 1 teaspoon
- one scallion
- soy sauce 1/4 cup
- Fresh grated ginger 1 teaspoon

### Instructions
- In the bowl, mix ginger, soy sauce, honey, balsamic, garlic, honey & sriracha & mix it well.
- Put half of (1/4 cup) marinade into the bowl with chicken, cover all marinate & meat minimum two hours/ overnight.
- The remaining sauce will be saved for later.
- Heat air fryer at 400F.
- Take chicken from marinade & transfer it to the basket of an air fryer.
- For fourteen minutes, cook in batch, flip halfway till cooked thru in the middle.
- In the meantime, put the remaining sauce in a pot & cook over med-low heat till it decreases a little & thickens around one to two minutes.
- For serving, sprinkle sauce on chicken & top with the scallions.

Cal 544 | Protein 40.6g | Carb 26.6g | Fat 30.2g

## PERSIAN JOOJEB KABABS
*Prep time:15 min | Cook time:20 min | Serves: 2*

### Ingredients
- Kosher Salt 1 teaspoon
- Chicken breasts 1.5 lbs., cut into large.
- Full-Fat Greek Yogurt 1/4 cup
- Smoked Paprika 1/2 teaspoon
- Ground Black Pepper 1/2 teaspoon
- Saffron water 2 tablespoon s.
- Onion 1/4 cup, chopped.
- Oil 1 tablespoon
- Turmeric 1 teaspoon

### Instructions
- Make a Saffron Water
- In the mortar & pestle, grind saffron & sugar equally.
- 1/2 teaspoon of this powder is mixed with 1 cup of water to make saffron water so that you can season the cakes, meat, and desserts.
- Put the chicken in the bowl.
- In a blender, put oil, salt, paprika, Greek yogurt, black pepper, and onion. Blend till you get a smooth mixture.
- Put all the smooth mixture on the chicken.
- Add saffron water & turmeric blend till chicken is coated well with the flavoring. Accumulate these two ingredients far ahead to keep the blender bowl from being permanently marked yellow.
- Let the chicken be left in a marinated bowl for 30 minutes or in the refrigerator until 24 hours.
- Now remove the chicken from the marinated bowl and put all the chicken in the air fryer basket.
- Set the air fryer's heat at 370 F at fifteen minutes, and after that, turn the chicken on both sides to cook well.
- You must ensure that the meat temperature must be at 165F before it serves.
- Joojeh kabab will be served with plain rice & butter and saffron water on the rice's top.

Cal 159 | Carb 1g | Protein 25g | Fat 5g

## CHICKEN STUFFED WITH PROSCIUTTO AND FONTINA

*Prep time:6 min | Cook time:10 min | Serves: 2*

### Ingredients
- Lemon ½, juiced.
- Prosciutto two-slice
- To taste salt
- Boneless chicken 2breast halves
- Rosemary three sprigs
- Baby arugula one bunch
- Unsalted butter 4 tablespoon s.
- Olive oil 2 tablespoon s.
- Fontina cheese 4 ounces cut into two inches sticks; rind removed.
- To taste, ground black pepper.
- Portabella sliced mushrooms 1 cup.
- Dry white wine ½ cup

### Instructions
- Put halves of chicken breast b/w sheets of the wax paper & using the rolling pin/mallet, lb. thin.
- Cover every fontina cheese stick along with the one slice prosciutto & put in the middle of every half-flattened chicken breast. Roll the chicken around cheese, prosciutto & secure with the butcher's twine /toothpicks. Flavor chicken rolls along with the salt, black pepper & salt.
- In the heavy skillet, warm two tablespoon s. of butter & one tablespoon of olive oil. Speedily rolls of brown chicken on med heat, two to three minutes each side. Put chicken rolls in the air fryer basket. Adjust temp to 350 F & air fry for seven minutes. Remove chicken rolls to the cutting board & allow them rest for 5 minutes. Cut the rolls at an angle into the six slices.
- Reheat skillet & put remaining butter, wine, mushrooms & rosemary; sprinkle with pepper & salt; & boil for ten minutes.
- In a bowl, toss leaves of arugula in the remaining lemon juice, olive oil, pepper & salt. To serve, place chicken & mushrooms on the bed of arugula.

Cal 381 | Fat 14g | Protein 46.6g | Carb 14.1g

## UN-FRIED CHICKEN

*Prep time:10 min | Cook time:1 hr. 10 min | Serves: 4*

### Ingredients
- Buttermilk 1 cup
- Flakes red pepper 1 teaspoon.
- Boneless 4, chicken breasts skinless
- Kosher salt/black pepper
- Breadcrumbs multi-grain panko 1 1/2 cups
- Grated Parmesan 3 tablespoon s.
- Hot sauce 1 tablespoon, as Louisiana Hot Sauce
- Lemon 1, quartered, plus lemon zest 1 tablespoon.

### Instructions
- Mix buttermilk & hot sauce in the bowl. Flavor chicken with the pepper & salt & dip in a mixture of buttermilk.
- Mix parmesan, breadcrumbs, red pepper flakes & pinch of pepper & salt in the dish. Remove chicken from the mixture of buttermilk, allow the extra drip off & dredge in a mixture of breadcrumb until evenly coated. Put pieces flat on the nonstick baking sheet & chill it uncovered at least for 30 minutes.

- Warm the air fryer to 400 F. Bake the chicken till just cooked thru, twenty to twenty-five minutes. Split the chicken into four plates & crush the lemon on the chicken.

Cal 560 | Fat 41g | Carb 6g | Protein 39g

## CHICKEN WINGS

*Prep time:5 min | Cook time:20 min | Serves:2*

### Ingredients
- 1 tablespoon olive oil
- 1 teaspoon lemon pepper
- 2 teaspoon garlic salt
- 1 lb. chicken wings

### Instructions
- Make sure the chicken wings are completely dry by dabbing them with a paper towel. Combine the chicken wings, baking powder, and spices in a zip-lock container. Close the bag (adding air if necessary) and throw it together until the wings are fully coated.
- Spread the chicken wings out in a single sheet.
- Set the Air Fry temp at 400°F and cook for 20 minutes. Make the sweet chili sauce while the chicken wings are cooking.
- After 10 minutes, remove the lid and toss or turn the chicken wings with tongs to prevent sticking. Enable them to cook for another 10 minutes with the lid closed
- When the timer goes off, check the internal temperature to make sure they're finished. Allow for 5 minutes of rest before adding the sweet chili sauce.
- In a small saucepan, combine all ingredients and heat over medium heat on the burner. Bring the sauce to a boil, then reduce to a low heat and continue to stir until the sauce has reduced and thickened slightly. Heat the sauce until the chicken wings are finished.
- Throw the fried chicken wings in the sauce or dip them in it. I like to double-check that they're fully coated.
- Arrange the sauced chicken wings on an oiled cookie sheet with wire rack insert in a single layer. Broil the chicken wings for 2-4 minutes on the top rack. Keep an eye on the wings and keep them close to the air fryer; they will burn fast! Remove the wings from the air fryer until the sauce has thickened and the wings have developed some colour. Serve hot with Sriracha Ranch and optional garnishes.

Cal 648 | Carb 25.4g | Protein 47.8g | Fat 35.6g

## AIR FRIED TURKEY

*Prep time:10 min | Cook time:45 min | Serves: 1*

### Ingredients
- Poultry seasoning, as needed
- Olive oil
- 1 Turkey breast
- Pepper
- Salt

- Sage

**Instructions**

- Sprinkle the turkey breast with rub seasonings, olive oil all over the turkey breast & lay it in the air fryer basket.
- Set the air fryer temp at 325 F & also set a timer for thirty minutes.
- When the timer ends, turn the turkey breast & set another timer for 15 to 30 minutes.
- Please ensure that the internal temp is 180 F. Let it rest for fifteen minutes, slice & serve.

Cal 263 | Protein 4 | Carb 0.3g | Fat 10.1g

## TANDOORI CHICKEN

*Prep time:30 min | Cook time:15 min | Serves: 4*

**Ingredients**

- Garlic paste 1 tablespoon
- Oil 1 tablespoon
- Lemon wedges 4
- For marinade
- Thick yogurt 1/4 cup
- Chicken drumsticks (de-skinned) 5
- Dried fenugreek leaves 1 t tablespoon.
- Salt 1 teaspoon
- Lime juice 1 tablespoon
- Ginger paste 1 tablespoon
- Cayenne 1 teaspoon
- Ground turmeric 1/2 teaspoon
- Garam masala 1/2 teaspoon
- Ground cumin 1 teaspoon

**Instructions**

- Make 3 to 4 slits on every drumstick.
- Combine all of the ingredients for a marinade.
- Put equally to chicken drumsticks & allow them to marinate for one hour in the freezer.
- Take marinated chicken from the freezer once ready to cook. In the air fryer pan, arrange in a single layer. Baste with a few cooking oils.
- Cook in an air fryer over 360 F for ten minutes. Turn over the chicken & baste with the oil. After this cook for the next five minutes.
- Put it on the serving plate. Top with coriander. Serve with sliced onion & lemon wedges.

Cal 178 | Carb 2g | Protein 25g | Fat 6g

## CRISPY CHICKEN BREAST

*Prep time:10 min | Cook time:10 min | Serves: 4*

**Ingredients**

- Salt ½ teaspoon
- 2 (Sliced into cutlets) boneless skinless chicken breasts
- black pepper ¼ teaspoon.
- Garlic powder ¼ teaspoon
- Onion powder ¼ teaspoon
- Oil olive oil, canola, 1 tablespoon
- Dried bread crumbs ½ cup
- Paprika ½ teaspoon
- Dried chili powder ¼ teaspoon
- Cayenne pepper ¼ teaspoon

**Instructions**

- Breaded version:
- Place your chicken breasts in the bowl & sprinkle with oil. Please ensure that they are very well coated.
- In the dish, combine dried bread crumbs with spices till well mixed.
- Coat every chicken breast in the bread crumbs & move it to the air fryer basket.
- Air fry in an air fryer at 390 F for 10 to 12 minutes. After seven minutes, open your air fryer & turn the chicken on the second side. After this, continue cooking.
- Sprinkle oil on the boneless & skinless chicken breasts, & top with your preferred seasonings.
- Put your seasoned chicken breasts in an air fryer basket & air fry for 12 to 15 minutes, turning midway through the kitchen tongs.
- Once Cook time:is over, take it from the air fryer so that your chicken does not dry out. Let it rest for five minutes before serving.

Cal 200 | Fat 0.4g | Carb 37g | Protein 102g

## CHICKEN DRUMSTICKS

*Prep time:30 min | Cook time:20 min | Serves: 6*

**Ingredients**

- Chicken drumsticks 6
- Teriyaki sauce 1 cup

**Instructions**

- Mix drumsticks with teriyaki sauce in a gallon size zip lock bag. Let marinate for 30 minutes
- Preheat air fryer to 360 F. Place drumsticks in one layer in the air fryer basket and cook for 20 minutes. Shake the basket couple times through cooking.
- Garnish with sesame seeds and chopped green onions.

Cal 163 | Carb 7g | Protein 16g | Fat 7g

## GARLIC PARMESAN CHICKEN WINGS

*Prep time:5 min | Cook time:30 min | Serves: 3*

**Ingredients**

- Dried parsley 1 teaspoon
- Chicken wings 1.5 lbs.
- Baking powder 1 tablespoon
- Wings sauce garlic parmesan
- Black pepper 1/2 teaspoon
- Smoked paprika 1/2 teaspoon.
- Grated parmesan 1/2 cup
- Onion powder 1 teaspoon
- Garlic powder 1 teaspoon
- Sea salt 1/2 teaspoon
- Garlic powder 1/2 teaspoon
- Onion Powder 1/2 teaspoon
- Melted & unsalted butter 1/4 cup.
- Black pepper 1/4 teaspoon

**Instructions**

- Take your chicken wing parts from a fridge & pat dry.
- Mix the black pepper, paprika, sea salt, garlic powder, baking powder & onion powder in the dish/ramekin.
- Drizzle the mixture of seasoning on the wings & toss to coat.
- In the air fryer, put wings on the flat layer.
- Using an air-fryer programmed settings for the chicken, cook for 25 to 30 minutes. Set your timer for around 15 minutes, turn the wings, then check your wings at 5 minutes' intervals till the skin

becomes crispy. To make the wings crispy very quickly requires turning them around halfway thru.

- In the bowl, mix all the components for the sauce of the garlic parmesan.
- Toss your wings in the mixture of garlic parmesan & serve immediately.

Cal 438 | Fat 34g | Carb 12.6g | Protein 20g

## BRAZILIAN CHICKEN

*Prep time:15 min | Cook time:25 min | Serves: 4*

### Ingredients

- Lime juice 1/4 cup
- Oil 2 tablespoon
- Chicken drumsticks 1.5 lbs.
- Cumin seeds 1 teaspoon
- Turmeric 1 teaspoon
- Kosher salt 1 teaspoon
- Dried oregano 1 teaspoon
- Dried parsley 1 teaspoon
- Coriander seeds 1/2 teaspoon
- Black peppercorns 1/2 teaspoon
- Cayenne pepper 1/2 teaspoon

### Instructions

- Grind together the oregano, cumin, parsley, kosher salt, turmeric, coriander seeds, peppercorns & cayenne pepper in the clean coffee grinder.
- In a med bowl, mix the ground spices with lime juice & oil. Put the chicken drumsticks & flip them, coating well with the marinade. Let the chicken marinate for thirty minutes or can be for one day in the refrigerator.
- Once you are prepared to cook, put the chicken legs into an air fryer basket.
- Set the air fryer temp to 390 f & timer for 20 to 25 minutes for meaty chicken legs. Halfway thru, turn the chicken legs over.
- Remove & serve with enough napkins.

Cal 345 | Protein 29.3g | Carb 11.5g | Fat 19.9g

## CRISPY CHICKEN WINGS

*Prep time:5 min | Cook time:35 min | Serves: 4*

### Ingredients

- Black pepper 1/4 teaspoon
- Sea salt 3/4 teaspoon
- Chicken wings 2 lb.
- Baking powder 2 teaspoon

### Instructions

- In the bowl, toss your wings with the sea salt, black pepper & baking powder.
- Put the wings onto an oiled rack or put only enough wings into a basket to be in the single layer.
- Put the racks/basket into an air fryer & cook for fifteen minutes at 250 F
- Turn the wings & switch the trays. Increase temp to 430. Air fry for around 15- 20 minutes, till chicken wings, are cooked & crispy.

Cal 227 | Carb 2g | Protein 19g | Fat 12g

## BASIC CHICKEN BREASTS

*Prep time:5 min | Cook time:11 min | Serves: 2*

### Ingredients

- Paprika 1 teaspoon

- Chicken breasts 2
- Salt 1 pinch
- Olive oil 1 tablespoon
- Garlic powder 1 teaspoon

### Instructions

- Rub the olive oil & coat them with a mix of salt, garlic powder, & paprika onto the chicken breasts.
- Place into your air fryer, making sure there is some space between them.
- Set the air fryer to 400f and let it cook for 7 minutes before flipping the chicken and cooking for another 4 minutes.

Cal 133 | Fat 3g | Carb 1g

## CHICKEN NUGGETS

*Prep time:10 min | Cook time:14 min | Serves: 4*

### Ingredients

- Chicken breast 2 6 oz.
- Oil to spray
- Pickle juice 1 cup
- Black pepper 1/4 teaspoon
- Garlic powder 1/4 teaspoon
- Onion Powder 1/4 teaspoon
- All-purpose flour 3/4 cup
- Corn starch 3 tablespoon
- Egg 1
- Milk 3 tabs
- Powdered sugar 2 tablespoon
- Salt 1 1/2 teaspoon
- Paprika 3/4 teaspoon

### Instructions

- In a plastic bag, put chicken slices & pickle juice. Close & put in the freezer for 20 to 30 minutes.
- Therefore, in the bowl, stir together the egg & milk.
- In the other bowl, stir together corn starch, flour, salt, powdered sugar, paprika, powder, onion, garlic powder & black pepper. Set aside.
- Take the chicken pieces from the freezer. Oil your air fryer basket with a little bit of oil. Coat the chicken pieces in the mixture of an egg; after this, coat it in the mixture of flour; shake off the extra flour & put it in a basket. Repeat till the bottom of your air fryer basket is full. Ensure that no pieces are overlapping.
- Close your air fryer basket & cook at 360 F for twelve minutes, turning halfway. Spray the flour spots when turning.
- After twelve minutes, increase the air fryer heat to 400 F & cook for another two minutes.
- Remove & serve with your preferable dipping sauce.

Cal 166 | Carb 33g | Protein 4g | Fat 2g

## JALAPENO POPPER STUFFED CHICKEN

*Prep time:10 min | Cook time:12 min | Serves: 12*

### Ingredients

- Onion Powder 1/4 teaspoon
- Boneless & skinless chicken thighs 12
- Onion Powder 1/2 teaspoon
- Chili powder 1/2 teaspoon
- Fresh ground pepper 1/4 teaspoon
- Salt 1 teaspoon
- Seeded & cut lengthwise jalapenos 6.

- Cream cheese 125g
- Minced garlic three cloves
- Oil mixture
- Avocado oil 4 tablespoon
- Chili powder 1/4 teaspoon

**Instructions**

- In the med bowl, mix the garlic, cream cheese, chili powder, onion powder, salt & pepper. Set aside.
- Remove a stem of jalapenos, slice them lengthwise, & remove the seeds.
- Use the butter knife & add the cream cheese to each half of the twelve jalapenos.
- Roll out the piece of a chicken thigh. Put the jalapeno popper on your chicken & roll it up. To hold it secure. Use the toothpick.
- Do the above step again till all the ingredients are used.
- In the bowl, mix all the ingredients for the mixture of oil.
- Brush the mixture of oil on each side of every piece of the chicken.

Cal 654 | Carb 2g | Protein 62g | Fat 42g

## BUFFALO CHICKEN EGG ROLLS

*Prep time:60 min | Cook time:10 min | Serves: 12*

**Ingredients**

- Chopped green onions 2.
- Softened cream cheese 4oz
- Blue cheese crumbles ½ cup
- Egg roll wrappers 12
- Shredded chicken 1 ½
- Buffalo wing sauce ½ cup
- Shredded cheddar cheese ½ cup

**Instructions**

- In the bowl, mix cream cheese, buffalo wing sauce, blue cheese crumbles & cheddar cheese till well combined. Whisk in chopped green onions & shredded chicken. Combine well.
- As per the egg roll package instructions, assemble the egg rolls by using around two tablespoon of filling for every egg roll.
- In the air fryer basket, put wrapped egg rolls, leave the space b/w egg rolls. Spray lightly with the non-stick cooking spray.
- Cook in an air fryer over 370 F for ten minutes, turning halfway thru cooking time.
- Serve warm with the blue cheese dressing.

Cal 231.5 | Protein20 g | Fat6 g | Carb24.5 g

## CRISPY CHICKEN

*Prep time:10 min | Cook time:40 min | Serves: 5*

**Ingredients**

- Celery salt 1 teaspoon
- Pepper & salt
- Full chicken
- Thyme 2 teaspoon
- Pepper & salt
- Oxo cube chicken 1
- Paprika 1 tablespoon
- Chicken rub
- Olive oil 1 tablespoon
- Paprika 1 tablespoon

**Instructions**

- Into the freezer bag, put all the brine ingredients. Put the whole chicken & then add cold water till the chicken is fully covered. Put it in your fridge for a night.
- Once you are ready to cook the air fryer rotisserie chicken the next day, remove your chicken from the bag, remove the brine stock, remove the giblets, & pat dry the full chicken with the towel.
- In a bowl, make the chicken rub.
- Place the whole chicken & rub ½ olive oil & ½ of a chicken rub into every visible skin in the air fryer.
- Cook your chicken for twenty minutes on 360f.
- After twenty, turn over with the kitchen tongs; after this, add the remaining oil & your chicken rub onto the other chicken side.
- Cook for an additional twenty minutes.
- Serve hot.

Cal 475 | Fat 36g | Carb 0g | Protein 35g

## AIR FRYER GRILLED CHICKEN BREASTS

*Prep time: 5 min | Cook time: 14 min | Serves: 4*

**Ingredients**

- ½ teaspoon garlic powder
- salt and black pepper to taste
- 1 teaspoon dried parsley
- 2 tablespoons olive oil, divided
- 3 boneless, skinless chicken breasts

**Directions**

- Preparing the Ingredients. In a small bowl, combine together the garlic powder, salt, pepper, and parsley. Using 1 tablespoon of olive oil and half of the seasoning mix, rub each chicken breast with oil and seasonings. Place the chicken breast in the air fryer basket.
- Set the temperature of your Air Fryer to 370°F. Set the timer and grill for 7 minutes.
- Using tongs, flip the chicken and brush the remaining olive oil and spices onto the chicken. Reset the timer and grill for 7 minutes more. Check that the chicken has reached an internal temperature of 165°F. Add Cooking Time if needed.
- When the chicken is cooked, transfer it to a platter and serve.

Cal 182 | Carb 0g | Fat 9g | Protein 26g

## CHICKEN TENDER "HOT DOGS"

*Prep time:10 min | Cook time:30 min | Serves: 1*

**Ingredients**

- Yellow mustard 2 teaspoon
- Stoneground mustard 2 teaspoon
- Diced red onion ¼ cup.
- Homemade hot dog buns 8 (gluten-free)
- Chicken tenderloins 1.25 lb.
- Celery salt 1 teaspoon

- Garlic powder ½ teaspoon
- Onion powder ½ teaspoon
- Buttermilk 1 cup
- Gluten-free breadcrumbs 1½ cup
- Cayenne ¼ teaspoon
- Crushed black pepper ½ teaspoon.
- Honey 3 tablespoon

### Instructions

- In the buttermilk, soak your chicken tenders for ten to fifteen minutes.
- In the bowl, mix the breadcrumbs, celery salt, onion powder, garlic powder, cayenne & black pepper. Stir well.
- Please pick up the one tender of chicken, shake off the extra buttermilk & roll it in your seasoned breadcrumbs. Set aside on a separate plate.
- Repeat these steps with the leftover tenders.
- Put some slices in a lightly oiled air fryer basket in a single layer. Spray the prepared tenders lightly.
- Air fry on 370 f for fifteen minutes, turning at the midway mark.
- Do again with all of the prepared tenders of chicken.
- Whereas the tenders of chicken are air frying, mix yellow, stoneground mustard & honey then combine it well in the bowl.
- To serve: cut open the hot dog buns(warm) lengthwise.
- Put the air fried chicken tender in it & finish with the honey mustard(prepared) & minced red onion. Serve it immediately.

Cal 259 | Protein 8.4g | Carb 18.7g | Fat 16.6g

## TURKEY MEATBALLS

*Prep time:5 min | Cook time:16 min | Serves: 4*

### Ingredients

- Moroccan spice 1 tablespoon
- Coriander 1 tablespoon
- Pepper & salt
- Leftover turkey 30 g
- Soft cheese 30 g
- Couscous 1/2 cup
- Turkey stock 30 ml
- Cooked vegetables 150 g
- Greek yogurt 1 tablespoon
- Desiccated coconut 20 g
- Cumin 1 tablespoon

### Instructions

- In the blender, put the cooked vegetables, turkey leg meat, Greek yogurt (soft cheese), turkey stock, & seasoning. Blend for some minutes or till the mixture resembles the thick.
- Move the blender ingredients into the mixing bowl, put in a couscous & combine well.
- Form the combination into balls & roll in desiccated coconut.
- Put in your air fryer for sixteen minutes on 360f & then serve.

Cal 220 | Carb 2g | Protein 42g | Fat 4g

## CORNISH HEN

*Prep time:5 min | Cook time:25 min | Serves: 3*

### Ingredients

- Salt
- Paprika
- Cornish hen 1
- Black pepper

### Instructions

- With spices, rub the Cornish hen. Spray your air fryer basket with olive/coconut oil spray.
- Put the Cornish hen into the air fryer at 390f for around 25 minutes. Turning halfway thru
- Safely remove & serve.

Cal 300 | Protein 25g | Fat 21g |

## BASIL PESTO CHICKEN

*Prep time:5 min | Cook time:15 min | Serves: 4*

### Ingredients

- Cherry tomatoes 1/2 cup
- Pesto 1/2 cup
- Grated parmesan cheese 1/4 cup
- Red pepper flakes 1/2-1 teaspoon
- Boneless & skinless chicken thighs 1 lb.
- Sliced onion 1/2 cup.
- Sliced red bell pepper 1/4 cup.
- Sliced bell peppers 1/4 cup.

### Instructions

- Oil a six x three heatproof pan & set aside.
- In the bowl, combine the pesto, parmesan cheese, pepper flakes & cream. Put in the chicken & turn to coat well with the sauce.
- Put the sauce & chicken into the oiled pan.
- Scatter the peppers, tomatoes & onions on top.
- Put the pan in an air fryer basket. Adjust the air fryer temp to 360f for around fifteen minutes till the chicken is fully cooked.

Cal 299 | Fat 13g | Carb 12g | Protein 30g

## PEANUT CHICKEN

*Prep time:15 min | Cook time:20 min | Serves: 4*

### Ingredients

- Bone-in skin-on chicken thighs 1 lb.
- Minced Garlic 1 teaspoon
- Minced Ginger 1 teaspoon
- Kosher salt 1/2 teaspoon
- Hot water 1/2 cup
- Thai sweet chili sauce 2 tablespoon
- Lime juice 2 tablespoon
- For the sauce
- Creamy peanut butter 1/4 cup
- Sriracha sauce 1 tablespoon
- Soy sauce 1 tablespoon

**For the garnish**

- Finely chopped coriander 5 to 6 teaspoon
- Chopped green scallions 1/4 cup.
- Crushed peanuts 2-3 tablespoon

### Instructions

- Mix the sriracha, peanut butter, sweet chili sauce, soy sauce, lime juice, & salt. Place in hot water & mix till you have a smooth combination.
- Put the chicken in the zip-top bag. Place in half sauce & mix till the chicken is well coated. Let the chicken marinate for thirty minutes or up to one day in the freezer.
- Take the chicken from the bag. Put the coated chicken in an air fryer basket.
- Adjust the air fryer temp to 350f for 20 to 22 minutes.

- Season with coriander, peanuts & onion. Serve it with the remaining sauce for dipping.

Cal 361 | Carb 10g | Protein 22g | Fat 27g

## CHEESY CHICKEN TENDER'S

*Prep time:15 min | Cook time:30 min | Serves: 4*

### Ingredients

- Paprika 1/4 teaspoon
- Onion Powder 1/2 teaspoon
- Milk 2 cups
- Boneless & skinless chicken tenders 2- 2.5 lbs.
- Pulverized cheese crackers 2 cups cooking spray olive oil

### Instructions

- In the bowl, soak the thawed chicken tenders filled with the milk for one hour. It could be soaked for a night or a whole day.
- Pulverize your crackers in the electric food chopper.
- Place the chopped cheese crackers into the resalable bag (gallon size).
- Put the seasonings on your crackers & shake to mix.
- Drain the tenders of chicken.
- Put around 2/3 tenders at one time in a bag with the cracker combination & shake to coat.
- Put the coated tenders into an air fryer basket.
- Drizzle each one with the cooking spray.
- Set the temp at 400 F & also set the timer for 12 minutes & cook.
- Test the tenders at the end of the first twelve minutes, flip over & drizzle this side with the cooking spray.
- Cook for another 10 to 15 minutes.
- Now enjoy it with your favorite toppings.

Cal 253 | Protein 26.2g | Carb 9.8g | Fat 11.4g

## BUFFALO CHICKEN

*Prep time:5 min | Cook time:25 min | Serves:3*

### Ingredients

- 2 Tablespoons Ghee,
- 1/4 Cup Frank's Red Hot Original Sauce
- 2 Lbs. Chicken Drumsticks

### Instructions

- Preheat the air fryer to 400 F for 2-3 minutes. Oil should be sprayed on the air fryer basket.
- Place drumsticks in a basket and air fry for 15 minutes at 400°F.
- Flip the drumsticks and continue to air fried at 400°F for another 5 minutes.
- In a big mixing bowl, combine melted ghee and hot sauce. Toss the drumsticks in the sauce in a mixing dish. Return the drumsticks to the basket and spoon the remaining sauce over the end. Air fry for another 5 minutes, or until the internal temperature of the chicken exceeds 165°F.

Cal 983 | Fat55g

## PARMESAN CHICKEN WINGS

*Prep time:10 min | Cook time:30 min | Serves: 8*

### Ingredients

- 1 teaspoon paprika
- 1 teaspoon Herbs
- salt
- 2 lbs chicken wings
- ½ cup grated Parmesan Cheese

- salt
- black pepper ground

### Instructions

- Dry the chicken wings and put them in a bowl.
- Mix well after seasoning with salt and pepper.
- Preheat the air fryer to 350 F and spray the basket with cooking spray.
- Cook the chicken wings for 15 minutes in batches, turning halfway through.
- Check the temperature of the chicken wing with a meat thermometer to ensure it has reached 165 F.

Cal 328 | Protein 27g | Fat 23g

## CHICKEN COCONUT MEATBALLS

*Prep time:10 min | Cook time:15 min | Serves:4*

### Ingredients

- 1 tablespoon Hoisin Sauce
- 1 tablespoon Soy Sauce
- 1 teaspoon Sriracha Sauce
- 1 teaspoon Sesame Oil
- 1-pound Ground Chicken
- 2 Chopped Green Scallions, finely chopped
- 1/2 cup Cilantro, chopped
- 1/4 cup Unsweetened Shredded Coconut
- Kosher Salt, to taste
- Ground Black Pepper

### Instructions

- Preheat the air fryer to 350 F .
- Gently combine all of the ingredients. It results in a sticky, wet mixture.
- Using foil, line a cookie sheet. Drop rounds of the mixture onto the foil-lined baking sheet with a small scoop or a teaspoon.
- Bake for 15-20 minutes, or until they hit an internal temperature of 150-160F.
- Move the sheet closer to the broiler and brown the tops for a few minutes if desired.
- Instructions for using an air fryer
- In an air fryer, these turned out beautifully; the only issue is that I could only fit 6-8 at a time, so you'd have to do them in batches.
- Cook for 10 minutes at 350°F, rotating once, or until an internal temperature of 150-165°F is reached.
- Brown for 2-3 minutes at 400°F.

Cal 223 | Carb 3g | Protein 20g | Fat 14g

## JAPANESE DUCK BREASTS

*Prep time:15 min | Cook time:25 min | Serves: 8*

### Ingredients

- 25 ounces' chicken stock
- Salt and black pepper according to your taste
- 4 tablespoons honey
- 2 and ½ teaspoon five-spice powder
- 2 teaspoon sesame oil
- 8 duck breasts, boneless
- 6 tablespoons hoisin sauce
- 6 ginger slices
- 6 tablespoons soy sauce

### Instructions

- Mix your soy sauce, five-spice powder, pepper, salt, and honey in a small bowl, mix, add your duck breasts, shake to cover, and set aside for the time being.
- Warm a pan over a medium-high flame with the stock, ginger, hoisin sauce, and sesame oil, mix well, cook for about 2-3 more minutes, turn off the heat and set it aside.
- Place the duck breasts in your air fryer and cook them for about 15 minutes at around 400 F F.
- Split and serve between dishes, drizzle some more hoisin on top and some ginger sauce all over them. cooking
- Enjoy!

Cal 132 | Protein 14.8g | Carb 3.5g | Fat 6.4g

## DUCK AND PLUM SAUCE
*Prep time:15 min | Cook time:40 min | Serves: 4*

### Ingredients
- 4 duck breasts
- 4 tablespoons red wine
- 4 tablespoons sugar
- 2 shallots, chopped
- 2 tablespoons olive oil
- 2-star anise
- 2 cup beef stock
- 14 ounces red plumps, stoned, cut into small wedges
- 2 tablespoon butter, melted

### Instructions
- Over medium flame, warm the pan with some olive oil, add the shallot, mix well and simmer for about 5 minutes,
- Stir in the sugar and plums, blend and simmer until the sugar is dissolved.
- for now, add some stock and wine, whisk, simmer for another 15 minutes, take off the flame and keep it warm.
- Season with some salt and black pepper, brush with melted butter, switch to a heat-proof dish that suits your air fryer, add star anise and plum sauce, place it in the air fryer, and cook for about 12 minutes at around 360 F.
- Split and serve all on dishes. Enjoy!

Cal 370　 | Fat 12 g | Carb 33 g | Protein 27 g

## CHICKEN AND CREAMY MUSHROOMS
*Prep time:15 min | Cook time:35 min | Serves: 10*

### Ingredients
- ½ cup parmesan, grated
- 2 cup chicken stock
- 6 tablespoons butter, melted
- 6 garlic cloves, minced
- 10 ounces cremini mushrooms, halved
- Salt and black pepper according to your taste
- 10 chicken thighs
- 2 tablespoon mustard
- 1 teaspoon oregano, dried
- 1 teaspoon thyme, dried
- 1 teaspoon basil, dried
- ½ cup heavy cream

### Instructions
- Rub the chicken bits with 2 tablespoons of butter, season with some salt and black pepper, place in the basket of your air fryer, cook for about 5 minutes at around 370 F and leave in a bowl for now.

- In the meantime, over medium-high flame, prepare, heat a skillet with the remainder of the butter, including the mushrooms and garlic, mix and simmer for about 5 minutes.
- Add pepper, salt, thyme, oregano, stock, and basil, mix well, and move to an air-fryer-friendly heat-proof bowl.
- Add the chicken, toss it, bring the air fryer in and cook for about 20 minutes at around 370 F.
- Add the parmesan, mustard, and heavy cream, toss it all over again, simmer for an additional 5 minutes, split between plates and eat. Enjoy!

Cal 326 | Carb 3g | Protein 26g | Fat 22g

## CHICKEN AND CAPERS
*Prep time:14 min | Cook time:25 min | Serves: 4*

### Ingredients
- 3 tablespoons butter, melted
- 5 garlic cloves, minced
- 3 tablespoons capers
- 5 chicken thighs
- 6 green onions, chopped
- 2 lemons, sliced
- 1 cup chicken stock
- Salt and black pepper according to your taste

### Instructions
- Rub the butter on the meat, sprinkle the salt and black pepper to taste, and put them in a baking pan that's perfect for your air fryer.
- Add chicken stock, garlic, capers, and lemon slices as well, toss to cover, put in your air fryer and cook for about 20 minutes at around 370 F, turning midway.
- Sprinkle with green onions, split between dishes, and eat. Enjoy!

Cal 180 | Protein 14g | Carb 1g | Fat 5g

## CHICKEN THIGHS AND BABY POTATOES
*Prep time:15 min | Cook time:40 min | Serves: 5*

### Ingredients
- 4 teaspoons oregano, dried
- 2-pound baby potatoes halved
- 3 tablespoons olive oil
- 10 chicken thighs
- 4 teaspoons thyme, chopped
- 2 red onions, chopped
- 3 garlic cloves, minced
- Salt and black pepper according to your taste
- 1 teaspoon sweet paprika
- 4 teaspoons rosemary, dried

### Instructions
- Mix the chicken thighs, pepper, salt, paprika, thyme, rosemary, onion, oregano, garlic, and oil in a small bowl.
- Toss to cover, scatter everything in a heat-proof pan that suits your air fryer, and cook for about 30 minutes at around 400 F, rotating midway.
- Split and serve between dishes. Enjoy!

Cal 364 | Fat 15.4g | Carb 21.7g | Protein 34.3g

## CHINESE STUFFED CHICKEN
*Prep time:20 min | Cook time:50 min | Serves: 10*

### Ingredients
- 6 ginger slices

- 4 red chilies, chopped
- 20 wolfberries
- 2 whole chicken
- 5 teaspoons sesame oil
- Salt and white pepper according to your taste
- 2 teaspoon soy sauce
- 2 yams, cubed

**Instructions**

- Season the chicken with some salt, black pepper, sesame oil, soy sauce, yam cubes, wolfberries, chilies, and ginger to taste.
- Put it in your air fryer, cook for about 20 minutes at around 400 F, then for another 15 minutes at around 360 F.
- Carve the chicken, split it between bowls, and eat. Enjoy!

Cal 353.2 | Fat 5.8g | Carb 50.7g | Protein 22.6g

## BARBECUE WITH CHORIZO AND CHICKEN

*Prep time: 5 min | Cook time: 35 min | Serves: 4*

**Ingredients**

- 4 chicken thighs
- 2 Tuscan sausages
- small onions

**Directions**

- Preheat the fryer to 400°F for 5 minutes. Season the meat the same way you would if you were going to use the barbecue.
- Put in the fryer, lower the temperature to 320°F and set for 30 minutes.
- After 20 minutes, check if any of the meat has reached the point of your preference. If so, take whichever is ready and return to the fryer with the others for another 10 minutes, now at 400°F. If not, return them to Air Fryer for the last 10 minutes at 400°F.

Cal 135 | Carb 0g | Fat 5g | Protein 6g

## CHINESE DUCK LEGS

*Prep time:15 min | Cook time:40 min | Serves: 4*

**Ingredients**

- 2 bunch spring onions, chopped
- 4-star anise
- 2 tablespoons olive oil
- 4 dried chilies, chopped
- 2 tablespoon rice wine
- 18 ounces' water
- 2 teaspoon sesame oil
- 2 tablespoon soy sauce
- 2 tablespoon oyster sauce
- 4 ginger slices
- 4 duck legs

**Instructions**

- Heat the pan over medium-high heat with the oil, mix in the chili, star anise, rice wine, sesame oil, soy sauce, oyster sauce, ginger, water, and simmer for 6 minutes.
- Add the spring onions and the legs of the duck, toss to cover, move to a pan that suits your air fryer, bring the air fryer in and cook for about 30 minutes at around 370 F.
- Split and serve between dishes. Enjoy!

Cal 442 | Carb 7g | Protein 50g | Fat 21g

## ITALIAN CHICKEN

*Prep time:12 min | Cook time:20 min | Serves: 5*

**Ingredients**

- 4 garlic cloves, minced
- 2 tablespoons olive oil
- 5 chicken thighs
- Salt and black pepper according to your taste
- 4 tablespoons basil, chopped
- 1 cup sun-dried tomatoes
- ½ cup parmesan, grated
- 2 teaspoon red pepper flakes, crushed
- 1 cup chicken stock
- 1 cup heavy cream
- 2 tablespoon thyme, chopped

**Instructions**

- Add salt and pepper to the meat, brush with half of the oil, put in your preheated 350 F air fryer, and cook for about 4 minutes.
- In the meantime, over medium-high heat, heat a pan with the rest of the oil, add garlic, thyme, pepper flakes, heavy cream, sun-dried tomatoes, parmesan, salt, stock, and pepper, mix, bring to a boil, take off flame and switch to an air-fryer-friendly dish.
- Add the top of the chicken thighs, place them in your air fryer and cook for about 12 minutes at around 320 F.
- Split between dishes and serve with the top sprinkled with basil. Enjoy!

Cal 344 | Protein 27.5g | Carb 7.7g | Fat 22.4g

## HONEY DUCK BREASTS

*Prep time:15 min | Cook time:30 mins | Serves: 3*

**Ingredients**

- 2 bunch spring onions, chopped
- 1 teaspoon apple vinegar
- 2 tablespoon mustard
- 2 teaspoon tomato paste
- 2 teaspoon honey
- 2 smoked duck breast, halved

**Directions**

- Mix honey with some mustard, tomato paste, and vinegar in a small bowl, whisk good, adds pieces of duck breast, mix to cover well, move to your air fryer and cook for about 15 minutes at around 370 F.
- Take the duck breast out of your fryer, apply it to the honey blend, toss it again, return it to the air fryer, and steam for another 6 more minutes at around 370 F.
- Split it into dishes and serve it with a side salad. Enjoy!

## MEXICAN CHICKEN

*Prep time:15 min | Cook time:25 min | Serves: 5*

**Ingredients**

- Salt and black pepper according to your taste
- 2 tablespoons olive oil

- 18 ounces' salsa Verde
- 2 teaspoon garlic powder
- ½ cup cilantro, chopped
- 2 and ½ cup Monterey Jack cheese, grated
- 2-pound chicken breast, boneless and skinless

**Nutrition**

- Season the chicken with salt, garlic powder, pepper, spray with olive oil and put it over your salsa Verde. Pour the salsa Verde into a baking dish that suits your air fryer.
- Put it in an air fryer and cook for about 20 minutes at around 380 F.
- Sprinkle on top of cheese and roast for an additional 2 minutes.
- Split between plates and serve once heated. Enjoy!

Cal 264 | Protein 35.4g | Carb 4.9g | Fat 11.1g

## CREAMY CHICKEN, RICE AND PEAS

*Prep time:15 min | Cook time:45 min | Serves: 6*

**Ingredients**

- 4 garlic cloves, minced
- 2 tablespoons olive oil
- Salt and black pepper to the taste
- 2 cup white rice, already cooked
- 2-pound chicken breasts, skinless, boneless, and cut into quarters
- 2 and ½ cups parmesan, grated
- 4 cups peas, frozen
- ½ cup parsley, chopped
- 2 cup chicken stock
- ½ cup heavy cream
- 1 cup white wine
- 2 yellow onion, chopped

**Instructions**

- Season the chicken breasts with some salt and black pepper, drizzle half the oil over them, rub gently, place them in the basket of your air fryer and cook them for about 6 minutes at around 360 F.
- Heat the pan over a medium-high flame with the remainder of the oil, add the onion, pepper, garlic, stock, wine, salt, and heavy cream, mix, bring to boil and cook for another 9 minutes.
- Move the chicken breasts to a heat-proof tray that suits your air fryer, cover them with peas, rice and cream blend, mix some parmesan and parsley and scatter all over, put in your air fryer and cook for about 10 minutes at around 420 F.
- Split between plates and serve once heated. Enjoy!

Cal 766 | Fat 45g | Carb 53g | Protein 35g

## LOW CARB CHICKEN ENCHILADAS

*Prep time:15 min | Cook time:5 min | Serves: 4*

**Ingredients**

- ¼ cup cheese Mexican blend cheese
- 3/4 teaspoon garlic powder
- 1/2 teaspoon red pepper
- 1/4 teaspoon salt
- 1 cup salsa can use tomato sauce
- 12 6-inch carb-conscious tortillas
- 2 teaspoons ground cumin
- 1 15-ounce can black beans
- 1 cup chopped tomato
- 6 tablespoons sour cream

- 1 cup chopped onion
- 1 cup chicken stock
- 1/4 cup fresh cilantro
- 3 cups boneless rotisserie chicken breast
- 1 1/2 tablespoons chili powder

**Instructions**

- Preheat the Air Fryer to 350 F .
- Combine that the ingredients expect chicken a cheese in a medium saucepan, and cook them for 2-3 minutes.
- 1 1/2 cups sauce mixture should be set aside. In the pan with the beans, cook for 2 minutes, or until the chicken is completely cooked.
- Stack tortillas, cover in damp paper towels, and microwave for 25 seconds on Warm. Serve with the remaining sauce and cheese on top.
- Fill each tortilla with around 1/3 cup chicken mixture and roll it up. Place tortillas in the bottom glass and spray cooking oil.
- 3 minutes under the broiler, or until the cheese is lightly browned and the sauce is bubbling. Toss with tomato and cilantro before serving. Serve with sour cream on the side.

Cal 500 | Fat 29g | Carb 25g | Protein 42g

## HERBED CHICKEN

*Prep time:35 min | Cook time:45 min | Serves: 5*

**Ingredients**

- 2 teaspoon garlic powder
- Salt and black pepper according to your taste
- 2 whole chicken
- 4 tablespoons olive oil
- 2 tablespoon lemon juice
- 2 teaspoon rosemary, dried
- 1 teaspoon thyme, dried
- 2 teaspoon onion powder

**Instructions**

- Add salt and pepper to the chicken, combine with rosemary, thyme, garlic powder and onion powder, cook with lemon juice and olive oil and let stand for at least 30 minutes.
- Put your chicken in an air fryer and cook each side for about 20 minutes at around 360 F.
- Leave the chicken aside, carve and serve to cool off. Enjoy!

Cal 176 | Carb 5g | Protein 26g | Fat 4g

## CHINESE CHICKEN WINGS

*Prep time:2 hours 30 min | Cook time:20 min | Serves: 8*

**Ingredients**

- 6 tablespoons lime juice
- 4 tablespoons honey
- 18 chicken wings
- Half teaspoon white pepper
- Salt and black pepper according to your taste
- 4 tablespoons soy sauce

**Instructions**

- Mix honey with some salt, soy sauce, black and white pepper and some lime juice in a tiny bowl, mix well, add pieces of meat, cover and refrigerate for at least 2 hours.
- Move the chicken to your fryer, cook on each side for about 6 minutes at around 370 F, and raise the fire to 400 F, and cook for another 3 minutes.
- Serve it warm. Enjoy!

Cal 256 | Protein 15.6g | Carb 28g | Fat 9.2g

## APPLE CHEDDAR STUFFED CHICKEN

*Prep time:10 min | Cook time::25 min | Serves: 2*

**Ingredients**

- 1 tablespoon fine bread crumbs
- 1/2 cup chicken broth
- chopped fresh parsley for serving
- 1 tablespoon butter
- 2 chicken breasts flattened to 1/4"
- 1/2 cup apple peeled and diced
- 1/4 cup shredded cheddar cheese

**Instructions**

- Preheat your air fryer to 350°F with the BAKE setting.
- Set aside the chicken after seasoning it with salt and pepper.
- Combine the bread crumbs apple, and cheese, in a small cup. Mix thoroughly.
- In the middle of the chicken breast, spread half of the apple mixture and roll it up. Toothpicks are used to keep everything together.
- Place the chicken in a pan and cook it. Pour in the chicken broth into the pan. Only enough to reach the bottom of the container. Cover the pan with tin foil or use our build a simple cover method. Cooking time is 20 minutes. Check the temperature. Cook, uncovered, until the internal temperature exceeds 165°F. Cook for another 10 minutes if necessary. The length of time depends on the thickness of the material.
- Remove from the air fryer and set aside for 5 minutes. Serve garnished with chopped new parsley.

Cal 379 | Protein 37.7g | Carb 12.3g | Fat 18.9g

## BACON RANCH CHICKEN BURGERS

*Prep time:5 min | Cook time:15 min | Serves: 4*

**Ingredients**

- 1/2 cup bread crumbs
- 1 tablespoon ranch seasoning
- 8 pieces' bacon pre-cooked
- salt and pepper
- 4 slices cheese
- 1/2 cup parmesan cheese shredded -
- 1-pound ground chicken

**Instructions**

- Preheat your air fryer to 390 F .
- In a mixing bowl, combine the ground chicken, bacon, bread crumbs, and seasoning. It's important to be firm. If necessary, add a little more bread crumbs before patties can be formed.
- Cook on the lowest rack for 5 minutes. Cook for another five minutes on the other side.
- The 165' test has been completed. If it isn't done yet, flip it and cook for a few minutes more.
- To make amazing sandwiches, gather buns, lettuce, more bacon honey mustard, and whatever else your heart desires.

Cal 571 | Carb 13g | Protein 39g | Fat 40g

## ROTISSERIE CHICKEN NUGGETS

*Prep time:10 min | Cook time:7 min | Serves: 6*

**Ingredients**

- 1 boneless skinless chicken breast cut into 1/2 inch chunks
- 1 egg
- 1/4 cup milk

- 1/4 teaspoon salt
- 1/8 teaspoon black pepper
- 1 cup Panko breadcrumbs
- 2 tablespoons grated Parmesan optional

**Instructions**

- In a single dish, whisk together the egg and the milk.
- Place Panko crumbs in another bowl, making sure it can hold a skewer. It works well with a paper plate.
- Season the chicken pieces with salt and pepper before placing them in the egg mixture.
- Remove the bits from the pan and skewer them. Then, when all of them are finished, dip them in the Panko mixture.
- Preheat the air fryer to 390°F.
- Attach the rotisserie tray and cook for 7 minutes once it has heated up. Check the temperature. The temperature should be about 165 F . If not, continue to cook for a few more minutes until golden brown.

Cal 85 | Carb 8g | Protein 7g | Fat 3g

## MALL STYLE BOURBON CHICKEN

*Prep time:10 min | Cook time:10 min | Serve:: 4*

**Ingredients**

- 4 ounces' soy sauce
- 1/2 teaspoon garlic powder
- 1/2 cup Jim Beam Bourbon Whiskey
- 1/2 cup brown sugar
- 2 tablespoons dried minced onion
- 1 teaspoon powdered ginger
- 1-pound chicken leg or thigh meat

**Instructions**

- Preheat your air fryer to 350°F using the BAKE setting.
- In a mixing bowl, combine powdered ginger, soy sauce, garlic powder, dried minced onion, brown sugar, garlic powder, and whiskey; pour over chicken pieces in pan. Second, double-check that the pan can fit inside your air fryer.
- Refrigerate for several hours or overnight, sealed. Cooking time is 20 minutes. Check the internal temperature, which should be about 165 F. If not, continue cooking for another 5 minutes until finished. If you want a thicker sauce, thicken with a pinch of corn starch.

Cal 208 | Carb 8g | Protein 15g | Fat 10g

## CHICKEN LEGS

*Prep time:10 min | Cook time:20 min | Serves:4*

**Ingredients**

- 1 teaspoon garlic powder
- 1 teaspoon paprika
- 1 teaspoon onion
- 2 tablespoon BBQ sauce
- 2 lbs chicken legs 6-8 drumsticks
- 1 tablespoon olive oil
- 1 teaspoon salt
- 1 teaspoon pepper

**Instructions**

- Drizzle olive oil and seasoning over drumsticks in a large mixing bowl. Toss to evenly coat.
- Place the basket in the air fryer with the chicken legs. Because loading the fryer when it's hot is difficult, I put these in before it heats up.

- Preheat your Air Fryer to 375 F .
- Cook for 5-10 minutes before checking the temperature. When the temperature reaches 165°F, turn off the air fryer. Allow the basket to cool for a few minutes.
- Remove the basket from the room. It'll still be hot, so be careful!
- Brush with a small amount of BBQ sauce before serving as an option.

Cal 209 | Carb 1g | Protein 14g | Fat 16g

## ROASTED THIGH

*Prep time: 5 min | Cook time: 30 min | Serves: 1*

### Ingredients
- 3 chicken thighs and thighs
- 2 red seasonal bags
- 1 clove garlic
- ½ tsp of salt
- 1 pinch of black pepper

### Directions
- Season chicken with red season, minced garlic, salt, and pepper. Leave to act for 5-10 minutes to obtain the flavor.
- Put the chicken in the basket of the air fryer and bake at 390°F for 20 minutes.
- After that time, remove the Air Fryer basket and check the chicken spot. If it is still raw or not golden enough, turn it over and leave it for another 10 minutes at 350°F.
- After the previous step, your chicken will be ready on the Air Fryer! Serve with doré potatoes and leaf salad.

Cal 278 | Carb 0.1g | Fat 18g | Protein 31g

## CRACKER CHICKEN STRIPS

*Prep time:10 min | Cooking: 5 min | Serves: 4*

### Ingredients
- ½ teaspoon garlic powder
- ½ teaspoon pepper
- ½ cup butter cut into pieces
- 1.5 pounds' boneless skinless chicken breast cut into strips
- 2 eggs
- ¼ cup milk
- 1 cup crushed butter crackers Ritz

### Instructions
- Preheat the Air Fryer to 375°F.
- Whisk the eggs and milk together in a shallow dish.
- Add the crushed crackers to a separate bowl. Garlic powder and pepper to taste.
- Each chicken strip should be dipped in the egg mixture before being dipped in the cracker mixture. To secure the chicken, press the cracker crumbs into it.

- Place each coated chicken strip in the baking dish that has been prepared. Place a slice of butter on top of each chicken strip.
- Bake for 30 to 40 minutes in the Air Fryer, or until chicken is cooked through and golden brown.

Cal 544 | Carb 11g | Protein 43g | Fat 36g

## CRISPY CRUNCHY CHICKEN TENDERS

*Prep time:5 min | Cook time:10 min | Serves: 4*

### Ingredients
- 1 teaspoon Paprika
- 1 teaspoon Salt
- 1/4 teaspoon Pepper
- 4 cups Bread Crumbs
- 3 Uncooked Chicken Breasts
- 1 Egg
- 2 tablespoon Milk

### Instructions
- Preheat your air fryer to 350 F on the AIR FRY setting.
- Chicken breasts should be cut into strips.
- In one mug, whisk together the milk and the egg.
- In a separate bowl, combine bread crumbs, paprika, salt, and pepper.
- Dredge the chicken strips in the egg mixture, then the bread crumbs
- Arrange one inch apart on the pan.
- Cook for ten minutes in the air, turning halfway through.
- Use a thermometer to check the temperature. Cook until the internal temperature reaches 165°F, then continue to cook for a few minutes longer until finished.

Cal 64 | Carb 79g | Protein 52g | Fat 11g

## WHOLE CHICKEN

*Prep time:10 min | Cook time: 60 min | Serves: 4*

### Ingredients
- 1 tablespoon salt and pepper
- 2 tablespoons olive oil
- 1 Whole Chicken
- 1 tablespoon paprika

### Instructions
- Don't wash the chicken, just pat it dry.
- Season and coat with olive oil. Incorporate into the oil
- Place the chicken in the basket after tying it up.
- Preheat the air fryer to 350 F; you can air fry or bake. Preheat the air fryer before adding the chicken. You don't want to get burnt!
- Cook for 60 minutes, or until the internal temperature reaches 165 F.

Cal 476 | Carb 1g | Protein 36g | Fat 36g

## SPICY PARMESAN WINGS

*Prep time:5 min | Cook time:15 min | Serves: 6*

### Ingredients
- 1 teaspoon lemon juice
- 1 teaspoon apple cider vinegar
- 1 teaspoon dried oregano
- 1 teaspoon dried basil
- salt and pepper to taste
- 2 lbs. Bone-in chicken wings
- 2 large cloves of garlic minced or pressed
- 2 tablespoons olive oil

- 1/2 cup mayonnaise
- 1 tablespoon honey
- 3 tablespoons grated parmesan cheese

**Instructions**

- Preheat the air fryer to 390°F on the air fry level, with the rack in the middle position if you aren't using the rotisserie.
- In a big mixing bowl, whisk together all of the ingredients except the chicken wings.
- Toss the wings in the bowl with the mixture and coat evenly.
- Place the wings on the racks for rack cooking. Cook for 5 minutes before rotating racks or flipping the pan. Cook for another 5 minutes and then switch back. Preheat air fryer to 165°F.
- Place the wings in the basket and place the basket in the air fryer for rotisserie cooking. Cook at 390°F in an air fryer. Check the temperature after 10 minutes by putting the thermometer into the basket. When you get to 1605', remove it.
- Serve immediately with dipping sauce.

Cal 791 | Carb 5g | Protein 43g | Fat 65g

## CHICKEN JALAPENO POPPER CASSEROLE
*Prep time:30 min | Cook time:20 min | Serves:* **6**

**Ingredients**

- Mozzarella cheese: 4 tbsp., shredded
- Shredded cheddar cheese: half cup
- 3 jalapenos
- Cream cheese: 1 ½ cups
- 6 slices of bacon
- Mayonnaise: ¼ cup
- Boneless chicken thighs, 2 lbs., no bones
- Hot sauce: ¼ cup
- Salt & black pepper, to taste

**Instructions**

- Let the Kalorik Air Fryer Oven preheat to 375 F.
- Season the chicken with salt and pepper, air fry for ten minutes. Take out in a casserole dish (remove skin).
- In a pan, add the rest of the ingredients with salt.
- Cook until mixed well and pour in a casserole dish.
- Add cheese on top.
- Air fry for 4 to 5 minutes, until warmed through and cheese melts.

Cal 457 | Fat 12.4 g | Protein 41 g | Carb 4g

## MISO CHICKEN
*Prep time:20 min | Cook time:20 min | Serves:2-3*

**Ingredients**

- Salt & pepper
- 2 chicken breasts with no skin & bones

**For the Miso sauce**

- Olive oil: 1 tsp.
- Minced ginger: ½ tbsp.
- Rice vinegar: ¼ cup
- 2 chopped garlic cloves
- 1 diced green onion
- Honey: 1 tbsp.
- Miso paste: 2 tbsp.
- Fish sauce: 1 tsp.

**Instructions**

- Let the air fry preheat to 350 F.
- Season chicken with salt and pepper, air fry for 7 to 8 minutes, flip halfway through.
- In a dish, add all the sauce's ingredients and mix.
- Pour over chicken, air fry for 8 to 10 minutes more until the internal temperature reaches 165 F.
- Serve right away.

Cal 304 | Fat 25 g | Protein 32 g | Carb 11 g

## ALMOND COATED CHICKEN TENDERS
*Prep time:20 min | Cook time:10 min | Serves:* **4**

**Ingredients**

- 1 lb. Chicken tenders
- Paprika: 1 tbsp.
- Almonds: 1½ cups
- Chili powder: 1 tbsp.
- Cumin powder: 1 tbsp.
- 2 whole eggs

**Instructions**

- Let the air fry preheat to 375 F.
- Add all ingredients, except for chicken and eggs in the food processor. Transfer to a bowl.
- In a bowl whisk the eggs.
- Dip chicken in eggs and then in the almond-spice bowl.
- Air fry for 8 to 10 minutes.
- Serve

Cal 258 | Fat 18 g | Protein 32 g | Carb 3.4 g

## ARTICHOKE CHICKEN
*Prep time:10 min | Cook time:20 min | Serves: 4*

**Ingredients**

- Quartered artichoke hearts: 2 (6 oz.) jars marinated with no liquid
- Chicken broth: 2 cups
- Mushrooms: 1 jar (~5 oz.), with no liquid
- Diced onion: half cup
- Dried rosemary: 1 to 1/2 tsp.
- 8 chicken breast, halved (skinless & boneless)
- Flour: 1/3 cup
- Salt & pepper

**Instructions**

- Season the chicken with salt and pepper, air fry at 375 F.
- Take out on a baking dish, add artichoke and mushrooms on top.
- In a pan, add the rest of the ingredients cook until reduced to half.
- Pour over chicken and air fry for 10-12 minutes at 35o F.
- Serve right away

Cal 269 | Fat 9.6 g | Protein 21 g | Carb 4 g

## PISTACHIO CHICKEN BREASTS
*Prep time:20 min | Cook time:20 min | Serves:* **4**

**Ingredients**

- 6 chicken breasts
- Lemon juice: ¼ cup plus 1 tbsp.
- Dijon mustard: half tbsp. (grainy)
- 1 garlic clove
- pistachios: 1 cup
- Oil: 2 tbsp.

**Instructions**

- Let the air fry preheat to 375 F.

- In a food processor, add garlic, mustard, ¼ cup of lemon juice, and pistachios. Pulse until smooth.
- Pound the chicken with a mallet, and spread the mixture on chicken.
- Roll and secure with tooth pick, season the rolls with salt, oil, lemon juice and pepper.
- Place in a dish, and air fry for 12 minutes, flip halfway through.

Cal 226 | Fat 11 g | Protein 27 g | Carb 5 g

## CHIPOTLE CHICKEN TINGA
*Prep time:15 min | Cook time:10 min | Serves: 4-6*

**Ingredients**
- 2 chopped garlic cloves
- Sweetener: 2 tbsp.
- Chipotle chili paste: 2-3 tbsp.
- 2 onions, sliced thin
- 6 chicken thighs, boneless, skinless
- Chopped tomatoes: 14 oz.

**Instructions**
- Season the chicken with salt. Air fry for 7-8 minutes at 375 F.
- In a pan, add the rest of the ingredients with ¼ cup of water. Cook until reduced.
- Pour over chicken and air fry for 7 to 8 minutes.
- Serve with rice.

Cal 166 | Fat 8.2 g | Protein 16 g | Carb 6 g

## PERUVIAN CHICKEN SOUP (AGUADITO)
*Prep time:6 min | Cook time:9 min | Serves: 8*

**Ingredients**
- 2 tablespoon oil
- 1/3 cup rice
- 1/2 cup peas
- 1 teaspoon cumin
- 1/2 teaspoon salt
- Black pepper
- 2 tablespoon lime juice
- 2 cups shredded chicken
- 1 onion chopped
- 1 large Poblano pepper chopped
- 4 garlic cloves chopped
- 1 Jalapeno pepper
- 1 1/2 cups hot water
- 5 1/2 cups chicken stock
- 2 carrots diced into small cubes
- 1 stalk celery cut into small Cubes
- 1 bunch fresh cilantro leaves
- 1 medium Yukon gold potato

**Instructions**
- Cook for 4 minutes, stirring regularly to avoid browning the onions, with the, jalapeno, Poblano pepper, garlic oil, onions and 2 halved green onions in the inner pot. Set aside in a food processor or blender's mixing bowl. In the inner pot, bring 1.2 cup (118ml) hot water to a boil. With a wooden spoon, scrape the pan's bottom clean. To cancel, press the Cancel button.
- Combine the chicken stock, the remaining water, the potatoes, carrots, celery, rice, peas, and cumin in the same jar. Cook for 5 minutes

Cal 290 | Fat18g | Carb19g | Protein16g

## JUICY CHICKEN BREAST
*Prep time:2 min | Cook time:20 min | Serves: 4*

**Ingredients**
- 4 chicken breasts raw, boneless skinless
- Dried oregano: half tsp.
- Salt: half tsp.
- Black pepper: 1/8 tsp.
- Garlic powder: half tsp.

**Instructions**
- In a bowl, add all spices and herbs.
- Oil spray the chicken and sprinkle the spice mixture and rub.
- Let the Kalorik Air Fryer Oven preheat to 360 F.
- Air fry the chicken for ten minutes.
- Flip halfway through, let it rest for five minutes, slice and serve.

Cal 185 | Carb 2g | Protein 22g | Fat 10g

## EVERYTHING BAGEL BBQ CHICKEN WINGS
*Prep time:3 min | Cook time:18 min | Serves: 6*

**Ingredients**
- 1 cup Water
- 1 cup Barbeque Sauce
- 1/2 teaspoon black pepper
- 3 teaspoon Everything Bagel spice divided
- 3 lbs chicken wings

**Instructions**
- Fill the inner pot halfway with water, then add the steam rack. Stack the wings on top of each other.
- Make sure the steam release handle is in the Sealing position before closing the lid. Click the Pressure Cook button and select a 5-minute cooking time.. Turn the steam release handle to the Venting place when the Cook time:is finished to easily release the pressure. Preheat the broiler in the air fryer. Close the lid and press Cancel.
- Place the wings on a baking sheet. Toss the chicken with the barbeque sauce and pepper to cover. Half of the All Bagel spice should be sprinkled on top. Place the pan in the top third of the air fryer, but not on the air fryer rack closest to the fire. 5 minutes under the broiler Broil for another 5 minutes, or until desired browning, after flipping the wings and adding the remaining All Bagel spice.

Cal 330 | Fat 24g | Carb 4g | Protein 24g

## CHICKEN POUTINE
*Prep time:10 min | Cook time: 50 min | Serves: 4*

**Ingredients**
- 2 lb potatoes cut into 1-inch wedges
- 1 cup shredded cooked chicken heated
- 1/2 cup shredded aged Cheddar cheese
- 1 cup cheese curds
- 1/4 cup crumbled blue cheese
- 1/3 cup Frank's Red Hot
- 1/4 teaspoon each salt and pepper
- 2 tablespoon canola oil
- 1/2 cup ranch dressing divided
- 2 cups carrot and celery sticks for serving

**Instructions**
- Sprinkle salt and pepper on the potato wedges.
- Fill the basket with potato wedges in two batches; do not overfill. Drizzle half of the oil over each batch.

- Air fry at 400°F for 22 to 24 minutes (turning basket halfway through cooking time), or until wedge fries are golden brown and cooked through, using the Air Fryer Lid
- In a serving bowl, arrange the potato wedges. Serve with chicken on top. Cheddar, cheese curds, and blue cheese are sprinkled on top. Drizzle with 2 tablespoon ranch dressing and buffalo wing sauce. Serve with carrot and celery sticks for dipping and the remaining ranch dressing.
- You can also make Buffalo Chicken Poutine in a small air fryer-safe baking dish. Place trivet on top of inner pot with sling. Broil for 2 to 3 minutes, or until cheese is golden and bubbling, using the Air Fryer Cap.

Cal 640 | Fat 39g | Carb 47g | Protein 27g

## EASY CHICKEN BREAST
*Prep time:1 min | Cook time:8 min | Serves: 4*

### Ingredients
- 5 chicken breasts
- 1 teaspoon pepper
- 1 cup water or chicken broth
- 1 teaspoon salt

### Instructions
- Season the chicken breasts with salt and pepper, as well as any other seasonings to taste.
- Fill the inner pot with water or chicken broth.
- Place the chicken breasts in a bowl of water or on a trivet.
- Choice 1: Fresh Chicken Press Pressure Cook/Manual and set for 8 minutes using the +/- keys. Set the steam release to "venting" for Fast Release once the Cook time:is over.
- If you want a crispier finish, use an Air Fryer Lid instead of the pressure cooker lid and cook for 1 minute, or sauté for 1 minute on each side.
- Choice 2: Shredded Chicken Press Pressure Cook/Manual and set the timer for 10 minutes using the +/- keys. Set the steam release to "venting" for Fast Release once the time is up. Drain the liquid and use forks to shred the chicken breasts.
- Option 3: Frozen Chicken Breast Press Pressure Cook/Manual and set the timer for 12 minutes using the +/- buttons. Set the steam release to "venting" for Fast Release once the Cook time:is over. If you want a crispier finish, use an Air Fryer Lid instead of the pressure cooker lid and cook for 1 minute, or sauté for 1 minute on each side.

Cal 284 | Carb 0g | Fat 6.2g | Protein 31g

## BRUSCHETTA CHICKEN
*Prep time:20 min | Cook time:20 min | Serves: 2*

### Ingredients
- Olive oil: 2 tbsp.
- Chopped Fresh basil: ⅓ cup
- Garlic powder: 2 tsp.
- 4 chicken breasts (boneless & skinless)
- Italian seasoning: 1 tsp.
- 4 chopped tomatoes
- Half red onion, diced
- 2 chopped garlic cloves
- Salt & pepper

### Instructions
- With salt, garlic powder, pepper, oil (1 tbsp.) and Italian seasoning, season the chicken.
- Air fry for 5 to 7 minutes at 375 F, or until cooked through.

- In a bowl, add the rest of the ingredients and mix well.
- Top the chicken with bruschetta mixture and serve with parmesan cheese on top.

Calories 325 | Fat 18 g | Protein 42 g | Carb 4 g

## ORANGE CHICKEN
*Prep time:10 min | Cook time:20 min | Serves: 4-6*

### Ingredients
- 2 lbs chicken tenders, cut into 4 pieces
- 1 tablespoon orange zest
- 1 cup orange juice
- 1/3 cup Hoisin Sauce
- 3 tablespoons white sugar
- 1/2 teaspoon salt
- 1/2 teaspoon pepper
- 1 1/2 tablespoon water
- 1 tablespoon cornstarch
- 3 medium carrots thinly sliced
- 3 minced garlic cloves

### Instructions
- In a pot, stir the carrots, garlic, zest, orange juice, hoisin sauce, sugar, salt, and pepper until the sugar dissolves and the mixture is uniform.
- air fry the chicken for 10 to 12 minutes at 375 F.
- In a small cup, whisk together the water and cornstarch until smooth.
- Add chicken and slurry to the pot, cook for 1 to 2 minutes
- Serve right away.

Cal 490 | Fat 23g | Carb51 g | Protein19g

## MAPLE MISO WINGS
*Prep time:10 min | Cook time: 60 min | Serves: 4*

### Ingredients
- 2 lb split chicken wings
- 2 tablespoon canola oi
- 1/4 cup maple syrup
- 2 tablespoons white miso paste
- 2 tablespoon sriracha hot sauce
- 2 cloves garlic minced
- 1/2 teaspoon salt
- 1/2 teaspoon pepper
- 1/4 cup all-purpose flour

### Instructions
- Season wings with salt and pepper, then roll in flour.
- Place them air-fryer basket. Fill the basket with wings in three batches; do not overfill. Drizzle one-third of the canola oil over each batch.
- Pick Air Fry at 400°F for 20 minutes
- Combine maple syrup, miso, hot sauce, and garlic in a mixing bowl. Toss hot wings with sauce in a big mixing bowl and serve right away.

Cal 390 | Fat 23g | Carb 24g | Protein 23g

## MOJO ROAST CHICKEN
*Prep time:4 hours | Cook time:45 min | Serves: 4*

### Ingredients
- 2 teaspoon ground cumin
- 1 small onion quartered
- 1/4 cup orange juice

- 1/4 cup lime juice
- 1/4 cup lemon juice
- 1/4 cup olive oil divided
- 1/2 Serrano chili pepper seeded and diced
- 1 tablespoon Dijon mustard
- 4 cloves garlic minced
- 2 cups chicken broth
- 2 teaspoons coarse salt
- 2 teaspoon dried oregano
- 2 teaspoon chili powder
- 1 teaspoon brown sugar
- 1 teaspoon pepper
- 1 whole chicken about 3 lbs
- 2 bay leaves

**Instructions**

- Combine cumin, salt, oregano, chili powder, brown sugar, and pepper in a mixing bowl; rub spice mixture all over the chicken and within the cavity. Place the chicken, bay leaves, and onion in a large resalable plastic bag.
- Combine orange juice, lime juice, lemon juice, 3 tablespoons oil, Serrano peppers, mustard, and garlic in a bag. Place the bag on a tray or in a bowl and seal it. Refrigerate for at least 4 hours or overnight in the refrigerator.
- Remove the chicken from the marinade and set aside. In the inner pot of the Air Fryer, position the chicken breast side down. Add the broth and the marinade that was set aside.
- Cook for 20 minutes on 375 F.

Cal 560 | Fat 38g | Carb 11g | Protein 45g

## CRISPY PARMESAN ROAST CHICKEN
*Prep time:10 min | Cook time:50 min | Serves: 6*

**Ingredients**

- 2 lemons small
- 6 rosemary sprigs
- 2 teaspoon red pepper flakes plus more for serving, optional
- 1 whole chicken about 3 pounds
- 1/3 cup parmesan finely grated
- 4 cups chicken stock
- 3 teaspoons kosher salt plus more to taste
- 3 teaspoons black pepper
- 2 teaspoons rosemary chopped

**Instruction**

- Finely grate 2 teaspoons lemon zest into a small cup.
- Combine 3 teaspoons salt, pepper, chopped rosemary, and red pepper flakes in a large mixing bowl (if using). Set aside the chicken after seasoning it both inside and out with the salt mixture. 2 rosemary springs should be stuffed into the cavity of the chicken.
- Place the chicken breast-side down in the air fryer, cook for 20 minutes, flip halfway through.

Cal 663 | Fats 50g | Carb 20g | Protein 30g

## FALL OFF THE BONE CHICKEN
*Prep time:5 min | Cook time: 70 min | Serves: 4*

**Ingredients**

- 1 tablespoon packed brown sugar
- 1 teaspoon freshly chopped thyme
- 1 whole small chicken
- kosher salt

- black pepper
- 1 tablespoon olive oil
- 2/3 cup low-sodium chicken broth
- 2 tablespoons freshly chopped parsley
- 1 tablespoon chili powder
- 1 tablespoon smoked paprika

**Instructions**

- Combine brown sugar, chili powder, paprika, and thyme in a small bowl.
- Dry the chicken with paper towels before seasoning liberally with salt and pepper. The brown sugar mixture should be rubbed all over the chicken.
- Air fry the chicken for 20 minutes at 375 F, flip halfway through.
- Sprinkle with parsley and serve immediately.

Cal 224 | Fat 7.0 g | Carb 1.1 g | Protein 39 g

## BREADED NUGGET IN DORITOS

*Prep time: 10 min | Cook time: 15 min | Serves: 4*

**Ingredients**

- ½ lb. boneless, skinless chicken breast
- ¼ lb. Doritos snack
- 1 cup of wheat flour
- 1 egg
- Salt, garlic and black pepper to taste.

**Directions**

- Cut the chicken breast in the width direction, 1 to 1.5 cm thick, so that it is already shaped like pips.
- Season with salt, garlic, black pepper to taste and some other seasonings if desired.
- You can also season with those seasonings or powdered onion soup.
- Put the Doritos snack in a food processor or blender and beat until everything is crumbled, but don't beat too much, you don't want flour.
- Now bread, passing the pieces of chicken breast first in the wheat flour, then in the beaten eggs and finally in the Doritos, without leaving the excess flour, eggs or Doritos.
- Place the seeds in the Air Fryer basket and program for 15 minutes at 400°F, and half the time they brown evenly.

Cal 42 | Carb 1.65g | Fat 1.44g | Protein 5.29g

## HASSEL BACK FAJITA CHICKEN
*Prep time:10 min | Cook time:14 min | Serves: 2*

**Ingredients**

- Cumin: half tsp.
- 2 chicken breasts, boneless & skinless
- Salt & pepper
- Mexican cheese: half cup, shredded
- Garlic powder: half tsp.

- Half red bell pepper, sliced thin
- Chipotle chili powder: half tsp.
- 1/4 red onion, sliced thin

**Instructions**
- Make 5-6 slits along with chicken, not all the way through.
- Season with salt and pepper.
- Add the rest of the spices to the chicken and rub them in the slits.
- Add onion and bell peppers in the slits.
- Let the Kalorik Air Fryer Oven preheat to 350 F.
- Oil spray the air fryer basket, air fry for 13 minutes.
- Add cheese on top, air fry for 1-2 minutes.
- Serve with fresh herbs on top.

Cal 250 | Fat 11g | Carb 5g | Protein 31g

## CHICKEN PAD THAI
*Prep time:5 min | Cook time: 25 min | Serves: 4*

**Ingredients**
- 8 oz. pad Thai noodle
- ¼ cup shallot
- ¾ cup pad Thai sauce
- 1 cup bean sprout
- ½ cup peanuts crushed
- ¼ cup green onion,
- ¼ cup fresh cilantro
- 2 tablespoons sesame oil, divided
- 2 eggs
- 1 chicken breast, diced

**Instructions**
- Cook the noodles according to the package instructions.
- Toss with 1 tablespoon of sesame oil and set aside.
- Add ½ teaspoon of sesame oil to a pot with the lightly beaten eggs. When the eggs are finished cooking, set aside.
- Pour the remaining ½ tablespoon of sesame oil into the pot
- Air fry the chicken for 8 to 10 minutes, add to the noodles.
- Add the shallots to the pot and cook until lightly browned and fragrant. Then, add the noodles, eggs, and chicken back into the pot.
- Pour in the pad Thai sauce and toss to coat.
- Top with the bean sprouts, crushed peanuts, green onions, and cilantro, and stir until well blended.
- Dish up and garnish with extra peanuts, green onions, and cilantro.

Cal 554 | Fat 21g | Carb 56g | Protein 36g

## REUBEN HASSEL BACK CHICKEN
*Prep time:5 min | Cook time:18 min | Serves: 2*

**Ingredients**
- Deli corned beef: 4 thin slices
- 2 chicken breasts, boneless & skinless
- Sauerkraut: half cup, moisture squeezed
- Salt & pepper
- Swiss cheese: 6 slices

**Sauce**
- Ketchup: 1 tbsp.
- Mayonnaise: ¼ cup
- Chopped cucumber: 1 tbsp.

**Instructions**

- Make 5-6 slits along with chicken, not all the way through.
- Season with salt and pepper.
- Add cheese and beef slices in the slits. Add sauerkraut on top of slits.
- Let the Kalorik Air Fryer Oven preheat to 350 F.
- Oil spray the basket of the air fryer, air fry for 18 minutes.
- In a bowl, mix all ingredients of the sauce. Pour over chicken and serve.

## QUICK MEATBALL PARMIGIANA
*Prep time:5 min | Cook time: 10 min | Serves: 4*

**Ingredients**
- 1 lb frozen prepared meatballs
- 1 1/2 cups tomato sauce
- 1/4 cup basil pesto
- 2 cups shredded mozzarella cheese
- 1/2 cup grated parmesan cheese

**Instructions**
- Air fry the meatballs for 7 to 9 minutes, at 375 F.
- In a pan, add the rest of the ingredients on medium flame.
- Add the air fried meatballs in the pan, cook for five minutes and serve.

Cal 660 | Fat 49g | Carb 19g | Protein 40g

## GREEK CHICKEN
*Prep time:5 min | Cook time:12 min | Serves: 2*

**Ingredients**
- 1 chicken breast, boneless & skinless
- Half bell pepper, chopped
- Dried parsley: half tsp.
- Half zucchini, chopped
- Half red onion, chopped
- Feta cheese: 2 tbsp.
- Dried oregano: 1 tsp.
- Olive oil: 1 1/2 tbsp.
- Garlic powder: half tsp.
- Dried thyme: ¼ tsp.
- salt and pepper

**Instructions**
- Slice the chicken into one" cubes.
- In a bowl, add vegetables and chicken.
- Add spices, olive oil and herbs.
- Toss to coat.
- Let the Kalorik Air Fryer Oven preheat to 380 F.
- Air fry for 12-15 minutes, shake the basket halfway through.
- Add feta cheese and serve.

Cal 234 | Fat 16g | Carb 7g | Protein 16g

## JALAPENO POPPER HASSEL BACK CHICKEN
*Prep time:10 min | Cook time:15 min | Serves: 2*

**Ingredients**
- Cooked bacon: 4 slices, crumbled
- 2 chicken breasts, boneless & skinless
- Pickled jalapenos: 1/4 cup, chopped
- Cream cheese: 2 oz., softened
- Shredded cheddar cheese: half cup

**Instructions**

- In a bowl, mix jalapenos, bacon, cheddar (1/4 cup) and cream cheese.
- Make six slits on top of the chicken, not all the way through.
- Add the cheddar mixture to the slits.
- Air fry the chicken for 15 minutes at 350 F.
- Add the rest of the cheese on top, air fry for 1 minute and serve.

Cal 530 | Fat 30g | Carb 2g | Protein 41g

## SRIRACHA-HONEY CHICKEN WINGS

*Prep time:10 min | Cook time:30 min | Serves: 2*

### Ingredients
- 1 pound of chicken wings
- Lime juice, as needed
- Sriracha sauce: 2 tbsp.
- Soy sauce: 1 1/2 tbsp.
- Honey: 1/4 cup
- Butter: 1 tbsp.

### Instructions
- Let the Kalorik Air Fryer Oven preheat to 360 F.
- Air fry wings for 25-30 minutes, flip after every 7 minutes.
- In a pan, add the rest of the ingredients, boil for three minutes.
- Add cooked wings, toss and serve.

Cal 78 | Carb 21 g | Protein 23 g | Fat 8 g

## TURKEY BREAST TENDERLOIN

*Prep time:5 min | Cook time:25 min | Serves: 3-4*

### Ingredients
- 1 turkey breast tenderloin
- Pink salt: half tsp.
- Paprika: half tsp.
- Black pepper, to taste
- Sage: half tsp.
- Dry Thyme: half tsp.
- Instructions
- Let the Kalorik Air Fryer Oven preheat to 350 F.
- In a bowl, mix all spices. Coat turkey well in the spice blend.
- Oil spray the air fryer basket. Cook turkey for 25 minutes, flip halfway through and serve.

Cal 62 | Carb 1g | Protein 14g | Fat 1g

## BAGEL CHICKEN TENDERS

*Prep time:10 min | Cook time:15 min | Serves: 2-3*

### Ingredients
- 2 whole eggs
- Dry panko: ¾ cup
- 4 chicken breasts, cut into wide strips
- Salt & pepper
- Bagel Seasoning: 4 tbsp.

### Instructions
- Let the air fry preheat to 375 F.
- In a dish, add all spices and mix. In a bowl, whisk eggs.
- In a dish, add the bagel seasoning.
- Coat the chicken strips in spices, then in egg and lastly in bagel seasonings.
- Air fry for 11-12 minutes, flip halfway through.

Cal 112 | Carb 4 g | Protein 17 g | Fat 3 g

## BBQ CHICKEN BREASTS

*Prep time: 5 min | Cook time: 15 min | Serves: 4*

### Ingredients
- Boneless, skinless chicken breast – 4, about 6 oz. each
- BBQ seasoning – 2 tbsps.
- Cooking spray

### Directions
- Rub the chicken with BBQ seasoning and marinate in the refrigerator for 45 minutes. Preheat the air fryer at 400°F. Grease the basket with oil and place the chicken.
- Then spray oil on top. Cook for 13 to 14 minutes. Flipping at the halfway mark. Serve.

Cal 131 | Carb 2g | Fat 3g | Protein 24g

## ROTISSERIE CHICKEN

*Prep time: 5 min | Cook time: 1 hour | Serves: 4*

### Ingredients
- Whole chicken – 1, cleaned and patted dry
- Olive oil – 2 tbsps.
- Seasoned salt – 1 tbsp.

### Directions
- Remove the giblet packet from the cavity. Rub the chicken with oil and salt. Place in the air fryer basket, breast-side down. Cook at 350°F for 30 minutes.
- Then flip and cook another 30 minutes. Chicken is done when it reaches 165°F.

Cal 534 | Carb 0g | Fat 36g | Protein 35g

## HONEY-MUSTARD CHICKEN BREASTS

*Prep time: 5 min | Cook time: 25 min | Serves: 6*

### Ingredients
- Boneless, skinless chicken breasts – 6 (6-oz, each)
- Fresh rosemary – 2 tbsps. minced
- Honey – 3 tbsps.
- Dijon mustard – 1 tbsp.
- Salt and pepper to taste

### Directions
- Combine the mustard, honey, pepper, rosemary and salt in a bowl. Rub the chicken with this mixture.
- Grease the air fryer basket with oil. Air fry the chicken at 350°F for 20 to 24 minutes or until the chicken reaches 165°F. Serve.

Cal 236 | Carb 9.8g | Fat 5g | Protein 38g

## CHICKEN PARMESAN WINGS

*Prep time: 5 min | Cook time: 15 min | Serves: 4*

### Ingredients
- Chicken wings – 2 lbs. cut into drumettes, pat dried
- Parmesan – ½ cup, plus 6 tbsps. grated
- Herbs de Provence – 1 tsp.
- Paprika – 1 tsp.
- Salt to taste

### Directions
- Combine the parmesan, herbs, paprika, and salt in a bowl and rub the chicken with this mixture. Preheat the air fryer at 350°F.
- Grease the basket with cooking spray. Cook for 15 minutes. Flip once at the halfway mark. Garnish with parmesan and serve.

Cal 490 | Carb 1g | Fat 22g | Protein 72g

## AIR FRYER CHICKEN

*Prep time: 5 min | Cook time: 30 min | Serves: 4*

**Ingredients**

- Chicken wings – 2 lbs.
- Salt and pepper to taste
- Cooking spray

**Directions**

- Flavor the chicken wings with salt and pepper. Grease the air fryer basket with cooking spray. Add chicken wings and cook at 400°F for 35 minutes.
- Flip 3 times during cooking for even cooking. Serve.

Cal 277 | Carb 1g | Fat 8g | Protein 50g

## CREAMY COCONUT CHICKEN

*Prep time: 5 min | Cook time: 20 min | Serves: 4*

**Ingredients**

- Big chicken legs – 4
- Turmeric powder – 5 tsps.
- Ginger – 2 tbsps. grated
- Salt and black pepper to taste
- Coconut cream – 4 tbsps.

**Directions**

- In a bowl, mix salt, pepper, ginger, turmeric, and cream. Whisk. Add chicken pieces, coat and marinate for 2 hours.
- Transfer chicken to the preheated air fryer and cook at 370°F for 25 minutes. Serve.

Cal 300 | Carb 22g | Fat 4g | Protein 20g

## TERIYAKI WINGS

*Prep time: 5 min | Cook time: 20 min | Serves: 4*

**Ingredients**

- Chicken wings – 2 pounds
- Teriyaki sauce – ½ cup
- Minced garlic – 2 tsp.
- Ground ginger - ¼ tsp.
- Baking powder – 2 tsp.

**Directions**

- Except for the baking powder, place all ingredients in a bowl and marinate for 1 hour in the refrigerator. Place wings into your air fryer oven basket and sprinkle with baking powder.
- Gently rub into wings. Cook at 400°F for 25 minutes. Shake the basket two- or three-times during cooking. Serve.

Cal 446 | Carb 3.1g | Fat 29.8g | Protein 41.8g

## LEMONY DRUMSTICKS

*Prep time: 5 min | Cook time: 20 min | Serves: 2*

**Ingredients**

- Baking powder – 2 tsps.
- Garlic powder – ½ tsp.
- Chicken drumsticks – 8
- Salted butter – 4 tbsps. melted
- Lemon pepper seasoning – 1 tbsp.

**Directions**

- Sprinkle garlic powder and baking powder over drumsticks and rub into chicken skin. Place drumsticks into your air fryer oven basket. Cook at 375°F for 25 minutes. Flip the drumsticks once halfway through the Cooking Time.
- Remove when cooked. Mix seasoning and butter in a bowl. Add drumsticks to the bowl and toss to coat. Serve.

Cal 532 | Carb 1.2g | Fat 32.3g | Protein 48.3g

## PARMESAN CHICKEN TENDERS

*Prep time: 5 min | Cook time: 10 min | Serves: 4*

**Ingredients**

- 1 pound chicken tenderloins
- 3 large egg whites
- ½ cup Italian-style bread crumbs
- ¼ cup grated Parmesan cheese

**Directions**

- Preparing the Ingredients. Spray the air fryer basket with olive oil. Trim off any white fat from the chicken tenders. In a bowl, whisk the egg whites until frothy. In a separate small mixing bowl, combine the bread crumbs and Parmesan cheese. Mix well.
- Dip the chicken tenders into the egg mixture, then into the Parmesan and bread crumbs. Shake off any excess breading. Place the chicken tenders in the greased air fryer basket in a single layer. Generously spray the chicken with olive oil to avoid powdery, uncooked breading.
- Set the temperature of your Air Fryer to 370°F. Set the timer and bake for 4 minutes. Using tongs, flip the chicken tenders and bake for 4 minutes more. Check that the chicken has reached an internal temperature of 165°F. Add Cooking Time if needed. Once the chicken is fully cooked, plate, serve, and enjoy.

Cal 210 | Fat 4g | Carb 10g | Fiber 1g | Sugar 1g | Protein 33g

## EASY LEMON CHICKEN THIGHS

*Prep time: 5 min | Cook time: 10 min | Serves: 4*

**Ingredients**

- Salt and black pepper to taste
- 2 tablespoons olive oil
- 2 tablespoons Italian seasoning
- 2 tablespoons freshly squeezed lemon juice
- 1 lemon, sliced

**Directions**

- Place the chicken thighs in a medium mixing bowl and season them with the salt and pepper. Add the olive oil, Italian seasoning, and lemon juice and toss until the chicken thighs are thoroughly coated with oil. Add the sliced lemons. Place the chicken thighs into your air fryer oven basket in a single layer.
- Set the temperature of your Air Fryer to 350°F. Set the timer and cook for 10 minutes. Using tongs, flip the chicken. Reset the timer and cook for 10 minutes more. Check that the chicken has reached an internal temperature of 165°F. Add Cooking Time if needed.
- Once the chicken is fully cooked, plate, serve, and enjoy.

Cal 325 | Carb 1g | Fat 26g | Protein 20g

## CRISPY AIR FRYER BUTTER CHICKEN

*Prep time: 5 min | Cook time: 15 min | Serves: 4*

**Ingredients**

- 2 (8-ounce) boneless, skinless chicken breasts
- 1 sleeve Ritz crackers
- 4 tablespoons (½ stick) cold unsalted butter, cut into 1-tablespoon slices

**Directions**

- Preparing the Ingredients. Spray the air fryer basket with olive oil, or spray an air fryer–size baking sheet with olive oil or cooking spray.

- Dip the chicken breasts in water. Put the crackers in a resealable plastic bag. Using a mallet or your hands, crush the crackers. Place the chicken breasts inside the bag one at a time and coat them with the cracker crumbs.
- Place the chicken in the greased air fryer basket, or on the greased baking sheet set into your air fryer oven basket. Put 1 to 2 dabs of butter onto each piece of chicken.
- Set the temperature of your Air Fryer to 370°F. Set the timer and bake for 7 minutes.
- Using tongs, flip the chicken. Spray the chicken generously with olive oil to avoid uncooked breading. Reset the timer and bake for 7 minutes more.
- Check that the chicken has reached an internal temperature of 165°F. Add Cooking Time if needed. Using tongs, remove the chicken from the air fryer and serve.

Cal 750 | Fat 40g | Carb 38g | Protein 57g

## LIGHT AND AIRY BREADED CHICKEN BREASTS

*Prep time: 5 min | Cook time: 15 min | Serves: 2*

**Ingredients**

- 2 large eggs
- 1 cup bread crumbs or panko bread crumbs
- 1 teaspoon Italian seasoning
- 4 to 5 tablespoons vegetable oil
- 2 boneless, skinless, chicken breasts

**Directions**

- Preparing the Ingredients. Preheat the air fryer to 370°F. Spray the air fryer basket with olive oil or cooking spray. In a small bowl, whisk the eggs until frothy. In a separate small mixing bowl, mix together the bread crumbs, Italian seasoning, and oil. Dip the chicken in the egg mixture, then in the bread crumb mixture. Place the chicken directly into the greased air fryer basket, or on the greased baking sheet set into the basket.
- Air Frying. Spray the chicken generously and thoroughly with olive oil to avoid powdery, uncooked breading. Set the timer and fry for 7 minutes. Using tongs, flip the chicken and generously spray it with olive oil. Reset the timer and fry for 7 minutes more. Check that the chicken has reached an internal temperature of 165°F. Add Cooking Time if needed. Once the chicken is fully cooked, use tongs to remove it from the air fryer and serve.

Cal 833 | Fat 46g | Carb 40g | Protein 65g

## CHICKEN MEATBALLS

*Prep time: 5 min | Cook time: 15 min | Serves: 2*

**Ingredients**

- ½ lb chicken breast
- 1 tbsp of garlic
- 1 tbsp of onion

- ½ chicken broth
- 1 tbsp of oatmeal, whole wheat flour or of your choice

**Directions**

- Place all of the ingredients in a food processor and beat well until well mixed and ground.
- If you don't have a food processor, ask the butcher to grind it and then add the other ingredients, mixing well.
- Make balls and place them in the Air Fryer basket.
- Program the Air Fryer for 15 minutes at 400°F.
- Half the time shake the basket so that the meatballs loosen and fry evenly.

Cal 45 | Carb 1.94g | Fat 1.57g | Protein 5.43g

## CHICKEN FILLETS, BRIE & HAM

*Prep time: 5 min | Cook time: 15 min | Serves: 4*

**Ingredients**

- 2 Large Chicken Fillets
- Freshly Ground Black Pepper
- 4 Small Slices of Brie (Or your cheese of choice)
- 1 Tbsp Freshly Chopped Chives
- 4 Slices Cured Ham

**Directions**

- Preparing the Ingredients. Slice the fillets into four and make incisions as you would for a hamburger bun. Leave a little "hinge" uncut at the back. Season the inside and pop some brie and chives in there. Close them, and wrap them each in a slice of ham. Brush with oil and pop them into the basket.
- Heat your fryer to 350°F. Roast the little parcels until they look tasty (15 min)

Cal 850 | Carb 43g | Fat 50g | Protein 76 g

## AIR FRYER CORNISH HEN

*Prep time: 5 min | Cook time: 30 min | Serves: 2*

**Ingredients**

- 2 tablespoons Montreal chicken seasoning
- 1 (1½- to 2-pound) Cornish hen

**Directions**

- Preheat the air fryer to 390°F. Rub the seasoning over the chicken, coating it thoroughly.
- Put the chicken in the basket. Set the timer and roast for 15 minutes.
- Flip the chicken and cook for another 15 minutes. Check that the chicken has reached an internal temperature of 165°F. Add Cooking Time if needed.

Cal 520 | Fat 36g | Carb 0g | Protein 45g

## AIR FRIED TURKEY WINGS

*Prep time: 5 min | Cook time: 26 min | Serves: 4*

**Ingredients**

- 2 pounds turkey wings
- 3 tablespoons olive oil or sesame oil
- 3 to 4 tablespoons chicken rub

**Directions**

- Put the turkey wings in a large mixing bowl. Pour the olive oil into the bowl and add the rub. Using your hands, rub the oil mixture over the turkey wings. Place the turkey wings in the air fryer basket.
- Fix the temperature of your Air Fryer to 380°F. Set the timer and roast for 13 minutes.

- Using tongs, flip the wings. Reset the timer and roast for 13 minutes more. Remove the turkey wings from the air fryer, plate, and serve.

Cal 521 | Fat 34g | Carb 4g | Protein 52g

## CAESAR MARINATED GRILLED CHICKEN

*Prep time: 10 min | Cook time: 25 min | Serves: 4*

**Ingredients**

- ¼ cup crouton
- 1 teaspoon lemon zest. Form into ovals, skewer and grill.
- 1/2 cup Parmesan
- 1/4 cup breadcrumbs
- 1-pound ground chicken
- 2 tablespoons Caesar dressing and more for drizzling
- 2-4 romaine leaves

**Directions**

- In a shallow dish, mix well chicken, 2 tablespoons Caesar dressing, parmesan, and breadcrumbs. Mix well with hands. Form into 1-inch oval patties. Thread chicken pieces in skewers. Place on skewer rack in air fryer.
- For 12 minutes, cook on 360°F. Halfway through Cooking Time, turnover skewers. If needed, cook in batches. Serve on a bed of lettuce and sprinkle with croutons and extra dressing.

Cal 342 | Fat 12g | Carb 8g | Protein 36g

## MUSTARD CHICKEN TENDERS

*Prep time: 5 min | Cook time: 20 min | Serves: 4*

**Ingredients**

- ½ C. coconut flour
- 1 tbsp. spicy brown mustard
- 2 beaten eggs
- 1 pound of chicken tenders

**Directions**

- Season tenders with pepper and salt.
- Place a thin layer of mustard onto tenders and then dredge in flour and dip in egg.
- Add to your air fryer oven, set temperature to 390°F, and set time to 20 minutes.

Cal 346 | Fat 10g | Carb 12g | Protein 31g

## CHEESY CHICKEN TENDERS

*Prep time: 10 min | Cook time: 30 min | Serves: 4*

**Ingredients**

- 1 large white meat chicken breast
- 1 cup of breadcrumbs
- 2 medium-sized eggs
- Pinch of salt and pepper
- 1 tablespoon of grated or powdered parmesan cheese

**Directions**

- Cover the basket of the Air fryer with a layer of tin foil, leaving the edges open to allow air to flow through the basket.
- Preheat the air fryer to 350°F.
- In a bowl, whisk the eggs until fluffy and until the yolks and whites are fully combined, and set aside. In a separate bowl, mixt he breadcrumbs, parmesan, salt and pepper, and set aside. One by one, dip each piece of raw chicken into the bowl with dry ingredients, coating all sides; then submerge into the bowl with wet ingredients, then dip again into the dry ingredients. Put the coated chicken pieces on the foil covering the Air fryer basket, in a single flat layer.
- Set the air fryer timer for 15 minutes.
- After 15 minutes, the air fryer will turn off and the chicken should be mid-way cooked and the breaded coating starting to brown. Flip each piece of chicken over to ensure a full all over fry.
- Reset the air fryer to 320°F for another 15 minutes. After 15 minutes, when the air fryer shuts off, remove the fried chicken strips using tongs and set on a serving plate. Eat once cool enough to handle, and enjoy.

Cal 278 | Fat 15g | Protein 29g | Sugar 7g

## MINTY CHICKEN-FRIED PORK CHOPS

*Prep time: 10 min | Cook time: 30 min | Serves: 4*

**Ingredients**

- 4medium-sized pork chops
- 1 cup of breadcrumbs
- 2 medium-sized eggs
- Pinch of salt and pepper
- ½ tablespoon of mint, either dried and ground; or fresh, rinsed, and finely chopped

**Directions**

- Preparing the Ingredients. Cover the basket of the Air fryer with a layer of tin foil, leaving the edges open to allow air to flow through the basket.
- Preheat the air fryer to 350°F. In a mixing bowl, whisk the eggs until fluffy and until the yolks and whites are fully combined, and set aside. In a separate bowl, mix the breadcrumbs, mint, salt and pepper, and set aside.
- One by one, dip each raw pork chop into the bowl with dry ingredients, coating all sides; then submerge into the bowl with wet ingredients, then dip again into the dry ingredients. Lay the coated pork chops on the foil covering the Air fryer basket, in a single flat layer.
- Set the air fryer timer for 15 minutes.
- After 15 minutes, the Air fryer will turn off and the pork should be mid-way cooked and the breaded coating starting to brown. Using tongs, turn each piece of steak over to ensure a full all-over fry.
- Reset the air fryer to 320°F for 15 minutes. After 15 minutes remove the fried pork chops using tongs and set on a serving plate.

Cal 262 | Fat 17g | Carb 7g | Protein 32g

## BACON LOVERS' STUFFED CHICKEN

*Prep time: 10 min | Cook time: 20 min | Serves: 4*

**Ingredients**

- 4 (5-ounce) boneless, skinless chicken breasts, sliced into ¼ inch thick
- 2 packages Boursin cheese
- 8 slices thin-cut bacon or beef bacon
- Sprig of fresh cilantro, for garnish

**Directions**

- Preparing the Ingredients. Spray the air fryer basket with avocado oil.
- Preheat the air fryer to 400°F. Put one of the chicken breasts on a cutting board. With a sharp knife held parallel to the cutting board, make a 1-inch-wide incision at the top of the breast.

- Carefully cut into the breast to form a large pocket, leaving a ½-inch border along the sides and bottom. Repeat with the other 3 chicken breasts. Snip the corner of a large resealable plastic bag to form a ¾-inch hole. Place the Boursin cheese in the bag and pipe the cheese into the pockets in the chicken breasts, dividing the cheese evenly among them. Wrap 2 slices of bacon around each chicken breast and secure the ends with toothpicks.
- Air Frying. Place the bacon-wrapped chicken in the air fryer basket and cook until the bacon is crisp and the chicken's internal temperature reaches 165°F, about 18 to 20 minutes, flipping after 10 minutes.
- Garnish with a sprig of cilantro before serving, if desired.

Cal 446 | Fat 17g | Carb 13g | Protein 36g

## AIR FRYER TURKEY BREAST

*Prep time: 5 min | Cook time: 60 min | Serves: 6*

### Ingredients

- Pepper and salt
- 1 oven-ready turkey breast
- Turkey seasonings of choice

### Directions

- Preheat the air fryer to 350°F.
- Season turkey with pepper, salt, and other desired seasonings.
- Place turkey in air fryer basket.
- Set temperature to 350°F, and set time to 60 minutes. Cook 60 minutes. The meat should be at 165°F when done. Allow to rest 10-15 minutes before slicing. Enjoy.

Cal 212 | Fat 12g | Protein 24g | Sugar0g

## BREADED CHICKEN WITHOUT FLOUR

*Prep time: 10 min | Cook time: 15 min | Serves: 6*

### Ingredients

- 1 1/6 oz. of grated parmesan cheese
- 1 unit of egg
- 1 lb of chicken (breast)
- Salt and black pepper to taste

### Directions

- Cut the chicken breast into 6 fillets and season with a little salt and pepper.
- Beat the egg in a bowl.
- Pass the chicken breast in the egg and then in the grated cheese, sprinkling the fillets.
- Non-stick and put in the air fryer at 400°F for about 30 minutes or until golden brown.

Cal 114 | Carb 13g | Fat 5.9g | Protein 2.3g | Sugar 3.2g

## DUCK THIGHS

*Prep time: 5 min | Cook time: 50 min | Serves: 4*

### Ingredients

- 2pcs. Duck legs
- 1 tsp salt
- 1 tsp spice mixture (for ducks and geese)
- 1 tsp olive oil

### Directions

- For the duck legs of the Air fryer the duck leg wash and pat dry. Mix the oil with the salt and the spice mixture and rub the duck legs around with it.

- Place the spiced duck legs on the rack of the hot air fryer and cook at 390°F in 40 minutes. After 20 minutes, turn the legs once. Enjoy!

## CHICKEN BREAST

*Prep time: 30 min | Cook time: 25 min | Serves: 6*

### Ingredients

- 1 lb. diced clean chicken breast
- ½ lemon
- Smoked paprika to taste
- Black pepper or chili powder, to taste
- Salt to taste

### Directions

- Flavor the chicken with salt, paprika and pepper and marinate.
- Store in Air fryer and turn on for 15 minutes at 350°F.
- Turn the chicken over and raise the temperature to 390°F, and turn the Air Fryer on for another 5 minutes or until golden. Serve immediately.

Cal 124 | Carb 0g | Fat 1.4g | Protein 26.1g | Sugar 0g

## COXINHA FIT

*Prep time: 10 min | Cook time: 10-15 min | Serves: 4*

### Ingredients

- ½ lb. seasoned and minced chicken
- 1 cup light cottage cheese
- 1 egg
- Condiments to taste
- Flaxseed or oatmeal

### Directions

- In a bowl, mix all of the ingredients together except flour.
- Knead well with your hands and mold into coxinha format.
- If you prefer you can fill it, add chicken or cheese.
- Repeat the process until all the dough is gone.
- Pass the drumsticks in the flour and put them in the fryer.
- Bake for 10 to 15 minutes at 390°F or until golden. Enjoy!

Cal 220 | Carb 40g | Fat 18g | Protein 100g | Sugar 5g

## SPICED CHICKEN WINGS IN AIR FRYER

*Prep time: 15 min | Cook time: 30 min | Serves: 4*

### Ingredients

- 1 kg chicken wings
- Salt
- Ground pepper
- Extra virgin olive oil
- Spices, I put roasted chicken or roast chicken spices.

### Directions

- Clean the wings and chop, throw the tip and place in a bowl the other two parts of the wings that have more meat.
- Season and add some extra virgin olive oil threads.
- Sprinkle with spices
- Flirt well and leave for 30 minutes to rest in the refrigerator.
- Put the wings in the basket of the Air fryer and select 360°F, about 30 minutes. From 20 minutes, check if you have to remove them before.
- From time to time, shake the basket so that the wings move and are made all over their faces. Serve and enjoy!

Cal 170 | Fat 6g | Carb 8g | Protein 15g

## CHICKEN IN BEER

*Prep time: 5 min | Cook time: 10 min | Serves: 4*

**Ingredients**

- 2 ¼ lbs chicken thigh and thigh
- ½ can of beer
- 4 cloves of garlic
- 1 large onion
- Pepper and salt to taste

**Directions**

- Wash the chicken pieces and, if desired, remove the skin to be healthier.
- Place on an ovenproof plate.
- In the blender, beat the other ingredients: beer, onion, garlic, and add salt and pepper, all together.
- Cover the chicken with this mixture; it has to stay like swimming in the beer.
- Take to the preheated air fryer at 390°F for 45 minutes.
- It will roast when it has a brown cone on top and the beer has dried a bit.

Cal 674 | Carb 5.47g | Fat 41.94g | Protein 61.94g

## ROLLED TURKEY BREAST

*Prep time: 5 min | Cook time: 10 min | Serves: 4*

**Ingredients**

- 1 box of cherry tomatoes
- ¼ lb. turkey blanket

**Directions**

- Wrap the turkey and blanket in the tomatoes, close with the help of toothpicks.
- Take to Air Fryer for 10 minutes at 390°F.
- You can increase the filling with ricotta and other preferred light ingredients.

Cal 172 | Carb 3g | Fat 2g | Protein 34g | Sugar 1g

## CRISPY OLD BAY CHICKEN WINGS

*Prep time: 10 min | Cook time: 15 min | Serves: 4*

**Ingredients**

- Olive oil
- 2 tablespoons Old Bay seasoning
- 2 teaspoons baking powder
- 2 teaspoons salt
- 2 pounds chicken wings

**Directions**

- Spray a fryer basket lightly with olive oil.
- In a big resealable bag, combine together the Old Bay seasoning, baking powder, and salt.
- Pat the wings dry with paper towels.
- Place the wings in the zip-top bag, seal, and toss with the seasoning mixture until evenly coated.
- Place the seasoned wings in the fryer basket in a single layer. Lightly spray with olive oil.
- Air fry for 7 minutes. Turn the wings over, lightly spray them with olive oil, and air fry until the wings are crispy and lightly browned, 5 to 8 more minutes. Using a meat thermometer, check to make sure the internal temperature is 165°F or higher.

Cal 501 | Fat 36g | Carb 1g | Protein 42g

## CHICKEN WINGS WITH PROVENCAL HERBS

*Prep time: 15 min | Cook time: 20 min | Serves: 4*

**Ingredients**

- 1kg chicken wings
- Provencal herbs
- Extra virgin olive oil
- Salt
- Ground pepper

**Directions**

- Put the chicken wings in a bowl, clean and chopped.
- Add a few threads of oil, salt, ground pepper and sprinkle with Provencal herbs.
- Linked well and let macerate 15 minutes.
- Take to the preheated air fryer at 360°F for 20 minutes.
- From time to time, remove so that they are done on all their faces.
- If see that they have been little golden, put a few more minutes.
- Serve and enjoy!

Cal 160 | Fat 6g | Carb 8g| Protein 13g

# MEAT RECIPES

## BEEF EMPANADAS
*Prep time:20 min | Cook time:15 min | Serves: 15*

### Ingredients
- Puff pastry, as needed
- Egg wash

**Filling**
- olive oil: 1 tbsp.
- 2 minced garlic cloves
- 1 yellow onion, diced
- Cumin: 1 tsp.
- Ground beef: 1 lb.
- Salt & black pepper, to taste
- Tomato paste: 1 tbsp.
- Monterey jack: 1 1/4 cup, shredded
- Oregano: 1 tsp.
- Paprika: half tsp.
- Shredded cheddar: 1 1/4 cup
- Pickled jalapeños: half cup, chopped
- Tomatoes: half cup, chopped

### Instructions
- In a pan, sauté onion in oil for five minutes, add garlic and cook for 1 minute.
- Add beef and cook for five minutes, drain any liquids.
- Add tomato paste, cook for 1 minute. Add the rest of the ingredients, except for cheese, cook for 3 to 4 minutes.
- Turn off the heat and let it cool
- Cut the dough into 4.5 inches of circles, with a cookie cutter
- Add 2 tbsp. of beef mixture and cheese on the dough circles. Fold the circle in half, seal the edges with water.
- Brush the empanadas with egg wash.
- Air fry for 10 minutes.
- Serve with sour cream.

## SWEET & SOUR PORK
*Prep time:25 min | Cook time:20 min | Serves: 5-6*

### Ingredients
- Crushed pineapple unsweetened: half cup, with liquid
- Cider vinegar: half cup
- Packed dark brown sugar: 1/4 cup
- 1 3/4 pound, pork tenderloin, cut in half
- Ketchup: 1/4 cup
- Sugar: 1/4 cup
- Soy sauce: 1 tbsp.
- Dijon mustard: 1 1/2 tsp.
- Garlic powder: half tsp.
- Salt & Pepper: 1/8 tsp. each

### Instructions
- In a saucepan, add all ingredients except for the pork. Let it come to a boil, turn the heat to a low simmer for 6 to 8 minutes.
- Let the Kalorik Air Fryer Oven preheat to 350 F.
- Season the pork with salt and pepper. Oil spray the pork and air fry for 7 to 8 minutes.
- Flip, add 2 tbsp. of sauce over pork cook for 10 to 12 minutes, until the internal temperature reaches 145 F.

- Rest it for five minutes, slice and serve with sauce.

Cal 502 | Fat 7g | Carb 72g | Protein 35g

## SEASONED PORK CHOPS

*Prep time: 10 min | Cook time: 12 min | Serves: 4*

### Ingredients
- 4 (6-ounce) boneless pork chops
- 2 tablespoons pork rub
- 1 tablespoon olive oil

### Directions
- Coat both sides of the pork chops with the oil and then, rub with the pork rub.
- Place the pork chops onto the lightly greased cooking tray.
- Arrange the drip pan in the bottom of Air Fryer Oven cooking chamber.
- Take to the preheated air fryer at 400°F for 12 minutes in the center position.
- After 6 minutes turn the pork chops.
- When cooking time is complete, remove the tray from Air Fryer and serve hot.

Cal 285 | Fat 9.5g | Carb 1.5 g | Fiber 0 g| Sugar 0.8g | Protein 44.5 g

## SPICY CHEESEBURGER
*Prep time:10 min | Cook time:30 min | Serves: 4*

### Ingredients
- Ground beef: 1 lb.
- Salt & black pepper, to taste
- 2 minced garlic cloves
- 4 hamburger buns
- Soy sauce: 1 tbsp.
- American cheese, 4 slices

### Instructions
- In a bowl, add beef, soy sauce and garlic, mix and make into 4 patties.
- Season with salt and pepper.
- Let the Kalorik Air Fryer Oven preheat to 375 F.
- Air fry for four minutes on each side.
- Serve in buns with cheese and other desired toppings.

## TACO TWISTS
*Prep time:15 min | Cook time:25 min | Serves: 4*

### Ingredients
- Ground beef: 1/3 pound
- Hot pepper sauce: 1/4 tsp.
- Shredded cheddar cheese: 2/3 cup
- Salsa: 1/3 cup
- Crescent rolls: 8 oz.
- 1 onion, diced

126

- Canned green chilies: 3 tbsp., chopped
- Garlic powder: 1/4tsp.
- Salt: 1/8 tsp.
- Ground cumin: 1/8 tsp.

**Instructions**

- Let the Kalorik Air Fryer Oven preheat to 300 F.
- In a skillet, cook onion and beef on medium flame.
- Add garlic powder, cumin, cheese, pepper sauce, salt and salsa.
- Cut the dough into 4 rectangles, add half a cup of beef mixture in each dough piece.
- Grab all edges and twist, seal it.
- Air fry for 18 to 22 minutes
- Serve with desired toppings.

Cal 371 | Fat 21g | Carb 30g | Protein 16g

## MOZZARELLA-STUFFED MEATBALLS

*Prep time:10 min | Cook time:40 min | Serves: 4*

**Ingredients**

- Dried oregano: 1 tsp.
- Ground beef: 1 lb.
- 1 egg
- Bread crumbs: half cup
- Mozzarella: 3 oz., cut into 16 cubes
- Freshly grated parmesan: 1/4 cup
- Chopped fresh parsley: 1/4 cup
- 2 minced garlic clove
- Salt & black pepper, to taste

**Instructions**

- In a bowl, add all ingredients, except for cheese cubes, mix and make into 2 tbsp. of meal balls, flatten into patties.
- In each patty, add one cube and make it into a ball.
- Let the Kalorik Air Fryer Oven preheat to 370 F.
- Air fry the balls for 12 minutes, serve with marinara sauce.

## BEEF WELLINGTON WONTONS

*Prep time:35 min | Cook time:10 min | Serves: 24*

**Ingredients**

- Olive oil: 1 tbsp.
- Lean ground beef: half pound
- Butter: 1 tbsp.
- 2 minced garlic cloves
- Water: 1 tbsp.
- Dry red wine: 1/4 cup
- Minced fresh parsley: 1 tbsp.
- Chopped shallot: 1 ½ tsp.
- Chopped different mushrooms: 3 cups
- Wonton wrappers: 12 oz., 1 pack
- Salt: half tsp.
- Pepper: ¼ tsp.
- 1 egg

**Instructions**

- Let the Kalorik Air Fryer Oven preheat to 325 F.
- In a skillet, cook meat until no longer pink; for 4 to 5 minutes, take the beef out. Add butter, olive oil on medium flame. Add shallot, garlic, cook for 1 minute. Add wine and mushrooms. Cook for 8 to 10 minutes, until tender, add the beef back. Add parsley and salt, and black pepper.

- In every wonton wrapper, add some filling. Seal the edges with egg wash, and fold tightly.
- Oil spray the air fryer basket and air fry the wontons for 4 to 5 minutes, flip, oil spray and cook for 4 to 5 minutes, serve right away.

Cal 42 | Fat 1g | Carb 5g | Protein 2g

## RASPBERRY BALSAMIC SMOKED PORK CHOPS

*Prep time:15 min | Cook time:15 min | Serves: 4*

**Ingredients**

- 2 eggs
- Balsamic vinegar: 1/3 cup
- Panko bread crumbs: 1 cup
- Chopped pecans: 1 cup
- Raspberry jam: 2 tbsp.
- 4 smoked pork bone-in chops
- Orange juice concentrate: 1 tbsp.
- Milk: 1/4 cup
- All-purpose flour: 1/4 cup
- Brown sugar: 2 tbsp.

**Instructions**

- Let the Kalorik Air Fryer Oven preheat to 400 F.
- In a bowl, whisk eggs with milk. In another bowl, add bread crumbs and pecans.
- Coat the chops in flour, then in eggs and lastly in crumbs mixture.
- Place in the air fryer oil sprayed basket and spray with oil.
- Air fry for 12 to 15 minutes until the internal temperature of the meat reaches 145 F, flip halfway through and spray with oil.
- In a pan, add the rest f the ingredients and let it come to a boil. Cook for 6 to 8 minutes, serve with pork chops.

Cal 579 | Fat 36g | Carb 36g | Protein 32g

## CHEESEBURGER ONION RINGS

*Prep time:25 min | Cook time:15 min | Serves: 8*

**Ingredients**

- Lean ground beef: 1 pound
- Mustard: 2 tbsp.
- Garlic powder: 2 tsp.
- Salt: half tsp.
- 1 onion
- Ketchup: 1/3 cup
- Cheddar cheese: 4 oz., cut into squares
- Panko bread crumbs: 1-1/2 cups
- All-purpose flour: 3/4 cup
- 2 eggs, whisked

**Instructions**

- Let the Kalorik Air Fryer Oven preheat to 335 F
- In a bowl, add meat, salt, ketchup, and mustard mix lightly.
- Slice the onion into half-inch slices and separate into circles.
- In eight slices, add the beef mixture.
- Add cheese and put more beef mixture on top.
- In a bowl, add garlic powder and flour.
- In different bowls, add eggs and bread crumbs.
- Coat the onion-filled rings in flour, then in egg and lastly in crumbs.

- Oil spray the basket and place the ring inside and oil spray it and air fry for 12 to 15 minutes until the internal temperature reaches 160 F.
- Serve right away.

Cal 258 | Fat 11g | Carb 19g | Protein 19g

## EASY GLAZED PORK CHOPS

*Prep time:5 min | Cook time:20 min | Serves: 4*

### Ingredients
- 4 thick cut, bone-in pork chops
- Soy sauce: 3 tsp.
- Smoked paprika: 2 tsp.
- Salt & pepper
- Dijon mustard: 3 tsp.
- Flour: 2 tbsp.
- Olive oil
- White wine vinegar: 3 tbsp.
- Brown sugar: 3 tbsp.

### Instructions
- In a bowl, add flour, black pepper, salt and paprika. Coat the chops in this flour mixture.
- Let the Kalorik Air Fryer Oven preheat to 350 F.
- Sear the chops in olive oil for 2 minutes on each side.
- Air fry the chops for 8-10 minutes until the internal temperature of the meat reaches 145 F.
- In a pan, mix mustard, sou sauce, brown sugar and vinegar, boil and turn the heat low, place the air fried chops in the pan.
- Coat in sauce well and serve.

## RIB EYE WITH HERB ROASTED MUSHROOMS

*Prep time: 135 min | Cook time:20 min | Serves: 4*

### Ingredients
- Worcestershire sauce: 2 tbsp.
- Thyme fresh leaves: 1 tsp.
- 2 rib-eye steaks, boneless
- Cremini mushrooms: 8 oz., without stems & caps halved
- Red wine: ¼ cup
- Olive oil: 2 tbsp.
- Salt & black pepper

### Instructions
- Season the steaks with black pepper.
- In a zip lock bag, add red wine and Worcestershire sauce. Mix and add steaks (pierce the steaks with a fork before adding to the bag). Keep in the fridge for 2 hours.
- Let the Kalorik Air Fryer Oven preheat to 400 F.
- In a bowl, add mushrooms, salt, pepper, olive oil, thyme, and parsley, toss to coat.
- Place the steaks in the air fryer basket, sprinkle salt and top with mushrooms.
- Air fry for ten-15 minutes. Flip halfway through.
- Serve with mushrooms and rice.

## HONEY MUSTARD PORK CHOPS

*Prep time:10 min | Cook time:15 min | Serves: 2*

### Ingredients
- Lemon juice: 1 tbsp.
- 2 pork chops, bone-in
- Brussels sprouts: 10 oz., halved
- Honey: ¼ cup
- Worcestershire sauce: 1 tsp.
- Whole grain mustard: 2 tbsp.
- Mini gold potatoes: ¾ pound, cut in half
- Smoked paprika: ¼ tsp.
- Olive oil
- Salt & black pepper

### Instructions
- In a casserole dish, mix the paprika, Worcestershire, honey, lemon juice and mustard.
- Pierce the chops with a fork all over and coat in the honey mixture. Keep in the fridge for 3 hours. Flip once or twice.
- Before cooking, let them come to room temperature.
- Let the Kalorik Air Fryer Oven preheat to 400 F.
- Oil spray the vegetables and season with salt and pepper, air fry for 13 minutes, shaking the basket a few times and take out in a bowl. Keep warm.
- Air fry the chops for 10-12 minutes until the internal temperature reaches 155 F.
- Serve the chops with roasted vegetables.

## PINEAPPLE GLAZED STUFFED PORK LOIN

*Prep time:20 min | Cook time:47 min | Serves: 4*

### Ingredients
- Hawaiian sweet bread: 4 cups, cubed
- Grated onion: ¼ cup
- Dried pineapple: half cup, diced
- 1 egg whisked
- Dried sage: half tsp.
- Pork loin roast: 1 1/2 pound
- Fresh parsley: 2 tbsp.
- Warm chicken stock: 1/3 cup
- Dried mango: half cup, diced
- Chopped mixed nuts: 1/3 cup
- Pineapple preserves: 8 oz.
- Salt: half tsp.
- Soy sauce: 1 tbsp.
- Brown sugar: 1 tbsp.
- Black pepper, to taste
- Broccoli florets: half head
- Cauliflower florets: half head

### Instructions
- Let the Kalorik Air Fryer Oven preheat to 380 F.
- In a bowl, add onion, bread, and stock. Mix and add nuts, mango, parsley, dried pineapple, pepper, sage, salt and egg. Mix well.
- Double butter the pork loin; ask your butcher to do so.
- Pound the meat to even thickness.
- Season the meat with salt and pepper from inside, spread the bread mixture on top, roll the meat and tie with twine in 3-4 place.
- Spray the outside generously with olive oil and season with salt and pepper.
- In a bowl, add soy sauce, brown sugar and pine apple preserves.
- Air fry the pork for 35 minutes, keep glazing with the soy sauce mixture and rotate every 8-10 minutes.
- Slice and serve.

## BOURBON BACON BURGER
*Prep time:10 min | Cook time:25 min | Serves: 4*

### Ingredients
- Bourbon: 1 tbsp.
- BBQ sauce: 2 tbsp.
- Brown sugar: 2 tbsp.
- 3 strips of maple bacon, halved
- Ground beef: ¾ pound
- Black pepper, to taste
- Minced onion: 1 tbsp.
- Salt: half tsp.
- Monterey Jack: 2 slices
- 2 Kaiser rolls

### Instructions
- Let the Kalorik Air Fryer Oven preheat to 390 F, add some water in the bottom drawer to prevent smoke.
- In a bowl, mix sugar and bourbon, brush the bacon strips with this mixture and air fry for 4 minutes, flip brush with mixture and cook for 4 minutes.
- In a bowl, add the rest of the ingredients, except for cheese slices, buns, and mix until combined. Make into 2 patties
- Air fry the burgers for 15-20 minutes at 370 F, flipping halfway through.
- Serve the burgers on rolls with bacon and other desired toppings.

## MINI SWEDISH MEATBALLS
*Prep time:15 min | Cook time:10 min | Serves: 16*

### Ingredients
- White bread: 2 slices
- Ground allspice: ¾ tsp.
- Milk: half cup
- Ground beef: 8 oz.
- Salt & black pepper, to taste
- Ground pork: 8 oz.
- ¼ onion, grated
- 1 egg

### Instructions
- In a bowl, add bread and milk, let it rest for five minutes, take out the bread and squeeze the milk.
- In a bowl, add the bread and the rest of the ingredients. Mix until combined and make into small meatballs.
- Let the Kalorik Air Fryer Oven preheat to 360 F. oil spray the basket of the air fryer.
- Air fry meatballs for ten minutes, shake the basket halfway through.
- Serve with spicy sauce.

## SPARERIBS
*Prep time:20 min | Cook time:40 min | Serves: 2-3*

### Ingredients
- Salt & black pepper, to taste
- St. Louis-style pork ribs: 1 rack, separated (2 ½-3 pounds)
- Dark brown sugar: 1/3 cup, packed
- Ketchup: 2 cups
- Worcestershire sauce: 2 tbsp.
- Paprika: 3 tsp.
- Apple cider vinegar: 1/3 cup
- White vinegar: 1/3 cup

- Hot sauce: 1-2 tsp.

### Instructions
- In a dish, add paprika (1 tsp.), salt (1 tbsp.) and pepper (2 tbsp.) mix and coat the rib rack well in this spice mixture.
- Let the Kalorik Air Fryer Oven preheat to 350 F.
- Air fry the ribs for 40 minutes.
- In a saucepan, add the rest of the ingredients with salt, pepper and ¾ cup of water.
- Cook on a medium flame for 2 minutes. Keep warm on low flame.
- Coat the ribs in this sauce and serve.

## HERB & CHEESE-STUFFED BURGERS
*Prep time:20 min | Cook time:15 min | Serves: 4*

### Ingredients
- 2 green onions, sliced
- Ketchup: 2 tbsp.
- Minced fresh parsley: 2 tbsp.
- Dijon mustard: 4 tsp.
- Ground beef: 1 pound
- Dry bread crumbs: 3 tbsp.
- Salt: half tsp.
- 4 hamburger buns, split
- Dried rosemary: half tsp.
- Dried sage leaves: ¼ tsp.
- Cheddar cheese: 2 oz., sliced

### Instructions
- Let the Kalorik Air Fryer Oven preheat to 375 F
- In a bowl, add parsley, green onion and mustard (2 tsp.).
- In a different bowl, mix the mustard (2 tsp.), crumbs, seasonings and ketchup. Mix and add beef mix until combined.
- Make into 8 patties, add cheese on 4 patties and add onion mixture on top of the cheese.
- Add one Pattie on top of the onion mixture, seal the edges.
- Air fry for 8 minutes, on each side, until the internal temperature of the meat reaches 160 F.
- Serve in buns with desired toppings.

Cal 369 | Fat 14g | Carb 29g | Protein 29g

## HAM STEAK WITH BROWN SUGAR GLAZE
*Prep time:10 min | Cook time:20 min | Serves: 2*

### Ingredients
- Fresh pineapple: 2 cups., diced
- Maple syrup: half cup
- Ham steak: half-pound, half-inch-thick
- Apple cider vinegar: 1/3 cup
- Brown sugar: ¾ cups
- Dijon mustard: 2 tbsp.
- Black pepper: 1 tsp.

### Instructions
- In a bowl, whisk vinegar, mustard, sugar, maple syrup and black pepper, whisk well.
- Let the Kalorik Air Fryer Oven preheat to 400 F.
- Toss the pineapple with sugar glaze and air fry for 8 minutes, shake the basket for few times. Take out and keep the pineapple warm.
- Brush the steak with sugar glaze, and air fry for 18 minutes at 380 F. baste with glaze a few times, flip halfway through.

- Serve the steak with pineapple cubes.

## FLAT IRON STEAK WITH LEMON HAZELNUT COUSCOUS

*Prep time:2 hours & 15 min | Cook time:15 min | Serves: 4*

**Ingredients**

- 1 flat iron steak, 1 pound
- Olive oil: ¼ cup
- Sun-dried tomatoes: half cup, packed in oil
- Salt, to taste
- Oregano fresh leaves: 2 tbsp.
- Red wine: half cup
- Black pepper, to taste
- 1 minced garlic clove

**Lemon hazelnut couscous**

- Dried couscous: 1 cup
- Salt: half tsp.
- Butter: 1 tbsp.
- Black pepper, to taste
- Fresh parsley: ¼ cup, chopped
- Lemon zest: 1 tbsp.
- Boiling water: 1 ½ cups
- Toasted hazelnuts: 1/3 cup, chopped
- Lemon juice: 1 tbsp.

**Instructions**

- In a food processor, add oregano and sun-dried tomatoes and pulse until fine.
- Add olive oil, red wine and pulse until smooth.
- In a zip lock bag, add this mixture with garlic and black pepper.
- With a knife, pierce the steak and place in the zip lock bag, coat well and keep in the fridge for 2 hours.
- Let the steak come to room temperature before cooking.
- Let the Kalorik Air Fryer Oven preheat to 400 F.
- Take the steak out, season with salt and pepper.
- Air fry for 8-14 minutes, flipping halfway through.
- Let it rest for five minutes before slicing.
- In a bowl, add couscous, salt and zest. Add boiling water, stir and cover for five minutes, fluff with a fork and add parsley, lemon juice, butter and hazelnut.
- Serve with steak.

## SWEET & SOUR PINEAPPLE PORK

*Prep time:25 min | Cook time:15 min | Serves: 4-6*

**Ingredients**

- Crushed pineapple: 8 oz., undrained & unsweetened
- Dark brown sugar: half cup, packed
- Garlic powder: 1 tsp.
- Ketchup: half cup
- Cider vinegar: 1 cup
- Soy sauce: 2 tbsp.
- Sugar: half cup
- Pepper: ¼ tsp.
- Dijon mustard: 1 tbsp.
- 2 pork tenderloins, cut in half
- Salt: ¼ tsp.

**Instructions**

- Season the pork with salt and pepper.

- In a saucepan, add the rest of the ingredients, let it come to a boil, turn the heat low and simmer for 15 to 20 minutes.
- Let the Kalorik Air Fryer Oven preheat to 350 F.
- Air fry the pork for 7 to 8 minutes, flip and pour sauce (1/4 cup) over pork. Air fry for 10 to 12 minutes until the internal temperature of the meat reaches 145 F.
- Rest it for a few minutes, slice and serve

Cal 489 | Fat 6g | Carb 71g | Protein 35g

## LAMB BURGERS

*Prep time: 15 min | Cook time: 8 min | Serves: 6*

**Ingredients**

- 2 pounds ground lamb
- 1 tablespoon onion powder
- Salt and ground black pepper, as required

**Directions**

- In a bowl, add all the ingredients and mix well.
- Make 6 equal-sized patties from the mixture and arrange the patties onto a cooking tray.
- Arrange the drip pan in the bottom of Air Fryer Oven cooking chamber.
- Take to the preheated air fryer at 360°F for 8 minutes. Turn the burgers after 4 minutes.
- When cooking time is complete, remove the tray from Air Fryer and serve hot.

Cal 285 | Fat 11.1g | Carb 0.9g | Fiber 0.1g | Sugar 0.4g | Protein 42.6 g

## BEEF & BEAN BURRITOS

*Prep time:25 min | Cook time:25 min | Serves: 12*

**Ingredients**

- Ground beef: 1 pound
- 1 jalapeño, chopped without seeds
- Chili powder: 1 tbsp.
- Water: half cup
- Half onion diced
- Ground cumin: 2 tsp.
- Salt: 1 tsp.
- Cheddar cheese: 3 cups
- Black pepper, to taste
- Taco sauce: ¼ cup
- Canned black beans: 15 oz., rinsed
- 24 tortillas (8") shells

**Instructions**

- Cook the beef and onion on medium flame, until no longer pink, drain any liquids.
- Add beans, Jalapeño, salt, pepper, cumin, chili powder, water and taco sauce. Mix and simmer for two minutes. Turn off the heat and let it cool.
- Add 2 tbsp. of beef mixture in each tortilla, add cheese and fold tightly. Spray the tortillas with oil.

- Let the Kalorik Air Fryer Oven preheat to 400 F.
- Air fry the tortillas for five minutes, flip and oil spray and air fry for five minutes more.
- Serve with sour cream.

Calories 217 | Fat 11g | Carb 20g | Protein 10g

## SALT & PEPPER FILETS MIGNON

*Prep time:10 min | Cook time:15 min | Serves: 4*

### Ingredients

- Kosher salt & coarse black pepper
- Filets mignons: 24 oz.

**Horseradish sauce**

- Prepared horseradish: 3 tbsp.
- Chopped fresh parsley: 1 tbsp.
- Sour cream: ¾ cup
- Lemon juice: 2 tbsp.
- Chopped fresh thyme: 1 tsp.

### Instructions

- Let the Kalorik Air Fryer Oven preheat to 400 F.
- Season the steaks with salt and pepper, and place in the air fryer.
- Air fry for 15 minutes, flipping halfway through.
- In a bowl, add all the ingredients of horseradish cream, mix and serve with steaks.

Cal 557 | Fat 46g | Carb 3g | Protein 32g

## PUMPKIN & PORK EMPANADAS

*Prep time:30 min | Cook time:15 min | Serves: 3-4*

### Ingredients

- Ground pork: 1 pound
- Half onion diced
- Olive oil: 2 tbsp.
- Pumpkin purée: 1½ cups
- Dried thyme: half tsp.
- Water: 3 tbsp.
- 1 red chili pepper minced
- 10 empanada dough discs
- Cinnamon: half tsp.
- Salt: 1 tsp.
- Black pepper

### Instructions

- Cook pork, onion on a medium flame for five minutes, drain any liquids.
- Add the rest of the ingredients, mix and simmer for ten minutes, turn off the heat and let it cool.
- In each dough, disc adds 2-3 tbsp. of filling and seal the edges with water.
- Brush the empanadas with oil.
- Let the Kalorik Air Fryer Oven preheat to 370 F.
- Air fry for 3-5 minutes; on each side, serve right away.

Cal 290 | Fat 16g | Carb 28g | Protein 12g

## INSIDE OUT CHEESEBURGERS

*Prep time:5 min | Cook time:20 min | Serves: 2*

### Ingredients

- Lean ground beef: 12 oz.
- Yellow mustard: 2 tsp.
- Minced onion: 3 tbsp.
- 8 dill pickle chips
- Ketchup: 4 tsp.
- Salt & black pepper, to taste
- Cheddar cheese: 4 slices, cut into smaller pieces

### Instructions

- In a bowl, add all ingredients except for cheese and dill pickles. Mix and divide into 4 portions.
- Make each portion in a patty, add four dill pickles on top, add cheese on 2 patties.
- Add the rest of the two patties on top and seal the edges.
- Let the Kalorik Air Fryer Oven preheat to 370 F.
- Air fry for 20 minutes, flipping halfway through.
- Serve in buns with desired toppings.

Cal 482 | Fat 27g | Carb 5g | Protein 51g

## HONEY GARLIC PORK CHOPS

*Prep time:10 min | Cook time:20 min | Serves: 4*

### Ingredients

- Salt & pepper, to taste
- Sweet chili sauce: 1 tbsp.
- Honey: ¼ cup
- 4 pork chops
- 2 minced garlic cloves
- Olive oil: 1 tbsp.
- Lemon juice: 2 tbsp.

### Instructions

- Let the Kalorik Air Fryer Oven preheat to 400 F
- Season the chops with salt and pepper.
- Air fry for 10 to 15 minutes, flip halfway through until the internal temperature of the meat reaches 145 F.
- In a pan, add olive oil, saute garlic for 30 seconds.
- Add the rest of the ingredients and mix well. Simmer for 3 to 4 minutes.
- Serve the chops with glaze sauce on top.

Cal 435 | Fat 21g | Carb 21g | Protein 40g

## STUFFED PORK CHOPS

*Prep time:40 min | Cook time:20 min | Serves: 4*

### Ingredients

- Olive oil: half tsp.
- Chopped onion: 1/4 cup
- Rubbed sage: 1/8 tsp.
- Bread: 4 slices, cubed
- 1 celery rib, diced
- Fresh parsley: 2 tbsp., chopped
- Salt: 1/8 tsp.
- White pepper: 1/8 tsp.
- Chicken broth: 1/3 cup
- Dried marjoram: 1/8 tsp.
- Dried thyme: 1/8 tsp.

**Pork chops**

- 4 pork rib chops
- Salt & pepper: ¼ tsp. each

### Instructions

- In a skillet, add oil, onion and celery and cook for 4 to 5 minutes. Turn off the heat.
- In a bowl, add seasonings and bread, broth and celery mixture. Mix well.
- Make a deep pocket in each pork chop, stuff with the celery mixture and secure with toothpicks.

- Let the Kalorik Air Fryer Oven preheat to 325 F.
- Season the chops with salt and pepper.
- Air fry the chops for ten minutes, flip and cook for 5 to 8 minutes until the internal temperature of the meat reaches 165 F.

Cal 274 | Fat 10g | Carb 16g | Protein 28g

## JERK PORK

*Prep time: 4 hours & 10min | Cook time: 20min | Serves: 4*

**Ingredients**
- Jerk paste: ¼ cup
- Pork butt: 1.5 lbs., cut into 3" pieces

**Instructions**
- Coat the pork well in the jerk paste and let it marinate for 4 to 24 hours in the fridge.
- Let the Kalorik Air Fryer Oven preheat to 390 F. oil spray the basket of the air fryer.
- Let the pork come to room temperature before cooking, air fry for 20 minutes, flipping halfway through.
- Slice and serve

Cal 234 | Protein 31g | Fat 9g

## REUBEN STROMBOLI

*Prep time: 10 min | Cook time: 15 min | Serves: 6*

**Ingredients**
- Pizza dough: 12 oz.
- Swiss cheese: 6 slices
- Island dressing: 1 tbsp.
- Garlic salt: 1/4 tsp.
- Corned beef: half-pound, sliced thin
- Sauerkraut: 1 cup, liquid squeezed

**Instructions**
- Roll the pizza dough into a ten-inch long rectangle, add island dressing on top.
- Add beef, cheese, and sauerkraut, in layers on top.
- Roll the dough and tuck the edges. Oil spray the log and sprinkle garlic salt on top.
- Let the Kalorik Air Fryer Oven preheat to 350 F.
- Air fry for 13 to 15 minutes.
- Slice and serve.

Cal 335 | Carb 30g | Protein 18g | Fat 16g

## BACON-WRAPPED STEAK

*Prep time: 15 min | Cook time: 20 min | Serves: 2*

**Ingredients**
- 2 rib eye steaks
- Pepper: 1/4 tsp.
- Bacon: 6 strips
- Onion powder: half tsp.
- Coarse salt to taste
- Chili powder: 1/4 tsp.
- Garlic powder: 1 tsp.

**Instructions**
- In a bowl, add all seasonings and mix.
- Coat the steak with this seasoning mix.
- Wrap the steak in bacon strips, do not overlap.
- Let the Kalorik Air Fryer Oven preheat to 375 F.
- Air fry for 18 minutes, flipping halfway through.
- Rest it, slice and serve.

Cal 377 | Fat 29g | Carb 10g | Protein 27g

## ITALIAN PORK CHOPS

*Prep time: 10 min | Cook time: 18 min | Serves: 3*

**Ingredients**
- 3 pork chops
- Garlic powder, to taste
- Marinara sauce: 1 cup, heated
- Smoked paprika, to taste
- Salt & black pepper, to taste
- Breadcrumbs: half cup
- Parmesan cheese: half cup, grated
- 1 egg
- Chopped italian parsley: 2 tbsp.
- Mozzarella cheese: half cup, grated

**Instructions**
- Coat the chops in paprika, salt, garlic powder and black pepper.
- In a bowl, add parsley, crumbs and parmesan cheese mix.
- In another bowl, whisk the egg.
- Coat the pork chops in egg, and then in crumb mixture, oil sprays the breaded chops.
- Let the Kalorik Air Fryer Oven preheat to 380 F.
- Air fry the chops for 8 to 12 minutes, flip after 6 minutes, air fry until the internal temperature of the meat reaches 145 to 160 F.
- Add cheese on top, air fry for two minutes more.
- Serve with marinara sauce

Cal 495 | Carb 18g | Protein 53g | Fat 22g

## ITALIAN SAUSAGE & VEGETABLES

*Prep time: 5 min | Cook time: 14 min | Serves: 4*

**Ingredients**
- One bell pepper
- One small onion
- Italian Sausage: 4 pieces
- Mushrooms: ¼ cup

**Instructions**
- Let the air fryer pre-heat to 400 F.
- Put Italian sausage in a single layer in the air fryer basket and let it air fry for 6 minutes.
- Slice the vegetables.
- After 6 minutes, change the temperature to 360 F. flip the sausage. Add the mushrooms, onions, and peppers to the basket around the sausage.
- Cook for 8 minutes. After half halfway, mix the sausage and vegetables.
- The sausage temperature should be 160 F.
- Take vegetables and sausage out and serve hot with brown rice.

Cal 291 | Fat 21g | Carb 10g | Protein 16g

## BACON-WRAPPED SCALLOPS

*Prep time: 15 min | Cook time: 20 min | Serves: 9*

**Ingredients**
- ½ cup of mayonnaise
- 2 tablespoons. Sriracha sauce
- 1 lb. bay scallops
- 1 pinch of coarse salt
- 1 pinch of black pepper freshly cracked
- 12 slices bacon
- 1 serving olive oil cooking spray

**Instructions**

- In a small mixing bowl, combine mayonnaise and Sriracha sauce. Keep the Sriracha mayo refrigerated until ready to use.
- Preheat the air fryer to 390°F
- Place the scallops on a plate or cutting board and pat them dry with a paper towel. Salt and pepper to taste. Wrap a third of a slice of bacon around each scallop and secure with a toothpick.
- Using cooking spray, coat the air fryer basket. Place the bacon-wrapped scallops in a single layer in the basket; if necessary, divide into two batches.

Cal 222 | Carb3.3g | Protein 17.3g | Fat 15.3g

## SMOKED BBQ RIBS
*Prep time:15 min | Cook time:15 min | Serves: 4*

### Ingredients
- Ribs one rack
- Liquid smoke 1 tablespoon
- Pork rubs 2-3 tablespoons.
- Salt & pepper
- BBQ sauce 1/2 cup

### Instructions
- Remove membrane from the back of ribs. It's a tinny layer that is not easy to remove. Occasionally it will be peeled right off. Easily you can cut & peel off. Cut the ribs in the centre so that the ribs can easily adjust in the air fryer.
- Sprinkle liquid smoke on each side of the ribs.
- Flavor each side with pork rub, pepper & salt.
- Cover ribs & let ribs at room temp for thirty minutes.
- Put ribs in an air fryer.
- Cook for fifteen minutes at 360 F
- Open-air fryer. Turn the ribs. Cook for an extra fifteen minutes.
- Remove ribs from air fryer. Sprinkle ribs with the BBQ sauce.

Cal 576 | Carb 22g | Protein 42g | Fat 36g

## CHIPOTLE STEAK TACOS
*Prep time: 60 min | Cook time:8 min | Serves: 4*

### Ingredients
**The Steak**
- Garlic 2 cloves crushed & peeled.
- 1 Chipotle Chile
- Ancho Chile Powder 1 tablespoon
- Flank steak 1.5 lbs.
- Ground Cumin 1 teaspoon
- Dried Oregano 1 teaspoon
- Water 2 tablespoon
- Kosher Salt 1.5 teaspoon
- Red Onion 1/2 cup
- Olive Oil 1 tablespoon
- Ground Black Pepper 1/2 teaspoon

**For Serving**
- Cheese 1/2 cup, crumbled.
- Salsa 1 cup
- Tortillas 8 flour, tortillas 6-inch, warmed.

### Instructions
- Put beef strips in the large bowl/ resalable bag of plastic. In the blender/ food processor, mix chipotle Chile, onion, oregano, Chile powder, garlic, cumin, olive oil, water, pepper, adobo sauce & salt. Blend till smooth. Put marinade on meat & mix/ seal bag & massage bag to thoroughly coat & mix. Marinate at room temp for thirty minutes/cover & refrigerate for twenty-four hours.

- Use tongs, remove beef strips from the bag & lay the basket of an air fryer. Minimize overlap as possible; remove marinade. Adjust air fryer at 400°F for eight minutes, flip beef strips in the centre. Do this in the batches.
- Put a steak on the sheet pan in a single layer.
- Adjust air fryer to the broil & cook steak for three to four minutes.
- Turn & allow cook for an extra two minutes.

## ZA'ATAR LAMB CHOPS
*Prep time:1 hour 5 min | Cook time:10 min | Serves: 4*

### Ingredients
- Lamb loin chops 8, trimmed.
- Black pepper
- Za'atar 1 tablespoon
- Kosher salt 1 1/4 teaspoon
- Fresh lemon 1/2
- olive oil 1 teaspoon
- Garlic three cloves, crushed.

### Instructions:
- Lamb chops rub with garlic & oil.
- Squash lemon on each side & season with za'atar, black pepper & salt.
- Preheat the air fryer at 400F. Uneven layer & in batches cook to the desired, around four to five minutes on every side.
- On every bone, chops must have raw meat 2 1/2 oz.

Cal 206 | Protein 29 g | Fat 8 g | Carb 1.5 g

## BEEF STEAK KABOBS
*Prep time:30 min | Cook time:10 min | Serves: 4*

### Ingredients
- Beef chuck ribs, 1-pound cut into one" pieces
- Soy sauce: 2 tbsp.
- Sour cream: 1/3 cup
- 1 bell peppers
- Half onion

### Instructions
- In a bowl, add soy sauce, and sour cream. Mix and add beef cubes, keep in the fridge for half an hour.
- Slice the onion and bell pepper in one" cubes.
- Thread the vegetables and meat onto skewers, sprinkle salt and pepper.
- Air fry for ten minutes at 375 F.

Cal 251 | Carb 4g | Protein 22g | Fat 15g

## PERFECT STEAK
*Prep time:15 min | Cook time:12 min | Serves: 2*

### Ingredients
- Fresh chopped parsley 2 tablespoon
- Minced Garlic 2 teaspoon
- Worcestershire Sauce 1 teaspoon
- Salt 1/2 teaspoon
- Ribeye steak 2 8 oz.
- Salt
- Black pepper freshly cracked.
- Olive oil
- Garlic Butter
- Softened unsalted butter one stick.

### Instructions

- Combine the parsley garlic, butter, salt & Worcestershire sauce until well mixed, prepare the garlic butter.
- Put in bakery release paper & roll it into the log. Please put it in the fridge till ready.
- Remove the steak from the fridge & allow it to rest for 20 minutes at room temp. Rub all sides of the steak with a little bit of olive oil & sprinkle with salt & freshly cracked black pepper.
- Air Fryer Preheated to 400 ° F. Place the steaks in an air fryer when preheated, cook for 12 minutes, turning halfway thru.
- Take it from the air-fryer & allow 5 minutes to relax. Garnish with garlic butter.

Cal 301 | Fat 23g | Carb 0.0g | Protein 23g

## HOT DOGS

*Prep time:5 min | Cook time:5 min | Serves: 5*

**Ingredients**
- Ketchup
- Mustard
- Hotdogs 4
- Buns hotdog 4

**Instructions**
- Before frying, make a few minor cuts (or poke the hot dogs) to keep your hot dogs from exploding. In the air fryer, arrange your hot dogs.
- Cook for six minutes at 390f.
- Take out the hot dogs. Now place the bread buns in your air fryer & fry them for another 2 minutes for toasted & crunchy buns!

Cal 269 | Protein 9.1g | Carb 23.1g | Fat 15.2g

## AIR FRYER MEATBALLS

*Prep time:10 min | Cook time:20 min | Serves: 4*

**Ingredients**
- Minced garlic two cloves
- Italian seasoning 1/2 teaspoon
- Salt 3/4 teaspoon
- Pepper 1/4 teaspoon
- Ground beef 1 lb.
- Dried bread crumbs 1/2 cup
- Parmesan cheese grated 1/2 cup
- Milk 1/4 cup

**Instructions**
- In the bowl, mix all the ingredients & form them into 1.5-inch meatballs.
- Place the meatballs in a single sheet into the air fryer basket without touching them.
- At 375F, air fry your meatballs for fifteen minutes.

Cal 96 | Protein 7.9g | Carb 2g | Fat 6.1g

## TACO MEATBALLS

*Prep time:10 min | Cook time:15 min | Serves: 4*

**Ingredients**
- Blend Shredded Cheese (Mexican) 1/2 cup
- Eggs 1
- Kosher Salt
- Ground Black Pepper
- Lean Ground Beef 1 lb.
- chopped onions 1/4 cup.
- chopped Cilantro 1/4 cup.

- Minced Garlic 1 tablespoon
- Taco Seasoning 2 tablespoon
- For Dipping Sauce
- salsa 1/2 cup
- Cholula hot sauce 1-2
- sour cream 1/4 cup

**Instructions**
- Put all the ingredients in a mixing bowl on the stand. Stir till it becomes a sticky paste, around 2-3 minutes, using a paddle attachment.
- Form them into Twelve meatballs. Put the meatballs in the basket of an air fryer. For ten minutes, set the air fryer at 400 F.
- Meanwhile, blend the sauce: mix the salsa, hot sauce & sour cream in a bowl. Now enjoy it with the meatballs.

Cal 323 Carb 5g | Protein 33g | Fat 18g

## ASIAN BEEF & VEGGIES

*Prep time:10 min | Cook time:8 min | Serves: ; 4*

**Ingredients**
- Rice vinegar 1/4 cup
- Sesame oil 1 teaspoon
- Brown sugar 1/3 cup
- Chinese 5 spice 1 teaspoon
- Water 1/4 cup
- Cut into strips sirloin steak 1 lb.
- Cornstarch 2 tablespoon
- Sliced yellow onion 1/2 med.
- Sliced into strips red pepper one med.
- Minced garlic three cloves
- Grated ginger 2 tablespoon
- Red chili flakes 1/4 teaspoon
- Soy sauce 1/2 cup

**Instructions**
- On a gallon shaped zip bag, Put all the ingredients. Make sure that all the ingredients are mixed. For up to four months, mark & freeze.
- Overnight, thaw the zip bag in the freezer.
- Remove the vegetables & steak using tongs & move them to the Air Fryer. Take the marinade away.
- Preheat the air fryer to 400 F & set the timer to 8 minutes.
- Serve with rice, then garnish with scallions & sesame seeds.

Cal 289 | Carb 27g | Protein 31g | Fat 7g

## MEATLOAF

*Prep time:10 min | Cook time:50 min | Serves: 3-4*

**Ingredients**
- Salt 1 teaspoon
- Thick-cut bacon 1/2 lb.
- Celery salt 1/2 teaspoon
- Cayenne pepper 1/4 teaspoon
- Egg 1

For the sauce:
- Ketchup 1/2 cup
- Maple syrup 2–3 tablespoon
- Ground beef 1/2 lb.
- Ground pork 1/2 lb.
- Almond flour 1 cup
- Diced yellow onion 1/2

- Diced red bell pepper 1.
- Ketchup 2 tablespoon
- Spicy brown mustard 1 tablespoon
- Garlic powder 1 teaspoon
- White pepper 1/2 teaspoon

**Instructions**

- Preheat your air fryer to 350 F.
- In a bowl, whisk together the meatloaf ingredients till thoroughly mixed. In the other bowl, stir the sauce ingredients together & set aside.
- Top a 9-to-5 loaf pan with mildly overlapping bacon strips. Put the meatloaf combination on top of the bacon to fully cover the meatloaf, wrap the strips near the meat. After this, tip the pan on to remove your meatloaf.
- In an air fryer, put the meatloaf. Heat the air fryer to 350 F and set the timer for approximately 50 minutes.
- When the timer reaches the mark of 30 minutes, click pause & brush around Three tablespoon of the sauce over top of a meatloaf by using the basting brush. Slightly cover the piece of tin rolls with the meatloaf.
- Cook for Sixteen more minutes, now remove a foil, baste your meatloaf once again in around three tablespoons of sauce, then cook for the next 4 minutes without the foil.
- When cooked, before slicing & serving, allow the meatloaf rest for ten minutes. Only a head up, it's certainly a little tough to pull the meatloaf out. You'll be able to gently press up and lift the wire rack from the basket till the wire rack has chilled.

Cal 297 | Protein 24.8g | Carb 5.9g | Fat 18.8g

### MUSTARD GLAZED PORK TENDERLOIN
*Prep time:10 min | Cook time:18 min | Serves: 4*

**Ingredients**

- Yellow mustard ¼ cup
- Brown sugar 3 tablespoon
- Italian seasoning 1 teaspoon
- Dried rosemary 1 teaspoon
- Pork tenderloin 1 1.5 lb.
- Minced garlic 1 tablespoon
- Salt ¼ teaspoon
- Black pepper fresh cracked ⅛ teaspoon

**Instructions**

- Rinse & dry tenderloin of pork. Slice the top of the pork tenderloin into slits. In the slits, put chopped garlic. Sprinkle the pork with pepper & salt.
- Whisk the Italian seasoning, rosemary & mustard brown sugar in a small bowl till well mixed. Pour and cook the mustard combination over the whole pork. Put it in the refrigerator for at least 2hrs to marinate.
- In the oiled air fryer basket, put the pork tenderloin. Cook for 18 to 20 minutes at 400 ° F until a fast-read meat thermometer reports a 145 F temp.
- Take it from the Air Fryer & let it rest before slicing for five minutes.

Cal 286 | Protein 25.4g | Carb 31.4g | Fat 6.5g

### BREADED PORK CHOPS
*Prep time:10 min | Cook time:12 | Serves: 4*

**Ingredients**

- Dried parsley 2 teaspoon
- Garlic powder 1/2 teaspoon
- Black pepper 1/2 teaspoon
- Cayenne pepper 1/4 - 1/2 teaspoon
- Dry mustard 1/4 teaspoon
- Salt 1/2 teaspoon
- Cut pork chops 4, around 24 oz.
- Cooking spray non-Fat
- Liquid Dredge Station:
- Beaten one egg.
- Water 1/4 cup
- Dry Dredge Station:
- Panko breadcrumbs 1 cup
- Paprika 4 teaspoon

**Instructions**

- Prepare your chops: Trim the chops with all the Fat. To extract some bone particles, clean them with water.
- Prepare a station of dredge: Beat an egg with water in a dish/baking pan. Combine the Panko bread crumbs & the spices in some other bowl/baking pan.
- Set up the 3rd pan with flour if you add an Extra flour dredge.
- Coat your Chops: First, gently coat a chop in flour if the optional flour step is used. Shake off the extra flour. This move allows the egg wash to adhere to a pork chop. Skip to the next stage if the flour is not used.
- Put the chops in the mixture of egg wash & switch the two sides to wet. Then, roll the chops in the crumb combination to cover all sides.
- Onto the Fryer: Into the Air Fryer pan, put the chops. Using non-stick cooking oil, spray gently. To make the second tier of pork chops, add a wire rack if required and close the drawer into the fryer.
- Cook your Chops: Set the time for twelve minutes and & temp at 380 F. Cook your Chops: Set the time for twelve minutes and & temp at 380 F. Midway thru the cooking time, flip the chops & brush gently with cooking spray. Please shut the drawer & continue to cook. Once the internal temperature exceeds 145 ° F & the middle is not pink anymore, the chops are cooked.
- Giving it a rest: Let the chops sit before serving for 3 minutes.

Cal 394 | Protein 44.7g | Carb 10g | Fat 18.1g

### STEAK TIPS
*Prep time:5 min | Cook time:20 min | Serves: 4*

**Ingredients**

- Garlic powder 1/2 teaspoon
- Salt
- Black pepper
- Minced parsley for garnish
- Potatoes 1/2 lb.
- Steaks 1 lb.
- Butter 2 tablespoon
- Worcestershire sauce 1 teaspoon

**Instructions**

- Carry a pot of water to a simmer & after this, add the potatoes. Cook for five minutes or till almost soft. Place away & drain
- Combine the tips for steaks with blanched potatoes. Mix the melted butter, garlic powder, Worcestershire sauce, salt, and pepper.
- Preheat your Air Fryer for four minutes at 400 °F.

- In the air fryer basket, scatter the steak & potatoes in a layer. Air fry for 10 to 18 minutes at 400 ° F, shaking & flipping & the steak & potatoes two cycles during the cooking process.
- To see how well cooked it is, see the steak. If you want to do something about the steak, put an additional 2 to 5 minutes of cooking time
- Sprinkle with parsley. If needed, drizzle with extra salt and pepper. Serve hot.

Cal 526 | Fat 34g | Carb 6g | Protein 49g

## CHINESE SALT & PEPPER PORK CHOPS
*Prep time:10 min | Cook time:15 min. | Serves: 1-2*

### Ingredients
- Sliced (stems removed) Jalapeño Pepper 2
- Sliced Scallions 2
- Canola Oil 2 tablespoon
- Sea Salt 1 teaspoon
- Black Pepper 1/4 teaspoon
- Pork Chops
- White Egg 1
- Sea Salt 1/2 teaspoon
- Black Pepper 1/4 teaspoon
- Potato Starch 3/4 cup
- Oil Mister 1
- Stir Fry
- Chicken Fryer Cast Iron

### Instructions
- Lightly coat the air fryer basket with a little bit of oil.
- Whisk salt, pepper & egg white together in a med bowl till foamy. Cut pork chops into cutlet slices, leave a little on the bones & pat dry. Put pork chop pieces in a combination of egg white. Cover completely. Marinate for at least twenty minutes.
- Move pork chops into a big bowl & put Potato Starch. Dredge your pork chops into a Potato Starch. Shake off the pork & put it into the ready Air Fryer Basket. With oil, Spray the pork.
- Cook for Nine minutes at 360 F, sometimes shaking the basket & spraying b/w shakes with oil. Cook at 400 F for an extra six minutes, or till the pork becomes brown & crispy.

Cal 351 | Fat 14g | Carb 51g | Protein 5g

## PORK SCHNITZEL
*Prep time:10 min | Cook time:10 min | Serves: 4*

### Ingredients
- Sirloin cutlets four pork cooking spray
- Dill sauce:
- All-purpose flour 1 tablespoon
- Chicken pork 3/4 cup
- Sour cream 1/2 cup
- Dill weed 1/4 teaspoon.
- All-purpose flour 1/4 cup
- Seasoned salt 1 teaspoon
- Pepper 1/4 teaspoon
- Egg 1
- Milk 2 tablespoon
- Dry bread crumbs 3/4 cup
- Paprika 1 teaspoon

### Instructions

- Air fryer preheated to 375 F. In the bowl, combine seasoned salt, pepper & flour. In the other bowl, whisk egg & milk till well blended. In the 3rd bowl, combine bread crumbs & paprika.
- Pound pork cutlets along with the meat mallet to 0.25inch thickness. Dip cutlets in the flour combination to coat all sides; shake off extra. Dip in a mixture of egg, after this in crumb combination, patting it to coating adhere.
- Put the pork in the single layer on an oiled tray in an air-fryer basket, drizzled with cooking spray. Cook till golden brown, 4 to 5 minutes. Flip; drizzle with cooking spray. Cook till golden brown, 4 to 5 minutes. Remove to the serving plate; keep hot.
- Whereas, in a saucepan, stir flour & broth till smooth. Carry to a simmer, stirring regularly; cook & stir two minutes or till thickened. Lower the heat. Stir in sour cream & dill; heat thru (do not simmer). Serve it with pork.

Cal 309 | Fat 13g | Carb 17g | Protein 30g

## BEEF TENDERLOIN

*Prep time: 5 min | Cook time: 30 min | Serves: 6*

### Ingredients
- 1 (2-poundbeef tenderloin, trimmed of visible fat
- 2 tbsp. salted butter; melted.
- 2 tsp. minced roasted garlic
- 3 tbsp. ground 4-peppercorn blend

### Directions
- In a small bowl, mix the butter and roasted garlic. Brush it over the beef tenderloin.
- Place the ground peppercorns onto a plate and roll the tenderloin through them, creating a crust. Place tenderloin into your air fryer oven basket
- Adjust the temperature to 400 F and set the timer for 25 minutes. Flip the tenderloin halfway through cooking. Set aside for 10 minutes before slicing.

Cal 289 | Protein 37g | Fiber 9g | Fat 18g | Carb 5g

## BEEF PAPAS RELLENAS
*Prep time:1 hour | Cook time:15 min | Serves: 3*

### Ingredients
- Peeled and cut into wedges potatoes 2-1/2 lbs.
- Lean ground beef 1 lb.
- Finely chopped green pepper, one small
- Finely chopped onion, one small
- Tomato sauce 1/2 cup
- Paprika 1/2 teaspoon
- Garlic powder 1 teaspoon
- Lightly beaten eggs two large
- Seasoned bread crumbs 1 cup cooking spray
- Sliced green olives with pimientos 1/2 cup.
- Raisins 1/2 cup
- Divided salt 1-1/4 teaspoon
- Divided pepper 1-1/4 teaspoon

**Instructions**

- Put potatoes in a big saucepan & fill with water. Carry to a simmer. Lower the heat; cover & cook till soft, 15 to 20 minutes.
- In a big skillet, cook green pepper, onion & beef on med heat till meat is no further pink; drain. Stir in olives, raisins, tomato sauce, 1/4 teaspoon salt, paprika & 1/4 teaspoon pepper: heat through.
- Drain the potatoes; mash with the remaining 1 teaspoon salt, pepper & garlic powder. Shape 2 tablespoon potatoes into the patty; put the heaping tablespoon of filling in the middle. Form potatoes around filling, forming the ball. Repeat.
- Put eggs & bread crumbs in the different bowls. Dip the balls of potato into eggs; after this, roll in bread crumbs. Air fryer preheated to 400 F. In the batches, put in a single layer on an oiled tray in the air-fryer basket, Drizzle with cooking spray. Cook till golden brown, 14 to 16 minutes.

Cal 380 | Protein 14.3g | Carb 45.3g | Fat 15.8g

## BEEF MINI CHIMICHANGAS

*Prep time:15 min | Cook time:10 min | Serves: 14*

**Ingredients**

- Sour cream 1 cup
- Drained chopped green chills one can.
- Roll wrappers 14 egg.
- Lightly beaten egg white, one large cooking spray
- Salsa
- Ground beef 1 lb.
- Chopped onion one med.
- Taco seasoning one envelope.
- Water 3/4 cup
- Shredded Monterey jack cheese 3 cups

**Instructions**

- In the big skillet, cook beef & onion on med heat till meat is no further pink; drain. Stir in water & taco seasoning. Carry to a simmer. Lower the heat; boil, uncovered, for five minutes, stirring often. Take it from the heat; cool it lightly.
- Air fryer preheated to 375 F. In a big bowl, mix sour cream, chills & cheese. Whisk in beef combination. Put the egg roll wrapper on a work surface with one point facing you. Put 1/3 cup filling in the middle. Fold the bottom of one-third of the wrapper on filling; fold its insides.
- Coat the highest point with white egg; roll up to cover. Repeat with leftover wrappers & filling.
- In the batches, put chimichangas in the single layer on an oiled tray in the air-fryer basket, Drizzle with cooking spray. Cook till golden brown for 3 to 4 minutes on both sides. Serve hot with salsa & extra sour cream.

Cal 455 | Protein 2 | Carb 41g | Fat 20.6g

## LOADED PORK BURRITOS

*Prep time: 20 min | Cook time:10 min | Serves: 6*

**Ingredients**

- Lime juice 1 tablespoon
- Garlic powder 1/4 teaspoon
- Uncooked long-grain rice 1 cup
- Shredded Monterey jack cheese 3 cups
- Warmed tortillas six flour
- Rinsed & drained black beans, one can.
- Sour cream 1-1/2 cups cooking spray
- Thawed limeade concentrates 3/4 cup.

- Olive oil 1 tablespoon
- Divided salt 2 teaspoon
- Divided pepper 1-1/2 teaspoon
- Boneless pork loin 1-1/2 lbs.
- Chopped seeded plum tomatoes 1 cup.
- Chopped green pepper, one small.
- Chopped onion, one small.
- Minced fresh coriander 1/4 cup + 1/3 cup.
- Seeded & chopped jalapeno pepper, 1.

**Instructions**

- In a big dish, mix the limeade concentrate, oil, 1/2 teaspoon pepper & 1 teaspoon salt; put pork. Flip to coat; cover & refrigerate for twenty minutes.
- In a bowl, salsa combine tomatoes, onion, green pepper, 1/4 cup cilantro, jalapeno, garlic powder, lime juice, and remaining salt & pepper. Set aside.
- Whereas cook rice as per the package instructions. Stir in leftover coriander; keep hot.
- Drain pork & discard the marinade. Air fryer preheated to 350 F. In batches, put pork in the single layer on an oiled tray in an air-fryer basket, Drizzle with cooking spray. Cook till pork is no further pink, 8 to 10 minutes, flipping halfway through.
- Drizzle 1/3 cup cheese off-centre on every tortilla. Layer every with 1/2 cup rice combination, 1/4 cup salsa, 1/4 cup black beans & 1/4 cup sour cream, finish with around 1/2 cup pork. Fold sides & ends on filling. Serve with leftover salsa.

Cal 910 | Fat 42g | Carb 82g | Protein 50g

## BEEFY SWISS BUNDLES

*Prep time:15 min | Cook time:10 min | Serves: 4*

**Ingredients**

- Minced garlic 1-1/2 teaspoon
- Ground beef 1 lb.
- Mashed potatoes 2/3 cup.
- Shredded Swiss cheese 1 cup.
- Egg one large
- Water 2 tablespoon
- Paprika 3/4 teaspoon
- Salt 1/2 teaspoon
- Sliced fresh mushrooms 1-1/2 cups.
- Chopped onion 1/2 cup.
- Worcestershire sauce 4 teaspoon
- Crushed dried rosemary 3/4 teaspoon.
- Pepper 1/4 teaspoon
- Thawed frozen puff pastry one-sheet.

**Instructions**

- Air fryer preheated to 375 F. In a big skillet, cook mushrooms, onion & beef, on med heat till meat is no further pink & veggies are softer, 8 to 10 minutes. Put garlic; cook one minute further. Drain. Whisk in Worcestershire sauce & seasonings. Take it from the heat; set aside.
- On a lightly floured surface, roll the puff pastry into a 15 into a 13-inch rectangle. Cut into rectangles. Put around two tablespoon potatoes on every rectangle: scatter to within one in of edges. Drizzle each with a 3/4 cup beef combination; season with 1/4 cup cheese.
- Beat egg & water; brush a few on pastry edges. Carry opposite pastry corners on each bundle; put a pinch of seams to seal.

137

Brush with leftover egg combination. In batches, put pastries in the single layer on a tray in an air-fryer basket; cook till color changes to a golden brown.

- Freeze option: Freeze your unbaked pastries on the parchment-lined cookie sheet till hard. Move it to an airtight jar, back to the freezer. To use it, cook frozen pastries till their color changes to a golden brown & heated fully

Cal 706 | Fat 42g | Carb 44g | Protein 35g

## BEEF BULGOGI
*Prep time:10 min | Cook time:12 min | Serves: 6*

### Ingredients
- Sesame Oil 2 tablespoon
- Sesame Seeds 2 tablespoon
- Minced Garlic 2 teaspoon
- Ground Black Pepper 1/2 teaspoon
- Sirloin Steak 1.5 lbs.
- Minced Green Scallions 3
- Shredded carrots 1 cup
- Soy Sauce 3 tablespoon
- Brown Sugar 2 tablespoon

### Instructions
- Put sliced carrots, green onions & beef into the zip-top bag (plastic). Put brown sugar, soy sauce, sesame oil, garlic, ground pepper & sesame seeds. Squish a bag well to get the meat & sauce mixed well.
- Let the beef marinate for thirty minutes or up to one day in the freezer.
- Put the meat and vegetables into the air fryer basket, leave behind the marinade as you can. Heat the air fryer to 400 F for about 12 minutes, shaking halfway thru.
- Serve with rice cauliflower, steamed rice.

Cal 232 | Protein 16.2g | Cards 12.4g | Fat 13.2g

## FRIED PORK CHOPS
*Prep time:15 min | Cook time:20 min | Serves: 4*

### Ingredients
- Pepper
- Ziploc bag 1 cooking oil spray
- Pork chops 4
- Buttermilk 3 tablespoon
- All-purpose flour 1/4 cup
- Seasoning salt

### Instructions
- Pat your pork chops to dry.
- Sprinkle the pork chops with the seasoning of salt & pepper.
- Sprinkle the buttermilk on the pork chops.
- Put the pork chops in the Ziploc bag with flour. Shake it to thoroughly coat.
- Put the pork chops in an air fryer. Cook in batches if necessary.
- Spray your pork chops with the cooking oil.
- Cook your pork chops for fifteen minutes at 380 F. Turn the pork chops on to the different side after ten minutes.

Cal 173 | Carb 7g | Protein 22g | Fat 6g

## HONEY & MUSTARD PORK MEATBALLS
*Prep time:5 min | Cook time:10 min | Serves: 4*

### Ingredients
- Minced Pork 500 g

- Red Onion 1 Small
- Mustard 1 teaspoon
- Honey 2 teaspoon
- Garlic Puree 1 teaspoon
- Pork Seasoning 1 teaspoon
- Salt and Pepper

### Instructions
- Peel & thinly cut the red onion.
- Put all of the ingredients into a food processor & mix well till the pork chops are well seasoned.
- By Using the meatball press, make the meatballs. If required, add some oat flour to mix them.
- Put your pork meatballs into an air fryer & cook for ten minutes at 360 F.
- Serve while still warm.

Cal 357 | Carb 7g | Protein 22g | Fat 27g

## PORK CHOPS & BROCCOLI
*Prep time:5 min | Cook time:10 min | Serves: 3*

### Ingredients
- Divided salt 1 teaspoon
- Broccoli florets 2 cups
- Minced garlic two cloves
- Bone-in pork chops 2 5 ounce
- Divided avocado oil 2 tablespoon.
- Paprika 1/2 teaspoon
- Onion Powder 1/2 teaspoon
- Garlic powder 1/2 teaspoon

### Instructions
- Air fryer preheated to 350 F. With non-stick spray, Spray basket.
- Sprinkle one tablespoon of oil on both sides of the chops of the pork.
- Garnish the pork chops on each side with the onion powder, paprika, garlic powder, & 1/2 teaspoon of salt.
- Put pork chops into the air fryer basket & cook for five minutes.
- Whereas chops of pork are cooking, put the garlic, broccoli, leftover 1/2 teaspoon of salt, & leftover tablespoon of oil to the bowl & toss to coat.
- Open your air fryer & carefully turn the pork chops.
- Put the broccoli in a basket & back to the air fryer.
- Cook for five extra minutes, stirring the broccoli midway thru.
- Safely take the food from the air fryer & serve.

Cal 483 | Fat 30g | Carb 12g | Protein 40g

## BEEF MUSHROOM STEAK
*Prep time:10 min | Cook time:10 min | Serves:4*

### Ingredients
- Garnish with minced parsley
- Optional: melted butter for finishing
- Finish with chili flakes, if desired.
- 1 pound steaks, sliced into half-inch cubes
- Worcestershire sauce, 1 teaspoon
- Optional: 1/2 teaspoon (2.5 mL) garlic powder
- Mushrooms, 8 oz. (227 g) (cleaned, washed and halved)
- 2 Tablespoons (30 ml) melted butter (or olive oil)
- a pinch of flaky salt, to taste
- black pepper, freshly cracked, to taste

### Instructions

- Rinse and pat dry the steak cubes thoroughly. In a mixing dish, combine the steak cubes and mushrooms. After brushing with melted butter, season with Worcestershire sauce, additional garlic powder, and a generous amount of salt and pepper.
- Preheat the Air Fryer for 4 minutes at 400°F.
- In the air fryer basket, arrange the steak and mushrooms in an even layer. Air fry for 10-18 minutes at 400°F, shaking and tossing the steak and mushrooms twice during the cooking process (time depends on your preferred doneness, thickness of the steak, size of air fryer).
- Examine the steak to see how well it has been prepared. Cook the steak for an additional 2-5 minutes if you like it more cooked.
- Drizzle with optional melted butter and/or optional chili flakes and garnish with parsley. If needed, season with more salt and pepper. Heat the dish before serving.

Cal 401 | Carb 3g | Protein 32g | Fat 29g

## RACK OF LAMB
*Prep time:5 min | Cook time:15 min | Serves:* **4**

### Ingredients
- 2 teaspoons minced garlic
- Salt
- Pepper
- 4 tablespoons olive oil
- 1 rack of lamb
- 2 tablespoons dried rosemary dried thyme

### Instructions
- By combining the rosemary, thyme, garlic, salt, pepper, and olive oil in a small mixing bowl.
- Make a good mix.
- Then coat the lamb with the mixture.
- In an air fryer, position the rack of lamb.
- Preheat the air fryer to 360 F and keep it there for 10 minutes.
- After 10 minutes, use the method mentioned above to check the internal temperature of the rack of lamb.
- 150 F is rare.
- Then take it out, and serve

Cal 481 | Protein 22.2g | Carb 5.6g | Fat 40.8g

## GLAZED STEAKS
*Prep time:4 hours 20 min | Cook time:20 min | Serves:2*

### Ingredients
- 1/2 tablespoon Worcestershire Sauce
- 1 tablespoon Grated Peeled Ginger
- 1 tablespoon Garlic Crushed
- 1 teaspoon Seasoned Salt
- 2 Sirloin Steaks at least 6oz
- 2 tablespoon Soy Sauce
- 2 tablespoon Brown Sugar
- Salt/Pepper to Taste

### Instructions
- Combine the steaks and the remaining ingredients in a big eatable container.
- Allow it to marinate in the refrigerator for at least 8 hours.
- Place foil in the bottom of the air fryer and spray it with nonstick cooking spray before placing the steaks on it.
- Steaks should be cooked for 10 minutes at 400°F.
- Cook for another 10-15 minutes, or until steaks are cooked to your liking.

Cal 271 | Protein 25g | Fat 12g

## BACON WRAPPED HOT DOGS
*Prep time:5 min | Cook time:15 min | Serves: 8*

### Ingredients
- 8 Hot Dogs
- Bacon: 8 strips

### Instructions
- On each hot dog wrap the bacon.
- Preheat air fry to 360 F.
- Cook for 15 minutes, flip halfway through and serve.
- Wrap the desired quantity of bacon around each hot dog.

Cal 203 | Carb 9g | Protein 8g | Fat 15g

## BACON-WRAPPED SWEET POTATO ROUNDS
*Prep time:5 min | Cook time:12 min | Serves: 6*

### Ingredients
- 2 thin sweet potatoes
- Melted butter: 1 tbsp.
- 6 slices bacon
- Paprika: ¼ tsp.
- Salt
- Cayenne pepper: ¼ tsp.

### Instructions
- Peel and cut the sweet potatoes into half-inch-thick slices.
- Slice every bacon piece in half lengthwise.
- Around each slice of potato, wrap the bacon, secure with a toothpick.
- Sprinkle salt on top.
- Air fry for ten minutes at 375 F.
- In a bowl, add the rest of the ingredients, mix and brush the potatoes with this mixture.
- Air Fry for 2-3 minutes.

Cal 146 | Fat 10g | Carb 9g | Protein 3g

## AIR FRYER MONGOLIAN BEEF
*Prep time:20 min | Cook time:20 min | Serves:3*

### Ingredients
**Meat**
- 3/4 Cup Brown Sugar Packed
- Cooked Rice
- Green Beans
- Green Onions
- 1 Lb. Flank Steak
- 1/4 Cup Corn Starch
- Sauce
- 2 teaspoon Vegetable Oil
- 1/2 teaspoon Ginger
- 1 tablespoon Minced Garlic
- 1/2 Cup Soy Sauce or Gluten Free Soy Sauce
- 1/2 Cup Water

### Instructions
- Cover the steak in corn starch after thinly slicing it into long sections.
- Cook for 5 minutes on each side in the Air Fryer at 390°F. (Start with 5 minutes and increase as necessary.) I cook it for 10 minutes on each side; however, some have said that's too long.)
- Heat all sauce ingredients in a medium-sized saucepan over medium-high heat as the steak cooks.

- Combine all of the ingredients in a small saucepan and bring to a low boil.
- Place the steak in a bowl with the sauce and let it soak in for 5-10 minutes after both the steak and the sauce have been cooked.
- Remove the steak with tongs when ready to eat, allowing the excess sauce to drip off.
- Place the steak on top of the cooked rice and green beans, and drizzle with more sauce if desired.

Cal 554 | Fat 16g | Protein 44g

## GROUND BEEF WELLINGTON

*Prep time:30 min | Cook time:20 min | Serves: 2*

### Ingredients
- Ground beef 1/2 lb.
- Refrigerated crescent rolls 1 tube (4 ounces)
- Large egg 1, lightly beaten optional.
- Dried parsley flakes 1 teaspoon
- Butter 1 tablespoon
- Chopped fresh mushrooms 1/2 cup.
- All-purpose flour 2 teaspoon s.
- Pepper 1/4 teaspoon, divided.
- Half-&-half cream 1/2 cup
- Large egg yolk 1
- Finely chopped onion 2 tablespoon s.
- Salt 1/4 teaspoon

### Instructions
- Preheat the fryer to 300 F. Heat the butter over med-high heat in a saucepan. Add mushrooms; cook & mix for 5-6 minutes until soft. Stir in the flour and 1/8 teaspoon of pepper till combined. Add cream gradually. Put to a boil; cook & stir until thickened, or for 2 minutes. Remove & set aside from the heat.
- Combine egg yolk, 2 tablespoons. of mushroom sauce, onion, salt, and 1/8 teaspoon of pepper left in a bowl. Crumble the beef over the mixture and blend properly. Shape into two loaves. Unroll and separate the crescent dough into two rectangles; press the perforations to close. Place each rectangle with the meatloaf. Bring together the edges & pinch to seal. Brush the beaten egg if desired.
- In the air-fryer basket, put the Wellingtons in one layer on the oiled tray. Cook until a thermometer placed into the meatloaf reads 160 F, 18-22 minutes, till golden brown.
- Meanwhile, over less heat, heat the remaining sauce; mix in the parsley. With Wellingtons, serve the sauce.

Cal 585 | Fat 38g | Carb 30g | Protein 29g

## JAMAICAN JERK MEATBALLS

*Prep time:3 min | Cook time:14 min | Serves: 4*

### Ingredients
- Breadcrumbs 100 g
- Jerk dry rub 1 tablespoon.
- Chicken mince 1 kg

### Jamaican Sauce
- Soy sauce 1 tablespoon
- Jerk dry rub 1 teaspoon.
- Honey 4 tablespoon

### Instructions
- Along with the breadcrumbs and the jerk seasoning, put the chicken in a mixing bowl and combine well. Using a meatball press or make meatball forms.

- Put the Meatballs in the air fryer & on 360f cook for 14 minutes.
- Combine the honey, soy sauce, and the remaining jerk dry rub in a bowl. Mix thoroughly.
- In the sauce, toss them and on sticks serve them when the meatballs are cooked.

Cal 527 | Carb 36g | Protein 48g | Fat 22g

## SIMPLE BEEF PATTIES

*Prep time: 10 min | Cook time: 13 min | Serves: 4*

### Ingredients
- 1 lb. ground beef
- ½ tsp garlic powder
- ¼ tsp onion powder
- Pepper
- Salt

### Directions
- Preheat the Air Fryer oven to 400°F.
- Add ground meat, garlic powder, onion powder, pepper, and salt into the mixing bowl and mix until well combined.
- Make even shape patties from meat mixture and arrange on air fryer pan.
- Place pan in Air Fryer oven.
- Cook patties for 10 minutes. Turn patties after 5 minutes.
- Serve and enjoy.

Cal 212 | Fat 7.1g | Carb 0.4g | Protein 34.5 g

## CHAR SIU PORK

*Prep time:10 min | Cook time:20 min | Serves: 4*

### Ingredients
- 4 tbsp. of Honey
- 2 tbsp. of soy sauce
- Pork belly: 1-pound
- 1 tbsp. of hoisin sauce
- 4 tbsp. of Ginger & garlic Minced
- 1 tbsp. of Sugar
- 1 tbsp. of Chinese 5 Spice
- 1 tbsp. of Shaoxing Wine

### Instructions:
- Poke the pork with a fork all over.
- In a bowl, add the rest of the ingredients and mix.
- In a zip lock bag, add half of the sauce with pork. Keep in the fridge for half an hour.
- Preheat the air fryer at 390 F.
- Cook pork for 15 minutes, flip halfway through.

Cal 226 | Carb 20g | Protein 26g | Fat 4g

## RANCH PORK CHOPS

*Prep time:5 min | Cook time:10 min | Serves: 4*

### Ingredients
- 4 centre-cut pork chops, boneless, 1-inch thick

- 2 teaspoons. Dry ranch salad dressing mix

**Instructions**

- Spray both sides of the pork chops with cooking spray and place on a tray. Allow 10 minutes at room temperature after sprinkling both sides with ranch seasoning mix.
- Preheat an air fryer to 390 F by spraying the basket with cooking spray
- Place the chops in the preheated air fryer in batches if possible, to avoid overcrowding the fryer.
- Cook for a total of 5 minutes. Cook for another 5 minutes after flipping the chops.
- Allow to rest for 5 minutes on a foil-covered plate before serving.

Cal 260 | Carb 0.6g; | Protein 40.8g | Fat 9.1g

## BACON RANCH POPPERS
*Prep time:5 min | Cook time:15 min | Serves: 2*

### Ingredients

- 1 teaspoon salt & pepper
- 1/4 cup Ranch for dipping
- 6 slices bacon
- 1/4 cup Mexican cheese
- 1/4 cup ground pork rinds
- 1 egg beaten
- 1 teaspoon garlic - minced
- 1 teaspoon onion powder
- 1 teaspoon dill

### Instructions

- Preheat your Air Fryer to 400 F .
- Chop the bacon and beat the egg
- In a large mixing bowl, add all of the ingredients.
- To thoroughly blend, use your hands.
- Balls, such as meatballs, should be possible. If necessary, add a few more pork rinds.
- 15 minutes in the air fryer Temperature should be 165 F . If not, cook for a few more minutes until finished. Don't overcook your food!

Cal 96 | Fat 6g | Carb 2g | Protein 8g

## PIGS IN A BLANKET
*Prep time:1 min | Cook time:8 min | Serves: 4*

### Ingredients

- 1 Can Crescent Rolls
- 1 Pig Little Smokiest

### Instructions

- Preheat the air fryer to 400°F for the Air Fryer. Place your rack in the centre of the room.
- Roll out the crescent rolls after opening the bags.
- Create triangles out of them.
- Fill the crescent rolls with the little smokiest.
- Bake for 5 minutes, flipping halfway through.

Cal 107 | Fat 8g | Carb 6g | Protein 3g

## STEAKS
*Prep time:30 min | Cook time:10 min | Serves: 1*

### Ingredients

- 1 teaspoon garlic
- 1 tablespoon parsley
- 1 lb. Steaks
- 3 tablespoon softened butter
- 3 tablespoon Worcestershire sauce
- salt and pepper to taste

### Instructions

- In a cup, combine the butter, a pinch of Worcestershire, parsley, and garlic.
- Roll into a tube on wax paper or parchment paper. While preparing/cooking steaks, place it in the freezer.
- Dry the steaks with a paper towel. Season the steaks with salt and pepper, then drizzle with Worcestershire sauce. To tenderize the steaks, pierce them with a fork to drive the seasoning in.
- Refrigerate the steaks for at least 30 minutes after marinating them in Worcestershire sauce.
- Remove the steaks from the pan and set them aside for 30 minutes. The highest temperature is room temperature!
- Preheat your Air Fryer to 400 F with the grate in place (if you have one). If you're using a grate, set the rack to the LOW setting. If not, place the rack on the MIDDLE level and place the steak directly on it.
- OPEN THE FRYER CAREFULLY and put the steaks on the grate.
- Cook for 5 minutes before flipping.
- Remove the steak from the pan and set it aside for five minutes before serving.
- Place a sliver of garlic butter on top of the sizzling steak.

Cal 652 | Protein 44g | Carb 7.5g | Fat 49.1g

## BACON CAULIFLOWER MAC & CHEESE
*Prep time:5 min | Cook time:20 min | Serves: 6*

### Ingredients

- 1 teaspoon salt
- ¼ teaspoon cayenne pepper
- green onions or parsley (chopped)
- 2 cups shredded cheddar cheese
- 4 strips bacon
- 1 cup water
- 1 cauliflower diced small
- 4 oz. cream cheese
- 1 teaspoon paprika
- 1/4 cup heavy cream

### Instructions

- In your air fryer, cook the bacon for 5 minutes. Cut up the dice into small bits.
- Cauliflower should be diced into small pieces.
- Add one cup of water and the cauliflower to a microwave-safe dish. 5 minutes in the microwave Tenderness should be tested. Cook for a few more minutes if it's still too hard. Drain the water.
- Preheat your Air Fryer to 400 F on Air Fry mode. During cooking, the rack will be set to the LOWEST position.
- Combine the cream cheese, heavy cream, one cup of cheese, salt, cayenne pepper, bacon, and paprika in the same dish. 1 minute more in the microwave
- Fill a Vortex-safe dish halfway with the cauliflower mixture. Place on the lowest shelf and, if you have one, cover with a fast cover to prevent the top from browning too quickly.
- 4 minutes in the air fryer Remove the top and cook for another 2 minutes, or until golden brown.

- Enjoy Garnish with green onions or parsley.

Cal 505 | Carb 8g | Protein 25g | Fat 42g

## SWEET BACON WRAPPED PORK TENDERLOIN

*Prep time:5 min | Cook time:20 min | Serves: 4*

### Ingredients

- 5 slices bacon approximately 10 ounces
- 1 pork tenderloin about 1 pound
- 3 tablespoon honey mustard
- ¼ cup brown sugar
- ½ teaspoon salt
- ¼ teaspoon black pepper

### Instructions

- Preheat the air fryer to 400 F on AIR FRY. The rack should be set to the LOWEST position.
- Cook the bacon in long strips for a few minutes, or until they are halfway through.
- Preheat the air fryer to 300 F on bake mode.
- Using paper towels, pat the pork dry.
- Combine mustard, brown sugar, salt, and pepper in a small cup. Stir in the sugar until it is fully dissolved in the mustard.
- Arrange the pork loin on a tray. Using a few tablespoons of the sauce, drizzle it over the pork.
- Wrap the bacon around the tenderloin of pork.
- On the lowest rack, bake for 10 minutes. Check the temperature and add a few minutes if it isn't 145'.
- Shift the bacon to the top rack for a minute or two if it isn't crispy enough.

Cal 48 | Carb 18g | Protein 55g | Fat 19g

## BOURBON GOUDA STUFFED MEAT LOAVES

*Prep time:20 min | Cook time:20 min | Serves: 4*

### Ingredients

- 1 Tablespoons Bourbon
- 6 oz. Gouda Either slices or cut into strips
- FOR THE SAUCE
- 1/4 cup ketchup
- 1/4 cup brown sugar
- 2 Tablespoons bourbon
- 1 teaspoon crushed red pepper flakes
- 1-pound ground beef'
- 1/4 cup panko bread crumbs
- 1/4 medium red onion grated
- 2 cloves garlic minced
- 1 egg lightly beaten
- 1 Tablespoon Chili Sauce
- 1 Tablespoon Worcestershire sauce

### Instructions

- Preheat your Air Fryer to BAKE at 400 F . The rack will be set to the LOWEST setting.
- Combine the bourbon and bread crumbs in a large mixing bowl. Allow the bourbon to soak into the bread crumbs for a few minutes. Combine the ground beef, chili sauce, red onion, garlic, eggs, and Worcestershire sauce in a large mixing bowl.
- Gently blend with your hands until it is well mixed. Don't overwork the meat; otherwise, your meatloaf would be tough and chewy.
- In the bowl, divide the meat into four pieces. Make a patty with half of one beef. Place the cheese in the centre of the meatloaf,

leaving an inch of meatloaf on all sides. Cover with the remaining meatloaf mixture and press the edges together to tightly seal the sandwich. Any exposed holes would allow the cheese to leak out during the cooking process.

- Rep until you've completed all four and put them on a shelf. Add them to the air fryer on the lowest setting once it has heated up. Cook for 10 minutes, or until well browned on the outside.
- In a small bowl, combine all of the ingredients. Combine the sauce ingredients and pour over the top of the meatloaf, allowing it to run down the sides a little.
- Remove the pan from the air fryer and cover with the sauce. Return to the air fryer for another 1-2 minutes, or until the mixture is bubbly.
- Serve with mashed potatoes or vegetables as a side dish!

Cal 372 | Fat 21g; | Carb 11g; | Protein 31g

## STUFFED ZUCCHINI BOATS

*Prep time:15min | Cook time:10 min | Serves: 7*

### Ingredients

- Ground pork: 1 lb.
- Mushrooms: 1 cup
- Yellow onion: 1/2
- 4 chopped garlic cloves
- 4 zucchinis
- 1 bell pepper chopped without seeds

### Instructions

- Slice the zucchinis in half and take the middle part out.
- In a food processor, add vegetable, garlic and zucchini middle part.
- Pulse until chopped.
- Cook pork in a pan on medium flame, when it is half cooked add vegetable mixture.
- Cook for 3 to 4 minutes.
- Let the air fry preheat to 375 F.
- Add the pork mixture in zucchini boats.
- Air fry for 7 to 10 minutes.
- Serve.

Cal 269 | Fat 13g | Protein 27g | Carb 4g

## SAUSAGE BALLS

*Prep time:15min | Cook time:10 min | Serves: 7*

### Ingredients

- Breakfast sausage: 1 lb.
- Minced onions: 1 tbsp., Dried
- Baking powder: 2 tsp.
- cheddar cheese: 1 cup, grated
- ½ cup cream cheese, softened
- Salt
- 1 egg
- Almond flour: ¾ cup

### Instructions

- Let the air fry preheat to 350 F.
- Add all ingredients in a bowl, and mix well.
- make small meatballs from the mixture.
- Air fry for 8 to 10 minutes.
- Serve with sauce

Cal 62 | Fat 4 g | Protein 5 g | Carb 1 g

## GARLIC THYME PORK CHOPS

*Prep time:15 min | Cook time:15 min | Serves: 2*

### Ingredients
- Pork chops: 1 ¾ pounds
- Fresh thyme: 3 sprigs
- Fresh rosemary, 1 sprig
- Oil: 2 tbsp.
- Salt & black pepper
- 2 garlic cloves

### Instructions
- Let the pork chops come to room temperature before cooking. Season with salt and pepper.
- Let the air fry preheat to 350 F.
- Sear pork chops in a pan for 3 to 4 minutes in hot oil. Take the chops out.
- Add the rest of the ingredients in the pan, cook for 2 to 3 minutes, pour over chops.
- Air fry for 8 to 10 minutes, until the pork's internal temperature reaches 145 F.
- Serve right away.

Cal 299 | Fat 13 g | Protein 31 g | Carb 3 g

## GRANDMA'S STUFFED CABBAGE

*Prep time:10 min | Cook time:30 min | Serves: 8*

### Ingredients
Sauce
- 1 tablespoon oil
- 1 tablespoon honey
- 1/2 teaspoon salt
- 1/4 teaspoon black pepper
- 1/3 cup golden raisins 50g
- 1 large green apple peeled and cut into 3/4-inch (2cm) cubes
- 2 medium onions chopped into small dice
- 1 can crushed tomatoes 28-ounce [828ml]
- 1 cup Water 236ml
- 1/4 cup fresh lemon juice from 1–2 lemons, 59ml
- 5 tablespoon light brown sugar 60g

Cabbage Rolls
- 1 head Napa cabbage
- 1 large egg
- 1/4 cup Water 59ml
- 1/2 teaspoon salt
- 1/4 teaspoon black pepper
- 1 onion
- 1 lb ground beef
- 1/3 cup white rice 65g

### Instructions
- Cut the cabbage in half and separate the 17 leaves. On the stovetop, bring a medium or big saucepan of water to a boil. Over a bowl near the saucepan, put a colander. Cook the leaves for 4 minutes per batch, about 6 at a time, with the water boiling the entire time. Raise the cooked leaves with tongs and put them in a colander to drain. Make an effort not to tear the leaves. Allow to dry on paper towels or a clean dishtowel.
- To make the sauce, press Sauté and add the oil, chopped onions, and apples when the show reads "Hot." Cook, stirring often, for around 5 minutes, or until they begin to soften but do not brown.

- In the meantime, make the cabbage filling. By hand or in a food processor, finely chop the onion. Place in a big mixing bowl. Mix well with your hands the beef, rice, egg, water, salt, and pepper. In front of you, fan out a cabbage leaf with the stem facing you. Scoop up a quarter cup of the meat and rice mixture and position it at the bottom of each cabbage leaf, near the stem.
- Fold the bottom of the leaf over the meat and roll it up, then fold the sides of the leaf toward the centre to cover the meat and roll it up.
- Bring the crushed tomatoes, water, lemon juice, brown sugar, and honey to a boil after the onions and apple have been cooked. Season with salt and pepper.
- Transfer the sauce to a big mixing bowl. Boil 1/2 cup (118ml) hot water in the inner pot, then scrape the bottom of the pot clean with a wooden spoon. On top of that, put the steam rack. Place one layer of rolls on the rack, then one ladle of sauce, then another layer of rolls, and so on, finishing with any remaining sauce. On top, scatter the golden raisins.
- Close the lid and make sure the steam release handle is set to Sealing. Click the Pressure Cook button and select an 18-minute cooking time. Enable the pot to sit for 15 minutes after the Cook time:has ended to allow the pressure to naturally release. To relieve any residual pressure, turn the valve to the Venting position. Delete the lid by pressing Cancel.

Cal 468 | Protein 28.1g | Carb 21.7g | Fat 29.8g

## HONEY DIJON PORK SCHNITZEL

*Prep time:20 min | Cook time:12 min | Serves: 4*

### Ingredients
- 2 tablespoons lemon juice
- 1/2 teaspoon salt
- 1/4 teaspoon black pepper
- 1 lb boneless pork chops pounded thin,
- sauerkraut warmed
- 3 tablespoon liquid honey
- 1 tablespoon Dijon mustard
- 2/3 cup dry seasoned bread crumbs
- 1/4 cup grated parmesan cheese

### Instructions
- Combine the lemon juice, sugar, and mustard in a mixing bowl. Combine bread crumbs, cheese, salt, and black pepper in a shallow dish. Pork should be dipped in the lemon juice mixture, then breadcrumbs, and put on two baking trays. Spray all sides of the pork schnitzels with cooking spray.
- Place the drip pan in the cooking chamber's bottom. Select Air Fry on the display screen, then set the Temperature to 375°F and the Time to 12 minutes. Start by pressing the Start button. Preheat the Vortex until the display says "Add Food."
- If only one tray is being used, slip the cooking tray into the middle spot. Switch the schnitzel over when the show says to. If you're using two trays, placing one in the middle and the other in the bottom. When the show says Turn Food, flip the schnitzels over and move the bottom tray to the top and the middle tray to the bottom.
- Cook until the meat is no longer pink inside and the internal cooked temperature exceeds 160°F when measured with a meat thermometer. Allow for a 5-minute rest period before serving. Serve with soft sauerkraut on the side.

Cal 309 | Fat 13g, | Carb 17g | Protein 30g

## MEAT & MUSHROOMS

*Prep time:10 min | Cook time:18 min | Serves: 3*

### Ingredients

- 1 lb. steaks, cut into half inch cubes
- Melted Butter: 2 tbsp.
- salt & pepper
- Worcestershire sauce: 1 tsp.
- 8 oz. mushrooms, cut in half
- Garlic powder: half tsp.

### Instructions

- In a bowl, add mushrooms and steak cubes, add the rest of the ingredients, toss to coat.
- Let the Kalorik Air Fryer Oven preheat to 400 F.
- Place the steak and mushrooms in the air fryer basket, air fry for 10 to 18 minutes. Shake the basket twice.
- Add fresh herbs on top and serve with rice.

Cal 483 | Fat 30g | Carb 30g | Protein 25g

## EASY BABY BACK RIBS

*Prep time:5 min | Cook time:40 min | Serves: 4*

### Ingredients

- 2 tablespoon brown sugar
- 1 rack of baby back pork ribs membrane removed
- 1/4 teaspoon liquid smoke
- 1/4 cup BBQ sauce
- 1 tablespoon chili powder
- 2 teaspoon garlic salt

### Instructions

- In a bowl, add all ingredients and coat the ribs.
- Keep in the fridge for 30 minutes
- Air fry the ribs for 10 to 12 minutes at 375 F

Cal 216 | Fat 6g | Carb 35g | Protein 5g

## PARTY CASSOULET

*Prep time:20 min (+ 8 hours soaking time) | Cook time:70 min | Serves: 4*

### Ingredients

- 1 cup dried white navy beans
- 2 tablespoon tomato paste
- 1/2 cup dry white wine
- 2 thyme sprigs
- 2 bay leaves
- 1 lb pork stewing meat
- 8 oz. kielbasa sausage cut into large chunks
- 2 1/2 cups chicken broth
- 1 cup packed French bread torn into 1/2 inch pieces
- 1/4 cup grated parmesan cheese
- 3 tablespoons olive oil
- 2 tablespoons finely chopped fresh chives
- 4 bone-in chicken thighs
- 1/2 teaspoon each salt and pepper divided
- 4 thick bacon slices chopped
- 1 onion diced
- 1 celery stalk diced
- 1 carrot chopped
- 1 leek chopped
- 3 garlic cloves chopped
- 1/2 teaspoon herbs de Prair fryerce

### Instructions

- Soak the beans overnight in water. Set aside after draining and rinsing.
- Season chicken thighs with 1/4 teaspoon salt and 1/4 teaspoon pepper; set aside.
- Air fry the chicken for 8 to 12 minutes at 375 F.
- Place the chicken on a tray.
- Combine the onion, celery, carrot, leek, garlic, herbes de Prair fryerce, and the remaining salt and pepper in a large mixing bowl. Cook for 3–5 minutes, or until the vegetables soften. Toss in the tomato paste. 1 minute of cooking Bring to a boil with the wine, thyme sprigs, and bay leaves.
- Press the Cancel button. Over the top, layer-soaked beans, chicken, pork stewing beef, kielbasa, and bacon that has been set aside. Add the broth.
- Put the lid on the pot and tighten it to seal it. a lot of pressure Cook for 30 minutes on high pressure.
- When the pressure cooking is over, release the pressure naturally. Remove the lid until the pressure has been released. Bay leaves should be discarded.
- Combine the bread, Parmesan cheese, and olive oil in a mixing bowl. Sprinkle the topping on top of the casserole. Pick Roast at 400°F for 3 to 5 minutes, or until golden brown and toasted, using the Air Fryer Lid. Serve with chives on top.

Cal 1150 | Fat 73g | Carb 48g | Protein 69g

## HONEY MESQUITE PORK CHOPS

*Prep time:30 min | Cook time:15 min | Serves: 2*

### Ingredients

- Olive oil: 1 1/2 tbsp.
- Mesquite seasoning: 1 1/2 tbsp.
- 2 center-cut pork chops, with bone, medium thickness
- Honey: 2 tbsp.
- Black pepper: ¼ tsp.

### Instructions

- In a dish, add all ingredients and coat the pork chops.
- Cover and let it rest for 20 minutes.
- Let the Kalorik Air Fryer Oven preheat to 380 F.
- Air fry the chops for 8 minutes, flipping halfway through. Pour the spice mixture and air fry for 4-8 minutes more.

Cal 382 | Fat 21g | Carb 20g | Protein 30g

## SWEET AND SOUR PINEAPPLE PORK

*Prep time:25 min | Cook time:15 min | Serves: 4*

### Ingredients

- Crushed pineapple: 1 can (8 ounce), with liquid
- Garlic powder: 1 tsp.
- Sugar: ½ cup
- Ketchup: half cup
- Apple cider vinegar: 1 cup
- Brown sugar: half cup
- Dijon mustard: 1 tsp.
- 2 pork tenderloins, cut in half
- Soy sauce: 2 tbsp.
- Black pepper & salt

### Instructions

- In a pan, add all ingredients except for pork. Simmer for 15 to 20 minutes, until thickness.
- Let the Kalorik Air Fryer Oven preheat to 350 F.
- Sprinkle salt and pepper on the pork.

- Air fry for 7 to 8 minutes, flip and pour some sauce over.
- Air fry for 10 to 12 minutes more, until the internal temperature of the meat reaches 145 F.
- Slice and serve with sauce

Cal 489 | Carb 72 g | Protein 35 g | Fat 7 g

## GINGERY PORK MEATBALLS
*Prep time:10 min | Cook time:15 min | Serves: 3 to 4*

### Ingredients
- 1 whole egg
- honey: 1 1/2 tbsp.
- 1 jalapeño, chopped, seeded
- lime zest: 2 tsp.
- lime juice: 2 tbsp.
- ground pork: 1 lb.
- 2 scallions, chopped
- fish sauce: 1 tsp.
- minced ginger: 1 tbsp.
- salt, to taste
- dry Panko: half cup
- 1 chopped garlic clove
- Cilantro: 1/4 cup, minced

### Instructions
- In a large dish, add all the ingredients. Mix well.
- Make into meatballs
- Air fry for 8 to 12 minutes, at 400 F, flip halfway through.
- Serve with rice.

## BBQ PORK RIBS
*Prep time: 10 min | Cook time: 12 min | Serves: 6*

### Ingredients
- 1 slab baby back pork ribs, cut into pieces
- ½ cup BBQ sauce
- ½ tsp paprika
- Salt

### Directions
- Add pork ribs in a mixing bowl.
- Add BBQ sauce, paprika, and salt over pork ribs and coat well and set aside for 30 minutes.
- Preheat the Air Fryer oven to 350°F.
- Arrange marinated pork ribs on Air Fryer oven pan and cook for 10-12 minutes. Turn halfway through.
- Serve and enjoy.

Cal 145 | Fat 7g | Carb 10g | Protein 9 g

## EASY ROSEMARY LAMB CHOPS
*Prep time: 10 min | Cook time: 6 min | Serves: 4*

### Ingredients
- 4 lamb chops
- 2 tbsp dried rosemary
- ¼ cup fresh lemon juice
- Pepper
- Salt

### Directions
- In a small bowl, mix together lemon juice, rosemary, pepper, and salt.
- Brush lemon juice rosemary mixture over lamb chops.

- Place lamb chops on air fryer oven tray and air fry at 400°F for 3 minutes.
- Turn lamb chops to the other side and cook for 3 minutes more.
- Serve and enjoy.

Cal 267 | Fat 21.7g | Carb 1.4g | Protein 16.9 g

## JUICY STEAK BITES
*Prep time: 10 min | Cook time: 9 min | Serves: 4*

### Ingredients
- 1 lb sirloin steak, sliced into bite-size pieces
- 1 tbsp steak seasoning
- 1 tbsp olive oil
- Pepper
- Salt

### Directions
- Preheat the air fryer oven to 390°F.
- Add steak pieces into the large mixing bowl. Add steak seasoning, oil, pepper, and salt over steak pieces and toss until well coated.
- Transfer steak pieces on Air Fryer pan and air fry for 5 minutes.
- Turn steak pieces to the other side and cook for 4 minutes more.
- Serve and enjoy.

Cal 241 | Fat 10.6g | Carb 0g | Protein 34.4 g

## SPICED BUTTERNUT SQUASH
*Prep time: 10 min    Cook time: 15 min | Serves: 4*

### Ingredients
- 4 cups 1-inch-cubed butternut squash
- 2 tablespoons vegetable oil
- 1 to 2 tablespoons brown sugar
- 1 teaspoon Chinese five-spice powder

### Directions
- Preparing the Ingredients. In a bowl, combine the oil, sugar, squash, and five-spice powder. Toss to coat.
- Place the squash in the air fryer basket.
- Air Frying. Set the air fryer to 400°F for 15 minutes or until tender.

Cal 160 | Fat 5g | Carbs 9g | Protein 6g

## EASY BEEF ROAST
*Prep time: 10 min | Cook time: 45 min | Serves: 6*

### Ingredients
- 2 ½ lbs. beef roast
- 2 tbsp Italian seasoning

### Directions
- Arrange roast on the rotisserie spite.
- Rub roast with Italian seasoning then insert into your air fryer oven.
- Air fry at 350°F for 45 minutes or until the internal temperature of the roast reaches to 145 F.
- Slice and serve.

Cal 365 | Fat 13.2g | Carb 0.5g | Sugar 0.4g | Protein 57.4 g

## BEEF JERKY
*Prep time: 10 min | Cook time: 4 hours | Serves: 4*

### Ingredients
- 2 lbs. London broil, sliced thinly
- 1 tsp onion powder

- 3 tbsp brown sugar
- 3 tbsp soy sauce
- 1 tsp olive oil

**Directions**

- Add all ingredients except meat in the large zip-lock bag.
- Mix until well combined. Add meat in the bag.
- Seal bag and massage gently to cover the meat with marinade.
- Let marinate the meat for 1 hour.
- Arrange marinated meat slices on Air Fryer tray and dehydrate at 160°F for 4 hours.

Cal 133 | Fat 4.7g | Carb 9.4g | Sugar 7.1g | Protein 13.4 g

## PORK TAQUITOS

*Prep time: 10 min | Cook time: 16 min | Serves: 8*

**Ingredients**

- 1 juiced lime
- 10 whole wheat tortillas
- 2 ½ c. Shredded mozzarella cheese
- 30 ounces of cooked and shredded pork tenderloin

**Directions**

- Preparing the ingredients. Ensure your air fryer is preheated to 380°F.
- Drizzle pork with lime juice and gently mix.
- Heat up tortillas in the microwave with a dampened paper towel to soften.
- Add about 3 ounces of pork and ¼ cup of shredded cheese to each tortilla. Tightly roll them up.
- Grease the air fryer basket with a drizzle of olive oil.
- Air frying. Set temperature to 380°F, and set time to 10 minutes. Air fry taquitos 7-10 minutes till tortillas turn a slight golden color, making sure to flip halfway through cooking process.

Cal 309 | Fat 11g | Protein 21g

## PANKO-BREADED PORK CHOPS

*Prep time: 5 min | Cook time: 12 min | Serves: 6*

**Ingredients**

- 5 (3½- to 5-ounce) pork chops (bone-in or boneless)
- salt and pepper
- ¼ cup all-purpose flour
- 2 tablespoons panko bread crumbs
- Cooking oil

**Directions**

- Preparing the Ingredients. Season the pork chops with salt and pepper to taste.
- Sprinkle the flour on both sides of the pork chops, then coat both sides with panko bread crumbs.
- Put the pork chops in the air fryer. Stacking them is okay.
- Air Frying. Spray the pork chops with cooking oil. Cook for 6 minutes.
- Halfway through, flip the pork chops. Cook for an additional 6 minutes
- Cool before serving.
- Typically, bone-in pork chops are juicier than boneless. If you prefer really juicy pork chops, use bone-in.

Cal 246 | Fat 13g | Protein 26g | Fiber 0g

## GREEK LAMB CHOPS

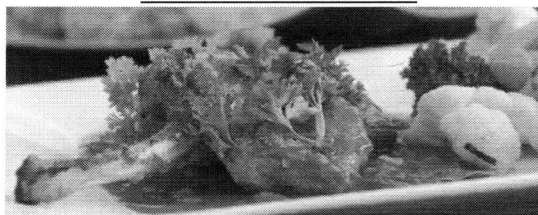

*Prep time: 10 min | Cook time: 10 min | Serves: 4*

**Ingredients**

- 2 lbs. lamb chops
- 2 tsp garlic, minced
- 1 ½ tsp dried oregano
- ¼ cup fresh lemon juice
- salt and pepper

**Directions**

- Add lamb chops in a mixing bowl. Add remaining ingredients over the lamb chops and coat well.
- Arrange lamb chops on the air fryer oven tray and cook at 400°F for 5 minutes.
- Turn lamb chops and cook for 5 minutes more.
- Serve and enjoy.

Cal 538 | Fat 29.4g | Carb 1.3g | Sugar 0.4g | Protein 64 g

## CRISPY ROAST GARLIC-SALT PORK

*Prep time: 5 min | Cook time: 45 min | Serves: 4*

**Ingredients**

- 1 teaspoon Chinese five spice powder
- 1 teaspoon white pepper
- 2 pounds pork belly
- 2 teaspoons garlic salt

**Directions**

- Preparing the Ingredients. Preheat the air fryer to 390°F.
- Mix all of the seasonings in a bowl to create the dry rub.
- Score the skin of the pork belly with a knife and season the entire pork with the spice rub.
- Air Frying. Place in the air fryer and cook for 40 to 45 minutes until the skin is crispy.
- Chop before serving.

Cal 785 | Fat 80.7g | Protein 14.2g

## BEEF ROLLS

*Prep time: 10 min | Cook time: 14 min | Serves: 4*

**Ingredients**

- 2 pounds beef steak, opened and flattened with a meat tenderizer
- Salt and black pepper to the taste
- 3 ounces red bell pepper, roasted and chopped
- 6 slices provolone cheese
- 3 tablespoons pesto

**Directions**

- Arrange flattened beef steak on a cutting board, spread pesto all over, add cheese in a single layer, add bell peppers, salt and pepper to the taste.
- Roll your steak, secure with toothpicks, season again with salt and pepper, place roll in your air fryer's basket and cook at 400°F for 14 minutes, rotating roll halfway.

- Leave aside to cool down, cut into 2-inch smaller rolls, arrange on a platter and serve them as an appetizer.
- Enjoy!

Cal 230 | Fat 1g | Fiber 3g | Carb 12g | Protein 10g

## HOMEMADE CORNED BEEF WITH ONIONS

*Prep time: 5 min | Cook time: 50 min | Serves: 4*

**Ingredients**
- Salt and pepper to taste
- 1 cup water
- 1-pound corned beef brisket, cut into chunks
- 1 tablespoon Dijon mustard
- 1 small onion, chopped

**Directions**
- Preheat the air fryer to 400°F.
- Place all ingredients in a baking dish that will fit in the air fryer.
- Cover with foil.
- Cook for 35 minutes.
- Remove foil, mix well, turnover beef, and continue cooking for another 15 minutes.

Cal 238 | Carb 3.1g | Protein 17.2g | Fat 17.1g | Fiber 0.6g

## ROAST BEEF

*Prep time: 10 min | Cook time: 35 min | Serves: 4*

**Ingredients**
- 2 lb. beef roast top
- oil for spraying
- Rub
- salt and pepper to taste
- 2 teaspoon garlic powder
- 1 teaspoon summer savory

**Directions**
- Whisk all the rub ingredients in a small bowl.
- Liberally rub this mixture over the roast.
- Place in the Air Fryer Basket and layer it with cooking oil.
- Set the seasoned roast in the Air Fryer Basket.
- Take to the preheated air fryer at 370°F for 20 minutes.
- Turn the roast and continue Air fryer for another 15 minutes.
- Serve warm.

Cal 427 | Fat 14.2g | Carb 1.4g | Fiber 0.3g | Protein 69.1g

## SIMPLE BREADED PORK CHOPS

*Prep time: 10 min | Cook time: 18 min | Serves: 4*

**Ingredients**
- 4 boneless, center-cut pork chops, 1-inch thick
- 1 teaspoon Cajun seasoning
- 1 1/2 cups garlic-flavored croutons
- 2 eggs
- cooking spray

**Directions**
- Grind croutons in a food processor until it forms crumbs.
- Season the pork chops with Cajun seasoning liberally.
- Beat eggs in a shallow tray then dip the pork chops in the egg.
- Coat the dipped chops in the crouton crumbs.
- Spray the chops with cooking oil.
- Take to the preheated air fryer at 380°F for 18 minutes.
- Serve.

Cal 301 | Fat 12.4g | Carb 12.2g | Fiber 0g | Protein 32.2g

## BASIC PORK CHOPS

*Prep time: 10 min | Cook time: 15 min | Serves: 4*

**Ingredients**
- 4 pork chops, bone-in
- 1 tablespoon olive oil
- 1 teaspoon kosher salt
- 1/2 teaspoon black pepper

**Directions**
- Liberally season the pork chops with olive oil, salt, and black pepper.
- Spray the chops with cooking oil.
- Take to the preheated air fryer at 380°F for 15 minutes.
- Serve.

Cal 287 | Fat 23.4g | Carb 0.2g | Fiber 0.1g | Protein 18g

## BEEF AND BALSAMIC MARINADE

*Prep time: 5 min | Cook time: 40 min | Serves: 4*

**Ingredients**
- 4 medium beef steaks
- 3 garlic cloves; minced
- 1 cup balsamic vinegar
- 2 tbsp. olive oil
- Salt and black pepper to taste.

**Directions**
- Take a bowl and mix steaks with the rest of the ingredients and toss.
- Transfer the steaks to your air fryer's basket and cook at 390°F for 35 minutes, flipping them halfway
- Divide among plates and serve with a side salad.

Cal 273 | Fat 14g | Fiber 4g | Carb 6g | Protein 19g

## HONEY MUSTARD PORK TENDERLOIN

*Prep time: 15 min | Cook time: 25 minutes | Serves: 3*

**Ingredients**
- 1-pound pork tenderloin
- 1 tablespoon garlic, minced
- 2 tablespoons soy sauce
- 2 tablespoons honey
- 1 tablespoon Dijon mustard
- 1 tablespoon grain mustard
- 1 teaspoon Sriracha sauce

**Directions**
- In a large bowl, add all the ingredients except pork and mix well.
- Add the pork tenderloin and coat with the mixture generously.
- Refrigerate to marinate for 2-3 hours.
- Remove the pork tenderloin from bowl, reserving the marinade.
- Place the pork tenderloin onto the lightly greased cooking tray.
- Arrange the drip pan in the bottom of Air Fryer Oven cooking chamber.
- Take to the preheated air fryer at 380°F for 25 minutes.
- After 12 minutes When the display shows "Turn Food" turn the pork and oat with the reserved marinade.
- When cooking time is complete, remove the tray from Air Fryer and place the pork tenderloin onto a platter for about 10 minutes before slicing.
- With a sharp knife, cut the pork tenderloin into desired sized slices and serve.

Cal 277 | Fat 5.7g | Carb 14.2g | Fiber 0.4g | Sugar 11.8g | Protein 40.7 g

## AIR FRYER MEATLOAF
*Prep time: 10 min | Cook time: 25 min | Serves: 4*

**Ingredients**

- 1-pound lean beef
- 1 lightly beaten egg
- 3 tablespoons. bread crumbs
- 1 small, finely chopped onion
- 1 tablespoon. chopped fresh thyme
- 1 teaspoon salt
- 1 pinch ground black pepper to taste
- 2 thickly sliced mushrooms
- 1 tablespoon. olive oil

**Directions**

- Preheat an air fryer up to 390°F.
- In a bowl, combine ground beef, egg, bread crumbs, ointment, thyme, salt, and pepper. Knead and mix well.
- Move the mixture of beef into a baking pan and smooth the rim—press chestnuts into the top and coat with olive oil. Place the saucepan in the basket of the air fryer and slide into your air fryer oven.
- Set 25-minute air fryer timer and roast meatloaf until well browned.
- Set aside the meatloaf for at least 10 minutes before slicing and serving into wedges.

Cal 296.8 | Protein 24.8g | Carb 5.9 g

## BEEF AND RADISHES
*Prep time: 5 min | Cook time: 15 min | Serves: 2*

**Ingredients**

- 1 lb. radishes, quartered
- 2 cups corned beef, cooked and shredded
- 2 spring onions; chopped
- 2 garlic cloves; minced
- A pinch of salt and black pepper

**Directions**

- In a pan that fits your air fryer, mix the beef with the rest of the ingredients, toss.
- Put the pan in the fryer and cook at 390°F for 15 minutes
- Divide everything into bowls and serve.

Cal 267 | Fat 13g | Fiber 2g | Carb 5g | Protein 15g

## HERBED PORK CHOPS
*Prep time: 5 min | Cook time: 25 min | Serves: 4*

**Ingredients**

- 4 pork chops
- 2 tsp. basil; dried
- ½ tsp. chili powder
- 2 tbsp. olive oil
- A pinch of salt and black pepper

**Directions**

- In a pan that fits your air fryer, mix all the ingredients, toss.
- Introduce in the fryer and cook at 400°F for 25 minutes. Divide everything between plates and serve

Cal 274 | Fat 13g | Fiber 4g | Carb 6g | Protein 18g

## CRISPY BRATS
*Prep time: 5 min | Cook time: 15 min | Serves: 4*

**Ingredients**

- 4 (3-oz. beef bratwursts

**Directions**

- Place brats into your air fryer oven basket.
- Adjust the temperature to 375 Degrees F and set the timer for 15 minutes.

Cal 286 | Protein 18g | Fiber 0g | Fat 28g | Carb 0g

## CAJUN BACON PORK LOIN FILLET
*Prep time: 10 min | Cook time: 20 min | Serves: 6*

**Ingredients**

- 1½ pounds pork loin fillet or pork tenderloin
- 3 tablespoons olive oil
- 2 tablespoons Cajun Spice Mix
- Salt
- 6 slices bacon
- Olive oil spray

**Directions**

- Preparing the Ingredients. Cut the pork in half so that it will fit in the air fryer basket.
- Place both pieces of meat in a resealable plastic bag. Add the oil, Cajun seasoning, and salt to taste, if using. Seal the bag and massage to coat all of the meat with the oil and seasonings. Marinate in the refrigerator for at least 1 hour or up to 24 hours.
- Air Frying. Remove the pork from the bag and wrap 3 bacon slices around each piece. Spray the air fryer basket with olive oil spray. Place the meat in the air fryer. Set the air fryer to 350°F for 15 minutes. Increase the temperature to 400°F for 5 minutes.
- Use a meat thermometer to ensure the meat has reached an internal temperature of 145°F.
- Let the meat rest for 10 minutes. Slice into 6 medallions and serve.

Cal 355 | Protein 34.83g | Fat 22.88 g | Carb 0.6 g

## PORCHETTA-STYLE PORK CHOPS
*Prep time: 10 min | Cook time: 15 min | Serves: 2*

**Ingredients**

- 1 tablespoon extra-virgin olive oil
- Grated zest of 1 lemon
- 2 cloves garlic, minced
- 2 teaspoons chopped fresh rosemary
- 1 teaspoon finely chopped fresh sage
- 1 teaspoon fennel seeds, lightly crushed
- ¼ to ½ teaspoon red pepper flakes
- 1 teaspoon kosher salt
- 1 teaspoon black pepper
- (8-ounce) center-cut bone-in pork chops, about 1 inch thick

**Directions**

- Preparing the Ingredients. In a small bowl, combine the olive oil, zest, garlic, rosemary, sage, fennel seeds, red pepper, salt, and black pepper. Stir, crushing the herbs with the back of a spoon, until a paste forms. Spread the seasoning mix on both sides of the pork chops.
- Air Frying. Place the chops in the air fryer basket. Set the air fryer to 375°F for 15 minutes. Use a meat thermometer to ensure the chops have reached an internal temperature of 145°F.

Cal 200 | Protein 23.45g | Fat 9.7g | Carb 4.46 g

## BASIL PORK CHOPS

*Prep time: 5 min | Cook time: 30 min | Serves: 4*

**Ingredients**

- 4 pork chops
- 2 tsp. basil; dried
- ½ tsp. chili powder
- 2 tbsp. olive oil
- A pinch of salt and black pepper

**Directions**

- In a pan that fits your air fryer, mix all the ingredients, toss.
- Introduce in the fryer and cook at 400°F for 25 minutes. Divide everything between plates and serve

Cal 274 | Fat 13g | Fiber 4g | Carb 6g | Protein 18g

## APRICOT GLAZED PORK TENDERLOINS

*Prep time: 5 min | Cook time: 30 min | Serves: 3*

**Ingredients**

- 1 teaspoon salt
- 1/2 teaspoon pepper
- 1-lb pork tenderloin
- 2 tablespoons minced fresh rosemary or 1 tablespoon dried rosemary, crushed
- 2 tablespoons olive oil, divided
- 1 garlic cloves, minced
- Apricot Glaze Ingredients
- 1 cup apricot preserves
- 3 garlic cloves, minced
- 4 tablespoons lemon juice

**Directions**

- Preparing the Ingredients. Mix well pepper, salt, garlic, oil, and rosemary. Brush all over pork. If needed cut pork crosswise in half to fit in air fryer. Lightly grease baking pan of air fryer with cooking spray. Add pork.
- Air Frying. For 3 minutes per side, brown pork in a preheated 390°F air fryer. Meanwhile, mix well all glaze Ingredients in a small bowl. Baste pork every 5 minutes. Cook for 20 minutes at 330°F. Serve and enjoy.

Cal 454 | Protein 43.76g | Fat 16.71 g | Carb 33.68 g

## SWEET & SPICY COUNTRY-STYLE RIBS

*Prep time: 10 min | Cook time: 25 min | Serves: 4*

**Ingredients**

- 2 tablespoons brown sugar
- 2 tablespoons smoked paprika
- 1 teaspoon garlic powder
- 1 teaspoon onion powder
- 1 teaspoon dry mustard
- 1 teaspoon ground cumin
- 1 teaspoon kosher salt
- 1 teaspoon black pepper
- ¼ to ½ teaspoon cayenne pepper
- 1½ pounds boneless country-style pork ribs
- 1 cup barbecue sauce

**Directions**

- Preparing the Ingredients. In a small bowl, stir together the brown sugar, paprika, garlic powder, onion powder, dry mustard, cumin, salt, black pepper, and cayenne. Mix until well combined.

- Pat the ribs dry with a paper towel. Generously sprinkle the rub evenly over both sides of the ribs and rub in with your fingers.
- Air Frying. Place the ribs in the air fryer basket. Set the air fryer to 350°F for 15 minutes. Turn the ribs and brush with ½ cup of the barbecue sauce. Cook for an additional 10 minutes. Use a meat thermometer to ensure the pork has reached an internal temperature of 145°F. Serve with remaining barbecue sauce.

Cal 416 | Protein 38.39g | Fat 12.19 g | Carb 36.79 g

## FLAVORFUL STEAK

*Prep time: 10 min | Cook time: 18 min | Serves: 2*

**Ingredients**

- 2 steaks, rinsed and pat dry
- ½ tsp garlic powder
- 1 tsp olive oil
- Pepper
- Salt

**Directions**

- Brush steaks with olive oil and season with garlic powder, pepper, and salt.
- Preheat the Air Fryer oven to 400°F.
- Place steaks on air fryer oven pan and air fry for 10-18 minutes. Turn halfway through.
- Serve and enjoy.

Cal 361 | Fat 10.9g | Carb 0.5g | Sugar 0.2g | Protein 61.6 g

## PORK TENDERS WITH BELL PEPPERS

*Preparation Time: 5 min | Cook time: 15 min | Serves: 4*

**Ingredients**

- 11 Oz Pork Tenderloin
- 1 Bell Pepper, in thin strips
- 1 Red Onion, sliced
- 2 Tsps. Provencal Herbs
- Black Pepper to taste
- 1 tbsp. Olive Oil
- 1/2 tbsp. Mustard

**Directions**

- Preparing the Ingredients. Preheat the air fryer to 390°F.
- In the oven dish, mix the bell pepper strips with the onion, herbs, and some salt and pepper to taste.
- Add half a tablespoon of olive oil to the mixture
- Cut the pork tenderloin into four pieces and rub with salt, pepper and mustard.
- Thinly coat the pieces with remaining olive oil and place them upright in the oven dish on top of the pepper mixture
- Air Frying. Place the bowl into your air fryer oven. Set the timer to 15 minutes and cook the meat and the vegetables
- Turn the meat and mix the peppers halfway through
- Serve with a fresh salad

Cal 220 | Protein 23.79g | Fat 12.36 g | Carb 2.45 g

## WONTON MEATBALLS

*Prep time: 15 min | Cook time: 10 min | Serves: 4*

**Ingredients**

- 1-pound ground pork
- 2 large eggs
- ¼ cup chopped green onions (white and green parts)
- ¼ cup chopped fresh cilantro or parsley
- 1 tablespoon minced fresh ginger
- 3 cloves garlic, minced
- 2 teaspoons soy sauce
- 1 teaspoon oyster sauce
- ½ teaspoon kosher salt
- 1 teaspoon black pepper

**Directions**

- Preparing the Ingredients. In the bowl of a stand mixer fitted with the paddle attachment, combine the pork, eggs, green onions, cilantro, ginger, garlic, soy sauce, oyster sauce, salt, and pepper. Mix on low speed until all of the ingredients are incorporated, 2 to 3 minutes.
- Form the mixture into 12 meatballs and arrange in a single layer in the air fryer basket.
- Air Frying. Set the air fryer to 350°F for 10 minutes. Use a meat thermometer to ensure the meatballs have reached an internal temperature of 145°F.
- Transfer the meatballs to a bowl and serve.

Cal 402 | Protein 32.69g | Fat 27.91 g | Carb 3.1 g

## BARBECUE FLAVORED PORK RIBS

*Prep time: 5 min | Cook time:15 min | Serves: 6*

**Ingredients**

- ¼ cup honey, divided
- ¾ cup BBQ sauce
- 2 tablespoons tomato ketchup
- 1 tablespoon Worcestershire sauce
- 1 tablespoon soy sauce
- ½ teaspoon garlic powder
- Freshly ground white pepper, to taste
- 1¾ pound pork ribs

**Directions**

- Preparing the ingredients. In a large bowl, mix together 3 tablespoons of honey and remaining ingredients except pork ribs. Refrigerate to marinate for about 20 minutes. Preheat the air fryer to 355°F. Place the ribs in the Air fryer basket.
- Air Frying. Cook for about 13 minutes. Remove the ribs from the Air fryer and coat with remaining honey. Serve hot.

Cal 265 | Protein 29.47g | Fat 9.04g | Carb 15.87 g

## MARINATED PORK TENDERLOIN

*Prep time: 70 min | Cook time: 30 min | Serves: 4*

**Ingredients**

- ¼ cup olive oil
- ¼ cup soy sauce
- ¼ cup freshly squeezed lemon juice
- 1 garlic clove, minced
- 1 tablespoon Dijon mustard
- 1 teaspoon salt
- ½ teaspoon freshly ground black pepper
- 2 pounds pork tenderloin

**Directions**

- Preparing the Ingredients. In a large mixing bowl, make the marinade. Mix together the olive oil, soy sauce, lemon juice, minced garlic, Dijon mustard, salt, and pepper. Reserve ¼ cup of the marinade.
- Place the tenderloin in a large bowl and pour the remaining marinade over the meat. Cover and marinate in the refrigerator for about 1 hour. Place the marinated pork tenderloin into your air fryer oven basket.
- Set the temperature to 400°F. Set the timer and roast for 10 minutes. Using tongs, flip the pork and baste it with half of the reserved marinade. Reset the timer and roast for 10 minutes more.
- Using tongs, flip the pork, then baste with the remaining marinade.
- Reset the timer and roast for another 10 minutes, for a total cooking time of 30 minutes.

Cal 345 | Protein 41.56g | Fat 17.35 g | Carb 3.66 g

## STEAK SUPREME

*Prep time: 10 min | Cook time: 30 min | Serves: 8*

**Ingredients**

- ½ pound beef-bottom round, sliced into strips
- 1 cup of breadcrumbs
- 2 medium-sized eggs
- Pinch of salt and pepper
- ½ tablespoon of ground thyme

**Directions**

- Preparing the Ingredients. Cover the basket of the Air fryer with a layer of tin foil, leaving the edges open to allow air to flow through the basket.
- Preheat the air fryer to 350°F. In a bowl, whisk the eggs until fluffy and until the yolks and whites are fully combined, and set aside. In a separate bowl, mix the breadcrumbs, thyme, salt and pepper, and set aside.
- One by one, dip each piece of raw steak into the bowl with dry ingredients, coating all sides; then submerge into the bowl with wet ingredients, then dip again into the dry ingredients. This double coating will ensure an extra crisp air fry. Lay the coated steak pieces on the foil covering the air-fryer basket, in a single flat layer.
- Set the air fryer timer for 15 minutes. After 15 minutes, the air fryer will turn off and the steak should be mid-way cooked and the breaded coating starting to brown. Using tongs, turn each piece of steak over to ensure a full all-over fry.
- Reset the air fryer to 320 F for 15 minutes. After 15 minutes, when the air fryer shuts off, remove the fried steak strips using tongs and set on a serving plate. Eat once cool enough to handle and enjoy.

Cal 421 | Fat 26g | Carb 8g | Protein 46g

# VEGETARIAN RECIPES

## FRIED RICE WITH SESAME-SRIRACHA SAUCE

*Prep time:10 min | Cook time:20 min | Serves: 1-2*

### Ingredients
- Cooked white rice: 2 cups
- Salt & black pepper, to taste
- Sriracha: 1 tsp.
- Peas and carrots: 1 cup
- Toasted sesame oil: 2 tsp.
- Soy sauce: 1 tsp.
- Vegetable oil: 1 tbsp.
- Sesame seeds: half tsp.
- 1 egg, whisked

### Instructions
- In a bowl, add rice, sesame oil (1 tsp.), water (1 tbsp.), salt and pepper. Mix the rice.
- Transfer in a cake pan.
- Let the Kalorik Air Fryer Oven preheat to 350 F, cook the rice for 12 minutes, rotate halfway through.
- In a bowl, add sesame seeds, sriracha, sesame oil and soy sauce and mix.
- Pour over rice and air fry for 4 minutes, add carrots, peas, and egg. Mix and cook for 2 minutes more.
- Serve right away.

## FRIED AVOCADO TACOS

*Prep time:30 min | Cook time:20 min | Serves: 4*

### Ingredients
- Shredded coleslaw mix: 2 cups
- Minced fresh cilantro: 1/4 cup
- Greek yogurt: 1/4 cup
- Lime juice: 2 tbsp.
- Honey: 1 tsp.
- Salt: to taste
- Ground chipotle pepper: to taste
- Pepper: ¼ tsp.
- 1 egg, whisked
- Cornmeal: 1/4 cup
- Garlic powder: half tsp.
- 2 avocados, sliced
- 8 tortillas (six inches)
- 1 tomato, chopped

### Instructions
- Let the Kalorik Air Fryer Oven preheat to 400 F.
- In a bowl, add the egg.
- In another bowl, add chipotle pepper, cornmeal, garlic powder and salt, mix.
- Coat the avocado slices in egg, then in cornmeal mixture. Oil spray the slices.
- Add the rest of the ingredients with chipotle pepper in a bowl, mix and keep in the fridge.
- Oil spray the air fryer basket, air fry the avocado slices for 4 minutes, flip, oil spray and cook for 3 to 4 minutes.
- Serve the slices in tortillas and salsa on top.

Cal 407 | Fat 21g | Carb 48g | Protein 9g

## HONEY CINNAMON BUTTERNUT SQUA

*Prep time:10 min | Cook time:15 min | Serves: 4*

### Ingredients
- Ground cinnamon: half tsp.
- 1 peeled butternut squash, cut into one" chunks
- Honey: 2 tbsp.
- Olive oil: 2 tbsp.
- Fine sea salt: ¼ tsp.
- Honey: 1 tsp.

### Instructions
- Let the Kalorik Air Fryer Oven preheat to 400 F.
- In a bowl, add squash, and the rest of the ingredients, toss well.
- Add this to the air fryer, do not crowd it. Air fry for 14 to 16 minutes shake every five minutes.
- Serve right away.

## FALAFEL

*Prep time:15 min | Cook time:30 min | Serves: 6*

### Ingredients
- 1 can of (15 oz.) chickpeas, rinsed
- 3 minced garlic cloves
- Chopped cilantro: 1/3 cup
- Red pepper flakes: 1/8 tsp.
- Chopped scallions: 1/3 cup
- Cumin: 1 tsp.
- Chopped parsley: 1/3 cup
- All-purpose flour: 4 tbsp.
- 1 yellow onion, quartered
- Kosher salt: half tsp.
- Baking powder: 1 tsp.

### Instructions
- In a food processor, add cilantro, parsley, pepper flakes, scallions, salt and cumin. Pulse 3 to 4 times until roughly chopped.
- Add flour, baking powder and the rest of the ingredients, pulse 2 to 3 times.
- Take out in a bowl, cover and keep in the fridge for 2-3 hours.
- Make into 12 balls; use flour if it is too sticky.
- Let the Kalorik Air Fryer Oven preheat to 350 F.
- Oil spray the falafel, air fry for 14 minutes, flip halfway through.

Cal 134 | Carb 24g | Protein 6g | Fat 2g

## CAJUN FRIES

*Prep time:15 min | Cook time:25 min | Serves: 4*

### Ingredients
- Cajun seasoning: 1 tbsp.

peeled Russet potatoes large, half" sticks
Canola oil: 2 tsp.

**Cajun seasoning**

- Dried thyme: half tsp.
- Salt: 2 tsp.
- Garlic powder: 1 tsp.
- Black pepper: 1 tsp.
- Cayenne pepper: 1 tsp.
- Paprika: 1 tsp.
- Dried oregano: half tsp.
- Onion powder: half tsp.

**Instructions**

- Boil the potatoes for four minutes in salted boiling water.
- Take them out and wash with cold water, and pat dry.
- Let the Kalorik Air Fryer Oven preheat to 400 F.
- Toss the potatoes with oil and air fry for 25 minutes, shake the basket a few times.
- Sprinkle the Cajun seasoning on potatoes, oil spray and air fry for 5 minutes.
- Oil spray again and fry for 5 more minutes serve right away.

## BROCCOLI WITH SWEET SOY DRIZZLE
*Prep time:5 min | Cook time:20 min | Serves: 4*

**Ingredients**

- Sugar: 1 cup
- 2 green onions, sliced
- Soy sauce: 1 cup
- Black whole peppercorns: 1 tsp.
- 1 cinnamon stick
- Water: half cup
- 1 garlic clove, sliced
- Peeled fresh ginger: half inch piece, sliced
- Broccoli: 1 head, broken in florets

**Instructions**

- In a pan, add water and sugar, stir until sugar dissolves. Let it come to a boil, turn the heat low and simmer for 20 minutes.
- Turn off the heat and add the green onion, soy sauce, garlic, cinnamon, Ginger and peppercorns.
- Cook on low heat until it turns syrupy.
- Let the Kalorik Air Fryer Oven preheat to 400 F.
- In a bowl, add broccoli, oil, salt and pepper, toss to combine.
- Air fry for ten minutes, shake the basket a few times.
- Serve with warm syrup drizzled on top.

## STIR FRIED ZOODLES AND VEGETABLES WITH TOFU
*Prep time:20 min | Cook time:30 min | Serves: 4*

**Ingredients**

- Canola oil: 1 tbsp.
- 2 carrots, sliced
- Honey: 2 tbsp.
- Sriracha chili sauce: 2 tbsp.
- Rice wine vinegar: 2 tbsp.
- Soy sauce: 2 tbsp.
- 1 red bell pepper sliced
- Half onion sliced
- Sesame oil: 1 tbsp.

- Minced ginger: 1 tsp.
- Zucchini zoodles: 8 oz.
- Snow peas: 1 cup, sliced lengthwise
- Baby corn: 1 cup
- Fresh cilantro leaves

**Instructions**

- In a bowl, add honey, oil, soy sauce, ginger, vinegar, sesame oil, and sriracha chili sauce. Mix and add tofu and let it marinate for 15 minutes.
- Let the Kalorik Air Fryer Oven preheat to 400 F.
- Air fry the tofu for 15 minutes shake the basket a few times. Take the tofu out.
- Add carrots, onion to the air fryer, cook for five minutes.
- Add corn, peas, and red pepper and cook for five minutes, shake the basket.
- Add tofu back and pour the marinade over. Toss to coat and air fry for few minutes.
- Take out in a bowl, pour over the juice from the bottom drawer serve with zoodles.

## SPINACH ARTICHOKE WHITE PIZZA
*Prep time:10 min | Cook time:18 min | Serves: 4*

**Ingredients**

- 1 minced garlic clove
- Artichoke hearts: ¼ cup, chopped
- Pizza dough: 8 oz.
- Fresh spinach: 3 cups
- Mozzarella cheese: half cup, grated
- Dried oregano: ¼ tsp.
- Fontina cheese: ¼ cup
- Parmesan cheese: 2 tbsp., grated
- Salt & black pepper

**Instructions**

- Sauté garlic and spinach on medium flame, until spinach wilts. Take out on a plate.
- Let the Kalorik Air Fryer Oven preheat to 390 F.
- Cover the air fryer basket with oil, leave some space around.
- Oil spray the foil and place the dough inside, pierce with a fork several times.
- Oil spray the dough air fry for 6 minutes, flip the dough, oil spray and cook for 4 minutes.
- Add half cheese on top, add artichoke and spinach, dried herbs, the rest of the cheese, olive oil drizzle on top.
- Air fry for 8 minutes at 350 F.
- Slice and serve.

Cal 489 | Fat 19g | Carb 59g | Protein 23g

## ROASTED TOMATO WITH CAPERS & BASIL
*Prep time:15 min | Cook time:18 min | Serves: 4*

**Ingredients**

- Cherry tomatoes: 3 cups, halved
- White wine vinegar: 1 tbsp.
- Italian seasoning: 1 tsp.
- 1 minced garlic clove
- 1 shallot, chopped
- Chopped fresh basil: ¼ cup
- Olive oil: 2 tbsp.
- Capers: 2 tbsp.

- Dried pasta: half-pound, cooked

**Instructions**

- Let the Kalorik Air Fryer Oven preheat to 400 F.
- Toss the tomatoes with the rest of the ingredients, except for pasta.
- Transfer to the air fryer basket.
- Air fry for 20 minutes, shake the basket a few times, lightly crush the tomatoes.
- Add pasta, and toss. Use the liquid from the bottom drawer toss to combine and serve with a sprinkle of salt and pepper on top.

Cal 626 | Fat 16g | Carb 103g | Protein 19g

## VEGGIE CHIP MEDLEY
*Prep time:15 min | Cook time:40 min | Serves: 4*

**Ingredients**

- 1 sweet potato
- 2 tablespoons olive oil: 2 tbsp.
- 1 golden beet
- 1 purple potato
- salt & black pepper, to taste
- 1 red beet

**Instructions**

- Wash and scrub the vegetables, and thinly slice with a mandolin into 1/6" thick.
- Keep the vegetables slices' separate.
- Wash with cold water, and water runs clear; pat dries the slices.
- Place in a dry bowl, toss with oil, salt and pepper. Toss to coat.
- Let the Kalorik Air Fryer Oven preheat to 320 F.
- Place the potatoes slices in the basket of the air fryer; it can overlap.
- Air fry for 20-25 minutes, flip and shake.
- Air fry beets for half an hour, tossing every five minutes.
- Take out in a bowl, add more salt if needed.

Serve right away.

## CRISPY AIR-FRYER TOFU
*Prep time:15 min | Cook time:20 min | Serves: 4*

**Ingredients**

- 1 block extra-firm tofu, 1 pound
- White wine vinegar: 1 tsp.
- Soy sauce: 2 tbsp.
- Kosher salt, to taste
- Toasted sesame oil: 2 tbsp.
- 1 teaspoon honey: 1 tsp.

**Instructions**

- Drain and wrap the tofu in towels, place something heavy on top for 15 minutes.
- Slice into 1 inch of cubes.
- In a bowl, add the rest of the ingredients whisk well.
- Add tofu cubes, and toss to coat. Let it rest for 15 minutes.
- Let the Kalorik Air Fryer Oven preheat to 375 F.
- Place tofu in one even layer in the air fryer basket, air fry for 15-20 minutes. Shake the basket a few times.

Serve with any dipping sauce and rice.

## CHILI-GARLIC TOFU WITH GREEN BEANS
*Prep time:15 min | Cook time:40 min | Serves: 4*

**Ingredients**

- 2 packages (14 oz.) extra-firm tofu

- Green beans: 1 pound
- Soy sauce: 1/3 cup
- Brown sugar: 1 tbsp.
- Olive oil: 2 tbsp.
- Salt & black pepper, to taste
- Rice wine vinegar: 2 tbsp.
- Mirin: 2 tbsp.
- 2 scallions, sliced
- Chili-garlic paste: 1-2 tsp.
- Cornstarch: 1 tsp.
- 3 minced garlic cloves

**Instructions**

- Drain and wrap the tofu in towels, place something heavy on top for 15 minutes.
- Cut each block into 6 half-inch slices.
- Brush the tofu slices with oil and season with salt and pepper.
- Let the Kalorik Air Fryer Oven preheat to 400 F.
- Air fry the tofu slices for 20 minutes, flipping halfway through. Take out on a plate.
- Trim and toss the beans with oil, salt and pepper.
- Air fry for ten minutes, shake the basket a few times.
- In a pan, add the rest of the ingredients with water (3 tbsp.), cook on low flame for 5-7 minutes, until thickens slightly.
- Serve the beans and tofu with glaze sauce on top.

## GNOCCHI AND SQUASH
*Prep time:15 min | Cook time:40 min | Serves: 2*

**Ingredients**

- Kosher salt & pepper, to taste
- Unsalted butter: 6 tbsp.
- Fresh or frozen gnocchi: 1 pound
- Shaved parmesan: half cup
- 1 delicata squash
- Chopped walnuts: half cup
- 8 fresh sage leaves, sliced thin

**Instructions**

- Cook the gnocchi as per package instructions.
- Let the Kalorik Air Fryer Oven preheat to 375 F.
- Slice the squash in half, cut into ¼" thick half-moons.
- In a bowl, add squash with olive oil (1 tbsp.), salt and pepper.
- Air fry for 15 minutes, shake the basket a few times. Take out in a bowl.
- In a bowl, add boiled gnocchi toss with olive oil (2 tsp.), salt and pepper.
- Air fry for ten minutes, shake the basket a few times.
- In a pot, add butter and melt until it becomes nutty and lightly golden, for 2-3 minutes.
- Add the sage and walnuts cook for 2 minutes.
- Pour over gnocchi, cheese, and squash, toss and serve.

## EGGPLANT STICKS
*Prep time:10 min | Cook time:15 min | Serves: 2*

**Ingredients**

- Eggplant: 10 oz.
- Italian seasoned breadcrumbs: half cup
- Olive oil: 1 tsp.
- 1 egg white

- Salt & pepper, to taste
- Parmesan cheese: 2 tbsp.

**Instructions**

- Let the Kalorik Air Fryer Oven preheat to 350 F
- Cut the eggplant into strips and coat it with oil, salt and pepper.
- In a bowl, add egg white.
- In another bowl, add cheese and breadcrumbs.
- Coat the strips in egg white, then in breadcrumbs.
- Oil spray the strips and air fry for ten minutes, flip halfway through.

Cal 87│Carb 12g│Protein 4.5g│Fat 3g

## POTATO GALETTE

*Prep time:25 min│Cook time:30 min│Serves: 4-5*

**Ingredients**

- Butter melted: ¼ cup
- Salt & black pepper, to taste
- Fresh thyme sprigs
- Half shallot, chopped
- Yukon gold potatoes: 1 pound
- Fresh thyme leaves: 2 tbsp.
- Gruyère cheese: 4 oz., grated

**Instructions**

- Slice the potatoes with a mandolin, and add the rest of the ingredients, except for cheese. Toss to coat.
- Let the Kalorik Air Fryer Oven preheat to 380 F.
- Make a foil bowl smaller than the air fryer basket, overlap the potatoes, add some cheese; add 2 more layers of potato and cheese.
- Air fry for half an hour, change the temperature to 340, drain some Fat by poking holes in the foil.
- Air fry for five minutes more.
- Serve right away.

## POTATOES & GREEN BEANS

*Prep time:20 min│Cook time:40 min│Serves: 2-4*

**Ingredients**

- Thick cut bacon: 4 slices, diced
- Olive oil: ¼ cup
- Brown sugar: 1 tbsp.
- Apple cider vinegar: 2 tbsp.
- Russet potatoes: 2-3, cut into large chunks
- 2 shallots chopped
- Dijon mustard: 1 tbsp.
- Salt & black pepper, to taste
- Green beans: 12 oz., halved

**Instructions**

- Let the Kalorik Air Fryer Oven preheat to 400 F.
- Air fry bacon for ten minutes, flip halfway through. take out on a plate.
- In the bacon Fat, sauté the onion and brown sugar for 2-3 minutes.
- Turn off the heat and add Dijon mustard, cider vinegar, whisk until it dissolves.
- Add olive oil while whisking, add salt and pepper
- In a bowl, add potatoes, oil, salt and pepper, toss to coat.
- Air fry for 20 minutes, shake the basket a few times. Add green beans and air fry for ten minutes.

- Serve the potatoes, beans with bacon and sauce.

## HERB & LEMON CAULIFLOWER

*Prep time:20 min│Cook time:20 min│Serves: 4*

**Ingredients**

- Cauliflower florets: 6 cups
- Minced fresh parsley: 1/4 cup
- Minced fresh thyme: 1 tbsp.
- Olive oil: 4 tbsp.
- Lemon zest: 1 tsp.
- Minced fresh rosemary: 1 tbsp.
- Lemon juice: 2 tbsp.
- Salt: half tsp.
- Red pepper flakes: ¼ tsp.

**Instructions**

- Let the Kalorik Air Fryer Oven preheat to 350 F.
- In a bowl, toss cauliflower with olive oil (2 tbsp.).
- Air fry the cauliflower for 8 to 10 minutes. Shake the basket a few times.
- In a bowl, add the rest of the ingredients with 2 tbsp. of oil whisk and pour over cauliflower, and serve.

Cal 161│Fat 14g│Carb 8g│Protein 3g

## CAULIFLOWER RICE BALLS

*Prep time:5 min│Cook time:25 min│Serves: 4*

**Ingredients**

- 1 sausage link (Italian chicken), without casing (2 3/4 oz.)
- Marinara: 2 tbsp.
- Shredded mozzarella: half cup
- Riced cauliflower: 2 1/4 cups
- Kosher salt: ¼ tsp.
- Grated parmesan: 1 tbsp.
- 1 egg, whisked
- Bread crumbs: ¼ cup

**Instructions**

- Break and Cook sausage on a medium flame for 4-5 minutes
- Add marinara, cauliflower and salt, cook for six minutes.
- Turn off the heat and add cheese, mix and let it cool for 3-4 minutes.
- Make into six big cauliflower balls.
- In a bowl, add the egg.
- In another bowl, add the breadcrumbs and parmesan.
- Coat the balls in egg and then in breadcrumbs mixture.
- Let the Kalorik Air Fryer Oven preheat to 400 F.
- Air fry for nine minutes, flip halfway through.
- Serve with marinara sauce

Cal 257 │ Protein 21.5g│Carb 15.6g│Fat 11.5g

## ZUCCHINI, CORN & HALOUMI FRITTERS

*Prep time:10 min│Cook time:25 min│Serves: 10*

**Ingredients**

- 2 medium zucchini, grated
- Block halloumi: 8 oz., grated
- Fresh oregano leaves: 3 tsp.
- 2 eggs, whisked
- Corn kernels: 1 cup
- Self-rising flour: 2/3 cup

**Instructions**

- Squeeze the moisture out of the zucchini, add it to a bowl.
- Add corn and halloumi; mix well.
- Add oregano, eggs and flour, salt and pepper, mix.
- Let the Kalorik Air Fryer Oven preheat to 390 F.
- Add foil to the air fryer basket, leaving some space around.
- Add a spoonful of mixture on the foil, air fry for 8 minutes, flip if necessary.
- Serve with a drizzle of olive oil, black pepper.

## GREEN BEANS

*Prep time:3 min | Cook time:10 min | Serves: 4*

### Ingredients
- 2 cups Green beans
- 1/2 teaspoon Oil

### Instructions
- Wash the green beans & cut the ends off if necessary. With oil, toss the beans.
- Place the beans in an air fryer. Cook for 10 minutes at 390 ° F.

Cal 45 | Carb 3g | Protein 1g | Fat3g

## RANCH ZUCCHINI CHIPS

*Prep time:20 min | Cook time:20 min | Serves: 2*

### Ingredients
- 2/3 cup panko breadcrumbs
- 1 tablespoon Ranch dressing
- 10 oz. Zucchini
- 1/4 cup of Egg whites

### Instructions:
- Mix the breadcrumbs in a large bowl with the seasoning.
- Split zucchini into coins that are a quarter-inch wide. Put in another large bowl. Place an egg on top, & flip to coat.
- Shake the zucchini coins one at a time to extract the excess egg, then gently cover with the breadcrumb mixture.
- In one layer, put the zucchini in an air fryer & top with any leftover seasoned crumbs.
- Set the air fryer to 390 F
- Cook till golden brown, 8 to 10 minutes, working in batches.

Cal 243 | Protein 5.3g | Carb 16.5g | Fat 17.8g

## LOADED CAULIFLOWER HASH BROWNS

*Prep time:15 min | Cook time:20 min | Serves: 8*

### Ingredients
- Thick-cut bacon: 4 slices, diced
- Diced onion: half cup
- Paprika: half tsp.
- Red & green bell pepper: half cup, diced
- Salt: 1 tsp.
- 1 egg
- Cauliflower: 1 head
- Chickpea almond: half cup

- Grated cheddar cheese: 1 cup
- Black pepper, to taste

### Instructions
- Let the Kalorik Air Fryer Oven preheat to 400 F.
- Air fry onion, bacon for 8-10 minutes, shake the basket a few times.
- In a food processor, grate the cauliflower. Squeeze the moisture out of grated cauliflower.
- Take out in a bowl, add the rest of the ingredients with bacon and onion. Mix and make into oval 8 patties, and keep in the freezer for 60 minutes.
- Let the Kalorik Air Fryer Oven preheat to 400 F again.
- Oil spray the air fryer basket and air fry the hash browns for ten minutes, flip halfway through.
- Sprinkle salt and pepper, and serve.

## QUINOA BURGERS

*Prep time:30 min | Cook time:40 min | Serves: 4*

### Ingredients
- Quinoa: 1 cup
- Water: 1 ½ cups
- Black pepper
- Rolled oats: 1 ½ cups
- Salt: 1 tsp.
- Chopped fresh chives: ¼ cup
- 3 eggs, whisked
- Minced onion: ¼ cup
- Crumbled feta cheese: half cup
- 4 buns

### Instructions
- Rinse and drain the quinoa, add in a pan, dry on medium flame. Add water, salt and pepper. Let it come to a boil, turn the heat low and simmer for 20-23 minutes.
- Turn off the heat, and cover with the lid. Spread on a sheet and cool.
- In a bowl, add onion, quinoa, herbs, oats, salt, cheese, pepper, and eggs. Mix and make into 4 patties; add some water if required.
- Oil sprays the patties and place them in the basket of the air fryer.
- Let the Kalorik Air Fryer Oven preheat to 400 F.
- Air fry the burgers for ten minutes, flip halfway through.
- Serve in buns with desired toppings.

Cal 561 | Fat 18g | Carb 73g | Protein 26g

## EGGPLANT PARMESAN PANINI

*Prep time:30 min | Cook time:25 min | Serves: 2*

### Ingredients
- 1 eggplant, 1 pound, half-inch slices
- Dried parsley: 2 tsp.
- Italian seasoning: half tsp.
- Black pepper
- Garlic powder: half tsp.
- Breadcrumbs: half cup
- Onion powder: half tsp.
- Salt: half tsp.
- Italian bread: 4 slices
- Milk: 2 tbsp.

- Parmesan cheese: 2 tsp.
- Mayonnaise: half cup
- Tomato sauce: ¾ cup
- Mozzarella cheese: 1 ½ cups

**Instructions**

- Sprinkle the eggplant slices with salt, and Let the eggplant slices sit on paper towels for half an hour.
- In a dish, add Italian seasoning, black pepper, garlic powder, breadcrumbs, salt, onion powder, and parsley mix.
- In a bowl, whisk mayo and milk.
- Let the Kalorik Air Fryer Oven preheat to 400 F.
- Brush any salt off of eggplant slices, and coat in egg mixture, then in breadcrumbs. Oil spray the breaded slices.
- Air fry for 15 minutes, flipping halfway through.
- Toasted the bread slices, add air-fried eggplant, add cheese on top.
- Add tomato sauce and the rest of the cheese, place another slice of bread on top.
- Grill for ten minutes until cheese is melted.
- Serve right away.

### ROASTED VEGETABLE PASTA SALAD
*Prep time:20 min | Cook time:20 min | Serves: 8*

**Ingredients**

- 1 orange, green & red pepper, sliced into large chunks
- 1 yellow squash, cut in half moons
- Brown mushrooms: 4 oz., halved
- Olive oil: ¼ cup
- 1 zucchini, cut in half moons
- Italian seasoning: 1 tsp.
- salt & black pepper
- rigatoni: 1 pound, cooked
- 1 onion, sliced
- balsamic vinegar: 3 tbsp.
- grape tomatoes: 1 cup, halved
- Kalamata olives: half cup, halved
- chopped fresh basil: 2 tbsp.

**Instructions**

- Let the Kalorik Air Fryer Oven preheat to 380 F.
- In a bowl, add all vegetables and toss with olive oil.
- Add Italian seasoning, pepper and salt. Toss to coat.
- Air fry for 12-15 minutes. shake the basket a few times.
- In a bowl, add cooked pasta and air fried vegetables, add balsamic vinegar, olive oil, and toss. Add salt and pepper.
- Serve chilled after adding fresh basil.

Cal 320 | Fat 9g | Carb 50g | Protein 9g

### MUSHROOM ROLL-UPS
*Prep time:30 min | Cook time:10 min | Serves: 8*

**Ingredients**

- Olive oil: 2 tbsp.
- Ricotta cheese: 4 oz.
- Large portobello mushrooms: 8 oz., without gills, finely chopped
- Dried oregano: 1 tsp.
- Red pepper flakes: half tsp.
- Salt: ¼ tsp.
- Dried thyme:1 tsp.
- 1 pack of (8 oz.) cream cheese, softened

- 10 flour tortillas (8")

**Instructions**

- Sauté mushrooms for four minutes, add herbs and spices. Cook for 4 to 6 minutes, turn off the heat and let it cool.
- In a bowl, add all cheeses, add mushrooms and mix.
- In each tortilla, add some mixture and roll tightly.
- Let the Kalorik Air Fryer Oven preheat to 400 F.
- Oil spray the tortillas and air fry for 9 to 11 minutes.
- Slice and serve.

Cal 291 | Fat 16g | Carb 31g | Protein 8g

### LATKES
*Prep time:10 min | Cook time:16 min | Serves: 10*

**Ingredients**

- Half yellow onion
- Russet potatoes: 2 to 3
- Kosher salt: 2 tsp.
- 2 eggs
- Matzo meal: ¼ cup
- Black pepper: half tsp.

**Instructions**

- Peel and grate the potatoes; grate the onion too with larger holes.
- Squeeze moisture out of the vegetables, and place in a bowl.
- Add eggs and the rest of the ingredients, mix.
- Let the Kalorik Air Fryer Oven preheat to 375 F. Oil spray the air fryer basket.
- Add 2 tbsp. of latkes in the air fryer, flatten into a patty. Spray with oil.
- Air fry for 8 minutes, flipping halfway through.
- Serve with sour cream.

Cal 206 | Fat 13.0 g | Carb 19.2 g | Protein3.5 g

### CAULIFLOWER GNOCCHI
*Prep time:10 min | Cook time:15 min | Serves: 2*

**Ingredients**

- 1 pack of cauliflower gnocchi
- Kosher salt & black pepper
- Vegetable stock: 1/3 cup
- Diced red onion: half cup
- Olive oil: 2 tbsp.
- 3 minced garlic clove
- Fresh spinach: 1 cup
- Baby belle mushrooms: 2 cups
- Dried oregano: 1 tbsp.
- Grated parmesan cheese: half cup
- Coconut milk: 1 cup
- Fresh chopped parsley: 1/4 cup

**Instructions**

- Cook the gnocchi as per package instructions, sprinkle salt and pepper.
- Sauté onion, mushroom and garlic in olive oil for 4 to 5 minutes.
- Add spinach and cook for 1 to 2 minutes.
- Add vegetable stock, herbs, salt and pepper, simmer for 2 to 3 minutes.
- Add coconut milk and cook for two minutes.
- In a dish, add gnocchi on the bottom, add the coconut milk mixture on top. Top with cheese air fry for 3 to 6 minutes.
- Serve right away.

## CAULIFLOWER WINGS

*Prep time:15 min | Cook time:15 min | Serves: 4*

**Ingredients**

- 3 eggs
- Cauliflower: 1 head
- panko bread crumbs: 2 cups

**Korean BBQ Sauce**

- Honey: 1/3 cup
- Sesame oil: 1 tsp.
- Water cold: 1/4 cup
- Rice vinegar: 1 tbsp.
- Hoisin sauce: 1/4 cup
- Ketchup: 1 tbsp.
- Ground ginger: 1/4 tsp.
- Soy sauce: 1 tbsp.
- 2 minced garlic cloves
- Corn starch: 2 tsp.

**Instructions**

- Let the Kalorik Air Fryer Oven preheat to 400 F
- Cut the cauliflower into bite-size pieces.
- In a bowl, whisk the eggs. In another bowl, add bread crumbs.
- Coat cauliflower in egg then in bread crumbs.
- Air fry for 15 minutes.
- In a bowl, mix cornstarch with water.
- In a bowl, add all ingredients of the sauce, whisk well on medium flame. Pour the cornstarch mixture and whisk, cook for 2 to 3 minutes, until it thickens.
- Toss the cauliflower in the sauce and serve.

## CHILI GARLIC TOFU

*Prep time:10 min | Cook time:15 min | Serves: 5*

**Ingredients**

- Super firm tofu: 1 pack
- Olive oil: 1 tbsp.
- Chili garlic sauce: 2 tbsp.
- Rice vinegar: 1 tbsp.
- Cornstarch: half cup
- Soy sauce: 1/4 cup
- Sesame seeds: half tsp.
- Brown sugar: 1 1/2 tbsp.
- 2 minced garlic cloves
- Grated ginger: 1 tsp.
- Sesame oil: 1 tsp.
- 2 green onions, sliced

**Instructions**

- Drain and wrap the tofu in towels, place something heavy on top for 15 minutes.
- Slice the tofu into cubes.
- In a zip lock bag, add cornstarch and tofu, toss and place in a bowl, toss with 1 tbsp. of olive oil.
- Air fry for 12-15 minutes at 370 F. Oil spray halfway through if required.
- In a pan, add the rest of the ingredients and mix, let it come to a boil, turn the heat low and simmer for 1 minute.
- Add tofu and toss. Serve with green onion on top.

Cal 165 | Fat 7g | Carb 21g | Protein 7g

## BREADED SUMMER SQUASH

*Prep time:15 min | Cook time:10 min | Serves: 4*

**Ingredients**

- Yellow summer squash: 4 cups, thinly sliced
- Cayenne pepper: 1/8 tsp.
- Olive oil: 3 tbsp.
- Salt: half tsp.
- Panko bread crumbs: 3/4 cup
- Pepper: half tsp.
- Grated parmesan cheese: 3/4 cup

**Instructions**

- Let the Kalorik Air Fryer Oven preheat to 350 F
- Toss the squash with oil and seasonings.
- In a bowl, add cheese and crumbs.
- Add squash in the crumbs pat to adhere.
- Air fry for ten minutes.
- Serve right away.

Cal 203 | Fat 14g | Carb 13g | protein 6g

## TOFU WITH PEANUT SAUCE

*Prep time:15 min | Cook time:30 min | Serves: 4*

**Ingredients**

**Peanut sauce**

- Powdered peanut butter: 6 tbsp.
- Soy sauce: 1 tbsp.
- 1 minced garlic clove
- Chinese cooking wine: half tsp.
- Grated ginger: half tsp.
- Toasted sesame oil: 1 tsp.

**Noodles**

- 1 block extra firm tofu, cut into cubes after pressing
- 2 zucchinis, spiralized
- Garlic powder: ¼ tsp.
- Soy sauce: 2 tbsp.
- Shiitake mushrooms: 6-8 oz., caps sliced with no stems
- Toasted sesame oil: 1 tsp.
- Cornstarch: 1 tbsp.
- 2 yellow squash, spiralized

**Instructions**

- In a bowl, add water (3 tbsp.) with powdered peanut butter, mix well.
- Add the rest of the sauce's ingredients and mix. Heat in a pan, and set it aside.
- In a bowl, add cornstarch, soy sauce, sesame oil mix and add sesame seeds.
- Let the Kalorik Air Fryer Oven preheat to 390 F.
- Air fry the tofu for 8-10 minutes, take out on a plate.
- Air fry the mushrooms for 4 minutes.
- Sauté the zoodles in olive oil and garlic powder for 7-8 minutes.
- Serve the zoodles with tofu and mushrooms and fresh herbs on top.

## SPICY ZUCCHINI

*Prep time: 10 min | Cook time: 15 min | Serves: 4*

**Ingredients**

- Zucchini – 1 lb. cut into ½-inch thick slices lengthwise
- Olive oil – 1 tbsp.
- Garlic powder – ½ tsp.
- Cayenne pepper – ½ tsp.
- Salt and ground black pepper, as required

**Directions**

- Put all of the ingredients into a bowl and toss to coat well.
- Arrange the zucchini slices onto a cooking tray.
- Arrange the drip pan in the bottom of the Air Fryer Oven cooking chamber.
- Take to the preheated air fryer at 400°F for 12 minutes.
- Serve hot.

Cal 67 | Carb 5.6g | Fat 5g | Protein 2g

## ZUCCHINI CORN FRITTERS

*Prep time:10 min | Cook time:12 min | Serves: 4*

**Ingredients**

- Corn kernels: 1 cup
- Olive oil: 1 to 2 tsp.
- 2-3 minced garlic cloves
- 1 medium cooked potato
- 2 medium zucchinis
- Chickpea flour: 2 tbsp.
- Salt & pepper

**Instructions**

- Grate the zucchini and mix with some salt, let it rest for 10 to 15 minutes, squeeze any moisture.
- Grate the potato in a bowl. Add all the ingredients with zucchini and grated potato.
- Mix and make into patties (2 tbsp.)
- Oil spray the air fryer basket.
- Let the Kalorik Air Fryer Oven preheat to 360 F.
- Air fry for 8 minutes, flipping halfway through.
- Serve with dipping sauce.

## VEGETARIAN STUFFED PEPPERS

*Prep time:10 min | Cook time:15 min | Serves: 4*

**Ingredients**

- 4 to 6 Bell Peppers
- Italian Seasoning: 1 to 2 tbsp.
- Diced tomatoes: 15 oz.
- Cooked rice: 1 cup
- Parmesan cheese: 1 tbsp.
- Kidney beans: 1 cup, rinsed
- Mozzarella cheese: half cup

**Instructions**

- Cut the tops of bell peppers, take the seeds out.
- Chop the lids of bell peppers.
- In a bowl, add tomatoes, seasonings, rice, chopped bell pepper, and beans.
- Stuff the bell peppers with this mixture.
- Let the Kalorik Air Fryer Oven preheat to 360 F.
- Air fry for 12 minutes.
- Add cheese and air fry for three minutes, serve right away.

Cal 156 | Carb 23g | Protein 6g | Fat 4g

## CAULIFLOWER TACOS

*Prep time:15 min | Cook time:15 min | Serves: 6*

**Ingredients**

- 2 eggs
- Panko bread crumbs: 1 cup
- Chili powder: 2 tsp.
- 12 tortillas
- Cumin: 1 tsp.
- Cauliflower: 1 head, florets

**Instructions**

- In a bowl, add eggs and spices, and whisk.
- In a different bowl, add breadcrumbs.
- Dip the florets in egg, then in crumbs, oil spray the florets.
- Let the Kalorik Air Fryer Oven preheat to 350 F.
- Air fry the florets for 14 minutes; halfway through, shake the basket.
- Add the air fried florets in the tortilla, add desired toppings and serve.

Cal 67 | Carb 10g | Protein 2g | Fat 2g

## CRISPY VEGETABLE QUESADILLAS

*Prep time:15 min | Cook time:20 min | Serves: 4*

**Ingredients**

- Canned black beans: 1 cup, rinsed
- Cheddar cheese, shredded: 1 cup
- 4 whole flour tortillas, (6")
- Fresh cilantro: 2 tbsp.
- Greek yogurt: 4 tbsp.
- Sliced zucchini: 1 cup
- Bell pepper, sliced: 1 cup
- 1 tsp. Lime zest & 1 tbsp. of lime juice
- Half cup Pico de Gallo
- Ground cumin: 1/4 tsp.

**Instructions**

- Add 2 tbsp. of shredded cheese on half of each tortilla.
- Add black beans, pepper slices, zucchini slices, and more cheese.
- Fold the tortilla. Coat with oil spray and close with toothpicks.
- Oil spray the air fryer's basket. Place 2 quesadillas in the air fryer.
- Air fry for ten minutes.
- In a bowl, mix yogurt, cumin, lime zest and lime juice.
- Slice and serve the quesadilla with sauce.

Cal 294 | Carb 36 g | Protein 17 g | Fat 8 g

## BUFFALO MUSHROOM POPPERS

*Prep time:15 min | Cook time:20 min | Serves: 8*

**Ingredients**

- Apple cider vinegar: 3 tbsp.

- Button mushrooms: 1 pound
- Buffalo hot sauce: 1/4 cup
- 1 cup of panko breadcrumbs
- Salt
- Buttermilk: half cup
- 1 chopped jalapeño pepper, without seeds
- 2 eggs, whisked
- 1/4 tsp. Black pepper
- Chopped fresh chives: 2 tbsp.
- Softened cream cheese: 3 tbsp.
- Crumbled blue cheese: half cup
- 1/4 cup of all-purpose flour
- Plain yogurt: half cup

**Instructions**

- Cut the stems of mushrooms, and chop them finely.
- In a bowl, mix cream cheese, mushroom stems, salt, pepper, and jalapenos.
- Stuff this mix into the caps of the mushroom.
- In a bowl, add panko. In a different bowl, add flour, and in a separate bowl, whisk the eggs.
- Dip the mushroom balls in flour, then coat in egg, and lastly coat in panko mix.
- Spray the mushroom with cooking spray.
- Place these in the basket of the air fryer.
- Let the Kalorik Air Fryer Oven preheat to 350 F.
- Air fry for 20 minutes.
- Drizzle the mushrooms with buffalo sauce. Serve with chives on top.
- In a bowl, mix the rest of the ingredients and mix. Serve the mushroom with sauce.

Cal 134 | Carb 16 g | Protein 7 g | Fat 4 g

## DELICATA SQUASH
*Prep time:15 min | Cook time:10 min | Serves: 2*

**Ingredients**

- Olive oil: half tbsp.
- One delicata squash
- Salt: half tsp.
- Rosemary: half tsp.

**Instructions**

- Chop the squash in slices of ¼" of thickness
- In a bowl, add olive oil, salt, rosemary with squash slices. Toss well.
- Let the Kalorik Air Fryer Oven preheat to 400 F.
- Air fry the squash for ten minutes. flip the squash halfway through.
- Serve right away

Cal 69 | Fat 4g | Carb 9g | Protein 1g

## ASPARAGUS WITH GARLIC AND PARMESAN
*Prep time:5 min | Cook time:10 min | Serves: 4*

**Ingredients**

- 1 bundle of Asparagus
- 1 teaspoon of Olive oil
- 1/8 teaspoon of Garlic salt
- 1 tablespoon (grated or powdered)
- Parmesan cheese
- Pepper

**Instructions**

- Clean the Asparagus & pat dry. To take the woody stems off, cut off 1 " off the bottom.
- In an air fryer, lay the Asparagus in a layer & spritz with oil.
- Evenly sprinkle on top of the Asparagus with garlic salt. Season with pepper & then finish it with some Parmesan cheese.
- Cook for 7-10 minutes at 400 F. Thinner Asparagus can be quicker to cook.
- Add some more Parmesan cheese to top it off after the Asparagus is removed from the air fryer.
- Enjoy.

Cal 18 | Fat 2g | Carb 1g | Protein 1g

## CORN ON THE COB
*Prep time:5 min | Cook time:15 min | Serves: 1-2*

**Ingredients**

- Corn
- Cilantro
- Salt & Pepper
- Butter

**Optional toppings:**

- Sriracha
- Basil & parmesan cheese
- Bacon

**Instructions:**

- If needed, extract the husk & trim it. Lay flat the cobs in one layer in an air fryer.
- Use the favorite cooking spray to spray corn and cook for 10-15 minutes at 400 until mildly charred.
- In a cup, add the butter, salt, & pepper, and microwave until the butter is melted.
- Sprinkle with Cilantro and add butter to the corn.

Cal 72; | Fat 8.4g | Carb 1g | Protein 10mg

## SWEET POTATO
*Prep time:5 min | Cook time:35 min | Serves: 3*

**Ingredients**

- 3 Sweet potatoes
- 1 tablespoon Olive oil
- 1-2 teaspoons Kosher salt

**Instructions**

- Clean the sweet potatoes, then make air holes in the potatoes with a fork.
- Sprinkle with olive oil and salt and rub on the potatoes evenly.
- If the potatoes are coated, put them in the Air Fryer & place them in the machine.
- Cook the potatoes for 35-40 minutes at 392 F or until the fork-tender.

Cal 84 Protein 1.2g | Carb 12.1g | Fat 4g

## AIR FRYER EGGPLANT
*Prep time:10 min | Cook time:20 min | Serves: 1-2*

**Ingredients**

- Two tablespoons Olive oil
- 1 teaspoon Garlic powder
- 1/2 teaspoon Red pepper
- 1 teaspoon optional Sweet paprika
- 1/2 teaspoon Italian seasoning
- 1 cut into 1" pieces. Eggplant

**Instructions**

- Combine all the ingredients and toss till the bits of eggplant are filled with spices and olive oil. Place the eggplant in the air fryer.
- The eggplant is air fried for 20 minutes at 375F
- Serve.

Cal 96.2 | Fat 3.0 g | Carb 17.0 g | Protein 2.7 g

## BACON WRAPPED ASPARAGUS

*Prep time:10 min | Cook time:10 min | Serves: 6*

**Ingredients**

- 1 lb bacon cut in half.
- 1 lb Asparagus trimmed.
- Salt, pepper, & Creole seasoning/seasoned salt to taste
- 1 tablespoon Olive oil

**Instructions**

- Slice the bacon in two, and the asparagus ends are trimmed.
- Drizzle the Asparagus with olive oil. Add salt, pepper, & Creole seasoning to season. To coat evenly, toss.
- Bacon half slice is wrapped around two asparagus spears.
- Cook for ten minutes in an air fryer, then switch & cook for a further ten minutes. You can cook your bacon for less time, depending on how crispy you like it.
- Serve promptly, or store for up to a week in an airtight jar.

Cal 350 | Carb 3g | Protein 11g

## CAJUN SWEET POTATO FRIES

*Prep time:5 min | Cook time:30 min | Serves: 2*

**Ingredients**

- 1 med Sweet Potato Yam
- 1 teaspoon Cajun Seasoning
- 2 tablespoons Cornstarch
- 3 tablespoons Olive oil

**Cajun mayo**

- 1 cup Hellman's mayonnaise
- 2 tablespoons Dijon Mustard
- 1 Lime
- 1/2 teaspoon Cajun Seasoning
- Cayenne pinch

**Instructions**

- Chop the yam to 1/4 " fries on a wide cutting board.
- Place them in a wide bowl and soak them in water.
- Soak for at least 30 minutes, strain, and put in a different bowl.
- Season it with cornstarch & toss it to coat.
- Drizzle over the top with olive oil & season.
- Bake for 30 minutes at 400 f.
- Create the spicy mayo as it's frying, eat alongside & enjoy.

Cal294 | Protein 3.9g | Carb 47.4g | Fat 10.5g

## ROASTED RAINBOW VEGETABLES

*Prep time:15 min | Cook time:10 min | Serves: 4*

**Ingredient**

- Red bell pepper 1, seeded & cut into 1" pieces.
- Yellow summer squash 1, cut into 1" pieces.
- Zucchini 1 cut into 1" pieces.
- 4 ounces, halved Fresh mushrooms
- ½, cut into 1" wedges Sweet onion
- 1 tablespoon olive oil
- Salt & Pepper

**Instructions**

- According to recommendations from the manufacturer, preheat the air fryer.
- Put in a wide bowl the red bell pepper, zucchini, mushrooms, summer squash, and onion. To combine, add olive oil, black pepper, and salt and shake.
- Place the vegetables in a layer in the air fryer. Air-fry vegetables till roasted, stirring halfway through the cooking time, around 20 minutes.

Cal 69 | Protein 2.6g | Carb 7.7g | Fat 3.8g

## GARLIC ROASTED GREEN BEANS

*Prep time: 5 min | Cook time:8 min | Serves: 4*

**Ingredients**

- 3/4-1 lb Fresh green beans (trimmed)
- 1 tablespoon Olive oil
- 1 teaspoon Garlic powder
- Salt and Pepper

**Instructions**

- Drizzle the green beans with olive oil. Toss it to coat it.
- Put green beans in the air fryer.
- Cook green beans at 370 F for 7-8 minutes. Toss halfway through cooking . Serve.

Cal 45 | Carb 3g | Protein 1g | Fat 3g

## ROASTED CAULIFLOWER

*Prep time:8 min | Cook time:12 min | Serves: 4*

**Ingredients**

- 4 cups Chopped cauliflower
- 1 tablespoon Olive oil
- 1 teaspoon Parsley
- 1 teaspoon thyme
- 1 teaspoon Minced Garlic
- 1 teaspoon salt
- ¼ cup Parmesan cheese
- Salt & Pepper

**Instructions**

- Combine the cauliflower, olive oil, parsley, minced garlic, thyme, and salt in a wide bowl.
- Toss to mix, and it is well coated with cauliflower.
- In an air-fryer, put the cauliflower. For 20 minutes, adjusted to 400 F.
- After 10 minutes, mix the cauliflower and add the parmesan cheese.
- Season with salt & pepper to taste and serve immediately.

Cal 53 | Fat 4g | Carb 4g | Protein 2g

## SWEET AND SPICY BRUSSELS SPROUTS

*Prep time:5 min | Cook time:20 min | Serves: 4*

**Ingredients**

- 1 lb cut in half of Brussels sprouts
- 2 tablespoons Honey
- 1 1/2 tablespoons Vegetable oil
- 1 tablespoon Gochujang
- ½ teaspoon Salt

**Instructions**

- In a bowl, mix the honey, gochujang, vegetable oil, and salt and stir. Set around 1 tablespoon of the sauce aside. Add the sprouts to the bowl and mix until all the sprouts are fully coated.

- In the Air Fryer, put the Brussels sprouts, ensure that they do not overlap, and cook for 15 minutes at 360 ° F, shaking the bucket halfway through. Set the bowl aside.
- Increase the temperature to 390 ° F after 15 minutes and cook for five more minutes. Place in a bowl when the sprouts are finished and cover with remaining sauce and stir. Enjoy, enjoy.

Cal 83 | Carb 10g | Protein 3g | Fat 3g

## ROASTED ASPARAGUS
*Prep time:2-3 min | Cook time:10 min | Serves: 4*

### Ingredients
- 1 bunch Fresh Asparagus
- 1 tablespoon Olive oil
- Salt & Pepper
- 1 1/2 teaspoons. Herbes de Prair fryerce seasoning optional
- Optional fresh lemon wedge

### Instructions
- Wash & trim Asparagus hard ends.
- Drizzle the olive oil & the seasonings with the Asparagus. Cooking oil spray may also be used.
- In an air fryer, add the Asparagus.
- Cook at 360 F for 6-10 minutes until crisp. Drizzle over the roasted Asparagus with lemon.
- Begin to track it closely after Asparagus is cooked for 5 minutes.

Cal 94 | Protein 9g | Carb 10.1g | Fat 3.3g

## ROASTED BROCCOLI
*Prep time:3-4 min | Cook time:10 min | Serves: 4*

### Ingredients
- 3-4 cups broccoli florets
- 1 tablespoon Olive oil
- Salt & Pepper
- herbs de Prair fryerce seasoning 1 teaspoon

### Instructions
- Drizzle with olive oil on the broccoli or spray with the cooking oil. The seasonings are sprinkled throughout.
- Spray the air fryers with cooking oil. Load up the broccoli. Cook at 360 F for 5-8 minutes.
- Open the air fryer and check the broccoli once the broccoli is cooked for five minutes. Each type of air fryer cooks differently. To make sure the broccoli is not overcooked, use your judgment.

Cal 61 | Fat4 g | Carb 6 g | Protein3 g

## CUMIN CARROTS

*Prep time:5 min | Cook time:15 min | Serves: 4*

### Ingredients
- 2 teaspoons Coriander seeds
- 2 teaspoons Cumin seeds
- Carrots 1 lb, peeled & cut into 4x1/2" sticks.

- 1 tablespoon Melted coconut oil/butter
- 2 Garlic cloves, minced.
- 1/4 teaspoon salt
- 1/8 teaspoon Pepper
- Optional minced fresh Cilantro

### Instructions
- Preheat the fryer to 325 F. Toast the coriander & cumin seeds in some small dry skillet over med heat for 45-60 secs until it's aromatic, stirring regularly. Slightly cool. Grind in some spice grinder until finely ground, or by a mortar & pestle.
- Place the carrots in a wide bowl. Mix melted coconut oil, salt, garlic, crushed spices, and pepper; toss to cover.
- Cook, stirring regularly, until crisp-tender & lightly browned, 12 to 15 minutes. Sprinkle it with Cilantro if necessary.

Cal 86 | Fat 4g | Carb 12g | Protein 1g

## CRISPY BALSAMIC BRUSSELS SPROUTS
*Prep time:5 min | Cook time:10 min | Serves: 5*

### Ingredients
- 1 1/2 -2 cups. Fresh Brussels sprouts, halved
- 1/2 cup sliced red onions
- 1 tablespoon Balsamic vinegar
- 1 tablespoon Olive oil
- Salt & Pepper

### Instructions
- In a bowl, add the Brussels sprouts & sliced red onions. Olive oil and balsamic vinegar are drizzled throughout.
- Sprinkle salt & pepper to taste. To coat uniformly, stir.
- Spray the air fryers with cooking oil.
- Add onions and Brussels sprouts.
- Cook at 350 F for 5 minutes.
- Open the air fryer and use tongs to shake/toss the vegetables.
- For an extra 3-5 minutes, cook. Each type of air fryer is cooked differently. To determine the optimum cooking period, use your judgment.
- Before serving, cool it.

Cal 71 | Fat4g | Carb8.1g | Protein3g

## GENERAL TSO'S CAULIFLOWER
*Prep time:5-8 min | Cook time:20 min | Serves: 4*

### Ingredients
- 1/2 cup all-purpose flour
- 1/2 cup Cornstarch
- 1 teaspoon salt
- 1 teaspoon Baking powder
- 3/4 cup Club soda
- 6 cups Head cauliflower 1 medium, cut into 1" florets

**Sauce:**
- 3 tablespoons vegetable broth
- 3 tablespoons Sugar
- 2 tablespoons Rice vinegar
- 2 teaspoons Sesame oil
- 2 teaspoons Cornstarch
- 2 tablespoons Canola oil
- 2 to 6 Dried pasilla
- 1/4 cup Orange juice
- 3 Green onions, green part thinly sliced white part minced.
- 3, minced. Garlic cloves

- 1 teaspoon grated fresh ginger root
- 1/2 teaspoon grated orange zest
- 4 cups Hot cooked rice
- 3 tablespoons Soy sauce

**Instructions**

- Preheat the fryer to 400 F. Mix the flour, salt, cornstarch, and baking powder together. Stir in the club soda when combined. (batter will be thin). Toss the florets in the batter, transfer over a baking sheet to a wire rack. Let it stand for 5 minutes. Cook till tender & golden brown, 10-12 minutes.
- Meanwhile, whisk the first six ingredients of the sauce together: whisk in the cornstarch till smooth.
- Heat the canola oil over med to high heat in a wide saucepan. Add chills; cook & mix for 1-2 minutes until fragrant. Add the white onions, ginger, garlic, and orange zest; simmer for around 1 min, until fragrant. Stir in the mixture of orange juice; add to the saucepan. Take to a boil; cook & stir for 2-4 minutes till thickened.
- To the sauce, add cauliflower; toss to coat. Now Serve with rice & sprinkle with green onions, thinly sliced.

Cal 528 | Fat 11g | Carb 17g | Protein 11g

### GARLIC-HERB FRIED PATTY PAN SQUASH

*Prep time:15 min | Cook time:15 min | Serves: 4*

**Ingredients**

- patty pan squash 5 cups
- 1 tablespoon Olive oil
- Garlic cloves 2, minced
- 1/2 teaspoon salt
- 1/4 teaspoon Dried oregano
- 1/4 teaspoon Dried thyme
- 1/4 teaspoon Pepper
- 1 tablespoon minced fresh parsley

**Instructions**

- Preheat the fryer to 375 F. Put your squash in a wide bowl. Mix together the oil, the garlic, the salt, the oregano, the thyme, and the pepper, drizzle over the squash. Toss it to coat it.
- Place the squash in an air-fryer. Cook until soft, 10-15 minutes, occasionally stirring. With parsley, sprinkle.

Cal 79 | Protein 1.5g | Carb 4.4g | Fat 6.6g

### BLOOMING ONION

*Prep time:5 min | Cook time:25 min | Serves: 4*

**Ingredients**

- For the onion
- 1 Large yellow onion
- 3 large eggs
- 1 cup Breadcrumbs
- 2 teaspoons Paprika
- 1 teaspoon Garlic powder
- 1 teaspoon. Onion powder
- 1 teaspoon Kosher salt
- 3 tablespoons.  olive oil

**For the sauce**

- Kosher salt
- 2/3 c. Mayonnaise
- 2 tablespoons. Ketchup
- 1 teaspoon. Horseradish

- 1/2 teaspoon Paprika
- 1/2 teaspoon Garlic powder
- 1/4 teaspoon dried oregano

**Instructions**

- Slice off the stem of the onion and place the onion on the flat side. Into 12 - 16 sections, cut an inch down from the root, being cautious not to cut across all the way. To separate petals, turn over and softly take sections of onion out.
- Whisk together 1 tablespoon of water and eggs in a small bowl. Whisk the breadcrumbs & spices together in another small bowl. Dip the onion into the egg wash, dredge it in the breadcrumb mix, then coat it fully with a spoon. Sprinkle the onion with some oil.
- Cook 20 to 25 minutes at 375 ° until the onion is tender. Drizzle as needed with more oil.
- Meanwhile, mix the mayonnaise, horseradish, paprika, ketchup, garlic powder, & dried oregano in a med bowl.  Season it with salt.
- For dipping, serve the onion with sauce.

Cal 117 | Carb 22g | Protein 4g | Fat 0g

### VEGGIE BURGERS

*Prep time:20 min | Cook time:5 min | Serves: 6*

**Ingredients**

- Sweet Potato: 17 oz.
- Cauliflower: 28 oz.
- Carrots: 6.7 oz.
- 1 Cup Chickpeas
- 2 Cups Breadcrumbs
- 1 Cup Grated Mozzarella Cheese
- 1 tablespoon Mixed Herbs
- 1 tablespoon Basil
- Salt & Pepper

**Instructions**

- Peel and cut the vegetables and put them at the Instant air fryer. Cook manually for 10 minutes.
- Drain the vegetables & strain out the extra moisture with a tea towel such that the vegetables are dry.
- The chickpeas are added, and the vegetables are mashed.
- Add the breadcrumbs & blend well.
- The seasoning is added & make into the shape of a veggie burger.
- Roll the grated cheese in such a manner that it is fully coated in cheese.
- Put the veggie burgers in an air fryer and cook at 360f for 10 minutes.
- Serve hot with bread buns or a salad (or both).

Cal 161  | Fat 11g | Carb 8g | Protein 8g

### BUTTERNUT SQUASH & KIELBASA SAUSAGE

*Prep time:10 min | Cook time:25 min | Serves: 4*

**Ingredients**

- 1 cup diced butternut squash
- 1/2 tablespoon olive oil
- 1/4 teaspoon garlic salt
- 1/2 cup diced pre-cooked kielbasa
- 1/4 diced medium red or white onion

**Instructions**

- Preheat the air fryer to 370 F.

- Butternut squash should be cut into one-inch cubes. In a mixing bowl, combine the butternut squash, onion, oil, and seasoning. Coat, to be precise.
- Arrange the butternut squash in a single layer on a rack. Both of them should be able to be laid flat.
- Squash should be cooked for 10 minutes.
- Remove the rack, add the kielbasa, and cook for another 5 minutes, or until all is crispy and done. The size of the sausage and squash will determine how long it takes to cook. The total time should be about 20 minutes.

Cal 261 | Carb 10g | Protein 9g | Fat 21g

## SAUSAGE, HASH POTATO & BELL PEPPER

*Prep time:10 min | Cook time:1 hour 55 min*

### Ingredients
- 2 potatoes peeled and cubed
- 1 link sausage
- ½ tablespoon olive oil
- ½ onion diced
- 1/2 green bell pepper diced
- ¼ teaspoon garlic powder
- 1/2 teaspoon Cajun seasoning
- Salt and black pepper

### Instructions
- Preheat the air fryer to 350 F.
- Place the potatoes in a cup, diced. Season with 1 teaspoon olive oil and a pinch of salt and pepper.
- Cook for 5 minutes, turning the potatoes once in the centre.
- The rest of the vegetables and sausage as they're cooking. Place them in a mixing bowl. Season with 1 teaspoon olive oil and a pinch of salt and pepper.

Cal 611 | Fat38g | Carb 43g | Protein 26g

## ITALIAN PORTOBELLO MUSHROOM CAPS

*Prep time:10 min | Cook time:12 min | Serves: 4*

### Ingredients
- 4 Tablespoons
- 4 Tablespoons Balsamic vinegar
- kosher salt and Pepper
- 1 cup Shredded Mozzarella Cheese
- 1 Cup Crushed pork rinds
- 1 Cup Shredded Parmesan Cheese
- 1/2 Tablespoon Italian seasoning
- 4-inch Portobello Mushroom
- 2 Tablespoons Melted Butter

### Instructions:
- Preheat the air fryer to 400 F.
- Apply avocado oil and balsamic vinegar to the inside of each mushroom cap.
- Salt and pepper the insides of each one.
- In the centre of the mushroom caps, position the mozzarella cheese.
- Combine the pork rinds, parmesan, Italian seasoning, and melted butter in a big mixing bowl.
- Fill the mushroom caps uniformly with the pork rind mixture.
- Cook for 12 minutes or until the tops are brown and crisp and the mushrooms are tender, spraying the air fryer's interior with cooking spray. Put the mushrooms in the air fryer, 2 at a time

(unless all 4 can fit), and cook for 12 minutes or until the tops are brown and crisp and the mushrooms are tender.

Calories:416 | Carb6g | Protein 20g | Fat 36g

## ROASTED GARLIC & ROSEMARY POTATOES

*Prep time:5 min | Cook time:10 min | Serves:2*

### Ingredients
- 2 pounds mini-Yukon potatoes
- 4 tablespoons extra virgin olive oil
- 6 garlic cloves minced or pressed
- 1 teaspoon dried thyme
- 1 teaspoon dried rosemary
- 1 teaspoon of salt
- 1 teaspoon of pepper

### Instructions
- Preheat your Air Fryer to 350 F. During cooking, the rack should be set to the MIDDLE position.
- Rinse and cut your potatoes in half.
- Combine olive oil, garlic, thyme, rosemary, salt, and pepper in a big mixing bowl.
- Toss the potatoes with the herb mixture in a big mixing bowl.
- Distribute the potatoes uniformly around the racks.
- Cook for 5 minutes on the lowest setting. Cook for another 5 minutes after tossing and switching the racks (move one up and one down). You may have to do this again to get the potatoes to the perfect doneness.

Cal 276 | Fat20g | Carb24.1g | Protein2g

## SNAP PEAS

*Prep time: 2 min | Cook time:5 min | Serves: 2*

### Ingredients
- 2 cups Snap Peas
- 2 tablespoons olive oil
- salt and Pepper
- 1 teaspoon minced garlic or garlic powder

### Instructions
- Preheat your air fryer to 390 F.
- Toss the peas in a bowl with olive oil and seasonings.
- Cook for 4 minutes before tossing. Cook for another 3 minutes, or until they achieve the perfect tenderness.

Cal 165 | Carb 7g | Protein 3g | Fat 14g

## STUFFED TWICE "BAKED" POTATOES

### Ingredients
- 2 Potatoes
- 2 teaspoons olive oil
- 1 Avocado
- ⅓ Cup sour cream
- 1 tablespoon lime juice
- 1 teaspoon garlic powder
- ¼ teaspoon onion powder
- 4 tablespoon bacon crispy and chopped
- 1 tablespoon chives chopped
- Salt and pepper to taste

### Instructions:
- Preheat the air fryer to 350°F and bake on BAKE. During the cooking process, the rack will be set to the LOWEST position.

- Poke potatoes a couple of times with a fork. Drizzle with olive oil and season with salt. Cook for 30 minutes, or until the potatoes are tender.
- Start preparing the filling in the meantime. Mash the avocado in a small cup, add the lime juice, garlic powder, onion powder, heavy cream, salt, and pepper to taste. Mix until all of the ingredients are well combined.
- Remove the potatoes from the air fryer and cut them in half. Stuff the tortillas with guacamole, bacon, and chives.

Cal 240 | Fat4.5 g | Carb4 g | Protein 180g

## PARMESAN CRUSTED SWEET POTATOES
*Prep time:5 min | Cook time:10 min | Serves: 4*

### Ingredients
- 2 Sweet potatoes scrubbed and cut into wedges
- ½ Cup parmesan cheese
- ½ teaspoon garlic powder
- ½ teaspoon onion powder
- 1 teaspoon paprika
- 3 tablespoons olive oil
- Salt and pepper to taste

### Instructions
- Cover sweet potato wedges in cold water in a big mixing bowl. Allow for an hour of soaking to extract the excess starch.
- Preheat your Air Fryer to 400 F using the AIRFRY setting. During cooking, the rack will be on the MIDDLE floor.
- Meanwhile, mix parmesan cheese, onion powder, garlic powder, and paprika in a small cup.
- Drain the wedges dry with a paper towel. And then brush them and serve.

Cal 236 | Fat 18g | Carb 15g | Protein 4g

## GREEN CHIPS

*Prep time:5 min | Cook time:5 min | Serves: 2*

### Ingredients
- 1 tablespoon olive oil
- 1 teaspoon salt
- 1 bunch kale
- Garlic, Pepper, Lemon, Cajun

### Instructions
- Preheat your air fryer to 375°F with the AIR FRY mode.
- Remove the leaves from the spine and break them into chip-sized pieces.
- Drizzle olive oil over the leaves and season with salt.
- One layer should be placed on the middle level of the rack. To prevent them from going, place the other rack above it.
- Cook for an additional two minutes. Cook for a few minutes more on the other side. If they aren't crispy enough, add more. Keep your eyes open for them!
- To make them extra crispy, make many batches.

- Season to taste with salt (if desired) or any other seasonings.
- For up to a week, store in a paper bag. A plastic bag lined with paper towels may also be used. If they lose their crispiness, return them to the air fryer.

Cal 187 | Carb 11g | Protein 6g | Fat 15g

## POTATO WEDGES
*Prep time:5 min | Cook time:8 min | Serves: 3-4*

### Ingredients
- 1/2 teaspoon paprika
- 1/8 teaspoon ground black pepper
- 2 medium potatoes cut into wedges
- 1/2 teaspoon sea salt
- 1 1/2 tablespoons olive oil

### Instructions
- Preheat the air fryer to 400 F.
- Make wedges out of the potatoes. Every potato should be quartered and then cut into eight pieces.
- In a big mixing bowl, position the potato wedges. Season with salt and pepper and stir well to mix.
- Cook the wedges for 8 minutes, rotating once, on a rack in the centre of the air fryer.

Cal 386 | Carb 43g | Protein 9g | Fat 21g

## CRUSTED SWEET POTATO FRIES
*Prep time:5 min | Cook time:10 min | Serves: 4*

### Ingredients
- 1 teaspoon paprika
- 2 Sweet potatoes, cut into wedges
- ½ Cup parmesan cheese
- ½ teaspoon garlic powder
- 3 tablespoons olive oil
- ½ teaspoon onion powder

### Instructions
- Cover sweet potato wedges in cold water in a big mixing bowl. Enable for an hour of soaking to extract the excess starch.
- Preheat your Air Fryer to 400 F using the AIRFRY mode. During cooking, the rack will be on the MIDDLE floor.
- Meanwhile, mix parmesan cheese and all the powders in a small cup.
- Drain and pat the wedges dry with a paper towel. Brush the potatoes with olive oil and put them 5 minutes in the air fryer. Set the timer for 5 minutes after shaking the potatoes.

Cal 393 | Fat 18g | Carb 53g | Protein 7g

## ROASTED BUTTER GARLIC CARROTS
*Prep time:20 min | Cook time:13 min | Serves: 6*

### Ingredients
- 16 oz. Baby Carrots
- 1/4 cup Melted Butter
- 1/2 Teaspoon Salt
- 1/2 Teaspoon Pepper
- Parsley for garnish
- 1 tablespoon Garlic

### Instructions
- Preheat the air fryer to 400 F
- Place baby carrots in a small baking dish.
- In a small cup, melt the butter and add the garlic.
- Salt and pepper according to your taste

- Create a proper mixture. Pour the butter mixture over the carrot
- Blend it all to make a uniform layer
- Stir, then roast for another 5 minutes, or until the vegetables are tender.
- Remove from the air fryer and top with parsley before serving!

Cal 97 | Carb 7g | Protein 1g | Fat 8g

## CARROT FRIES
*Prep time:5 min | Cook time:8 min | Serves:2-3*

### Ingredients
- 3 carrots sliced into sticks
- 2 tablespoons olive oil
- 1 teaspoon salt and pepper
- 1/4 cup mayo
- 2 tablespoon honey
- 1 teaspoon Sriracha add extra if you like things spicy

### Instructions
- Preheat the air fryer to 400 F using the AIRFRY configuration. During cooking, the rack will be in the MIDDLE and LOWEST positions.
- Cut the carrots into fries and arrange them on a rack in a single layer.
- At a time, you can do two racks.
- Cook for 4 minutes, stirring periodically. You can also drive one rack up and one rack down if you have two racks. Cooking would be more even as a result of this.
- Until golden brown, check every 4 minutes. You may have to shift the racks around and rotate them again before they're done enough for your family! Place the fries on the top rung for about a minute to make them super crunchy.

Cal 831 | Carb 53g | Protein 2g | Fat 70g

## ROASTED TRI-COLOR CARROTS
*Prep time:5 min | Cook time:6 min | Serves: 4*

### Ingredients
- 3 Tri-Color Carrots Cut into pieces
- 2 tablespoons olive oil
- 1 teaspoon salt and pepper

### Instructions
- Preheat the air fryer to 375 F using the AIRFRY setting. When cooking, the rack will be in the MIDDLE and LOWEST positions.
- Carrots should be peeled and sliced. Season with olive oil and salt, and pepper. Place them on a rack to dry.
- At the same time, you can do two shelves.
- Cook for 4 minutes, rotating the fries halfway through. You can also move one rack up and one rack down (if you have two). This aids inconsistent cooking.
- Every 4 minutes, double-check. You may have to rotate the racks and shift them around before they're done.

Cal 831 | Protein2g | Carb 53g | Fat 70g

## EGGPLANT PARMESAN
*Prep time:20 min | Cook time:30 min | Serves: 6*

### Ingredients
- 1 Eggplant Medium sliced into 1/2-inch rounds
- 1/2 cup Italian bread crumbs
- 1/4 cup freshly grated Parmesan cheese
- 1 teaspoon Italian seasoning
- 1 teaspoon salt
- ½ teaspoon basil
- ½ teaspoon garlic
- ½ teaspoon onion powder
- ½ teaspoon black pepper
- 1/2 cup flour
- 1 egg beaten
- 1 cup marinara sauce or bolognas
- 6 slices mozzarella cheese, possibly more if you get more slices out of the eggplant

### Instructions
- Preheat the Vortex on AIRFRY to 360°F. The rack should be set to the MIDDLE position.
- Using a knife, cut the eggplant into 1/2-inch thick slices.
- Take three bowls and fill one with bread crumbs and parmesan cheese. In a separate bowl, whisk together the egg and milk. The third layer contains rice, salt, pepper, garlic, and onion powder.
- First, coat the sliced eggplant in flour, then in beaten eggs, and then in the bread crumb mixture.
- Enable to sit for a few minutes on the racks. Six should fit on two racks. Make certain they aren't in touch. You may need to do two batches.
- Cook for another 4 minutes before flipping. Depending on the thickness, an extra minute or two will be needed.
- 1 slice mozzarella cheese and marinara sauce on top of each eggplant round. Return to the air fryer for a minute or two more, or until the cheese has melted. If required, repeat with any remaining slices.

Cal 219 | Carb 23g | Protein 13g | Fat 9g

## HOME FRIED POTATOES
*Prep time:5 min | Cook time:10 min | Serves: 4*

### Ingredients
- 2 Potatoes Sliced
- 1 teaspoon vegetable oil
- Salt and Pepper to taste

### Instructions
- Preheat your air fryer to 400 F.
- Breaks potatoes into slices
- Drizzle with oil and season with salt and pepper.
- Cook for another 5 minutes before flipping. Check for doneness by inserting a fork into the middle. If not, cook for a few more minutes.

Cal 91 | Carb 19g | Protein 2g | Fat 1g

## GINGER ASPARAGUS
*Prep time:5 min | Cook time:0 min | Serves: 4-6*

### Ingredients
- 1 bunch asparagus
- 1 cup Water
- 2 tablespoons olive oil
- 1 1/2 - 3 teaspoon lemon juice
- 1/2 - 1 teaspoon salt
- 1/2 - 3/4 teaspoon grated peeled fresh ginger

### Instructions
- Place the Asparagus in the Air fryer.
- Air fry for 8-10 minutes at 350 F
- Combine the oil, lemon juice, 1/2 teaspoon salt, and 1/2 teaspoon ginger in a serving cup.

- Carefully remove the lid from the bowl and add the Asparagus. Toss all together. Taste and adjust with more lemon juice and ginger, if necessary.

Cal 84 | Fat 7g | Carb 5g | Protein 3g

## EGGPLANT FRIES

*Prep time:15 min | Cook time:10 min | Serves: 6*

### Ingredients

- 2 large eggs
- Italian spices: 1 tsp.
- Parmesan cheese: half cup
- Toasted wheat germ: half cup
- Garlic salt: ¼ tsp.
- Pasta sauce: 1 cup

### Instructions

- In a bowl, whisk eggs.
- In a different bowl add the rest of the ingredients except for eggplant.
- Let the Kalorik Air Fryer Oven preheat to 375 F.
- Cut the eggplant into half-inch strips.
- Coat in eggs then in spice mixture.
- Air fry for 4 to 5 minutes.

Cal 134 | Fat 5g | Protein 9g | Carb 15g

## COCONUT CURRY LENTIL CHICKPEA AND KALE

*Prep time:10 min | Cook time:8 min | Serves: 4*

### Ingredients

- 1 teaspoon turmeric
- 3/4 cup red lentils
- 1 cup of onion juice
- 1 cup vegetable broth
- 1 teaspoon peeled and grated fresh ginger
- 1 teaspoon salt
- 13.66 oz. coconut milk
- 15 oz. can chickpeas drained and rinsed, 1 can
- 4 cups deveined kale finely chopped
- 1 tablespoon lime juice
- 15 oz. diced tomatoes with garlic
- 1 tablespoon curry powder

### Instructions

- In the inner pot, mix all of the ingredients, lime juice, and cilantro leaves except the kale, and stir well to combine. Close the cover.
- Set the timer to 8 minutes.
- When the timer beeps, let the pressure naturally escape before the float valve decreases, then open the lid.
- Add the kale and lime juice and mix well. Serve topped with Cilantro and spooned into bowls.

Cal 328 | Fat 8g | Protein 15g | Carb 48g

## BOWLS WITH CARROT GINGER DRESSING

*Prep time:20 min | Cook time:26 min | Serves: 4*

### Ingredients

- 1 cup brown rice
- 1/2 tablespoon olive oil
- 2 large carrots thinly sliced
- 1 tablespoon ginger chopped
- 1/4 teaspoon pure stevia powder
- 2 avocados peeled

- 1/2 tablespoon apple cider vinegar
- 1 tablespoon fresh lime juice
- 3/4 teaspoon toasted sesame oil
- 1/8 teaspoon salt
- 1 1/2 cups frozen shelled edamame thawed
- 4 cups red cabbage thinly sliced
- 2 scallions thinly
- 1 1/4 cups vegetable stock divided
- 1 1/2 cups broccoli florets thinly sliced
- 2 tablespoon sesame seeds
- 1 medium cucumber thinly sliced

### Instructions

- In the inner pot, combine the rice and 1 cup of stock. Close the cover.
- Set the timer to 24 minutes and press the Manual or Pressure Cook button.
- Prepare the dressing while the rice is cooking. Blend the olive oil, vinegar, half of the carrot slices, ginger, lime juice, stevia, sesame oil, and salt in a high-powered blender until fully smooth. Remove from the equation.
- When the timer beeps, let the pressure naturally escape before the float valve decreases, then open the lid. Fluff the rice with a fork. To cancel, press the Cancel button.
- Add 1/4 cup stock, along with the edamame and broccoli, to the Sauté button. Gently stir them in and cook for about 2 minutes, or until they are hot.
- Spoon a quarter of the rice mixture into each of the four bowls to create the Vegetable Buddha Bowls. Divide the remaining carrot slices, cabbage, cucumber, and avocado slices into quarters in each bowl, keeping the ingredients separate. Drizzle one-quarter of the Carrot Ginger Dressing over each bowl and sprinkle with sesame seeds and scallions.

Cal 462 | Fat 17g | Protein 17g | Carb 64g

## JAMAICAN MIXED VEGETABLE CURRY

*Prep time:10 min | Cook time:30 min | Serves: 6*

### Ingredients

- 1 stemmed, seeded, and sliced Scotch bonnet pepper
- 2 tablespoon vegetable oil
- 3 garlic cloves minced
- 3 sprigs fresh thyme
- 1 tablespoon minced fresh ginger
- 1 cup chopped onion
- 1 tablespoon plus 1
- 1 teaspoon kosher salt
- 1/2 teaspoon ground allspice
- 4 cups peeled pumpkin 1-inch cubes
- 1 1/2 cups peeled potatoes 1-inch cubes
- 2 cups stemmed, seeded, and diced red, yellow, or orange bell peppers
- 1 cup Water
- Cooked rice for serving
- 1/2 teaspoon Jamaican curry powder

### Instructions

- sauté the onion. Combine the curry powder, Scotch bonnet pepper, thyme, cinnamon, and allspice in a large mixing cup.
- Combine the pumpkin, potatoes, bell peppers, and water in a large mixing bowl.

- Air fry the vegetables for 8 to 10 minutes at 375 F and transfer to the onion pot.
- Mash some vegetables with the back of a spoon to thicken the curry.
- To eat, ladle the curry into individual bowls over rice.

Cal 259 | Fat 0g | Protein 7.9g | Carb 42g

## AVOCADO CORN SALAD

*Prep time:5 min | Cook time:10 min | Serves: 6*

### Ingredients

- 1 1/2 cups Water
- Three fresh ears corn shucked and halved
- Juice and zest of 1 medium lime
- 1/4 cup olive oil
- 1/4 teaspoon salt
- 1/4 teaspoon ground black pepper
- 2 ripe medium avocados peeled, pitted, and diced
- 1/2 cup diced English cucumber
- 1 cup halved cherry tomatoes

### Instructions

- Air fry the corn for 5 to 8 minutes at 375 F.
- Move the corn to a serving dish and set it aside to cool. Remove the kernels from the cobs.
- Combine lime juice and zest, oil, salt, and pepper in a wide mixing bowl. Combine corn, avocados, cucumbers, and tomatoes in a mixing dish.
- Refrigerate until ready to eat, sealed. Chill before serving.

Cal 210 | Fat 16g | Protein 3g | Carb 16g

## ASIAN MUSHROOM SWEET POTATO NOODLES

*Prep time:5 min | Cook time:3 min | Serves: 4*

### Ingredients

- 2 tablespoon coconut aminos
- 1 tablespoon White vinegar
- 2 teaspoon olive oil
- 1 teaspoon sesame oil
- 1 tablespoon honey
- 1/4 teaspoon red pepper flakes
- 3 garlic cloves minced
- 1 large sweet potato peeled and spiraled
- 1 lb. shiitake mushrooms sliced
- 1 cup vegetable broth
- 1/4 cup chopped fresh parsley

### Instruction

- Combine coconut aminos, vinegar, olive oil, sesame oil, butter, red pepper flakes, and garlic in a big mixing bowl.
- Toss the sweet potato with the shiitake mushrooms in the sauce. Refrigerate for 30 minutes, sealed.
- Air fry for 8 to 10 minutes at 35o F.

Cal 244 | Fat 13g | Carb 24g | Protein 9g

## CAULIFLOWER PUREE

*Prep time:5 min | Cook time:15 min | Serves: 4-6*

### Ingredients

- 1 small cauliflower head cut into florets
- 1 tablespoon olive oil
- ¼ teaspoon ground turmeric
- ½ teaspoon smoked paprika
- ½ teaspoon salt

- ¼ teaspoon ground black pepper

### Instructions

- Air fry the cauliflower for 8 to 10 minutes at 375.
- In a bowl, add the roasted cauliflower and the rest of the ingredients.
- Puree with a stick blender and serve.

Cal 204 | Fat 17g | Protein 6.5g | Carb0g

## PUMPKIN SPICE BREAD

*Prep time:15 min | Cook time:70 min | Serves: 6-8*

### Ingredients

- 1 cup chicken broth
- 1 head cauliflower, cut into large chunks
- 1/2 cup milk
- 2 tablespoon salted butter 1/4 stick
- salt and black pepper to taste

### Instructions

- Combine baking powder and flour in a medium mixing bowl. Remove from the equation.
- Spray a 6-cup Bundt pan with a non-stick spray inside and out. Remove from the equation.
- In a large bowl, mix cream, butter, and sugar with a mixer until completely mixed. One at a time, add the eggs and beat until smooth.
- Combine the pumpkin, vanilla, herbs, and salt in a mixing bowl. The mixture may have a grainy appearance.
- Kindly fold in the flour/baking powder mixture with a rubber spatula until uniform. Do not overmix the ingredients.
- Pour the batter into the Bundt pan and cover tightly with foil.
- Add to the Instant air fryer. Lower the Bundt pan
- Air fry for 10 to 15 minutes at bake.

Cal 140. | Protein 3 g. | Carb 32 g | Fat 1 g

## SEASONED VEGGIES

*Prep time: 5 min | Cook time: 12 min | Serves: 4*

### Ingredients

- Baby carrots – 1 cup
- Broccoli florets – 1 cup
- Cauliflower florets – 1 cup
- Olive oil – 1 tbsp.
- Italian seasoning – 1 tbsp.
- Salt and ground black pepper, as required

### Directions

- Gather all of the ingredients into a bowl and toss to coat well.
- Place the vegetables in the rotisserie basket and attach the lid.
- Arrange the drip pan in the bottom of the Air Fryer Oven cooking chamber.
- Take to the preheated air fryer at 380°F for 18 minutes.
- Serve

Cal 66 | Carb 5.7g | Fat 4.7g | Protein 1.4g

## SWEET POTATO CHILI
*Prep time:10 min | Cook time:35 min | Serves: 4*

### Ingredients
- 2 teaspoon canola oil
- 1 cup yellow onion chopped
- 1 clove garlic finely chopped
- 1-1/2 teaspoon chili powder
- 1/2 teaspoon ground cumin
- 28 ounces diced tomatoes 1 can
- 15 ounces' black beans 1 can rinse and drained
- 1 medium green bell pepper seeded and diced
- 1 medium sweet potato peeled and diced
- 1 teaspoon kosher salt
- 3/4 cup frozen corn kernels

### Instructions
- In the inner container, choose Sauté and pour in the canola oil. Combine the onion and garlic in a mixing dish. Sauté for 2 minutes, or until the onion is soft and translucent and the garlic is fragrant.
- Toss in the tomatoes, black beans, bell pepper, sweet potato, and kosher salt, followed by the chili powder and cumin. Stir all together thoroughly.
- Close the lid, lock it, and turn the steam release handle to the seal spot. Select Pressure Cook (High) and 15 minutes as the cooking time. Enable the pressure to naturally release after the Cook time:is over (about 20 minutes).
- Take off the cover and add the corn. Fill serving bowls halfway with chili. Serve immediately.

Cal 250 | Protein 16g | Carb 32.5g | Fa t7.4g

## DUM ALOO - BABY POTATOES CURRY
*Prep time:5 min | Cook time:20 min | Serves: 3-4*

### Ingredients
- 15 baby potatoes
- 2 tablespoon oil or ghee
- 1 tablespoon cumin seeds
- 1/2 onion thinly sliced
- 1 1/2 tablespoon Ginger-Garlic paste
- 4 medium tomatoes chopped
- 2 teaspoon garam masala
- 1 teaspoon turmeric powder
- 1 1/2 tablespoon coriander powder
- red chili powder to taste
- salt to taste
- 1/3 cup cashews (soaked and grind into a smooth paste)
- 1 cup water or as needed
- cilantro to garnish

### Instructions
- In a pan, Add the ghee and heat it.
- Throw in the cumin seeds and cook for 1 minute, then add the onions and cook until golden brown.
- Fry for 2 minutes with the ginger garlic paste, then add the tomatoes and cook until mushy.
- Once the potatoes are mushy, stir in the garam masala, coriander powder, red chili powder, and turmeric powder. Season with salt to taste.

- Stir in the cashew paste, cook for 2 minutes, then stir in the washed and peeled potatoes.
- Pour in enough water to barely cover the potatoes. Switch off the sauté feature.
- Transfer in a dish, air fry for 7 to 8 minutes, at 350 F.
- Garnish with Cilantro and serve immediately with rice, roti, or naan.

Cal 364 | Carb | Protein 35g | Fat 7g

## EGGPLANT CURRY
*Prep time:5 min | Cook time:15 min | Serves: 4*

### Ingredients
- 1 big Eggplant
- 1 small onion chopped
- 2 cloves garlic chopped
- 2 teaspoon oil of choice
- 1 teaspoon mustard seeds
- 1 teaspoon cumin seeds
- 1 sprig of curry leaves
- 2 tomatoes chopped
- 1 teaspoon turmeric powder
- chili powder to taste
- salt to taste
- 1 tablespoon coriander powder
- 1 tablespoon curry powder of choice
- 1 cup Water
- cilantro to garnish

### Instructions
- In the oil Fry the mustard and cumin seeds together.
- Toss in the garlic and curry leaves and cook until fragrant. Toss in the onions and cook for a few minutes.
- Toss in the tomatoes and cook for 2 minutes. Mix in all of the spice powders as well as the salt.
- Mix in the cubed eggplant and water once more.
- Transfer in a dish, top with cheese.
- Air fry for 6 to 7 minutes at 350 F.

Cal 167.4 | Fat7.7 g | Carb 22.3 g | Protein 5.0

## SPINACH-POTATO TACOS
*Prep time:10 min | Cook time:15 min | Serves: 6*

### Ingredients
- 16 ounces' spinach
- 2 large Yukon gold potatoes cubed
- 1 yellow onion diced
- 2 cloves garlic minced
- 14-ounce diced tomatoes with juice
- 2 teaspoons ground cumin
- 1/4 cup milk
- 3 tablespoons nutritional yeast
- 1 teaspoon sea salt
- 1/4 teaspoon black pepper ground
- 1/2 cup Cilantro fresh, chopped
- 12 Corn tortillas or flour tortillas

### Instructions
- In a bowl, add all ingredients except for tacos.
- Toss to coat, air fry for 10 to 12 minutes at 360 F.
- Serve in warm tortillas.

Cal 251 | Fat 4g | Carb 51g | Protein 6g

## INSTANT VEGETABLE MEDLEY

*Prep time:5 min | Cook time:2 min | Serves: 4*

**Ingredients**

- 1 lb. assorted non-starchy vegetables
- 2 tablespoons olive oil
- 1 clove garlic minced
- Fine sea salt and black pepper

**Instructions**

- In a bowl, add all ingredients toss to coat.
- Air fry for 10 minutes at 360 F. Serve with rice

Cal45 | Fat9.8g | Carb 2g | Protein 0mg

## VEGAN ZUCCHINI LASAGNA

*Prep time:9 min | Cook time:21 min | Serves: 1*

**Ingredients**

- 2 lasagna egg-free noodles
- Fresh basil leaves: 1/4 cup chopped
- Shredded zucchini: 3 tbsp.
- Salt
- Pasta sauce: half cup
- Tofu ricotta: ¼ cup
- Baby spinach leaves: 1/4 cup chopped

**Instructions**

- Break noodles into 2 pieces to get 4 noodles for five".
- Cook the noodles as per package instructions, then dry on kitchen towels.
- In a mini loaf pan, add 2 tbsp. of pasta sauce, add one noodle, add 1 tbsp. of ricotta, herbs, spinach, zucchini.
- Repeat the layers.
- Add ricotta cheese on top.
- With aluminum foil, cover the pan.
- Let the Kalorik Air Fryer Oven preheat to 400 F.
- Air fry for ten minutes, take the foil off and cook for 3 to 5 minutes.

Cal 344 | Carb 52g | Protein 14g | Fat 9g

## BUTTERNUT SQUASH FALAFEL

*Prep time:20 min | Cook time:30 min | Serves: 2*

**Ingredients**

- Half onion, chopped
- Cayenne pepper: 1 tsp.
- 1 can of chickpeas
- Cumin powder: 1 tsp.
- Sea salt
- Coriander powder: 1 tsp.
- Cilantro chopped: 3 tbsp.
- 1 butternut squash

**Instructions**

- Let the Kalorik Air Fryer Oven preheat to 375 F.
- Peel and cut the squash into cubes, oil spray them and air fry for 15 minutes, till tender.
- In a bowl, add the butternut squash to a bowl with rest of the ingredients and mix well.
- Make into ten balls and air fry them for 15 minutes, shake the basket halfway through

Cal 182 | Carb 36g | Protein 7g | Fat 2g

## GARLIC PARMESAN CARROT FRIES

*Prep time:10 min | Cook time:16 min | Serves: 4*

**Ingredients**

- 6-7 medium carrots
- Parmesan cheese: 3 tbsp., grated
- Olive oil: 1 1/2 tbsp.
- 1 garlic clove, crushed
- Kosher salt
- Black pepper: ¼ tsp.

**Instructions**

- Slice the carrots into three" pieces, slice each piece lengthwise to get 2-3 skinny pieces.
- Toss with olive oil.
- Mash the garlic with salt to make a paste.
- Toss with carrots. Add cheese and pepper, toss to coat.
- Let the Kalorik Air Fryer Oven preheat to 360 F.
- Air fry for 16-18 minutes, shake the basket halfway through.

Cal 102 | Fat 7g | Carb 9g | Protein 2g

## SPICY CHICKPEAS

*Prep time: 5 min | Cook time: 20 min | Serves: 4*

**Ingredients**

- Olive oil
- ½ teaspoon ground cumin
- ½ teaspoon chili powder
- ¼ teaspoon cayenne pepper
- ¼ teaspoon salt
- 1 (19-ounce) can chickpeas, drained and rinsed

**Directions**

- Spray a fryer basket lightly with olive oil.
- In a bowl, combine the chili powder, cumin, cayenne pepper, and salt.
- In a medium bowl, add the chickpeas and lightly spray them with olive oil. Add the spice mixture and toss until coated evenly.
- Transfer the chickpeas to the fryer basket. Air fry until the chickpeas reach your desired level of crunchiness, 15 to 20 minutes, making sure to shake the basket every 5 minutes.

Cal 122 | Fat 1g | Carb 22g | Protein 6g | Fiber 6g

## SEASONED YELLOW SQUASH

*Prep time: 5 minutes | Cook time: 10 minutes | Serves: 4*

**Ingredients**

- Large yellow squash – 4, cut into slices
- Olive oil – ¼ cup
- Onion – ½, sliced
- Italian seasoning – ¾ tsp.
- Garlic salt – ½ tsp.
- Seasoned salt – ¼ tsp.

**Directions**

- In a bowl, mix all the ingredients together. Place the veggie mixture in the greased cooking tray.
- Arrange the drip pan in the bottom of the Air Fryer Oven cooking chamber.
- Take to the preheated air fryer at 400°F for 10 minutes.
- Serve hot.

Cal 113 | Carb 8.1g | Fat 9g | Protein 4.2g

## BUTTERED ASPARAGUS

*Prep time: 5 min | Cook time: 10 min | Serves: 4*

**Ingredients**

- Fresh thick asparagus spears – 1 lb. trimmed
- Butter – 1 tbsp. melted
- Salt and ground black pepper, as required

**Directions**

- Put all of the ingredients into a bowl and toss to coat well. Arrange the asparagus onto a cooking tray.
- Arrange the drip pan in the bottom of the Air Fryer Oven cooking chamber.
- Take to the preheated air fryer at 350°F for 10 minutes.
- Serve hot.

Cal 64 | Carb 5.9g | Fat 4g | Protein 3.4g

## GARLIC THYME MUSHROOMS

*Prep time: 5 min | Cook time: 10 min | Serves: 4*

**Ingredients**

- 3 tablespoons unsalted butter, melted
- 1 (8-ounce) package button mushrooms, sliced
- 2cloves garlic, minced
- 3sprigs fresh thyme leaves
- ½ teaspoon fine sea salt

**Directions**

- Preparing the Ingredients. Grease the basket with avocado oil. Preheat the air fryer to 400°F.
- Place all the ingredients in a medium-sized bowl. Use a spoon or your hands to coat the mushroom slices.
- Air Frying. Put the mushrooms in the basket in one layer; work in batches if necessary. Cook for 10 minutes, or until slightly crispy and brown. Garnish with thyme sprigs before serving.
- Reheat in a warmed up 350°F air fryer for 5 minutes, or until heated through.

Cal 82 | Fat 9g | Protein 1g | Carb 1g | Fiber 0.2g

## SEASONED CARROTS WITH GREEN BEANS

*Prep time: 5 min | Cook time: 10 min | Serves: 4*

**Ingredients**

- Green beans – ½ lb. trimmed
- Carrots – ½ lb. peeled and cut into sticks
- Olive oil – 1 tbsp.
- Salt and ground black pepper, as required

**Directions**

- Gather all the ingredients into a bowl and toss to coat well.
- Place the vegetables in the rotisserie basket and attach the lid.
- Arrange the drip pan in the bottom of the Air Fryer Oven cooking chamber. Take to the preheated air fryer at 400°F for 10 minutes.

- Serve hot.

Cal 94 | Carb 12.7g | Fat 4.8g | Protein 2g

## SWEET POTATO WITH BROCCOLI

*Prep time: 5 min | Cook time: 20 min | Serves: 4*

**Ingredients**

- Medium sweet potatoes – 2, peeled and cut in 1-inch cubes
- Broccoli head – 1, cut in 1-inch florets
- Vegetable oil – 2 tbsps.
- Salt and ground black pepper, as required

**Directions**

- Grease a baking dish that will fit in the Air Fryer Oven.
- Gather all of the ingredients into a bowl and toss to coat well. Place the veggie mixture into the prepared baking dish in a single layer.
- Arrange the drip pan in the bottom of the Air Fryer Oven cooking chamber.
- Take to the preheated air fryer at 415°F for 20 minutes.
- Serve hot

Cal 170 | Carb 25.2g | Fat 7.1g | Protein 2.9g

## POTATO GRATIN

*Prep time: 5 min | Cook time: 20 min | Serves: 4*

**Ingredients**

- Large potatoes – 2, sliced thinly
- Cream – 5½ tbsps.
- Eggs – 2
- Plain flour – 1 tbsp.
- Cheddar cheese – ½ cup, grated

**Directions**

- Arrange the potato cubes onto the greased rack.
- Arrange the drip pan in the bottom of the Air Fryer Oven cooking chamber. Take to the preheated air fryer at 355°F for 10 minutes
- Meanwhile, in a bowl, add cream, eggs and flour and mix until a thick sauce form.
- Once cooking is done, remove the tray from the Air Fryer Oven. Divide the potato slices into 4 lightly greased ramekins evenly and top with the egg mixture, followed by the cheese.
- Arrange the ramekins on top of a cooking rack.
- Take to your air fryer oven at 390°F for 10 minutes.
- Serve warm.

Cal 233 | Carb 31.g | Fat 8g | Protein 9.7g

## GARLIC EDAMAME

*Prep time: 5 min | Cook time: 10 min | Serves: 4*

**Ingredients**

- Olive oil
- 1 (16-ounce) bag frozen edamame in pods
- salt and freshly ground black pepper
- ½ teaspoon garlic salt
- ½ teaspoon red pepper flakes (optional)

**Directions**

- Spray a fryer basket lightly with olive oil.
- In a medium bowl, add the frozen edamame and lightly spray with olive oil. Toss to coat.

- In a bowl, combine together the garlic salt, salt, black pepper, and red pepper flakes (if using). Add the mixture to the edamame and toss until evenly coated.
- Place half the edamame in the fryer basket. Do not overfill the basket.
- Air fry for 5 minutes. Shake the basket and cook until the edamame is starting to brown and get crispy, 3 to 5 more minutes.
- Repeat with the remaining edamame and serve immediately.

Cal 100 | Fat 3g | Carb 9g | Protein 8g | Fiber 4g

## EGG ROLL PIZZA STICKS

*Prep time: 10 min | Cook time: 5 min | Serves: 4*

### Ingredients
- Olive oil
- 8 pieces reduced-fat string cheese
- 8 egg roll wrappers
- 24 slices turkey pepperoni
- Marinara sauce, for dipping (optional)

### Directions
- Spray a fryer basket lightly with olive oil. Fill a small bowl with water.
- Place each egg roll wrapper diagonally on a work surface. It should look like a diamond.
- Place 3 slices of turkey pepperoni in a vertical line down the center of the wrapper.
- Place 1 mozzarella cheese stick on top of the turkey pepperoni.
- Fold the top and bottom corners of the egg roll wrapper over the cheese stick.
- Fold the left corner over the cheese stick and roll the cheese stick up to resemble a spring roll. Dip a finger in the water and seal the edge of the roll
- Repeat with the rest of the pizza sticks.
- Place them in the fryer basket in a single layer, making sure to leave a little space between each one. Lightly spray the pizza sticks with oil.
- Air fry until the pizza sticks are lightly browned and crispy, about 5 minutes.
- These are best served hot while the cheese is melted. Accompany with a small bowl of marinara sauce, if desired.

Cal 362 | Fat 8g | Carb 40g | Protein 23g | Fiber 1g

## BUTTERED BROCCOLI

*Prep time: 5 min | Cook time: 15 min | Serves: 4*

### Ingredients
- Broccoli florets – 1 lb.
- Butter – 1 tbsp. melted
- Red pepper flakes – ½ tsp. crushed
- Salt and ground black pepper, as required

### Directions
- Gather all of the ingredients in a bowl and toss to coat well.
- Place the broccoli florets in the rotisserie basket and attach the lid.
- Arrange the drip pan in the bottom of the Air Fryer Oven cooking chamber.
- Take to the preheated air fryer at 400°F for 15 minutes.
- Serve immediately.

Cal 55 | Carb 6.1g | Fat 3g | Protein 2.3g

## PESTO GNOCCHI

*Prep time: 5 min | Cook time: 15 min | Serves: 4*

### Ingredients:
- 1 tablespoon olive oil
- 1 onion, finely chopped
- cloves garlic, sliced
- 1 (16-ounce) package shelf-stable gnocchi
- 1 (8-ounce) jar pesto
- ⅓ cup grated Parmesan cheese

### Directions:
- Combine the oil, onion, garlic and gnocchi in a 6-by-6-by-2-inch pan. Put into your air fryer oven.
- Bake for 10 minutes, then remove the pan and stir.
- Return the pan to the Air Fryer and cook for 5 to 10 minutes or until the gnocchi are lightly browned and crisp.
- Remove the pan from the air fryer. Stir in the pesto and Parmesan cheese, and serve immediately.

Cal 646 | Fat 32g | Carb 69g | Fiber 2g | Protein 22g

## CRISP & SPICY CABBAGE

*Prep time: 5 Min | Cook time: 10 Min | Serves: 2*

### Ingredients
- 1/2 Head White Cabbage, Chopped & Washed
- 1 Tablespoon Coconut Oil, Melted
- ¼ Teaspoon Cayenne Pepper
- ¼ Teaspoon Chili Powder
- ¼ Teaspoon Garlic Powder

### Directions
- Turn on your air fryer to 390°F.
- Mix your cabbage, spices and coconut oil together in a bowl, making sure your cabbage is coated well.
- Place it in the fryer and cook for 10 minutes.

Cal 100 | Fat 2g | Carb 3g | Protein 5g

## CAULIFLOWER RICE

*Prep time: 10 min | Cook time: 7 min | Serves: 4*

### Ingredients
- 14 ounces cauliflower heads
- 1 tablespoon coconut oil
- 2 tablespoons fresh parsley, chopped

### Directions
- Wash the cauliflower heads carefully and chop them into small pieces of rice.
- Place the cauliflower in the air fryer and add coconut oil.
- Stir carefully and cook for 5 min at 370° F.
- Then add the fresh parsley and stir well.
- Cook the cauliflower rice for 2 min more at 400° F.
- After this, gently toss the cauliflower rice and serve immediately.

Cal 55 | Fat 3.5g | Fiber 2.5g | Carbs 5.4g | Protein 2g

## BALSAMIC KALE
*Prep time: 2 min | Cook time: 12 min | Serves: 6*

**Ingredients**
- 2 tablespoons olive oil
- 3 garlic cloves, minced
- 2 and ½ pounds kale leaves
- Salt and black pepper to the taste
- 2 tablespoons balsamic vinegar

**Directions**
- In a pan that fits the air fryer, combine all the ingredients and toss.
- Put the pan in your air fryer and cook at 300°F for 12 minutes.
- Divide between plates and serve.

Cal 122 | Fat 4g | Fiber 3g | Carb 4g | Protein 5g

## CAJUN ZUCCHINI CHIPS

*Prep time: 10 min | Cook time: 15 min | Serves: 4*

**Ingredients**
- Olive oil
- 2 large zucchinis, cut into ⅛-inch-thick slices
- 2 teaspoons Cajun seasoning

**Directions**
- Spray a fryer basket lightly with olive oil.
- Put the zucchini slices in a medium bowl and spray them generously with olive oil.
- Sprinkle the Cajun seasoning over the zucchini and stir to make sure they are evenly coated with oil and seasoning.
- Place slices in a single layer in the fryer basket, making sure not to overcrowd.
- Air fry for 8 minutes. Flip the slices over and air fry until they are as crisp and brown as you prefer, an additional 7 to 8 minutes.

Cal 26 | Fat <1g | Carb 5g | Protein 2g | Fiber 2g

## CREAMY CABBAGE
*Prep time: 10 min | Cook time: 20 min | Serves: 2*

**Ingredients**
- ½ green cabbage head, chopped
- ½ yellow onion, chopped
- Salt and black pepper, to taste
- ½ cup whipped cream
- 1 tablespoon cornstarch

**Directions**
- Put cabbage and onion in the air fryer.
- In a bowl, mix cornstarch with cream, salt, and pepper. Stir and pour over cabbage.
- Toss and cook at 400°F for 20 minutes.
- Serve.

Cal 208 | Fat: 10g | Carb: 16g | Protein: 5g

## CINNAMON AND SUGAR PEACHES
*Prep time: 10 min | Cook time: 13 min | Serves: 4*

**Ingredients**
- Olive oil
- 2 tablespoons sugar
- ¼ teaspoon ground cinnamon
- 4 peaches, cut into wedges

**Directions**
- Spray a fryer basket lightly with olive oil.
- In a bowl, combine the cinnamon and sugar. Add the peaches and toss to coat evenly.
- Place the peaches in a single layer in the fryer basket on their sides.
- Air fry for 5 minutes. Turn the peaches skin side down, lightly spray them with oil, and air fry until the peaches are lightly brown and caramelized, 5 to 8 more minutes.
- Make it Even Lower Calorie: Use a zero-calorie sugar substitute such as NutraSweet or monk fruit sweetener instead of granulated sugar.

Cal 67 | Fat <1g | Carb 17g | Protein 1g | Fiber 2g

## SPICY CABBAGE
*Prep time: 5 min | Cook time: 7 min | Serves: 4*

**Ingredients**
- 1 head cabbage, sliced into 1-inch-thick ribbons
- 1 tablespoon olive oil
- 1 teaspoon garlic powder
- 1 teaspoon red pepper flakes
- 1 teaspoon salt
- 1 teaspoon freshly ground black pepper

**Directions**
- Toss the cabbage with the olive oil, garlic powder, red pepper flakes, salt, and pepper in a large mixing bowl until well coated.
- Transfer the cabbage to the baking pan.
- Slide the baking pan into Rack Position 1, select Convection Bake, set temperature to 350ºF and set time to 7 minutes.
- Flip the cabbage with tongs halfway through the cooking time.
- When cooking is complete, the cabbage should be crisp. Remove from the oven to a plate and serve warm.

Cal 172 | Fat 9.8g | Carb 17.5g | Protein 3.9g

## SPICY BROCCOLI WITH HOT SAUCE
*Prep time: 5 min | Cook time: 14 min | Serves: 6*

**Ingredients**
**Broccoli:**
- 1 medium-sized head broccoli, cut into florets
- 1½ tablespoons olive oil
- 1 teaspoon shallot powder
- 1 teaspoon porcini powder
- ½ teaspoon freshly grated lemon zest
- ½ teaspoon hot paprika
- ½ teaspoon granulated garlic
- ⅓ teaspoon fine sea salt
- ⅓ teaspoon celery seeds

**Hot Sauce:**
- ½ cup tomato sauce

172

- 1 tablespoon balsamic vinegar
- ½ teaspoon ground allspice

**Directions**

- In a mixing bowl, combine all the ingredients for the broccoli and toss to coat. Transfer the broccoli to your air fryer oven basket.
- Put in the air fryer basket and cook at 360°F for 14 minutes.
- Meanwhile, make the hot sauce by whisking together the tomato sauce, balsamic vinegar, and allspice in a small bowl.
- When cooking is complete, remove the broccoli from the oven and serve with the hot sauce.

Cal 191 | Fat 6g | Carb 31.4g | Protein 3.7g

## ROSTI (SWISS POTATOES)

*Prep time: 10 min | Cook time: 15 min | Serves: 4*

**Ingredients**

- 250 g peeled white potatoes
- 1 tablespoon finely chopped chives
- Freshly ground black pepper
- 1 tablespoon of olive oil
- 2 tablespoons of sour cream

**Directions**

- Preheat the air fryer to 360°F. Grate the thick potatoes in a bowl and add three quarters of the chives and salt and pepper to taste. Mix it well.
- Grease the pizza pan with olive oil and spread the potato mixture evenly through the pan. Press the grated potatoes against the pan and spread the top of the potato cake with some olive oil.
- Place the pizza pan inside the fryer basket and insert it into your air fryer oven. Set the timer to 15 mins and fry the rosti until it has a nice brownish color on the outside and is soft and well done inside.
- Cut the rosti into 4 quarters and place each quarter on a plate. Garnish with a spoonful of sour cream. Spread the remaining of the scallions over the sour cream and add a touch of ground pepper.

## COCONUT OIL ARTICHOKES

*Prep time: 10 min | Cook time: 8 min | Serves: 4*

**Ingredients**

- 1-pound artichokes
- 1 tablespoon coconut oil
- 1 tablespoon water
- ½ teaspoon minced garlic
- ¼ teaspoon cayenne pepper

**Directions**

- Trim the ends of the artichokes, sprinkle them with the water, and rub them with the minced garlic.
- Sprinkle with the cayenne pepper and the coconut oil.

- After this, wrap the artichokes in foil and place in the air fryer basket.
- Cook for 5 minutes at 370° F.
- Then remove the artichokes from the foil and cook them for 3 minutes more at 400° F.
- Transfer the cooked artichokes to serving plates and allow to cool a little. Serve.

Cal 83 | Fat 3.6g | Fiber 6.2g | Carbs 12.1g | Protein 3.7g

## CHEESY BROCCOLI GRATIN

*Prep time: 5 min | Cook time: 14 min | Serves: 2*

**Ingredients**

- ⅓ cup fat-free milk
- 1 tablespoon all-purpose or gluten-free flour
- ½ tablespoon olive oil
- ½ teaspoon ground sage
- ¼ teaspoon kosher salt
- ⅛ teaspoon freshly ground black pepper
- 2 cups roughly chopped broccoli florets
- 6tablespoons shredded Cheddar cheese
- 2 tablespoons panko bread crumbs
- 1 tablespoon grated Parmesan cheese
- Olive oil spray

**Directions**

- Spritz the baking pan with olive oil spray.
- Mix the milk, flour, olive oil, sage, salt, and pepper in a medium bowl and whisk to combine. Stir in the broccoli florets, Cheddar cheese, bread crumbs, and Parmesan cheese and toss to coat.
- Pour the broccoli mixture into the prepared baking pan.
- Select Convection Bake set temperature to 330°F and set time to 14 minutes.
- When cooking is complete, the top should be golden brown and the broccoli should be tender. Remove from the oven and serve immediately.

Cal 172 | Fat 9.8g | Carb 17.5g | Protein 3.9g

## VEGGIES ON TOAST

*Prep time: 12 min | Cook time: 10 min | Serves: 4*

**Ingredients:**

- 1 red bell pepper, cut into ½-inch strips
- 1 cup sliced button or cremini mushrooms
- 1 small yellow squash, sliced
- green onions, cut into ½-inch slices
- Extra light olive oil for misting
- to 6 pieces sliced French or Italian bread
- tablespoons softened butter
- ½ cup soft goat cheese

**Directions:**

- Combine the red pepper, mushrooms, squash, and green onions in the air fryer and mist with oil. Roast for 5 to 9 minutes or until the vegetables are tender, shaking the basket once during cooking time.
- Remove the vegetables from the basket and set aside.
- Spread the bread with butter and place in the air fryer, butter-side up. Toast for 2 to 4 minutes or until golden brown.
- Spread the goat cheese on the toasted bread and top with the vegetables; serve warm.

- Variation tip: To add even more flavor, drizzle the finished toasts with extra-virgin olive oil and balsamic vinegar.

Cal 162 | Fat 11g | Carb 9g | Fiber 2g | Protein 7g

## JUMBO STUFFED MUSHROOMS
*Prep time: 10 min | Cook time: 8 min | Serves: 4*

**Ingredients**:
- jumbo portobello mushrooms
- 1 tablespoon olive oil
- ¼ cup ricotta cheese
- tablespoons Parmesan cheese, divided
- 1 cup frozen chopped spinach, thawed and drained
- ⅓ cup bread crumbs
- ¼ teaspoon minced fresh rosemary

**Directions**:
- Wipe the mushrooms with a damp cloth. Remove the stems and discard. Using a spoon, gently scrape out most of the gills.
- Rub the mushrooms with the olive oil. Put in the air fryer basket, hollow side up, and bake for 3 minutes. Carefully remove the mushroom caps, because they will contain liquid. Drain the liquid out of the caps.
- In a medium bowl, combine the ricotta, 3 tablespoons of Parmesan cheese, spinach, bread crumbs, and rosemary, and mix well.
- Stuff this mixture into the drained mushroom caps. Sprinkle with the remaining 2 tablespoons of Parmesan cheese. Put the mushroom caps back into the basket.
- Bake for 4 to 6 minutes or until the filling is hot and the mushroom caps are tender.

Cal 117 | Fat 7g | Carb 8g | Fiber 1g | Protein 7g

## HEALTHY CARROT FRIES
*Prep time: 5 Min | Cook time: 12-15 Min | Serves: 2*

**Ingredients**
- 5 Large Carrots
- 1 Tablespoon Olive Oil
- ½ Teaspoon Sea Salt

**Directions**
- Heat your air fryer to 390°F, and then wash and peel your carrots. Cut them in a way to form fries.
- Combine your carrot sticks with your olive oil and salt, coating evenly.
- Place them into your air fryer oven, cooking for twelve minutes. If they're not as crispy as you desire, then cook for two to three more minutes.
- Serve with sour cream, ketchup or just with your favorite main dish.

Cal 140 | Fat 3g | Carb 6g | Protein 7g

## SIMPLE ROASTED CARROTS
*Prep time: 5 Min | Cook time: 35 Min*

**Ingredients**
- 4 Cups Carrots, Chopped
- 1 Teaspoon Herbs de Provence
- 2 Teaspoons Olive Oil
- 4 Tablespoons Orange Juice

**Directions**
- Start by preheating your air fryer to 320°F.
- Combine your carrot pieces with your herbs and oil.

- Cook for twenty-five to twenty-eight minutes.
- Take it out and dip the pieces in orange juice before frying for an additional seven minutes.

Cal 125 | Fat 2g | Carb 5g | Protein 6g

## BROCCOLI & CHEESE
*Prep time: 5 Min | Cook time: 9 Min*

**Ingredients**
- 1 Head Broccoli, Washed & Chopped
- Salt & Pepper to Taste
- 1 Tablespoon Olive oil
- Sharp Cheddar Cheese, Shredded

**Directions**
- Start by putting your air fryer to 360°F.
- Combine your broccoli with your olive oil and sea salt.
- Place it in the air fryer, and cook for six minutes.
- Take it out, and then top with cheese, cooking for another three minutes.
- Serve with your choice of protein.

Cal 170 | Fat 5g | Carb 9g | Protein 7g

## PARMESAN ASPARAGUS FRIES
*Prep time: 15 min | Cook time: 6 min | Serves: 4*

**Ingredients**
- 2egg whites
- ¼ cup water
- ¼ cup plus 2 tablespoons grated Parmesan cheese, divided
- ¾ cup panko bread crumbs
- ¼ teaspoon salt
- 12 ounces (340 g) fresh asparagus spears, woody ends trimmed
- Cooking spray

**Directions**
- In a shallow dish, whisk together the egg whites and water until slightly foamy. In a separate shallow dish, thoroughly combine ¼ cup of Parmesan cheese, bread crumbs, and salt.
- Dip the asparagus in the egg white, then roll in the cheese mixture to coat well.
- Place the asparagus in the air fryer basket in a single layer, leaving space between each spear. Spritz the asparagus with cooking spray.
- Put in the air fryer and cook at 390°F for 6 minutes.
- When cooking is complete, the asparagus should be golden brown and crisp. Remove from the oven. Sprinkle with the remaining 2 tablespoons of cheese and serve hot.

Cal 191 | Fat 6g | Carb 31.4g | Protein 3.7g

## CAULIFLOWER HASH
*Prep time: 10 min | Cook time: 15 min | Serves: 6*

**Ingredients**
- 1-pound cauliflower
- 2 eggs
- 1 teaspoon salt
- ½ teaspoon ground paprika
- 4-ounce turkey fillet, chopped

**Directions**
- Wash the cauliflower, chop, and set aside.
- In a different bowl, crack the eggs and whisk well.
- Add the salt and ground paprika; stir.

- Place the chopped turkey in the air fryer basket and cook it for 4 minutes at 365° F, stirring halfway through.
- After this, add the chopped cauliflower and stir the mixture.
- Cook the turkey/cauliflower mixture for 6 minutes more at 370° F, stirring it halfway through.
- Then pour in the whisked egg mixture and stir it carefully.
- Cook the cauliflower hash for 5 minutes more at 365° F.
- When the cauliflower hash is done, let it cool and transfer to serving bowls. Serve and enjoy.

Cal 143 | Fat 9.5g | Fiber 2g| Carb 4.5g | Protein 10.4g

## AIR FRIED ROASTED CORN ON THE COB

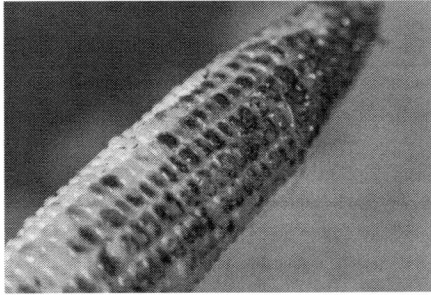

*Prep time: 5 min | Cook time: 10 min | Serves: 4*

### Ingredients
- 1 tablespoon vegetable oil
- 4 ears of corn
- Unsalted butter, for topping
- Salt, for topping
- Freshly ground black pepper, for topping

### Directions
- Preparing the Ingredients. Rub the vegetable oil onto the corn, coating it thoroughly.
- Set the temperature to 400°F. Set the timer and grill for 5 minutes.
- Using tongs, flip or rotate the corn.
- Reset the timer and grill for 5 minutes more.
- Serve with a pat of butter and a generous sprinkle of salt and pepper.

Cal 265 | Fat 17g | Carb 29g | Sugar 5g | Protein 5g

## SWEET POTATO & ONION MIX

*Prep time: 10 min | Cook time: 10 min | Serves: 4*

### Ingredients
- 2 sweet potatoes, peeled
- 1 red onion, peeled
- 1 white onion, peeled
- 1 teaspoon olive oil
- ¼ cup almond milk

### Directions
- Chop the sweet potatoes and the onions into cubes.
- Sprinkle the sweet potatoes with olive oil.
- Place the sweet potatoes in the air fryer basket and cook for 5 minutes at 400° F.
- Then stir the sweet potatoes and add the chopped onions.
- Pour in the almond milk and stir gently.
- Cook the mix for 5 minutes more at 400° F.
- When the mix is cooked, let it cool a little and serve.

Cal 56 | Fat 4.8g | Fiber 0.9g | Carbs 3.5g | Protein 0.6g

## CHILI BROCCOLI

*Prep time: 5 min | Cook time: 15 min | Serves: 4*

### Ingredients
- 1-pound broccoli florets
- 2 tablespoons olive oil
- 2 tablespoons chili sauce
- Juice of 1 lime
- A pinch of salt and black pepper

### Directions
- Combine all of the ingredients in a bowl, and toss well.
- Put the broccoli in your air fryer's basket and cook at 400°F for 15 minutes.
- Divide between plates and serve.

Cal 173 | Fat 6g | Fiber 2g | Carb 6g | Protein 8g

## AIR FRIED ROASTED CABBAGE

*Prep time: 5 min | Cook time: 10 min | Serves: 4*

### Ingredients
- 1 head cabbage, sliced in 1-inch-thick ribbons
- 1 tablespoon olive oil
- salt and freshly ground black pepper
- 1 teaspoon garlic powder
- 1 teaspoon red pepper flakes

### Directions
- Preparing the Ingredients. In a bowl, combine the olive oil, cabbage, salt, pepper, garlic powder, and red pepper flakes. Make sure that the cabbage is thoroughly coated with oil. Place the cabbage in the air fryer basket.
- Set the temperature of your Air Fryer to 350°F. Set the timer and roast for 4 minutes.
- Using tongs, flip the cabbage. Reset the timer and roast for 3 minutes more.

Cal 100 | Fat 1g | Carb 3g| Protein 3g

## CARAMELIZED BROCCOLI

*Prep time: 5 minutes | Cook time: 10 min | Serves: 4*

### Ingredients
- 4 cups broccoli florets
- 3 tablespoons melted ghee or butter-flavored coconut oil
- 1½ teaspoons fine sea salt or smoked salt
- Mayonnaise, for serving (optional; omit for egg-free)

### Directions
- Preparing the Ingredients. Grease the basket with avocado oil. Preheat the air fryer to 400°F. Place the broccoli in a large bowl. Drizzle it with the ghee, toss to coat, and sprinkle it with the salt.
- Air Frying. Transfer the broccoli to your air fryer oven basket and cook for 8 minutes, or until tender and crisp on the edges.

Cal 120 | Fat 2g | Carb 4g | Protein 3g

## CHARRED GREEN BEANS WITH SEEDS

*Prep time: 5 min | Cook time: 8 min | Serves: 4*

### Ingredients
- 1 tablespoon reduced-sodium soy sauce or tamari
- ½ tablespoon Sriracha sauce
- 4 teaspoons toasted sesame oil, divided
- 12 ounces (340 g) trimmed green beans
- ½ tablespoon toasted sesame seeds

### Directions

- Whisk together the soy sauce, Sriracha sauce, and 1 teaspoon of sesame oil in a small bowl until smooth. Set aside.
- Toss the green beans with the remaining sesame oil in a large bowl until evenly coated.
- Place the green beans in the air fryer basket in a single layer.
- Put the air fryer basket, set temperature to 375°F and set time to 8 minutes.
- Stir the green beans halfway through the cooking time.
- When cooking is complete, the green beans should be lightly charred and tender. Remove from the oven to a platter. Pour the prepared sauce over the top of green beans and toss well. Serve sprinkled with the toasted sesame seeds.

Cal 191 | Fat 6g | Carb 31.4g | Protein 3.7g

## AIR FRIED HONEY ROASTED CARROTS

*Prep time: 5 min | Cook time: 15 min | Serves: 4*

### Ingredients
- 3 cups baby carrots
- 1 tablespoon extra-virgin olive oil
- 1 tablespoon honey
- Salt
- Freshly ground black pepper
- Fresh dill (optional)

### Directions
- Preparing the Ingredients. In a bowl, combine honey, olive oil, carrots, salt, and pepper. Make sure that the carrots are thoroughly coated with oil. Place the carrots in the air fryer basket.
- Set the temperature to 390°F. Set the timer and roast for 12 minutes, or until fork-tender.
- Remove the air fryer drawer and release the air fryer basket. Pour the carrots into a bowl, sprinkle with dill, if desired, and serve.

Cal 140 | Fat 3g | Carb 7g | Protein 9g

## BRUSSELS SPROUTS WITH BALSAMIC OIL

*Prep time: 5 min | Cook time: 15 min | Serves: 4*

### Ingredients
- ¼ teaspoon salt
- 1 tablespoon balsamic vinegar
- 2 cups Brussels sprouts, halved
- 3 tablespoons olive oil

### Directions
- Preparing the Ingredients. Preheat the air fryer for 5 minutes. Mix all ingredients in a bowl until the Brussels sprouts are well coated.
- Air Frying. Place in the air fryer basket. Close and cook for 15 minutes for 350°F.

Cal 82 | Fat 6.8g | Protein 1.5g

## SHREDDED CABBAGE

*Prep time: 10 min | Cook time: 15 min | Serves: 4*

### Ingredients
- 15 ounces cabbage
- ¼ teaspoon salt
- ¼ cup chicken stock
- ½ teaspoon paprika

### Directions
- Shred the cabbage and sprinkle it with the salt and paprika.
- Stir the cabbage and let it sit for 10 minutes.
- Then transfer the cabbage to your air fryer oven basket and add the chicken stock.
- Cook the cabbage for 5 minutes at 250° F, stirring halfway through.
- When the cabbage is soft, it is done.
- Serve immediately, while still hot

Cal 132 | Fat 2.1g | Carbs 32.1g | Protein: 1.78g

## ZUCCHINI CURRY

*Prep time: 5 Min | Cook time: 8-10 Min | Serves: 2*

### Ingredients
- 2 Zucchinis, Washed & Sliced
- 1 Tablespoon Olive Oil
- Pinch Sea Salt
- Curry Mix, Pre-Made

### Directions
- Turn on your air fryer to 390°F.
- Combine your zucchini slices, salt, oil, and spices.
- Put the zucchini into your air fryer oven, cooking for eight to ten minutes.
- You can serve alone or with sour cream.

Cal 100 | Fat 1g | Carb 4g | Protein 2g

# DESSERT RECIPES

## CHOCOLATE CHIP OATMEAL COOKIES

*Prep time:20 min | Cook time:10 min | Serves: 24*

**Ingredients**

- Butter: 1 cup, softened
- Sugar: 3/4 cup
- Instant vanilla pudding mix: 1 pack, 3.4 oz.
- All-purpose flour: 1-1/2 cups
- 2 eggs
- Vanilla extract: 1 tsp.
- Packed brown sugar: 3/4 cup
- Quick-cooking oats: 3 cups
- Semisweet chocolate chips: 2 cups
- Baking soda: 1 tsp.
- Salt: 1 tsp.
- Chopped nuts: 1 cup

**Instructions**

- Let the Kalorik Air Fryer Oven preheat to 325 F.
- In a bowl, cream the sugars and butter for 5 to 7 minutes.
- Add vanilla and eggs.
- In a different bowl, add flour, baking soda, oats, pudding mix, salt. Mix and add into the creamed mix.
- Add nuts and chocolate chips.
- Place spoon full of dough on the air fryer tray bake for 8 to 10 minutes.
- Serve warm.

1 cookie: Cal 102 | Fat 5g | Carb 13g | Protein 2g

## CRESTLESS CHEESECAKE

*Prep time:10 min | Cook time:10 min | Serves: 2*

**Ingredients**

- Vanilla extract: 1 tsp.
- Sweetener: 3/4 cup
- Sour cream: 2 tbsp.
- Cream cheese: 16 oz. Softened
- 2 eggs
- Lemon juice: half tsp.

**Instructions**

- Let the Kalorik Air Fryer Oven preheat to 350 F.
- Add all the ingredients in the blender, pulse until smooth.
- Pour into two spring forms (4-inch), air fry for 8 to 10 minutes.
- serve chilled

## SPICED APPLES

*Prep time:5 min | Cook time:10 min | Serves: 4*

**Ingredients**

- Sugar: 2 tbsp.
- 4 small apples, thinly sliced
- Apple pie spice: 1 tsp.
- Coconut oil: 2 tbsp., melted

**Instructions**

- In a bowl, add apples.
- Add coconut oil, pie spice and sugar. Toss to coat.
- Let the Kalorik Air Fryer Oven preheat to 350 F.
- Air fry the apples for ten minutes. Serve warm with ice cream.

## CARAMEL APPLE

*Prep time:10 min | Cook time:8 min | Serves: 2*

**Ingredients**

- caramel sauce: 4 tsp.
- 8 graham cracker
- 4 marshmallows
- 1 green apple, thinly sliced

**Instructions**

- On each graham cracker, add 3 to 4 apple slices.
- Add caramel sauce. Put marshmallow on top
- Air fry at 350 F for 4-8 minutes and serve.

## CHOCOLATE Covered STRAWBERRY S'MORES

*Prep time:5 min | Cook time:10 min | Serves: 4*

**Ingredients**

- 8 chocolate graham crackers
- 4 marshmallows
- 8 slices of strawberries
- Nutella: 4 tbsp.

**Instructions**

- On each graham crackers add 2 slices of strawberries.
- Add Nutella and place marshmallow on top.
- Air fry for 4 to 7 minutes at 350 F.
- Serve right away.

## CHEESECAKE EGG ROLLS

*Prep time:20 min | Cook time:10 min | Serves: 15*

**Ingredients**

- egg roll wrappers: 15
- Sugar: 1/4 cup
- cream cheese: 2 packs, 16 oz., softened
- unsalted butter: 2 tbsp. melted
- fig jam: 8/5 oz.
- lemon juice: 1 tbsp.
- vanilla extract: 1 tsp.
- 1 egg + 1 tbsp. water
- ground cinnamon: 1 tsp.

**Instructions**

- In a bowl, cream the cream cheese, vanilla extract, lemon juice, and sugar. Whip on medium speed for two minutes. Add into a pastry bag and cut the tip.
- Place the egg roll and add the cream cheese mixture (2 tbsp.), add jam (1 tbsp.), fold and seal the edges with egg wash.
- Oil spray the egg rolls
- Let the Kalorik Air Fryer Oven preheat to 370 F.
- Air fry the egg roll for 5 to 7 minutes, serve warm.

## BANANA S'MORES

*Prep time:10 min | Cook time:6 min | Serves: 4*

### Ingredients

- Mini chocolate chips:  3 tbsp.
- Graham cracker cereal: 3 tbsp.
- 4 bananas
- peanut butter chips, mini: 3 tbsp.
- Marshmallow mini: 3 tbsp.

### Instructions

- Let the Kalorik Air Fryer Oven preheat to 400 F.
- Do not peel the bananas, slice inside the curve lengthwise, do not slice all the way through.
- Open the banana to make a pocket.
- In each egg, add the marshmallows, all chips and cereal.
- Place the bananas on the air fryer tray.
- Air fry for six minutes, until marshmallows have melted.
- Serve warm.

## SUGARED DOUGH DIPPERS

*Prep time:25 min | Cook time:16 min | Serves: 12*

### Ingredients

- Bread dough: 1 pound
- Heavy cream: 1 cup
- Butter melted: half cup
- Almond extract: 2 tbsp.
- Sugar: 1 cup
- Semi-sweet chocolate chips: 12 oz.

### Instructions

- Make the dough into 2 fifteen inch logs. Slice each log into 20 pieces.
- Slice every piece in half and twist the halves 3-4 times.
- Place the twists on the air fryer tray and brush with butter. Add sugar on top.
- Let the Kalorik Air Fryer Oven preheat to 350 F.
- Air fry for 5 minutes. Flip, brush with butter and air fry for 3 minutes more.
- In a pan, add heavy cream on the medium flame.
- In a bowl, add chocolate chips and add the cream.
- Mix and melt add the almond.
- Serve the sauce with bread twists.

## RASPBERRY ALMOND FRUIT SQUARES

*Prep time:20 min | Cook time:30 min | Serves: 8*

### Ingredients

- Almond paste: 2 oz.
- All-purpose flour: 1 cup
- Unsalted butter: ¼ cup, softened
- 1 egg
- Baking powder: ¼ tsp.
- Baking soda: ¼ tsp.
- Raspberries: 2 cups
- Sugar: 1/3 cup
- Raspberry jam: 1/3 cup
- Salt: 1/8 tsp.

### Topping layer:

- Oatmeal: 1/3 cup
- Butter: 3 tbsp., melted
- Brown sugar: 1/3 cup
- All-purpose flour: 1/3 cup
- Sliced almonds: 1/3 cup

### Instructions

- Let the Kalorik Air Fryer Oven preheat to 350 F on bake.
- Place parchment paper in the 7" cake pan.
- In a food processor, add butter and almond paste pulse to combine.
- Add egg, sugar, pulse until smooth.
- Add the rest of the ingredients until dough forms.
- Press this mixture in the lined cake pan.
- Bake for ten minutes.
- Whisk the jam, add raspberries.
- Pour this mixture over the crust.
- In a bowl, add all the ingredients of toppings. Sprinkle all over the jam.
- Cover the pan with aluminum foil and bake for ten minutes.
- Take the foil off and air fry for ten more minutes.
- Serve warm.

## PISTACHIO PAVLOVA WITH STRAWBERRIES

*Prep time:15 min | Cook time:30 min | Serves: 4*

### Ingredients

- 2 egg whites
- Heavy cream: half cup
- Cornstarch: 1 ½ tsp.
- Salted & shelled roasted pistachios: ¼ cup
- Vanilla extract: half tsp.
- Sugar: half cup
- Sliced strawberries: 1 cup
- White vinegar: half tsp.

### Instructions

- Chop the pistachios in a chopper until fine crumbs forms.
- Whisk the egg with a stand mixer until fluffy. Add sugar (1 tbsp.) at a time until stiff.
- Strain the fine crumbs of pistachios in the egg whites.
- Add vanilla, vinegar and corn-starch and fold.
- Let the Kalorik Air Fryer Oven preheat to 250 F.
- Pour half the mixture into a parchment-lined baking pan.
- Air fry for half an hour. Let it cool in the air fryer for 30 minutes more.
- Repeat with the rest of the mixture.
- Whisk the heavy cream to soft peaks.
- Add the cream in between two pavlova circles, add strawberries and pistachios.
- Serve right away.

## PEACH & BLUEBERRY COBBLER

*Prep time:10 min | Cook time:60 min | Serves: 4*

### Ingredients

- Sugar: 1/3 cup
- Peeled peaches sliced: 3 cups
- Cornstarch: 3 tbsp.
- Half lemon's juice
- Salt, a pinch
- Blueberries:  2 cups

### Topping

- Butter cold: 3 tbsp.

- Baking powder: 1 tsp.
- Turbinado sugar
- Salt: ¼ tsp.
- All-purpose flour: ¾ cup
- Sugar: 4 tbsp.
- Buttermilk: 2/3 cup

**Instructions**

- In a bowl, add corn-starch, salt and sugar. Mix and add peaches, lemon juice, and blueberries toss to coat.
- Place this mixture to a baking dish.
- In a bowl, add the baking powder, sugar, flour and salt, grate the cold butter and mix.
- Add buttermilk and make dough (wet).
- Let the Kalorik Air Fryer Oven preheat to 380 F.
- Pour the dough over fruits do not cover the whole fruits, leave some space in between.
- Add turbinado sugar on top.
- Place aluminium foil on top and air fry for 65 minutes.
- Remove the foil, change the temperature to 330 F, air fry for 15 minutes.
- Rest for ten minutes and serve.

## PEANUT BUTTER DOUGHNUT HOLES

*Prep time: 3 hours | Cook time:5 min | Serves: 12*

**Ingredients**

- Active dry yeast: 1 tsp.
- Salt: ¼ tsp.
- Warm milk: half cup
- 24 mini peanut butter cups
- Sugar: 1 tbsp.
- Vanilla extract: half tsp.
- Bread flour: 1½ cups
- 2 egg yolks
- Melted butter: 2 tbsp.

**Instructions**

- In a bowl, add sugar, yeast and flour.
- Add butter, milk, egg yolks, and vanilla. Mix until dough forms. Knead with hands for 2 minutes.
- Place this dough in an oiled bowl and cover with a towel. Place in a warm place for 60-90 minutes.
- Make 24" log from the dough. Slice into 24 pieces.
- Add 1 piece of peanut butter cup in each dough piece and make it into a ball.
- Keep them in a warm place for half an hour.
- Let the Kalorik Air Fryer Oven preheat to 400 F.
- Oil spray the dough balls and air fry for four minutes, flip halfway through.
- Serve right away.

Cal 141 | Fat 7g | Carb 17g | Protein 3g

## CHERRY PIES

*Prep time:5 min | Cook time:10 min | Serves: 6*

**Inredients**

- Cherry pie filling: half cup
- Package pie crusts: 14 oz.

**Instructions**

- Let the Kalorik Air Fryer Oven preheat to 350 F.
- Roll the pie crust and cut it into six pies.

- In each piece of dough, add 1 ½ tbsp. of cherry pie filling.
- Fold the dough in half. Seal the edges. Make three cuts on top.
- Oil spray the pies and air fry for ten minutes.
- Serve warm.

## CHURROS WITH MEXICAN CHOCOLATE SAUCE

*Prep time:10 min | Cook time:10 min | Serves: 6*

**Ingredients**

**Churros**

- Cinnamon: 1 tbsp.
- 1 can of (8 oz.) Crescent rolls
- Melted butter: 2 tbsp.
- Sugar: 2 tbsp.

**Chocolate sauce**

- Heavy cream: 1/4 cup
- Cinnamon: 1 tsp.
- Dark chocolate chips: half cup
- Cayenne pepper: 1/8 tsp.

**Instructions**

- Let the Kalorik Air Fryer Oven preheat to 330 F.
- In a bowl, add cinnamon and sugar and mix.
- Slice the dough into four rectangles.
- Brush each piece of dough with melted butter.
- On each piece of dough, sprinkle sugar mix.
- Cut each rectangle into four strips.
- Twist the dough pieces and place on the air fryer tray.
- Air fry for 5-6 minutes, until crispy and brown.
- In a pan, add cream on medium flame. Turn off the heat
- Add the rest of the ingredients and mix.
- Serve with chorus.

## APPLE PIE EGG ROLLS

*Prep time:25 min | Cook time:15 min | Serves: 8*

**Ingredients**

- Chopped tart apples, peeled: 3 cups
- Ground cinnamon: 2 1/2 tsp.
- Corn-starch: 1 tsp.
- Caramel ice cream: 2/3 cup
- 8 egg roll wrappers
- Packed brown sugar: half cup
- Cream cheese: half cup, softened
- Sugar: 1 tbsp.

**Instructions**

- Let the Kalorik Air Fryer Oven preheat to 400 F.
- In a bowl, add corn-starch, apples, cinnamon (2 tsp.) and brown sugar. Toss well.
- Spread egg roll wrappers, add cream cheese and apple mixture. Roll and seal the edges with water. Oil spray the rolls.
- Air fry the rolls for 5 to 6 minutes on each side.
- Serve with ice cream.

1 roll: Cal 273 | Fat 4g | Carb 56g | Protein 5g

## PUFF PASTRY DANISHES

*Prep time:25 min | Cook time:10 min | Serves: 12*

**Ingredients**

- Sugar: ¼ cup
- Raspberry jam: 2/3 cup
- All-purpose flour: 2 tbsp.

- 1 pack of puff pastry
- Cream cheese: 8 oz., softened
- Vanilla extract: half tsp.
- 2 egg yolks
- Water: 1 tbsp.

**Instructions**

- Let the Kalorik Air Fryer Oven preheat to 325 F.
- With a stand mixer, whisk the vanilla, cream cheese, flour, sugar and one egg yolk.
- In a bowl, whisk the egg yolk with water.
- Unroll the puff pastry, and cut into 9 squares.
- In each square add cream cheese mixture with jam.
- Seal the edges with egg yolk, and brush the top with egg yolk mixture.
- Air fry for 8 to 10 minutes.
- Serve warm.

1 pastry: Cal 197 | Fat 12g | Carb 20g | Protein 3g

## MINI LEMON TARTLETS

*Prep time:30 min | Cook time:20 min | Serves :12*

**Ingredients**

- 1 box of lemon dessert mix
- Raspberries
- 12 mini tart shells

**Instructions**

- Preheat the Air Fryer to 350°F on the BAKE level.
- Make the dessert mix according to the product directions.
- On a shelf, place the mini tart shells.
- Bake for 1-2 minutes the empty mini tart shells. Don't overcook the food.
- Take the mini tart shells out of the air fryer and fill them with your dessert filling.
- Bake for 5 minutes filled mini-tarts. If you haven't finished yet, add a few minutes.
- Take out of the air fryer and set aside to cool.
- Serve with your favourite fruit (we used raspberries) and a dusting of icing sugar.

Cal 229 | Protein 2.9g | Carb 28.6g | Fat 11.9g

## BRAZILIAN GRILLED PINEAPPLE

*Prep time:5 min | Cook time:10 min | Serves: 4*

**Ingredients**

- 2 teaspoon of ground cinnamon
- 1 peeled & cored pineapple (cut into spears)
- 3 tablespoons of Melted butter
- 1/2 cup (110 g) brown sugar

**Instructions**

- In the bowl, combine cinnamon & brown sugar.
- Coat the pineapple spears with softened butter. Drizzle cinnamon sugar on the spears, gently pressing to make sure it adheres well.
- Put your spears into an air fryer in a single layer. Set the air fryer temp to 400 F and set the timer for ten minutes for the first. Midway through, brush with any leftover butter.
- Now the pineapples are done; once they are heated thru & the sugar starts bubbling.

Cal 255 | Protein 1.3g | Carb 66.4g | Fat 0.3g

## FRUIT HAND PIES

*Prep time:8 min | Cook time:35 min | Serves: 2*

**Ingredients**
**For crust**

- 1.5 cups All-purpose
- 1/4 cup Shortening
- 62.5 g Coldwater
- 1/4 cup Butter
- 1/2 teaspoon Kosher salt

**For the fruit filling**

- 1 teaspoon Coarse sugar
- 1 large Egg
- 1 tablespoon of Water

**Instructions**

- Air fryer preheated to 320 F.
- On the piece of eight 1/2 x 11-inch paper, trace about a six-inch round cooking pan. Cut the circle out. Set aside.
- In the medium bowl, whisk together the salt & flour. By using the pastry blender, cut in a shortening & butter. Drizzle 1 tablespoon of cold water on the part of a mixture of flour. Toss with the fork. Transfer the moistened pastry to a side of a bowl. Repeat with leftover flour, 1 tablespoon water till everything becomes moist. Fold the flour combination into the ball & knead nicely.
- Slightly flatten the pastry, then roll it from the middle to an edge into the thirteen-inch circle on the lightly floured surface. Put a pattern over a pastry near one edge. Use a subtle knife & cut out a six-inch circle of the pastry. Repeat this step to make two circles. Discard the scraps of dough.
- Put half of a fruit filling on the half of a pastry circle, leave the ¼-inch border. With water, brush a bare edge. Fold an empty pastry half on the filling. Use the fork & press around the pastry edge to cover it. Poke a top in some places with the fork. Repeat this with leftover filling & pastry.
- In the bowl, mix the egg & water. Brush on the tops & drizzle the pies with coarse sugar.
- Put the pies in an air fryer & cook for thirty-five minutes, or the pies colour changes to a golden brown.
- Before serving, cool pies on the wire rack for twenty minutes.

Cal 554 | Fat 29g; | Carb 68g | Protein 7g

## MINI-NUTELLA DOUGHNUT HOLES

*Prep time:8 min | Cook time:8 -10 min | Serves: 3*

**Ingredients**

- Big refrigerated flaky biscuits one tube
- 2/3 cup Nutella
- 1 tablespoon Water
- 1 large Egg
- Sugar
- Oil

**Instructions**

- Air fryer preheated to 300 F. Beat egg with water. Roll every biscuit into the six-in. Circle on the lightly floured surface; cut every into four wedges. Brush gently with the mixture of an egg; top every wedge with one teaspoon of Nutella. Carry up the corners over the filling, pinch edges tightly to seal.
- Arrange biscuits in a single layer on the tray in an air-fryer in the batches. Cook till its colour changes to a golden brown, 8 to 10

minutes, flipping once. Brush with confectioners' sugar; serve hot.

Cal 94 |Fat 6g| Carb 4g | Protein 1g

## Strawberry Upside-Down Cake

*Prep time:5 min | Cook time:45 min | Serves:* **4**

### Ingredients

- 1 teaspoon of baking soda
- 2 cups strawberries, diced
- 1 tablespoon granulated sugar plus 1/3 cup granulated sugar divided
- 1 cup all-purpose flour plus 1 tablespoon all-purpose flour, divided
- 2 tablespoon melted unsalted butter
- 1 pound of ricotta
- 2 teaspoons of baking powder
- 1 1/2 quarts a body of water
- 1 teaspoon extract vanilla
- An egg
- 1/8 teaspoon of salt

### Instructions

- Oil and flour a 6-inch cake pan. In the bottom, place a circle of parchment paper.
- Toss strawberries with 1 tablespoon flour and 1 tablespoon sugar in a medium mixing dish. Place strawberries in an even layer
- In a medium mixing cup, whisk together the egg. In a separate bowl, whisk together the butter, 1/3 cup sugar, and vanilla extract until smooth. Except for the water, combine the remaining ingredients, including the remaining flour. Pour the batter over the strawberry layer
- Place the cake pan on top of the steam rack in an air fryer. Close the cover.
- Change the time to 35 minutes by pressing the Manual or Pressure Cook button. Quickly release pressure before the float valve decreases when the timer beeps. The lid should be unlocked.
- Remove the cake pan from the pot and set it aside to cool for 30 minutes. Place the cake on a serving platter and flip it over. Remove the parchment paper from the pan. Cut into slices and serve.

Cal 404 |Fat 14g| Carb 51g| Protien:13g

## Cheesecake Chimichanga

*Prep time:5 min | Cook time:6 min | Serves:5*

### Ingredients

- 1 *teaspoon* vanilla extract
- 1 (8 ounces) brick of cream cheese
- 1/4 cup sour cream
- 8 medium strawberries
- 8 soft flour tortillas
- 8 teaspoons Nutella
- cinnamon sugar
- 1 medium banana, peeled and sliced
- olive oil spray
- 2 tablespoons melted butter

### Instructions

- Cream together the softened cream cheese, sour cream, sugar, and vanilla in a medium mixing bowl until smooth.

- Throw quartered strawberries in one medium bowl and sliced bananas in the other with the cream cheese mixture. To merge, gently stir (or omit completely).
- On a clean work surface, place a soft flour tortilla. 1/4 of the strawberry mixture should be placed on the tortilla just to the left of the centre. After that, stir in a teaspoon of Nutella.
- Fold the tortilla's left side over the filling. Roll like a burrito by folding the short ends in.
- Proceed with the remaining strawberry mixture, and afterward, do the banana mixture in the same manner.
- Preheat your air fryer to 360° and spray oil.
- Function in batches, putting the chimichangas seam-side down in an even layer and air frying for 8 to 10 minutes, or until the tortilla is a rich golden brown, depending on the size of your air fryer. My air fryer can accommodate 4 at a time.
- Move the chimichangas to a wire rack placed over a rimmed baking sheet once they've been fried. Brush both sides, including nooks and crannies, with butter before rolling in cinnamon sugar. Repetition is essential.
- Get ready to fall head over heels in love.

Cal 308 | Fat 14g | Carb 39g | Protein 7g

## Carrot Coffee Cake

*Prep time:15 min | Cook time:35 min | Serves: 6*

### Ingredients

- Lightly beaten egg one large
- 1/2 cup Buttermilk
- 1/3 cup + 3 tablespoons Canola oil
- 1 teaspoon grated orange zest
- 1 teaspoon Vanilla extract
- 1/3 cup Wheat flour (white whole)
- 2/3 cup All-purpose flour
- 2 teaspoon Pumpkin pie spice
- 1/4 teaspoon Baking soda
- 1/4 teaspoon Salt
- 1 cup Shredded carrots
- 1/4 cup Dried cranberries
- 1/3 cup of Toasted chopped walnuts
- 1 teaspoon Baking powder

### Instructions

- Air fryer preheated to 350 F; oil & flour the 6-in. Round cooking pan. In the bowl, stir egg, 1/3 cup sugar, buttermilk, oil, orange zest, vanilla & brown sugar. In the other bowl, stir flours, 1 teaspoon of pumpkin pie spice, baking soda, baking powder, & salt. Slowly beat into egg combination. Fold in the carrots & dried cranberries. Place into the prepared pan.
- In the bowl, mix walnuts, the remaining one teaspoon of pumpkin spice & the remaining two tablespoons of sugar. Drizzle equally on the batter. Nicely put the pan in the big air fryer.

- Cook till the toothpick inserted in the middle comes out clean, 35 to 40 minutes. If the top gets too dark, then seal firmly with foil; before removing it from the pan, cool it in the pan over the wire rack for ten minutes. Serve warm.

Cal 316 | Fats 13g | Carb 46g | Protein 6g

## PIZOOKIE

*Prep time:5 min | Cook time:10 min | Serves:3*

### Ingredients
- teaspoon vanilla
- 1/2 cup butter, softened
- 1/2 cup sugar
- 1/2 cup brown sugar1/2 cup mini chocolate chips
- 1/2 cup Mini-M&Ms
- 1 1/2 cups flour
- 1 egg
- 1/2 teaspoon baking soda
- 1/2 teaspoon salt

### Instructions
- 1. Preheat the air fryer to 350 F
- 2. Cream together the butter and sugars.
- 3. Mix in the egg and vanilla extract. Blend until fully smooth
- 4. Combine the baking soda, salt, and flour in a mixing bowl.
- 5. Stir in the mini chocolate chips and M&Ms
- Fry in the air fryer, bake for 8-10 minutes.

Cal 312 | Carb 110g | Protein 10g | Fat 36g

## FRENCH TOAST CUPS

*Prep time:1 hour | Cook time:20 min | Serves: 2*

### Ingredients
- 1/2 cup Fresh/frozen raspberries
- Two slices of Italian bread (Cut into 1/2-inch cubes)
- 2 large Eggs
- 1/2 cup Milk
- 1 tablespoon Maple syrup
- 2 ounces Cream cheese

### Raspberry syrup
- 2 teaspoons Corn-starch
- Water 1/3 cup
- 2 cups Fresh/frozen raspberries
- 1 tablespoon Lemon juice
- 1 tablespoon Maple syrup
- 1/2 teaspoon Grated lemon zest

### Instructions
- Split half bread cubes b/w two oiled custard cups (8-oz). Sprinkle with cream cheese & raspberries. Top with the leftover bread. In the bowl, stir milk, syrup & eggs, place over bread. Cover & refrigerate for one hour.
- Air fryer preheated to 325 F. Put custard cups on the tray in an air-fryer. Cook till its color changes to golden brown & puffed, 12 to15 minutes.
- Therefore, in the saucepan, mix water & corn-starch till smooth. Put 1.5 cup raspberries, syrup, lemon zest & lemon juice carries to a simmer; lower the heat. Cook & whisk till thickened, around two minutes. Strain & discard seeds; chill them slightly.
- Nicely whisk leftover 1/2 cup berries into the syrup. If required, drizzle cinnamon on French toast cups; serve with the syrup.

Cal 406 | Fat 18g | Carbs 50g | Protein 14g

## HOMEMADE CANNOLI

*Prep time:45 min | Cook time:2hrs 50min | Serves: 20*

### Ingredients
### For the filling:
- 1/2 c Powdered sugar
- 1 Container ricotta
- 3/4 c Heavy cream
- 1 teaspoon Pure vanilla extract
- 1 teaspoon Orange zest
- 1/4 teaspoon Kosher salt
- 1/2 c Mini chocolate chips
- 1/2 c Mascarpone cheese

### For the shells:
- Kosher salt 1 teaspoon
- 2 c All-purpose flour
- 1/2 teaspoon Cinnamon
- 4 tablespoons Cold butter
- 6 tablespoons White wine
- 1 large Egg
- Vegetable oil to fry
- 1/4 c Granulated sugar

### Instruction
- In batches, put moulds in the air fryer & cook at 350 F for twelve minutes.
- Once it's cool enough to handle or use the towel to hold, remove the twist shells off the moulds nicely.
- Put filling in the pastry bag. Pipe the filling into the shells. After this dip ends in the mini chips of chocolate.

Cal 219.7 | Fat 7.8 g | Carb 30.3 g | Protein 6.9 g

## CARAMELIZED BANANAS

*Prep time:5 min | Cook time:6 min | Serves: 1*

### Ingredients
- 1 tablespoon Coconut sugar
- 1/4 Juiced lemon
- 2 Bananas

### Instructions:
- With the peel on, wash the bananas, after which slice them from the middle, lengthwise.
- Drizzle juice of the lemon on the top of every banana
- If using the cinnamon, then mix within the coconut sugar, & sprinkle on top of each banana till coated
- Put into the air fryer (parchment lined) for 6 to 8 minutes on 400F.
- Remove from the air fryer, & now serve it.

Cal 107 | Protein 1.3g | Carb 27g | Fat 0.7g

## SUPER-EASY CINNAMON ROLLS

*Prep time:10 min | Cook time:7 min | Serves: 8*

### Ingredients
### Cinnamon rolls:
- One-sheet Thawed puff pastry
- 1 tablespoon Ground cinnamon
- 6 tablespoon Brown sugar
- ¾ stick. Softened unsalted butter

### Icing:
- 2 teaspoons Fresh lemon juice
- ½ cup Powdered sugar

- 1 tablespoon Milk

**Instructions**

- In the bowl, mix softened butter, sugar & cinnamon. Combine well.
- Air fryer preheated to 400 F for four minutes.
- Nicely roll out the pastry & spread the cinnamon mixture around the whole sheet – in the thin layer.
- Roll it nicely & loosely.
- With the serrated knife/flavor-free dental floss, cut your pastry into around one-inch pieces.
- Move them to the heated air fryer & cook at 400 F for seven minutes or till the rolls are puffed & golden brown.
- Once ready, remove them from the air fryer, cool slightly, then top them with the icing made by mixing powdered sugar, lemon juice & milk.
- Serve warm

Cal 310 | Protein 3.9g | Carb 44.2g | Fat 13.6g

## PEPPERMINT LAVA CAKE

*Prep time:5 min | Cook time:25 min | Serves: 4*

### Ingredients

- 1 cup Confectioners' sugar
- 2/3 cup Semisweet chocolate chips
- 2 large Eggs
- 1 teaspoon Peppermint extract
- 6 tablespoon All-purpose flour
- Butter 1/2 cup

### Instructions

- Preheated air fryer to 375 F. In the microwave-safe bowl, melt butter & chocolate chips for about 30 seconds, whisk till smooth. Stir in the confectioners' sugar, egg yolks, eggs & extract till well blended. Fold in the flour.
- Gently oil & flour four ramekins put the batter into the ramekins. Don't overfill. On the tray in an air-fryer, put ramekins; cook till the thermometer reaches 160 F & edges of cakes are set, 10 to 12 minutes.
- Take it from the; let it sit for five minutes. Safely run the knife around the sides of ramekins sometimes to loosen the cake, invert onto the dessert plates. Drizzle with the crushed candies. Now serve immediately.

Cal 563 | Fat 36g | Carbs 57g | Protein 7g

## CUPCAKES

*Prep time:20 min | Cook time:12 min | Serves: 3-4*

### Ingredients

- 1 tablespoon Olive Oil
- Self-Raising Flour: 14 oz.
- Caster Sugar: 15.8 oz.
- 4 Eggs
- 1 tablespoon Vanilla Essence
- Butter room temperature: 7 oz.
- Skimmed Milk: 16.9 oz.

### Chocolate Buttercream:

- 1 tablespoon Maple Syrup
- Butter: 8 oz.
- Cocoa Powder: 1.5 oz.
- 3 tablespoon Single Cream
- Icing Sugar: 14.8 oz.
- 2 teaspoon Vanilla Essence

**Instructions**

- Combine the butter and sugar in a mixing bowl and beat the butter into the sugar with a hand mixer. In a mixing bowl, break eggs, apply vanilla extract, extra virgin olive oil, and whisk again with a hand mixer. Mix in the cocoa powder, flour, and milk with a wooden spoon until it's creamy. Use a stand mixer instead of a hand mixer to avoid overmixing. Adjust the consistency with a little more skimmed milk or water if it's too thick.
- Fill muffin cups halfway with batter and bake for 12 minutes at 320°F in the air fryer. Place on a plate and set aside to cool.
- Make your chocolate buttercream as it cools. Mix the icing sugar into the butter with a hand mixer. Mix in the remaining ingredients until you have a creamy buttercream. Refrigerate your cupcakes while they cool.
- Make a fist with your piping bag from the bottom. Then open it up over your hand to form a funnel. Then spoon your mixture into the piping bag with your other hand. But first, make sure you've got the correct nozzle for piping; otherwise, you'll have to start over, which is a hassle. When the piping bag is nearly full, twist it close, gently squeeze to release some air, then squeeze with gentle pressure and swirl it on top.

Cal 1113 | Carb 157g | Protein 14g | Fat 52g

## FRIED OREOS

*Prep time:5 min | Cook time:4 min | Serves: 9*

### Ingredients

- 1 roll Crescent sheets
- 9 Oreo cookies

### Instructions

- Pop crescent & spread it over the table. Line & cut with your knife nine even squares.
- Get nine cookies & cover them in squares.
- Air fryer preheated to 360 F. Put wrapped cookies in one layer & cook for around four minutes, shaking & turning halfway.
- Season with powder sugar/cinnamon if you like & enjoy.

Cal 77 | Protein 1.2g | Carb 13.7g | Fat 2.1g

## STRAWBERRY POP-TARTS

*Prep time:10 min | Cook time:10 min | Serves: 6*

### Ingredients

- 1 teaspoon Sugar sprinkles
- 2 crusts of Freeze pie
- 1/3 cup Strawberry cooking oil
- 1/2 cup Vanilla Greek yogurt
- 1 teaspoon Corn-starch
- 1 oz. Cream cheese
- 1 tablespoon Sweetener

### Instructions

- Lay the pie crust on the flat cutting board.
- Use the knife/pizza cutter to cut the two pie crusts into six rectangles. Each must be quite long as you have to fold it to close a pop tart.
- Add your preserves & corn-starch to the bowl & combine well.
- Put the preserves tablespoon to the crust. Put the preserves in the upper part of a crust.
- Fold your pop tarts.
- Use the fork to make the imprints in each pop tart, to make vertical & horizontal lines with the edges.
- Put the pop tarts in an air fryer. Cook in the batches, if required. Spray with the cooking oil.

- Cook at 370 F for around 10 minutes.
- Mix the cream cheese, sweetener & Greek yogurt in the bowl to make the frosting.
- Let the pop tarts chill before taking them from an air fryer. If you do not allow them to cool, they will break.
- Take the pop tarts from an air fryer. Top every with the frosting. Drizzle sugar sprinkles throughout.

Cal 794 | Carb 114g | Protein 8g | Fat 35g

## DESSERT EMPANADAS

*Prep time:4-5 min | Cook time:10 min | Serves: 12*

### Ingredients
- 12 empanada wrappers
- 2 tablespoon honey
- 1 teaspoon Vanilla extract
- 1 teaspoon Cinnamon
- 1/8 teaspoon Nutmeg
- 2 teaspoon Corn-starch
- 1 teaspoon Water
- 1. Beaten egg
- 2 Apples

### Instructions
- Put the saucepan on med-high heat. Put the cinnamon, apples, nutmeg, vanilla & honey. Whisk & cook for 2 to 3 minutes till the apples are soft.
- Combine the corn-starch & water in the bowl. Put it in the pan & stir. Cook for around 30 seconds.
- Before loading it onto empanada wrappers, allow the filling to cool for five minutes.
- Put the empanada wrappers on the flat surface. In water, dip the cooking brush. Glaze each empanada wrapper with a wet brush.
- Put the mixture of apples to each. Put 1 tablespoon of apple mix per empanada. Flatten out the combination with the help of a spoon.
- 6. Make indents in the crust with a spoon to seal the empanadas around the sides. Along the edge of each crust, press a fork into it
- Put the empanadas in an air fryer.
- Using the cooking brush, brush the top of every empanada with the egg (beaten).
- Put the air fryer at 400 F. Cook it for around 8 to 10 minutes or till crisp.
- Cool it before serving.

Cal 320 | Protein 5.2g | Carb 44.5g | Fat 15.4g

## CHOCOLATE CHIP COOKIES

*Prep time:3-4 min | Cook time:18 min | Serves: 10*

### Ingredients
- 1/2 cup. Chopped walnuts
- 8 tablespoon Softened butter
- 1/3 cup Light brown sugar (packed)
- 1 large Egg
- 1 teaspoon Vanilla extract
- 1/8 1 teaspoon Squeezed lemon juice
- 1 cup Flour
- 1/4 cup Rolled oats
- 1/2 teaspoon Baking soda
- Salt 1/2 1 teaspoon
- 1/4 teaspoon Cinnamon

- 1/2 cups Sweet chocolate chips
- 1/3 cup Granulated sugar

### Instructions
- Put sugar, brown sugar & cream butter in the mixing bowl.
- Put vanilla, lemon juice & egg; use the mixer & blend for thirty seconds. Then blend on med for some minutes or till light & fluffy, scraping the down bowl.
- Put flour, baking soda, oats, salt & cinnamon, blend for around 45 seconds. Don't overmix it.
- Fold it in the chocolate chips & walnuts.
- Line your air fryer with bakery release paper. Scoop your cookie dough into the balls & put them in an air fryer around 1 1/2 to 2 inches apart. Use moist hands & flatten the top of your cookies.
- Now air fry for around 6 to 8 minutes at 300 F.
- Let the cookies cool for five minutes before taking them from the air fryer.
- Move your cookies to the wire rack to cool for a further ten minutes.

Cal 268 | Fat 15g | Carbs 34.0g | Protein 3g

## MOLTEN LAVA CAKE

*Prep time:20 min | Cook time:20 min | Serves: 4*

### Ingredients
- Confectioner's sugar: 3.5 tbsp.
- 2 whole eggs
- Unsalted Butter, unsalted: 3.5 oz.
- Flour: 1.5 tbsp.
- Dark chopped Chocolate: 3.5 oz.

### Instructions
- Let the Kalorik Air Fryer Oven preheat to 375 F.
- Oil spray and lightly sprinkle four ramekins with flour.
- Melt the chocolate and stir.
- Cream the sugar and eggs until frothy.
- Add the melted chocolate to egg mixture. Add flour and mix.
- Pour into ramekins and bake in air fry for ten minutes.
- Cool for five minutes and serve.

## LEMON CAKE

*Prep time:10 min | Cook time:20 min | Serves: 6*

### Ingredients
- 1 teaspoon Vanilla extract
- 1/2 c All-purpose flour
- 1/2 teaspoon Salt
- 1/2 c Unsalted butter
- 1 Sweetener
- 1 tablespoon Lemon zest
- 2 tablespoons Squeezed lemon juice
- 2/3 cup Plain Greek yogurt
- 1 teaspoon Baking powder
- 4 Eggs

### Instructions
- Butter & flour a six-cup Bundt pan.
- Mix the salt, baking powder & flour in a med bowl.
- Put the butter & sweetener in the mixing bowl. And use your mixer to cream the butter. Stir till creamy.
- Put in two eggs & mix with the hand mixer. Put in the leftover eggs, & mix.

- Put the lemon zest, dry flour mix, yogurt, vanilla & lemon juice in a mixing bowl. Blend till the batter is smooth.
- Place the batter into a Bundt pan.
- Cover a Bundt pan with foil. Air fry for around fifteen minutes at 320 deg.
- Open your air fryer & remove the foil. Air fry for a further 15 to 20 minutes.
- Let the cake chill for ten minutes.
- Put the cake stand on the Bundt pan & turn the Bundt pan to release the cake.

Cal 82 | Protein 0.8g | Carb 14.3g | Fat 2.8g

## BROILED GRAPEFRUIT
*Prep time:10 min | Cook time:6 min | Serves: 2*

**Ingredients**
- 1 tablespoon Brown sugar
- ½ teaspoon of Ground cinnamon
- 2 teaspoon of Brown sugar
- 1 tablespoon Softened butter
- 1 red grapefruit, refrigerated

**Instructions:**
- Preheat the air fryer to 400 F
- If the grapefruit isn't sitting flat, cut it in half crosswise and slice a thin sliver off the bottom of each half. To make the grapefruit easier to eat until cooked, cut around the outside edge and between each segment with a sharp paring knife.
- In a small mixing bowl, add softened butter and 1 tablespoon brown sugar. Apply the mixture to each half of a grapefruit. The remaining brown sugar should be sprinkled on top.
- Cut two 5-inch squares of aluminium foil and put each grapefruit half on one; fold up the edges to capture any juices. Place in the air fryer to cook.
- 6–7 minutes in the air fryer before the sugar mixture is bubbling. Until serving, sprinkle the fruit with cinnamon.

Cal 150 | Carb 25.5g | Protein 1.1g | Fat 5.9g

## CHOCOLATE ZUCCHINI BREAD
*Prep time:10 min | Cook time:50 min | Serves:12*

**Ingredients**
- 2 tablespoon vegetable oil
- ½ teaspoon baking soda
- 1/3 teaspoon salt
- 1 egg, room temperature
- 2 tablespoon butter, melted and slightly cooled
- ½ cup all-purpose flour
- ½ teaspoon vanilla extract
- ½ cup semisweet chocolate chips, divided
- 6 tablespoon light brown sugar, packed
- ¼ cup cocoa powder
- ¾ cup shredded zucchini

**Instructions:**
- Set aside a mini baking pan that has been sprayed with cooking spray.
- Whisk together the flour, salt, baking soda, and cocoa powder in a bowl.
- Combine the egg, melted butter, brown sugar, oil, and vanilla in a larger mixing bowl. Whisk until the mixture is almost smooth.

- Mix the dry ingredients into the wet ingredients until all is well mixed. Fold in the zucchini and the rest of the chocolate chips, leaving a few for the tip.
- Sprinkle the remaining chocolate chips on top of the mixture in the prepared mini baking tray. Then bake at 310°F for 30-35 minutes, or until a toothpick inserted in the centre comes out clean.

Cal 212 | Fat 10.40g | Carb 49g

## BROWN SUGAR AND PECAN ROASTED APPLES
*Prep time:10 min | Cook time:10 min | Serves: 2*

**Ingredients**
- 1 tablespoon butter, melted
- 2 tablespoons coarsely chopped pecans
- ¼ teaspoon of apple pie spice
- 2 medium apples, cored & cut into wedges
- 1 teaspoon of all-purpose flour
- 1 tablespoon brown sugar

**Instructions**
- Preheat the air fryer to 360 F
- In a small mixing bowl, add pecans, brown sugar, flour, and apple pie spice. In a medium mixing bowl, toss apple wedges with butter and toss to cover. In the air fryer, arrange the apples in a single layer and top with the pecan mixture.
- Cook for 10 to 15 minutes in a preheated air fryer until apples are tender.

Cal 204 | Carb 27.9g | Protein 1.2g | Fat 11.3g

## PANCAKES
*Prep time:10 min | Cook time:10 min | Serves: 4 to 6*

**Ingredients**
- Baking soda: 1 1/2 tsp.
- Flour: 2 cups
- Baking powder: 1 1/2 tsp.
- Salt, a pinch
- Sugar: 3 1/2 tbsp.
- Buttermilk: cups
- 2 eggs
- Butter: 3 tbsp.

**Instructions**
- In a bowl, whisk butter and milk until fluffy.
- Let the Kalorik Air Fryer Oven preheat to 375 F.
- In a bowl, add the dry ingredients. Mix and add the wet ingredients. Mix until just combined.
- Place the aluminum foil on the air fryer basket, oil spray it.
- Pour the batter and cook for 2-3 minutes on each side.
- Serve with syrup.

## CINNAMON-SUGAR DOUGHNUTS
*Prep time:10 min | Cook time:10 min | Serves: 8*

**Ingredients**
- 1 teaspoon ground cinnamon
- ¼ cup of butter, melted
- ¼ teaspoon ground nutmeg (Optional)
- 1 (16.3 ounces) package of refrigerated flaky biscuit dough
- ¼ cup of brown sugar
- ½ cup of white sugar

**Instructions**

- In a mixing bowl, melt the butter. In a separate cup, add white sugar, brown sugar, cinnamon, and nutmeg.
- 2. To create a doughnut shape, separate the biscuit dough into biscuits shape and use a biscuit cutter to cut out the centres. Placed doughnuts in the air fryer.
- 4 to 6 minutes at 350 F before golden brown. Cook for an additional 1 to 3 minutes after flipping the doughnuts.
- Take the doughnuts out of the air fryer. Dip of doughnut in melted butter (ensuring that the top, bottom, and sides are all covered), then in the sugar-cinnamon mixture until completely coated. Serve right away.

***Note from the Chef:***
*Microwave doughnuts for 8 to 10 seconds to reheat, only long enough to soften them up again.*

Cal 310 | Carb 44.2g | Protein 3.9g | Fat 13.6g

## CHURROS
*Prep time:5 min | Cook time:15 min | Serves: 6*

### Ingredients
- ¼ Cup of butter
- 1 pinch salt
- ¼ cup of white sugar
- ½ cup of milk
- 2 eggs
- ½ teaspoon Ground cinnamon
- ½ cup all-purpose flour

### Instructions
- In a saucepan over medium-high heat, melt the butter. Pour in the milk and season with salt. Reduce heat to medium and bring to a boil, constantly stirring with a wooden spoon. Put the flour all at once. Stir the dough before it comes together.
- Remove from the heat and set aside for 5 to 7 minutes to cool. With a wooden spoon, mix in the eggs before the pastry comes together. Fill a pastry bag with the dough and a large star tip right into the air fryer, pipe dough into strips.
- Air fried churros for 5 minutes at 340 F
- Meanwhile, in a small cup, mix the sugar and cinnamon and pour onto a shallow plate.
- Take the fried churros out of the air fryer and roll them in the cinnamon-sugar mix.

Cal 173 | Carbs 17.5g | Protein 3.9g | Fat 9.8g

## OREOS
*Prep time:5 min | Cook time:5 min | Serves: 9*

### Ingredients
- 1 tablespoon. Confectioners' sugar
- ½ Cup of complete pancake mix cooking spray
- 9 chocolate sandwich cookies
- ⅓ cup of water

### Instructions
- Combine the pancake mix and water in a large mixing bowl.
- Using parchment paper, line an air fryer. Using non-stick cooking spray, cover parchment paper. Place each cookie in the air fryer after dipping it in the pancake batter. Make sure they're not touching and, if possible, cook them in batches.
- Preheat your air fryer to 400 F. Cook for 4 to 5 minutes on the one hand, then flip and cook for another 2 to 3 minutes.

Cal 77 | Carb 13.7g | Protein 1.2g | Fat 2.1g

## APPLE PIES
*Prep time:30 min | Cook time:15 min | Serves: 4*

### Ingredients
- 1 teaspoon of Milk
- 1 teaspoon of Ground cinnamon
- 1 teaspoon of Corn-starch
- 4 tablespoon Butter
- 2 med granny smith apples, diced
- 2 teaspoon Cold water
- ½ (14 ounces) package pastry for a 9-inch double-crust pie cooking spray
- ½ tablespoon of Grapeseed oil
- ¼ cup of powdered sugar
- 6 tablespoon Brown sugar

### Instructions
- In a non-stick skillet, combine the apples, butter, brown sugar, and cinnamon. Cook for 5 minutes over medium heat or until apples has softened.
- Corn-starch should be dissolved in cold water. Cook, stirring continuously, until the sauce thickens, around 1 minute. As you prepare the crust, remove the apple pie filling from the heat and set it aside to cool.
- Unroll the pie crust on a lightly floured surface and gently roll it out to smooth the surface. Cut the dough into rectangles that will fit into your air fryer two at a time. Continue with the remaining crust until you have 8 equal rectangles, re-rolling scraps of dough as required.
- Wet the outer edges of four rectangles with water and fill the middle with apple filling about 1/2-inch from the edges. Roll out the remaining four rectangles slightly larger than the filled rectangles. Place these rectangles on top of the filling and use a fork to seal the edges. Cut four narrow slits in the pies' tops.
- Using a spatula, brush the tops of two pies with grapeseed oil and move to the air fryer.
- Preheat the air fryer to 385 F. Bake for about 8 minutes, or until golden brown. Remove the pies from the air fryer and repeat the process with the remaining two pies.
- In a small cup, combine powdered sugar and milk. Enable too dry after brushing glaze on warm pies. Warm or room temperature pies may be served.

Cal 497 Carb 59.7g | Protein 3.2g | Fat 28.6g

## BEIGNETS
*Prep time:10 min | Cook time:15 min | Serves: 5*

### Ingredients
- 2 tablespoon Confectioners' sugar cooking spray
- 1 pinch salt
- ¼ cup of white sugar
- ⅛ cup of water
- 1 ½ teaspoon Melted butter
- ½ teaspoon Baking powder
- ½ teaspoon Vanilla extract
- ½ cup of all-purpose flour
- 1 large egg, separated

### Instructions
- Preheat the air fryer to 370 F
- In a wide mixing bowl, combine flour, water, egg, butter, baking powder, vanilla, sugar, yolk, extract, and salt. To mix, stir all together.

- In a small mixing bowl, beat egg whites on medium speed with an electric hand mixer until soft peaks form. Toss into the batter. Using a small hinged ice cream scoop, scoop mixture into the prepared mold.
- Fill the silicone mold with batter and put it in the air fryer.
- Cook for 10 minutes in a preheated air fryer. Remove the beignets from the pan and put them on a parchment paper round.
- Return the parchment round with the beignets to the air fryer. Cook for another 4 minutes. Dust the beignets with confectioners' sugar after removing them from the air fryer.

Cal 88 | Carb16.2g | Protein 1.8g: | Fat 1.7g

## BANANA CAKE
*Prep time:10 min | Cook time:30 min | Serves: 4*

### Ingredients
- 1 pinch salt
- 2 tablespoon Honey cooking spray
- 3 ½ tablespoon Butter, at room temperature
- 1 banana, mashed
- 1 egg
- 1 cup of self-rising flour
- ½ teaspoon Ground cinnamon
- ⅓ cup of brown sugar

### Instructions
- Preheat your air fryer to 320 F. Using cooking spray, cover a small fluted tube pan.
- Using an electric mixer, cream together the sugar and butter in a mixing bowl. In a separate cup, combine the banana, egg, and honey. Blend the banana mixture into the butter mixture until it is fully smooth.
- Combine the flour, cinnamon, and salt in a sifter and sift into the banana-butter mixture. Blend the batter until it is smooth. Transfer to the prepared pan and use the back of a spoon to level the surface.
- In the air fryer, position the cake pan. Set the timer for 30 minutes on the air fryer. Cook until a toothpick inserted into the cake comes out clean.
- Please keep in mind that
- If you don't have an air fryer, you can use a toaster air fryer or a standard air fryer to make this recipe. Cook time:should be increased by 5 minutes.

Cal 347 | Carb 56.9g | Protein 5.2g | Fat 11.8g

## BUTTER CAKE
*Prep time:10 min | Cook time:15 min | Serves: 4*

### Ingredients
- 6 tablespoon Milk cooking spray
- ¼ cup of white sugar
- 2 tablespoon White sugar
- 1 egg
- 1 ⅔ cups of all-purpose flour
- 1 pinch salt
- 7 tablespoon Butter, at room temperature

### Instructions
- Preheat your air fryer to 350 F. Using cooking spray, cover a small fluted tube pan.
- In a bowl, mix cream butter and 2 tablespoons of sugar with a mixer until light and fluffy. Mix in the egg until it is smooth and

fluffy. Combine flour and salt in a mixing bowl. Add the milk and thoroughly blend the batter. Transfer the batter to the prepared pan and smooth the top with the back of a spoon.
- In the air fryer, position the pan. Make a 15-minute timer. Cook until a toothpick inserted into the centre of the cake comes out clean.
- Remove the cake from the pan and set it aside to cool for 5 minutes.

Cal 470 | Carb 59.7g | Protein 7.9g | Fat 22.4g

## AIR FRYER S'MORES
*Prep time:5 min | Cook time:8 min | Serves: 4*

### Ingredients
- 1 milk chocolate chip from Hershey's
- 4 marshmallows
- 4 Graham Crackers halved

### Instructions
- Place four graham crackers halves in the basket of air fryer.
- Add marshmallow on top.
- Air fry at 375 F for 7 to 8 minutes.
- Add one graham cracker on top and chocolate.
- Air fry for 2 minutes.

## DONUT STICKS
*Prep time:20 min | Cook time:15 min | Serves: 8*

### Ingredients
- ½ cup of white sugar
- 1 (8 ounces) package refrigerated crescent roll dough
- 2 teaspoon ground cinnamon
- ½ cup of any flavor fruit jam
- ¼ cup of butter, melted

### Instructions
- Unroll the crescent roll dough sheet into an 8x12-inch rectangle. With a pizza cutter, cut the dough in half lengthwise and then crosswise into 1/2-inch thick "sticks." Dip doughnut sticks in melted butter and put them in the air fryer one by one.
- Cook for 4 to 5 minutes in an air fryer at 380 F until well browned.
- In a pie plate or shallow dish, combine the sugar and cinnamon. Take the doughnut sticks out of the air fryer and roll them in the cinnamon-sugar mix. Rep with the rest of the dough.
- Doughnut sticks should be served with jelly.

Cal 266 | Carb 37.6g | Protein2.2g | Fat 11.8g

## SHORTBREAD COOKIE FRIES
*Prep time:20 min | Cook time:10 min | Serves: 24*

### Ingredients
- 3 tablespoons of white sugar
- 1 ¼ cups of all-purpose flour
- ⅓ cup of strawberry jam
- ⅛ teaspoon ground dried chipotle pepper (Optional)
- ⅓ cup of lemon curd
- ½ cup of butter

### Instructions
- In a medium mixing dish, add flour and sugar. Using a cutter, cut in the butter. Create a ball out of the mixture and knead it until smooth.
- Preheat your air fryer to 350°F.

- On a lightly floured surface, roll out the dough to a 1/4-inch thickness. Split into 3- to 4-inch long "fries" with a 1/2-inch deep slit. Sprinkle with more sugar if desired.
- In the air fryer, arrange the fries on a single sheet. Cook for 3 to 4 minutes, or until lightly browned. Enable to cool in the air dryer until solid enough to move to a wire rack to finish cooling. Rep with the rest of the dough.
- Using the back of a spoon, press strawberry jam through a fine-mesh sieve to make strawberry "ketchup." Stir in the chipotle powder. To make the "mustard," whip the lemon curd.
- Sugar cookie fries can be eaten with strawberry ketchup and lemon curd mustard.

Cal 88 | Carb 12.4g | Protein 0.7g | Fat 4.1g

## CHOCOLATE CAKE

*Prep time:10 min | Cook time:15 min | Serves: 4*

### Ingredients
- 1 tablespoon Apricot jam
- 3 ½ tablespoon Butter, softened
- 6 tablespoon All-purpose flour
- 1 tablespoon Unsweetened cocoa powder
- 1 egg
- ¼ cup of white sugar
- Salt

### Instructions
- Preheat an air fryer to 320 F. Using cooking spray, cover a small fluted tube pan.
- Cream together the sugar and butter with an electric mixer in a mixing bowl until light and fluffy. Mix in the egg and jam until it is well mixed. Mix thoroughly after sifting in the flour, cocoa powder, and salt. Pour the batter into the pan that has been prepared. With the back of a spoon, level the batter's surface.
- Preheat the air fryer and place the pan inside. Cook for 15 minutes, or until a toothpick inserted in the centre of the cake comes out clean.

Cal 214 | Carb 25.5g | Protein 3.2g | Fat 11.7g

## EASY FRENCH TOAST STICKS

*Prep time:10 min | Cook time:10 min | Serves: 2*

### Ingredients
- 1 pinch ground nutmeg
- 1 teaspoon Vanilla extract
- 4 slices slightly stale thick bread, like Texas toast
- 2 large eggs,
- ¼ cup of milk
- 1/2 teaspoon Cinnamon
- Parchment paper

### Instructions
- To make the sticks, cut the bread into slices and cut butter paper to match the air fryer's rim.
- Preheat the air fryer to 360°F.
- In a mixing bowl, whisk together the eggs, milk, vanilla extract, cinnamon, and nutmeg until well mixed. Make sure each piece of bread is fully submerged in the egg mixture. Shake each bread stick to extract any excess liquid before putting it in an air fryer in a single layer. If possible, cook in batches to prevent overcrowding the fryer.
- Cook for 5 minutes, then switch the bread pieces and cook for another 5 minutes.

Cal 232 | Carb 28.6g | Protein 11.2g | Fat 7.4g

## PEANUT BUTTER & JELLY S'MORES

*Prep time:5 min | Cook time:5 min | Serves: 1*

### Ingredients
- 1 teaspoon Seedless raspberry jam
- 1 chocolate-covered peanut butter cup
- 1 large marshmallow
- 2 chocolate graham cracker squares,

### Instructions
- Preheat the air fryer to 400 F
- Place peanut butter cup on 1 graham cracker square. Top with jelly and marshmallow. Carefully place in an air fryer.
- Preheated air fryer and cook the marshmallow until they get browned and softened, about a minute.
- Serve

Cal 249 | Carb 41.8g | Protein 3.9g | Fat 8.2g

## CHOCOLATE CHIP COOKIE BITES

*Prep time:10 min | Cook time:30 min | Serves: 17*

### Ingredients
- ½ teaspoon of salt
- ½ cup of butter softened
- ¼ cup of white sugar
- ½ teaspoon of baking soda
- 1 egg
- 1 ½ teaspoon vanilla extract
- 1 cup of miniature semisweet chocolate chips
- ½ cup of packed brown sugar
- 1 ⅓ cups of all-purpose flour

### Instructions
- To use in an air fryer, cut a piece of parchment paper to match.
- In a big mixing bowl, beat butter for 30 seconds at medium to high speed with an electric mixer. Mix in brown sugar, white sugar, baking soda, and salt for 2 minutes on medium pressure, scraping bowl periodically. Combine the egg and vanilla extract in a mixing bowl. Blend in as much flour as possible. Combine any leftover flour, chocolate chips, and pecans in a mixing bowl.
- Drop the dough onto the parchment paper 1 inch apart. Move the parchment paper to the air fryer with care.
- Preheat the air fryer to 300 F and cook for around 8 minutes, or until golden brown and set. Cool the parchment paper on a wire shelf. Rep with the rest of the cookie dough.

Cal 188 | Carb 23.6g | Protein 2g | Fat 10.4g

## APPLE CIDER DONUT

*Prep time:10 min | Cook time:10 min | Serves: 21*

### Ingredients
- 1 (4 ounces) container unsweetened applesauce
- 1 teaspoon apple cider vinegar
- 2 ¼ cups of all-purpose flour
- 1 ½ teaspoon apple pie spice
- 4 teaspoon baking powder
- ½ cup of sparkling apple cider
- 3 tablespoons white sugar
- ½ teaspoon salt
- 1 large egg

### Glaze:
- 1 teaspoon caramel extract (optional)
- 2 cups of powdered sugar

- ¼ cup of sparkling apple cider
- ½ teaspoon apple pie spice

**Instructions**

- Preheat the air fryer for 5 minutes at 400 F
- In a wide mixing bowl, add flour, sugar, baking powder, apple pie seasoning, and salt. Combine all ingredients in a mixing bowl.
- In a small mixing bowl, whisk together sparkling applesauce egg, apple cider, melted butter, and vinegar. Mix the wet and dry ingredients and blend until just mixed. Fill each with 2 tablespoons batter using an ice cream scoop. In the air fryer, position the mold.
- Reduce the temperature to 350°F and cook for 8 minutes. Cook for an additional 2 minutes after carefully turning out the donut bites.
- When the donut bites are cooked, remove them from the air fryer and cool fully on a wire rack before glazing, about 30 minutes. In a small cup, whisk together powdered sugar and apple pie seasoning. Whisk together the sparkling apple cider and caramel extract until the glaze is smooth.
- Dip each donut bite into the glaze and roll it around so that both sides are coated. Enable the glaze to dry and harden on a wire rack before serving.

Cal 132 | Carb 25.9g | Protein1.7g | Fat 2.6g

### TONGA TOAST
*Prep time:20 min | Cook time:10 min | Serves: 4*

**Ingredients**

- Heavy cream: 1 cup
- Unsliced white bread: 1 loaf
- Vanilla extract: 1 tsp.
- 4 eggs
- Sugar: 1 tsp.
- 2 bananas, sliced
- Cinnamon: 1 tsp.
- Instructions
- Slice the bread into 2 to 3 slices.
- On one side of the slices, cut the circle and add banana slices.
- In a bowl, mix eggs, vanilla, milk, sugar and cinnamon.
- Soak the bread into this mixture.
- Air fry for 6 to 7 minutes at 375 F.

### CHOCOLATE HAZELNUT PASTRY
*Prep time:10 min | Cook time:15 min | Serves: 4*

**Ingredients**

- 1 tablespoon of water
- 2 tablespoons of turbinado sugar
- 4 tablespoons of hazelnut spread
- 4 teaspoons slivered almonds plus more for garnish
- (8 oz.)1 layer frozen puff pastry
- 1 beaten egg

**Instructions**

- On a lightly floured surface, thaw and open the puff pastry according to the package instructions.
- Break the puff pastry into four squares. Fill each square with a heaping tablespoon of hazelnut spread. Slivered almonds should be sprinkled on top.
- To make a rectangle, wet the edges of each pastry and fold them together. To seal the edges, use a fork to press them together.

- Combine the egg and 1 tablespoon of water in a small mixing cup. Apply the egg wash to the top of the puff pastry.
- Sprinkle the turbinado sugar over the pastries' tops. To finish, sprinkle a few slivered almonds on top of each pastry.
- Move the pastries to two baking trays with care.
- Place the drip pan in the cooking chamber's rim. Select AIRFRY from the display panel then set the temperature to 330°F and the time to 10 minutes, then press START.
- Insert one cooking tray in the middle position and one tray in the bottom-most position when the show says "Add Food."
- When the show says "Switch Food," don't flip the food; instead, swap the cooking trays so that the one in the middle is now in the bottom-most position, and the one in the bottom-most position is now in the top-most position.
- Keep an eye on the pastries and take them out when they've turned a dark golden brown. Heat the dish before eating.

### CRUST LESS CHEESECAKE
*Prep time:20 min | Cook time:10 min | Serves: 2*

**Ingredients**

- Any sweetener: 3/4 cup
- Sour cream: 2 tbsp.
- 2 eggs
- Vanilla extract: 1 tsp.
- Softened cream cheese: 16 oz.
- Lemon juice: 1 tsp.

**Instructions**

- Let the Kalorik Air Fryer Oven preheat to 350 F.
- In a food processor, mix the lemon juice, eggs, sweetener and vanilla. Pulse till smooth, add cream cheese and mix.
- Pour into 2 four" spring form pans, bake in air fryer for 8 to 10 minutes, until set.
- Let it cool completely then remove and serve.

### VEGAN BEIGNETS
*Prep time:30 min | Cook time:6 min | Serves:3-4*

**Ingredients**

- For the powdered baking blend:
- 1 cup Whole Earth Sweetener Baking Blend
- 1teaspoon organic corn starch

**For the proofing**

- 1/2 teaspoons active baking yeas
- cup full-Fat coconut milk from a can
- tablespoons powdered baking blend

**For the dough**

- 3 cups unbleached white flour
- 2 teaspoons vanilla
- 2 tablespoons melted coconut oil
- 2 tablespoons aquafaba

**Instructions**

- Combine the corn starch Whole Earth Baking Blend and process until it gets smooth in a blender.
- Heat the coconut milk until it is warm but not hot enough to burn your finger in. If the temperature is too high, the yeast will die. Combine it with the sugar and yeast in your mixer. Allow for a 10-minute rest period, or before the yeast starts to foam.
- Add the coconut oil, vanilla, and aquafaba to the mixer. Then, apply the flour.

- If you have a dough hook, switch to it until the flour has been incorporated and the dough has begun to pull away from the sides of the mixer. (If you don't have a paddle, keep using it.
- Knead the dough for about 3 minutes in your mixer. While the dough will be wetter than for a loaf of bread, you should be able to scrape it out and roll it into a ball without it sticking to your hands.
- Put the dough in a mixing bowl, cover with a clean dishtowel, and set aside for one hour to rise.
- Sprinkle some flour on a wide cutting board and roll out the dough into a 13-inch-thick rectangle. Until cooking, cut the dough into 24 squares and let it proof for 30 minutes.
- Preheat the air fryer to 390 F . You can cook 3 to 6 beignets at a time, depending on the size of your air fryer
- Cook on one side for 3 minutes. Cook for another 2 minutes after flipping. Since air fryers vary, you will need to cook them for an additional minute or two to make them golden brown.
- Finish with a generous sprinkling of the powdered baking mix you made earlier, and enjoy!
- Continue to cook them in batches until all of them are finished.
- Preheat the oven to 350 F . Place the beignets on a parchment-paper-lined baking sheet.
- Bake for 15 minutes or until golden brown on top. Enjoy a generous sprinkling of the powdered baking mix you created earlier!

Cal 102 | Fat 3g | Carb 15g | Protein 3g

## PERFECT BANANA MUFFINS
*Prep time:10 min | Cook time:10 min | Serves: 12*

### Ingredients
- 1 teaspoon baking soda
- 1 teaspoon baking powder
- 1/2 teaspoon salt
- 3 large bananas mashed
- 1 1/2 cups all-purpose flour
- 1 teaspoon cinnamon
- 1/3 cup butter melted
- 3/4 cup white sugar
- 1 egg

### Instructions
- Allow the butter to soften
- Preheat the air fryer to 350 F
- Combine all ingredients in a mixer or a mixing bowl. Mix until it is well blended. It's meant to be fluffy.
- Put muffin cups on a rack and cook half of the muffins at a time.
- Fill the cups with the mixture and cover with the bottom drip tray.
- 5 minutes in the air fryer
- Cook for another 5 minutes after uncovering.

Cal 182 | Carb 31g | Protein 2g | Fat 6g

## SWEET POTATO ORANGE CUPS
*Prep time:10 min | Cook time:30 min*

### Ingredients
- 8 oranges
- 3 large sweet potatoes
- 2 tablespoons butter
- 1/8 cup Cream
- 3/4 cup miniature marshmallows
- 1/4 cup brown sugar packed

### Instructions
- Bring the sweet potatoes to a boil in a big saucepan. Reduce heat to low, cover, and cook for 25-30 minutes, or until vegetables are tender. Drain the water. If you prefer, you can simply use canned Yams. Three cans are equivalent to two cans.
- Preheat the Air Fryer to 350 F and Bake mode.
- Beat sugar, milk, concentrate, sweet potatoes, and butter in a large bowl until it smooth.
- Peel the oranges and cut them in half.
- Cut a small piece of the bottom of the orange off so they can stand up straight.
- Remove the pulp from the oranges and discard the shell. If you have a juicer, use it, just keep the shells.
- Fill the shells with sweet potato mixture and with mini marshmallows. The more information you can cram into that room, the better!
- Cook it for the other 4 minutes, or until the top is lightly toasted. It gives them a S'mores-like crunch!

Cal 119 | Protein 1.1g | Carb 13.5g | Fat 7.1g

## JELLY DONUT
*Prep time:5 min | Cook time:5 min*

### Ingredients
- 1 tablespoon butter, melted
- 1 package Pillsbury Grands
- 1/2 cup sugar
- 1/2 cup seedless raspberry jelly

### Instructions
- Preheat the air fryer to 320 F.
- Cook the Grand Rolls in a single layer in the air fryer for 5-6 minutes, or until golden brown.
- Remove the rolls from the air fryer and place them on a plate to cool.
- Sugar should be placed in a large bowl with a flat bottom.
- Brush the donut with butter on all sides and roll it in sugar to fully cover it. Finish with the remaining donuts.
- Pipe 1-2 tablespoons of raspberry jelly into each donut with a long cake edge.
- Enjoy right away or shop for up to 3 days.

Cal 250 | Fat 7g | CarbS 502mg | Protein 3g

## APPLE FRITTERS
*Prep time:10 min | Cook time:6-7min*

### Ingredients
- 1 teaspoon baking powder
- 2 apples, cored and diced
- 1 cup all-purpose flour
- 1/2 teaspoon salt
- 1/2 teaspoon ground cinnamon
- 1/4 teaspoon ground nutmeg
- 1/3 cup milk
- 2 tablespoons butter, melted
- 1/2 teaspoon lemon juice
- 1 egg

### Cinnamon glaze
- 1/2 cup confectioners' sugar
- 2 tablespoons milk
- 1/2 teaspoon ground cinnamon

- Pinch of salt

**Instructions**

- Set aside the apples, sliced into tiny cubes. If needed, peel them.
- In a large mixing bowl, add the flour, sugar, baking powder, salt, ground cinnamon, and ground nutmeg.
- Combine the milk, butter, egg, and lemon juice in a separate cup.
- Combine the wet and dry ingredients in a mixing bowl and stir only until mixed. Refrigerate the mixture for anywhere from 5 minutes to 2 days after adding the apples (covered).
- Preheat the air fryer to 370 F
- Scoop out apple fritters into 2-tablespoon balls and place a parchment round on the bottom of them. Cook for 6-7 minutes in the air fryer with apple fritters.
- To make the glaze, whisk together the confectioner's sugar, milk, cinnamon, and salt while the chicken is cooking.
- Remove the apple fritters from the air fryer, put them on a wire rack, and drizzle the glaze over them right away

Cal 100 | Carb 18g | Protein 2g.

## DESSERT FRIES

*Prep time:5 min | Cook time:15 min | Serves:2*

**Ingredient**

- 1 tablespoon butter, melted
- 2 sweet potatoes
- 2 tablespoons sugar
- 1 teaspoon butter, melted and separated from the above

**Instructions**

- Preheat the air fryer to 380 F
- 2. Sweet potatoes should be peeled and cut into thin fries.
- 3. Using 1 tablespoon of butter, coat the fries.
- 4. Cook fries for 15-18 minutes in a preheated air fryer. They can overlap, but your air fryer should not be more than half full.
- 5. Place the sweet potato fries in a bowl after removing them from the air fryer.
- Add the sugar and cinnamon to the remaining butter and coat. To coat, mix everything.

Cal 150 | Carb; 18g | Protein 1g

## PUMPKIN PIE TWIST

*Prep time:5 min | Cook time:6 min*

**Ingredients**

- 1/2 cup sugar
- 2 teaspoons pumpkin pie spice
- 1 can Pillsbury crescent rolls
- 1/8 teaspoon salt
- 3 tablespoons unsalted butter
- 2 and 1/4 teaspoons milk
- 1/2 cup pumpkin puree
- 2 tablespoons melted butter

**Instructions**

- Roll out the crescent roll dough and press any perforated lines flat.
- Make a lengthwise cut and then a width wise cut to divide the dough into sections. If used in a smaller air fryer, cut into eighths.
- Mix in the pumpkin puree, half of the pumpkin pie spice, and the salt.
- On top of the crescent roll dough, spread the pumpkin puree.

- Place two of the crescent dough sheets, pumpkin side down, on top of the other two. Make sure the corners and sides are as close as possible to each other.
- Cut each pumpkin twist sheet into four long strips with a dough or pizza cutter for a total of eight.
- Preheat the air fryer for 2-3 minutes at 320 F.
- Twist each strip a couple of times on the bottom and a couple of times on top.
- Brush the pumpkin pie twists with melted butter and sprinkle with the remaining pumpkin pie spice.
- Place the pumpkin twists in the air fryer in a single layer, not touching, in the air fryer. 6 minutes in the air fryer
- In a separate cup, whisk together the confectionery sugar, melted butter, and milk to make the icing.
- Inventive+ phrasing Remove the Air Fryer Pumpkin Pie Twists from the air fryer and ice them.
- Enjoy right away or keep refrigerated for up to 3 days.

Cal 219 | Fat 13g | Carb 25g | Protein 2g

## AIR FRYER APPLES

*Prep time:10 min | Cook time:5 min*

**Ingredients**

- 1 teaspoon ground cinnamon
- 3 Granny Smith Apples
- 1/4 cup sugar
- 1 cup graham cracker crumbs
- 3 eggs, whisked
- 1 cup flour
- Caramel sauce for dipping

**Instructions**

- Preheat the air fryer to 380 F
- Remove the core from the apples and cut them into wedges.
- Place the flour in the first bowl, the egg in the second bowl, and the graham cracker crumbs, sugar, and cinnamon in the third bowl, using three cups.
- Dip an apple wedge into the flour, then the egg, and finally the graham cracker mixture, coating the apple as thoroughly as possible each time.
- Rep with the rest of the apple slices.
- Place the apples in a single layer in the air fryer and cook for 5-6 minutes, flipping after one minute.
- Take the apples out of the air fryer and eat them! If needed, top with caramel sauce.

Cal 219 | Fat 13g | Carb 25g | Protein 2g

## S'MORES

*Prep time:2 min | Cook time:8 min | Serves:2-3*

**Ingredients**

- 4 graham crackers broken in half
- 1 milk chocolate bar,
- 4 large marshmallows

**Instructions**

- Line the air fryer with four graham cracker halves.
- Cut a small slice from the bottom of each marshmallow and adhere it to the graham cracker. It will keep it safe throughout the cooking process.
- Bake for 7-8 minutes at 375 F or until the marshmallow is golden brown.

- Top with the remaining graham cracker and desired quantity of Hershey's chocolate.
- Return to the air fryer for another 2 minutes or until the chocolate melts.

Cal 50 g | Carb 26g | Protein 2g | Fat 4g

## OREOS WITH CRESCENT ROLLS
*Prep time:5 min | Cook time:5 min | Serves:2-3*

### Ingredients
- 8 Oreo cookies
- Powdered sugar for dusting
- 1 package of Pillsbury Crescents Rolls

### Instructions
- On a cutting board or table, spread out the crescent dough.
- Press down into each perforated line with your finger to create one wide sheet
- Cut the dough into eighths with a sharp knife.
- In the centre of each crescent roll square, place an Oreo cookie and roll each corner up
- Roll up the remaining crescent roll to fully cover the Oreo cookie. The crescent roll should not be stretched too thinly, or it will crack.
- Preheat the air fryer to 320°F for 2-3 minutes.
- Gently position the Air Fried Oreos in one even row inside the air fryer, making sure they do not strike. Cook in batches if you have a smaller air fryer.
- Bake Oreos for 5-6 minutes at 320 F until golden brown on the outside.
- Carefully remove the Air Fryer Oreos from the air fryer and, if necessary, immediately brush with powdered sugar.

Cal 172 | Fat 4g | Carb 32g | Protein 2g

## BROWNIES
*Prep time:5 min | Cook time:20 min | Serves:3*

### Ingredient
- 4 tablespoon s Salted Butter
- ¼ cup White Sugar
- ¼ cup Cocoa Powder
- ½ teaspoon Vanilla
- ¼ cup All Purpose / Plain Flour
- ¼ cup Brown Sugar
- 1 Egg
- 1/3 cup Chocolate Chips

### Instructions
- Preheat air fryer to 350°F. Line 2 mini loaf pans or 1 standard loaf pan with baking paper.
- In a microwave-safe cup, add the butter, brown sugar, white sugar, and cocoa powder. Microwave in 20-second intervals, stirring well after each until butter is fully melted and mixed.
- Whisk in the vanilla extract until fully mixed. Enable for a minute for the bowl to cool slightly.
- Beat in the egg, then stir in the flour until all is well mixed.
- Combine the chocolate chips and fold them in (and the optional chocolate chunks if using).
- Divide the mixture between the pans and bake for 20-25 minutes in the air fryer.
- Allow 10 minutes for the brownies to cool in the loaf pans before transferring to a wire rack to cool fully.

Cal 342 | Fat 15g | Carb 47g | Protein 5g

## CHOCOLATE GLAZE DONUTS
*Prep time:5 min | Cook time:5 min | Serves: 8*

### Ingredients
### Donuts
- 1 package Grand Flaky Biscuits
- Chocolate Glaze Recipe
- teaspoon Vanilla
- 1/2 tablespoons Water
- Sprinkles optional
- 1/2 tablespoons Cocoa Powder
- 1 cup Powdered Sugar

### Instructions
- Cut a hole in the biscuits with a small donut cutter after opening them.
- Preheat the air fryer to 350 F and cook the biscuit donuts for 3-4 minutes on the lower rack.
- Turn the donuts and cook for another minute in the air fryer.
- When the donuts are cool enough to treat, dip them in the chocolate glaze and decorate as desired.
- Glazed in chocolate
- In a mixing bowl, combine all of the ingredients for the chocolate glaze and swirl to combine.
- If it's too thick, add 1 teaspoon of water at a time until the desired consistency is reached.

Cal 276 | Carb 44g | Protein 4g | Fat 10g

## CINNAMON BREAD TWISTS
*Prep time:15 min | Cook time:15 min | Serves:3*

### Ingredients
### For the Bread Twists Dough
- 1 teaspoon Baking Powder
- 1 C All-Purpose Flour
- 1/4 teaspoon Kosher Salt
- 2/3 C Fat-Free Greek Yogurt

### For Brushing on the Cooked Bread Twists
- 1-2 teaspoon Ground Cinnamon, to taste
- 2 tablespoon (28g) Light Butter*
- 2 tablespoon (24g) Granulated Sugar*

### Instructions
- Before adding the Greek yogurt, whisk together the flour, baking powder, and salt. Stir all together and make dough forms.
- Then turn the dough form into a ball shape. Make six 45-gram bits out of the dough. Roll the dough into thin strips, about 8" long, between your palms or on a flat surface.
- To make a ribbon shape, fold one end of each strip over and place in an air fryer sprayed with cooking spray. Close the lid until all six bread twists are in it.
- Air fry for 15 minutes at 350°F. (Alternatively, bake at 375°F for 25-30 minutes on a baking sheet.)
- At the end of the cooking time, melt the light butter in the microwave and stir in the granulated sugar and cinnamon. As soon as the bread twists come out of the air fryer, brush them with the cinnamon-sugar butter. Heat the dish before serving.

Cal 105 | Fat 2g | Carb 16g | Protein 5g

## STRAWBERRY NUTELLA PIES
*Prep time:10 min | Cook time:20 min | Serves: 3*

### Ingredients
- 1Pillsbury refrigerated pie crust

- 3 to 4 strawberries
- coconut oil cooking spray
- sugar
- 3-inch heart cookie cutter
- Nutella

**Instructions**

- Roll out the pie crust and place it on a baking sheet. Cut out hearts as near as possible with the cutter. Gather the scraps into a ball and roll it out thinly to make a few more heart shapes.
- Set aside a baking tray lined with parchment paper.
- Put aside the strawberries, which have been finely chopped. Spread a dollop of Nutella (about 1 teaspoon) on one of the hearts. Add a few strawberry bits to the mix. Add a pinch of sugar to the top.
- Place another heart on top and use a fork to crimp the edges firmly. Gently poke holes in the top of the pie with a fork. Place on a baking sheet.
- Both of the pies on the tray should be sprayed with coconut oil. Rather than tossing the pies, pass them around the tray to get more coconut oil.
- Preheat the air fryer for 3 minutes at 400 F to bake in the air fryer. Place pie hearts in the air fryer. 5–7 minutes in the air fryer, or until well browned. There's no need to turn the hearts over.

## EASY BEIGNETS

*Prep time:6min | Cook time:15-16 min | Serves:3-4*

**Ingredients**

- 1 teaspoon Vanilla
- 2 tablespoon Sugar
- 2 tablespoon Melted unsalted butter
- Cup Plain Greek Yogurt
- 1/2 Cup Powdered Sugar
- 1 Cup Self-Rising Flour

**Instructions**

- In a mixing bowl, add the yogurt, sugar, and vanilla extract.
- Stir in the flour until the mixture begins to form a dough.
- Knead the dough on a floured work surface.
- Fold the dough in half a couple of times.
- Cut out a 1-inch-thick rectangle. It should be cut into 9 bits. Using a light dusting of flour, gently coat each piece.
- Set aside for 15 minutes.
- Preheat the air fryer to 350 F
- A spray of your air fryer with canola spray.
- Using melted butter, clean the tops of your pastry.
- Place your tray or with the butter side down. Brush the dough's tops with sugar
- Air fry for approximately 6-7 minutes, or until the edges begin to brown.
- Cook for another 6-7 minutes on the other hand.
- Finish with a dusting of powdered sugar.

Cal 123 | Fat 3g | Carbs 20g | Protein 4g

## APPLE PIE BOMB

*Prep time:6 min | Cook time:15-16 min | Serves: 3*

**Ingredients**

- 3 teaspoons ground cinnamon
- 1 can Grands canned biscuits
- 1 cup apple pie filling
- ½ cup butter

- ¾ cup sugar

**Instructions**

- Using a knife and a fork, cut the pie filling into small parts.
- Divide the biscuits into two layers and put them on a clean surface. With a rolling pin, roll to a 4-inch circle or flatten with your fingertips.
- Preheat the air fryer to 350 F for 5 minutes.
- Fill each dough ball with filling, then pinch the edges together to seal. Shape the dough into balls.
- Put apple pie bombs about 2 inches apart in an air fryer, cooking in batches depending on how many you can carry.
- Cook, occasionally stirring, for 8 minutes or until golden brown.
- Melt the butter as the first batch bakes.
- Add sugar and cinnamon to a medium mixing bowl.
- Drizzle melted butter over cooked apple pie bombs on all sides, allowing excess to drip off
- Roll into the cinnamon-sugar mixture and set on a wire rack to cool.
- Continue with the remaining ingredients.
- Serve hot or cold, depending on your choice.

Cal 124 | Carb 16g | Protein 1g

## MINI S'MORES PIE

*Prep time:2 min | Cook time:6min | Serves:* **4-5**

**Ingredients**

- 6 Mini Graham Ready Crust
- 12 Snack Sized Hershey's Bars (broken in half)
- Cup Mini Marshmallows

**Instructions**

- Preheat the Air Fryer to 320 F.
- Fill each mini crust with 4 broken Hershey bar bits.
- Sprinkle mini marshmallows on top, making sure they fully cover the Hershey bars.
- Air fried marshmallows at 320°F for 5-7 minutes, depending on how toasty you like them.
- Serve right away, and enjoy

Cal 562 | Fat 28g | Carb 71g | Protein 8g

## TWIX CHEESECAKE

*Prep time:15 min | Cook time: 75 min | Serves:* **4**

**Ingredients**

**Cookie Crust**

- ½ sticks Butter melted
- 1 ½ cups Flour
- 1 cup Powdered Sugar

**Cheesecake**

- 1 teaspoon Lemon Juice
- ½ cup Powdered Sugar
- 32 oz. Cream Cheese softened
- ½ package Jell-O Instant Cheesecake Pudding 3 oz. size
- Eggs
- ¼ cup Heavy Cream

**Topping**

- 3 squares Chocolate Almond Bark Melting Chocolate
- jar Caramel Ice Cream Topping
- ⅓ cup Heavy Cream

**Instructions**

- In a mixing dish, combine the flour and powdered sugar. Microwave the butter until it melts, then pour it into the flour/powdered sugar mixture. In a mixing bowl, combine the flour, butter, and salt.

- Using parchment paper, line the bottom of a 7-inch Spring-form pan and press the flour mixture tightly into the pan.
- Preheat the Air Fryer to 350 F and cook the pan for six minutes.
- Put the softened cream cheese in the mixing bowl of a stand mixer and blend until smooth while the crust is baking.
- Combine the lemon juice and eggs in a small mixing bowl and whisk until thoroughly combined. Mix in the heavy cream until the Instant pudding is almost smooth.
- Pour the pudding into the mixing bowl and stir to blend. Mix in the powdered sugar at low speed until smooth.
- Scrap down the sides of the bowl and stir until it is well combined. Remove the cheesecake mixture from the Air Fryer and pour it into the Spring form pan. Preheat the air fryer to 350 F and bake the cheesecake for 55 minutes.
- After about 10 minutes, remove the cheesecake from the Air Fryer and cover it loosely with foil. Send it to the Air Fryer to finish cooking.
- When the cheesecake is finished, remove it from the Air Fryer and set it aside for 30 minutes (with the Air Fryer switched off). Enable to cool on a wire rack.
- Once the cheesecake has cooled, wrap it in foil and put it in the refrigerator to set up overnight. Remove the cheesecake from the refrigerator the next day, spoon the caramel topping on top, and return it to the fridge.
- Cal: 632 | Carb 49g | Protein 7g

## GLAZED DONUTS
*Prep time:5 min | Cook time:6 min | Serves: 3-4*

### Ingredients
- 1 cup powdered sugar
- 2 tablespoon milk
- ½ teaspoon use extract
- ¼ teaspoon vanilla extract
- 1 can (16.3 ounces) Grands

### Instructions
- Preheat the air fryer to 350 F
- Combine sugar, all the ingredients in a small mixing bowl. Whisk all together until it's fully smooth.
- Take a board and put biscuits from biscuit can. Cut out the middle hole of the donuts with a 1-inch round cookie cutter.
- Coat the air fryer with non-stick cooking spray. Place donuts in an air fryer with enough room between them. It's best to stop piling these when they're cooking. You may have to cook these in two batches. 3 minutes in the air fryer
- Open the drawer and turn the donuts over after the three minutes are up. Close the drawer and continue to air fry for an additional 2-3 minutes.
- Remove the donuts from the air fryer and set them aside to cool slightly. Then dip the donut in the used glaze and set it aside to cool fully on a wire cooling rack set over a cookie sheet to catch any drips.
Cal 236 | Fat 6g | Carb 27g | Protein 4g

## APPLE PIES
*Prep time:5 min | Cook time:10 min | Serves:3-4*

### Ingredients
- 1 Egg
- Pre Made Pie Crusts

- 5 oz. Can Apple Pie Filling

**Instructions**
- Lay out the pie crust and cut out circles with a cookie cutter.
- Spoon a half teaspoon of apple pie filling into the centre of half of your circles.
- Roll out the remaining circles with a rolling pin to make a slightly wider tab than the apple circles.
- Place the larger circle on top and mend the edges with a fork.
- Brush each apple pie with an egg wash.
- Cook for 12-15 minutes at 350°F in an air fryer.
- Assemble the dish and serve.
Cal 497 | Protein 3.2g | Carb 59.7g | Fat 28.6g

## BAKED APPLES
*Prep time:5 min | Cook time:20 min | Serves:3-4*

### Ingredients
- 1 tablespoon butter, melted
- 2 granny smith apples, halved and cored
- 2 tablespoon brown sugar
- Whipped cream for topping (optional)
- ½ teaspoon cinnamon
- ¼ cup old fashioned oats (not the instant kind)

### Instructions
- In the Air Fryer, arrange cored apple halves in a single sheet (the apple's flesh should be pointing up).
- Air fried plain apple halves for 10 minutes at 350 F
- In the meantime, make the topping by combining the oats, melted butter, brown sugar, and cinnamon.
- Top apple halves with topping and continue air frying at 350 F for 5-10 minutes more, or until apples are tender and topping is crispy. When you poke an apple in the centre with a fork, it should be tender.
- Serve hot, with whipped cream or ice cream on top if desired.
Cal 98 | Fat 3g | Carb 17g | Protein 1g

## BLUEBERRY MINI PIES
*Prep time:10 min | Cook time:48 min | Serves:*

### Ingredients
- Blueberry Pie Filling
- 1 teaspoon Cinnamon
- 2 tablespoon Cornstarch
- ½ cup Water
- 1 teaspoon Lemon juice
- ½ cup White sugar
- 2 cups Blueberries
- Pie Dough cooking spray
- 2 Pillsbury Pie Crusts thawed and

**Vanilla Glaze**
- 2 cups Confectioner's sugar
- 3 tablespoon Milk
- 1 teaspoon Vanilla

**Instructions**
- Blueberry Filling
- Cornstarch and sugar should be whisked together in a large saucepan.
- Cook over medium heat with the remaining ingredients.
- Stir constantly, squeezing the blueberries as you do so.

- Remove from heat once the mixture has thickened (about 10-12 minutes), and set aside to cool as you prepare the dough

**Dough for pies**

- Bring two refrigerated or frozen store-bought pie crusts to room temperature according to package directions.
- Roll out the dough on a clean surface until it has reached room temperature.
- Cut circles out of the dough with a four-inch diameter cookie cutter (or a drinking cup).
- Mini Blueberry Pies with Blueberry Filling
- Scoop one levelled scoop into the middle of one dough circle with a small to medium-sized cookie scoop. (Depending on the size of cookie cutter/cup you used and the size of scoop you have, you'll have to judge for yourself.)
- To make a perfect half-moon-shaped pie, lift half of the dough circle over.
- Crimp the edges with a fork. (If the filling begins to ooze out, you have too much filling; remove some filling and continue; put a little less filling in the other pies going forward.)
- Continue filling, folding over dough, and crimping the remaining pies.
- If you're going to use an air fryer, here's what you should do.
- Using a cooking oil spray such as Pam, gently coat both sides of the dough.
- Place four pies into the air fryer with care. (Depending on the size of your air fryer, you might be able to fit fewer or more pies in.) Do not overlap or touch the pies.
- Preheat the air fryer to 375°F and cook for 6 minutes.
- Cook for 6 minutes more on the other hand, or until the pies are well browned.
- Continue with the remaining pies.

Cal 185 | Carb 48g | Protein 2g | Fat 2g

## BREAD PUDDING
*Prep time:10 min | Cook time:15 min | Serves:3*

**Ingredients**

- 2 cups bread cubed
- 1/4 cup chocolate chips optional
- 1/4 cup sugar
- 1/2 teaspoon vanilla extract
- 2/3 cup heavy cream
- 1 egg

**Instructions**

- Sprays the inside of a baking dish that fits inside the air fryer.
- 2. In a baking dish, place bread cubes. Sprinkle chocolate chips on top of the bread if used.
- 3. Combine the egg, whipped cream, vanilla, and sugar in a separate dish.
- 4. Enable 5 minutes for the egg mixture to soak into the bread cubes.
- In the air fryer, position the baking dish. Cook for 15 minutes in the air fryer at 350°F or until the bread pudding is cooked through.

Cal 375 | Carb 53g | Protein 9g | Fat 14g

## GIANT COOKIE
*Prep time:8 min | Cook time:10 min | Serves:4-5*

**Ingredients**

- 1 teaspoon vanilla

- 1/2 cup butter softened
- 1/2 cup light brown sugar
- 1/2 teaspoon baking soda
- 1/4 teaspoon salt
- 1 1/2 cups all-purpose flour
- 1 cup chocolate chips or chocolate chunks
- 1 egg
- 1/2 cup sugar

**Instructions**

- Preheat the Air Fryer to 350°F.
- In a mixing bowl, cream together the butter, sugar, and brown sugar. Mix in the egg and vanilla extract. Combine the baking soda, salt, and flour in a mixing bowl. Add chocolate chips or cubes to the mix.
- Press cookie dough into the oiled pan's sides. Bake for 10-12 minutes, one at a time, until lightly browned around the edges.

Cal 39g | Fat 19g | Carb 56g | Protein 4g

## CRISPY APPLE CHIPS
*Prep time:2 min | Cook time: 6 min | Serves:3*

**Ingredients**

- Cinnamon
- 1-2 apples red delicious

**Instructions**

- Slice the apples on the thinnest setting (2.5mm) on a mandolin.
- In the air fryer, put the apples. If using, sprinkle with cinnamon. Cover the apple slices with a metal rack, so they don't fly up into the fan when cooking.
- Cook for 16 minutes at 300 F, tossing and turning the apples every 5 minutes.
- Remove the apples after 16 minutes and set them aside to cool for 5-10 minutes on a plate until crisp. Take pleasure in it.

Cal 95 | Carb 25g | Protein 1g | Fat 1g

## GRILLED PEACHES
*Prep time:5 min | Cook time:10 min | Serves: 2-3*

**Ingredients**

- 2 yellow peaches
- Whipped Cream or Ice Cream
- 1/4 cup butter diced into tiny cubes
- 1/4 cup brown sugar
- 1/4 cup graham cracker crumbs

**Instructions**

- Remove the pits from the peaches and cut them into wedges.
- Place a piece of parchment paper on top of the rack in the air fryer.
- Place peach wedges on parchment paper, skin side up (on the side).
- 5 minutes at 350°F in an air fryer
- Combine the crumbs, brown sugar, and butter in a mixing bowl.
- Turn the peaches over to the skin hand.
- Spread crumb mixture on top of peaches, attempting to bring the butter as close to the peaches as possible.
- Continue to air fry at 350°F for another 5 minutes.
- Spoon peaches onto plates with a large spoon.
- Finish with whipped cream.
- Remove any leftover butter/topping mixture from the parchment and put it on top of the whipped topping.

Cal 85 | Fat 1g | Carb 20.9g | Protein 2g

## APPLE TURNOVERS
*Prep time:20 min | Cook time:20 min | Serves:* **4**

### Ingredients
- 1 teaspoon Maple Syrup
- 1 teaspoon Cinnamon
- 2 Apples skin removed and diced
- 2 tablespoon Water

### For turnovers
- 1 Egg, lightly whisked into an egg wash
- 1 sheet Frozen Puff Pastry
- Thickened Cream, whipped

### Instructions
- Take the puff pastry sheet out of the freezer and let it thaw slightly. Then cut the sheet into four squares and use the egg to brush the edges of each square.
- Fill each puff pastry square with apples, fold the pastry over from corner to corner into a triangle shape and seal the edges with a fork.
- Brush the tops of each turnover with the egg, then put two turnovers in the air fryer and cook for 15 minutes at 350 F, or until golden brown. Cook the remaining turnovers in the same manner.
- Serve plain or with a dollop of thickened milk

Cal 154 | Carb 18g | Protein 4g | Fat1 g

## DEEP-FRIED SNICKERS
*Prep time:10 min | Cook time:6 min | Serves* 4

### Ingredients
- 1 Tablespoon Butter, melted
- 10 Fun Size Snickers Bars
- 8 oz. Crescent Rolls Tube

### Instructions
- Remove the crescent rolls from the tube, unroll the dough, and roll it out slightly thinner and longer with a rolling pin or wide bottle. Cut out 10 squares of dough and wrap the Snickers in each one. To completely seal the seams and cuts and smooth out the dough, pinch them together tightly.
- Apply a thin layer of melted butter to the dough using a pastry brush. Place on a baking sheet and air fry for 6 minutes at 370°F or until golden brown (no need to flip halfway through). Sprinkle with powdered sugar, whipped cream, and chocolate sauce.

Cal 205 | Carb 20g | Protein 3g | Fat 12g

## BANANA BREAD
*Prep time:20 min | Cook time:20 min | Serves:* **4**

### Ingredients
- ¼ teaspoon baking soda
- ½ cup granulated sugar
- ½ cup chopped walnuts
- ¾ cup all-purpose flour
- 1 large egg
- ½ teaspoon pure vanilla extract
- ¼ cup sour cream
- ¼ teaspoon salt
- 2 ripe bananas
- ¼ cup vegetable oil

### Instructions
- Combine flour, salt, and baking soda in a large mixing bowl.

- Mash bananas with a fork or potato masher in a medium bowl until very smooth.
- Whisk together the sugar, oil, sour cream, vanilla, and egg until fully mixed.
- Fold dry ingredients into wet ingredients until just mixed. Don't over-mix the ingredients.
- If needed, whisk in walnuts gently.
- Pour the batter into a non-stick 6- to 7-inch round baking pan and put it in the air fryer. (Alternatively, you may use the square, tall-sided pan that came with your air fryer or any other air fryer-safe pan of similar size.)
- Bake at 310°F for 33–37 minutes, or until a toothpick inserted in the centre of the bread comes out clean.
- Cool for at least 20 minutes in the baking pan on a wire rack before removing.

Cal 184 | Fat6g | Carb 29.2g | Protein 4g

## MONKEY BREAD
*Prep time:10 min | Cook time:7 min | Serves:* **2-4**

### Ingredients
- 1 teaspoon of sugar
- 1 cup self-rising flour
- 1/2 teaspoon cinnamon
- 1 cup non-Fat Greek yogurt

### Instructions
- Combine yogurt and self-rising flour in a mixing bowl. It will initially appear crumbly but keep going, and the dough will shape.
- Roll the dough into a round ball. After that, cut it into fourths.
- Shape a flattened circular disc out of a wedge of dough (as shown in the previous photo). Split into eight equal bits (like a pizza). Each wedge should be rolled into a ball.
- In a plastic Ziploc container, combine cinnamon and sugar, then add your dough balls. To uniformly coat them, seal the bag and shake it well.
- Lightly coat a mini loaf pan in non-stick cooking oil. Sprinkle a small amount of the cinnamon-sugar mixture on top of your dough balls.
- Preheat air fryer to 375°F and bake mini loaf pan for 7 minutes.

Cal 250 | Fat 14g | Carb 32g | Protein 2g

## RASPBERRY MUFFIN
*Prep time:10 min | Cook time:22 min | Serves:2-3*

### Ingredients
- 1 teaspoon baking powder
- 1 cup plain flour
- 1/2 tablespoon vanilla sugar
- 1/2 teaspoon vanilla essence
- 1 egg
- 1/8 teaspoon salt
- vegetable oil
- 1/3 cup milk
- 1/2 cup raspberries
- 1/2 teaspoon orange zest
- 1/3 cup sugar

### Instructions
- 1. Line each muffin cup in a muffin tray with a paper muffin liner.
- 2. Combine the flour, baking powder, and salt in a big mixing bowl.

- 3. Whisk together the oil, milk, egg, vanilla, and sugar in a separate bowl until well mixed.
- 4. Whisk in the wet ingredients until just mixed; fold in the raspberries gently so they don't split.
- 5. Spoon the batter into the muffin cups and sprinkle with vanilla sugar
- 6. Bake for 12-15 minutes in the air fryer, or until a skewer inserted into a muffin comes out clear
- Let the muffins cool in the pan for a few minutes before moving them to a cooling rack to cool fully.

Cal 196 | Carb 29g | Protein 3g | Fat 7g

## HEAVENLY FRENCH TOAST
*Prep time:10 min | Cook time:7 min | Serves:* **2-4**

### Ingredients
- 1 teaspoon of vanilla
- 4 slices of bread
- 1/2 teaspoon of cinnamon
- 2 eggs
- 2/3 cup of milk

### Instructions
- Combine the eggs, milk, cinnamon, and vanilla in a small mixing bowl. After that, beat until the eggs are broken up, and all is thoroughly combined.
- Next, dip each piece of bread into the mixture and shake off any excess before placing them in your prepared pan.
- Cook for 3 minutes at 320°F in an air fryer. Then turn them over and repeat the process for another 3 minutes.
- Drizzle with maple syrup and eat

Cal 260 | Fat 12 | Carb 28g | Protein 10g

## STRAWBERRY SCONES
*Prep time:3 min | Cook time:12 min | Serves:4-5*

### Ingredients
- 1 tablespoon Homemade Strawberry Jam
- Butter: 1.7 oz.
- Caster Sugar: 1.7 oz.
- Fresh Strawberries: 1.7 oz.
- Self-Rising Flour: 7.9 oz.
- Milk: 2.1 oz.
- 4 tablespoon Whipped Cream

### Instructions
- 1. In a mixing bowl, combine the flour, butter, and sugar. Combine the butter, sugar, and flour in a mixing bowl until it resembles breadcrumbs. Then add enough milk to make a soft dough, followed by the vanilla extract.
- 2. Divide the dough into four equal-sized scone-shaped balls.
- 3. Cook for 10 minutes at 356°F in the Air fryer inside your baking pan.
- 4. Allow cooling on a cooling rack for a few minutes after cooking.
- Finally, split them in half and stuff them with fresh strawberries, whipped cream, and strawberry jam.

Cal 361 | Carb 55g | Protein 7g | Fat 12g

## FRESH CHERRY CRUMBLE
*Prep time:15 min | Cook time:15 min | Serves:4-5*

### Ingredients
- Cherries: 3 cups, pitted
- White sugar: 10 tbsp.

- Cinnamon powder: 1 tsp.
- Powdered vanilla: 1 tsp.
- Lemon juice: 2 tsp.
- Melted butter: 1/3 cup
- Baking flour: 1 cup
- Nutmeg powder: 1 tsp.

### Instructions
- Let the Kalorik Air Fryer Oven preheat to 325 F.
- In a bowl, mix lemon juice, sugar (4 tbsp.) and cherries, transfer to a baking dish.
- In a bowl, mix sugar and flour. Add butter and rest of the ingredients and mix.
- Spread the flour mixture on top of the cherry mixture.
- Bake in air fryer for 20 to 25 minutes.

Cal 459 | Protein 4.9g | Carb 76.4g | Fat 17.8g

## TRIPLE-CHOCOLATE OATMEAL COOKIES
*Prep time:15 min | Cook time:10 min | Serves:6-7*

### Ingredients
- 1 teaspoon baking soda
- 1 ½ cups all-purpose flour
- 1 cups quick-cooking oatmeal
- 1 cup butter softened
- teaspoon salt
- 1 teaspoon vanilla extract
- 2 eggs
- 2cups chocolate chip
- ¼ cup cocoa powder
- 1 (3.4 ounces) package instant chocolate pudding mix
- ¾ cup brown sugar
- ¾ cup white sugar
- 1 cup chopped walnuts (optional)

### Instructions
- Preheat an air fryer to 350 F. Using non-stick cooking spray, coat the air fryer.
- In a mixing bowl, add the flour, pudding mix, cocoa powder, baking soda, oatmeal and salt.
- Using an electric mixer, cream together butter, brown sugar, and white sugar in a separate bowl. Combine the eggs and vanilla extract in a mixing bowl. Mix in the oatmeal mixture thoroughly. Combine the chocolate chips and walnuts in a mixing bowl.
- Using a large cookie scoop, drop dough into the air fryer; flatten out and leave about 1 inch between each cookie.
- Cook for 6 to 10 minutes, or until lightly browned. Until serving, cool on a wire rack.

Cal 199 | Protein 2.9g | Carbs 24.7g | Fat 10.9g

## CHOCOLATE PEANUT BUTTER OATMEAL
*Prep time:5 min | Cook time:20 min | Serves:5*

- 1 teaspoon maple syrup
- 1/2 cup rolled oats
- 1/2 tablespoon peanut butter
- 1/3 cup milk of choice
- 1/4 teaspoon vanilla extract
- 1/8 teaspoon salt
- 1/2 banana
- 1/2 teaspoon baking powder

### Instructions

- Preheat the air fryer to 350 F
- In a food processor, grind the oats into a floury consistency. Then, except for the chocolate, combine all of the remaining ingredients in a smooth batter.
- Taste and adjust some of the ingredients to your preferences, such as adding more sweeteners or peanut butter.
- Put peanut oatmeal butter banana batter into a heat-resistant bowl and mix them.
- Before adding the chocolate chips, swirl some chocolate sauce, chocolate syrup, or Nutella into the batter to make the chocolate swirl topping.
- Bake the chocolate peanut butter baked oatmeal for 20 to 25 minutes. Cook for 20 minutes for a slightly gooey final result; for a cake-like result, cook for 25 minutes.
- Maintain the same temperature in an air fryer and bake for 15-20 minutes.
- Let the cake cool down and serve.

Cal 328 | Carb 52g | Protein 10g | Fat 10g

## COOKIES
*Prep time:10 min | Cook time:15 min | Serves:3-4*

**Ingredients**
- 1 teaspoon vanilla extract
- 1 cup oats
- 1/2 teaspoon baking soda
- 1/4 teaspoon salt
- 1/3 cup brown sugar
- 1/2 cup sea salt caramel chips
- 1/4 cup milk
- 1 cup whole wheat flour2 tablespoon butter melted
- 1 large egg

**Instructions**
- Preheat the air fryer to 330°F.
- Combine the oats, flour, baking soda, and salt in a small mixing bowl. Whisk together brown sugar, melted butter, vanilla, milk, and the egg in a larger mixing bowl.
- Fold the dry ingredients into the wet ingredients slowly until they are uniformly mixed. Combine the caramel chips and fold them in.
- Use parchment paper to line the bottom of an air fryer-safe baking pan. Scoop the cookie dough into the pan and smooth it out evenly with the back of a spatula
- Cook for 15 minutes with the air fryer (or until the top is brown and a toothpick inserted comes out clean.
- Carefully remove the pan from the air fryer and serve nice.
- Keep refrigerated for up to 5 days or frozen for up to 3 months in an airtight jar.

Cal 181 | Carb 27g | Protein 4g | Fat 7g

## STRAWBERRY SHORTCAKE
*Prep time:10 min | Cook time:8 min | Serves: 3-4*

**Ingredients**
**Strawberry Topping**
- strawberries sliced: 2 cups
- 1/2 cup confectioner's sugar

**Shortcake**
- sugar-free whipped cream, as needed
- 2/3 cup water
- 1/2 cup confectioner's sugar substitute

- 1/4 cup butter cold, cube
- 2 cups Carbic

**Instructions**
- Add the strawberries and 1/2 cup sugar substitute to a big mixing bowl
- Smash a few strawberries against the side of the bowl to help them start producing juices
- Set aside, stirring regularly to prevent the strawberries from releasing their juices
- In a separate bowl, blend the butter and completely add the mixture into the butter.
- Combine the sugar substitute and salt in a mixing bowl
- Stir in enough water to make a dough
- Cut dough into 6 biscuits of similar size
- Place biscuits in the air fryer and air fry (or air crisp) at 400 F for 8 to 9 minutes, or until doughy
- After removing the biscuits from the air fryer, we like to let them rest for 3 minutes
- Serve upside-down shortcakes with strawberries spooned on top and sugar-free whipped cream on the side, if needed.

Cal 315 | Carb 45g | Protein 15g | Fat 23g

## DOUBLE CHERRY MINI EGGROLLS
*Prep time:10 min | Cook time:15-18 min | Serves: 1*

**Ingredients**
- ½ teaspoon ground cinnamon
- ½ 8-ounce package cream cheese,
- ¼ cup dried tart red cherries,
- Nonstick cooking spray or 1 tablespoon butter,
- 3 tablespoons sugar
- ⅓ cup cherry jam
- 16 wonton wrappers (about 3-1/2x3-1/2-inch squares

**Instructions**
- Preheat the air fryer to 400 F . Cream together cream cheese and cherry jam in a small mixing bowl. Add the dried cherries and blend well. Place a wonton wrapper with a corner pointing toward you on a work surface. Using mist, dampen the edges. Just below the centre of the wrapper, place a rounded teaspoon of cherry mixture. Fold the bottom corner over the filling and tuck the other side under. Roll the egg roll into the remaining corner, folding the side corners over the filling. Rep with the rest of the wrappers and filling. Using nonstick cooking spray or melted butter, coat all sides of the egg rolls. In a shallow dish, combine the sugar and cinnamon; set aside.
- Arrange egg rolls in a single layer in the fryer, if possible in batches. Cook for an additional 4 to 5 minutes, or until well browned. Turn off the air fryer from the oven. Immediately roll in cinnamon sugar with two forks on a wire rack, cool for 5 to 10 minutes. Heat the dish before serving.

Cal 84 | Fat 3g | Carb 14g | Protein 1g

## COCONUT DONUTS
*Prep time: 5 min | Cook time: 15 min | Serves: 4*

**Ingredients**
- 8 ounces coconut flour
- 1 egg, whisked
- and ½ tablespoons butter, melted
- 4 ounces coconut milk
- 1 teaspoon baking powder

**Directions**

- In a bowl, put all of the ingredients and mix well.
- Shape donuts from this mix, place them in your air fryer's basket and cook at 370°F for 15 minutes.
- Serve warm.

Cal 190 | Protein 6g | Fat 12g | Carb 4g

## BLUEBERRY CREAM

*Prep time: 4 min | Cook time: 20 min | Serves: 6*

### Ingredients

- 2 cups blueberries
- Juice of ½ lemon
- 2 tablespoons water
- 1 teaspoon vanilla extract
- 2 tablespoons swerve

### Directions

- In a large bowl, put all ingredients and mix well.
- Divide this into 6 ramekins, put them in the air fryer and cook at 340°F for 20 minutes
- Cool down and serve.

Cal 123 | Protein 3g| Fat 2g | Carb 4g

## BLACKBERRY CHIA JAM

*Prep time: 10 min | Cook time: 30 min | Serves: 12*

### Ingredients

- 3 cups blackberries
- ¼ cup swerve
- 4 tablespoons lemon juice
- 4 tablespoon schia seeds

### Directions

- In a pan that suits the air fryer, combine all the ingredients and toss.
- Put the pan in the fryer and cook at 300°F for 30 minutes.
- Divide into cups and serve cold.

Cal 100 | Protein 1g | Fat 2g | Carb 3g

## MIXED BERRIES CREAM

*Prep time: 5 min | Cook time: 30 min | Serves: 6*

### Ingredients

- 12 ounces blackberries
- 6 ounces raspberries
- 12 ounces blueberries
- ¾ cup swerve
- 2 ounces coconut cream

### Directions

- In a bowl, put all the ingredients and mix well.
- Divide this into 6 ramekins, put them in your air fryer and cook at 320°F for 30 minutes.
- Cool down and serve it.

Cal 100 | Protein 2g | Fat 1g | Carb 2g

## CINNAMON-SPICED ACORN SQUASH

*Prep time: 5 min | Cook time: 15 min | Serves: 2*

### Ingredients

- 1 medium acorn squash, halved crosswise and deseeded
- 1 teaspoon coconut oil
- 1 teaspoon light brown sugar
- Few dashes of ground cinnamon
- Few dashes of ground nutmeg

### Directions

- On a clean work surface, rub the cut sides of the acorn squash with coconut oil. Scatter with the brown sugar, cinnamon, and nutmeg.
- Put the squash halves in the air fryer basket, cut-side up.
- Put in the air fryer basket and cook at 325°F for 15 minutes.
- When cooking is complete, the squash halves should be just tender when pierced in the center with a paring knife. Remove from the oven. Rest for 5 to 10 minutes and serve warm.

Cal 172 | Fat 9.8g | Carb 17.5g | Protein 3.9g

## SWEETENED PLANTAINS

*Prep time: 5 min | Cook time: 8 min | Serves: 4*

### Ingredients

- 2 ripe plantains, sliced
- 2 teaspoons avocado oil
- Salt to taste
- Maple syrup

### Directions

- Toss the plantains in oil.
- Season with salt.
- Cook in the air fryer basket at 400°F for 10 minutes, shaking after 5 minutes.
- Drizzle with maple syrup before serving.

Cal 125 | Protein 1.2g | Fat 0.6g | Carb 32g

## PEAR CRISP

*Prep time: 10 min | Cook time: 25 min | Serves: 2*

### Ingredients

- 1 cup flour
- 1 stick vegan butter
- 1 tablespoon cinnamon
- ½ cup sugar
- 2 pears, cubed

### Directions

- Mix flour and butter to form crumbly texture.
- Add cinnamon and sugar.
- Put the pears in the air fryer.
- Pour and spread the mixture on top of the pears.
- Cook at 350°F for 25 minutes.

Cal 544 | Protein 7.4g | Fat 0.9g | Carb 132.3g

## CINNAMON ROLLS

*Prep time: 2 hours| Cook time: 15 min | Serves: 8*

### Ingredients

- 1 pound vegan bread dough
- ¾ cup coconut sugar
- 1 and ½ tablespoons cinnamon powder
- 2 tablespoons vegetable oil

### Directions

- Roll dough on a floured working surface, shape a rectangle and brush with the oil.
- In a bowl, mix cinnamon with sugar, stir, sprinkle this over dough, roll into a log, seal well and cut into 8 pieces.
- Leave rolls to rise for 2 hours, place them in your air fryer's basket, cook at 350°F for 5 minutes, flip them, cook for 4 minutes more and transfer to a platter.
- Enjoy!

Cal 170 | Protein 6g | Fat 1g | Carb 7g

## EASY PEARS DESSERT
*Prep time: 10 min | Cook time: 25 min | Serves: 12*

**Ingredients**

- 6 big pears, cored and chopped
- ½ cup raisins
- 1 teaspoon ginger powder
- ¼ cup coconut sugar
- 1 teaspoon lemon zest, grated

**Directions**

- In a container that fits your air fryer, mix pears with raisins, ginger, sugar and lemon zest, stir, introduce in the fryer and cook at 350°F for 25 minutes.
- Divide into bowls and serve cold.

Cal 200 | Protein 6g | Fat 3g | Carb 6g

## RAISINS CINNAMON PEACHES
*Prep time: 10 min | Cook time: 15 min | Serves: 4*

**Ingredients**

- 4 peaches, cored and cut into chunks
- 1 tsp vanilla
- 1 tsp cinnamon
- ½ cup raisins
- 1 cup of water

**Directions**

- Put all of the ingredients in the pot and stir well.
- Seal pot and cook on high for 15 minutes.
- As soon as the cooking is done, let it release pressure naturally for 10 minutes then release remaining using quick release. Remove lid.
- Stir and serve.

Cal 118 | Protein 2g | Fat 0.5g | Carb 29 g

## SWEET BANANAS AND SAUCE
*Prep time: 10 min | Cook time: 20 min | Serves: 4*

**Ingredients**

- Juice of ½ lemon
- 3 tablespoons agave nectar
- 1 tablespoon coconut oil
- 4 bananas, peeled and sliced diagonally
- ½ teaspoon cardamom seeds

**Directions**

- Arrange bananas in a pan that fits your air fryer, add agave nectar, lemon juice, oil and cardamom, introduce in the fryer and cook at 360°F for 20 minutes
- Divide bananas and sauce between plates and serve.
- Enjoy!

Cal 210 | Protein 3g | Fat 1g | Carb 8g

## VANILLA STRAWBERRY MIX
*Prep time: 10 min | Cook time: 20 min | Serves: 10*

**Ingredients**

- 2 tablespoons lemon juice
- 2 pounds strawberries
- 4 cups coconut sugar
- 1 teaspoon cinnamon powder

- 1 teaspoon vanilla extract

**Directions**

- In a pot that fits your air fryer, mix strawberries with coconut sugar, lemon juice, cinnamon and vanilla, stir gently, introduce in the fryer and cook at 350°F for 20 minutes
- Divide into bowls and serve cold.

Cal 140 | Protein 2g | Fat 0g | Carb 5g

## CINNAMON APPLES AND MANDARIN SAUCE
*Prep time: 10 min | Cook time: 20 min | Serves: 4*

**Ingredients**

- 4 apples, cored, peeled and cored
- 2 cups mandarin juice
- ¼ cup maple syrup
- 2 teaspoons cinnamon powder
- 1 tablespoon ginger, grated

**Directions**

- In a pot that fits your air fryer, mix apples with mandarin juice, maple syrup, cinnamon and ginger, introduce in the fryer and cook at 365°F for 20 minutes
- Divide apples mix between plates and serve warm.
- Enjoy!

Cal 170 | Protein 4g | Fat 1g | Carb 6g

## COCOA BERRIES CREAM
*Prep time: 10 min | Cook time: 10 min | Serves: 4*

**Ingredients**

- 3 tablespoons cocoa powder
- 14 ounces coconut cream
- 1 cup blackberries
- 1 cup raspberries
- 2 tablespoons stevia

**Directions**

- In a bowl, whisk cocoa powder with stevia and cream and stir.
- Add raspberries and blackberries, toss gently, transfer to a pan that fits your air fryer, introduce in the fryer and cook at 350°F for 10 minutes.
- Divide into bowls and serve cold.
- Enjoy!

Cal 205 | Protein 2g | Fat 34g | Carb 6g

## COCOA PUDDING

*Prep time: 10 min | Cook time: 20 min | Serves: 2*

**Ingredients**

- 2 tablespoons water
- ½ tablespoon agar
- 4 tablespoons stevia
- 4 tablespoons cocoa powder

- 2 cups coconut milk, hot

**Directions**

- In a bowl, mix milk with stevia and cocoa powder and stir well.
- In a bowl, mix agar with water, stir well, add to the cocoa mix, stir and transfer to a pudding pan that fits your air fryer.
- Introduce in the fryer and cook at 356°F for 20 minutes.
- Serve the pudding cold.
- Enjoy!

Cal 170 | Protein 3g | Fat 2g | Carb 4g

## CHOCOLATE VANILLA BARS

*Prep time: 10 min | Cook time: 7 min | Serves: 12*

**Ingredients**

- 1 cup sugar free and vegan chocolate chips
- 2 tablespoons coconut butter
- 2/3 cup coconut cream
- tablespoons stevia
- ¼ teaspoon vanilla extract

**Directions**

- Put the cream in a bowl, add stevia, butter and chocolate chips and stir
- Leave aside for 5 minutes, stir well and mix the vanilla.
- Transfer the mix into a lined baking sheet, introduce in your air fryer and cook at 356°F for 7 minutes.
- Leave the mix aside to cool down, slice and serve.
- Enjoy!

Cal 120 | Protein 1g | Fat 5g | Carb 6g

## RASPBERRY BARS

*Prep time: 10 min | Cook time: 6 min | Serves: 12*

**Ingredients**

- ½ cup coconut butter, melted
- ½ cup coconut oil
- ½ cup raspberries, dried
- ¼ cup swerve
- ½ cup coconut, shredded

**Directions**

- In your food processor, blend dried berries very well.
- In a bowl that fits your air fryer, mix oil with butter, swerve, coconut and raspberries, toss well, introduce in the fryer and cook at 320°F for 6 minutes.
- Spread this on a lined baking sheet, keep in the fridge for an hour, slice and serve.
- Enjoy!

Cal 164 | Protein 2g | Fat 22g | Carb 4g

## BLUEBERRY COCONUT CRACKERS

*Prep time: 10 min | Cook time: 30 min | Serves: 12*

**Ingredients**

- ½ cup coconut butter
- ½ cup coconut oil, melted
- 1 cup blueberries
- 3 tablespoons coconut sugar

**Directions**

- In a pot that fits your air fryer, mix coconut butter with coconut oil, raspberries and sugar, toss, introduce in the fryer and cook at 367°F for 30 minutes

- Spread on a lined baking sheet, keep in the fridge for a few hours, slice crackers and serve.
- Enjoy!

Cal 174 | Protein 7g | Fat 5g | Carb 4g

## SWEET VANILLA RHUBARB

*Prep time: 10 min | Cook time: 10 min | Serves: 4*

**Ingredients**

- 5 cups rhubarb, chopped
- 2 tablespoons coconut butter, melted
- 1/3 cup water
- 1 tablespoon stevia
- 1 teaspoon vanilla extract

**Directions**

- Put rhubarb, ghee, water, stevia and vanilla extract in a pan that fits your air fryer, introduce in the fryer and cook at 365°F for 10 minutes
- Divide into small bowls and serve cold.
- Enjoy!

Cal 103 | Protein 2g | Fat 2g | Carb 6g

## BLUEBERRY JAM

*Prep time: 10 min | Cook time: 11 min | Serves: 2*

**Ingredients**

- ½ pound blueberries
- 1/3 pound sugar
- Zest from ½ lemon, grated
- ½ tablespoon butter
- A pinch of cinnamon powder

**Directions**

- Put the blueberries in your blender, pulse them well, strain, transfer to your pressure cooker, add sugar, lemon zest and cinnamon, stir, cover and simmer on sauté mode for 3 minutes.
- Add butter, stir, cover the fryer and cook on High for 8 minutes.
- Transfer to a jar and serve.

Cal 211 | Protein 5g | Fat 3g | Carb 6g

## CAULIFLOWER PUDDING

*Prep time: 10 min | Cook time: 30 min | Serves: 4*

**Ingredients**

- 2½ cups water
- 1 cup coconut sugar
- 2 cups cauliflower rice
- 2 cinnamon sticks
- ½ cup coconut, shredded

**Directions**

- In a pot that fits your air fryer, mix water with coconut sugar, cauliflower rice, cinnamon and coconut, stir, introduce in the fryer and cook at 365°F for 30 minutes
- Divide pudding into cups and serve cold.
- Enjoy!

Cal 203 | Protein 4g | Fat 4g | Carb 9g

## PINEAPPLE PUDDING

*Prep time: 10 min | Cook time: 5 min | Serves: 8*

**Ingredients**

- 1 tablespoon avocado oil
- 1 cup rice
- 14 ounces  milk

- Sugar to the taste
- 8 ounces canned pineapple, chopped

**Directions**

- In your air fryer, mix oil, milk and rice, stir, cover and cook on High for 3 minutes.
- Add sugar and pineapple, stir, cover and cook on High for 2 minutes more.
- Divide into dessert bowls and serve.

Cal 154 | Protein 8g | Fat 4g | Carb 14g

## PLUM JAM

*Prep time: 20 min | Cook time: 8 min | Serves: 12*

**Ingredients**

- 3 pounds plums, stones removed and roughly chopped
- 2 tablespoons lemon juice
- 2 pounds sugar
- 1 teaspoon vanilla extract
- 3 ounces water

**Directions**

- In your air fryer, mix plums with sugar and vanilla extract, stir and leave aside for 20 minutes
- Add lemon juice and water, stir, cover and cook on High for 8 minutes.
- Divide into bowls and serve cold.

Cal 191 | Protein 13g | Fat 3g | Carb 12g

## APPLES AND RED GRAPE JUICE

*Prep time: 10 min | Cook time: 10 min | Serves: 2*

**Ingredients**

- 2 apples
- ½ cup natural red grape juice
- 2 tablespoons raisins
- 1 teaspoon cinnamon powder
- ½ tablespoons sugar

**Directions**

- Put the apples in your air fryer, add grape juice, raisins, cinnamon and stevia, toss a bit, cover and cook on High for 10 minutes.
- Divide into 2 bowls and serve.

Cal 110 | Protein 3g | Fat 1g | Carb 3g

## COCONUT PANCAKE

*Prep time: 10 min | Cook time: 20 min | Serves: 4*

**Ingredients**

- 2 cups self-rising flour
- 2 tablespoons sugar
- 2 eggs
- 1 and ½ cups coconut milk
- A drizzle of olive oil

**Directions**

- In a bowl, mix eggs with sugar, milk and flour and whisk until you obtain a batter.
- Grease your air fryer with the oil, add the batter, spread into the pot, cover and cook on Low for 20 minutes.
- Slice pancake, divide between plates and serve cold.

Cal 162 | Protein 8g | Fat 3g | Carb 7g

## CHERRIES AND RHUBARB BOWLS

*Prep time: 10 min | Cook time: 35 min | Servings: 4*

**Ingredients**

- 2 cups cherries, pitted and halved
- 1 cup rhubarb, sliced
- 1 cup apple juice
- 2 tablespoons sugar
- ½ cup raisins.

**Directions**

- In a pot that fits your air fryer, combine the cherries with the rhubarb and the other ingredients, toss, cook at 330°F for 35 minutes, divide into bowls, cool down and serve.

Cal 212 | Protein 7g | Fat 8g | Carbs 13g

## COCONUT AND AVOCADO PUDDING

*Prep time: 2 hours | Cook time: 2 min | Serves: 3*

**Ingredients**

- ½ cup avocado oil
- 4 tablespoons sugar
- 1 tablespoon cocoa powder
- 14 ounces canned coconut milk
- 1 avocado, pitted, peeled and chopped

**Directions**

- In a bowl, mix oil with cocoa powder and half of the sugar, stir well, transfer to a lined container, keep in the fridge for 1 hour and chop into small pieces.
- In your air fryer, mix coconut milk with avocado and the rest of the sugar, blend using an immersion blender, cover cooker and cook on High for 2 minutes.
- Add chocolate chips, stir, divide pudding into bowls and keep in the fridge until you serve it.

Cal 140 | Protein 4g | Fat 3g | Carb 3g

## 5-MINUTE BISCUIT PIZZAS

*Prep time:2 min | Cook time:5 min | Serves:2*

### Ingredients

- 1 can of regular refrigerated biscuits
- 1/4 cup pizza sauce

**Desired Toppings**

- Mini pepperonis, sliced olives
- 1 cup shredded mozzarella cheese

### Instructions

- Lightly brush your air fryer's bottom with olive oil spray. In the bottom of your air fryer, flatten each biscuit.
- Spread 1 tablespoon pizza sauce on top.
- Garnish with preferred toppings. Mini pepperonis and sliced olives were used.
- Finish with a sprinkling of Parmesan cheese.
- Preheat the air fryer to 350°F and bake for 5 minutes, or until golden brown.

Cal 255 | Carb29g | Protein7g | Fat13g

## BREAD CHEESE PIZZA

*Prep time:5 min | Cook time:5 min | Serves:3*

### Ingredients

- 1 piece of pita bread
- 1/2 cup pizza sauce
- 1/4 cup shredded mozzarella cheese

### Instructions

- Place the pita bread in the air fryer tray.
- Over the crust, spread the pizza sauce.
- Over the pizza sauce, sprinkle the mozzarella cheese.
- In the air fryer, position the pizza.

Cal 292 | Carb 33g | Protein 15g | Fat 10g

## 5-MINUTE GARLIC ROASTED GREEN BEANS

*Prep time:5 min | Cook time:5min | Serves:3*

### Ingredients

- 1 pound trimmed fresh green beans
- 2 tablespoons. extra virgin olive oil
- 2 garlic cloves, diced or sliced
- 1 tablespoon veggie mix seasoning

### Instructions

- Drizzle olive oil over green beans and season with seasoning mix.
- Coat the beans evenly with your fingers and spread them out on your baking sheet, so they don't overlap.
- Air fry for 5 minutes at 390 F in a preheated air fryer air fryer or until slightly wrinkled and lightly browned.

Cal 67 | Carb 8g | Protein 2g | Fat 4g

## SALSA MEAT TAQUITOS

*Prep time:5 min | Cook time:4-5 min | Serves: 10*

### Ingredients

- Ground cheese: 1 pound
- Cooked turkey shredded: 3-4 cups
- 20 flour tortillas
- Salsa, as needed

### Instructions

- In a bowl, toss the turkey with salsa.
- On a surface, place tortilla adds turkey mixture and some cheese.
- Roll tightly and oil spray them all.
- Air fry for 4 to 5 minutes on 350 F in the air fryer.
- Serve right away.

Cal 86 | Carb 93 g | Protein 43 g | Fat 35 g

## ROSEMARY POTATOES

*Prep time: 5 Min | Cook time: 5 Min | Serves: 2*

### Ingredients

- Three Large Red Potatoes, Cubed & Not Peeled
- 1 Tablespoon of Olive Oil
- Pinch Sea Salt
- ½ Teaspoon Rosemary, Dried

### Directions

- Start by preheating your fryer to 390.
- Combine your potatoes with olive oil, salt and rosemary. Make sure your potatoes are coated properly.
- Cook for 5 minutes, and then check them. If you'd like them to be crispier than you can cook them for another two to three minutes.
- You can serve them on their own or with sour cream.

Cal 150 | Fat 5g | Carb 9g | Protein 9g

## 5-MINUTE MINI CHEESE BISCUITS

*Prep time:5 min | Cook time:5 min | Serves:3*

### Ingredients

- 2 cups mini pretzels
- 2 cups mini cheddar biscuits
- 3/4 cup roasted unsalted peanuts
- 4 tablespoons raisins

### Instructions

- Combine all of the ingredients in a mixing bowl
- Serve.

Cal 232 | Carb 35g | Protein 7g | Fat 7g

## KALE CHIPS

*Prep time:2 min | Cook time:2-3 min | Serves:2*

### Ingredients

- 1 bunch kale
- 1 teaspoon olive oil
- ½ teaspoon salt

### Instructions

- Allow the kale to dry completely after washing.
- Preheat your air fryer to 375 F
- Remove the kale's tough stem and rip or cut the leaves into bite-size pieces. Combine them in a mixing bowl with salt and olive oil. Using your hands, uniformly coat the leaves in the seasoning.

- In the air fryer, place the kale. Depending on your air fryer's size, you may need to cook the chips in two or three batches; make sure the air fryer is not overcrowded.
- Air frying the kale chips for 2-3 minutes.
- When the chips are crispy or slightly golden around the edges, they are cooked.

Cal 25 | Carb 3g | Protein 1g | Fat 1g

## EASY 5-MINUTE MOIST PEANUT BUTTER MUG CAKE

*Prep time:4 min | Cook time:1 min*

### Ingredients
- 1 & 1/2 tablespoon butter melted
- 1 & 1/2 tablespoon peanut butter
- 1 egg yolk
- 2 tablespoon brown sugar
- 1 & 1/2 tablespoon milk
- 1/8 teaspoon vanilla extract optional
- 2 tablespoon flour
- 1/8 teaspoon baking powder
- vanilla frosting optional

### Instructions
- Melt the butter in the cup, then whisk in the peanut butter until well mixed. Stir in the egg yolk, brown sugar, milk, and vanilla until well combined.
- Mix in the flour and baking powder one more time until it is perfectly smooth.
- Air fry for 4-5 minutes, at bake and serve.

Cal 470 | Carb 33g | Protein 10g | Fat 35g

## 5-MINUTE CINNAMON ROLLS

*Prep time:2 min | Cook time:5 min | Serves:*

### Ingredients
- 1 can of cinnamon rolls

### Instructions
- Preheat the air fryer to 300°F. If your air fryer doesn't have a preheat button, you can run it at 300F for about 5 minutes to get it up to temperature!
- Spray the air fryer with non-stick cooking spray and arrange the cinnamon rolls 1-2 inches apart.
- Cook for a total of 5 minutes.
- Remove from the air fryer, set aside to cool slightly, and then frost!

Cal 160 | Fat 6g | Carb 23g | Protein 2g

## GRANOLA BITES

*Prep time:2 min | Cook time:2-3 min | Serves:2*

### Ingredients
- 1 1/2 cups oats (I used old fashioned)
- 1/2 cup dried blueberries
- 1/2 cup dried cranberries
- 1/2 cup chopped walnuts
- 1/4 cup mini chocolate chips
- 1/3 cup peanut butter
- 1/3 cup honey

### Instructions
- In a mixing bowl, combine the oats and the next four ingredients (through the chocolate chips).

- In a separate cup, whisk together the peanut butter and honey until smooth. (You can do this in a small saucepan over medium-low heat if your peanut butter is hard or cold.) Warming up the peanut butter and smoothing out the mixture takes just a minute.) Stir the peanut butter-honey mixture into the granola mix until it is evenly covered.
- Wet your hands with water and roll into 1-inch large balls - I did mine this way (a little bigger than a golf ball). Put the mixture in the fridge for 20-30 minutes to firm it up a little make it easier to roll. I'll do that step if I'm making these ahead of time. If I'm making them with M, we'll roll them up and eat them right away.
- Store in an airtight jar in the refrigerator. To keep the balls from sticking to each other, place wax paper between the layers. Have fun!

Cal 219 | Fat 10g | Carb 31g | Protein 5g

## 5-MINUTE QUESADILLA

*Prep time:2 min | Cook time:2-3 min | Serves: 1*

### Ingredients
- 1½ Cups Shredded Colby
- 2 Flour Tortillas

### Instructions
- Spray the air fryer air fryer with non-stick cooking spray.
- Toss the tortilla into the air fryer. Spread a thin layer of cheese on top of the tortilla, but not to the edges. Place the second tortilla on top and firmly push down.
- Air fried for 2 minutes at 350°F. Flip the quesadilla carefully and cook for another 2 minutes in the air fryer.
- Toss with sour cream, salsa, spicy sauce, guacamole, and cilantro before serving.

Cal 969 | Fat 60g | Carb 57g | Protein 49g

## CINNAMON HORNS

*Prep time:2 min | Cook time:2-3 min | Serves:1*

### Ingredients
- 5 tablespoons of butter melted
- 1/2 cup of white granulated sugar
- 2 teaspoons of ground cinnamon
- 4 cups of Bugles

### Instructions
- Combine all of the ingredients in a mixing bowl and put them on a baking sheet. Oil the baking sheet with non-stick cooking spray.
- Position sheet in Air Fryer and broil for 1 minute on high, then remove and stir the bugles before returning to the air fryer to broil for 30 seconds to a minute. So that they don't burn, keep a close eye on them. Allow cooling before serving or storing in an airtight jar.

Cal 220 | Protein2g | Carb 3g | Fats:3g

## TURKEY BACON

*Prep time:2 min | Cook time:5 min | Serves:1*

### Ingredients
- 8 slices of turkey bacon

### Instructions
- Preheat the air fryer to 400 F
- Cook the turkey bacon for 5 minutes in the air fryer. Halfway through cooking, flip the bacon.

Cal 60 | Fat 4g | Carb 1g | Protein 5g

## CHILI CHEESE DOGS

*Prep time:2 min | Cook time:5 min | Serves:1*

**Ingredients**

- 1/2 cup canned
- 2 sausage rolls
- 1/2 cup shredded cheddar cheese
- 2 hot dogs

**Instructions**

- Preheat the air fryer to 400 F
- In the air fryer, position the hot dogs and cook for 4 minutes, turning halfway through.
- Take the hot dogs out of the air fryer and stuff them into sausage rolls. Place each one in the air fryer gently and evenly distribute half of the cheddar cheese on top of the hot dogs.
- Top with the remaining cheddar cheese and chili
- Preheat the air fryer to 350°F and cook for 1-2 minutes, or until the cheese has melted and the chili is hot.
- Remove the chili cheese dogs from the air fryer with care and serve right away.

Cal 486 | Fat 37 g | Carb2 g | Protein 6g

## LEMON PARMESAN ASPARAGUS

*Prep time:2 min | Cook time:3 min | Serves:1*

**Ingredients**

- 1 bunch asparagus see note 1
- 1 tablespoon olive oil
- 1/8 teaspoon salt
- 1/2 lemon to squeeze over
- 1/2 cup parmesan cheese to sprinkle

**Instructions**

- Remove the woody ends of the asparagus spears by snapping or trimming them. This usually refers to the bottom two inches.
- Drizzle olive oil over the asparagus. Use your hands to massage it in, which is optional but beneficial.
- Preheat the air fryer to 400 F. Cook for 2-5 minutes on each hand, shaking and flipping halfway through.

Cal 103 | Carb 5g | Protein 7g | Fat 7g

## 5-MINUTE HEALTHY APPLE FRIES

*Prep time:2 min | Cook time:3 min | Serves:1*

**Ingredients**

- 1 medium apple sliced
- 1 tablespoon graham cracker crumbs
- 1 butter-flavored cooking spray
- 1/2 teaspoon cinnamon
- 1/2 teaspoon sugar

**Instructions**

- Spray the apple slices with the butter-flavored cooking spray and place them in a bowl.
- Add the Graham cracker crumbs and mix to combine.
- Arrange the slices in the air fryer of the air fryer.
- Drizzle cinnamon sugar over the slices.
- Bake 350°F for 15 minutes

Cal 121 | Fat1g | Carb 1g | Protein0g

## EASY CHEETOS

*Prep time:2 min | Cook time:3 min | Serves:1*

**Ingredients**

- 6 Frozen Cheddar Sticks

- 2 Eggs
- 8.5 oz. Bag Cheetos

**Instructions**

- Check to see if the cheddar sticks are frozen.
- Place the Cheetos in a big baggie and smash them with a rolling pin.
- Once the cheddar sticks are frozen, cut them in half and dip them in the egg.
- Finally, coat every egg-coated cheese stick in Cheetos dust.
- Return to freezer and preheat air fryer to 350 F.
- Remove from freezer and air fried for 3-5 minutes until preheated.
- Serve with a dipping sauce of your choice and enjoy.

Cal 220 | Fat 2g | Carb 2g | Protein 3g

## ASPARAGUS WITH ALMONDS

*Prep time: 5 min | Cook time: 5 min | Serves: 2*

**Ingredients**

- 9 ounces asparagus
- 1 teaspoon almond flour
- 1 tablespoon almond flakes
- 1/4 teaspoon salt
- 1 teaspoon olive oil

**Directions**

- Combine the almond flour and almond flakes; stir the mixture well.
- Sprinkle the asparagus with the olive oil and salt.
- Shake it gently and coat in the almond flour mixture.
- Place the asparagus in the air fryer basket and cook at 400°F for 5 minutes, stirring halfway through.
- Then cool a little and serve.

Cal 143 | Fat 11g | Fiber 4.6g | Carb 8.6g | Protein 6.4g

## FROZEN TEXAS TOAST

*Prep time:1 min | Cook time:5 min | Serves:1*

**Ingredients**

- 4 Frozen Texas Toasts (Cheese or Garlic)

**Instructions**

- Spread the frozen Texas toasts in an even layer in the air fryer (make sure they don't overlap). There's no need to use some oil spray.
- Texas cheese toast
- Air fry for 5 minutes at 360°F, or until the cheese is crispy and the toast is warmed through.

***Texas toast (without cheese)***

- Air fry for 5 minutes at 340°F. Overturn the garlic bread.
- Continue to Air Fry at 340°F for another 1–5 minutes, or until the golden crisp is achieved.
- If you're just making 1-2 pieces of garlic bread, the total time will be about 5-6 minutes, depending on how crisp you like your

toast. Test a piece first, and you'll have a better idea of your desired timing.

Cal 150 | Carb 17g | Protein 5g | Fat 7g

## 5-MINUTE SUGAR DOUGHNUT

*Prep time:3min | Cook time:5min | Serves:2-3*

**Ingredients**

- 5 Tablespoons Butter
- 1/2 Cup Sugar
- 1 Can Large Pillsbury Biscuits
- 1/2 Tablespoon Cinnamon

**Instructions**

- Preheat the air fryer to 330°F
- Combine the cinnamon and sugar in a medium mixing bowl. Remove from the equation.
- Take the biscuits out of the can and cut the centre of each one. (Because my doughnut cutter is too thin, I use a small heart-shaped cookie cutter.)
- In your air fryer, place the larger, outside part.
- Run at 330 F for 4-7 minutes. Depending on the model of your air fryer, you may need to change this slightly. After testing this recipe in three separate air fryers, I've discovered that the doughnuts will take anywhere from 4 to 7 minutes to cook completely When making the recipe for the first time, ensure that they are completely cooked in the centre.
- Melt the butter while the doughnuts are baking.
- Brush with melted butter using a brush. Then, using a spoon, brush the top of the cake in the cinnamon-sugar mixture.
- Shake off any extra cinnamon sugar gently.
- Serve the doughnuts warm.
- Set your timer for just 2-4 minutes while air frying the "holes" and top them with the butter and cinnamon/sugar as well.

Cal 135 | Fat 8g | Carb 16g | Protein 1g

## CHEESY LOADED NACHOS

*Prep time:3min | Cook time:2-3min | Serves:2-3*

**Ingredients**

- 1 tablespoon freshly chopped cilantro
- 6-7 oz. tortilla chips
- ¾ cup cooked black beans
- 4 oz. can dice green chilis
- 6 oz. freshly shredded cheddar
- sour cream for topping
- 1 jalapeno thinly sliced
- 1-2 scallions chopped
- 2-3 small tomatoes, diced

**Instructions**

- Tear a sufficient amount of aluminium foil and place it in the air fryer. Make sure it's long enough to allow your "handles" to pull with while you're removing it.
- Fold the foil or paper into a shape and put it on your counter top and [reheat your air fryer to 375°F and close yours.
- Layer half of the nachos onto the foil or parchment sheet as it's preheating. Half of your cheese, chilis, and beans should be sprinkled on top. Attach the rest of your nachos to the tip, along with your beans, chilis, and cheese.
- When your air fryer is set, carefully lift the entire sheet of nachos into your and air fry for 2 minutes, using the "handles."

- When the timer goes off, sneak a peek. If your cheese isn't fully melted, return it to the air fryer for another minute.
- Raise the nachos out of the with the handles and put them directly on your serving platter. I prefer to serve the nachos as-is while using parchment paper. (I think the paper is attractive.) If using foil, use a long spatula to slip the nachos off the foil.
- Toss the onions, jalapenos, scallions, a big dollop of sour cream, and freshly chopped cilantro on top of the nachos. Serve immediately!

Cal 400 | Protein 21g | Fat 15.8g | Carb3g

## FRENCH TOAST

*Prep time:2min | Cook time:2-3min | Serves:2-3*

**Ingredients**

- 2/3 cup dairy or non-dairy milk
- 4 tablespoons maple syrup
- 1 cup fresh blueberries, strawberries, or raspberries
- 2 eggs, beaten
- 3/4 teaspoon cinnamon
- 1 teaspoon vanilla extract
- 12 slices French or Italian bread

**Instructions**

- If your air fryer needs to be preheated, begin the process by setting the temperature to 350 F.
- A big pan, platter, or even pie dish, combine the eggs, milk, vanilla, and cinnamon. Using a whisk or fork, thoroughly mix the ingredients.
- Dip your bread into the mixture and leave it to soak for 5-10 seconds before turning it over and soaking the other side. Before putting each piece on the prepared rack, let any excess batter drip off.
- Preheat the air fryer to 350°F and air fry the French toast for 3 minutes. Cook for another 2-3 minutes on the other side after flipping the bits. You will need to do this in two batches, depending on the size of your air fryer.
- Drizzle maple syrup and new berries over your French toast.

Cal 170 | Fat 8g | 7g Protein 6g | Carb0g

## CHICKEN TAQUITOS

*Prep time:2min | Cook time:2-3min | Serves:2-3*

**Ingredients**

- 2 cups rotisserie chicken
- 1 cup Greek yogurt (or sour cream)
- ¾ cup shredded cheese (optional)
- Pico de Gallo
- ½ cup salsa
- Mission Carb Balance Soft Taco Flour Tortillas

**Instructions**

- Chop the rotisserie chicken into thin, bite-sized chunks. Combine the chicken with your favorite salsa.
- 1/4 cup of the chicken mixture should be added to the Carb Balance Flour Tortilla. If needed, top with shredded cheese. To keep the tortilla sealed, roll it tightly and spray the end with a little cooking spray. Continue rolling taquitos until you have enough for two servings, then set them aside.
- Cook for 5 minutes in an air fryer at 375 F, testing halfway through. When the taquitos are golden brown, they're ready.

Cal 174 | Protein 10.3g | Carb 12.9g | Fat 9.2g

## AIR FRYER SALMON (FRESH OR FROZEN)

*Prep time:1 min | Cook time:5 min | Serves:2-3*

### Ingredients

- 2 (6-ounce) wild-caught salmon fillets
- 2 teaspoons olive oil
- 1 tablespoon lemon juice
- 1 garlic clove, minced
- 1/2 teaspoon salt
- 1/4 teaspoon black pepper

### Instructions

- Preheat the air fryer to 400 F. In a small cup, combine the olive oil, lemon juice, and garlic while the air fryer is preheating. Place the mixture on top of the fish.
- Season each fillet with salt and pepper to taste. On top of each fillet, I sprinkle a quarter teaspoon of salt and a generous amount of black pepper. If needed, spray the bottom of the air fryer with oil to keep it from sticking. Place the two fillets in the air fryer and cook for 7 minutes at 400 F. Reduce the time by 2 minutes if your fish is thinner than 1 1/2 inches in the thickest section, just to make sure it doesn't overcook.
- Check the internal temperature of the salmon after the cooking cycle is over.  The thickest section should reach at least 140°F, and when you take it out to rest, it should reach 145°F. (The FDA's recommended safe temperature.) The fish should be opaque and easily flake with a fork. If it isn't finished yet, put it back in the air fryer for 1 minute at a time before it is.
- Serve the salmon with your favourite side dishes while it's still warm. Cooked salmon can be kept in an airtight jar in the refrigerator for up to 3 days.

Cal 28 | Carb 1g | Protein 34g | Fat 15g

## VEGETABLE STIR FRY WITH TOFU

*Prep time:1 min | Cook time:5 min | Serves:2-3*

### Ingredients

- ½ teaspoon sesame oil
- 4 stalks asparagus, ends trimmed and cut in half
- 4 Brussels sprouts, halved
- 3 brown mushrooms, sliced
- 2 cloves garlic, minced
- ¼ teaspoon soy sauce
- salt and pepper, to taste
- roasted white sesame seeds
- 1 teaspoon Italian seasoning
- 1 cup firm tofu, cut into strips

### Instructions

- Toss all of the ingredients together in a big mixing bowl.
- Place the vegetables in an air fryer and air fry for 7-8 minutes, depending on how well finished you like them. Halfway through, give a good shake.
- Remove from the air fryer, top with roasted white sesame seeds, and serve with rice on the side.

Cal 195 | Fat 3.7g | Carb 33.6g | Protein 18g

## HONEY GARLIC SALMON

*Prep time:1 min | Cook time:5 min | Serves:2-3*

### Ingredients

- 2 salmon fillets (5–8 oz. each)
- 2 tablespoons honey
- 1 1/2 tablespoons   soy sauce
- 1/4 teaspoon garlic powder/1 teaspoon fresh garlic, minced

**Optional Garnishes:**

- Black/white sesame seeds
- Green onions, sliced

### Instructions

- Whisk together the sugar, soy sauce, and garlic powder. Cut the sauce in half.
- Refrigerate the salmon fillet for 30 minutes after marinating it in half of the sauce.
- Preheat the air fryer to 400 F and add the salmon fillets. Brush the salmon fillets with the remaining marinade.
- Depending on the thickness of the salmon, air fry for 7-8 minutes.
- Plate and serve immediately with the remaining sauce drizzled on top.

Cal 111 | Fat 6.3g | Carb 19.2g | Protein 0g

## AIR FRYER FISH

*Prep time:1 min | Cook time:5 min | Serves:2-3*

### Ingredients

- 2 salmon filets
- 1 teaspoon olive oil
- 1/4 teaspoon chili lime seasoning blend
- salt and pepper to taste

### Instructions

- Using a paper towel, pat the salmon fillets dry on both sides.
- Brush all sides with olive oil. You may also use cooking spray as an alternative.
- Place the fillet in the fryer, skin side down. Season with salt and pepper.
- Bake for 5 minutes at 400 F.
- Serve right away.

Cal 259 | Fat 13g | Protein 34g | Carb 0g

## 5-MINUTE DONUTS

*Prep time:2 min | Cook time:5 min | Serves:2*

### Ingredients

- 2 tablespoons butter
- Biscuit dough, such as Pillsbury Grands
- 2 teaspoons cinnamon
- 1/2 cup sugar(icing)
- 2 tablespoons melted butter

### Instructions

- Separate the biscuits and position them on a cutting board or a flat surface. Cut holes in the middle of biscuits with a biscuit cutter (or small shot glass or plastic medicine cup).
- Place a few donuts at a time in the air fryer, making sure they don't hit.
- Preheat the air fryer to 350°F and cook for 4-5 minutes. They're done when they're flaky and slightly browned.
- Using an air fryer, brush donuts with melted butter before rolling them in powdered sugar or a cinnamon/sugar mixture.

Cal 238 | Fat 4g | Protein 5g | Carb 46

## HONEY LIME SHRIMP

*Prep time:5 min | Cook time:5 min | Serves: 2-4*

### Ingredients

- Olive oil: 1 ½ tbsp.
- 2 minced garlic cloves
- Lime juice: 1 ½ tbsp.

- 1 lb. shrimp, raw & shell removed
- Honey: 1 ½ tbsp.
- Salt: 1/8 tsp.

**Instructions**

- In a bowl, add all ingredients and toss to coat. Let it rest for 20 to 30 minutes.
- Let the Kalorik Air Fryer Oven preheat to 390 F
- Place the shrimps on the air fryer tray and air fry for 2 minutes, flip and cook for 2 to 3 minutes more.
- Serve right away with fresh herbs on top.

Cal 187 | Carb 7g | Protein 23g | Fat 7g

## CHEESY TUNA FLAUTAS

*Prep time:15 min | Cook time:5 min | Serves: 2*

**Ingredients**

- Cheddar cheese: half cup, shredded
- 8 flour tortillas
- Salt
- Fresh cilantro: 1 tbsp.
- Garlic powder: 2 pinches
- Ancho chili powder: 2 pinches
- 1 can of tuna

**Instructions**

- In a bowl, add all ingredients except for cheese and tortilla and mix.
- In each tortilla add cheese, and top with the tuna mixture.
- Roll tightly and secure with toothpick.
- Air fry for 5 minutes at preheat 350 F.
- Serve right away

Cal 57 | Fat 2g | Protein 14g | Carb 6g

## FRENCH ONION BEEF SLIDERS

*Prep time:12 min | Cook time:5 min | Serves: 12*

**Ingredients**

- melted butter: 2 tbsp.
- Worcestershire sauce: 1 tsp.
- Sweet Rolls: 12
- French-fried onions: 2/3 cup
- Dijon mustard: 2 tsp.
- Poppy seeds: ¼ tsp.
- Brown sugar: 1 tsp.
- roast beef: 3/4 pound, sliced thin
- Provolone cheese: 12 thin slices

**Instructions**

- In a bowl, mix Worcestershire, butter and sugar.
- On each roll's half, spread mustard, add beef on top, add onion and cheese slices.

- Top with the buns' other half. With a toothpick, secure it.
- Let the Kalorik Air Fryer Oven preheat to 350 F.
- Air fry the sliders for 4 to 5 minutes.
- Brush with the butter mixture and sprinkle poppy seeds, air fry for 1 minute and serve.

Cal 165 | Fat 7g | Carb 17g | Protein 9g

## CAJUN SHRIMP (NO BREADING)

*Prep time:5 min | Cook time:5min | Serves:2-3*

**Ingredients**

- 1 lb. raw, medium-large size shrimp
- 2 tablespoons olive oil
- garlic cloves
- 1/2 teaspoon sea salt
- 1 tablespoon Cajun seasoning

**Instructions**

- If necessary, devein and peel the shrimp; the tail may be left on or off. If you're using frozen shrimp, blot the excess moisture with paper towels after they've been defrosted.
- Preheat the air fryer for 5 minutes at 400 F.
- Combine the raw shrimp and oil in a medium-sized mixing bowl. Combine the minced garlic, sea salt, and Cajun seasoning in a bowl and mix well.
- In the air fryer, cook the shrimp for about 4 minutes or until they turn pink. Turn the shrimp or shake them. Following the first two minutes of cooking time. You want to cook the shrimp until the meat JUST turns yellow, which can take a little less or a little longer depending on your air fryer.

Cal42 | Fat4g | Carb2g | Protein1g

## FUNNEL CAKE

*Prep time:10 min | Cook time:5 min | Serves: 4*

**Ingredients**

- Flour: 1 cup
- Greek yoghurt: 1 cup
- Powder sugar: 1 ½ tbsp.
- Vanilla extract: 1 tsp.
- Ground Cinnamon: half tsp.

**Instructions**

- In a bowl, mix the flour, vanilla, yogurt and cinnamon. Mix and knead for two minutes with hands.
- Roll the dough and cut into 4 pieces.
- Cut each piece into six sections, and make each section in a long rope.
- Stack the ropes on top of each other in a cake shape.
- Do the same with all pieces.
- Preheat your air fryer for 375 F.
- Oil spray the air fryer basket, place cakes and oil spray them as well.
- Cook for five minutes.
- Sprinkle powder sugar and serve.

Cal 160 | Fat 1g | Carb 29g | Protein 9g

## FLOUNDER FISH

*Prep time:10 min | Cook time:5 min | Serves: 2*

**Ingredients**

- 2 flounder fillets
- Cayenne pepper: 1 tsp.
- Flour: half cup

- Red pepper: ¼ tsp.
- Salt
- Buttermilk: ¼ cup
- Corn-starch: 1 ½ tsp.
- Powdered onion: 1 tsp.
- Paprika: 1 tsp.

**Instructions**

- Soak the fish in buttermilk.
- In a bowl, add the rest of the ingredients and mix.
- Coat the fish in the flour mixture.
- Oil spray the fish and air fry for 3 to 5 minutes at 400 F.
- Serve.

Cal 500 | Fat 1g | Protein 12g | Carb 53g

## LEMONY APPLE BITES

*Prep time: 5 min | Cook time: 5 min | Serves: 4*

**Ingredients**

- big apples, cored, peeled and cubed
- teaspoons lemon juice
- ½ cup caramel sauce

**Directions**

- In your air fryer, mix all the ingredients; toss well.
- Cook at 340°F for 5 minutes.
- Divide into cups and serve as a snack.

Cal 180 | Fat 4g | Fiber 3g | Carb 10g | Protein 3g

## PLEASANT AIR-FRIED EGGPLANT

*Prep time: 5 min | Cook time: 5 min | Serves: 4*

**Ingredients**

- 2 thinly sliced or chopped into chunks eggplants
- 1 teaspoon of salt
- 1 teaspoon of black pepper
- 1 cup of rice flour
- 1 cup of white wine

**Directions**

- Using a bowl, add the rice flour, white wine and mix properly until it gets smooth.
- Add the salt, black pepper and stir again.
- Dredge the eggplant slices or chunks into the batter and remove any excess batter.
- Heat up your air fryer to 390°F.
- Grease your air fryer basket with a nonstick cooking spray.
- Add the eggplant slices or chunks into your air fryer and cook it for 5 minutes or until it has a golden brown and crispy texture, while still shaking it occasionally.
- Carefully remove it from your air fryer and allow it to cool off. Serve and enjoy!

  Cal 380 | Fat 15g | Protein 13g | Fiber 6.1g | Carb 51g

## SKY-HIGH ROASTED CORN

*Prep time: 5 min | Cook time: 5 min | Serves: 4*

**Ingredients**

- 4 ears of husk-less corn
- 1 tablespoon of olive oil
- 1 teaspoon of salt
- 1 teaspoon of black pepper

**Directions**

- Heat up your air fryer to 400°F.
- Sprinkle the ears of corn with the olive oil, salt and black pepper.
- Place it inside your air fryer and cook it for 5 minutes at 400°F.
- Serve and enjoy!

Cal 100 | Fat 1g | Protein 3g | Fiber 3g | Carb 22g

## GARLIC PRAWN

*Prep time: 5 min | Cook time: 5 min | Serves: 4*

**Ingredients**

- 15 fresh prawns
- 1 tablespoon olive oil
- 1 teaspoon chili powder
- 1 tablespoon black pepper
- 1 tablespoon chili sauce
- 1 garlic clove, minced
- Salt as needed

**Directions**

- Preheat your Air Fryer to 356°F
- Wash prawns thoroughly and rinse them
- Take a mixing bowl and add washed prawn, chili powder, oil, garlic, pepper, chili sauce and stir the mix
- Transfer prawn to Air Fryer and cook for 5 minutes
- Serve and enjoy!

Cal 140 | Fat 10g | Carb 5g | Protein 8g

## ZUCCHINI CUBES

*Prep time: 5 min | Cook time: 5 min | Serves: 2*

**Ingredients**

- 1 zucchini
- ½ teaspoon ground black pepper
- 1 teaspoon oregano
- 2 tablespoons chicken stock
- ½ teaspoon coconut oil

**Directions**

- Chop the zucchini into cubes.
- Combine the ground black pepper, and oregano; stir the mixture.
- Sprinkle the zucchini cubes with the spice mixture and stir well.
- After this, sprinkle the vegetables with the chicken stock.
- Place the coconut oil in the air fryer basket and preheat it to 360°F for 20 seconds.
- Then add the zucchini cubes and cook the vegetables for 5 minutes at 390°F, stirring halfway through.
- Transfer to serving plates and enjoy!

Cal 30 | Fat 1.5g | Fiber 1.6g | Carb 4.3g | Protein 1.4g

## TURMERIC CAULIFLOWER RICE

*Prep time: 5 min | Cook time:5 min | Serves:6*

**Ingredients**

- oz chive stems
- tablespoon butter
- 1 teaspoon salt
- 1-pound cauliflower
- 1 teaspoon turmeric
- 1 teaspoon minced garlic
- 1 teaspoon ground ginger
- 1 cup chicken stock

**Directions**

- Wash the cauliflower and chop it roughly.

- Then place the chopped cauliflower in the blender and blend it till you get the rice texture of the cauliflower.
- Transfer the cauliflower rice to the mixing bowl and add the diced chives.
- After this, sprinkle the vegetable mixture with the salt, turmeric, minced garlic, and ground ginger. Mix it up.
- Preheat the air fryer to 370°F.
- Put the cauliflower rice mixture there. Add the butter and chicken stock.
- Cook the cauliflower rice for 5 minutes.
- When the time is over – remove the cauliflower rice from the air fryer and strain the excess liquid.
- Stir it gently. Enjoy!

Cal 82 | Fat 1g | Fiber 0g | Carb 1.4g | Protein 0g

## PEPPERONI CHIPS

*Prep time: 2 min | Cook time: 5 min | Serves: 6*

### Ingredients
- oz pepperoni slices

### Directions :
- Place one batch of pepperoni slices in the air fryer oven basket.
- Cook for 5 minutes at 360°F.
- Cook remaining pepperoni slices using same steps.
- Serve and enjoy.

Cal 51 | Fat 1g | Carb 2g | Sugar 1.3g | Protein 0g

## ROASTED GARLIC HEAD
*Prep time: 5 min | Cook time: 5 min | Serves: 4*

### Ingredients
- 1-pound garlic head
- 1 tablespoon olive oil
- 1 teaspoon thyme

### Directions
- Cut the ends of the garlic head and place it in the air fryer basket.
- Then sprinkle the garlic head with the olive oil and thyme.
- Cook the garlic head for 5 minutes at 400°F.
- When the garlic head is cooked, it should be soft and aromatic.
- Serve immediately.

Cal 200 | Fat 4.1g | Fiber 2.5g | Carb 37.7g | Protein 7.2g

## SHIRATAKI NOODLES
*Prep time: 5 min | Cook time:5 min | Serves: 4*

### Ingredients
- cups water
- 1 teaspoon salt
- 1 tablespoon Italian seasoning
- 8 ozshirataki noodles

### Directions

- Preheat the air fryer to 365°F.
- Pour the water in the air fryer basket tray and preheat it for 3 minutes.
- Then add the shirataki noodles, salt, and Italian seasoning.
- Cook the shirataki noodles for 1 minute at the same temperature.
- Then strain the noodles and cook them for 2 minutes more at 360°F.
- When the shirataki noodles are cooked – let them chill for 1-2 minutes.
- Stir the noodles gently.
- Serve it!

Cal 16 | Fat 1g| Fiber 0g | Carb 1.4g | Protein 0g

## YAMS WITH DILL
*Prep time: 5 min | Cook time: 5 min | Serves: 2*

### Ingredients
- 2 yams
- 1 tablespoon fresh dill
- 1 teaspoon coconut oil
- ½ teaspoon minced garlic

### Directions
- Wash the yams carefully and cut them into halves.
- Sprinkle the yam halves with the coconut oil and then rub with the minced garlic.
- Place the yams in the air fryer basket and cook for 5 minutes at 400°F.
- After this, mash the yams gently with a fork and then sprinkle with the fresh dill.
- Serve the yams immediately.

Cal 25 | Fat 2.3g | Fiber 0.2g | Carb 1.2g | Protein 0.4g

## HONEY ONIONS
*Prep time: 5 min | Cook time: 5 min | Serves: 2*

### Ingredients
- 2 large white onions
- 1 tablespoon raw honey
- 1 teaspoon water
- 1 tablespoon paprika

### Directions
- Peel the onions and using a knife, make cuts in the shape of a cross.
- Then combine the raw honey and water; stir.
- Add the paprika and stir the mixture until smooth.
- Place the onions in the air fryer basket and sprinkle them with the honey mixture.
- Cook the onions for 5 minutes at 380°F.
- When the onions are cooked, they should be soft.
- Transfer the cooked onions to serving plates and serve.

Cal 102 | Fat 0.6g | Fiber 4.5g | Carb 24.6g | Protein 2.2g

## DELIGHTFUL ROASTED GARLIC SLICES
*Prep time: 5 min | Cook time: 5 min | Serves: 4*

### Ingredients
- 1 teaspoon coconut oil
- ½ teaspoon dried cilantro
- ¼ teaspoon cayenne pepper
- 12 ounces garlic cloves, peeled

### Directions

- Sprinkle the garlic cloves with the cayenne pepper and dried cilantro.
- Mix the garlic up with the spices, and then transfer to your air fryer oven basket.
- Add the coconut oil and cook the garlic for 5 minutes at 400°F, stirring halfway through.
- When the garlic cloves are done, transfer them to serving plates and serve.

Cal 137 | Fat 1.6g | Fiber 1.8g | Carb 28.2g | Protein 5.4g

## APPLE HAND PIES
*Prep time: 5 Min | Cook time: 5 Min | Serves: 6*

**Ingredients**
- 15-ounces no-sugar-added apple pie filling
- 1 store-bought crust

**Directions**
- Lay out pie crust and slice into equal-sized squares.
- Place 2 tablespoon filling into each square and seal crust with a fork.
- Pour into the Oven rack/basket. Place the Rack on the middle-shelf of the Air Fryer Oven. Set temperature to 390°F, and set time to 5 minutes until golden in color.

Cal 278 | Fat 10g | Protein 5g | Sugar 4g

## ROASTED MUSHROOMS
*Prep time:5 min | Cook time: 5 min | Serves: 2*

**Ingredients**
- 12 ounces mushroom hats
- ¼ cup fresh dill, chopped
- ¼ teaspoon onion, chopped
- 1 teaspoon olive oil
- ¼ teaspoon turmeric

**Directions**
- Combine the chopped dill and onion.
- Add the turmeric and stir the mixture.
- After this, add the olive oil and mix until homogenous.
- Then fill the mushroom hats with the dill mixture and place them in the air fryer basket.
- Cook the mushrooms for 5 minutes at 400°F.
- When the vegetables are cooked, let them cool to room temperature before serving.

Cal 73 | Fat 3.1g | Fiber 2.6g | Carb 9.2g | Protein 6.6g

## MASHED YAMS
*Prep time: 5 min | Cook time: 5 min | Serves: 5*

**Ingredients**
- 1 pound yams
- 1 teaspoon olive oil
- 1 tablespoon almond milk
- ¾ teaspoon salt
- 1 teaspoon dried parsley

**Directions**
- Peel the yams and chop.
- Place the chopped yams in the air fryer basket and sprinkle with the salt and dried parsley.
- Add the olive oil and stir the mixture.
- Cook the yams at 400°F for 5 minutes, stirring twice during cooking.

- When the yams are done, blend them well with a hand blender until smooth.
- Add the almond milk and stir carefully.
- Serve, and enjoy!

Cal 120 | Fat 1.8g | Fiber 3.6g | Carb 25.1g | Protein 1.4g

## BEEF AND MANGO SKEWERS
*Prep time: 5 min | Cook time: 5 min | Serves: 4*

**Ingredients**
- ¾ pound beef sirloin tip, cut into 1-inch cubes
- 2 tablespoons balsamic vinegar
- 1 tablespoon olive oil
- 1 tablespoon honey
- ½ teaspoon dried marjoram
- Pinch salt
- Freshly ground black pepper
- 1 mango

**Directions**
- Put the beef cubes in a medium bowl and add the balsamic vinegar, olive oil, honey, marjoram, salt, and pepper. Mix well, and then massage the marinade into the beef with your hands. Set aside.
- To prepare the mango, stand it on end and cut the skin off, using a sharp knife. Then carefully cut around the oval pit to remove the flesh. Cut the mango into 1-inch cubes.
- Thread metal skewers alternating with three beef cubes and two mango cubes.
- Grill the skewers in the air fryer basket for 5 minutes or until the beef is browned and at least 145°F.

Cal 242 | Fat 9g | Carb 13g | Protein 26g

## CHEESE BACON JALAPENO POPPERS
*Prep time: 5 min | Cook time: 5 min | Serves: 5*

**Ingredients**
- fresh jalapeno peppers, cut in half and remove seeds
- bacon slices, cooked and crumbled
- 1/4 cup cheddar cheese, shredded
- 6 oz cream cheese, softened

**Directions**
- In a bowl, combine together bacon, cream cheese, and cheddar cheese.
- Stuff each jalapeno half with bacon cheese mixture.
- Spray air fryer oven basket with cooking spray.
- Place stuffed jalapeno halved in air fryer oven basket and cook at 370°F for 5 minutes.
- Serve and enjoy.

Cal 195 | Fat 17.3g | Carb 3.2g | Sugar 1g | Protein 7.2 g

## BRUSSELS SPROUTS AND TOMATOES MIX
*Prep time: 5 min | Cook time: 5 min | Serves: 4*

**Ingredients**
- 1 lb. Brussels sprouts; trimmed
- 6 cherry tomatoes; halved
- 1/4 cup green onions; chopped.
- 1 tbsp. olive oil
- Salt and black pepper to the taste

**Directions**

- Season Brussels sprouts with salt and pepper, put them in your air fryer and cook at 350°F, for 5 minutes
- Transfer them to a bowl, add salt, pepper, cherry tomatoes, green onions and olive oil, toss well and serve.

Cal 121 | Fat 4g | Fiber 4g | Carb 11g | Protein 4g

## CRUNCHY BACON BITES

*Prep time: 5 min | Cook time: 5 min | Serves: 4*

**Ingredients**
- bacon strips, cut into small pieces
- 1/2 cup pork rinds, crushed
- 1/4 cup hot sauce

**Directions**
- Add bacon pieces in a bowl.
- Add hot sauce and toss well.
- Add crushed pork rinds and toss until bacon pieces are well coated.
- Transfer bacon pieces in air fryer oven basket and cook at 350°F for 5minutes.
- Serve and enjoy.

Cal 112 | Fat 9.7g | Carb 0.3g | Sugar 0.2g | Protein 5.2g

## FRIED LEEKS
*Prep time: 5 min | Cook time: 5 min | Serves: 4*

**Ingredients**
- 4 leeks; ends cut off and halved
- 1 tbsp. butter; melted
- 1 tbsp. lemon juice
- Salt and black pepper to the taste

**Directions**
- Coat leeks with melted butter, flavor with salt and pepper, put in your air fryer and cook at 350°F, for 5 minutes.
- Arrange on a platter, drizzle lemon juice all over and serve

Cal 100 | Fat 4g | Fiber 2g | Carb 6g | Protein 2g

## RADISH HASH RECIPE
*Prep time: 5 min | Cook time: 5 min | Serves: 4*

**Ingredients**
- 1/2 tsp. onion powder
- 1/3 cup parmesan; grated
- 4 eggs
- 1 lb. radishes; sliced
- Salt and black pepper to the taste

**Directions**
- In a bowl mix radishes with salt, pepper, onion, eggs and parmesan and stir well
- Transfer radishes to a pan that fits your air fryer and cook at 350°F, for 5 minutes
- Divide hash on plates and serve.

Cal 80 | Fat 5g | Fiber 2g | Carb 5g | Protein 7g

## BROCCOLI SALAD RECIPE
*Prep time: 5 min | Cook time: 5 min | Serves: 4*

**Ingredients**
- 1 broccoli head; florets separated
- 1 tbsp. Chinese rice wine vinegar
- 1 tbsp. peanut oil
- 6 garlic cloves; minced
- Salt and black pepper to the taste

**Directions**
- In a bowl mix broccoli with salt, pepper and half of the oil, toss, transfer to your air fryer and cook at 350°F, for 5 minutes; shaking the fryer halfway
- Transfer broccoli to a salad bowl, add the rest of the peanut oil, garlic and rice vinegar, toss really well and serve.

Cal 121 | Fat 3g | Fiber 4g | Carb 4g | Protein 4g

## PARMESAN BROCCOLI AND ASPARAGUS
*Prep time: 5 min | Cook time: 5 min | Serves: 4*

**Ingredients**
- 1 broccoli head, florets separated
- ½ pound asparagus, trimmed
- Juice of 1 lime
- Salt and black pepper to the taste
- 2 tablespoons olive oil
- 3 tablespoons parmesan, grated

**Directions**
- In a small bowl, combine the asparagus with the broccoli and all the other ingredients except the parmesan, toss, transfer to your air fryer's basket and cook at 400°F for 5 minutes.
- Divide between plates, sprinkle the parmesan on top and serve.

Cal 172 | Fat 5g | Fiber 2g | Carb 4g | Protein 9g

## BUTTER BROCCOLI MIX
*Prep time: 5 min | Cook time: 5 min | Serves: 4*

**Ingredients**
- 1-pound broccoli florets
- A pinch of salt and black pepper
- 1 teaspoon sweet paprika
- ½ tablespoon butter, melted

**Directions**
- In a small bowl, combine the broccoli with the rest of the ingredients, and toss.
- Put the broccoli in your air fryer's basket, cook at 350°F for 5 minutes, divide between plates and serve.

Cal 130 | Fat 3g | Fiber 3g | Carb 4g | Protein 8g

## KALE AND OLIVES
*Prep time: 5 min | Cook time: 5 min | Serves: 4*

**Ingredients**
- 1 an ½ pounds kale, torn
- 2 tablespoons olive oil
- Salt and black pepper to the taste
- 1 tablespoon hot paprika
- 2 tablespoons black olives, pitted and sliced

**Directions**
- In a pan that fits the air fryer, combine all the ingredients and toss.

- Put the pan in your air fryer, cook at 370°F for 5 minutes, divide between plates and serve.

Cal 154 | Fat 3g | Fiber 2g | Carb 4g | Protein 6g

## KALE AND MUSHROOMS MIX

*Prep time: 5 min | Cook time: 5 min | Serves: 4*

### Ingredients

- 1 pound brown mushrooms, sliced
- 1-pound kale, torn
- Salt and black pepper to the taste
- 2 tablespoons olive oil
- 14 ounces coconut milk

### Directions

- In a pot that fits your air fryer, mix the kale with the rest of the ingredients and toss.
- Put the pan in the fryer, cook at 380°F for 5 minutes, divide between plates and serve.

Cal 162 | Fat 4g | Fiber 1g | Carb 3g | Protein 5g

## SIMPLE GARLIC POTATOES

*Prep time: 5 Min | Cook time: 5 Min | Serves: 2*

### Ingredients

- 3 Baking Potatoes, Large
- 2 Tablespoons Olive Oil
- 2 Tablespoons Garlic, Minced
- 1 Tablespoon Salt
- ½ Tablespoon Onion Powder

### Directions

- Turn on your air fryer to 390.
- Create holes in your potato, and then sprinkle it with oil and salt.
- Mix your garlic and onion powder together, and then rub it on the potatoes evenly.
- Put it into your air fryer basket, and then bake for 5 minutes.

Cal 160 | Fat 6g | Carb 9g | Protein 9g

## OREGANO KALE

*Prep time: 5 min | Cook time: 5 min | Serves: 4*

### Ingredients

- 1-pound kale, torn
- 1 tablespoon olive oil
- A pinch of salt and black pepper
- 2 tablespoons oregano, chopped

### Directions

- In a pan that fits the air fryer, combine all the ingredients and toss.
- Put the pan in the air fryer and cook at 380°F for 5 minutes.

- Divide between plates and serve.

Cal 140 | Fat 3g | Fiber 2g | Carb 3g | Protein 5g

## KALE AND BRUSSELS SPROUTS

*Prep time: 5 min | Cook time: 5 min | Serves: 8*

### Ingredients

- 1-pound Brussels sprouts, trimmed
- 2 cups kale, torn
- 1 tablespoon olive oil
- Salt and black pepper to the taste
- 3 ounces mozzarella, shredded

### Directions

- In a pan that fits the air fryer, combine all the ingredients except the mozzarella and toss.
- Put the pan in the air fryer and cook at 380°F for 5 minutes.
- Divide between plates, sprinkle the cheese on top and serve.

Cal 170 | Fat 5g | Fiber 3g | Carb 4g | Protein 7g

## SPICY OLIVES AND AVOCADO MIX

*Prep time: 5 min | Cook time: 5 min | Serves: 4*

### Ingredients

- 2 cups kalamata olives, pitted
- 2 small avocados, pitted, peeled and sliced
- ¼ cup cherry tomatoes, halved
- Juice of 1 lime
- 1 tablespoon coconut oil, melted

### Directions

- In a pan that fits the air fryer, combine the olives with the other ingredients, toss, put the pan in your air fryer and cook at 370°F for 5 minutes.
- Divide the mix between plates and serve.

Cal 153 | Fat 3g | Fiber 3g | Carb 4g | Protein 6g

## OLIVES, GREEN BEANS AND BACON

*Prep time: 5 min | Cook time: 5 min | Serves: 4*

### Ingredients

- ½ pound green beans, trimmed and halved
- 1 cup black olives, pitted and halved
- ¼ cup bacon, cooked and crumbled
- 1 tablespoon olive oil
- ¼ cup tomato sauce

### Directions

- In a pan that fits the air fryer, combine all the ingredients, toss, put the pan in the air fryer and cook at 380°F for 5 minutes.
- Divide between plates and serve.

Cal 160 | Fat 4g | Fiber 3g | Carb 5g | Protein 4g

## SPICY KALE CHIPS WITH YOGURT SAUCE

*Prep time: 5 min | Cook time: 5 min | Serves: 4*

### Ingredients

- 1 cup Greek yogurt
- 3 tablespoons lemon juice
- 2 tablespoons honey mustard
- ½ teaspoon dried oregano
- 1 bunch curly kale
- 2 tablespoons olive oil
- ½ teaspoon salt
- ⅛ Teaspoon pepper

**Directions**

- In a small bowl, combine the yogurt, lemon juice, honey mustard, and oregano, and set aside.
- Remove the stems and ribs from the kale with a sharp knife. Cut the leaves into 2- to 3-inch pieces.
- Toss the kale with olive oil, salt, and pepper. Massage the oil into the leaves with your hands.
- Air-fry the kale in batches until crisp, about 5 minutes, shaking the basket once during cooking time. Serve with the yogurt sauce.

Cal 154 | Fat 8g | Carb 13g | Protein 8g

## ENGLISH MUFFIN TUNA SANDWICHES
*Prep time: 8 min | Cook time: 5 min | Serves: 4*

**Ingredients**:

- 1 (6-ounce) can chunk light tuna, drained
- ¼ cup mayonnaise
- tablespoons mustard
- 1 tablespoon lemon juice
- green onions, minced
- English muffins, split with a fork
- tablespoons softened butter
- thin slices provolone or Muenster cheese

**Directions**:

- In a small bowl, combine the tuna, mayonnaise, mustard, lemon juice, and green onions.
- Butter the cut side of the English muffins. Grill butter-side up in the air fryer for 2 to 3 minutes or until light golden brown. Remove the muffins from the air fryer basket.
- Top each muffin with one slice of cheese and return to your air fryer oven. Grill for 2 to 3 minutes or until the cheese melts and starts to brown.
- Remove the muffins from the air fryer, top with the tuna mixture, and serve.

Cal 389 | Fat 23g | Carb 25g | Fiber 3g | Protein 21g

## CAJUN SHRIMP
*Prep time: 5 min | Cook time: 5 min | Serves: 6*

**Ingredients**

- Tiger shrimp (16-20/1.25 lb.)
- Olive oil (1 tbsp.)
- Old Bay seasoning (.5 tsp.)
- Smoked paprika (.25 tsp.)
- Cayenne pepper (.25 tsp.)

**Directions**

- Set the Air Fryer at 390° F.
- Cover the shrimp using the oil and spices.
- Toss them into your air fryer oven basket and set the timer for 5 minutes.
- Serve.

Cal 356 | Fat 18g | Carb 5g | Protein 34g

## FLATBREAD
*Prep time: 5 min | Cook time: 5 min | Serves: 2*

**Ingredients**

- 1 cup shredded mozzarella cheese
- ¼ cup almond flour
- 1-ounce full-fat cream cheese softened

**Directions**

- Melt mozzarella in the microwave for 30 seconds. Stir in almond flour until smooth.
- Add cream cheese. Continue mixing until dough forms. Knead with wet hands if necessary.
- Divide the dough into two pieces and roll out to ¼-inch thickness between two pieces of parchment.
- Cover the air fryer basket with parchment and place the flatbreads into your air fryer oven basket. Work in batches if necessary.
- Cook at 320°F for 5 minutes. Flip once at the halfway mark.
- Serve.

Cal 296 | Fat 22.6g | Carb 3.3g | Protein 16.3g

## SHRIMP AND GRILLED CHEESE SANDWICHES
*Prep time: 5 min | Cook time: 5 min | Serves: 4*

**Ingredients**:

- 1¼ cups shredded Colby, Cheddar, or Havarti cheese
- 1 (6-ounce) can tiny shrimp, drained
- tablespoons mayonnaise
- tablespoons minced green onion
- slices whole grain or whole-wheat bread
- tablespoons softened butt

**Directions**:

- In a medium bowl, combine the cheese, shrimp, mayonnaise, and green onion, and mix well.
- Spread this mixture on two of the slices of bread. Top with the other slices of bread to make two sandwiches. Spread the sandwiches lightly with butter.
- Grill in the air fryer for 5 to 7 minutes or until the bread is browned and crisp and the cheese is melted. Cut in half and serve warm.

Cal 276 | Fat 14g | Carb 16g | Fiber 2g | Protein 22g

## VEGETABLE EGG ROLLS
*Prep time: 5 min | Cook time: 5 min | Serves: 8*

**Ingredients**

- ½ cup chopped mushrooms
- ½ cup grated carrots
- ½ cup chopped zucchini
- green onions, chopped
- tablespoons low-sodium soy sauce
- egg roll wrappers
- 1 tablespoon cornstarch
- 1 egg, beaten

**Directions**

- In a medium bowl, combine the mushrooms, carrots, zucchini, green onions, and soy sauce, and stir together.
- Place the egg roll wrappers on a work surface. Top each with about 3 tablespoons of the vegetable mixture.
- In a small bowl, combine the cornstarch and egg and mix well. Brush some of this mixture on the edges of the egg roll wrappers. Roll up the wrappers, enclosing the vegetable filling. Brush some of the egg mixture on the outside of the egg rolls to seal.
- Air-fry for 5 minutes or until the egg rolls are brown and crunchy.

Cal 112 | Fat 1g | Carb 21g | Fiber 1g | Protein 4g

## HASH BROWN BURCHETT

*Prep time: 5 min | Cook time: 5 min | Serves: 4*

**Ingredients**

- 4 frozen hash brown patties
- 1 tablespoon olive oil
- ⅓ cup chopped cherry tomatoes
- 3 tablespoons diced fresh mozzarella
- 2 tablespoons grated Parmesan cheese
- 1 tablespoon balsamic vinegar
- 1 tablespoon minced fresh basil

**Directions**

- Place the hash brown patties in the air fryer in a single layer. Air-fry for 5 minutes or until the potatoes are crisp, hot, and golden brown.
- Meanwhile, combine the olive oil, tomatoes, mozzarella, Parmesan, vinegar, and basil in a small bowl. When the potatoes are done, carefully remove from the basket and arrange on a serving plate. Top with the tomato mixture and serve.

Cal 123 | Fat 6g | Carb 14g | Protein 5g

## BROCCOLI WITH PARMESAN CHEESE

*Prep time: 5 min | Cook time: 4 min | Serves: 4*

**Ingredients**

- 1 pound broccoli florets
- 2 teaspoons minced garlic
- 2 tablespoons olive oil
- ¼ cup grated or shaved Parmesan cheese

**Directions**

- Preparing the Ingredients. Preheat the air fryer to 360°F. In a bowl, mix together the broccoli florets, garlic, olive oil, and Parmesan cheese.
- Place the broccoli in the air fryer basket in a single layer and set the timer and steam for 4 minutes.

Cal 130 | Fat 3g | Carb 5g | Protein 4g

## CINNAMON PEAR JAM

*Prep time: 5 min | Cook time: 4 min | Serves: 12*

**Ingredients**

- 8 pears, cored and cut into quarters
- 1 tsp cinnamon
- 1/4 cup apple juice
- 2 apples, peeled, cored and diced

**Directions**

- Put all of the ingredients in the air fryer and stir well.
- Seal pot and cook on high for 4 minutes.
- As soon as the cooking is done, let it release pressure naturally. Remove lid.

- Blend pear apple mixture using an immersion blender until smooth.
- Serve and enjoy.

Cal 103 | Protein 0.6g | Fat 0.3g | Carb 27.1g

## YELLOW SQUASH FRITTERS

*Prep time: 5 min | Cook time: 5 min | Serves: 4*

**Ingredients**

- 1 (3-ounce) package cream cheese, softened
- 1 egg, beaten
- ½ teaspoon dried oregano
- Pinch salt
- Freshly ground black pepper
- 1 medium yellow summer squash, grated
- ⅓ cup grated carrot
- ⅔ cup bread crumbs
- tablespoons olive oil

**Directions**

- In a medium bowl, combine the cream cheese, egg, oregano, and salt and pepper. Add the squash and carrot, and mix well. Stir in the breadcrumbs.
- Form about 2 tablespoons of this mixture into a patty about ½ inch thick. Repeat with remaining mixture. Brush the fritters with olive oil.
- Air-fry until crisp and golden, about 5 minutes.

Cal 234| Fat 17g | Carb 16g | Fiber 2g | Protein 6g

## ROASTED ALMONDS

*Prep time: 5 min | Cook time:5 min | Serves: 8*

**Ingredients**

- cups almonds
- 1/4 tsp pepper
- 1 tsp paprika
- 1 tbsp garlic powder
- 1 tbsp soy sauce

**Directions**

- Add pepper, paprika, garlic powder, and soy sauce in a bowl and stir well.
- Add almonds and stir to coat.
- Spray air fryer oven basket with cooking spray.
- Add almonds in air fryer oven basket and cook for 5 minutes at 320°F..
- Serve and enjoy.

Cal 143 | Fat 11.9g | Carb 6.2g | Sugar 1.3g | Protein 5.4 g

## WARM PEACH COMPOTE

*Prep time: 5 min | Cook time: 1 min | Serves: 4*

**Ingredients**

- 4 peaches, peeled and chopped
- 1 tbsp water
- 1/2 tbsp cornstarch
- 1 tsp vanilla

**Directions**

- Add water, vanilla, and peaches into your air fryer oven basket.
- Seal pot and cook on high for 1 minute.
- Once done, allow to release pressure naturally. Remove lid.
- In a small bowl, whisk together 1 tablespoon of water and cornstarch and pour into the pot and stir well.

- Serve and enjoy.

Cal 66 | Protein 1.4g | Fat 0.4g | Carb 15g

## MUSHROOM PITA PIZZAS

*Prep time:5 min | Cook time: 5 min | Serves: 4*

**Ingredients**

- (3-inch) pitas
- 1 tablespoon olive oil
- ¾ cup pizza sauce
- 1 (4-ounce) jar sliced mushrooms, drained
- ½ teaspoon dried basil
- green onions, minced
- 1 cup grated mozzarella or provolone cheese
- 1 cup sliced grape tomatoes

**Directions**

- Brush each piece of pita with oil and top with the pizza sauce.
- Add the mushrooms and sprinkle with basil and green onions. Top with the grated cheese.
- Bake for 5 minutes or until the cheese is melted and starts to brown. Top with the grape tomatoes and serve immediately.

Cal 231| Fat 9g | Carb 25g| Fiber 2g | Protein 13g

## PERFECT CRAB DIP

*Prep time: 5 min | Cook time: 5 min | Serves: 4*

**Ingredients**

- 1 cup crabmeat
- 1 tbsp parsley, chopped
- 1 tbsp fresh lemon juice
- 1 tbsp hot sauce
- 1/2 cup green onion, sliced
- cups cheese, grated
- 1/4 cup mayonnaise
- 1/4 tsp pepper
- 1/2 tsp salt

**Directions**

- In a 6-inch dish, mix together crabmeat, hot sauce, cheese, mayo, pepper, and salt.
- Place dish in air fryer oven basket and cook dip at 400°F for 5 minutes.
- Remove dish from air fryer oven.
- Drizzle dip with lemon juice and garnish with parsley.
- Serve and enjoy.

Cal 313 | Fat 23.9g | Carb 8.8g | Sugar 3.1g | Protein 16.2g

## HONEY FRUIT COMPOTE

*Prep time:5 min | Cook time: 3 min | Serves: 4*

**Ingredients**

- 1/3 cup honey

- 1 1/2 cups blueberries
- 1 1/2 cups raspberries

**Directions**

- Put all of the ingredients in the air fryer basket and stir well.
- Seal pot with lid and cook on high for 3 minutes.
- Once done, allow to release pressure naturally. Remove lid.
- Serve and enjoy.

Cal 141 | Protein 1g | Fat 0.5g | Carb 36.7g

## AIR FRIED BACON

*Prep time: 1 min | Cook time: 5 min | Serves: 6*

**Ingredients**

- 6 bacon slices

**Directions**

- Place the bacon slices in air fryer oven basket.
- Cook at 400°F for 5 minutes.
- Serve and enjoy.

Cal 103 | Fat 7.9g | Carb 0.3g | Sugar 0g | Protein 7g

## ROASTED BANANAS

*Prep time: 5 min | Cook time: 5 min | Serves: 2*

**Ingredients**

- 2 cups bananas, cubed
- 1 teaspoon avocado oil
- 1 tablespoon maple syrup
- 1 teaspoon brown sugar
- 1 cup almond milk

**Directions**

- Coat the banana cubes with oil and maple syrup.
- Sprinkle with brown sugar.
- Cook at 375 °F in the air fryer for 5 minutes.
- Drizzle milk on top of the bananas before serving.

Cal 107 | Protein 1.3g | Fat 0.7g | Carb 27g

# THANK YOU

Thanks for reading this book.

If you appreciated this book, I would be extremely grateful if you would take 1 minute of your time to leave a review on Amazon about my work using the QR code below.

If you didn't like it, I am very sorry. You can write me at *emilyfinnerwriter@gmail.com* to tell me how to improve it.

Thank you.

*Emily Finner*

**SCAN WITH YOUR MOBILE**

## Customer reviews

★★★★★ 4.9 out of 5

44 global ratings

| | | |
|---|---|---|
| 5 star | 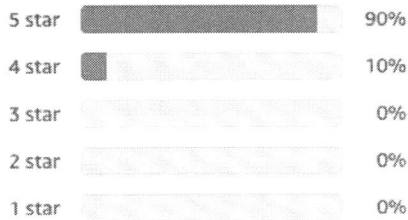 | 90% |
| 4 star | | 10% |
| 3 star | | 0% |
| 2 star | | 0% |
| 1 star | | 0% |

˅ How are ratings calculated?

# CONCLUSION

**The technology of the Kalorik MAXX Air Fryer Oven is exceptionally straightforward.** Fried foods get their crunchy feel because warm oil heats meals quickly and evenly onto their face. Oil is a superb heat conductor that aids with simultaneous and fast cooking across each ingredient. For decades' cooks have employed convection ovens to attempt and mimic the effects of cooking or frying the entire surface of the food.

However, the atmosphere never circulates quickly enough to precisely attain that yummy surface most of us enjoy in fried foods. With this mechanism, the atmosphere is spread high levels up to 400°F, into "air fry" any foods like poultry, fish or processors, etc. This technology has altered the entire cooking notion by decreasing the fat by around 80 percent compared to traditional fat skillet. There is also an exhaust fan directly over the cooking room, which offers the meals necessary airflow.

This also contributes to precisely the identical heating reaching every region of the food that's being cooked. This is the only grill and exhaust fan that helps the Smart Oven improve the air continuously to cook wholesome meals without fat. The inner pressure strengthens the temperature, which will be controlled by the exhaust system. Exhaust enthusiast releases filtered additional air to cook the meals in a far healthier way. Smart Oven doesn't have any odor whatsoever, and It's benign, making it easy and environment-friendly.

Hopefully, after going through this cookbook and trying out a couple of recipes, **you will get to understand the flexibility and utility of the air fryers**. The use of this kitchen appliance ensures that the making of some of your favorite snacks and meals will be carried out in a stress-free manner without hassling around, which invariably legitimizes its worth and gives you value for your money.

**We are so glad you leaped this healthier cooking format with us!**

The air fryer truly is not a gadget that should stay on the shelf. Instead, take it out and give it a whirl when you are whipping up one of your tried-and-true recipes or if you are starting to get your feet wet with the air frying method.

Regardless of appliances, recipes, or dietary concerns, we hope you have fun in your kitchen. Between food preparation, cooking time, and then the cleanup, a lot of time is spent in this one room, so it should be as fun as possible.

This is just the start. **There are no limits to working with the air fryer, and we will explore some more recipes as well.** In addition to all the great options that we talked about before, you will find that there are tasty desserts that can make those sweet teeth in no time, and some great sauces and dressing to always be in control over the foods you eat. There are just so many options to choose from that it won't take long before you find a whole bunch of recipes to use, and before you start to wonder why you didn't get the air fryer so much sooner. There are so numerous things to admire about the air fryer, and it becomes an even better tool to use when you have the right recipes in place and can use them. And there are so many fantastic recipes that work well in the air fryer and can get dinner on the table in no time.

We are pleased that you pursue this Air Fryer cookbook.

# RECIPES INDEX

Manufactured by Amazon.ca
Bolton, ON